Glencoe

Exploring Our World

People, Places, and Cultures

Western Hemisphere, Europe, and Russia

Boehm Armstrong Hunkins

NATIONAL GEOGRAPHIC

Mc Graw Hill **Glencoe**

New York, New York   Columbus, Ohio   Chicago, Illinois   Woodland Hills, California

About the Authors

NATIONAL GEOGRAPHIC

The National Geographic Society, founded in 1888 for the increase and diffusion of geographic knowledge, is the world's largest nonprofit scientific and educational organization. Since its earliest days, the Society has used sophisticated communication technologies, from color photography to holography, to convey geographic knowledge to a worldwide membership. The School Publishing Division supports the Society's mission by developing innovative education programs—ranging from traditional print materials to multimedia programs including CD-ROMs, videos, and software.

Senior Author
Richard G. Boehm

Richard G. Boehm, Ph.D., was one of seven authors of *Geography for Life*, national standards in geography, prepared under Goals 2000: Educate America Act. He was also one of the authors of the *Guidelines for Geographic Education*, in which the Five Themes of Geography were first articulated. Dr. Boehm has received many honors, including "Distinguished Geography Educator" by the National Geographic Society (1990), the "George J. Miller Award" from the National Council for Geographic Education (NCGE) for distinguished service to geographic education (1991), and "Gilbert Grosvenor Honors" in geographic education from the Association of American Geographers (2002). He was President of the NCGE and has twice won the *Journal of Geography* award for best article.

He has received the NCGE's "Distinguished Teaching Achievement" award and presently holds the Jesse H. Jones Distinguished Chair in Geographic Education at Texas State University in San Marcos, Texas.

Francis P. Hunkins

Francis P. Hunkins, Ph.D., is Professor of Education at the University of Washington. He began his career as a teacher in Massachusetts. He received his master's degree in education from Boston University and his doctorate from Kent State University with a major in general curriculum and a minor in geography. Dr. Hunkins has written numerous books and articles.

David G. Armstrong

David G. Armstrong, Ph.D., served as Dean of the School of Education at the University of North Carolina at Greensboro. A social studies education specialist with additional advanced training in geography, Dr. Armstrong was educated at Stanford University, University of Montana, and University of Washington.

Dinah Zike

Dinah Zike, M.Ed., is an award-winning author, educator, and inventor known for designing three-dimensional hands-on manipulatives and graphic organizers known as Foldables™. Dinah has developed educational books and materials and is the author of *The Big Book of Books and Activities*, which was awarded Learning Magazine's Teachers' Choice Award. In 2004 Dinah was honored with the CESI Science Advocacy Award. Dinah received her M.Ed. from Texas A&M, College Station, Texas.

 Glencoe

The McGraw-Hill Companies

Send all inquiries to:
Glencoe/McGraw-Hill
8787 Orion Place
Columbus, Ohio 43240-4027
ISBN: 978-0-07-874580-5
MHID: 0-07-874580-2
Printed in the United States of America.
2 3 4 5 6 7 8 9 079/055 14 13 12 11 10 09 08 07

Academic Consultants

Teacher Reviewers

Reading Consultant

Contents

▼ **Farming in Manitoba, Canada**

Contents

▼ **Celebration in Port-of-Spain, Trinidad**

▲ **Reed boat, Lake Titicaca**

Contents

The Danube River, Hungary

Contents

▼ **Breaking ice on the Arctic Ocean**

Features

Geography & History

World Literature

YOU Decide

◀ **Trans-Siberian
Railroad train**

TIME Features

▲ **Protesting in France**

TIME JOURNAL

Primary Sources

Ed. = Editor   Tr. = Translator   V = Volume

▲ **African Americans in Harlem during the 1930s**

Primary Sources

Toucan

◀ **Pan-American Highway, Panama**

UNIT 5

Skills Handbook

▲ **Brown bear cubs, Kamchatka Peninsula, Russia**

Maps

UNIT 1

The World

NATIONAL GEOGRAPHIC

The United Kingdom and Ireland

UNIT 2

The United States and Canada

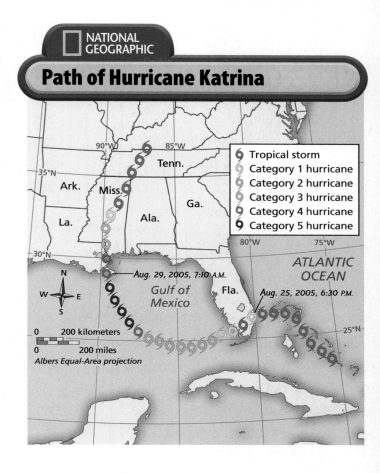

NATIONAL GEOGRAPHIC

Path of Hurricane Katrina

Tropical storm
Category 1 hurricane
Category 2 hurricane
Category 3 hurricane
Category 4 hurricane
Category 5 hurricane

90°W   85°W
35°N
Ark.   Tenn.
Miss.
La.   Ala.   Ga.
80°W   75°W
30°N
Aug. 29, 2005, 7:10 A.M.   ATLANTIC OCEAN
Gulf of Mexico   Fla.   Aug. 25, 2005, 6:30 P.M.
25°N

0   200 kilometers
0   200 miles
Albers Equal-Area projection

UNIT 3

Latin America

Maps

NATIONAL GEOGRAPHIC

Areas of the Netherlands Reclaimed From the Sea

Land Reclamation
- 1200–1600
- 1600–1900
- 1900–present
- Dike

North Sea

Wunseradiel

Stavoren

Andijk

Alkmaar

Amsterdam

Rotterdam

Rhine R.

Meuse R.

GERMANY

Rhine R.

BELGIUM

0   40 kilometers

0   40 miles

Lambert Conformal Conic projection

Exploring the Eastern Hemisphere

The Trans-Siberian Railroad

Diagrams, Charts, and Graphs

Comparing Population

United States and Selected Countries of Latin America

United States	
Brazil	
Mexico	
Argentina	
Peru	
Honduras	

= 30,000,000

Source: *World Population Data Sheet,* 2005.

Altitude Climate Zones

Tierra Helada
20˚F–55˚F
(-7˚C–13˚C)

— **10,000 feet**
(3,048 m)

Barley

Wheat

Potatoes   **Apples**

Tierra Fría
55˚F–65˚F
(13˚C–18˚C)

— **6,000 feet**
(1,829 m)

Coffee

Corn   **Citrus**

Tierra Templada
65˚F–75˚F
(18˚C–24˚C)

— **3,000 feet**
(914 m)

Bananas

Sugarcane

Tierra Caliente
75˚F–80˚F
(24˚C–27˚C)

Rice

Cacao

— **Sea Level**

![UNIT 3]

Latin America

![UNIT 4]

Europe

Diagrams, Charts, and Graphs

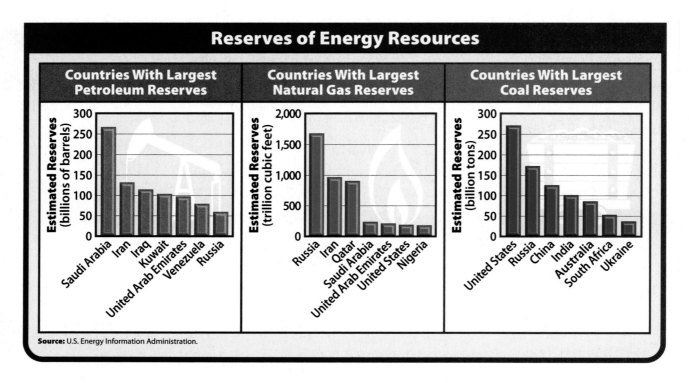

Reserves of Energy Resources

Countries With Largest Petroleum Reserves

Countries With Largest Natural Gas Reserves

Countries With Largest Coal Reserves

Source: U.S. Energy Information Administration.

Scavenger Hunt

Exploring Our World: People, Places, and Cultures contains a wealth of information. The trick is to know where to look to access all the information in the book. If you complete this scavenger hunt exercise with your teacher or parents, you will see how the textbook is organized and how to get the most out of your reading and study time. Let's get started!

1 How many units and how many chapters are in the book?

2 What does Unit 1 cover?

3 Where can you find facts about each country in each unit?

4 In what three places can you learn about the Big Ideas for each section?

5 What does the Foldables Study Organizer at the beginning of Chapter 2 ask you to do?

6 How are the content vocabulary terms throughout your book highlighted in the narrative?

7 Where do you find graphic organizers in your textbook?

8 You want to quickly find all the maps in the book about the world. Where do you look?

9 Where can you practice specific social studies skills in your textbook?

10 Where can you learn about the different types of map projections?

REFERENCE ATLAS

NATIONAL GEOGRAPHIC

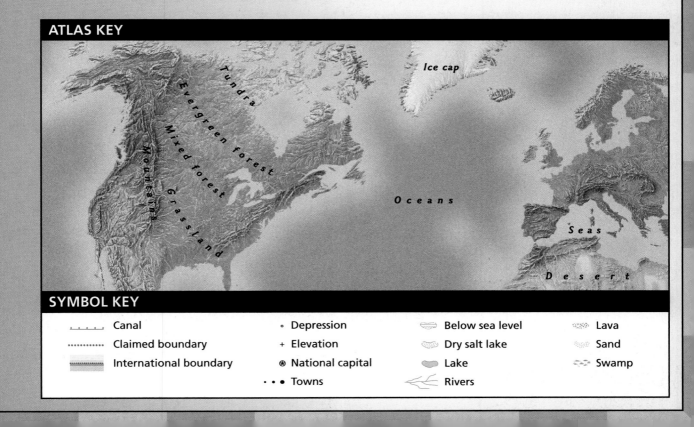

ATLAS KEY

Tundra
Evergreen forest
Mixed forest
Mountains
Grassland
Ice cap
Oceans
Seas
Desert

SYMBOL KEY

⌞⌞⌞⌞ Canal	∘ Depression	⬭ Below sea level	⬚ Lava
·········· Claimed boundary	+ Elevation	⬭ Dry salt lake	⬚ Sand
▓▓▓▓ International boundary	⊛ National capital	⬭ Lake	⤳ Swamp
	• • • Towns	⬳ Rivers	

WORLD
POLITICAL

0 mi   2000

0 km   2000

WINKEL TRIPEL PROJECTION

NATIONAL GEOGRAPHIC

ABBREVIATIONS

AUST.	AUSTRIA
B.&H.	BOSNIA & HERZEGOVINA
BELG.	BELGIUM
CROAT.	CROATIA
CZECH REP.	CZECH REPUBLIC
DEM. REP.	DEMOCRATIC
OF THE	REPUBLIC OF
CONGO	THE CONGO
EQ. GUINEA	EQUATORIAL GUINEA
EST.	ESTONIA
HUNG.	HUNGARY
LITH.	LITHUANIA
MACED.	MACEDONIA
MOLD.	MOLDOVA
NETH.	NETHERLANDS
SERB.	SERBIA
MONT.	MONTENEGRO
SLOV.	SLOVENIA
SWITZ.	SWITZERLAND
U.A.E.	UNITED ARAB EMIRATES

WORLD
PHYSICAL

0 mi — 2000

0 km — 2000

WINKEL TRIPEL PROJECTION

NATIONAL GEOGRAPHIC

**Map labels:**

A R C T I C

150°W 120°W 90°W 60°W 30°W 0°

Queen Elizabeth Islands
North Magnetic Pole
Oodaaq I.
Ellesmere Island
GREENLAND
Greenland Sea

Chukchi Sea
Siberia
Beaufort Sea
North Banks Island
Melville Island
Victoria Island
Baffin Island
Baffin Bay

Brooks Range
ALASKA
Mt. McKinley (Denali) 20,320 ft 6,194 m
60°N
Yukon
Alaska Range
Bering Sea
Aleutian Islands

Great Bear Lake
Great Slave Lake
Mackenzie
Hudson Bay

ARCTIC CIRCLE
Iceland

Alexander Archipelago
Queen Charlotte Islands
Vancouver Island
Coast Mountains

NORTH AMERICA

Nelson
Lake Winnipeg
Canadian Shield
Great Lakes

Labrador
Labrador Sea

British Isles
Ireland Great Britain

Cascade Range
Great Salt Lake
Missouri
Central Lowland
Appalachian Mountains

Island of Newfoundland
Nova Scotia

NORTH

Iberian Peninsula

30°N
Death Valley -282 ft -86 m
Colorado
Mississippi

ATLANTIC

Azores
Madeira Islands
Atlas

NORTH PACIFIC OCEAN

Hawaiian Islands

TROPIC OF CANCER
Hawaii

Baja California
Rio Grande
Gulf of Mexico
Bahama Islands
WEST INDIES
Cuba
Greater Antilles
Jamaica Hispaniola

OCEAN

Canary Islands

CENTRAL AMERICA
Caribbean Sea
Lesser Antilles
Trinidad

Cape Verde Islands

Upper

P O L Y N E S I A

Line Islands

EQUATOR

Galapagos Islands

Llanos
Orinoco
Guiana Highlands
Negro
Amazon
Amazon
Madeira

0°

Marquesas Islands

ANDES

Basin
SOUTH

Tocantins
São Francisco

Samoa Islands
Cook Islands
Tahiti
Society Is.
Tuamotu Archipelago

Lake Titicaca
Mato Grosso Plateau
AMERICA
Brazilian Highlights

SOUTH

Tonga Is.
Fiji Is.

TROPIC OF CAPRICORN

Atacama Desert
Gran Chaco
Paraguay
Paraná

ATLANTIC

Easter Island

Aconcagua 22,834 ft 6,960 m
30°S

Pampas

OCEAN

SOUTH PACIFIC

Chiloe Island
Valdes Peninsula -131 ft -40 m

OCEAN

Strait of Magellan
Tierra del Fuego
Falkland Islands
South Georgia
Scotia Sea
South Sandwich Islands

60°S

South Shetland Islands
South Orkney Islands

ANTARCTIC CIRCLE
Antarctic Peninsula

Bellingshausen Sea
Ellsworth Land
Weddell Sea
Ronne Ice Shelf

Ross Sea
Marie Byrd Land
Ross Ice Shelf
Vinson Massif 16,067 ft 4,897 m

TRANSANTARCTIC MOUNTAINS

PRIME MERIDIAN (MERIDIAN OF GREENWICH)

NORTH AMERICA

PHYSICAL

0 mi   1000

0 km   1000

AZIMUTHAL EQUIDISTANT PROJECTION

NATIONAL GEOGRAPHIC

UNITED STATES
POLITICAL

0 mi — 600
0 km — 600

OBLIQUE AZIMUTHAL EQUIDISTANT PROJECTION

NATIONAL GEOGRAPHIC

GREENLAND
(KALAALLIT NUNAAT)
Den.

ARCTIC CIRCLE

C A N A D A

MONTANA
Helena
•Billings

NORTH DAKOTA
⊙Bismarck

MINNESOTA

Lake Superior

MICHIGAN

Lake Huron

MAINE
Montpelier
⊙Augusta
•Portland
Concord, N.H.

SOUTH DAKOTA
Pierre⊙

Minneapolis
St. Paul
WISCONSIN
Milwaukee
Madison⊙
Lansing⊙

L. Michigan

Detroit
L. Erie
Cleveland
Buffalo

Lake Ontario
NEW YORK
Albany

Boston, MASS.
Providence, R.I.
Hartford, CONN.

WYOMING
•Casper
Cheyenne

SOUTH DAKOTA

Sioux City
Des Moines⊙
IOWA

NEBRASKA
Lincoln⊙
⊙Omaha

Chicago
ILLINOIS

IND.
Columbus
Indianapolis⊙
OHIO
Cincinnati

Toledo
Pittsburgh
Harrisburg
Dayton W. VA.

PA.
New York City
Trenton, N.J.
Philadelphia
Baltimore
Dover, DEL.
Annapolis, MD.
Washington, D.C.

Billings

COLORADO
Denver
Topeka⊙
Kansas City
MISSOURI
Springfield
St. Louis
Frankfort⊙
Louisville
KENTUCKY
Charleston
Richmond
VIRGINIA
Virginia Beach

KANSAS
Jefferson City⊙

Santa Fe⊙
•Albuquerque
NEW MEXICO

Oklahoma City
OKLAHOMA
⊙Tulsa
ARKANSAS
•Little Rock

Nashville
TENNESSEE
Memphis
Atlanta
Birmingham

Raleigh
NORTH CAROLINA
Charlotte
SOUTH CAROLINA
Columbia
Charleston

El Paso

Fort Worth
•Dallas
T E X A S
Austin
San Antonio

LOUISIANA
⊙Jackson
MISS.
ALABAMA
Montgomery
Baton Rouge
•New Orleans

GEORGIA
Savannah
Jacksonville
Tallahassee

M E X I C O

Rio Grande

Gulf of Mexico

FLORIDA
Tampa
Miami

BAHAMAS

Straits of Florida

CUBA

Caribbean Sea

JAMAICA

HAITI
DOMINICAN REPUBLIC

PUERTO RICO
U.S.
•San Juan

ANTIGUA & BARBUDA
ST. KITTS & NEVIS
DOMINICA

A T L A N T I C   O C E A N

Bermuda Is.
U.K.

CANADA

Lake of the Woods

Isle Royale
Lake Superior

Upper Peninsula

Lake Huron

Minneapolis

Mississippi

Milwaukee

Lake Michigan

Lower Peninsula

Detroit
Lake Erie

Chicago

Cleveland

CENTRAL
LOWLAND

Pittsburgh

Indianapolis

Ohio

St. Louis

Wabash

Flint
Hills

Ozark Plateau

Boston Mts.

Memphis

Tennessee

Ouachita Mts.

Mississippi

Appalachian Plateau
Cumberland Plateau
Cumberland
Allegheny Mts.
APPALACHIAN MOUNTAINS
Blue Ridge
Piedmont

Lake Champlain
Adirondack Mts.
Green Mts.
White Mts.
Gulf of Maine

Boston
Cape Cod

Lake Ontario
Niagara Falls

Connecticut
Hudson

Long Island
New York City

Philadelphia

Baltimore
Delaware Bay
Washington

Chesapeake Bay

ATLANTIC
OCEAN

Cape Hatteras

Mt. Mitchell
6,684 ft
2,037 m

Atlanta

Savannah

Black Belt

Red

Mississippi

COASTAL PLAIN

Jacksonville

Houston

New Orleans

Mississippi
River Delta

Gulf of Mexico

Cape Canaveral

Lake Okeechobee

The Everglades

Miami

Florida Keys

Straits of Florida

TROPIC OF CANCER

CUBA

UNITED STATES
PHYSICAL

0 mi   300
0 km   300

ALBERS CONIC EQUAL-AREA PROJECTION

NATIONAL GEOGRAPHIC

Niihau
Kauai
Oahu
Honolulu
Molokai
Lanai
Kahoolawe
Maui — 21°N

PACIFIC
OCEAN

Hawaii

Mauna Kea
13,796 ft
4,205 m

PRINCIPAL HAWAIIAN
ISLANDS

0 mi   100
0 km   100

N

9 10 11 12 13 14 15 16

Ellesmere
Island

Devon Island

GREENLAND
(KALAALLIT NUNAAT)
Den.

ICELAND

Baffin
Bay

Melville
Peninsula

Foxe
Basin

Baffin Island

NUNAVUT

Davis Strait

Southampton
Island

Hudson Strait

⊙ Iqaluit

Labrador

Sea

CANADA
PHYSICAL/POLITICAL

0 mi 400
0 km 400

AZIMUTHAL EQUIDISTANT PROJECTION

NATIONAL
GEOGRAPHIC

Ungava
Bay

H u d s o n

B a y

Belcher
Islands

James Bay

Schefferville

Smallwood
Reservoir

Cartwright

Happy Valley-
Goose Bay

"Churchill Falls"

NEWFOUNDLAND
AND LABRADOR

Island of
Newfoundland

QUEBEC

Manicouagan
Reservoir
Sept-Iles

Anticosti I.

⊙ St. John's
Avalon
Peninsula

St.-Pierre & Miquelon
Fr.

S H I E L D

ONTARIO

Lake
Nipigon

Rouyn-Noranda

Chicoutimi

Gaspe
Pen.

Gulf of
St. Lawrence

PRINCE
EDWARD
ISLAND

Cape Breton I.

ATLANTIC

Thunder
Bay
Lake
Superior

Sudbury

Quebec ⊙

Montreal

Ottawa ⊙

St. Lawrence

Fredericton ⊙

NEW
BRUNSWICK

Saint-John

⊙ Charlottetown

NOVA
SCOTIA

⊙ Halifax

Bay of Fundy

OCEAN

Lake
Huron

Toronto ⊙

Niagara Falls

London

L. Ontario

L. Erie

Lake Michigan

90°W 80°W 70°W 60°W

MIDDLE AMERICA
PHYSICAL/POLITICAL

0 mi   400

0 km   400

AZIMUTHAL EQUIDISTANT PROJECTION

NATIONAL GEOGRAPHIC

UNITED STATES

Tijuana
Mexicali

Sonoran Desert

30°N

BAJA CALIFORNIA

Gulf of California

Baja California

Ciudad Juárez

SONORA

CHIHUAHUA

Chihuahua

Rio Grande

COAHUILA

BAJA CALIFORNIA SUR

Nuevo Laredo

Sierra Madre Occidental

DURANGO

Monterrey

NUEVO LEON

Matamoros

Gulf of Mexico

La Paz

SINALOA

ZACATECAS

Sierra Madre Oriental

TAMAULIPAS

False Cape

Mazatlan

SAN LUIS POTOSI

20°N

NAYARIT

Ciudad Madero
Tampico

Cozumel Island

AGUASCALIENTES

San Luis Potosí

QUERETARO

Mérida

YUCATAN

Revillagigedo Islands
Mex.

Guadalajara

Leon

VERACRUZ

Yucatan Peninsula

JALISCO

HIDALGO

TLAXCALA

CAMPECHE

QUINTANA ROO

GUANAJUATO

Bay of Campeche

COLIMA

Mexico City

Orizaba
18,855 ft
+5,747 m

MICHOACAN

Popocatepetl
17,802 ft
5,426 m

PUEBLA

Veracruz

DISTRITO FEDERAL

TABASCO

Belize City

MEXICO

Sierra Madre del Sur

Isthmus of Tehuantepec

CHIAPAS

Belmopan

BELIZE

MORELOS

Acapulco

GUERRERO

OAXACA

Sierra Madre

Gulf of Honduras

Gulf of Tehuantepec

GUATEMALA

Guatemala

Tegucigalpa

HON

10°N

EL SALVADOR
San Salvador

Leon

CENTRAL

AMERICA

PACIFIC

OCEAN

Cocos Island
C.R.

0°

110°W

100°W

90°W

N

ATLANTIC

OCEAN

TROPIC OF CANCER

30°N

20°N

BAHAMAS

Freeport

Nassau

Andros Island

Straits of Florida

WEST INDI

Turks & Caicos Islands U.K.

ST. KITTS & NEVIS

ANTIGUA & BARBUDA

Havana

CUBA

Camaguey

Holguin

Santiago de Cuba

Isle of Youth

Cayman Islands U.K.

Santiago

HAITI

Port-au-Prince

Hispaniola

DOMINICAN REPUBLIC

Santo Domingo

San Juan

Puerto Rico U.S.

Virgin Islands U.S. & U.K.

Guadeloupe Fr.

DOMINICA

Bird I. Venez.

Martinique Fr.

ST. LUCIA

BARBADOS

ST. VINCENT & THE GRENADINES

Lesser Antilles

Greater Antilles

Montego Bay

JAMAICA

Kingston

Caribbean Sea

GRENADA

Neth.

Curacao

Bonaire

Aruba Neth.

TRINIDAD & TOBAGO

Port-of-Spain

Tobago

Trinidad

10°N

60°W

Lesser Antilles

DURAS

Coco

Mosquito Coast

NICARAGUA

Managua

Lake Nicaragua

COSTA

San Jose

RICA

Puerto Limon

Gulf of Mosquitos

Isthmus of Panama

Panama

PANAMA

David

Gulf of Panama

SOUTH

AMERICA

EQUATOR

0°

80°W

70°W

SOUTH AMERICA POLITICAL

C a r i b b e a n   S e a

80°W   60°W   50°W   40°W

A

N

10°N

Lake
Maracaibo
•Caracas

Orinoco
VENEZUELA   GUYANA
⊛Georgetown
Angel Falls   SURINAME
Total drop   ⊛Paramaribo
3,212 ft 979 m   Cayenne⊙
FRENCH
•Bogota   GUIANA
COLOMBIA   GUIANA   HIGHLANDS
Boundary claimed
by Suriname

ATLANTIC
OCEAN

B

Malpelo I.

Negro   Amazon   Marajo
0°   •Quito   Island   EQUATOR   0°
ECUADOR   A   M   A   Z   O   N

C

Amazon
Madeira
Tapajos
Xingu
S   e   l   v   a   s   Teles
B   A   S   I   N   Pires
Purus
Ucayali   Sao Francisco

D   B   R   A   Z   I   L   D
10°S   Lima⊛   Machu Picchu   B   R   A   Z   I   L   I   A   N   10°S
MATO GROSSO
Lake Titicaca   ⊛Brasilia
BOLIVIA   PLATEAU   H   I   G   H   L   A   N   D   S
•La Paz

E
⊛Sucre
Altiplano   Salar
de Uyuni   PARAGUAY   Iguazu
Falls
20°S   GRAN CHACO   ⊛Asuncion   20°S

F
TROPIC OF CAPRICORN   Paraguay
San Felix I.   San Ambrosio I.   Parana
Uruguay

G
Aconcagua   22,834 ft   Buenos   URUGUAY
6,960 m   Aires ⊛   ⊛Montevideo
30°S   Santiago⊛   Rio de la Plata   30°S
Juan Fernandez Is.   P   A   M   P   A   S

H
Negro
Chiloe Island   -131 ft   SOUTH
40°S   -40 m Valdes Peninsula   AMERICA   40°S
Gulf of   PHYSICAL
San Jorge   0 mi   800
Taitao   0 km   800
PACIFIC   Peninsula   AZIMUTHAL EQUIDISTANT PROJECTION

J
OCEAN   Wellington I.   Falkland Islands
(Islas Malvinas)   NATIONAL
⊙Stanley   GEOGRAPHIC
Strait of Magellan
Tierra del Fuego

K
50°S   Cape Horn   South Georgia I.   50°S

100°W   90°W   80°W   70°W   60°W   50°W   40°W   30°W   20°W
1   2   3   4   5   6   7

EUROPE
POLITICAL

0 mi   400
0 km   400

AZIMUTHAL EQUIDISTANT PROJECTION

NATIONAL GEOGRAPHIC

ICELAND
Akureyri
Reykjavík

ARCTIC CIRCLE

PRIME MERIDIAN (MERIDIAN OF GREENWICH)

Norwegian Sea

Tromso

NORWAY

Trondheim
Are
Alesund
Sundsvall
Bergen
Oslo
Uppsala
Stockholm

Faeroe Islands
Den.
Torshavn

Shetland
Islands
Lerwick

Rockall
U.K.

Isle of Lewis
Orkney Islands

Inverness

UNITED
SCOTLAND
Aberdeen
Glasgow
Edinburgh
NORTHERN
IRELAND
Belfast
IRELAND
Dublin
Irish
Sea
Liverpool
Manchester
KINGDOM
WALES
Birmingham
Cardiff
ENGLAND
London
Southampton

Cork

Celtic
Sea

Land's End

English Channel

Le Havre

Brest

Paris

Rennes

Stavanger

Skagerrak

North
Sea

DENMARK
Copenhagen

Kiel
Hamburg

The
Hague
Amsterdam
NETH.

Brussels
BELGIUM
LUX.
Bonn
Frankfurt

Berlin

GERMANY

Rhine

Goteborg
Gotland

Arhus
Malmo

Baltic

Gdansk

Bydgoszcz

POLAND
Lodz

Wroclaw

Prague
CZECH REP.
Bratislava
SLOVAKIA

Oder

ATLANTIC
OCEAN

Nantes

La Rochelle

Bay of
Biscay

Bordeaux

FRANCE

Strasbourg

Munich
Zurich
Bern
SWITZERLAND
Geneva
Lyon

LIECH.

Prague

Vienna
AUSTRIA
Budapest

ALPS

SLOVENIA
Ljubljana
Milan
Turin
Venice
Genoa

HUNGARY
Zagreb
CROATIA

BOSNIA &
HERZEGOVINA
Sarajevo

La Coruña
Vigo

Porto

Coimbra

Lisbon

Cape
St. Vincent

PORTUGAL

Donostia-
San Sebastian
Bilbao
Valladolid

Pyrenees

ANDORRA

Zaragoza

Madrid

SPAIN

Valencia

Cordoba

Seville
Cadiz
Malaga
GIBRALTAR
U.K.
Strait of Gibraltar

Toulouse

MONACO
Marseille
Nice

Corsica
Fr.

Palma

Murcia
Cartagena

Balearic
Islands
Sp.

Mediterranean

Sardinia
It.

Cagliari

SAN
MARINO

ITALY

Adriatic
Sea

VATICAN
CITY
Rome

Naples

MONTENEGRO
Podgorica

Tiranë
ALBANIA

Tyrrhenian
Sea

Ionian
Sea

Palermo
Sicily
Catania
Messina

Valletta
MALTA

AFRICA

A commonly accepted division between Asia and Europe—here marked by a gray line—is formed by the Ural Mountains, Ural River, Caspian Sea, Caucasus Mountains, and the Black Sea with its outlets, the Bosporus and the Dardanelles.

Barents Sea

Tobseda

ASIA

Europe-Asia boundary

Pechora

URAL MOUNTAINS

Murmansk
Kirovsk
Kola Peninsula
Umba
White Sea
Kem
Arkhangel'sk
Severodvinsk
Syktyvkar

Kiruna
Kemi
Lulea
Oulu
Umea
Vaasa
Kuopio
Pori
Tampere
Turku
Helsinki
LAPLAND
FINLAND
Bothnia
Ivalo

RUSSIA

Lake Onega
Lake Ladoga
St. Petersburg
Perm
Kirov
Ufa

Tallinn
ESTONIA
Velikiy Novgorod
Yaroslavl
Kazan
Orenburg

Riga
LATVIA
Daugavpils
Tver
Nizhniy Novgorod
Samara
Oral
KAZAKHSTAN

LITHUANIA
Vitsyebsk
Smolensk
Moscow
Ryazan
Volga
Saratov
Ural

RUSSIA
Kaunas
Vilnius
Minsk
Bryansk
Penza
BELARUS
Homyel
Kursk

Warsaw
Chernihiv
Sumy
Volgograd

Krakow
Kyiv (Kiev)
Kharkiv
Poltava
Astrakhan
Caspian Sea

Lviv
UKRAINE
Vinnytsya
Dniepropetrovsk
Donetsk
Rostov

Dniester
MOLDOVA
Chişinău
Odesa
Sea of Azov
Kerch
Stavropol
Grozny

Carpathian Mts.
ROMANIA
Crimea
Simferopol
Yalta
Sevastopol
Caucasus Mountains
GEORGIA
AZERBAIJAN
Baku

Belgrade
Bucharest
Constanta
Black Sea

SERBIA
Danube
Balkan Mts.
Varna

KOSOVO
BULGARIA
Sofia
Bosporus

Skopje
MACED.
Istanbul
TURKEY

Thessaloniki
Dardanelles
Sea of Marmara

GREECE
Aegean Sea
Athens
Peloponnesus

ASIA

Crete
Iraklio
Rhodes
Nicosia
CYPRUS

Sea

AFRICA
PHYSICAL

0 mi — 1000
0 km — 1000

AZIMUTHAL EQUIDISTANT PROJECTION

NATIONAL GEOGRAPHIC

EUROPE

ASIA

ATLANTIC OCEAN

Azores

Madeira Islands

Canary Islands

WESTERN SAHARA

Strait of Gibraltar

Algiers ⊛   Tunis ⊛
TUNISIA

Rabat ⊛
MOROCCO

⊛ Tripoli

Mediterranean Sea

ATLAS MOUNTAINS

ALGERIA

LIBYA

EGYPT

Cairo ⊛   *Sinai*

Suez Canal

Lake Nasser

TROPIC OF CANCER

S A H A R A

Ahaggar Mts.

Air

Tibesti

Libyan Desert

Red Sea

Nile

MAURITANIA

MALI

NIGER

CHAD

SUDAN

Boundary claimed by Sudan

Nouakchott ⊛

Khartoum ⊛

Asmara ⊛   ERITREA

DJIBOUTI ⊛
Djibouti ⊛

Gulf of Aden

Lake Assal -512 ft -156 m

Cape Verde
Dakar ⊛
SENEGAL
GAMBIA
Banjul ⊛
GUINEA-BISSAU
Bissau ⊛

Senegal

Bamako ⊛

BURKINA FASO

Niamey ⊛
Ouagadougou ⊛

Niger

N'Djamena ⊛

Lake Chad

Blue Nile

Lake Tana

Addis Ababa ⊛

ETHIOPIA

Boundary in dispute

SOMALIA

GUINEA
Conakry ⊛
SIERRA LEONE
Freetown ⊛
Yamoussoukro ⊛
Monrovia ⊛
LIBERIA
CÔTE D'IVOIRE
GHANA
Accra ⊛
Abidjan ⊛

UPPER GUINEA

BENIN
TOGO
Lomé ⊛
Porto-Novo ⊛

NIGERIA
Abuja ⊛

Malabo ⊛
EQUATORIAL GUINEA
SÃO TOMÉ & PRÍNCIPE
São Tomé ⊛

CAMEROON
Yaoundé ⊛

CENTRAL AFRICAN REPUBLIC

Bangui ⊛

White Nile

Lake Turkana

Mogadishu ⊛

INDIAN OCEAN

EQUATOR   0°

ATLANTIC OCEAN

Ascension Island

RIO MUNI
Libreville ⊛
GABON

LOWER GUINEA

Congo

CONGO

CONGO BASIN

DEM. REP. OF THE CONGO

CABINDA
Brazzaville ⊛
Kinshasa ⊛

Virunga Mts. 14,787 ft 4,507 m

Kigali ⊛
RWANDA
BURUNDI
Bujumbura ⊛

UGANDA
Kampala ⊛
Lake Victoria

KENYA
Nairobi ⊛

Kilimanjaro 19,340 ft 5,895 m

Great Rift Valley

Dodoma ⊛
TANZANIA
Dar es Salaam ⊛

Lake Tanganyika

SEYCHELLES

COMOROS
Moroni ⊛

Luanda ⊛

ANGOLA

Katanga Plateau

Zambezi

ZAMBIA

Lake Malawi

MALAWI
Lilongwe ⊛
Lusaka ⊛

MOZAMBIQUE

Mozambique Channel

MADAGASCAR
Antananarivo ⊛

Etosha Pan

Victoria Falls

Harare ⊛
ZIMBABWE

NAMIBIA

BOTSWANA

KALAHARI DESERT

Windhoek ⊛

Namib Desert

Gaborone ⊛

Drakensberg

Mbabane ⊛
Maputo ⊛
SWAZILAND

Tshwane (Pretoria) ⊛

Orange

SOUTH AFRICA

Bloemfontein ⊛
Maseru ⊛
LESOTHO

TROPIC OF CAPRICORN

Cape Town ⊛
Cape of Good Hope

Cape Agulhas

ATLANTIC OCEAN

ARCTIC

NORTH AMERICA

Norwegian Sea

ARCTIC CIRCLE

Franz Josef Land
Russ.

Barents Sea

Kara Sea

Gulf of Ob

Norilsk

EUROPE

A commonly accepted division
between Asia and Europe—here
marked by a gray line—is
formed by the Ural Mountains,
Ural River, Caspian Sea, Caucasus
Mountains, and the Black Sea
with its outlets, the Bosporus
and the Dardanelles.

⊛ Moscow

Europe-Asia
boundary

R   U   S   S   I   B

Ob

Ural

Mediterranean Sea

Istanbul

Black Sea

Ankara

TURKEY

Adana

LEBANON
Beirut ⊛
Damascus
⊛ SYRIA
Jerusalem
ISRAEL
Amman ⊛
JORDAN

Red Sea

Chelyabinsk
Omsk

Novosibirsk

Astana

KAZAKHSTAN

GEORGIA
Tbilisi ⊛
ARMENIA
Yerevan ⊛
AZERBAIJAN
Baku ⊛

Caucasus Mts.

Aral Sea

Syr Darya

Ili

Irtysh

Caspian Sea

TURKMENISTAN

UZBEKISTAN

Tashkent ⊛
Bishkek ⊛
KYRGYZSTAN
Almaty
Urumqi

SINKIANG

Euphrates

Tigris

Baghdad ⊛

IRAQ

Basra
KUWAIT
Kuwait ⊛

Tehran ⊛
Ashkhabad ⊛

IRAN

Amu Darya

Dushanbe ⊛
TAJIKISTAN

AFGHANISTAN
Kabul ⊛

Hindu Kush

KUNLUN

Himalaya

AFRICA

Jeddah
Makkah
(Mecca)

SAUDI

Riyadh ⊛
Manama
BAHRAIN
ARABIA   Doha
QATAR
Abu Dhabi ⊛
UNITED ARAB
EMIRATES

Rub al Khali

Sanaa ⊛
YEMEN

Aden

Gulf of Aden

Persian Gulf
(Arabian Gulf)

Zahedan ⊛

*Strait of
Hormuz*

Masqat ⊛

OMAN

Gulf of Oman

Islamabad ⊛
KASHMIR

Lahore

PAKISTAN

Karachi ⊛

Indus

Delhi
New Delhi ⊛
Jaipur

Boundary
claimed
by India

TIBET

NEPAL

Kathmandu ⊛
Thimphu
BHUTAN

Ganges

Indore
Bhopal

INDIA

Kolkata
(Calcutta)

Arabian Sea

Socotra
Yemen

Mumbai
(Bombay)

Godavari

Krishna

Hyderabad

*Bay
of
Bengal*

Bengaluru
(Bangalore)

Chennai
(Madras)

Lakshadweep
India

Madurai

SRI LANKA
Colombo ⊛

⊛ Male
MALDIVES

EQUATOR

I   N   D   I   A   N   O   C   E   A   N

Chagos Archipelago
Brit. Ind. Oc. Terr.

TROPIC
OF
CANCER

ASIA
POLITICAL

0 mi ────────────── 1000

0 km ────────────── 1000

TWO-POINT EQUIDISTANT PROJECTION

NATIONAL
GEOGRAPHIC

ASIA
PHYSICAL

0 mi — 1000

0 km — 1000

TWO-POINT EQUIDISTANT PROJECTION

NATIONAL GEOGRAPHIC

NORTH AMERICA

TROPIC OF CANCER

HAWAII
U.S.

Johnston Atoll
U.S.

N

P
O
L
Y
N
E
S
I
A

Kingman Reef
U.S.

Palmyra Atoll
U.S.

Howland Island
U.S.

Baker Island U.S.

KIRIBATI
Phoenix Is.

Line Islands

Kiritimati
(Christmas I.)

EQUATOR

Jarvis I.
U.S.

OCEANIA
PHYSICAL/POLITICAL

0 mi   1000

0 km
                 1000

MERCATOR PROJECTION

NATIONAL GEOGRAPHIC

TOKELAU
N.Z.

Wallis Is.
Fr.

SAMOA
Apia

AMERICAN
SAMOA
U.S.

Pago Pago

Samoa Is.

COOK ISLANDS
N.Z.

Marquesas Is.

Tuamotu Archipelago

TONGA

Niue

Tahiti
Papeete

Society Is.

FRENCH POLYNESIA
Fr.

Henderson I.
U.K.

Nukualofa

Austral Is.

TROPIC OF CAPRICORN

Pitcairn I.
U.K.

Ducie I.
U.K.

Kermadec
Islands
N.Z.

INTERNATIONAL DATE LINE

Chatham Islands
N.Z.

SOUTH PACIFIC OCEAN

MONDAY
SUNDAY

1 PM 2 PM 3 PM 4 PM 5 PM 6 PM 7 PM 8 PM 9 PM 10 PM 11 PM 12 AM

Franz Josef Land

ARCTIC OCEAN

Spitsbergen

Novyy Port

St. Petersburg

Yakutsk

Novosibirsk

Petropavlovsk Kamchatskiy

Aleutian Islands

NORTH PACIFIC OCEAN

Rome Istanbul

Tashkent

Baghdad

Kabul

Beijing

Vladivostok

Tokyo

Cairo

Makkah (Mecca)

Kolkata (Calcutta)

Hong Kong

INTERNATIONAL DATE LINE

Mumbai (Bombay)

Bangkok

Manila

Singapore

Marshall Is.

Kinshasa

Nairobi

INDIAN OCEAN

New Caledonia

Cape Town

Perth

Sydney

30°   60°   90°   120°   150°E   180°

ARCTIC OCEAN PHYSICAL

0 mi 800
0 km 800
AZIMUTHAL EQUIDISTANT PROJECTION

NATIONAL GEOGRAPHIC

RUSSIA

Ob
Yenisey
Gulf of Ob
White Sea
FINLAND
SWEDEN
NORWAY
GERMANY
LUX.
DENMARK NETH. BELGIUM FRANCE
North Sea
UNITED KINGDOM
IRELAND

Kara Sea
Barents Sea
Taymyr Peninsula
Novaya Zemlya
90°E
60°E
30°E
Svalbard
Norwegian Sea
ARCTIC CIRCLE
60°N
50°N

Lena
Laptev Sea
120°E
North Land
Franz Josef Land
0°
70°N
80°N
Greenland Sea
Denmark Strait
ICELAND
ATLANTIC OCEAN

New Siberian Islands
150°E
ARCTIC OCEAN
North Pole ★
Oodaaq Island
30°W
GREENLAND
Lincoln Sea

East Siberian Sea
180°
Queen
Ellesmere Island
Hayes Peninsula
60°W
Cape Farewell

Sea of Okhotsk
Wrangel Island
150°W
Elizabeth
90°W
Baffin Bay
Davis Strait

KAMCHATKA PENINSULA
120°W
Devon I.
Somerset I.
Baffin Island

Chukchi Sea
Islands
Melville Island
Prince of Wales I.
Boothia Peninsula
Melville Peninsula
Foxe Basin

Chukchi Peninsula
Bering Strait
Point Barrow
Banks Island
Victoria Island
Hudson Strait

Bering Sea
St. Lawrence Island
Seward Peninsula
North Slope
Brooks Range
Beaufort Sea
Southampton Island

Aleutian Islands
Nunivak Island
Yukon
ALASKA
Mackenzie
CANADA
Hudson Bay

PACIFIC OCEAN
Bristol Bay
Great Bear Lake

ANTARCTICA PHYSICAL

0 mi 600
0 km 600
AZIMUTHAL EQUIDISTANT PROJECTION

NATIONAL GEOGRAPHIC

SOUTH ATLANTIC OCEAN
60°W
60°S
South Orkney Is.
45°W
30°W
15°W
ANTARCTIC CIRCLE
0°
15°E
30°E
45°E
60°E

South Shetland Islands
ANTARCTIC PENINSULA
Weddell Sea
70°S
Ruser-Larsen Ice Shelf
Fimbul Ice Shelf
QUEEN MAUD LAND
ENDERBY LAND
INDIAN OCEAN

GRAHAM LAND
Larsen Ice Shelf
Mt. Jackson 13,747 ft 4,190 m
COATS LAND
75°E

SOUTH PACIFIC OCEAN
75°W
PALMER LAND
Alexander I.
Filchner Ice Shelf
Berkner Island
Ronne Ice Shelf
Amery Ice Shelf

Bellingshausen Sea
Vinson Massif 16,067 ft 4,897 m
Ellsworth Mts.
ANTARCTICA
AMERICAN HIGHLAND
West Ice Shelf

90°W
ELLSWORTH LAND
Polar Plateau
South Pole ★
TRANSANTARCTIC MOUNTAINS
EAST ANTARCTICA
90°E

Bentley Subglacial Trench -8,327 ft -2,538 m
WEST ANTARCTICA
105°E
Shackleton Ice Shelf

105°W
MARIE BYRD LAND
Ross Ice Shelf
Roosevelt I.
Dome Circe
WILKES LAND

120°W
VICTORIA LAND
INDIAN OCEAN

Ross I. Mt. Erebus 12,448 ft 3,794 m
135°W
Ross Sea
Talos Dome
120°E

135°E
150°W
165°W
180°
165°E
150°E

A WORLD OF EXTREMES

① The largest continent is Asia with an area of 12,262,691 sq. miles (31,758,898 sq. km).

② The smallest continent is Australia with an area of 2,988,888 sq. miles (7,741,184 sq. km).

③ The largest country is Russia with an area of 6,592,819 sq. miles (17,075,322 sq. km).

④ The smallest country is Vatican City with an area of 1 sq. mile (2.6 sq. km).

⑤ The longest river is the Nile River with a length of 4,160 miles (6,695 km).

⑥ The deepest freshwater lake is Lake Baikal with a maximum depth of 5,715 feet (1,742 m).

⑦ The highest waterfall is Angel Falls with a height of 3,212 feet (979 m).

⑧ The highest mountain is Mount Everest with a height of 29,028 feet (8,848 m) above sea level.

⑨ The largest desert is the Sahara with an area of 3,500,000 sq. miles (9,065,000 sq. km).

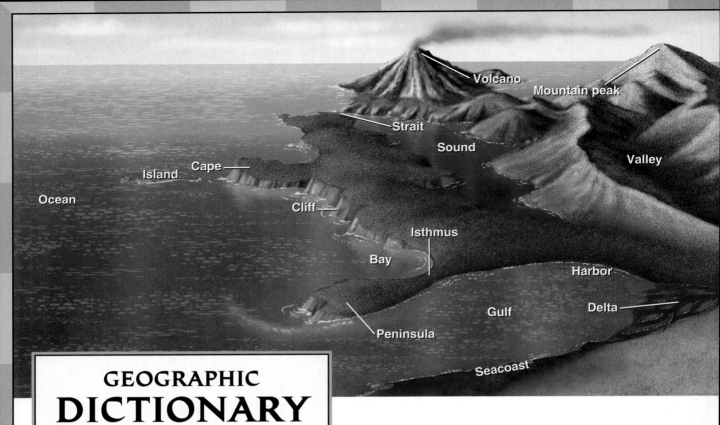

Volcano
Mountain peak
Strait
Sound
Valley
Island
Cape
Ocean
Cliff
Isthmus
Bay
Harbor
Peninsula
Gulf
Delta
Seacoast

GEOGRAPHIC DICTIONARY

As you read about the world's geography, you will encounter the terms listed below. Many of the terms are pictured in the diagram.

absolute location exact location of a place on the Earth described by global coordinates

basin area of land drained by a given river and its branches; area of land surrounded by lands of higher elevations

bay part of a large body of water that extends into a shoreline, generally smaller than a gulf

canyon deep and narrow valley with steep walls

cape point of land that extends into a river, lake, or ocean

channel wide strait or waterway between two landmasses that lie close to each other; deep part of a river or other waterway

cliff steep, high wall of rock, Earth, or ice

continent one of the seven large landmasses on the Earth

delta flat, low-lying land built up from soil carried downstream by a river and deposited at its mouth

divide stretch of high land that separates river systems

downstream direction in which a river or stream flows from its source to its mouth

elevation height of land above sea level

Equator imaginary line that runs around the Earth halfway between the North and South Poles; used as the starting point to measure degrees of north and south latitude

glacier large, thick body of slowly moving ice

gulf part of a large body of water that extends into a shoreline, generally larger and more deeply indented than a bay

harbor a sheltered place along a shoreline where ships can anchor safely

highland elevated land area such as a hill, mountain, or plateau

hill elevated land with sloping sides and rounded summit; generally smaller than a mountain

island land area, smaller than a continent, completely surrounded by water

isthmus narrow stretch of land connecting two larger land areas

lake a sizable inland body of water

latitude distance north or south of the Equator, measured in degrees

longitude distance east or west of the Prime Meridian, measured in degrees

lowland land, usually level, at a low elevation

Mountain range
Source of river
Channel
Glacier
Highland
Lake
Plateau
Hills
Mouth of river
Canyon
Desert
River
Upstream
Downstream
Plain
Lowland
Basin
Tributary

map drawing of the Earth shown on a flat surface

meridian one of many lines on the global grid running from the North Pole to the South Pole; used to measure degrees of longitude

mesa broad, flat-topped landform with steep sides; smaller than a plateau

mountain land with steep sides that rises sharply (1,000 feet or more) from surrounding land; generally larger and more rugged than a hill

mountain peak pointed top of a mountain

mountain range a series of connected mountains

mouth (of a river) place where a stream or river flows into a larger body of water

ocean one of the four major bodies of salt water that surround the continents

ocean current stream of either cold or warm water that moves in a definite direction through an ocean

parallel one of many lines on the global grid that circles the Earth north or south of the Equator; used to measure degrees of latitude

peninsula body of land jutting into a lake or ocean, surrounded on three sides by water

physical feature characteristic of a place occurring naturally, such as a landform, body of water, climate pattern, or resource

plain area of level land, usually at low elevation and often covered with grasses

plateau area of flat or rolling land at a high elevation, about 300 to 3,000 feet (90 to 900 m) high

Prime Meridian line of the global grid running from the North Pole to the South Pole at Greenwich, England; starting point for measuring degrees of east and west longitude

relief changes in elevation over a given area of land

river large natural stream of water that runs through the land

sea large body of water completely or partly surrounded by land

seacoast land lying next to a sea or an ocean

sound broad inland body of water, often between a coastline and one or more islands off the coast

source (of a river) place where a river or stream begins, often in highlands

strait narrow stretch of water joining two larger bodies of water

tributary small river or stream that flows into a large river or stream; a branch of the river

upstream direction opposite the flow of a river; toward the source of a river or stream

valley area of low land usually between hills or mountains

volcano mountain or hill created as liquid rock and ash erupt from inside the Earth

UNIT 1

The World

The world at night ▶

NATIONAL GEOGRAPHIC

World Atlas

The World
CLIMATE REGIONS

150°W 120°W 90°W 60°W 30°W

NORTH
AMERICA

ATLANTIC OCEAN

30°N

TROPIC OF CANCER

PACIFIC OCEAN

EQUATOR   0°

SOUTH
AMERICA

N
W   E
S

TROPIC OF CAPRICORN

30°S

ATLANTIC OCEAN

60°S   ANTARCTIC CIRCLE

Map Skills

1 **Place** What two climate zones are found in Antarctica?

2 **Regions** In general terms, how would you describe the world climate zones along the Equator?

ARCTIC OCEAN

30°E   60°E   90°E   120°E   150°E

EUROPE

ASIA

AFRICA

PACIFIC OCEAN

INDIAN OCEAN

AUSTRALIA

ANTARCTICA

Dry
Steppe
Desert
Midlatitude
Mediterranean
Humid subtropical
Marine west coast
Humid continental
Tropical
Tropical wet
Tropical dry
High latitude
Subarctic
Tundra
Ice cap

Highland (climate varies with elevation)

0   2,000 kilometers
0   2,000 miles
Winkel Tripel projection

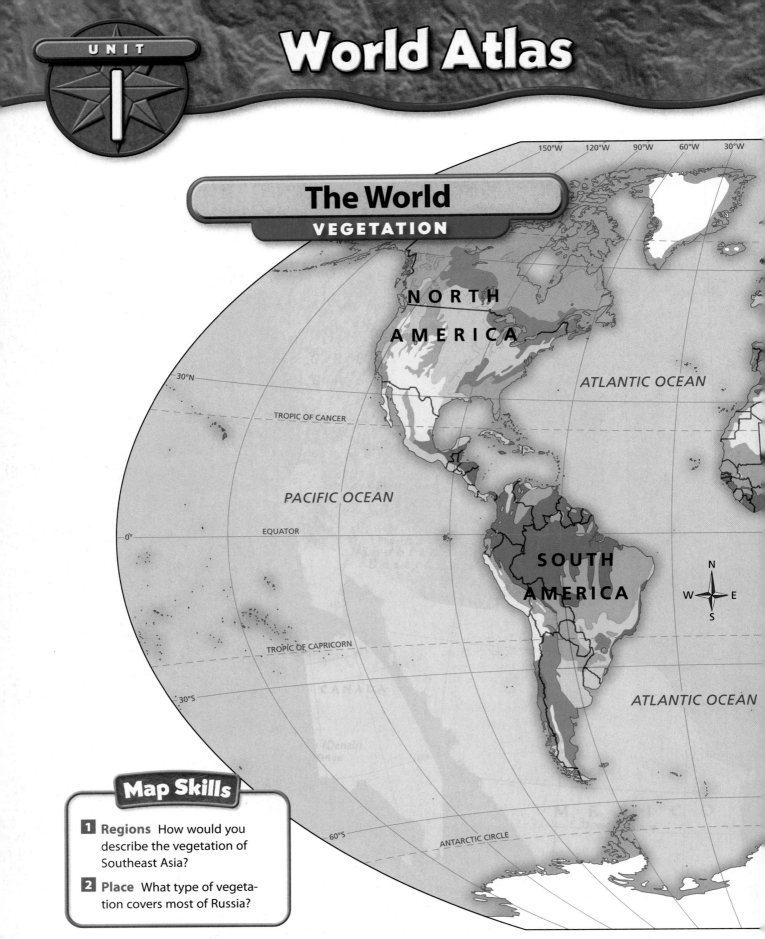

The World
VEGETATION

150°W   120°W   90°W   60°W   30°W

NORTH
AMERICA

ATLANTIC OCEAN

30°N

TROPIC OF CANCER

PACIFIC OCEAN

EQUATOR

0°

SOUTH
AMERICA

N
W   E
S

TROPIC OF CAPRICORN

30°S

ATLANTIC OCEAN

60°S

ANTARCTIC CIRCLE

Map Skills

1 **Regions** How would you describe the vegetation of Southeast Asia?

2 **Place** What type of vegetation covers most of Russia?

30°E 60°E 90°E 120°E 150°E

ARCTIC OCEAN

EUROPE

ASIA

AFRICA

PACIFIC OCEAN

INDIAN OCEAN

AUSTRALIA

Tropical rain forest
Tropical grassland (savanna)
Desert scrub and desert waste
Temperate grassland
Mediterranean scrub
Deciduous forest
Coniferous forest
Mixed forest (deciduous and coniferous)
Tundra
Ice cap
Highland (vegetation varies with elevation)

0   2,000 kilometers
0   2,000 miles
Winkel Tripel projection

ANTARCTICA

World Atlas

The World
POPULATION DENSITY

150°W   120°W   90°W   60°W   30°W

NORTH
AMERICA

Toronto

Chicago

New York

Lond

Madri

30°N

Los Angeles

ATLANTIC OCEAN

TROPIC OF CANCER

Mexico City

PACIFIC OCEAN

Caracas

Bogotá

EQUATOR

0°

SOUTH

Recife

N

Lima

AMERICA

W   E

S

Rio de
Janeiro

São
Paulo

TROPIC OF CAPRICORN

30°S

Santiago

Buenos
Aires

ATLANTIC OCEAN

60°S

ANTARCTIC CIRCLE

Map Skills

1 **Regions** What areas of the world are the most densely populated?

2 **Place** How are the population patterns of Australia and South America similar? How are they different?

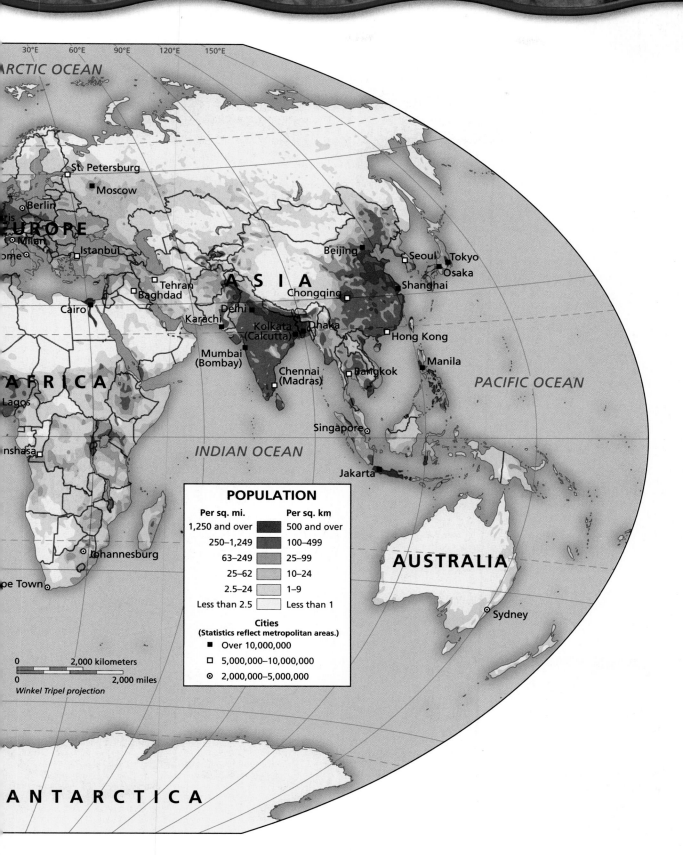

30°E 60°E 90°E 120°E 150°E

ARCTIC OCEAN

St. Petersburg

Moscow

Berlin

EUROPE

Paris

Milan

Rome

Istanbul

ASIA

Beijing

Seoul Tokyo
Osaka

Tehran

Baghdad

Chongqing

Shanghai

Cairo

Delhi

Karachi

Kolkata
(Calcutta)

Dhaka

Hong Kong

Mumbai
(Bombay)

Chennai
(Madras)

Bangkok

Manila

AFRICA

PACIFIC OCEAN

Lagos

Kinshasa

Singapore

INDIAN OCEAN

Jakarta

Johannesburg

AUSTRALIA

Cape Town

POPULATION

Per sq. mi.		Per sq. km
1,250 and over		500 and over
250–1,249		100–499
63–249		25–99
25–62		10–24
2.5–24		1–9
Less than 2.5		Less than 1

Cities
(Statistics reflect metropolitan areas.)
■ Over 10,000,000
□ 5,000,000–10,000,000
⊙ 2,000,000–5,000,000

Sydney

0 ___ 2,000 kilometers
0 ___ 2,000 miles
Winkel Tripel projection

ANTARCTICA

World Atlas

The World
RELIGIONS

150°W 120°W 90°W 60°W 30°W

NORTH
AMERICA

ATLANTIC OCEAN

30°N

TROPIC OF CANCER

PACIFIC OCEAN

EQUATOR   0°

SOUTH
AMERICA

N
W   E
S

TROPIC OF CAPRICORN

30°S

ATLANTIC OCEAN

60°S   ANTARCTIC CIRCLE

Map Skills

1 Place Where do you find the highest concentration of Hinduism?

2 Regions Compare the religions of Africa and North America.

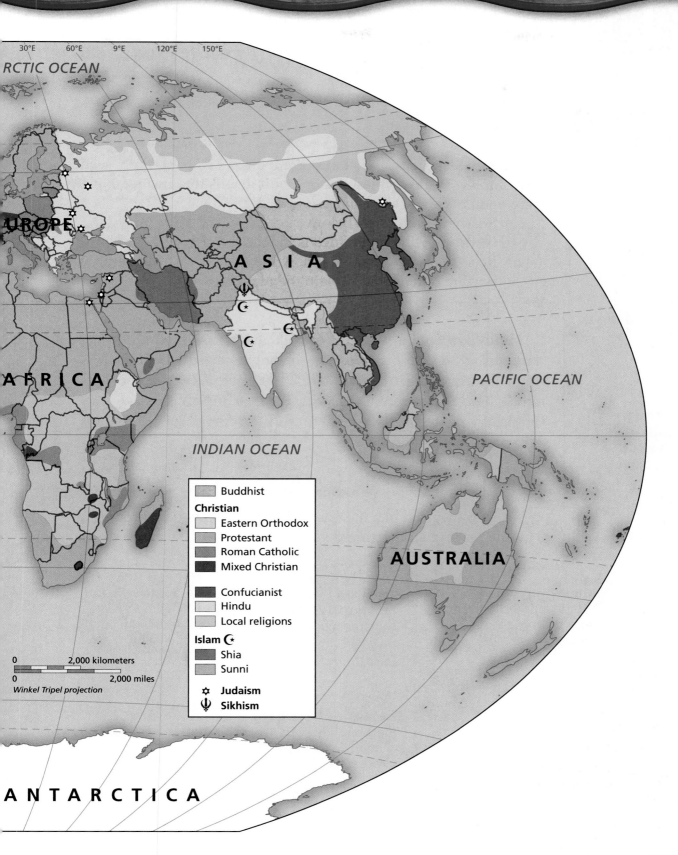

30°E 60°E 9°E 120°E 150°E

RCTIC OCEAN

EUROPE

ASIA

AFRICA

INDIAN OCEAN

PACIFIC OCEAN

AUSTRALIA

ANTARCTICA

Buddhist

Christian
Eastern Orthodox
Protestant
Roman Catholic
Mixed Christian

Confucianist
Hindu
Local religions

Islam ☪
Shia
Sunni

✡ **Judaism**
ੴ **Sikhism**

0   2,000 kilometers
0   2,000 miles
Winkel Tripel projection

Reading Social Studies

Identifying the Main Idea

Reading Skill

1 Learn It!

Main ideas are the most important ideas in a paragraph, section, or chapter. The examples, reasons, and details that further explain the main idea are called *supporting details*.

- Read the paragraph below.
- Notice how the main idea is identified for you.
- Read the sentences that follow the main idea. These are supporting details that explain the main idea.

Main Idea

Supporting Details

> Mountains are huge towers of rock and are the highest landforms. Some mountains may be only a few thousand feet high. Others can soar higher than 20,000 feet (6,096 m). The world's highest mountain is Mount Everest in South Asia's Himalaya ranges. It rises more than 29,028 feet (8,848 m), nearly five and a half miles high!
>
> —*from page 50*

A web diagram like the one below can help you record the main idea and supporting details.

Supporting Detail: Some mountains may be only a few thousand feet high.

Main Idea: Mountains are huge towers of rock and are the highest landforms.

Supporting Detail: Other mountains can soar higher than 20,000 feet (6,096 m).

Supporting Detail: The world's highest mountain, Mount Everest, rises more than 29,028 feet (8,848 m), nearly five and a half miles high.

Reading Tip

Main ideas often appear in the first sentence, but they can also be found in the middle or at the end of the paragraph.

2 Practice It!

Read the following paragraph from this unit.
- Draw a graphic organizer like the one shown below.
- Write the main idea for the paragraph in the center box.
- Write the supporting details in the ovals surrounding the box.

Remember that you do not need to include every word in the sentence when restating the main idea or supporting details.

Read to Write Activity

Read the main idea for Chapter 3, Section 2, and the paragraphs that follow. Using the main idea as a topic sentence, write a paragraph with supporting details. The supporting details should describe the elements that make up a culture.

People live on a surprisingly small part of the Earth. Land covers only about 30 percent of the Earth's surface, and only half of this land is usable by humans. Deserts, high mountains, and ice-covered lands cannot support large numbers of people.

—*from page 74*

Sparsely settled Mongolian plain ▶

Supporting Detail

Main Idea

Supporting Detail

Supporting Detail

3 Apply It!

Create several web diagrams like the ones found on these pages. As you read Chapters 1, 2, and 3, write the main idea for each section in the center box of the diagram. Write supporting details in ovals surrounding the center box. Use your diagrams to help you study for the chapter assessments.

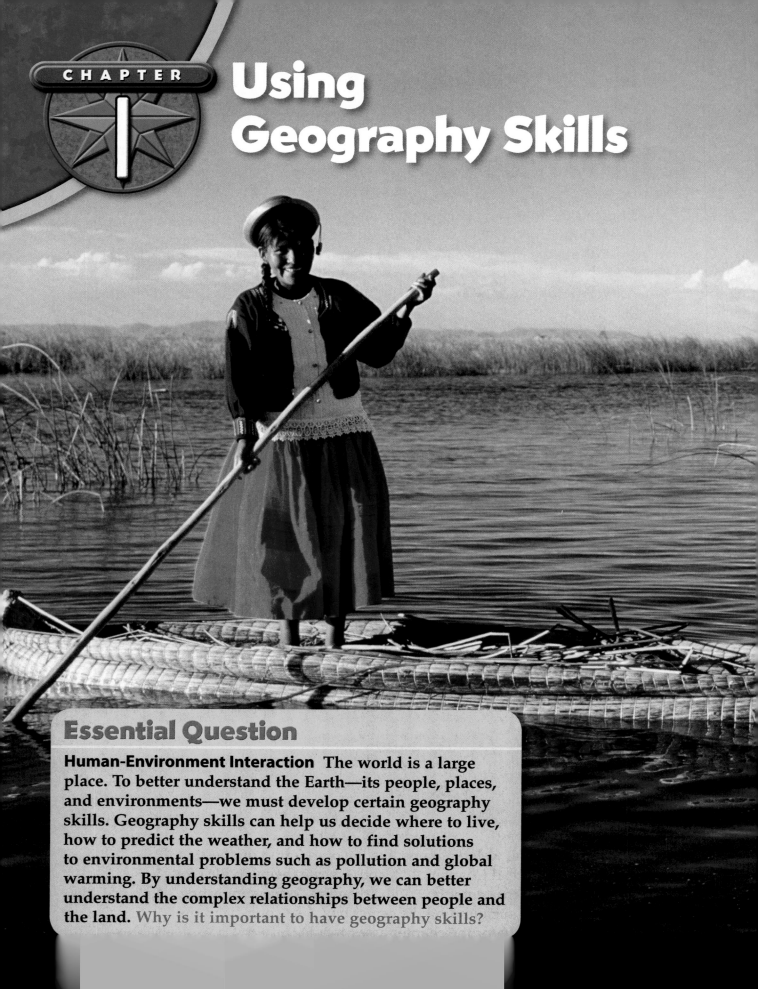

Using Geography Skills

Essential Question

Human-Environment Interaction The world is a large place. To better understand the Earth—its people, places, and environments—we must develop certain geography skills. Geography skills can help us decide where to live, how to predict the weather, and how to find solutions to environmental problems such as pollution and global warming. By understanding geography, we can better understand the complex relationships between people and the land. Why is it important to have geography skills?

BIG Ideas

Section 1: Thinking Like a Geographer

BIG IDEA Geography is used to interpret the past, understand the present, and plan for the future.
Geography is the study of the Earth. It is used to analyze the Earth's physical and human features. People can use geographic information to plan, make decisions, and manage resources.

◀ Lake Titicaca, Peru

Section 2: The Earth in Space

BIG IDEA Physical processes shape Earth's surface.
Earth has different seasons because of the way it tilts and the way it rotates around the sun. The warmth of the sun's rays makes life on Earth possible.

FOLDABLES™
Study Organizer

Organizing Information Make this Foldable to help you organize information about the uses of geography and about the Earth in space.

Step 1 Fold the sides of an 11x17 sheet of paper to meet in the middle, creating a shutter fold.

Step 2 Label your Foldable as shown.

Thinking Like a Geographer | The Earth in Space

Reading and Writing As you read the chapter, take notes under the appropriate flap of your Foldable. After you have completed your Foldable, use your notes to write a letter encouraging the study of geography by all students.

Social Studies ONLINE
To preview Chapter 1, go to glencoe.com.

Guide to Reading

BIG Idea

Geography is used to interpret the past, understand the present, and plan for the future.

Content Vocabulary

- geography *(p. 15)*
- absolute location *(p. 15)*
- relative location *(p. 15)*
- environment *(p. 15)*
- decade *(p. 16)*
- century *(p. 16)*
- millennium *(p. 16)*
- Global Positioning System (GPS) *(p. 17)*
- Geographic Information Systems (GIS) *(p. 17)*

Academic Vocabulary

- theme *(p. 15)*
- physical *(p. 15)*

Reading Strategy

Identifying Use a chart like the one below to identify two examples for each topic.

Themes of Geography
1.
2.
Types of Geography
1.
2.
Geographer's Tools
1.
2.

Thinking Like a Geographer

Picture This The Italian Research Center, also known as the Pyramid, allows researchers from around the world to study everything from the effects of altitude on humans to the impact of global warming on the Earth. The Pyramid is located at the base of Mount Everest in Nepal. It is completely self-contained and can house up to 20 people. To get to the Pyramid, scientists have to trek through a national park and allow their bodies time to adjust to the extremely high altitude. To learn more about how geographers use information about the world to plan for the future, read Section 1.

▼ **Research on Mount Everest**

The Five Themes of Geography

Main Idea Geographers use the Five Themes of Geography to help them study the Earth.

Geography and You Suppose a teacher tells you to pick a topic for a research paper. How do you organize your ideas? Read to discover how geographers use themes to help them organize ideas about geography.

Geography is the study of the Earth and its people. People who study geography are geographers. Geographers use five **themes,** or topics, to describe places and people. These themes are location, place, human-environment interaction, movement, and regions.

Location

Location is the position of a place on the Earth's surface. Geographers describe location in two ways. **Absolute location** is the exact spot on Earth where a geographic feature, such as a city or mountain, is found. **Relative location** describes where that feature is in relation to the features around it.

Place

Place describes the characteristics of a location that make it unique, or different. A place can be defined by **physical** features, such as landforms, plants, animals, and weather patterns. Other characteristics of a place describe the people who live there— such as what languages they speak.

Human-Environment Interaction

Human-environment interaction describes how people affect their **environment,** or natural surroundings, and how their environment affects them. People affect the environment by using or changing it to

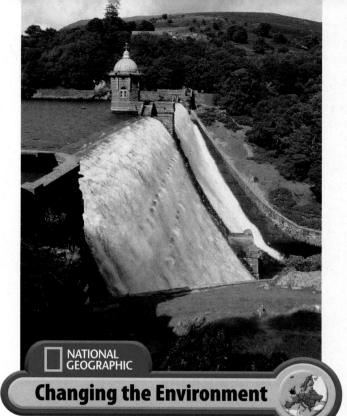

NATIONAL GEOGRAPHIC

Changing the Environment

Dams, like this one in Wales, can be built to control flooding, manage water flow, and supply electricity. **Human-Environment Interaction** How and why do people affect the environment?

meet their needs. Environmental factors that people cannot control, such as temperature and natural disasters, influence how people live.

Movement

Movement explains how and why people, ideas, and goods move from place to place. For example, people might leave a country that is involved in a war. Such movements can lead to great cultural change.

Regions

Regions refers to areas of the Earth's surface that have several common characteristics, such as land, natural resources, or population. For example, the alpine region in Europe is a large area known for mining and supplying hydroelectric power.

Reading Check **Explaining** Explain the difference between *place* and *location*.

A Geographer's Tools

Main Idea Geographers use many different tools to help them study and analyze Earth's people and places.

Geography and You Suppose a company wanted to build a new shopping center in your community. How would its managers know where to build it? Read to find out how geographers help make such decisions.

Geographers study the physical and human features of Earth. They rely on various tools to study people and places.

Types of Geography

When geographers study physical geography, they examine Earth's land areas, bodies of water, plant life, and other physical features. Physical geographers also study natural resources that are available in an area and the ways people use those resources. They help people make decisions about managing different types of resources such as water, forests, land, and even the wind.

Other geographers study human geography, focusing on people and their activities. Human geographers look at people's religions, languages, and ways of life. They may examine a specific location, or they may study entire countries or continents. They also compare different places to see how they are similar and different. Human geographers help plan cities and aid in international business.

Places in Time

Geographers use knowledge from other subject areas. History, for example, helps them understand how places appeared in the past. Geographers learn about places by studying the changes that have occurred over time.

NATIONAL GEOGRAPHIC

Using Geography

Surveyors, like this woman in Canada, use specialized equipment to measure land areas. ***Human-Environment Interaction*** **What tasks might geographers hired by the government carry out?**

History is divided into blocks of time known as periods. For example, a period of 10 years is called a **decade.** A period of 100 years is known as a **century.** A period of 1,000 years is a **millennium.**

In Western societies, it is common to group history into four long periods. The first of these periods is called Prehistory. Prehistory refers to the time before people developed writing, about 5,500 years ago. This time is followed by the period known as Ancient History, which lasted until about 1,500 years ago. The next thousand years is called the Middle Ages, or the medieval period. About 500 years ago, Modern History began and continues to the present.

Map Systems

Maps can provide geographers with different types of information about a place. Information for a map can be collected by using modern technology, or tools and methods that help people perform tasks. Satellites circling the Earth provide detailed digital images and photographs to create maps. Satellites can also measure changing temperatures and the amount of pollution in the air or land. This information can then be added to maps.

Another group of satellites makes up the **Global Positioning System (GPS)**. This system uses radio signals to determine the exact location of places on Earth. Hikers use GPS equipment to avoid getting lost. GPS is now built into some cars.

Geographic Information Systems (GIS) are computer hardware and software that gather, store, and analyze geographic information and then display it on a screen. It can display maps, but it also can show information that does not usually appear on maps, such as types of vegetation, types of soil, and even water quality.

Careers in Geography

Governments at all levels hire geographers for many kinds of tasks. Geographers help decide how land and resources might be used. For example, they analyze population trends, including why people live in certain areas and not in others.

In the business world, geographers often work as researchers and analysts. They can help companies decide where to locate new buildings. They also provide information about places and cultures where companies do business. Many geographers teach in high schools, colleges, and universities. As more schools recognize the importance of geography education, the demand for geography teachers is expected to grow.

✓ **Reading Check** **Explaining** How does modern technology make maps more precise?

Section Review

Social Studies ONLINE
Study Central™ To review this section, go to glencoe.com.

Vocabulary

1. **Explain** the significance of:
   a. geography
   b. absolute location
   c. relative location
   d. environment
   e. decade
   f. century
   g. millennium
   h. Global Positioning System (GPS)
   i. Geographic Information Systems (GIS)

Main Ideas

2. **Explaining** Use a web diagram like the one below to summarize information about the Five Themes of Geography.

Five Themes

3. **Contrasting** How is physical geography different from human geography?

Critical Thinking

4. **Drawing Conclusions** Describe how helpful you think GIS would be in deciding where to build a gas station.

5. **BIG Idea** What factors might influence where a city would develop?

6. **Challenge** Give three examples of how someone might use geography to plan for the future.

Writing About Geography

7. **Using Your FOLDABLES** Use your Foldable to write a paragraph that describes the uses of geography.

Geography Skills Handbook

How Do I Study Geography?

Geographers have created these broad categories and standards as tools to help you understand the relationships among people, places, and environments.

- **5 Themes of Geography**
- **6 Essential Elements**
- **18 Geography Standards**

5
Themes of Geography

1 Location

Location describes where something is. Absolute location describes a place's exact position on the Earth's surface. Relative location expresses where a place is in relation to another place.

2 Place

Place describes the physical and human characteristics that make a location unique.

3 Regions

Regions are areas that share common characteristics.

4 Movement

Movement explains how and why people and things move and are connected.

5 Human-Environment Interaction

Human-Environment Interaction describes the relationship between people and their environment.

6
Essential Elements

18
Geography Standards

I. The World in Spatial Terms
Geographers look to see where a place is located. Location acts as a starting point to answer "Where Is It?" The location of a place helps you orient yourself as to where you are.

1 How to use maps and other tools

2 How to use mental maps to organize information

3 How to analyze the spatial organization of people, places, and environments

II. Places and Regions
Place describes physical characteristics such as landforms, climate, and plant or animal life. It might also describe human characteristics, including language and way of life. Places can also be organized into regions. **Regions** are places united by one or more characteristics.

4 The physical and human characteristics of places

5 How people create regions to interpret Earth's complexity

6 How culture and experience influence people's perceptions of places and regions

III. Physical Systems
Geographers study how physical systems, such as hurricanes, volcanoes, and glaciers, shape the surface of the Earth. They also look at how plants and animals depend upon one another and their surroundings for their survival.

7 The physical processes that shape Earth's surface

8 The distribution of ecosystems on Earth's surface

9 The characteristics, distribution, and migration of human populations

10 The complexity of Earth's cultural mosaics

IV. Human Systems
People shape the world in which they live. They settle in certain places but not in others. An ongoing theme in geography is the movement of people, ideas, and goods.

11 The patterns and networks of economic interdependence

12 The patterns of human settlement

13 The forces of cooperation and conflict

14 How human actions modify the physical environment

V. Environment and Society
How does the relationship between people and their natural surroundings influence the way people live? Geographers study how people use the environment and how their actions affect the environment.

15 How physical systems affect human systems

16 The meaning, use, and distribution of resources

VI. The Uses of Geography
Knowledge of geography helps us understand the relationships among people, places, and environments over time. Applying geographic skills helps you understand the past and prepare for the future.

17 How to apply geography to interpret the past

18 How to apply geography to interpret the present and plan for the future

Understanding the **BIG Ideas** of Geography

The 15 Big Ideas will help you understand the information in *Exploring Our World: People, Places, and Cultures.* The Big Ideas are based on the Essential Elements and the Geography Standards. They help you organize important ideas, and they make it easier to understand patterns and relationships.

The World in Spatial Terms

- Geographers study how people and physical features are distributed on Earth's surface.

Places and Regions

- Places reflect the relationship between humans and the physical environment.
- Geographers organize the Earth into regions that share common characteristics.
- Culture influences people's perceptions about places and regions.

Physical Systems

- Physical processes shape Earth's surface.
- All living things are dependent upon one another and their surroundings for survival.

Human Systems

- The characteristics and movement of people impact physical and human systems.
- Culture groups shape human systems.
- Patterns of economic activities result in global interdependence.
- Geographic factors influence where people settle.
- Cooperation and conflict among people have an effect on the Earth's surface.

Environment and Society

- People's actions can change the physical environment.
- The physical environment affects how people live.
- Changes occur in the use and importance of natural resources.

The Uses of Geography

- Geography is used to interpret the past, understand the present, and plan for the future.

The World in Spatial Terms: Maps help you locate places on Earth's surface.

Physical Systems: Physical processes, such as hurricanes, shape the face of the Earth.

Human Systems: Technology impacts people and economies.

Environment and Society: Recycling is a choice people make to protect Earth's physical environment.

Using the BIG Ideas of Geography

You can find the Big Ideas throughout *Exploring Our World: People, Places, and Cultures*.

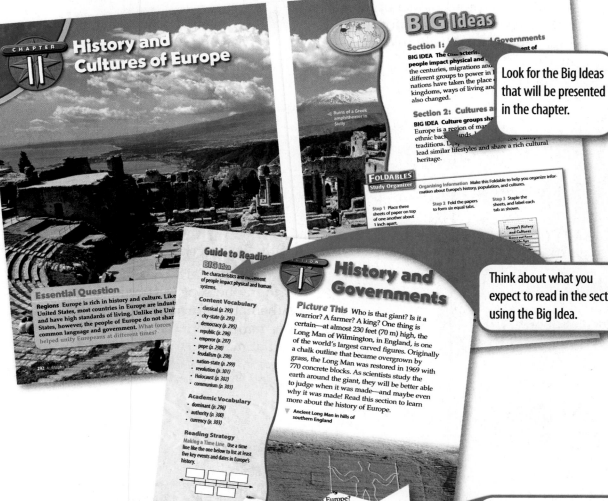

CHAPTER 11

History and Cultures of Europe

Ruins of a Greek amphitheater in Sicily

Essential Question

Regions Europe is rich in history and culture. Like the United States, most countries in Europe are industrialized and have high standards of living. Unlike the United States, however, the people of Europe do not share a common language and government. What forces have helped unify Europeans at different times?

292 · Chapter 11

BIG Ideas

Section 1: History and Governments

BIG IDEA The characteristics and movement of people impact physical and human systems. Over the centuries, migrations and wars brought different groups to power in Europe. Over time, nations have taken the place of early empires and kingdoms, ways of living and doing business also changed.

Section 2: Cultures and Lifestyles

BIG IDEA Culture groups share attitudes. Europe is a region of many peoples and ethnic backgrounds. Despite differences, Europeans lead similar lifestyles and share a rich cultural heritage.

> Look for the Big Ideas that will be presented in the chapter.

FOLDABLES
Study Organizer

Organizing Information Make this Foldable to help you organize information about Europe's history, population, and cultures.

Step 1 Place three sheets of paper on top of one another about 1 inch apart.

Step 2 Fold the papers to form six equal tabs.

Step 3 Staple the sheets, and label each tab as shown.

Europe's History and Cultures

Guide to Reading

BIG Idea
The characteristics and movement of people impact physical and human systems.

Content Vocabulary
- classical (p. 295)
- city-state (p. 295)
- democracy (p. 295)
- republic (p. 296)
- emperor (p. 297)
- pope (p. 298)
- feudalism (p. 298)
- nation-state (p. 299)
- revolution (p. 301)
- Holocaust (p. 302)
- communism (p. 303)

Academic Vocabulary
- dominant (p. 296)
- authority (p. 300)
- currency (p. 303)

Reading Strategy
Making a Time Line Use a time line like the one below to list at least five key events and dates in Europe's history.

SECTION 1

History and Governments

Picture This Who is that giant? Is it a warrior? A farmer? A king? One thing is certain—at almost 230 feet (70 m) high, the Long Man of Wilmington, in England, is one of the world's largest carved figures. Originally a chalk outline that became overgrown by grass, the Long Man was restored in 1969 with 770 concrete blocks. As scientists study the earth around the giant, they will be better able to judge when it was made—and maybe even why it was made! Read this section to learn more about the history of Europe.

▽ **Ancient Long Man in hills of southern England**

> Think about what you expect to read in the section using the Big Idea.

...and art... ...gion influ... ...n Europe?

Social Studies ONLINE
Study Central™ To review this section, go to glencoe.com.

Section 2 Review

Vocabulary

1. Explain how the terms *ethnic group, welfare state, fertility rate, urbanization,* and *secular* relate to Europe's population by writing a sentence containing each word.

Main Ideas

2. **Explaining** How do individual European countries deal with immigration?

3. **Describing** How does Europe's generally high level of education affect life there?

4. **Identifying** Use a chart like the one below to identify Europe's major religions, including the major forms of Christianity, and where each religion is generally located in Europe.

Major Religion	Where Found

Critical Thinking

5. **Challenge** Will immigration... ...t Europe in the future? Explain your... ...er.

6. **Drawing Conclusions** W...t factors have slowed economic deve...ment in certain areas of Europe?

7. **BIG Idea** What factors help unify Europe's different ethnic groups today?

Writing About Geography

8. **Expository Writing** Write a paragraph comparing European and American cultures.

> Use the section's Big Idea to help you answer assessment questions.

312 · Chapter 11

Globes and Maps

What Is a Globe? ▶

A **globe** is a round model of the Earth that shows its shape, landforms, and directions as they truly relate to one another.

◄ What Is a Map?

A **map** is a flat drawing of all or part of the Earth's surface. Cartographers, or mapmakers, use mathematical formulas to transfer information from the round globe to a flat map.

Globes and Maps ▶

Globes and maps serve different purposes, and each has advantages and disadvantages.

	Advantages	**Disadvantages**
Globes	• Represent true land shape, distances, and directions	• Cannot show detailed information • Difficult to carry
Maps	• Show small areas in great detail • Display different types of information, such as population densities or natural resources • Transport easily	• **Distort,** or change, the accuracy of shapes and distances

Map Projections

When the Earth's surface is flattened on a map, big gaps open up. Mapmakers stretch parts of the Earth to show either the correct shapes of places or their correct sizes. Mapmakers have developed different projections, or ways of showing the Earth on a flat piece of paper. Below are different map projections.

Goode's Interrupted Equal-Area Projection ▼

A map with this projection shows continents close to their true shapes and sizes. This projection is helpful to compare land area among continents.

Robinson Projection ▼

The Robinson projection has minor distortions. Continents and oceans are close to their sizes and shapes, but the North and South Poles appear flattened.

Mercator Projection ▼

The Mercator projection shows land shapes fairly accurately but not size or distance. Areas that are located far from the Equator are quite distorted. The Mercator projection shows true directions, however, making it useful for sea travel.

Winkel Tripel Projection ▼

This projection gives a good overall view of the continents' shapes and sizes. Land areas are not as distorted near the poles as they are in the Robinson projection.

Skills Practice

1 **Comparing and Contrasting** Explain similarities and differences between globes and maps.

2 **Describing** Why do map projections distort some parts of the Earth?

Location

To locate places on Earth, geographers use a system of imaginary lines that crisscross the globe. These lines are called *latitude* and *longitude*.

Latitude ▶

- Lines of **latitude** are imaginary circles that run east to west around the globe. They are known as *parallels*. These parallels divide the globe into units called degrees.

- The **Equator** circles the middle of the Earth like a belt. It is located halfway between the North and South Poles. The Equator is 0° latitude.

- The letter *N* or *S* that follows the degree symbol tells you if the location is north or south of the Equator. The North Pole, for example, is 90°N (north) latitude, and the South Pole is at 90°S (south) latitude.

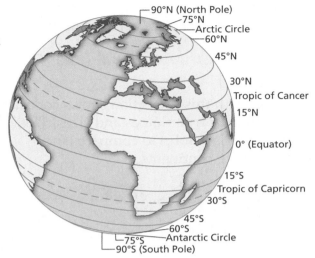

◀ Longitude

- Lines of **longitude,** also known as *meridians*, run from the North Pole to the South Pole. The **Prime Meridian** (also called the Meridian of Greenwich) is 0° longitude and runs through Greenwich, England.

- The letter *E* or *W* that follows the degree symbol tells you if the location is east or west of the Prime Meridian.

- On the opposite side of the Earth is the 180° meridian, also known as the International Date Line.

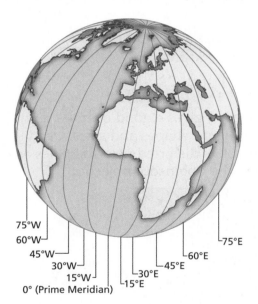

Absolute Location ▶

A place's exact location can be identified when you use both latitude and longitude. For example, Tokyo, Japan, is 36°N latitude and 140°E longitude.

Hemispheres

The Equator divides the Earth into Northern and Southern Hemispheres. Everything north of the Equator is in the Northern Hemisphere. Everything south of the Equator is in the Southern Hemisphere.

Northern Hemisphere   **Southern Hemisphere**

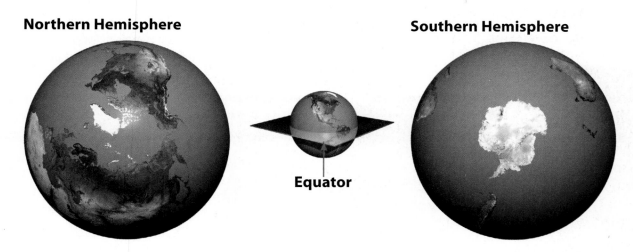

Equator

The Prime Meridian divides the Earth into Eastern and Western Hemispheres. Everything east of the Prime Meridian for 180 degrees is in the Eastern Hemisphere. Everything west of the Prime Meridian for 180 degrees is in the Western Hemisphere.

Eastern Hemisphere   **Western Hemisphere**

Prime Meridian

Skills Practice

1 **Identifying** What country is located at 30°S and 120°E?

2 **Analyzing Visuals** In which hemispheres is Europe located?

Parts of a Map

Title
The title tells you what information the map is showing.

Key
The key explains the symbols, colors, and lines on the map. The key is also called a *legend*.

Scale Bar
A measuring line, often called a **scale bar,** helps you figure distance on the map. The map scale shows the relationship between map measurements and actual distances on the Earth.

NATIONAL GEOGRAPHIC

Figure 2 **Europe: Political**

Boundary Lines
Boundary lines show the extent of an area's territory or political influence.

Compass Rose
The compass rose is a symbol that tells you where the **cardinal directions**—north, south, east, and west—are positioned.

Cities
Cities are symbolized by a solid circle (●). This symbol is found in the key and on the map.

Capitals
Capitals are symbolized by a star (✪). This symbol is found in the key and on the map.

Using Scale

All maps are drawn to a certain **scale.** The scale of a map is the size of the map compared to the size of the actual land surface. Thus, the scale of a map varies with the size of the area shown.

Small-Scale Maps ▼

A small-scale map, like this political map of Mexico, shows a large land area but little detail.

Large-Scale Maps ▼

A large-scale map, like this map of Mexico City, shows a small land area with a great amount of detail.

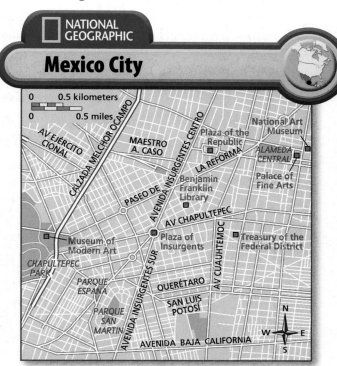

How Do I Use a Scale Bar?

Use the scale bar to find actual distances on a map. The scale bar tells you how many kilometers or miles are represented in that length. You can use a ruler, then, to calculate distances based on the scale bar's length.

About ½ of an inch equals 300 miles. A little more than ½ of a centimeter is equal to 300 kilometers.

Skills Practice

1 Defining What is scale?

2 Contrasting What is the difference between a small-scale map and a large-scale map?

3 Identifying What are the four cardinal directions?

4 Describing Would you use a small-scale or a large-scale map to plan a car trip across the United States? Why?

Types of Maps

General Purpose Maps

Maps are amazingly useful tools. You can use them to show information and to make connections between seemingly unrelated topics. Geographers use many different types of maps. Maps that show a wide range of information about an area are called **general purpose maps.** Two of the most common general purpose maps are physical maps and political maps.

Physical Maps ▼

Physical maps call out landforms and water features. The map key explains what each color and symbol stands for.

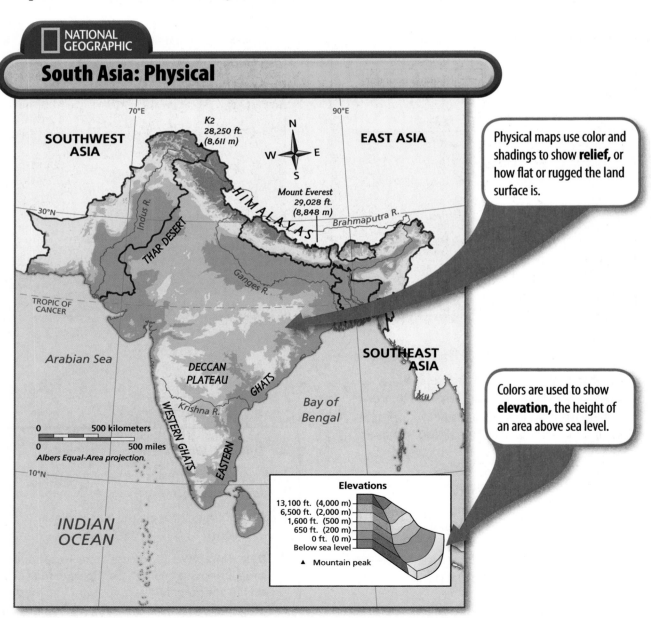

Physical maps use color and shadings to show **relief,** or how flat or rugged the land surface is.

Colors are used to show **elevation,** the height of an area above sea level.

Political Maps ▼

Political maps show the names and political boundaries of countries, along with human-made features such as cities or transportation routes.

NATIONAL GEOGRAPHIC

South Asia: Political

SOUTHWEST ASIA

Peshawar

Islamabad

EAST ASIA

Indus R.

30°N

BHUTAN

New Delhi

Brahmaputra R.

NEPAL

Kathmandu

Thimphu

PAKISTAN

Jaipur

Ganges R.

BANGLADESH

Karachi

TROPIC OF CANCER

Bhopal

Kolkata (Calcutta)

Dhaka

Arabian Sea

Mumbai (Bombay)

I N D I A

SOUTHEAST ASIA

⊕ National capital

● Major city

Krishna R.

Bay of Bengal

Bengaluru (Bangalore)

10°N

SRI LANKA

INDIAN OCEAN

Colombo

0   500 kilometers
0   500 miles
Albers Equal-Area projection

Male

MALDIVES

Solid lines outline political boundaries.

Major cities are shown on political maps.

Political maps can include major physical features such as bodies of water and mountains.

Capital cities are identified on political maps.

Skills Practice

1 Defining What is elevation?

2 Describing What type of map would you use to find the capital of a country?

Types of Maps

Special Purpose Maps

Some maps are made to present specific types of information. These are called **thematic** or **special purpose maps.** These maps usually show specific topics in detail. Special purpose maps may include information about:

- climate
- vegetation
- natural resources
- population density
- historical expansion

Look at some of the types of special purpose maps on these pages. The map's title is especially important for a special purpose map because it tells you the type of information that is being presented. Colors and symbols in the map key are also important tools to use when you read these types of maps.

Historical Maps ▼

Historical maps show events that occurred in a region over time. On the map below, you can see where Europeans settled on the North American continent in the past.

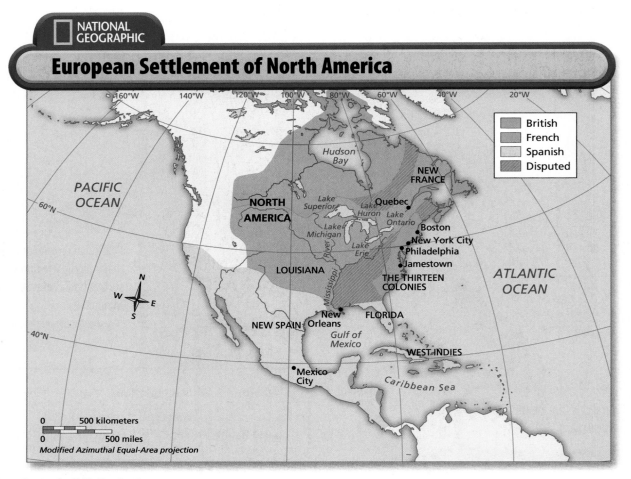

Contour Maps ▶

A contour map has **contour lines**—one line for each major level of elevation. All the land at the same elevation is connected by a line. These lines usually form circles or ovals—one inside the other. If contour lines are close together, the surface is steep. If the lines are spread apart, the land is flat or rises gradually.

NATIONAL GEOGRAPHIC

Sri Lanka: Contour

NATIONAL GEOGRAPHIC

Africa South of the Sahara: Vegetation

◀ **Vegetation Maps**

Vegetation maps are special purpose maps that show the different types of plants that are found in a region.

Skills Practice

1 Identifying What type of special purpose map might show battles during World War II?

2 Contrasting What is the difference between a general purpose map and a special purpose map?

Graphs, Charts, and Diagrams

Graphs

Graphs present and summarize information visually. Each part of a graph provides useful information. To read a graph, follow these steps:

- Read the graph's title to find out its subject.
- To understand bar and line graphs, read the labels along the **axes**—the vertical line along the left side of the graph and the horizontal line along the bottom of the graph. One axis will tell you what is being measured. The other axis tells you what units of measurement are being used.

Types of Graphs

There are many types of graphs. Listed below and on the next page are the types of graphs you will find in this textbook.

Bar Graphs ▶

Graphs that use bars or wide lines to compare data visually are called bar graphs.

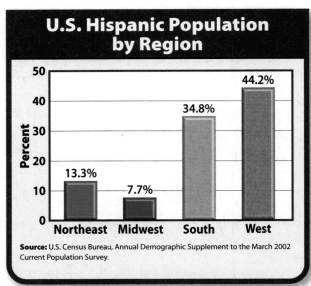

U.S. Hispanic Population by Region

Percent

- Northeast 13.3%
- Midwest 7.7%
- South 34.8%
- West 44.2%

Source: U.S. Census Bureau, Annual Demographic Supplement to the March 2002 Current Population Survey.

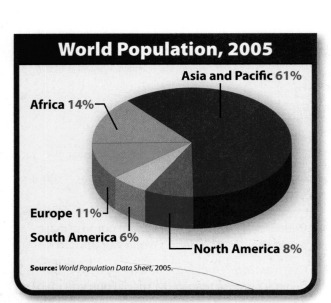

World Population, 2005

- Asia and Pacific 61%
- Africa 14%
- Europe 11%
- South America 6%
- North America 8%

Source: *World Population Data Sheet, 2005.*

◀ Circle Graphs

You can use circle graphs when you want to show how the whole of something is divided into its parts. Because of their shape, circle graphs are often called *pie graphs*. Each slice represents a part or percentage of the whole pie. The complete circle represents a whole group—or 100 percent.

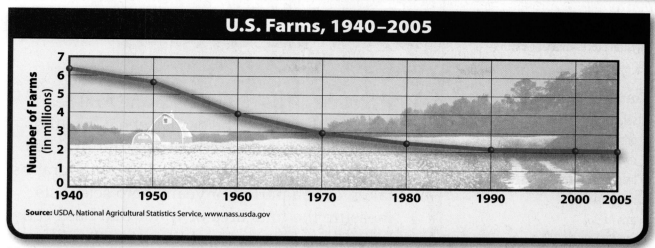

U.S. Farms, 1940–2005

Source: USDA, National Agricultural Statistics Service, www.nass.usda.gov

Line Graphs ▲

Line graphs help show changes over a period of time. The amounts being measured are plotted on the grid above each year and then are connected by a line.

Charts

Charts present related facts and numbers in an organized way. They arrange data, especially numbers, in rows and columns for easy reference.

Caribbean Island Populations

Aruba	71,891
Bermuda	65,773
British Virgin Islands	23,098
Jamaica	2,758,124

Source: *CIA World Factbook*, 2006.

NATIONAL GEOGRAPHIC

The Rain Shadow

WINDWARD SIDE

Cool moist air drops moisture

LEEWARD SIDE

Warm dry air in rain shadow

Warm moist air

Mountain range

Ocean

Diagrams

Diagrams are drawings that show steps in a process, point out the parts of an object, or explain how something works.

Skills Practice

1 Identifying What percentage does the whole circle in a circle graph represent?

2 Analyzing Information What type of graph would best show the number of Republicans and Democrats in the U.S. House of Representatives?

The Earth in Space

BIG Idea

Physical processes shape Earth's surface.

Content Vocabulary

- solar system *(p. 35)*
- orbit *(p. 35)*
- revolution *(p. 36)*
- leap year *(p. 36)*
- rotate *(p. 36)*
- axis *(p. 36)*
- atmosphere *(p. 36)*
- summer solstice *(p. 37)*
- winter solstice *(p. 38)*
- equinox *(p. 38)*
- Tropics *(p. 38)*

Academic Vocabulary

- significant *(p. 37)*
- reverse *(p. 38)*
- identical *(p. 38)*

Reading Strategy

Determining Cause and Effect
Use a diagram like the one below to show the effects of latitude on Earth's temperatures.

Picture This From space, the Aral Sea in Central Asia can be easily seen. Once the fourth-largest lake in the world, the Aral Sea has shrunk significantly. Satellite photographs, taken over a period of years, help scientists measure the total area of water that has been lost. These images, in addition to other information, help scientists understand what has caused the sea to change size. Scientists also continue to explore space and how the Earth's location in the solar system affects our planet. Read the next section to learn how the Earth's rotation, orbit, tilt, and latitude affect life on Earth.

▼ **The Aral Sea from space**

The Solar System

Main Idea The Earth is one of eight planets in the solar system. It rotates on its axis every 24 hours and takes a year to orbit the sun.

Geography and You Have you watched a sunrise or sunset and wondered why the sun seems to move across the sky each day? Read to find out about the Earth and its place in our solar system.

The sun provides the heat necessary for life on our planet. Earth, seven other major planets, and thousands of smaller bodies all revolve around the sun. Together with the sun, these bodies form our **solar system.**

Major Planets

The major planets differ from one another in size and makeup. Look at **Figure 1.** It shows that the inner planets—Mercury, Venus, Earth, and Mars—are relatively small and solid. The outer planets—Jupiter, Saturn, Uranus, and Neptune—are larger and composed mostly or entirely of gases. Pluto, once considered a major planet, is now called a minor planet.

Each planet follows its own path, or **orbit,** around the sun. The orbits vary from nearly circular to elliptical, or oval shaped.

Social Studies ONLINE

Student Web Activity Visit glencoe.com and complete the Chapter 1 Web Activity about the solar system.

NATIONAL GEOGRAPHIC

Figure 1   The Solar System

Neptune

Uranus

Moon

Venus   Earth

Mercury

Saturn

Mars

Sun

Jupiter

Diagram Skills

1 Identifying Which two planets are closest to the sun?

2 Identifying Which planets make up the outer planets?

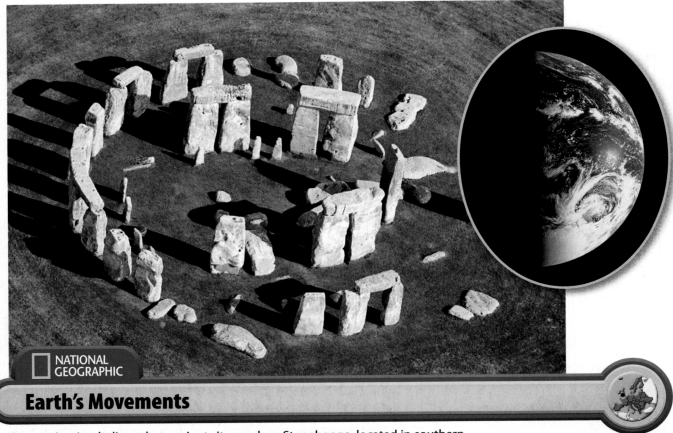

Earth's Movements

Some scientists believe that ancient sites such as Stonehenge, located in southern England, may have helped people track the Earth's revolution around the sun and the change of the seasons. From space, astronauts can see the Earth (inset) in light and shadow at the same time. **Movement** **Why do different parts of the Earth experience sunlight or darkness?**

The time necessary to complete an orbit differs, too. Mercury needs only 88 days to circle the sun, but faraway Neptune takes 165 years.

Earth's Movement

Earth takes almost 365¼ days to make one **revolution,** or a complete circuit, around the sun. This period is what we define as one year. Every four years, the extra fourths of a day are combined and added to the calendar as February 29th. A year that contains one of these extra days is called a **leap year.**

As Earth orbits the sun, it **rotates,** or spins, on its axis. The **axis** is an imaginary line that passes through the center of Earth from the North Pole to the South Pole. Earth rotates in an easterly direction, making one complete rotation every 24 hours. As Earth turns, different parts of the planet are in sunlight or in darkness. The part facing the sun experiences daytime, and the part facing away has night.

Why do we not feel Earth moving as it rotates? The reason is that the **atmosphere,** the layer of oxygen and gases that surrounds Earth, moves with it.

Reading Check **Explaining** Describe Earth's two principal motions—revolution and rotation.

Sun and Seasons

Main Idea **The tilt of Earth and its revolution around the sun lead to changing seasons during the year.**

Geography and You Did you know that when it is winter in the United States, it is summer in Australia? Read to learn why seasons differ between the Northern and Southern Hemispheres.

Earth is tilted 23½ degrees on its axis. As a result, seasons change as Earth makes its year-long orbit around the sun. To see why this happens, look at **Figure 2.** Notice how sunlight falls directly on the northern or southern half of Earth at different times of the year. Direct rays from the sun bring more warmth than indirect, or slanted rays. When the people in a hemisphere receive direct rays, they enjoy the warmth of summer. When they receive only indirect rays, they experience the cold of winter.

Solstices and Equinoxes

Four days in the year are **significant,** or important, because of the position of the sun in relation to Earth. These days mark the beginnings of the four seasons. On or about June 21, the North Pole is tilted toward the sun. On noon of this day, the sun appears directly overhead at the Tropic of Cancer (23½°N latitude). In the Northern Hemisphere, this day is the **summer solstice**– the day with the most hours of sunlight. It is the beginning of summer—but only in the Northern Hemisphere. In the Southern Hemisphere, that same day is the day with the fewest hours of sunlight and marks the beginning of winter.

NATIONAL GEOGRAPHIC   **Maps In Motion**   See StudentWorks™ Plus or <u>glencoe.com</u>.

Figure 2   The Sun and Earth's Seasons

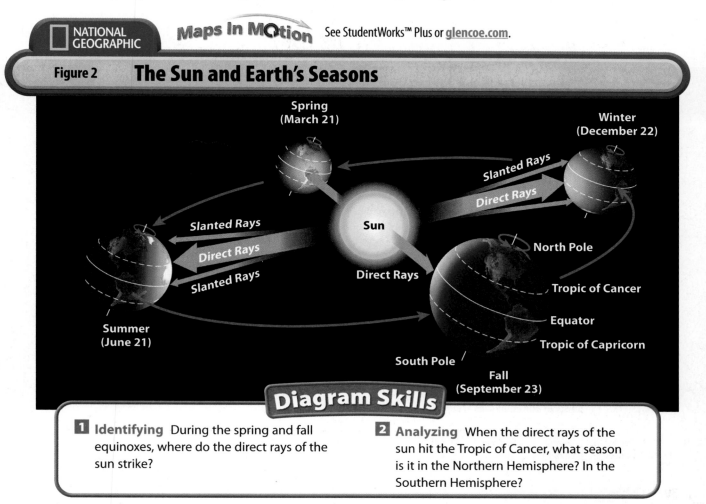

Diagram Skills

1. **Identifying** During the spring and fall equinoxes, where do the direct rays of the sun strike?

2. **Analyzing** When the direct rays of the sun hit the Tropic of Cancer, what season is it in the Northern Hemisphere? In the Southern Hemisphere?

Six months later—on or about December 22—the situation is **reversed,** or the opposite. The North Pole is tilted away from the sun. At noon, the sun's direct rays strike the Tropic of Capricorn. In the Northern Hemisphere, this day is the **winter solstice**—the day with the fewest hours of sunlight and the beginning of winter. This same day, however, marks the beginning of summer in the Southern Hemisphere.

Spring and autumn each begin on a day that falls midway between the two solstices. These two days are the **equinoxes,** when day and night are of **identical,** or equal, length in both hemispheres. On or about March 21, the spring equinox occurs. On or about September 23, the fall equinox occurs. On both days, the noon sun shines directly over the Equator.

Effects of Latitude

Earth's temperatures also are affected by the sun. Look again at **Figure 2.** The sun's rays directly hit places in the **Tropics,** the low-latitude areas near the Equator between the Tropic of Cancer and the Tropic of Capricorn. As a result, temperatures in the Tropics tend to be very warm.

At the high latitudes near the North and South Poles, the sun's rays hit indirectly. Temperatures in these regions are always cool or cold. In the midlatitudes—the areas between the Tropics of Cancer and Capricorn and the polar regions—temperatures, weather, and the seasons vary greatly. This is because air masses from both the high latitudes and the Tropics affect these areas.

✓ Reading Check **Analyzing Information** Why are the Tropics the Earth's warmest regions?

Social Studies ONLINE
Study Central™ To review this section, go to glencoe.com.

Section 2 Review

Vocabulary

1. **Explain** the significance of:
   - **a.** solar system
   - **b.** orbit
   - **c.** revolution
   - **d.** leap year
   - **e.** rotate
   - **f.** axis
   - **g.** atmosphere
   - **h.** summer solstice
   - **i.** winter solstice
   - **j.** equinox
   - **k.** Tropics

Main Ideas

2. **Identifying** Name the inner and outer planets, and describe the differences between the two groups.

3. **Comparing** Use a diagram like the one below to compare the days that mark the beginnings of the seasons.

Solstices and Equinoxes — Winter Solstice — Spring Equinox — Summer Solstice — Fall Equinox

Critical Thinking

4. **Analyzing** Why do we not feel the Earth's movement as it rotates?

5. **BIG Idea** What causes different seasons on Earth?

6. **Challenge** How might latitude affect the population of a region?

Writing About Geography

7. **Expository Writing** Write a paragraph explaining why seasons in the Southern Hemisphere are the opposite of those in the Northern Hemisphere.

CHAPTER 1

Visual Summary

Themes of Geography

- Geography is the study of the Earth and its people.

- In their study of people and places, geographers use five themes: location, place, human-environment interaction, movement, and regions.

Hiker using GPS

Geographers at Work

- To study the Earth, geographers use maps, globes, photographs, the Global Positioning System (GPS), and Geographic Information Systems (GIS).

- People can use information from geographers to plan, make decisions, and manage resources.

Sun and Seasons

- The Earth's tilt and its revolution around the sun cause the changes in seasons.

- Four days in the year mark the beginning points of the four seasons.

Luxembourg Palace, Paris, France

Seven Sisters Waterfall, Norway

Kinds of Geography

- Physical geography examines physical aspects of the Earth, such as land areas, bodies of water, and plant life.

- Human geography focuses on people and their activities, including religions, languages, and ways of life.

Solar System

- The sun, eight planets, and many smaller bodies form our solar system.

- Earth takes almost 365¼ days to make one revolution around the sun.

- Earth spins on its axis, causing day and night.

The Earth from space

STUDY TO GO Study anywhere, anytime! Download quizzes and flash cards to your PDA from **glencoe.com**.

STANDARDIZED TEST PRACTICE

TEST-TAKING

> Read every exam question twice to make certain you know exactly what it is asking.

Reviewing Vocabulary

Directions: Choose the word(s) that best completes the sentence.

1. _____ describes where a geographic feature is located by referring to other features around it.

   A Relative location

   B Absolute location

   C The Global Positioning System

   D A Geographic Positioning System

2. According to historians, the period known as Modern History began about five _____.

   A years ago

   B decades ago

   C centuries ago

   D millennia ago

3. The path each planet follows around the sun is called its _____.

   A axis

   B orbit

   C revolution

   D solar system

4. In the Northern Hemisphere, the day of the year with the fewest hours of sunlight is the _____.

   A fall equinox

   B winter solstice

   C spring equinox

   D summer solstice

Reviewing Main Ideas

Directions: Choose the best answer for each question.

Section 1 *(pp. 14–17)*

5. What geographic theme involves characteristics that make a location unique?

   A place

   B regions

   C location

   D movement

6. _____ provide(s) detailed photographs for creating maps.

   A A globe

   B A satellite

   C A Global Positioning System

   D Geographic Information Systems

Section 2 *(pp. 34–38)*

7. The Earth circles the sun every _____.

   A 24 hours

   B 365¼ days

   C 88 years

   D 165 years

8. Temperatures are always cool or cold near the North and South Poles because

   A the Poles face the sun in daytime.

   B the rays of the sun hit the Poles directly.

   C the Poles turn away from the sun at night.

   D the Poles receive only slanted rays from the sun.

GO ON ➤

Critical Thinking

Directions: Base your answers to questions 9, 10, and 11 on the map below and your knowledge of Chapter 1. Choose the best answer for each question.

The Earth

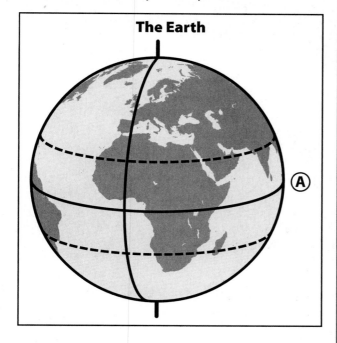

9. Label A is showing _____.

   A Earth's axis

   B the Equator

   C the Prime Meridian

   D the Tropic of Cancer

10. The Equator divides the Earth into

   A the North Pole and South Pole.

   B the Eastern and Western Hemispheres.

   C the Tropics of Cancer and Capricorn.

   D the Northern and Southern Hemispheres.

11. The sun's rays directly hit places in the _____.

   A midlatitudes

   B high latitudes

   C Tropics

   D spring equinox

Document-Based Questions

Directions: Analyze the following document and answer the short-answer questions that follow.

The following passage explains why scientists no longer consider Pluto a major planet.

> *Once known as the smallest, coldest, and most distant planet from the Sun, Pluto has a dual identity, not to mention being enshrouded in controversy since its discovery in 1930. On August 24, 2006, the International Astronomical Union (IAU) formally downgraded Pluto from an official planet to a dwarf planet. According to the new rules a planet meets three criteria: it must orbit the Sun, it must be big enough for gravity to squash it into a round ball, and it must have cleared other things out of the way in its orbital neighborhood. The latter measure knocks out Pluto and 2003UB313 (Eris), which orbit among the icy wrecks of the Kuiper Belt, and Ceres, which is in the asteroid belt.*
>
> —National Aeronautics and Space Administration, "Pluto"

12. In what two ways is Pluto like the major planets?

13. What other two bodies travel around the sun but are not considered planets?

Extended Response

14. Write a paragraph explaining how the concerns of physical geography and human geography often overlap.

STOP

Social Studies ONLINE

For additional test practice, use Self-Check Quizzes—Chapter 1 at glencoe.com.

Need Extra Help?														
If you missed question. . .	1	2	3	4	5	6	7	8	9	10	11	12	13	14
Go to page. . .	15	16	35	38	15	17	36	38	25	25	38	35	35	16

Earth's Physical Geography

Essential Question

Place Think about the characteristics of the area where you live. How does the land look? Is there a large body of water nearby? What is the climate like? Each place on the Earth is unique, with its own special characteristics. What kinds of geographic characteristics define the region where you live?

◀ Canyon on the Colorado Plateau, Arizona

BIG Ideas

Section 1: Forces Shaping the Earth

BIG IDEA Physical processes shape the Earth's surface. Forces from within and the actions of wind, water, and ice have shaped Earth's surface.

Section 2: Landforms and Water Resources

BIG IDEA Geographic factors influence where people settle. Physical features determine where people live.

Section 3: Climate Regions

BIG IDEA Geographers organize the Earth into regions that share common characteristics. Geographers use climate to define world regions.

Section 4: Human-Environment Interaction

BIG IDEA All living things are dependent upon one another and their surroundings for survival. Human actions greatly affect the natural world.

Study Organizer

Organizing Information Use this four-tab Foldable to help you record what you learn about the Earth's physical geography.

Step 1 Fold the top and bottom of a sheet of paper into the middle.

Step 2 Cut each flap at the midpoint to form 4 tabs.

Step 3 Label the tabs as shown.

Reading and Writing As you read the chapter, take notes about each section under the appropriate head. Use your Foldable to help you write a summary for each section.

Social Studies ONLINE
To preview Chapter 2, go to glencoe.com.

Forces Shaping the Earth

BIG Idea
Physical processes shape the Earth's surface.

Content Vocabulary

- core *(p. 45)*
- mantle *(p. 45)*
- magma *(p. 45)*
- crust *(p. 45)*
- continent *(p. 45)*
- plate tectonics *(p. 46)*
- earthquake *(p. 47)*
- fault *(p. 47)*
- weathering *(p. 47)*
- erosion *(p. 48)*

Academic Vocabulary

- release *(p. 45)*
- constant *(p. 47)*
- accumulate *(p. 48)*

Reading Strategy

Determining Cause and Effect
As you read, use a diagram like the one below to list the forces shaping the Earth and the effects of each.

Picture This This spectacular gash is California's San Andreas Fault. The San Andreas Fault is about 800 miles long and extends 10 miles beneath the Earth's surface. It is the source of the deadly earthquakes that occurred in California in 1906 and 1989. Read this section to learn more about processes that have shaped the surface of the Earth.

▼ **The San Andreas Fault, located 100 miles north of Los Angeles, California**

Inside the Earth

Main Idea **The Earth is made up of several layers that have different characteristics.**

Geography and You What do you see when you cut a melon in half? Like a melon, the Earth has distinct sections or layers.

The ground feels solid when you walk on it and downright hard if you should happen to fall. Yet Earth is not a large rock, solid through the middle. Beneath our planet's solid shell lies a center that is partly liquid. As **Figure 1** shows, the Earth has different layers, much like a melon or a baseball.

At the center of the Earth is a dense solid **core** of hot iron mixed with other metals and rock. The inner core lies about 3,200 miles (5,150 km) below the surface. Scientists think it is made up of iron and nickel. They also believe the inner core is under tremendous pressure. The next layer, the outer core, is so hot that the metal has melted into a liquid. The temperature in the outer core can reach an incredible 8,500°F (about 4,700°C).

Surrounding the core is the **mantle,** a layer of hot, dense rock about 1,770 miles (2,850 km) thick. Like the core, the mantle has two parts. The section nearest the core is solid. The rock in the outer mantle, however, can be moved, shaped, and even melted. If you have seen photographs of an active volcano, then you have seen this melted rock called **magma.** It flows to the surface during a volcanic eruption. Once it reaches the surface, magma is called lava. This movement of the matter in the mantle **releases** much of the energy generated in the Earth's interior.

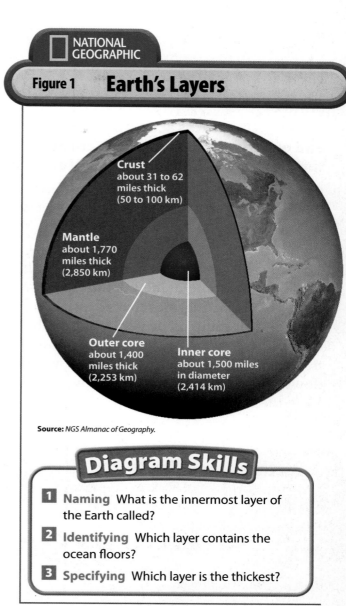

NATIONAL GEOGRAPHIC

Figure 1 **Earth's Layers**

Crust about 31 to 62 miles thick (50 to 100 km)

Mantle about 1,770 miles thick (2,850 km)

Outer core about 1,400 miles thick (2,253 km)

Inner core about 1,500 miles in diameter (2,414 km)

Source: *NGS Almanac of Geography.*

Diagram Skills

1 **Naming** What is the innermost layer of the Earth called?

2 **Identifying** Which layer contains the ocean floors?

3 **Specifying** Which layer is the thickest?

Earth's upper layer is the **crust,** a thin rocky shell that forms the surface. It reaches only 31 to 62 miles (50 to 100 km) deep. The crust includes ocean floors and seven large land areas known as **continents.** The continents are North America, South America, Europe, Asia, Africa, Australia, and Antarctica. The crust is just a few miles thick on the ocean floor, but is much thicker below the continents.

✓ **Reading Check** **Explaining** What is magma, and where does it originate?

Shaping the Earth's Surface

Main Idea Forces acting both inside and outside the Earth work to change the appearance of the Earth's surface.

Geography and You Have you been in an earthquake? Or, do you know anyone who has? Read on to discover what causes earthquakes.

The Earth's crust is not a fixed layer. It changes over time as new landforms are created and existing ones change forms. For hundreds of millions of years, the Earth's surface has been in constant motion, slowly transforming. Old mountains are worn down, while new mountains grow taller. Even the continents move.

Earthquake in Japan

NATIONAL GEOGRAPHIC

▲ City officials look over damage to an expressway that fell on one side during the 1995 earthquake in Kobe, Japan. **Location** Where in the world are **earthquakes common?**

Plate Movements

The theory of **plate tectonics** explains how the continents were formed and why they move. As **Figure 2** shows, each continent sits on one or more large bases called plates. As these plates move, the continents on top of them move. This movement is called continental drift.

The rate of movement varies from just under 1 inch (2.3 cm) to 7 inches (17 cm) per year. This movement is too slow for people to notice, but over millions of years, it can have dramatic effects.

Look at a map of the world. If you think of the eastern coast of South America as a giant puzzle piece, you will see that it seems to fit into the western coast of Africa. This is because these two continents were once joined together in a gigantic landmass that scientists call Pangaea. About 200 million years ago, however, the continents began to break and move apart because of tectonic activity.

When Plates Meet

The movements of Earth's plates have actually shaped the surface of the Earth. Sometimes the plates pull away from each other. Plates usually pull apart in ocean areas, but this kind of plate activity also occurs in land areas, such as Iceland and East Africa.

Plates can also collide. When two continental plates collide, they push against each other with tremendous force. This causes the land along the line where the plates meet to rise and form mountains. The Himalaya mountain ranges of Asia, the highest on Earth, were formed from such a collision.

Collisions of continental and oceanic plates produce a different result. The thinner ocean plate slides underneath the thicker continental plate. The downward

Figure 2 **Tectonic Plate Boundaries**

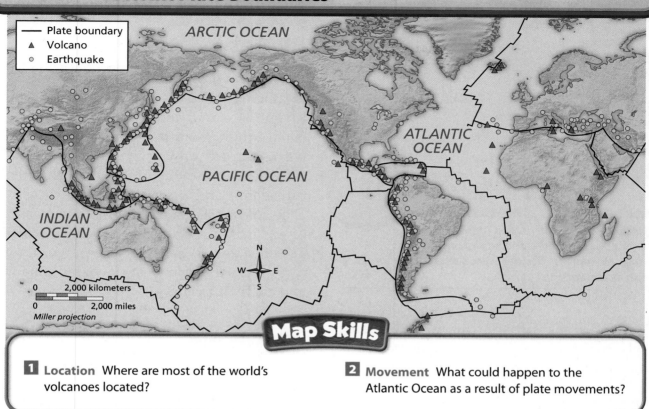

Map Skills

1 **Location** Where are most of the world's volcanoes located?

2 **Movement** What could happen to the Atlantic Ocean as a result of plate movements?

force of the lower plate causes magma to build up. Then the magma erupts and slowly hardens, forming volcanic mountains. This is how the Andes of South America were created.

Earthquakes are sudden and violent movements of the Earth's crust. They are common in areas where the collision of ocean and continental plates makes the Earth's crust unstable. For example, so many earthquakes and volcanoes occur around the edge of the Pacific Ocean that people call this region the Ring of Fire.

Sometimes two plates do not meet head-on but move alongside each other. This movement makes cracks in the Earth's crust called **faults.** Movements along faults do not take place **constantly,** but occur in sudden bursts that cause earthquakes. One of the most well-known faults in the United States is California's San Andreas Fault. A number of very destructive earthquakes have occurred in the region, and the threat of more still exists.

Weathering

The movement of tectonic plates causes volcanoes and earthquakes to change the Earth's landforms. Once created, however, these landforms will continue to change because of other forces that work on the Earth's surface.

One of these forces is called weathering. **Weathering** is when water and ice, chemicals, and even plants break rocks apart into smaller pieces. For example, water can run into cracks of rocks, freeze, and then expand.

Social Studies ONLINE
Student Web Activity Visit glencoe.com and complete the Chapter 2 Web Activity about plate tectonics.

NATIONAL GEOGRAPHIC
Erosion in Bangladesh

Heavy seasonal rains, called monsoons, lead to flooding and increased erosion in South Asia. *Movement* Besides water, what other forces can cause erosion?

These actions can split the rock. Chemicals, too, cause weathering when acids in air pollution mix with rain and fall back to Earth. The chemicals eat away rock and stone surfaces.

Erosion

Water, wind, and ice can move away weathered rock in a process called **erosion.** Rivers, streams, and even rainwater can cut through mountains and hills. Ocean waves can wear away coastal rocks. Wind can scatter loose bits of rock, which often rub against and wear down larger rocks.

In cold areas, giant, slow-moving masses of ice called glaciers form where water **accumulates.** When glaciers move, they carry rocks that can wear down mountains and carve out valleys.

✓ Reading Check   **Synthesizing** Why are earthquakes common where plates meet?

Social Studies ONLINE
Study Central™ To review this section, go to glencoe.com.

Section Review

Vocabulary

1. **Illustrate** the meaning of *core, mantle, magma, crust, continent, plate tectonics, earthquake, fault, weathering,* and *erosion* by drawing and labeling one or more diagrams.

Main Ideas

2. **Summarizing** Which layers of the Earth are solid? Which layers are liquid?

3. **Describing** Use a chart like the one below to list and describe the different results when plates meet.

Type of Plate Meeting	Results
1.	1.
2.	2.
3.	3.

Critical Thinking

4. **Drawing Conclusions** Where do you think an earthquake is more likely to occur—along North America's Pacific coast or along North America's Atlantic coast? Why?

5. **BIG Idea** How was the formation of the Himalaya and the Andes similar and different?

6. **Challenge** How do the shapes of South America and Africa support the theory of plate tectonics? Find another example of land areas that once might have been joined together but separated as plates moved apart.

Writing About Geography

7. **Using Your FOLDABLES** Use your Foldable to write a paragraph explaining how forces both beneath and on the surface help shape the surface of the Earth.

SECTION 2

Landforms and Water Resources

Content Vocabulary

- continental shelf *(p. 50)*
- trench *(p. 50)*
- groundwater *(p. 52)*
- aquifer *(p. 52)*
- water cycle *(p. 53)*
- evaporation *(p. 53)*
- condensation *(p. 54)*
- precipitation *(p. 54)*
- collection *(p. 54)*

Academic Vocabulary

- occur *(p. 50)*
- define *(p. 50)*
- availability *(p. 52)*

Reading Strategy

Identifying Use a diagram like the one below to identify the various bodies of water that can be found on the Earth's surface.

Picture This This fisherman in Indonesia uses a hand dredge to catch fish. He lowers the dredge into the water and drags it along the bottom of the shallow, sandy ocean floor. There it scoops up fish, scallops, and oysters. Read this section to learn how landforms and water influence human activities.

▲ Dredging for seafood, Indonesia

Types of Landforms

Main Idea Earth has a variety of landforms, and many of the landforms can be found both on the continents and the ocean floors.

Geography and You Do you know that there are mountains underwater? If the area where you live was underwater, what would it look like?

The Earth has a great variety of landforms—from mountains that soar miles high to lowlands that barely peek above the sea. These landforms appear not only on continents but also under the oceans.

On Land

Mountains are huge towers of rock and are the highest landforms. Some mountains may be only a few thousand feet high. Others can soar higher than 20,000 feet (6,096 m). The world's highest mountain is Mount Everest in South Asia's Himalaya ranges. It rises more than 29,028 feet (8,848 m), nearly five and a half miles high!

Hills are lower and more rounded than mountains. Between mountains and hills lie valleys. A valley is a long stretch of land that is lower than the land on either side. Flatlands **occur** in one of two forms, depending on their height above sea level. Plains are flat lowlands, typically found along coasts and lowland river valleys. Plateaus are flatlands at higher elevations.

Geographers **define** some landforms by their relationship to other landforms or to bodies of water. Look back at the geographic dictionary in the Reference Atlas to see examples of the following landforms.

An isthmus is a narrow strip of land that connects two larger landmasses and has water on two sides. An example is Central America, which connects North and South America. A peninsula, such as Florida, is a piece of land that is connected to a larger landmass on one side but has water on the other three sides. A body of land that is smaller than a continent and completely surrounded by water is an island.

Under the Oceans

Off each coast of a continent lies a plateau called a **continental shelf** that stretches for several miles underwater. At the edge of the shelf, the land drops down sharply to the ocean floor.

On the ocean floor, tall mountains thousands of miles wide line the edges of ocean plates that are pulling apart. Tectonic activity also makes deep cuts in the ocean floor called **trenches**. The Mariana Trench in the western Pacific Ocean is the deepest. It plunges 36,198 feet (11,033 m) below sea level.

Karakoram Range, South Asia

NATIONAL GEOGRAPHIC

▲ The Karakoram Range in South Asia is home to more than 60 peaks above 23,000 feet (7,000 m). *Location* Where is Mount Everest, the world's tallest peak, located?

ROUGHING IT

By Mark Twain

We jumped into the **stage,** the driver cracked his whip, and we bowled away.... It was a superb summer morning, and all the landscape was brilliant with sunshine. There was a freshness and breeziness, too, and an **exhilarating** sense of **emancipation** from all sorts of cares and responsibilities, that almost made us feel that the years we had spent in the close, hot city, toiling and slaving, had been wasted and thrown away. We were spinning along through Kansas, and in the course of an hour and a half we were fairly abroad on the great Plains. Just here the land was rolling—a grand sweep of regular elevations and depressions as far as the eye could reach—like the stately heave and swell of the **ocean's bosom** after a storm. And everywhere were cornfields, **accenting** with squares of deeper green this limitless expanse of grassy land. But presently this sea upon dry ground was to lose its "rolling" character and stretch away for seven hundred miles as level as a floor! . . .

There is not a tree of any kind in the deserts, for hundreds of miles—there is no vegetation at all . . . except the sage-brush and its cousin the "greasewood," which is so much like the sage-brush that the difference amounts to little. Camp-fires and hot suppers in the deserts would be impossible but for the friendly sage-brush.

From *Roughing It*, Mark Twain. New York: Harper & Brothers Publishers, 1899.

Mark Twain
(1835–1910)

Samuel Langhorne Clemens, who used the pen name "Mark Twain," was born in a Missouri river town along the banks of the Mississippi River. He held many jobs, including working as the pilot of a riverboat, before becoming a writer and humorist. He was one of the most popular American authors of the late 1800s.

Background Information

In *Roughing It*, Twain describes his experiences living and traveling in Nevada, California, and Hawaii in the 1860s. In this excerpt, he describes his trip from Missouri to Nevada. Twain traveled by stagecoach, a horse-drawn vehicle for carrying passengers.

Reader's Dictionary

stage: horse-drawn stagecoach

exhilarating: exciting

emancipation: freedom

ocean's bosom: ocean's surface

accenting: standing out

Analyzing Literature

1. **Making Inferences** What landform is Twain describing? What details make that clear?

2. **Read to Write** Think about the landforms in the area where you live. Write a letter describing what it would be like to travel over those landforms by foot or on a bicycle.

Humans and Landforms

Humans settle on all types of landforms. People choose a place to live based on a number of factors. Climate—the average temperature and rainfall of a region—is one factor that people must consider. The **availability** of resources is another factor. People settle where they can get freshwater and where they can grow food, catch fish, or raise animals.

✓ **Reading Check** **Explaining** What forces form ocean trenches?

Black River Delta, United States

NATIONAL GEOGRAPHIC

▲ The Black River forms a delta as it flows into the Mississippi River in Wisconsin. River deltas are often rich in wildlife, including birds and mammals. *Place* How are deltas formed?

The Water Planet

Main Idea **Water covers much of the planet, but only some of this water is usable.**

Geography and You Have you ever watched steam rise from a boiling pot of water? Read to learn how water changes from a solid, to a liquid, to a gas on Earth.

Earth is sometimes called the "water planet" because so much of it—about 70 percent of the surface—is covered with water. Water exists in many different forms. Streams, rivers, lakes, seas, and oceans contain water in liquid form. The atmosphere holds water vapor, or water in the form of gas. Glaciers and ice sheets are masses of water that have been frozen solid.

Salt Water

All of the oceans on Earth are part of a huge, continuous body of salt water. Almost 97 percent of the planet's water is salt water. Oceans have smaller arms or areas that are called seas, bays, or gulfs. These larger bodies of salt water can be linked to oceans by the more narrow bodies called straits or channels.

Freshwater

Only 3 percent of the water on Earth is freshwater. Much of this freshwater is frozen in ice that covers polar regions and parts of mountains. Some is **groundwater**, which filters through the soil into the ground. Groundwater often gathers in **aquifers** (A·kwuh·fuhrz). These are underground layers of rock through which water flows. People can pump the freshwater from aquifers. Only a tiny amount of all

Figure 3   The Water Cycle

Condensation

Clouds

Surface runoff

Evaporation from lakes and streams

Precipitation (snow, sleet, hail, rain)

Evaporation from ocean

Groundwater to rivers and oceans

Diagram Skills

1 **Identifying** In which step of the water cycle does water vapor form clouds?

2 **Explaining** How does the sun's heat drive the water cycle?

the water in the world is found in lakes and rivers. This water is often not safe to drink until it has been purified.

Large inland bodies of water are called lakes. Most lakes are freshwater lakes. Long, flowing bodies of water are called rivers. They begin at a source and end at a mouth. The mouth is the place where a river empties into another body of water, such as an ocean or a lake.

The largest rivers often have many tributaries, which are separate streams or rivers that feed into them. Many rivers form deltas at their mouths. A delta is an area where a river breaks into many different streams flowing toward the sea. Rivers often carry rich soil to their deltas and deposit it, building up the land.

The Water Cycle

The total amount of water on Earth does not change. It does not stay in one place, either. Instead the water moves constantly. In a process called the **water cycle**, the water goes from the oceans, to the air, to the ground, and finally back to the oceans.

Look at **Figure 3** to see how the water cycle works. The sun's heat drives the water cycle because it evaporates the water on the Earth's surface. This **evaporation** changes water from liquid to a gas, called water vapor. Water vapor rises from the Earth's oceans and other bodies of water, and then circulates in the atmosphere. The air's temperature determines how much water the air holds. Warm air holds more water vapor than cool air.

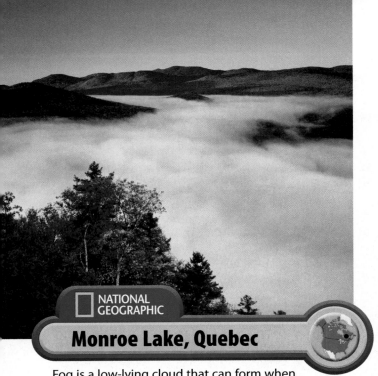

NATIONAL GEOGRAPHIC

Monroe Lake, Quebec

Fog is a low-lying cloud that can form when moist air blows over a cool surface. *Place* **How does air temperature affect water vapor in the air?**

When the air temperature drops low enough, **condensation** takes place. In this process, water changes from gas back to a liquid. Tiny droplets of water form in the air, although they are suspended in clouds.

When conditions in the atmosphere are right, these water droplets fall to the ground as some form of **precipitation.** This can be rain, snow, sleet, or hail. The form of precipitation depends on the temperature of the surrounding air.

Completing the cycle is the process called **collection.** The water collects on the ground and in rivers, lakes, and oceans. There it evaporates to begin the cycle again.

✓ **Reading Check**   **Making Inferences** Why is very little of the Earth's freshwater usable?

Section 2 Review

Social Studies ONLINE
Study Central™ To review this section, go to **glencoe.com**.

Vocabulary

1. **Explain** the meaning of the following terms by using each one in a sentence.
   a. continental shelf   **f.** evaporation
   b. trench   **g.** condensation
   c. groundwater   **h.** precipitation
   d. aquifer   **i.** collection
   e. water cycle

Main Ideas

2. **Contrasting** How do an isthmus, a peninsula, and an island differ?

3. **Summarizing** Use a diagram like the one below to summarize the water cycle.

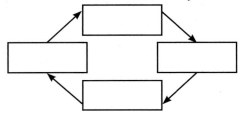

Critical Thinking

4. **Comparing and Contrasting** How are plains and plateaus similar and different?

5. **BIG Idea** Describe several factors that people consider when choosing a place to settle.

6. **Challenge** Which landforms do you think attracted people to settle in the area where you live? Which landforms, if any, may have kept people away?

Writing About Geography

7. **Expository Writing** Write a paragraph describing the major landforms found in the state where you live.

Guide to Reading

BIG Idea

Geographers organize the Earth into regions that share common characteristics.

Content Vocabulary

- weather (p. 56)
- climate (p. 56)
- prevailing wind (p. 57)
- current (p. 57)
- El Niño (p. 58)
- La Niña (p. 58)
- local wind (p. 59)
- rain shadow (p. 59)
- climate zone (p. 59)
- biome (p. 60)
- urban climate (p. 61)

Academic Vocabulary

- distribute (p. 56)
- alter (p. 57)

Reading Strategy

Identifying Central Issues Use a diagram like the one below to identify the effects of both El Niño and La Niña.

El Niño

La Niña

SECTION 3
Climate Regions

Picture This Residents rush to escape the swirling winds and pelting rain during the annual typhoon season in China. Typhoons are hurricanes that can topple buildings, snap power lines, and uproot trees. These violent thunderstorms draw their power from warm ocean waters and are common in the Tropics of southeast China. Read this section to learn about the variety of climates that are found on Earth.

▼ **Fleeing Typhoon Haitang, July 2005**

Effects on Climate

Main Idea Sun, wind, and water influence Earth's climate.

Geography and You What is the weather today in your area? Is it typical of the particular season you are in, or is it unusual? Read to find out about the difference between weather and climate.

When you turn on the television to find out the day's high and low temperatures, you are checking the local weather. **Weather** refers to the changes in temperature, wind direction and speed, and air moisture that take place over a short period of time. When geographers look at the usual, predictable patterns of weather in an area over many years, they are studying **climate**.

The Sun

Earth's climate is linked directly to the sun. As you recall from Chapter 1, the Earth does not heat evenly. The Tropics receive more of the sun's heat energy and the Poles receive less. The movement of air and water over the Earth helps to **distribute** the sun's heat more evenly around the globe.

NATIONAL GEOGRAPHIC **Maps In Motion** See StudentWorks™ Plus or glencoe.com.

Figure 4 **Prevailing Wind Patterns**

Map Skills

1 Movement In which general direction does the wind blow over North America and Europe?

2 Regions Which two areas of the world experience calm winds?

Winds

Air in the Tropics, which is warmed by the sun, moves north and south toward the Poles of the Earth. Colder air from the Poles moves toward the Equator. These movements of air are winds. Major wind systems follow patterns that are similar over time. These patterns, shown in **Figure 4,** are called **prevailing winds.**

Because the planet rotates, winds curve across Earth's surface. The winds that blow from east to west between the Tropics and the Equator are called the trade winds. Long ago sailing ships used these winds to carry out trade. The westerlies, which blow over North America, move from west to east in the area between the Tropics and about 60° north latitude.

Storms

When moist, warm air rises suddenly and meets dry, cold air, major storms can develop. In the summer, these storms can include thunder and lightning, heavy rain, and, sometimes, tornadoes. Tornadoes are violent, funnel-shaped windstorms with wind speeds up to 450 miles (724 km) per hour. In the winter, storms can become blizzards that bring much snow.

Other types of destructive storms are hurricanes and typhoons. Hurricanes occur in the western Atlantic and eastern Pacific Oceans. Typhoons occur in the western Pacific Ocean. These storms arise in the warm ocean waters of the Tropics and can reach great size and power. Some are as much as 300 miles (483 km) across and create strong winds and heavy rains.

Ocean Currents

The steadily flowing streams of water in the world's seas are called **currents.** Like winds, they follow patterns, which are shown in **Figure 5,** on the next page.

NATIONAL GEOGRAPHIC

Effects of El Niño

South America can experience dramatic changes in weather due to El Niño and La Niña. Forest fires, like this one in Brazil, occur during periods of drought. *Place* **How do El Niño and La Niña differ?**

Currents that carry warm water to higher latitudes can affect the climates in those latitudes. For example, the North Atlantic Current carries warm water from the Tropics to western Europe. Winds blowing over the warm water bring warmth and moisture to western Europe, which enjoys an unexpectedly mild climate.

El Niño and La Niña

Every few years, changes in normal wind and water patterns in the Pacific Ocean cause unusual weather in some places. In one of these events, weakened winds allow warmer waters to reach South America's coast. This change **alters** weather there and beyond.

These conditions are called **El Niño,** Spanish for "the boy."

In an El Niño, very heavy rains fall on western South America, causing floods. Meanwhile, little rain falls on Australia, southern Asia, and Africa. Also, North America may see severe storms.

In some years the opposite occurs, producing conditions called **La Niña,** Spanish for "the girl." La Niña causes unusually cool waters and low rainfall in the eastern Pacific. In the western Pacific, rains are heavy and typhoons can occur.

 Reading Check **Explaining** How are winds formed?

Landforms and Climate

Main Idea Landforms, especially mountains, can affect winds, temperature, and rainfall.

Geography and You Have you ever felt a cooling sea breeze on a hot summer's day? Read on to learn how the sea can affect climate.

Sun, wind, and water affect climate, but the shape of the land has an effect on climate as well. The distance between landforms as well as their nearness to water influence climate.

Figure 5 **World Ocean Currents**

Map Skills

1 **Movement** What kind of climate is the North Atlantic Current likely to bring to Europe?

2 **Regions** Which area generally has warmer waters, western South America or eastern South America?

Landforms and Local Winds

Some landforms cause **local winds,** or wind patterns that are typical only in a small area. Some local winds occur because land warms and cools more quickly than water does. As a result, cool sea breezes keep coastal areas cool during the day. After the sun sets, the opposite occurs. The air over the land cools more quickly than the air over the water. At night, then, a cool breeze blows from the land out to sea.

Local winds also occur near tall mountains. When the air along a mountain slope is warmer than the air in the valley below, it rises and a cool valley breeze moves up the mountain.

Mountains, Temperature, and Rainfall

The slopes of a mountain facing the sun can heat more quickly than nearby land. Higher up in the mountains, however, the air is thin and cannot hold the heat very well. As a result, mountain peaks are cold. This explains why some mountains in the Tropics are covered with snow.

Mountains have an effect on rainfall called a **rain shadow** that blocks rain from reaching interior regions. As warm, moist ocean air moves up the mountain slopes, it cools and releases its moisture. As a result, the side of mountains facing the wind, called the windward side, receives large amounts of rainfall.

As the air passes over the mountain peaks to the other side, called the leeward side, it becomes cool and dry. As a result, the land on the leeward side of the mountains is often very dry. Deserts can develop on the leeward side of mountain ranges.

✔ Reading Check **Determining Cause and Effect** How do mountains cause the rain shadow effect?

Climate Zones

Main Idea **The effects of wind, water, latitude, and landforms combine to create different climate zones.**

Geography and You Suppose you visited two islands that were thousands of miles apart. Read to find out how similar their climates might be.

As you have read, the effects of wind, water, latitude, and landforms combine to shape the climate of an area. Scientists have found that many parts of the world, even though they are very distant from one another, have similar climates. Southern California, for instance, has a warm, dry climate similar to that around the Mediterranean Sea in Europe. These areas have the same **climate zone,** or similar patterns of temperature and precipitation. These regions would also have similar vegetation.

NATIONAL GEOGRAPHIC

Figure 6 The Rain Shadow

WINDWARD SIDE

Cool moist air drops moisture

LEEWARD SIDE

Warm dry air in rain shadow

Warm moist air

Ocean

Mountain range

Diagram Skills

1 **Identifying** What type of air blows from the ocean toward the mountain?

2 **Explaining** Why is the land on the leeward side of the mountain dry?

Climate zones include **biomes,** or areas such as rain forest, desert, grassland, and tundra in which particular kinds of plants and animals have adapted to particular climates.

Major Climates

Scientists have identified five major climate zones, which are described in the chart below. Four of these zones have several subcategories. For example, the dry climate zone is subdivided into steppe and desert subcategories. These generally dry climates differ slightly in rainfall and temperature. Locations in the highland zone show great variation. In these areas, altitude, the position of a place toward or away from the sun, and other factors can make large differences in climate even though two locations may be near each other.

World Climate Zones

Category	Subcategory	Characteristics	Vegetation	Example
Tropical	Tropical rain forest	Warm temperatures; heavy rainfall throughout year	Dense rain forests	Amazon basin (South America); Congo basin (Africa)
	Tropical savanna	Warm temperatures throughout year; dry winter	Grasslands dotted by scattered trees	Southern half of Brazil; eastern Africa
Dry	Steppe	Temperatures can be warm or mild; rainfall low and unreliable	Grasses, shrubs	Western Great Plains (United States); Sahel region south of the Sahara (Africa)
	Desert	Temperatures can be warm or mild; rainfall very low and very unreliable	Drought-resistant shrubs and bushes	Sonoran Desert (southwestern United States, Mexico); Sahara (Africa)
Midlatitude	Marine west coast	Cool summers, mild winters; ample rainfall	Deciduous or evergreen forests	Northwestern United States; northwestern Europe
	Mediterranean	Warm, dry summers; mild, wet winters	Shrubs, low trees, drought-resistant plants	Southern California; Mediterranean region (Europe)
	Humid subtropical	Hot, wet summers; mild, wet winters	Mixed forests	Southeastern United States; eastern China
	Humid continental	Hot, wet summers; cold, somewhat wet winters	Deciduous forests	Northeastern United States; eastern Europe; western Russia
High Latitude	Subarctic	Short, mild summers; long, cold winters; light precipitation	Coniferous forests	Most of Alaska, Canada; western Russia
	Tundra	Short, cool summers; long, cold winters; precipitation varies	Low-lying grasses, mosses, shrubs	Extreme north of North America; Europe
	Ice cap	Cold all year long	None to very little	Greenland; Antarctica
Highland		Varies depending on local conditions	Changes with altitude	Northern Rocky Mountains (United States); the Himalaya (Asia)

Urban Climates

Large cities show significant climate differences from surrounding areas in their climate zone. These **urban climates** are marked by higher temperatures and other differences. Paved streets and stone buildings soak up and then release more of the sun's heat energy than areas covered by plants. This absorption leads to higher temperatures—as much as 10° to 20°F (6° to 11°C) higher—than in the nearby countryside. These different heat patterns cause winds to blow into cities from several directions instead of the prevailing direction experienced in rural areas. Some scientists believe cities also have more precipitation than rural areas.

✓ Reading Check **Drawing Conclusions** How do large cities affect climate?

NATIONAL GEOGRAPHIC

Shanghai, China: City Heat

City temperatures can soar in the summer. Buildings and pavement absorb the sun's heat, raising temperatures within the city. *Location* How does urban heat affect winds in the urban area?

Section 3 Review

Social Studies ONLINE
Study Central™ To review this section, go to glencoe.com.

Vocabulary

1. **Explain** the meaning of the following terms by writing three paragraphs that include all of the terms: *weather, climate, prevailing wind, current, El Niño, La Niña, local wind, rain shadow, climate zone, biome,* and *urban climate.*

Main Ideas

2. **Explaining** How do wind and water affect the Earth's climates?

3. **Reviewing** Describe two types of local winds and why they form.

4. **Identifying** Use a diagram like the one below to identify the main characteristics of the climate zone in which you live.

Local Climate Zone

Critical Thinking

5. **BIG Idea** Choose two climate zones, and compare and contrast their characteristics.

6. **Challenge** How might El Niño affect weather conditions in the central United States?

Writing About Geography

7. **Expository Writing** Choose a place in the world you would like to visit because of its climate. Write a paragraph describing the climate of that area.

Invaders From Another Land

When plants and animals move from their natural environment to one in which they do not belong, they can cause great harm.

How They Arrive In the 1800s, a settler in Australia released about a dozen European rabbits onto his land. He brought the rabbits to Australia in order to hunt other animals. Over the years, the number of rabbits grew beyond control. They eventually damaged plant and animal life throughout Australia.

The rabbits brought to Australia are an example of an invasive species. These are plants and animals introduced to new areas where they increase rapidly and crowd out local plants and animal life.

▲ **European rabbit**

Invasive species are a threat in other parts of the world as well as in Australia. Zebra mussels, for example, came to the United States during the 1980s attached to the bottoms of ships. They fell off the ships and spread throughout lakes, rivers, and streams. These mussels have blocked city water treatment systems and destroyed some fish populations.

▲ **Zebra mussels clustered on wood**

Finding a Solution The costs of invasive species can be great. Within a short time of arriving in a new location, invasive species can cause billions of dollars in damage. Costs to the environment are high too. Invasive species can cause the extinction of local animals and plants not used to them.

Experts believe that invasive species are becoming more common. Increasing world trade means more contact among the world's peoples and environments. This contact means more chances for species to move from one place to another. Some governments are working both to keep invasive species from arriving and to restore environments that have been harmed.

NATIONAL GEOGRAPHIC

The Spread of Zebra Mussels

- First detection, 1988
- 1991
- 2005

90°W · 85°W · 80°W · 75°W · 45°N · 40°N

L. Superior · L. Michigan · L. Huron · L. Ontario · L. Erie · Mississippi R. · Ohio R. · Missouri R.

N · W · E · S

0   200 kilometers
0   200 miles
Albers Equal-Area projection

Think About It

1. Why are some plants and animals called *invasive species*?
2. Why are invasive species becoming more common?

BIG Idea

All living things are dependent upon one another and their surroundings for survival.

Content Vocabulary

- smog *(p. 64)*
- acid rain *(p. 64)*
- greenhouse effect *(p. 64)*
- crop rotation *(p. 65)*
- deforestation *(p. 65)*
- conservation *(p. 66)*
- irrigation *(p. 66)*
- pesticide *(p. 66)*
- ecosystem *(p. 66)*
- biodiversity *(p. 66)*

Academic Vocabulary

- layer *(p. 64)*
- technique *(p. 65)*

Reading Strategy

Solving Problems Use a chart like the one below to identify environmental problems and what people are doing to solve them.

Problem	Solution
1.	1.
2.	2.
3.	3.

Human-Environment Interaction

Picture This Imagine guiding hundreds of logs through rough waters in a tugboat. In Deception Pass State Park in Washington, boats move newly cut logs along the waters of the park to reach the highway. The logs are loaded on trucks and taken to lumberyards. Read this section to learn about the effects of human activities on the Earth.

▽ **Logs moving through Deception Pass State Park in Washington**

The Atmosphere

Main Idea Human activity can have a negative impact on the air.

Geography and You Have you ever seen a blanket of dirty air hanging over a large city? Read to find out how human actions affect the atmosphere.

Throughout the world, people burn oil, coal, or gas to make electricity, to power factories, or to move cars. These actions often cause air pollution.

Air Pollution

Air pollution has serious effects on people and the planet. Some polluting chemicals combine with ozone, a form of oxygen, to create **smog.** This is a thick haze of smoke and chemicals. Thick smog above cities can lead to serious breathing problems.

Chemicals in air pollution can also combine with precipitation to form **acid rain.** Acid rain kills fish, eats away at the surfaces of buildings, and destroys trees and entire forests. Because the chemicals that form acid rain come from the burning of coal and oil, solving this problem has proved difficult.

Some human-made chemicals, particularly chlorofluorocarbons (CFCs), destroy the ozone **layer.** Ozone forms a shield high in the atmosphere against damaging rays from the sun that can cause skin cancer. Nations today are working to limit the release of CFCs.

The Greenhouse Effect

Like the glass in a greenhouse, gases in the atmosphere trap the sun's warmth. Without this **greenhouse effect**, the Earth would be too cold for most living things. **Figure 7** shows the greenhouse effect.

NATIONAL GEOGRAPHIC

Global Warming

Scientists are concerned that global warming might be harming wildlife, such as this polar bear. *Human-Environment Interaction* What human activities might contribute to global warming?

Some scientists, however, say that pollution is strengthening the greenhouse effect. They claim that the increased burning of coal, oil, and natural gas has released more gases into the atmosphere. These greenhouse gases have trapped more of the sun's heat near the Earth's surface, raising temperatures around the planet. Such warming could cause climate changes and melt polar ice. Ocean levels could rise and flood low-lying coastal areas.

The issue of global warming is debated. Critics argue that computer models showing global warming are unrealistic. Many nations, however, are addressing the problem. They are trying to use energy more efficiently, burn coal more cleanly, and adopt nonpolluting forms of energy such as wind and solar power.

✓ **Reading Check** **Explaining** Why do some scientists debate the issue of global warming?

The Lithosphere

Main Idea Some human activity damages our environment.

Geography and You How might your community have looked 200 years ago? Read to discover how human actions have affected the land.

The lithosphere is another name for the Earth's crust. It includes all the land above and below the oceans. Human activities, such as farming, logging, and mining can have negative effects on the lithosphere.

Rich topsoil is a vital part of the lithosphere that, if not carefully managed, can be carried away by wind or water. Some farmers use contour plowing to limit the loss of topsoil. With this **technique**, farmers plow along the curves of the land rather than in straight lines, preventing the soil from washing away. **Crop rotation**, or changing what is planted from year to year, also protects topsoil. Planting grasses in fields without crops holds the soil in place.

Deforestation, or cutting down forests without replanting, is another way in which topsoil is lost. When the tree roots are no longer there to hold the soil, wind and water can carry the soil away. Many rain forests, such as the Amazon rain forest, are being cut down at high rates. This has raised concerns because the forests support the water cycle and help replace the oxygen in the atmosphere. Forests also are home to many kinds of plants and animals.

✓ **Reading Check** **Identifying Central Issues** Why is deforestation a problem?

NATIONAL GEOGRAPHIC

Figure 7 **The Greenhouse Effect**

Sun

Some heat energy is reflected by the atmosphere back into space.

Some of the heat energy is reflected by the Earth. This reflected energy either escapes back into space or is reflected back downward by the atmosphere to the Earth. The trapped energy warms the Earth's surface and the lower atmosphere.

Some of the sun's heat energy passes through the atmosphere and is absorbed by the Earth.

Diagram Skills

1 Explaining How does the greenhouse effect get its name?

2 Describing What happens to the energy reflected by the Earth?

The Hydrosphere and Biosphere

Main Idea Water pollution poses a threat to a vital and limited resource.

Geography and You How much water do you use each day? How much of that water is wasted? Read to find out how people use water resources.

The hydrosphere refers to the Earth's surface water and groundwater. Water is vital to human life. Because the amount of freshwater is limited, people should practice **conservation,** the careful use of a resource, to avoid wasting water.

Throughout the world, farmers use **irrigation,** a process in which water is collected and distributed to crops. Irrigation is often wasteful, however, as much of the water evaporates or soaks into the ground before it reaches the crops. Pollution also threatens water supplies. Chemicals from industrial processes sometimes spill into waterways. **Pesticides,** or powerful chemicals that farmers use to kill crop-destroying insects, can also be harmful.

The biosphere is the collection of plants and animals of all types that live on Earth. The entire biosphere is divided into many **ecosystems.** An ecosystem is a place shared by plants and animals that depend on one another for survival.

Shrinking **biodiversity,** or the variety of plants and animals living on the planet, is also a concern. Changes to the environment can lead to decreasing populations of plants and animals in an ecosystem.

✔ **Reading Check** **Explaining** Why is the conservation of water important?

Section 4 Review

Social Studies ONLINE
Study Central™ To review this section, go to **glencoe.com**.

Vocabulary

1. **Explain** the significance of
   - **a.** smog
   - **b.** acid rain
   - **c.** greenhouse effect
   - **d.** crop rotation
   - **e.** deforestation
   - **f.** conservation
   - **g.** irrigation
   - **h.** pesticide
   - **i.** ecosystem
   - **j.** biodiversity

Main Ideas

2. **Organizing** Use a diagram like the one below to identify problems related to air pollution.

   Air Pollution

3. **Explaining** How do contour plowing and crop rotation preserve topsoil?

4. **Identifying** What is the biosphere?

Critical Thinking

5. **BIG Idea** What might happen to the animals of the rain forest if large areas of trees are cut down? Why?

6. **Challenge** Do you think countries should cooperate to solve problems like air and water pollution? Why?

Writing About Geography

7. **Persuasive Writing** Write a brief essay identifying the environmental issue you think is most important and what people can do about it.

Visual Summary

Inside the Earth

- Earth has four layers: the inner and outer cores, the mantle, and the crust.
- The continents are on large plates that move.
- Plates colliding or pulling apart reshape the land.

Shaping Landforms

- Water, chemicals, and plants break rock apart into smaller pieces.
- Water, wind, and ice can cause erosion.

Windstorm in West Africa

Types of Landforms

- Mountains, plateaus, valleys, and other landforms are found on land and under oceans.
- Climate and availability of resources affect where humans settle.

The Water Planet

- About 70 percent of the Earth's surface is water.
- In a process called the water cycle, water travels from the oceans to the air to the ground and back to the oceans.

Boaters on Inle Lake, South Asia

Climate

- Climate is the usual pattern of weather over a long period of time.
- Sun, winds, ocean currents, landforms, and latitude affect climate.
- Geographers divide the world into different climate zones.

Hawk in protected area, United States

AREA BEYOND THIS SIGN CLOSED
All public entry prohibited
By Foot, Bike, Or Vehicle
Violations Punishable

Humans and the Environment

- A delicate balance exists among the Earth's atmosphere, lithosphere, hydrosphere, and biosphere.
- Human actions, such as burning fuels and clearing rain forests, affect the environment.

Hills in Italy

STUDY TO GO Study anywhere, anytime! Download quizzes and flash cards to your PDA from glencoe.com.

STANDARDIZED TEST PRACTICE

TEST-TAKING **TIP**

> As you read the first part of a multiple-choice question, try to anticipate the answer before you look at the choices. If your answer is one of the choices, it is probably correct.

Reviewing Vocabulary

Directions: Choose the word(s) that best completes the sentence.

1. The theory of _____ explains how continents were formed and why they move.

   A magma formation

   B erosion

   C plate tectonics

   D mantle disbursement

2. A plateau called a _____ lies off the coast of each continent and stretches for several miles underwater.

   A continental aquifer

   B continental shelf

   C continental water cycle

   D continental trench

3. Areas that have similar patterns of temperature and precipitation are known as _____.

   A climate zones

   B biomes

   C El Niño

   D currents

4. Chemicals in air pollution can combine with precipitation to form _____.

   A chlorofluorocarbons

   B the ozone layer

   C the greenhouse effect

   D acid rain

Reviewing Main Ideas

Directions: Choose the best answer for each question.

Section 1 *(pp. 44–48)*

5. Surrounding Earth's core is a layer of hot, dense rock called the _____.

   A mantle

   B crust

   C magma

   D core

Section 2 *(pp. 49–54)*

6. Almost 97 percent of the planet's water is _____.

   A groundwater

   B freshwater

   C salt water

   D frozen in glaciers and ice sheets

Section 3 *(pp. 55–61)*

7. The usual, predictable patterns of weather in an area over many years are called _____.

   A climate

   B current

   C El Niño

   D biome

Section 4 *(pp. 63–66)*

8. The careful use of resources to avoid wasting them is called _____.

   A deforestation

   B biodiversity

   C irrigation

   D conservation

GO ON ➡

Critical Thinking

Directions: Base your answers to questions 9 and 10 on the graph below and your knowledge of Chapter 2. Choose the best answer for each question.

Global Temperature Changes (1880–2000)

Departure from Long-Term Average (°F)

Year

Source: U.S. National Climatic Data Center, 2001.

9. What is the overall trend of global temperature change in the twentieth century?

  A There has been a stable or flat trend throughout the century.

  B There has been an overall upward trend.

  C There has been an overall downward trend.

  D There was an upward trend early in the century followed by a downward trend.

10. During what twenty-year period of time did the sharpest rise in global temperatures take place?

  A 1880–1900

  B 1910–1930

  C 1950–1970

  D 1980–2000

Document-Based Questions

Directions: Analyze the document and answer the short-answer questions that follow.

> *Under the Kyoto Protocol, industrialized countries are to reduce their combined emissions of six major greenhouse gases during the five-year period 2008–2012 to below 1990 levels. The European Union, for example, is to cut its combined emissions by eight percent, while Japan should reduce emissions by six percent. For many countries, achieving the Kyoto targets will be a major challenge that will require new policies and new approaches. . . .*
>
> *Developing countries, including Brazil, China, India and Indonesia, are also Parties to the Protocol but do not have emission reduction targets. Many developing countries have already demonstrated success in addressing climate change.*
>
> —UNEP, "Kyoto Protocol to Enter into Force 16 February 2005"

11. According to this press release, what is the purpose of the Kyoto Protocol?

12. Compare how industrialized and developing countries would be affected by the Kyoto Protocol.

Extended Response

13. Which part of Earth's environment—the atmosphere, lithosphere, hydrosphere, or biosphere—do you feel is most threatened by human activity? In several paragraphs, define the part that you chose, explain why you think it is threatened, and describe what actions may help decrease the threat to that area.

STOP

Social Studies ONLINE

For additional test practice, use Self-Check Quizzes—Chapter 2 at glencoe.com.

Need Extra Help?													
If you missed question. . .	1	2	3	4	5	6	7	8	9	10	11	12	13
Go to page. . .	46	50	59	64	45	52	56	66	64	64	64	64	64

Earth's Human and Cultural Geography

Essential Question

Movement The human population is growing rapidly, but the world in which people live is, in many ways, becoming a smaller place. In the past, many cultures were isolated from each other. Today, individuals and countries are linked in a global economy and by forms of communication that can instantly bring them together. What factors bring about changes in cultures?

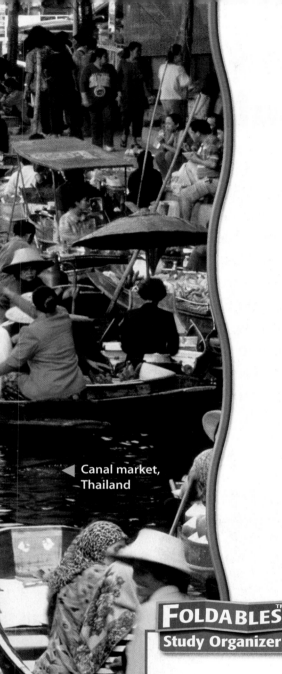

◀ Canal market, Thailand

BIG Ideas

Section 1: World Population

BIG IDEA Geographers study how people and physical features are distributed on Earth's surface. Although the world's population is increasing, people still live on only a small part of the Earth's surface.

Section 2: Global Cultures

BIG IDEA Culture influences people's perceptions about places and regions. The world's population is made up of different cultures, each of which is based on common beliefs, customs, and traits.

Section 3: Resources, Technology, and World Trade

BIG IDEA Patterns of economic activities result in global interdependence. Because resources are unevenly distributed, the nations of the world must trade with each other. New technologies make the economies of nations more dependent on one another.

FOLDABLES™
Study Organizer

Categorizing Information Make this Foldable to organize information about Earth's population; cultures; and resources, technology, and trade.

Step 1 Place two sheets of paper about 1 inch apart.

Step 2 Fold the paper to form four equal tabs.

Step 3 Staple the sheets, and label each tab as shown.

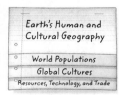

Earth's Human and Cultural Geography

World Populations

Global Cultures

Resources, Technology, and Trade

Reading and Writing As you read the chapter, take notes under the appropriate tab. Write a main idea for each section using your Foldable.

Social Studies ONLINE

To preview Chapter 3, go to glencoe.com.

World Population

Guide to Reading

BIG Idea

Geographers study how people and physical features are distributed on Earth's surface.

Content Vocabulary

- death rate *(p. 73)*
- birthrate *(p. 73)*
- famine *(p. 73)*
- population density *(p. 74)*
- urbanization *(p. 75)*
- emigrate *(p. 75)*
- refugee *(p. 76)*

Academic Vocabulary

- technology *(p. 73)*
- internal *(p. 75)*

Reading Strategy

Determining Cause and Effect
Use a diagram like the one below to show the causes and effects of global migration.

Causes   Effects

Global Migration

Picture This Forty years ago, for every car in China, there were 250 bicycles, earning the country the nickname "Bicycle Kingdom." Today, however, China, which is the world's most populous country, has a new love—the automobile. People are earning more money, and the number of people who own cars is increasing. Because of this, it is feared that China's cities will become more polluted and congested with traffic. Read this section to learn about the world's population and the effects it has on the Earth.

▼ **Residents of Shanghai, China**

Population Growth

Main Idea **The world's population has increased rapidly in the past two centuries, creating many new challenges.**

Geography and You Has the population in your community increased or decreased in recent years? Are new schools being built, for example? Read to find out why the world's population has grown so fast.

In the past 200 years, the world's population has increased rapidly. Around 1800, a billion people lived on Earth. Today the population is more than 6 billion.

Reasons for Population Growth

One reason the population has grown so fast in the last 200 years is that the death rate has gone down. The **death rate** is the number of deaths per year for every 1,000 people. Better health care and living conditions, as well as more plentiful food supplies, have decreased the death rate.

Another reason why the population has grown is high birthrates in Asia, Africa, and Latin America. The **birthrate** is the number of children born each year for every 1,000 people. High numbers of healthy births combined with lower death rates have increased the population growth, especially in these areas of the world.

Challenges of Population Growth

More food is needed for a growing population. Advances in **technology,** such as improved irrigation systems and the creation of hardier plants, will continue to increase food production. On the other hand, warfare and crop failures can lead to **famine,** or a severe lack of food. Some countries may also face shortages of water and housing. Additionally, growing populations require more services, like those provided by hospitals and schools.

✔ **Reading Check** **Identifying** What has caused population growth in the last 200 years?

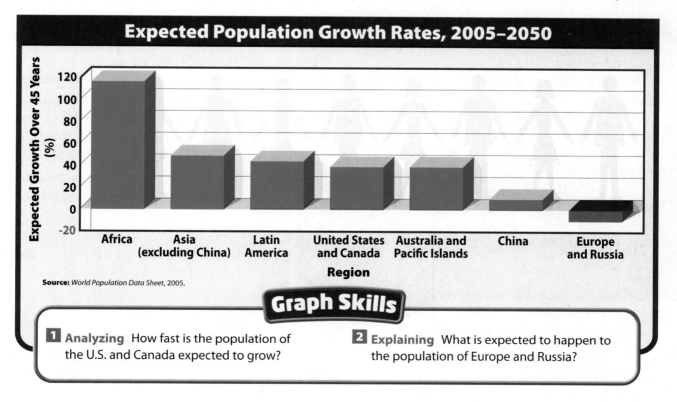

Expected Population Growth Rates, 2005–2050

Expected Growth Over 45 Years (%)

Region: Africa, Asia (excluding China), Latin America, United States and Canada, Australia and Pacific Islands, China, Europe and Russia

Source: *World Population Data Sheet, 2005.*

Graph Skills

1 **Analyzing** How fast is the population of the U.S. and Canada expected to grow?

2 **Explaining** What is expected to happen to the population of Europe and Russia?

Where People Live

Main Idea The Earth's population is not evenly distributed.

Geography and You Do you live in a city, a suburb, a small town, or a rural area? What are the advantages and disadvantages of your location? Read to find out where the world's people choose to live.

People live on a surprisingly small part of the Earth. Land covers only about 30 percent of the Earth's surface, and only half of this land is usable by humans. Deserts, high mountains, and ice-covered lands cannot support large numbers of people.

Population Distribution

On the usable land, population is not distributed, or spread, evenly. People nat-urally prefer to live in places that have fertile soil, mild climates, natural resources, and water resources, such as rivers and coastlines. Two-thirds of the world's people are clustered into five regions with these resources—East Asia, South Asia, Southeast Asia, Europe, and eastern North America. In most regions, more people live in cities than in rural areas because of the jobs and resources found there.

Population Density

Geographers have a way to figure out how crowded a country or region is. They measure **population density**—the average number of people living in a square mile or square kilometer. To arrive at this figure, the total population is divided by the total land area.

As you have just read, the world's population is not evenly distributed. Malaysia and Norway, for example, have about the same total land area, around 130,000 square miles (336,697 sq. km). Norway's population density is about 40 people per square mile (15 per sq. km). Malaysia, on the other hand, has a density of 205 people per square mile (79 per sq. km).

Population density represents an average. Remember that people are not distributed evenly throughout a country. Argentina, for example, has a population density of 36 people per square mile (14 per sq. km). However, the density around the city of Buenos Aires, where nearly one third of Argentina's people live, can be as high as 5,723 people per square mile (14,827 per sq. km).

Population Density

NATIONAL GEOGRAPHIC

▲ Population density is low on the grasslands of Mongolia. In contrast, Tokyo, Japan (inset), has a high population density. **Regions** In what regions are most of the world's people clustered?

Reading Check **Determining Cause and Effect** Why does much of the world's population live on a relatively small area of the Earth?

Population Movement

Main Idea Large numbers of people migrate from one place to another.

Geography and You Have you and your family ever moved? Read to learn some of the reasons why people all over the world move from one place to another.

Throughout history, millions of people have moved from one place to another. People continue to move today, sometimes as individuals, sometimes in large groups.

Types of Migration

Moving from place to place in the same country is known as **internal** migration. One kind of internal migration is the movement of people from farms and villages to cities. Such migrants are often in search of jobs. This type of movement results in **urbanization,** or the growth of cities. Urbanization has occurred rapidly in Asia, Africa, and Latin America.

Movement between countries is called international migration. Some people **emigrate,** or leave the country where they were born and move to another. They are emigrants in their homeland and immigrants in their new country. **Figure 1** shows the immigrant populations in regions of the world. Immigration has increased greatly in the past 200 years, partly due to better transportation.

NATIONAL GEOGRAPHIC

Figure 1 **World Immigrant Populations**

8.8%

13.5%

1.4%

1.9%

1.2%

15.1%

Immigrant population — Total population

Total population (millions)

Africa	905.7
Asia	3,920.5
Europe and Russia	730.2
Latin America	558.8
United States and Canada	328.8
Australia and Oceania	33.3

Map Skills

1 **Regions** Which region's population has the highest percentage of immigrants?

2 **Place** About how much of Africa's population is made up of immigrants?

Sources: *World Population Data Sheet,* 2005; *World Migrant Stock,* United Nations.

Reasons People Move

People migrate for a variety of reasons. Historians say that "push" factors convince people to leave their homes and "pull" factors attract them to another place. A shortage of farmland or few jobs in a region or country may "push" residents to emigrate. The lure of jobs has worked as a "pull" factor, attracting many immigrants to the United States.

People who are forced to flee to another country to escape wars, persecution, or natural disasters are called **refugees.** For example, 2 million refugees fled mass killings in Rwanda during the late 1990s.

Impact of Migration

Mass migrations of people have major impacts—both on the region they leave and on the region where they settle. When emigrants leave a country, its population decreases or does not increase as quickly. This can ease overcrowding. However, if skilled or educated workers leave, emigration may hurt the country's economy. Emigration can also divide families.

Migration also affects the country to which people move. Immigrants bring with them new forms of music, art, foods, and language. Some native-born citizens, however, fear or resent immigrants and the changes that they bring. This has led to violence and unjust treatment toward newcomers in some instances.

 Reading Check **Making Generalizations**
Why have so many rural citizens moved to cities in Asia, Africa, and Latin America?

Section Review

Social Studies ONLINE
Study Central™ To review this section, go to glencoe.com.

Vocabulary

1. **Explain** the meaning of the following terms by using each one in a sentence.
   - **a.** death rate
   - **b.** birthrate
   - **c.** famine
   - **d.** population density
   - **e.** urbanization
   - **f.** emigrate
   - **g.** refugee

Main Ideas

2. **Making Connections** How might the availability of food affect population growth?

3. **Explaining** What geographic factors lead people to live in certain areas of the world?

4. **Summarizing** Use a diagram like the one below to summarize the positive and negative effects of emigration on a country.

Critical Thinking

5. **BIG Idea** Discuss the factors that can cause a country's population to grow rapidly.

6. **Challenge** Explain the reasons people migrate. Identify which reasons are "push" factors and which are "pull" factors. Which factors do you think most strongly influence migrants? Explain.

Writing About Geography

7. **Expository Writing** Write a paragraph explaining how the Earth's population has changed in the past 200 years and how you think it will change in the next 50 years.

TIME
PERSPECTIVES

THE WORLD GOES GLOBAL

Technology and new methods of trade are affecting how the world interacts.

A local Inuit uses a laptop in the Canadian Arctic.

Around the world, technological advances are changing the way we live and work. Every day, new technologies make it possible for billions of e-mails and trillions of dollars to crisscross national borders. Communication between people and businesses and the movement of goods and money is done more quickly than ever before because of the Internet.

As technology continues to change, what might the world look like ten years from now? Inventions that create faster ways to communicate might make the world seem even smaller than it does today. And as globalization connects the world's economies as never before, people everywhere will learn about other nations and cultures.

Workers at a call center in India answer questions from American customers.

A GLOBAL MARKETPLACE

Venugopla Rao Moram is a highly sought after worker. Recently, the computer software engineer who lives in Bangalore, India, was offered five jobs during a two-week period. All of the offers were from companies whose headquarters are located thousands of miles from India.

Luckily, Moram will not have to travel that far to get to work. Computer companies from around the world are opening offices in Bangalore in order to hire Indian workers. Many Indians speak English and are well educated. This makes them valuable to foreign companies that are establishing workplaces in countries where labor is inexpensive. This type of labor helps manufacturers keep their production costs low.

As a result of **globalization**, a trend that is linking the world's nations through trade, thousands of Indians are working for foreign companies. In Moram's case, a business in California hired him to create software that makes the characters in video games jump and run. The software Moram produces becomes part of a product that is assembled in other countries and sold all over the world. All types of products, from toys to clothes to TVs, are being made and traded this way. As a result, economies are becoming much more connected—or global.

The Internet

The Internet has fueled globalization. The Internet is a giant electronic network that links computers all over the world. It was developed in the late 1960s when the U.S. military worked to connect its computers with those of college researchers so that they could share their ideas more easily. Over time, the Internet became available to everyone, and the way the world interacts changed forever.

The United States and the Global Economy

The United States trades with countries all over the world. It sells, or exports, some products, and buys, or imports, others. Here are the countries the U.S. did the most business with in 2005.

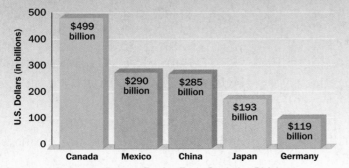

U.S. Dollars (in billions)

- Canada: $499 billion
- Mexico: $290 billion
- China: $285 billion
- Japan: $193 billion
- Germany: $119 billion

Source: U.S. Census Bureau, Foreign Trade Statistics Division.

INTERPRETING GRAPHS

Making Inferences Why might Canada and Mexico be the United States's top trading partners?

An anti-globalization demonstrator protests in Japan.

People all over the world can trade stocks on the New York Stock Exchange.

A Thai woman uses a bank machine.

The Internet also changed how people and companies buy goods. Today, just like you can shop online for games or CDs, so can businesses. For example, a business in need of computer software can use the Internet to research the products of computer companies from all over the world. With the click of a mouse, the buyer can research and compare prices for software products on a computer company's Web site or at an online store. Then, in seconds, the buyer can purchase the product.

Before the days of the Internet, a company in need of software could not have learned about suppliers and products as easily. As a result, business tended to be conducted more locally and at a slower pace. Today, a buyer can shop and trade online in minutes without leaving his or her desk. Companies can conduct business in less time and from anywhere in the world.

Sharing Globalization's Gains

The impact of globalization has been amazing, but its benefits have not been shared equally. **Developed countries**, or countries in which a great deal of manufacturing is carried out, have more goods to trade than **developing countries** that are still trying to industrialize. Also many companies prefer to build factories in wealthier countries rather than in poor ones, where support systems like roads and airports are often unavailable. As a result, some of the poorer nations in Asia and Africa have had a hard time creating any new jobs.

What steps can be taken to spread the benefits of globalization? International businesses and wealthy nations can be part of the solution. By 2002, businesses and countries had spent more than $3 trillion to help poorer countries build factories and transportation systems. Investing in such support systems could help businesses trade more effectively and grow. There is still much work to be done. Finding ways to help every nation share the gains of globalization is one of biggest challenges the world faces.

Lumber is processed at a Canadian mill for shipment to the United States.

EXPLORING THE ISSUE

1. Making Inferences Why do you think companies are concerned about how much money it costs to make a product?

2. Analyzing Information How might investing in transportation systems help developing countries?

The World Goes Global 79

MUSIC GOES GLOBAL

It has been said that music is the universal language. This has never been more true than in the Internet age. Today, music lovers can listen to music from all over the world. Online music stores and portable music players make it easy to listen to what you want, when you want.

In the past, listeners had much less control over the music they heard. Record producers and companies recorded the music of homegrown musicians, and radio stations played their songs. Artists and songs from different regions of the world were rarely played.

In the Internet age, however, music lovers are being exposed to sounds from around the world. West African drumming or Latin American dance music, for example, is available to anyone online. Listeners can just search for a **genre**, or style of music, and download a song for a small fee.

With such easy access to global sounds, it is not uncommon for a portable player to include a list of songs and artists from several countries. As a result, musicians are working to please the public by blending "international" material and elements into their acts. The American pop singer Christina Aguilera sings in English, but she has also recorded a CD completely in Spanish. Hip-hop artist Wyclef Jean mixes **Creole**, the language of Haiti, into his songs. Madonna has worn traditional costumes from Japan and Scotland during her tours.

In the twenty-first century, musicians and music lovers are no longer tied to the sounds of one nation. In fact, cross-cultural appeal in the music industry is becoming a key to success.

Wyclef Jean uses Haitian elements in his music.

REUTERS/GARY HERSHORN

EXPLORING THE ISSUE

1. **Determining Cause and Effect** How does the Internet help people learn about the music styles of performers from other countries?

2. **Making Inferences** List three reasons why it may be easier to buy music online than in a store that sells CDs.

REVIEW AND ASSESS

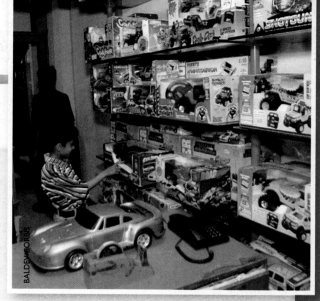

Many toys made in China are sold in other countries.

UNDERSTANDING THE ISSUE

1 **Making Connections** How has globalization affected the way some products are produced?

2 **Writing to Inform** Write a short article about how the Internet has changed the way that businesses shop for and buy goods.

3 **Writing to Persuade** Do you think that American musicians who combine music from other countries and cultures can become stars in the United States? Defend your answer in a letter to the president of a record company.

INTERNET RESEARCH ACTIVITIES

4 Go online to research the history of the Internet. Write an essay explaining why the Internet was created. Develop a time line that notes important developments.

5 With your teacher's help, use the Internet to research how many homes have access to the Internet in developed and developing nations. Compare the information and create a bar graph showing the top three countries in both categories.

BEYOND THE CLASSROOM

6 **Organize the class into three teams.** One group should represent developed nations, and another should represent developing nations. Debate this resolution: "Globalization is good for everyone." The third group of students will decide which team has the most convincing arguments.

7 **Take an inventory of your home.** Look for products that were made in other countries. Count the items that were imported from different countries. Make a chart to show how many countries are represented in your home.

The Universal Language

The Internet is changing the way people listen to music. In the Internet age, music lovers around the world are shopping online. Here is a look at the number of people visiting music sites.

125,648,125
110,729,189
96,095,620
73,049,912

Number of People (in millions)

130
120
110
100
90
80
70

June 2004   Dec. 2004   June 2005   Dec. 2005

Source: Nielsen/Net Ratings.

Building Graph Reading Skills

1. **Comparing** How many more people visited music Web sites in December 2005 than in December 2004?

2. **Making Inferences** How might the increase of shopping online for music affect traditional music stores?

The World Goes Global **81**

Guide to Reading

BIG Idea

Culture influences people's perceptions about places and regions.

Content Vocabulary

- culture (p. 83)
- ethnic group (p. 84)
- dialect (p. 84)
- democracy (p. 85)
- dictatorship (p. 86)
- monarchy (p. 86)
- civilization (p. 86)
- cultural diffusion (p. 87)
- culture region (p. 88)
- globalization (p. 89)

Academic Vocabulary

- widespread (p. 86)
- unique (p. 89)

Reading Strategy

Identifying Use a diagram like the one below to identify the elements of culture.

Elements of Culture

Global Cultures

Picture This The eagles that soar through the skies of the American southwest have long been sacred to the native peoples of the area. Many Native Americans believe that eagles have special qualities such as wisdom and courage. Eagle feathers are treated with respect and are often given as rewards for great deeds. Native American groups, such as the Tewa of New Mexico, perform dances to honor this beautiful bird. To learn more about how traditions reflect a culture's beliefs, read Section 2.

▼ **Honoring the eagle**

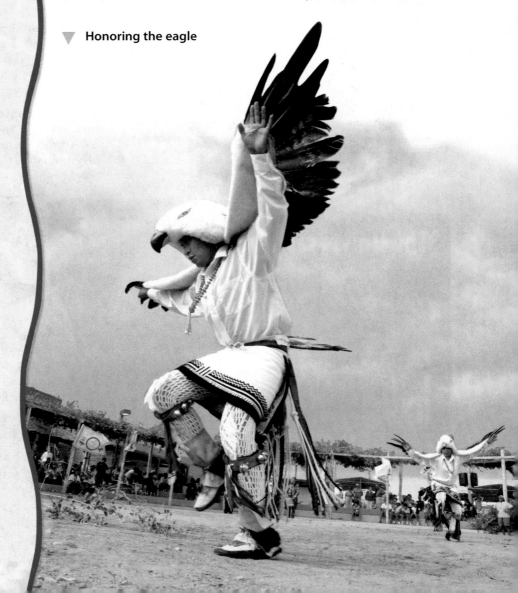

What Is Culture?

Main Idea **Culture refers to the many shared characteristics that define a group of people.**

Geography and You Think about the clothes you wear, the music you listen to, and the foods you eat. Read to learn about the many things that make up culture.

Culture is the way of life of a group of people who share similar beliefs and customs. A particular culture can be understood by looking at various elements: what languages the people speak, what religions they follow, and what smaller groups are part of their society. The study of culture also includes examining people's daily lives, the history they share, and the art forms they have created.

Geographers, anthropologists, and archaeologists all study culture. For example, geographers look at physical objects, such as food and housing. They also study elements such as religion, social groups, types of government, and economies. Anthropologists analyze cultures today to learn how different elements of culture are related. Archaeologists use the physical and historical objects of a culture, such as pottery and tools, to try to understand how people lived in the past. The work of all of these experts helps us better understand the world we live in.

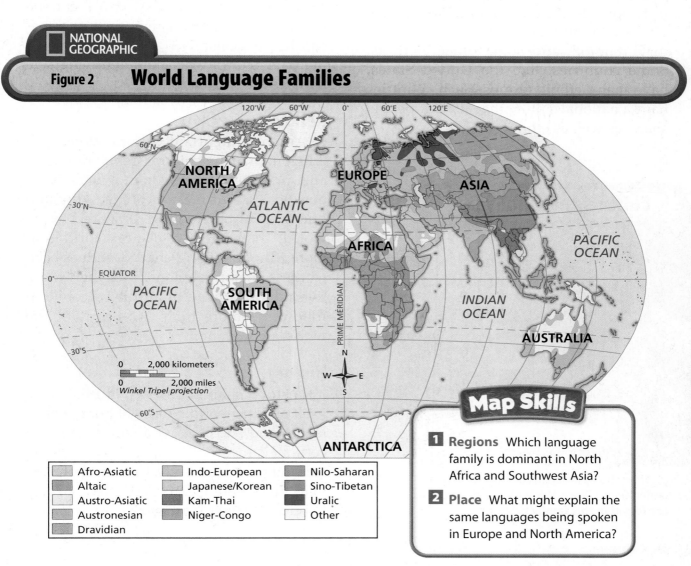

NATIONAL GEOGRAPHIC

Figure 2 **World Language Families**

Afro-Asiatic
Altaic
Austro-Asiatic
Austronesian
Dravidian
Indo-European
Japanese/Korean
Kam-Thai
Niger-Congo
Nilo-Saharan
Sino-Tibetan
Uralic
Other

Map Skills

1 Regions Which language family is dominant in North Africa and Southwest Asia?

2 Place What might explain the same languages being spoken in Europe and North America?

Social Groups

One way scientists study culture is by looking at different groups of people in a society. Each of us belongs to many social groups. For example, are you old or young? Male or female? A student, a worker, or both? Most social groups have rules of behavior that group members learn. The process by which people adjust their behavior to meet these rules is called socialization. Within society, each person has a certain status. Status refers to a person's importance or rank. In all cultures, the family is the most important social group. Although family structures vary from culture to culture, most of us first learn how to behave from our families.

People also belong to an **ethnic group.** This is a group that shares a language, history, religion, and some physical traits. Some countries, like the United States, have many ethnic groups. Such countries have a national culture that all their people share, as well as ethnic cultures.

Culture and Family Life

NATIONAL GEOGRAPHIC

▲ Households in Japan can include several generations. *Place* **What elements of culture are found in this family gathering?**

In some cases, people come to believe that their own culture is superior to, or better than, other cultures. This attitude is called ethnocentrism. If carried to extremes, ethnocentrism may cause hatred and persecution of other groups.

Language

Sharing a language is one of the strongest unifying forces for a culture. A language, however, may have different variations called dialects. A **dialect** is a local form of a language that may have a distinct vocabulary and pronunciation. Despite different dialects, speakers of the same language can usually understand one another.

More than 2,000 languages are spoken around the world today. Most can be grouped with related languages into a specific language family. **Figure 2** on the preceding page shows where different language families are spoken today.

Religion

Another important cultural element is religion. In many cultures, religious beliefs and practices help people answer basic questions about life's meaning. Although hundreds of religions are practiced in the world, there are five major world religions. The following chart describes each of these major religions. Together, these five religions have more than 4.5 billion followers—more than two-thirds of the world's population.

History

History shapes how a culture views itself and the world. Stories about the challenges and successes of a culture support certain values and help people develop cultural pride and unity. Cultural holidays mark important events and enable people to celebrate their heritage.

Major World Religions

Religion	Major Leader	Followers	Beliefs
Buddhism	Siddhartha Gautama, the Buddha	378.8 million	Buddhism is based on the teachings of Siddhartha Gautama, known as the Buddha. The Buddha taught that the goal of life is to escape the cycle of birth and death by achieving a state of spiritual understanding called nirvana. Buddhists believe that they must follow an eight-step path to achieve nirvana.
Christianity	Jesus Christ	2.1 billion	Christianity is based on the belief in one God and the teachings and life of Jesus as described in the New Testament of the Bible. Christians believe that Jesus was the Son of God and was sent to Earth to save people from their sins.
Hinduism	Unknown	860.1 million	Hinduism is based on the belief in a supreme spiritual force known as Brahman as recorded in sacred texts, including the Upanishads. Hindus believe that to unite with Brahman, they must first pass through many lives, being reborn into new forms. To move closer to Brahman they must make improvements in each of their lives.
Islam	Muhammad	1.3 billion	Islam is based on the belief in one God, Allah, as revealed through the prophet Muhammad. The Muslim sacred text is the Quran. Muslims follow five major acts of worship known as the Five Pillars of Islam.
Judaism	Abraham	15.1 million	Judaism is based on the belief in one God and the spiritual and ethical principles handed down by God. These principles, including the Ten Commandments, are presented in Jewish sacred texts collected in the Hebrew Bible.

Source: *Encyclopædia Britannica*, 2005.

Chart Skills

1 Identifying Which two religions include the belief that people are reborn into new forms?

2 Explaining What help do these religions give to their followers?

Daily Life

Food, clothing, and shelter are basic human needs. The type of food you eat and how you eat it reflect your culture. Do you use chopsticks, a fork, or bread to scoop up your food? The home you live in and the clothing that you wear reflect your culture and your physical surroundings. For example, the clothing people wear in the high, chilly Andes of South America differs greatly from the clothing people wear on the warm savannas of Africa.

Arts

Through music, painting, sculpture, dance, and literature, people express what they think is beautiful and meaningful. The arts can also tell stories about important figures and events in the culture.

Government

People need rules in order to live together without conflict. Governments fulfill this need. They can be either limited or unlimited. A limited government restricts the powers of its leaders. For example, in a **democracy,** power is held by the people.

Social Studies ONLINE

Student Web Activity Visit <u>glencoe.com</u> to learn more about forms of government around the world.

Most democracies today are called representative democracies because the people choose leaders to represent them and make decisions. In unlimited governments, leaders are all-powerful. In a **dictatorship**, for instance, the leader, or dictator, rules by force. Dictators often limit citizens' freedoms.

A **monarchy** is a government led by a king or queen who inherits power by being born into the ruling family. For much of history, monarchies had unlimited power. Today, most monarchies are constitutional monarchies in which elected legislatures hold most of the power.

Economy

People in every culture must earn a living. Geographers study economic activities to see how a culture uses its resources and trades with other places. An economy's success can be seen in people's quality of life—how well they eat and live and what kind of health care they receive.

✔**Reading Check** **Describing** Describe three elements that help unify a culture.

The Growth of Industry

NATIONAL GEOGRAPHIC

▲ Some of the earliest factories, like this one in Lowell, Massachusetts, used machines to make cloth. *Movement* **What recent technological advancements have led to cultural changes?**

Cultural Change

Main Idea **Cultures are constantly changing and influencing each other.**

Geography and You What influences from other cultures can you see in your community? Read on to see how cultures relate to each other and change.

Over time, all cultures experience change. Sometimes that change results from inventions and innovations, or technological improvements that bring about new ways of life. Sometimes change results from the influence of other cultures.

Inventions and Technology

Thousands of years ago, humans were hunters and gatherers who lived and traveled in small groups. After 8000 B.C., people learned to farm. Planting crops led to more reliable food supplies and larger populations. It also allowed people to settle in one place. Historians call this change the Agricultural Revolution. It had a huge impact on human culture because it led people to create **civilizations,** or highly developed cultures, in river valleys found in present-day Iraq, Egypt, India, and China. The people of these civilizations made a number of important advancements including building cities, forming governments, founding religions, and developing writing systems.

The world remained largely agricultural through the A.D. 1700s. Around that time, some countries began to industrialize, or use machines to make goods. The **widespread** use of machines made economies more productive. Industrial nations produced more food, goods, and wealth, which caused sweeping cultural changes.

The world has changed greatly in the past three decades. Computers have transformed businesses and households. Advances in communications allow people throughout the world to send and receive information almost instantly. Medical technology has dramatically increased human life expectancy. Each of these developments has sparked cultural changes.

Cultural Diffusion

The other major cause of cultural change is influence from other cultures. The process of spreading ideas, languages, or customs from one culture to another is called **cultural diffusion.** In the past, diffusion has taken place through trade, migration, and conquest. In recent years, new methods of communication have also led to cultural diffusion.

Historically, trade began with the exchange of goods, often over great distances. Soon trade also brought new ideas and practices to an area. Buddhist merchants brought their religion to China along trade routes, and Muslim traders shared their religious beliefs with people in West Africa. Trade continues to be a major means of cultural diffusion.

The movement of people from one place to another also leads to cultural diffusion. When Europeans arrived in North America, they brought horses, which were new to the continent. Native Americans living on the Great Plains quickly adopted the horse because it made hunting easier.

The conquest of one group by another is a third way culture can spread. Conquerors bring their culture to conquered areas. For example, the Romance languages, such as Italian, French, Spanish, and Portuguese, reflect the influence of the Roman Empire. These languages are based on Latin, the language of ancient Rome. In turn, conquered peoples can influence the culture of the conquerors. Christianity

NATIONAL GEOGRAPHIC

Cultural Influences

Children around the world, such as these students in China, anticipate each new Harry Potter book and movie. The books have been translated into 47 languages. *Movement* **What is cultural diffusion?**

arose among the Jews, a people conquered by the Roman Empire. In time, Christianity became a major religion in the empire.

Today television, movies, and the Internet contribute to cultural diffusion. For example, movies made in the United States, Mexico, Brazil, and India are seen around the world, introducing people to different ways of life. The Internet allows people to have contact with and be influenced by people from other cultures.

✓ **Reading Check** **Analyzing Information**
Describe one way that cultural diffusion takes place.

Regional and Global Cultures

Main Idea **As countries and regions share cultural traits, a global culture is emerging.**

Geography and You What do you have in common with a student who lives across town or across the country? Read to learn how similarities help to define cultural regions.

As you recall, geographers use the term *regions* for areas that share common physical characteristics. Likewise, geographers divide the world into several culture regions, as shown in **Figure 3**. A **culture region** is an area that includes different countries that share similar cultural traits.

Culture Regions

The countries in each culture region generally have similar social groups, governments, economic systems, religions, languages, ethnic groups, and histories. One example of a culture region is North Africa, Southwest Asia, and Central Asia. In that area, Islam is the dominant religion. Another culture region is Canada and the United States. These countries have similar languages, histories, and ethnic groups.

As you study the world, you will begin to recognize the characteristics shared by the

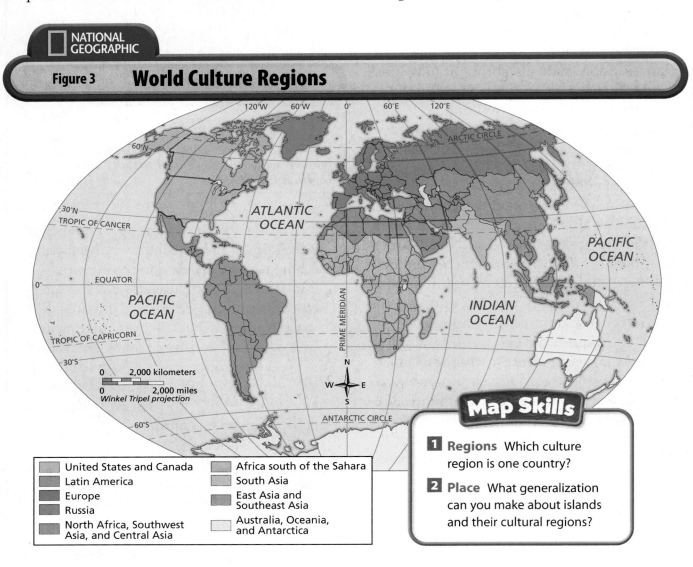

NATIONAL GEOGRAPHIC

Figure 3   **World Culture Regions**

Legend:
- United States and Canada
- Latin America
- Europe
- Russia
- North Africa, Southwest Asia, and Central Asia
- Africa south of the Sahara
- South Asia
- East Asia and Southeast Asia
- Australia, Oceania, and Antarctica

Map Skills

1 **Regions** Which culture region is one country?

2 **Place** What generalization can you make about islands and their cultural regions?

countries in each culture region. Although these countries are similar, they also have **unique** traits that set them apart.

Global Culture

Recent advances in communications and technology have helped break down barriers between culture regions. The result is **globalization,** or the development of a worldwide culture with an interdependent economy.

With globalization, individual economies rely greatly upon one another for resources and markets. Some people believe that as the global culture grows, local cultures will become less important. They point out that globalization might even erase the traditions and customs of smaller groups.

 Defining What are culture regions?

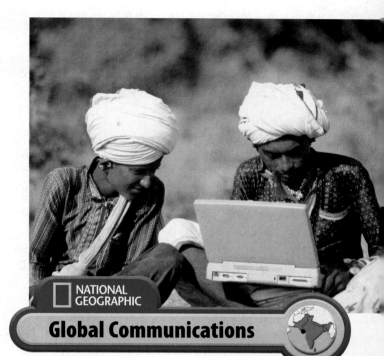

NATIONAL GEOGRAPHIC

Global Communications

The Internet and other forms of communications have helped link people around the world, such as these boys in rural India. **Movement** **What might happen as the global culture grows?**

Social Studies ONLINE
Study Central™ To review this section, go to glencoe.com.

Vocabulary

1. **Explain** the meaning of *culture, ethnic group, dialect, democracy, dictatorship, monarchy, civilization, cultural diffusion, culture region,* and *globalization* by writing three to four paragraphs that use all of the terms.

Main Ideas

2. **Explaining** What is an ethnic group, and how do ethnic groups relate to a region's culture?

3. **Summarizing** Use a diagram like the one below to identify the advancements made by the world's earliest civilizations.

```
        (   )            (   )
             \          /
              ( Earliest Civilizations )
             /          \
        (   )            (   )
```

4. **Explaining** Why is globalization occurring?

Critical Thinking

5. **BIG Idea** Explain the different ways that cultural change can occur.

6. **Challenge** How do local and national differences affect culture on a regional or global level?

Writing About Geography

7. **Personal Writing** Write a journal entry describing examples of globalization that you have witnessed. Then add your predictions about how globalization might affect your community in the future.

Is Globalization Good for Everyone?

Globalization is sometimes defined as the linking together of the world's nations through trade. This trade among nations allows people from different cultures to interact with each other. As a result, cultures begin sharing traits with others. People disagree about the effects of globalization on economies and cultures. Some people think that globalization helps countries by providing them with jobs and new technologies. However, others believe that globalization destroys the cultural traditions and customs of smaller groups.

 Globalization

One of the main restraints on liberty has always been "the tyranny [unjust use of power] of place." At its crudest, this has meant restrictions, both political and economic, on where people can live, but it also includes restrictions on where people can go, what they can buy, where they can invest, and what they can read, hear, or see. Globalization by its nature brings down these barriers, and it helps hand the power to choose to the individual.

—John Micklethwait and Adrian Wooldridge
A Future Perfect: The Essentials of Globalization

Against Globalization

For millions of people globalization has not worked. Many have been actually made worse off, as they have seen their jobs destroyed and their lives become more insecure. They have felt increasingly powerless against forces beyond their control. They have seen their democracies undermined, their cultures eroded.

If globalization continues to be conducted in the way that [it] has been in the past, if we continue to fail to learn from our mistakes, globalization will not only not succeed in promoting development but will continue to create poverty and instability.

—Joseph Stiglitz
Globalization and Its Discontents

You Be the Geographer

1. **Identifying** Choose a sentence from each opinion that best summarizes the authors' views about globalization.

2. **Critical Thinking** What does Stiglitz mean when he writes ". . . globalization . . . will continue to create poverty and instability"? Use the definition of *globalization* to explain your answer.

3. **Read to Write** Write one paragraph that identifies how globalization might benefit a nation. Then write a paragraph that describes how globalization might harm a nation.

SECTION 3

Resources, Technology, and World Trade

BIG Idea
Patterns of economic activities result in global interdependence.

Content Vocabulary

- natural resource *(p. 93)*
- renewable resource *(p. 93)*
- nonrenewable resource *(p. 93)*
- economic system *(p. 94)*
- developed country *(p. 94)*
- developing country *(p. 94)*
- newly industrialized country *(p. 94)*
- export *(p. 95)*
- import *(p. 95)*
- tariff *(p. 95)*
- quota *(p. 95)*
- free trade *(p. 96)*
- interdependence *(p. 96)*

Academic Vocabulary

- finite *(p. 93)*
- finance *(p. 95)*

Reading Strategy

Categorizing Information Use a diagram like the one below to list three specific examples of each type of natural resource.

Renewable Resources	Nonrenewable Resources
1.	
2.	
3.	

Picture This It might not have temperature controls, but this solar stove is one of the most important household appliances in Chinese homes. China is a world leader in the use of solar energy. As China's economy has grown, the demand for fuel has driven energy costs up, increasing the desire to use alternative energy sources. Read this section to learn more about other resources and how the world's people use them.

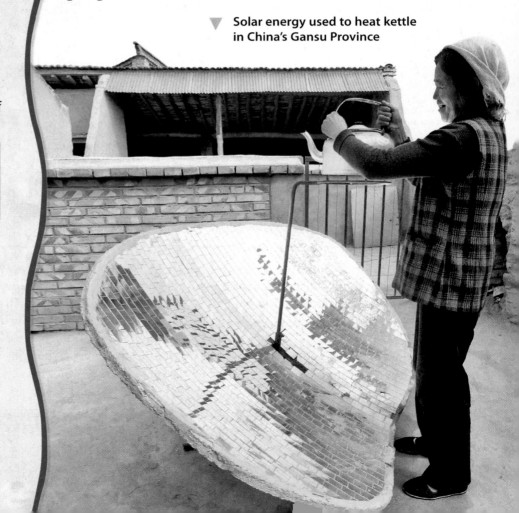

▼ **Solar energy used to heat kettle in China's Gansu Province**

Natural Resources

Main Idea **Earth's resources are not evenly distributed, nor do they all exist in endless supply.**

Geography and You What natural resources can you name? Read to learn about two kinds of natural resources.

Natural resources are materials from the Earth that people use to meet their needs. Soil, trees, wind, and oil are examples of natural resources. Such resources can provide food, shelter, goods, and energy.

Renewable resources are natural resources that cannot be used up or that can be replaced. For example, the sun, the wind, and water cannot be used up, and forests can replace themselves. Some renewable resources, such as rivers, the wind, and the sun, can produce electricity and are important sources of energy.

Most natural resources are **finite,** or limited in supply. They are called **nonrenewable resources.** Once humans use up these resources, they are gone. Minerals like iron ore and gold are nonrenewable, as are oil, coal, and other fossil fuels. Fossil fuels heat homes, run cars, and generate electricity.

✓ **Reading Check** **Identifying** Which energy resources are renewable? Nonrenewable?

NATIONAL GEOGRAPHIC **Maps In Motion** See StudentWorks™ Plus or glencoe.com.

Figure 4 **World Energy Production and Consumption**

- 🛢 Energy production (quadrillion Btus)
- 🛢 Energy consumption (quadrillion Btus)

111.8 88.5
92.9 60.3
72.7 27.4
101.0 70.6
49.2 29.1
36.0 28.7
19.6 11.0
10.2 14.0
10.3 5.1

Europe
Russia
Africa south of the Sahara
Australia, Oceania, and Antarctica
East Asia and Southeast Asia
North Africa, Southwest Asia, and Central Asia
United States and Canada
Latin America
South Asia

Map Skills

1 **Regions** Which region of the world consumes the least energy?

2 **Movement** Where do regions obtain the extra energy they need?

Source: Energy Information Administration, 2004.

Economies and Trade

Main Idea **An economy is the way people use and manage resources.**

Geography and You What kinds of goods and services do the people in your community produce? Read to find out about how economic decisions are made.

Economic Systems

To help make economic decisions, societies develop economic systems. An **economic system** is the method used to answer three key questions: what goods and services to produce, how to produce them, and who will receive them.

There are four kinds of economic systems. In a traditional economy, individuals decide what to produce and how to produce it. These choices are based on custom or habit. In these economies, people often do the same work as their parents and grandparents. Technology is often limited.

In a command economy, the government makes the key economic decisions about resources. It decides the costs of products and the wages workers earn, and individuals have little economic freedom.

In a market economy, individuals make their own economic decisions. People have the right to own property or businesses. Businesses make what they think customers want (supply). Consumers have choices about which goods and services to buy (demand). Prices are determined by supply and demand. People will buy less of an item as it gets more expensive. On the other hand, if the price is low, people will tend to buy more of an item.

Most nations have mixed economies, which is the fourth type of economic system. China, for example, has mostly a command economy, but the government allows some features of a market economy. The United States has mainly a market economy with some government involvement.

Developed and Developing Countries

Geographers look at economies in another way—how developed they are. A **developed country** has a mix of agriculture, a great deal of manufacturing, and service industries. Service industries, such as banking and health care, provide services rather than making products. Developed economies tend to rely on new technologies, and workers have relatively high incomes. Examples of developed countries include the United States, France, and Japan.

Countries with economies that are not as advanced are called **developing countries.** These countries have little industry. Agriculture remains important, and incomes per person are generally low. Developing countries include Sierra Leone, Cambodia, and Guatemala.

Still other countries are becoming more industrial. Geographers call these countries **newly industrialized countries.** South Korea, Thailand, and Singapore are all moving toward economies like those in developed countries. The chart below shows divisions in the economies of a developed, a developing, and a newly industrialized country.

Economic Divisions

Country	Agriculture	Industry	Services
United States	1%	20.4%	78.7%
Sierra Leone	49%	31%	21%
Thailand	9.9%	44.1%	46%

Source: *World Factbook*, 2006.

World Trade

Resources, like people, are not distributed evenly around the world. Because most countries have more than they need of some resources and not enough of others, trade is important.

Trade allows nations to **export**, or sell to other countries, the resources they have in abundance or the products made from those resources. They also **import**, or buy from other countries, the resources they do not have or the products they cannot make themselves.

Trade is important for both developed and developing nations. For example, the countries of Europe import what they need—food, energy resources, and minerals—to maintain their successful economies. The developing nations, in turn, rely on the sale of their products and resources to **finance**, or pay for, efforts to further industrialize and build their economies.

Barriers to Trade

Nations try to manage trade in order to boost their own economies. Some nations use **tariffs**, or taxes, to increase the price of imported goods. By making imported items more expensive, tariffs encourage consumers to buy less expensive items that are manufactured in their own country.

Quotas are another barrier to trade. A **quota** is a limit on how many items of a particular product can be imported from a certain nation.

TIME GLOBAL CITIZENS

NAME: BONO   **HOME COUNTRY:** Ireland

ACHIEVEMENT: The lead singer of the mega-rock band U2 has proven himself to be one of the world's most effective voices for the poor. In 2005, he convinced leaders from the world's wealthiest countries, such as the United States and Japan, to approve a $50 billion aid package—including $25 billion for Africa. Thanks largely to Bono, the leaders pledged to make lifesaving drugs available to poor people with HIV and also agreed that the 18 poorest African nations did not have to pay back money they had borrowed from several nations and organizations. Now they can spend the money on health care and schools rather than on paying back loans.

QUOTE: "There is a goal out there worthy of our generation. . . . It is the defeat of humanity's oldest foe: disease."

Bono sings for children in Ghana, while U.S. Treasury Secretary Paul O'Neil looks on.

CITIZENS IN ACTION How might Bono's actions today help people 10 years from now?

Free Trade

In recent years, many countries have agreed to get rid of trade barriers. The removal of trade limits so that goods flow freely among countries is called **free trade.** Often countries sign formal treaties agreeing to free trade. For example, in 1992 Canada, the United States, and Mexico signed the North American Free Trade Agreement (NAFTA). This pact removed most trade barriers between the three nations.

Interdependence and Technology

Growing trade among the world's countries has resulted in the globalization of the world's economies. As a result, the world's people and economies have become more interdependent. **Interdependence** means that countries rely on each other for ideas, goods, services, and markets, or places to sell their goods. When economies are linked together, a drought or a war in one region can cause price increases or shortages in another region far away.

Interdependence has come about in part because of new technologies. During the past 200 years, the invention of new technologies has occurred much faster than at any other time in history. Advances in transportation, such as trains and airplanes, and in communication, such as telephones and the Internet, have contributed greatly to globalization.

Reading Check **Explaining** Explain why trade barriers exist, and describe two types of trade barriers.

Section **3** Review

Social Studies ONLINE
Study Central™ To review this section, go to glencoe.com.

Vocabulary

1. **Explain** the significance of:
   a. natural resource
   b. renewable resource
   c. nonrenewable resource
   d. economic system
   e. developed country
   f. developing country
   g. newly industrialized country
   h. export
   i. import
   j. tarriff
   k. quota
   l. free trade
   m. interdependence

Main Ideas

2. **Explaining** Why do people need natural resources?

3. **Comparing and Contrasting** Use a Venn diagram like the one below to compare and contrast developed and developing countries.

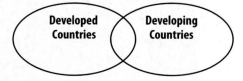

Critical Thinking

4. **Analyzing** Why has the world become more interdependent in recent years?

5. **BIG Idea** Explain how the distribution of natural resources relates to world trade.

6. **Challenge** In what ways might interdependence influence a place's cultural identity? Explain in two paragraphs.

Writing About Geography

7. **Using Your FOLDABLES** Use your Foldable to write a paragraph that predicts how population patterns might affect world resources in the future.

World Population

- Low death rates and high birthrates have led to rapid population growth.

- Some areas of the world are more densely populated than others.

- Nearly half of the world's population lives in cities.

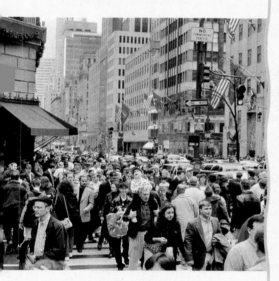

Commuters, New York City

Culture

- Culture is the way of life of a group of people who share similar beliefs and customs.

- Cultures change over time and influence one another.

- Modern technology has broken down barriers and helped create a global culture.

Oil worker, Iraq

Natural Resources

- Renewable resources either cannot be used up or can be replaced.

- Some resources—such as fossil fuels and minerals—are nonrenewable.

World Economies

- The four kinds of economic systems are traditional, command, market, and mixed.

- Developed countries use advanced technology and are highly productive.

- Developing countries have less advanced technology and are generally less productive.

World Trade

- In recent years, many countries have agreed to eliminate trade barriers.

- Growing trade among countries has made the world's people more interdependent.

Mexican president Vicente Fox (left), Canadian prime minister Jean Chrétien (center), and U.S. president George W. Bush (right) celebrate a trade agreement.

Grocery store in Yogakarta, Indonesia

STANDARDIZED TEST PRACTICE

TEST-TAKING **TIP**

Think of answers in your head before looking at the possible answers so that the choices on the test will not throw you off or trick you.

Reviewing Vocabulary

Directions: Choose the word(s) that best completes the sentence.

1. Geographers measure _____ to determine how crowded a country or region is.

A refugees

B population density

C death rates

D birthrates

2. _____ are people who are forced to flee to another country to escape wars, persecution, or natural disasters.

A Immigrants

B Free traders

C Refugees

D Importers

3. A(n) _____ group shares a language, history, religion, and some physical traits.

A democratic

B global

C social

D ethnic

4. Countries with a mix of agriculture and a great deal of manufacturing and service industries are called _____ countries.

A developed

B underdeveloped

C overdeveloped

D developing

Reviewing Main Ideas

Directions: Choose the best answer for each question.

Section 1 *(pp. 72–76)*

5. One reason for the rapid increase in world population over the last two centuries is _____ .

A increased migration

B increased population density

C improved health care

D urbanization

6. An example of a "push factor" for migration is _____ in the homeland.

A a shortage of jobs

B an abundance of jobs

C low population density

D an abundance of farmland

Section 2 *(pp. 82–89)*

7. In recent years more and more countries and regions are sharing cultural traits resulting in a(n) _____ culture.

A isolated

B global

C refugee

D ethnic

Section 3 *(pp. 92–96)*

8. To answer the questions of what goods and services to produce, how to produce them, and who will receive them, societies develop _____ .

A quota systems

B trading systems

C manufacturing systems

D economic systems

GO ON

Critical Thinking

Directions: Choose the best answer for each question.

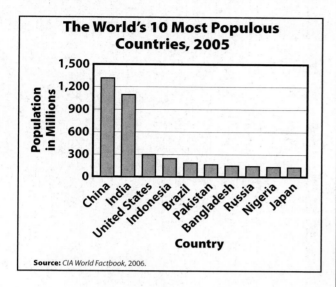

The World's 10 Most Populous Countries, 2005

Population in Millions: 1,500 / 1,200 / 900 / 600 / 300 / 0

Countries: China, India, United States, Indonesia, Brazil, Pakistan, Bangladesh, Russia, Nigeria, Japan

Country

Source: *CIA World Factbook*, 2006.

9. Based on the graph, what continent would likely be the most densely populated?

 A North America

 B South America

 C Asia

 D Africa

10. In which two countries would you expect to see the highest birthrates?

 A United States and Russia

 B India and China

 C Pakistan and Bangladesh

 D Brazil and Nigeria

Document-Based Questions

Directions: Analyze the document and answer the short-answer questions that follow.

[I]magine . . . that the world really is a 'global village.' . . . Say this village has 1,000 individuals, with all the characteristics of today's human race distributed in exactly the same proportions. . . .

Some 150 of the inhabitants live in [a wealthy] area of the village, about 780 in poorer districts. Another 70 or so live in a neighborhood that is [changing]. The average income per person is $6,000 a year. . . . But just 200 people [own] 86 percent of all the wealth, while nearly half of the villagers are eking out an existence on less than $2 per day. . . .

Life expectancy in the affluent district is nearly 78 years, in the poorer areas 64 years—and in the very poorest neighborhoods a mere 52 years. . . . Why do the poorest lag so far behind? Because in their neighborhoods there is a far higher incidence of infectious diseases and malnutrition, combined with an [serious] lack of access to safe water, sanitation, health care, adequate housing, education, and work.

—*Kofi Annan, Millennium Report, 2000*

11. Describe the differences in income in the village.

12. According to the writer, where is life expectancy higher and why is this so?

Extended Response

13. Write a letter to a government leader in which you try to persuade him or her to invest taxpayer money into research on how to better use our energy resources. Explain why you think either renewable or nonrenewable resources deserve more funds for research.

STOP

Social Studies ONLINE

For additional test practice, use Self-Check Quizzes—Chapter 3 at **glencoe.com**.

Need Extra Help?													
If you missed question...	1	2	3	4	5	6	7	8	9	10	11	12	13
Go to page...	74	76	84	94	73	76	89	94	73	73	94	94	93

TIME JOURNAL

It may be the middle of the night where you live, but in many parts of the world, people are well into their day. It's all because of the 24 time zones that divide up Earth. So while one part of the world sleeps, somewhere, kids are at school, workers are at their jobs, and some folks are having dinner. Take a look at what is happening on Earth at exactly the same moment during one day in April.

Monday, 7 a.m. LOS ANGELES, CALIFORNIA Some people are just waking up. Others are sitting down to breakfast. Early birds are headed to their jobs hoping to avoid traffic jams on the state's freeways. ▶

◀**Monday, 10 a.m. WASHINGTON, D.C.** Workers are at their desks. And at the White House, the wheels of government have been turning since 7 a.m. or even earlier, where 12-hour workdays are routine.

◀**Monday, 11 a.m. RIO DE JANEIRO, BRAZIL** Almost every day is a beach day in Rio. While beachgoers are enjoying sun and sand, traffic jams clog the city's streets, students are at their desks, and Rio's stores are filled with shoppers.

◀**Monday, 2 p.m. DAKAR, SENEGAL** Outdoor markets are packed in this west African nation. School is winding down for the day, and fishers are returning home with their day's catch from the Atlantic Ocean.

Monday, 5 p.m. CAIRO, EGYPT This capital city is filled with the sounds of people being called to prayer, vendors selling their goods at outdoor bazaars, and the blare of car and bus horns on traffic-clogged streets. Tourists and residents alike can marvel at the Pyramids of Giza built almost 5,000 years ago. ▼

Monday, 4 p.m. PARIS, FRANCE School is out and some kids are playing soccer, a favorite pastime. Other students are studying for exams to get into special high schools. Some tourists are having their pictures taken in front of the Eiffel Tower while others are visiting the city's famous museums, perhaps catching a glimpse of the *Mona Lisa*. ▶

Washington, D.C., U.S.

Moscow, Russia

Paris, France

Beijing, China

Los Angeles, U.S.

Cairo, Egypt

Dhaka, Bangladesh

Dakar, Senegal

Rio de Janeiro, Brazil

Wellington, New Zealand

Tuesday, 2 a.m. WELLINGTON, NEW ZEALAND
What do Kiwis (a nickname for New Zealanders) do when they can't sleep? They might count sheep. That's because the nation's 45 million woolly animals outnumber the island-nation's human inhabitants 11 to 1. ▶

Monday, 10 p.m. BEIJING, CHINA
The day is winding down for most of the 15 million residents of the nation's capital. China, with its more than one billion people, has one of the world's fastest growing economies. Night workers, including people who work with American companies, are starting their day, keeping to a U.S. time schedule. ▶

Monday, 6 p.m. MOSCOW, RUSSIA This huge country has 11 time zones. The nation, which has turned from communism to democracy, is undergoing a construction boom. Workers are going home for dinner. ▼

◀ **Monday, 8 p.m. DHAKA, BANGLADESH** Some residents of this city are sitting down to a dinner of fish or spicy curries. Meanwhile, fans of cricket, a popular sport in this country, are cheering for their favorite team.

Ice skating in Central
Park, New York City ▶

**NATIONAL
GEOGRAPHIC**

NGS ONLINE For more information about the region,
see www.nationalgeographic.com/education.

The United States and Canada

Where Is It?

A It is about 2,022 miles (3,254 km) from New York City to Edmonton.

B It is about 2,444 miles (3,933 km) from New York City to Los Angeles.

How Big Is It?

The land area of the region of the United States and Canada is about 7.7 million square miles (19.9 million sq. km). In area, Canada is the second-largest country in the world, and the United States is the third largest. The United States has many more people than Canada, however, and is the third-most-populous country in the world, after China and India.

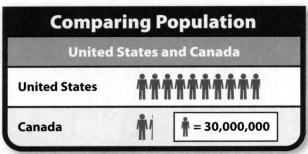

Comparing Population

United States and Canada

| United States | 👤👤👤👤👤👤👤👤👤👤 | |
| Canada | 👤 | 👤 = 30,000,000 |

Source: *World Population Data Sheet, 2005.*

GEO Fast Facts

Highest Point

Mount McKinley
(Alaska, United States)
20,320 ft. (6,194 m) high

Largest Lake

Lake Superior
(United States, Canada)
31,800 sq. mi.
(82,362 sq. km)

Lowest Point

Death Valley
(California, United States)
282 ft. (86 m)
below sea level

Longest River

Mississippi-Missouri
(United States)
3,877 mi. (6,238 km) long

Regional Atlas

The United States and Canada
PHYSICAL

RUSSIA

EUROPE

ARCTIC OCEAN

Chukchi Sea

Bering Strait

Bering Sea

Ellesmere Island

Greenland

ARCTIC CIRCLE

Mt. McKinley 20,320 ft. (6,194 m)

Brooks Range

Yukon R.

Beaufort Sea

Alaska Range

Aleutian Range

Gulf of Alaska

Mt. Logan 19,524 ft. (5,951 m)

YUKON PLATEAU

Mackenzie Mts.

Mackenzie R.

Great Bear Lake

Victoria Island

Baffin Island

Labrador Sea

Great Slave Lake

Lake Athabasca

Hudson Bay

COAST MOUNTAINS

ROCKY

Athabasca R.

Churchill R.

Saskatchewan R.

Nelson R.

James Bay

CANADIAN SHIELD

Gulf of St. Lawrence

Vancouver Island

PACIFIC OCEAN

Cascade Range

COLUMBIA PLATEAU

MOUNTAINS

Lake Winnipeg

Lake Superior

Laurentian Mts.

St. Lawrence R.

Mt. Shasta 14,162 ft. (4,317 m)

Snake R.

GREAT BASIN

Great Salt Lake

Platte R.

Missouri R.

GREAT PLAINS

Lake Michigan

Lake Huron

Lake Ontario

Lake Erie

APPALACHIAN MTS.

Chesapeake Bay

Sierra Nevada

Death Valley

Mojave Desert

COLORADO PLATEAU

Colorado R.

CENTRAL LOWLAND

Ohio R.

PIEDMONT

ATLANTIC OCEAN

Mt. Whitney 14,495 ft. (4,418 m)

Sonoran Desert

Rio Grande

Red R.

Arkansas R.

Mississippi R.

COASTAL PLAINS

Florida Keys

TROPIC OF CANCER

Gulf of Mexico

MEXICO

Hawaiian Islands

Niihau Kauai

Kaula

Oahu Molokai

Lanai Maui

Kahoolawe

Hawaii

PACIFIC OCEAN

0   200 kilometers

0   200 miles

Albers Equal-Area projection

Map Skills

1 **Place** What large bay lies north of the Canadian Shield?

2 **Location** Where is the highest point in the region?

0   600 kilometers

0   600 miles

Lambert Azimuthal Equal-Area projection

Elevations

13,100 ft. (4,000 m)

6,500 ft. (2,000 m)

1,600 ft. (500 m)

650 ft. (200 m)

0 ft. (0 m)

Below sea level

▲ Mountain peak

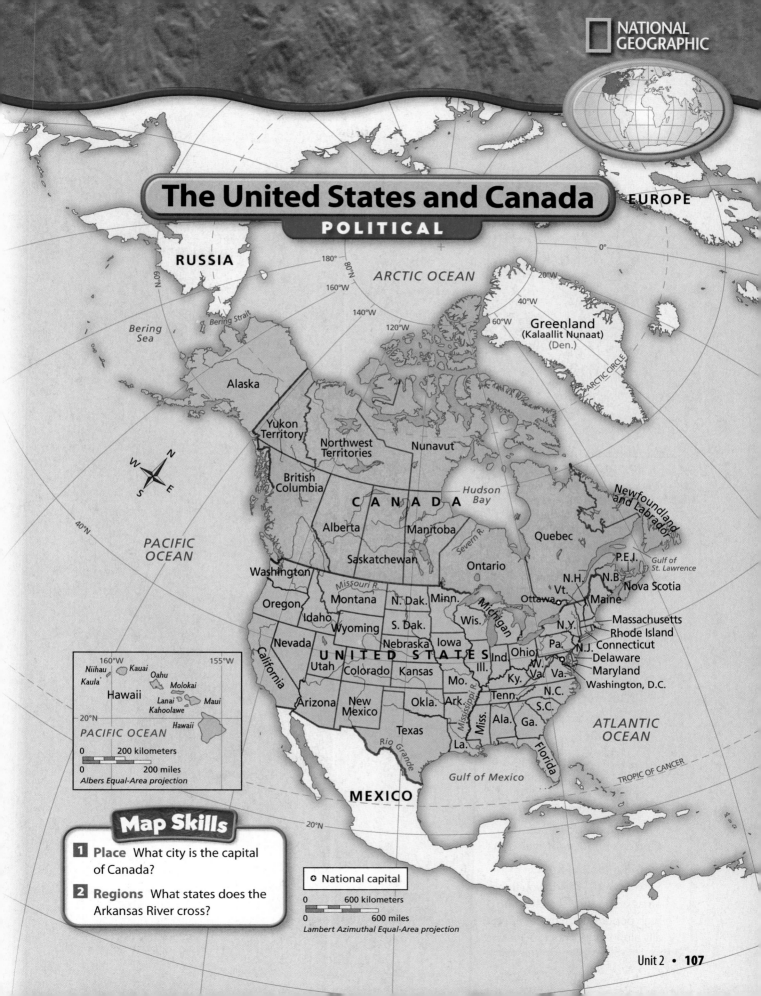

The United States and Canada
POLITICAL

EUROPE

RUSSIA

ARCTIC OCEAN

180°
80°N
160°W
140°W
120°W
0°
20°W
40°W
60°W

Bering Strait

Bering Sea

Greenland
(Kalaallit Nunaat)
(Den.)

ARCTIC CIRCLE

Alaska

Yukon Territory

Northwest Territories

Nunavut

60°N

Hudson Bay

Newfoundland and Labrador

British Columbia

C A N A D A

40°N

PACIFIC OCEAN

Alberta

Manitoba

Severn R.

Quebec

P.E.I.
Gulf of St. Lawrence

Saskatchewan

Ontario

N.H.
N.B.
Nova Scotia

Washington

Missouri R.

Montana

N. Dak.

Minn.

Michigan

Ottawa

Vt.
Maine

Oregon

Idaho

Wyoming

S. Dak.

Wis.

N.Y.

Massachusetts
Rhode Island

160°W   155°W

Niihau   Kauai
Kaula   Oahu
         Molokai
Hawaii   Lanai   Maui
         Kahoolawe
              Hawaii

20°N

PACIFIC OCEAN

0   200 kilometers
0   200 miles
Albers Equal-Area projection

Nevada

California

Utah

U N I T E D   S T A T E S

Nebraska

Colorado

Iowa

Kansas

Ind.

Ohio

Pa.

Ill.

Mo.

Mississippi R.

Ky.

W. Va.

Va.

N.J. Connecticut
Delaware
Maryland
Washington, D.C.

Arizona

New Mexico

Okla.

Ark.

Tenn.

N.C.

S.C.

Texas

Miss.

Ala.

Ga.

ATLANTIC OCEAN

Rio Grande

La.

Florida

MEXICO

Gulf of Mexico

TROPIC OF CANCER

20°N

1 Place What city is the capital of Canada?

2 Regions What states does the Arkansas River cross?

✧ National capital

0   600 kilometers
0   600 miles
Lambert Azimuthal Equal-Area projection

Regional Atlas

The United States and Canada
POPULATION DENSITY

EUROPE

RUSSIA

ARCTIC OCEAN

Bering Strait

ARCTIC CIRCLE

POPULATION

Per sq. mi.	Per sq. km
1,250 and over	500 and over
250–1,249	100–499
62–249	25–99
25–61	10–24
2.5–24	1–9
Less than 2.5	Less than 1

Hudson Bay

Gulf of St. Lawrence

Edmonton
Vancouver   Calgary
Seattle
Portland

Quebec
Ottawa–Gatineau   Montreal   Halifax
Minneapolis–St. Paul   Toronto   Boston
Milwaukee   Detroit   Providence
Sacramento   Chicago   Cleveland   New York–Newark
San Francisco-Oakland   Pittsburgh   Philadelphia
San Jose   Denver-Aurora   Indianapolis   Columbus   Baltimore
Kansas City   St. Louis   Cincinnati   Washington, D.C.
Las Vegas   Virginia Beach
Los Angeles
Riverside-San Bernardino   Memphis   Atlanta
San Diego   Phoenix-Mesa
Dallas-Ft. Worth
Austin   New Orleans   Orlando   ATLANTIC OCEAN
San Antonio   Houston   Tampa-St. Petersburg   Miami
TROPIC OF CANCER

160°W   155°W
Honolulu
20°N
PACIFIC OCEAN
0   200 kilometers
0   200 miles
Albers Equal-Area projection

PACIFIC OCEAN

MEXICO   Gulf of Mexico

0   600 kilometers
0   600 miles
Lambert Azimuthal Equal-Area projection

Map Skills

1 Place Where does most of Canada's population live?

2 Human-Environment Interaction Why do you think areas of the United States with high population densities are usually along large bodies of water?

Cities
(Statistics reflect metropolitan areas.)

- ■ Over 10,000,000
- □ 5,000,000–10,000,000
- ◉ 3,000,000–5,000,000
- ● 2,000,000–3,000,000
- ○ Under 2,000,000

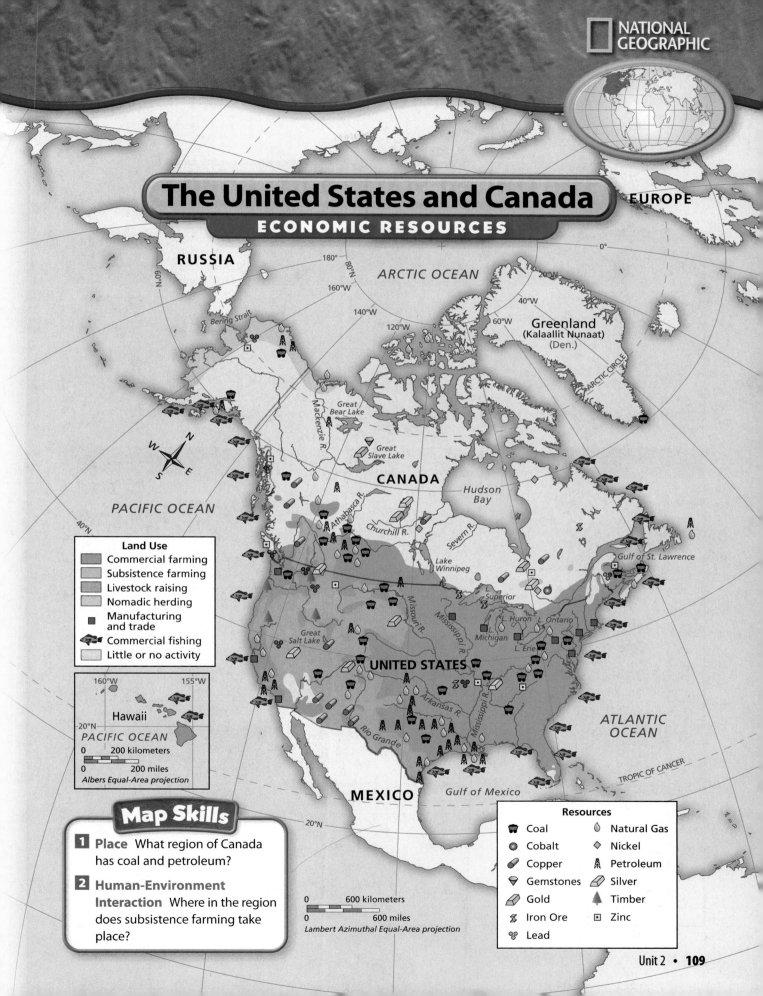

The United States and Canada
ECONOMIC RESOURCES

NATIONAL GEOGRAPHIC

RUSSIA

EUROPE

ARCTIC OCEAN

Bering Strait

Greenland
(Kalaallit Nunaat)
(Den.)

ARCTIC CIRCLE

Mackenzie R.

Great
Bear Lake

Great
Slave Lake

CANADA

Hudson
Bay

Athabasca R.

Churchill R.

Severn R.

Gulf of St. Lawrence

PACIFIC OCEAN

Lake
Winnipeg

L.
Superior

L. Huron L. Ontario

L.
Michigan

L. Erie

Missouri R.

Mississippi R.

Great
Salt Lake

UNITED STATES

Arkansas R.

Mississippi R.

ATLANTIC
OCEAN

Rio Grande

TROPIC OF CANCER

MEXICO

Gulf of Mexico

Land Use
- ▨ Commercial farming
- ▨ Subsistence farming
- ▨ Livestock raising
- ☐ Nomadic herding
- ▪ Manufacturing and trade
- 🐟 Commercial fishing
- ☐ Little or no activity

Hawaii
PACIFIC OCEAN
160°W   155°W
0   200 kilometers
0   200 miles
Albers Equal-Area projection
20°N

Map Skills

1 **Place** What region of Canada has coal and petroleum?

2 **Human-Environment Interaction** Where in the region does subsistence farming take place?

0   600 kilometers
0   600 miles
Lambert Azimuthal Equal-Area projection

Resources

🪨 Coal	◊ Natural Gas
⬤ Cobalt	◆ Nickel
⬭ Copper	⚒ Petroleum
▽ Gemstones	⬭ Silver
◸ Gold	🌲 Timber
🗡 Iron Ore	⊡ Zinc
❦ Lead	

Regional Atlas

The United States and Canada

Country and Capital	Literacy Rate	Population and Density	Land Area	Life Expectancy (Years)	GDP* Per Capita (U.S. dollars)	Television Sets (per 1,000 people)	Flag and Language
UNITED STATES Washington, D.C.	97%	296,500,000 80 per sq. mi. 31 per sq. km	3,717,796 sq. mi. 9,629,047 sq. km	78	$40,100	844	English
CANADA Ottawa	97%	32,000,000 8 per sq. mi. 3 per sq. km	3,849,670 sq. mi. 9,970,599 sq. km	80	$31,500	709	English, French

Sources: *CIA World Factbook*, 2005; Population Reference Bureau, *World Population Data Sheet*, 2005.

*Gross Domestic Product

U.S. State Names: Meaning and Origin

ALABAMA
Montgomery
"thicket clearers" (Choctaw)

ALASKA
Juneau
"the great land" (Aleut)

ARIZONA
Phoenix
"small spring" (O'odham/Pima)

ARKANSAS
Little Rock
"south wind" (Ohio Valley Native Americans' name for the Quapaws)

CALIFORNIA
Sacramento
named after Calafia, a place in a romantic Spanish story

COLORADO
Denver
"colored red" (Spanish)

CONNECTICUT
Hartford
"long river place" (Mohegan)

DELAWARE
Dover
named for Virginia's colonial governor, Thomas West, Baron De La Warr

FLORIDA
Tallahassee
"feast of flowers" (Spanish)

GEORGIA
Atlanta
named for England's King George II

HAWAII
Honolulu
unknown (Native Hawaiian)

IDAHO
Boise
unknown

ILLINOIS
Springfield
"tribe of superior men" (Algonquian)

INDIANA
Indianapolis
"land of Indians" (European American)

IOWA
Des Moines
name of a Native American group

KANSAS
Topeka
"people of the south wind" (Sioux)

KENTUCKY
Frankfort
"land of tomorrow," "cane and turkey lands," or "meadow lands" (Native American/ Iroquoian)

LOUISIANA
Baton Rouge
named for France's King Louis XIV

MAINE
Augusta
nautical term distinguishing the mainland from islands

MARYLAND
Annapolis
named in honor of the wife of England's King Charles I

MASSACHUSETTS
Boston
"at or about the great hill" (Native American)

MICHIGAN
Lansing
"great lake" (Ojibwa)

MINNESOTA
Saint Paul
"water that reflects the sky" (Dakota)

MISSISSIPPI
Jackson
"father of waters" (Chippewa)

Land areas and flags not drawn to scale

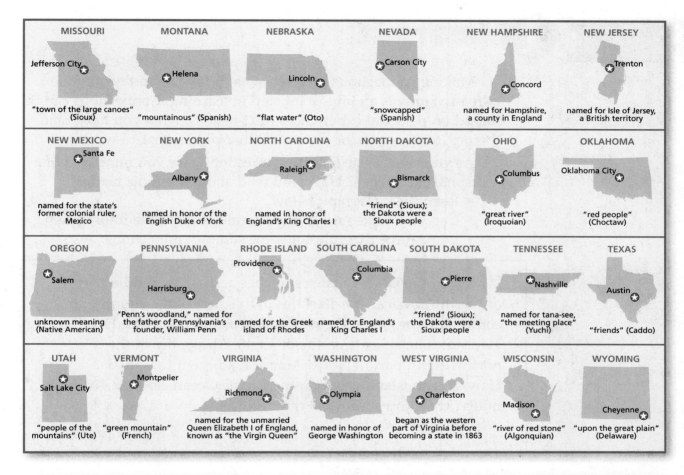

MISSOURI — Jefferson City — "town of the large canoes" (Sioux)

MONTANA — Helena — "mountainous" (Spanish)

NEBRASKA — Lincoln — "flat water" (Oto)

NEVADA — Carson City — "snowcapped" (Spanish)

NEW HAMPSHIRE — Concord — named for Hampshire, a county in England

NEW JERSEY — Trenton — named for Isle of Jersey, a British territory

NEW MEXICO — Santa Fe — named for the state's former colonial ruler, Mexico

NEW YORK — Albany — named in honor of the English Duke of York

NORTH CAROLINA — Raleigh — named in honor of England's King Charles I

NORTH DAKOTA — Bismarck — "friend" (Sioux); the Dakota were a Sioux people

OHIO — Columbus — "great river" (Iroquoian)

OKLAHOMA — Oklahoma City — "red people" (Choctaw)

OREGON — Salem — unknown meaning (Native American)

PENNSYLVANIA — Harrisburg — "Penn's woodland," named for the father of Pennsylvania's founder, William Penn

RHODE ISLAND — Providence — named for the Greek island of Rhodes

SOUTH CAROLINA — Columbia — named for England's King Charles I

SOUTH DAKOTA — Pierre — "friend" (Sioux); the Dakota were a Sioux people

TENNESSEE — Nashville — named for tana-see, "the meeting place" (Yuchi)

TEXAS — Austin — "friends" (Caddo)

UTAH — Salt Lake City — "people of the mountains" (Ute)

VERMONT — Montpelier — "green mountain" (French)

VIRGINIA — Richmond — named for the unmarried Queen Elizabeth I of England, known as "the Virgin Queen"

WASHINGTON — Olympia — named in honor of George Washington

WEST VIRGINIA — Charleston — began as the western part of Virginia before becoming a state in 1863

WISCONSIN — Madison — "river of red stone" (Algonquian)

WYOMING — Cheyenne — "upon the great plain" (Delaware)

Canadian Province and Territory Names: Meaning and Origin

ALBERTA — Edmonton — named for the daughter of England's Queen Victoria

BRITISH COLUMBIA — Victoria — named for the province's British heritage and the Columbia River

MANITOBA — Winnipeg — "the strait of the spirit" (Cree)

NEW BRUNSWICK — Fredericton — named for English royal family of Brunswick-Luneberg

NEWFOUNDLAND AND LABRADOR — St. John's — "new found land," named by explorer John Cabot in 1497; *lavrador*, "landholder" (Portuguese)

NORTHWEST TERRITORIES — Yellowknife — named for lands north and west of Lake Superior

NOVA SCOTIA — Halifax — Latin term for "New Scotland," based on province's Scottish heritage

NUNAVUT — Iqaluit — "our land" (Inuktitut)

ONTARIO — Toronto — "beautiful lake" or "sparkling beautiful water" (Native American)

PRINCE EDWARD ISLAND — Charlottetown — named for the son of England's King George III

QUEBEC — Quebec — "place where the river narrows" (Algonquian)

SASKATCHEWAN — Regina — "fast flowing river" (Cree)

YUKON TERRITORY — Whitehorse — "great river" (Native American)

For more country facts, go to the **Nations of the World Databank** at glencoe.com.

Making Connections

Reading Skill ❶ **Learn It!**

Making connections between what you read and what you already know is an important step in learning. Connections can be based on personal experiences (text-to-self), what you have read before (text-to-text), or events in other places (text-to-world).

As you read, ask connecting questions. Are you reminded of a personal experience? Have you read about the topic before?

- Read the paragraph below.
- Can you make one or more connections to the information?
- Look at the diagram for some sample connections.

Most of the United States stretches across the middle part of North America. The 48 states in this part of the country are contiguous, or joined together inside a common boundary. Two states lie apart from the other 48. Alaska lies in the northwestern part of North America, adjacent to Canada. Hawaii is an island group in the Pacific Ocean, about 2,400 miles (3,862 km) southwest of California.

—from page 117

Reading Tip

Make connections that relate to memorable times in your life. The stronger the connection is, the more likely it is that you will remember the information.

Topic

Most of the United States extends across the middle section of North America.

I know someone who is from Alaska.

Connection

I have seen maps of the United States, and I remember where Alaska, Hawaii, and the other 48 states are located.

Connection

I watched a television program about Hawaiian beaches and the Pacific Ocean.

Connection

Read to Write Activity

As you read Chapters 4, 5, and 6, choose five words or phrases from each chapter that make a connection to something you already know.

② Practice It!

Read the following paragraph from this unit.
- Draw a graphic organizer like the one below.
- List the topic of the reading along with connections to the information.
- Share your connections with a partner.
- Compare your list with your partner's, and discuss their similarities and differences.

Canadians are enthusiastic about hockey—a sport that began in Canada—as well as lacrosse, which began as a Native American game. Many Canadians also enjoy hunting and fishing.

—*from page 150*

▲ Ice hockey in Canada

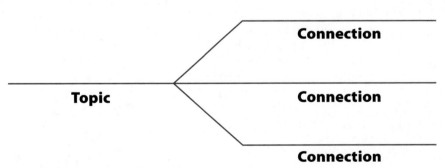

Topic — Connection
Connection
Connection

③ Apply It!

As you read the chapters in the unit, try to identify one concept that makes the following connections.

Chapter	Connection
4	Text-to-self:
5	Text-to-text:
6	Text-to-world:

CHAPTER 4

Physical Geography of the United States and Canada

Essential Question

Regions The United States and Canada cover most of the land area of North America, stretching from the Pacific Ocean to the Atlantic Ocean. These two huge countries share many of the same physical features, resources, and climates. How do landforms and climate help or hinder transportation in a vast region?

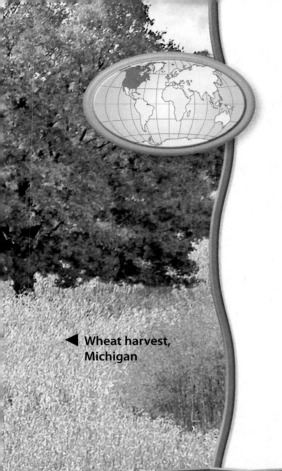

BIG Ideas

Section 1: Physical Features

BIG IDEA Geographers organize the Earth into regions that share common characteristics. The United States and Canada share a long border and many landforms. Their economies are closely linked by trade. Their governments have also worked together on major projects that have changed the land and benefited both countries.

Section 2: Climate Regions

BIG IDEA The physical environment affects how people live. A diversity of climates in the United States and Canada leads to different ways of life. Some parts of this region experience natural hazards that can threaten people's safety.

◀ Wheat harvest, Michigan

FOLDABLES™
Study Organizer

Organizing Information Make this Foldable to help you organize information about the physical features and climates of the United States and Canada.

Step 1 Fold a sheet of paper in half, leaving a ½-inch tab along one edge.

Step 2 Then fold into three sections.

Step 3 Draw a Venn diagram like the one below and then cut along the folds to create three tabs.

Step 4 Label your Foldable as shown.

Physical Geography — United States — Both — Canada

Reading and Writing Using the notes in your Foldable, write several short journal entries from an imaginary trip through Canada and the United States. In your entries, describe the landforms and climates you encounter.

Social Studies ONLINE

To preview Chapter 4, go to glencoe.com.

Guide to Reading

BIG Idea

Geographers organize the Earth into regions that share common characteristics.

Content Vocabulary

- contiguous *(p. 117)*
- megalopolis *(p. 117)*
- prairie *(p. 118)*
- cordillera *(p. 118)*
- canyon *(p. 119)*
- navigable *(p. 119)*
- glacier *(p. 119)*
- divide *(p. 120)*

Academic Vocabulary

- constrain *(p. 117)*
- route *(p. 119)*

Reading Strategy

Analyzing Information Use a Venn diagram like the one below to compare landforms in the eastern, western, and interior parts of the United States and Canada.

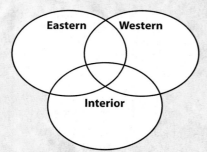

SECTION 1

Physical Features

Picture This Standing at the Grand Canyon's edge, you can see for miles. Its sheer size—277 miles (445 km) long, with walls rising up to 6,000 feet (1,829 m)—is almost mind-boggling. The Grand Canyon was formed by the Colorado River over a period of 6 million years. To learn more about the physical features of the United States and Canada, read Section 1.

▼ **Grand Canyon**

Major Landforms

Main Idea The region rises in elevation from east to west.

Geography and You Do you live in an area that is flat, hilly, or mountainous? Read to find out about the major landforms of the United States and Canada.

The United States and Canada form a region that covers most of North America. This region is bordered by the cold Arctic Ocean in the north, the Atlantic Ocean to the east, and the warm waters of the Gulf of Mexico in the southeast. The Pacific Ocean borders the western coast.

Canada occupies most of the northern part of North America. Canada's vast size makes it the second-largest country in the world, after Russia. The United States is the third-largest country. Most of the United States stretches across the middle part of North America. The 48 states in this part of the country are **contiguous,** or joined together inside a common boundary. Two states lie apart from the other 48. Alaska lies in the northwestern part of North America, adjacent to Canada. Hawaii is an island group in the Pacific Ocean, about 2,400 miles (3,862 km) southwest of California.

Eastern Lowlands and Highlands

The United States and Canada have a variety of landforms. A broad lowland runs along the Atlantic and the Gulf of Mexico coasts. In northeastern areas, the thin and

NATIONAL GEOGRAPHIC

New York City

New York City is one of several huge cities that developed along the Atlantic coastal plain. *Location* **Where is the area called the Piedmont located?**

rocky soil **constrains,** or limits, farming. A fertile, hilly area called the Piedmont, however, stretches inland from the coastal plain. Excellent harbors along the Atlantic coast have led to the growth of shipping ports.

The cities of Halifax, Boston, New York City, Philadelphia, and Washington, D.C., all lie along or near the Atlantic coast. In the United States, Atlantic coastal cities and their suburbs form an almost continuous line of settlement. Geographers call this connected area of urban communities a **megalopolis.** The Atlantic megalopolis has long been an important economic, cultural, and political center of the United States.

The coastal plain along the Gulf of Mexico is wider than the Atlantic plain. Soils in this region are better than those along the Atlantic coast. Large cities here include Houston and New Orleans.

West and north of the Atlantic coastal plain spread a number of highland areas.

Social Studies ONLINE

Student Web Activity Visit <u>glencoe.com</u> and complete the Chapter 4 Web Activity about the Piedmont.

The Rocky and Appalachian Mountains

NATIONAL GEOGRAPHIC

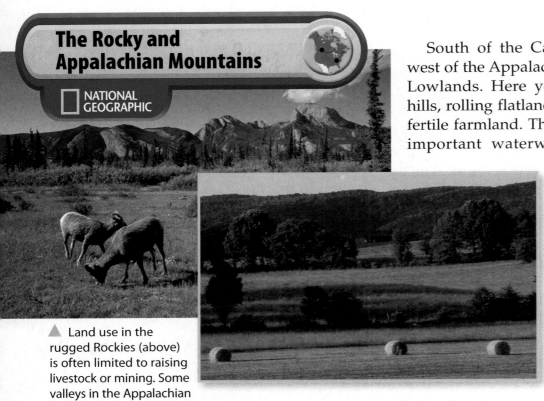

▲ Land use in the rugged Rockies (above) is often limited to raising livestock or mining. Some valleys in the Appalachian Mountains, like this one in Tennessee (right), have fertile soil and are good for farming. **Place** Why do the Appalachian and Rocky Mountains appear physically different?

These include the Appalachian Mountains, which run from eastern Canada to Alabama. The Appalachians are the oldest mountains in North America. Their rounded peaks show their age. Erosion has worn them down over time. The highest peak, Mount Mitchell in North Carolina, reaches 6,684 feet (2,037 m). Rich coal deposits in the Appalachians fueled industrial growth in the late 1800s and early 1900s.

Interior Lowlands

West of the eastern highlands are vast interior lowlands. In the north lies the Canadian Shield. This horseshoe-shaped area of rocky hills, lakes, and evergreen forests wraps around the Hudson Bay. With poor soil and a cold climate, the Canadian Shield is not farmable. It does, however, contain many mineral deposits, such as iron ore, copper, and nickel.

South of the Canadian Shield and west of the Appalachians lie the Central Lowlands. Here you will find grassy hills, rolling flatlands, thick forests, and fertile farmland. This area also contains important waterways, including the Great Lakes and the Mississippi River. Large cities, such as Chicago, Detroit, Cleveland, and Toronto, are located in the Central Lowlands.

The Great Plains stretch west of the Mississippi River, gradually rising in elevation from east to west. Much of this vast region is a **prairie,** or rolling inland grasslands with fertile soil. The Great Plains once provided food for millions of buffalo and the Native Americans who lived there. Today farmers grow grains, and ranchers raise cattle on the land. The Great Plains also have reserves of coal, oil, and natural gas.

Western Mountains and Plateaus

West of the Great Plains is a **cordillera,** which is a group of mountain ranges that run side by side. Millions of years ago, collisions between tectonic plates created these towering mountains. At the eastern edge of the cordillera, the Rocky Mountains begin in Alaska and run south to New Mexico. Although they are younger and higher than the Appalachians, the Rockies have not been a barrier to travel. The Rockies contain passes, or low areas in the mountains, that allow people to cross them.

Skiing in the Sierra Nevada

The Sierra Nevada are home to a number of popular ski resorts, including those around Lake Tahoe on the California-Nevada border. *Place* **What other mountain chains are found near the Pacific coast of North America?**

Near the Pacific coast is a series of mountain chains that make up the western part of the cordillera. They are the Sierra Nevada, the Cascade Range, the Coast Ranges, and the Alaska Range. Mount McKinley in the Alaska Range rises to 20,320 feet (6,194 m) and is the highest point in North America.

Between these Pacific ranges and the Rocky Mountains is a stretch of dry basins and high plateaus. In the southern part of this area, rivers have worn through rock to create magnificent **canyons,** or deep valleys with steep sides. The most famous of these is the Grand Canyon of the Colorado River.

In the Pacific Ocean, eight large islands and 124 smaller islands make up the American state of Hawaii. The islands of Hawaii extend over a distance of about 1,500 miles (2,400 km). Volcanoes on the ocean floor erupted and formed these islands.

✓**Reading Check** **Making Generalizations**
Describe the areas that make up the interior lowlands.

Bodies of Water

Main Idea The region's waterways provide transportation and electric power.

Geography and You Do you live near a river, lake, or ocean? What are the advantages and disadvantages of living by a body of water? Read to find out about the importance of waterways in the United States and Canada.

The United States and Canada have numerous freshwater lakes and rivers. Many of the region's rivers are **navigable,** or wide and deep enough to allow the passage of ships.

The Great Lakes

The Great Lakes—the world's largest group of freshwater lakes—lie in the central part of the region. Thousands of years ago, **glaciers,** or giant sheets of ice, formed Lake Superior, Lake Michigan, Lake Huron, Lake Erie, and Lake Ontario. The waters of these connected lakes flow into the St. Lawrence River, which empties into the Atlantic Ocean.

The St. Lawrence River is one of Canada's most important rivers. It flows for 750 miles (1,207 km) from Lake Ontario to the Gulf of St. Lawrence in the Atlantic Ocean. The Canadian cities of Quebec, Montreal, and Ottawa developed along the St. Lawrence River and its tributaries. They depend on the St. Lawrence as an important transportation link.

For many years, rapids, waterfalls, and other obstructions kept ships from navigating the entire **route,** or journey, from the Great Lakes to the Atlantic Ocean. Then, in the mid-1900s, the United States and Canada built the St. Lawrence Seaway. As shown in **Figure 1,** the Seaway links the Great Lakes and the Atlantic Ocean.

Duluth

St. Mary's River — Soo Locks

St. Clair River — Detroit River

Welland Canal

Iroquois Lock

Eisenhower Lock

Snell Lock

St. Lambert Lock

600 ft. (183 m)

579 ft. (176 m)

Lake Huron

Detroit

Lake Erie

570 ft. (174 m)

St. Lawrence River

245 ft. (75 m)

Sea Level

Lake Superior

Lake Ontario

Montreal

Melocheville Lock

Beauharnois Lock

Côte-Ste.-Catherine Lock

Map Skills

1 Human-Environment Interaction Which two bodies of water are connected by the Soo Locks?

2 Place How far is the largest drop in water level along the St. Lawrence Seaway? Where does that occur?

50°N   80°W   70°W   60°W

Lake Superior   **CANADA**

Duluth   St. Lawrence R.

Lake Michigan   Lake Huron   Montreal

Detroit   Lake Ontario

40°N   Lake Erie

UNITED STATES   **ATLANTIC OCEAN**

N   W   E   S

Today, ships carry raw materials and manufactured goods from Great Lakes cities, such as Chicago, Detroit, Cleveland, and Toronto, to the rest of the world.

The Mississippi River

The Mississippi River is North America's longest river. It flows 2,350 miles (3,782 km), beginning as a stream in Minnesota and enlarging to a width of 1.5 miles (2.4 km) before emptying into the Gulf of Mexico. Ships can travel on the Mississippi and some of its tributaries for great distances. Products from inland port cities, such as St. Louis and Memphis, are shipped down the river and on to foreign ports.

The Mississippi River system is the major waterway for the central part of the region. It drains about 1.2 million square miles (3.1 million sq. km) of land. This area includes all or part of 31 American states and much of central Canada.

The Continental Divide

Many rivers, such as the Colorado and Rio Grande, flow from the Rocky Mountains. A number of smaller rivers and streams connect with one of these rivers. The high ridge of the Rockies is called the Continental Divide. A **divide** is a high point that determines the direction that rivers flow. East of the Continental Divide, rivers flow toward the Arctic Ocean, the Atlantic Ocean, and the Mississippi River system into the Gulf of Mexico. To the west of the divide, rivers flow toward the Pacific Ocean.

Northeast of the Rockies, the Mackenzie River flows from the Great Slave Lake to the Arctic Ocean. It drains much of northern Canada's interior.

Reading Check   **Identifying** What are some inland ports along the Mississippi River?

Natural Resources

Main Idea The region has many energy, mineral, and other natural resources.

Geography and You Think about if you like to eat canned, frozen, or fresh vegetables. Where were these foods grown and processed? Read to learn about the natural resources that provide products for the United States and Canada.

In addition to major river systems, the United States and Canada have a great variety of other natural resources. Energy sources and raw materials have made it possible for both countries to develop strong industrial economies.

Energy and Mineral Resources

The United States and Canada have major energy resources, such as oil and natural gas. Texas ranks first in oil and natural gas reserves in the United States. Alaska also has major oil reserves. The United States, however, uses nearly three times the amount of oil that it produces. So, even though the United States has a large reserve of oil, it must import more to meet the nation's needs.

Canada exports both oil and natural gas. Much of Canada's energy exports go to the United States. Most of Canada's oil and natural gas reserves lie in or near the province of Alberta. This province has the world's largest reserves of oil in the form of oil mixed with sands. Obtaining oil from these sands is more costly than working with liquid crude oil.

The United States and Canada also have significant amounts of coal. Coal is mined in the Appalachian Mountains, Wyoming, and British Columbia. The region has enough coal to supply energy for about 400 years, but using this energy source adds to air pollution.

In eastern areas, highlands drop to the lower Atlantic plain. Along this fall line, rivers break into waterfalls that provide hydroelectric power. Niagara Falls is a major source of hydroelectric power for both Canada and the United States. The falls lie on the Niagara River, which flows north from Lake Erie to Lake Ontario. The falls also form part of the border between Ontario, Canada, and the state of New York.

Mineral resources are also plentiful in the United States and Canada. Parts of eastern Canada and the northern United States have large iron ore deposits. The Rocky Mountains yield gold, silver, and copper. Deep within the Canadian Shield are iron ore, copper, nickel, gold, and uranium. Minerals from the shield helped create a manufacturing region in southern Ontario and Quebec.

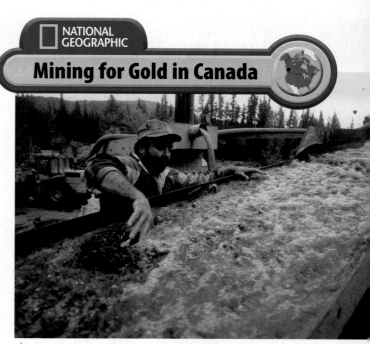

NATIONAL GEOGRAPHIC

Mining for Gold in Canada

▲ Gold is still mined in British Columbia. Here, a stream of rushing water is used to wash away mud and rocks to help find gold nuggets. *Place* What minerals are found in the Canadian Shield?

Soil, Timber, and Fish

Rich soil in parts of the United States and Canada is excellent for farming. Crops vary throughout the region, depending on the local climate. Farmers grow corn in the Central Lowlands, which receive plentiful rainfall, and wheat on the drier Great Plains. The wet, mild climate of western Washington and Oregon supports dairy farming and the growing of fruits and vegetables. Irrigation is used in the drier eastern areas of these two states to grow grain. The warm, wet valleys of central California yield more than 200 different crops. In the south central part of British Columbia, fruits and vegetables are grown on irrigated land.

Timber is another important resource in the region. Forests once covered much of the United States and Canada. Today, however, forests cover less than 50 percent of Canada and about one-third of the United States. Still, lumber and wood products, such as paper, are major Canadian exports. The timber industry is also strong in the states of Oregon and Washington.

Coastal waters are important to the region's economies. Large fishing industries depend on the fish and shellfish in these waters. In recent years, however, the region's Atlantic fishing grounds have suffered from overfishing. The Grand Banks, located off Canada's southeast coast, was once one of the world's richest fishing grounds. Overfishing has harmed the area, and the Canadian government has banned fishing here for some species.

✔ **Reading Check** **Explaining** What is unique about oil deposits in Alberta, Canada?

Section 1 Review

Social Studies ONLINE
Study Central™ To review this section, go to glencoe.com.

Vocabulary

1. **Explain** the significance of:
   a. contiguous
   b. megalopolis
   c. prairie
   d. cordillera
   e. canyon
   f. navigable
   g. glacier
   h. divide

Main Ideas

2. **Describing** Describe the Canadian Shield and its resources.

3. **Summarizing** Use a diagram like the one below to summarize important facts about the Mississippi River.

Mississippi River

4. **Comparing and Contrasting** Compare and contrast the agricultural conditions and crops grown in various parts of the region.

Critical Thinking

5. **BIG Idea** How did building the St. Lawrence Seaway change the land? How have the United States and Canada benefited from the St. Lawrence Seaway?

6. **Challenge** What conditions led to the formation of a megalopolis along the United States's Atlantic coast?

Writing About Geography

7. **Using Your FOLDABLES** Use your Foldable to make and write captions for a map of the region that describes the impact of landforms and waterways on people's lives.

Danger Zone

In August of 2005, a massive hurricane struck the southern United States. The damage it caused was overwhelming.

The Storm and the Damage Hurricane Katrina struck the Gulf coast of the United States on August 29, 2005. Katrina reached land as a category 4 hurricane, the second-strongest category of storm. The hurricane blasted the region with winds of more than 140 miles per hour (225 km/hr). It caused a storm surge—rising seas—of more than 30 feet (9 m) and brought as many as 16 inches (41 cm) of rainfall in a short time.

Storm conditions raged along the coasts of Louisiana, Mississippi, and Alabama. More than 1,800 people died, more than 500,000 were left homeless, and property damage exceeded $30 billion. Katrina was one of the worst natural disasters in American history.

▲ **Flooding from Hurricane Katrina, New Orleans**

Katrina and New Orleans The city of New Orleans suffered extensive damage from Katrina. The strength of the storm and the geography of the city helped lead to disaster. New Orleans lies below sea level, and the city is almost surrounded by water. Lake Pontchartrain lies to the north. The Mississippi flows to the west and south of town. Many years ago, a complex system of high walls, called levees, was built along the lake and river to protect the city from flooding.

The power of Katrina overwhelmed the levees, some of which had weakened with age. Water rushed through breaks in the barriers. Floodwaters rose as high as 20 feet (6 m) in parts of the city. Fortunately, most of New Orleans's 450,000 residents were evacuated before the storm hit. Many months after Katrina, fewer than half of the city's people had returned to their homes.

NATIONAL GEOGRAPHIC

Path of Hurricane Katrina

🌀	Tropical storm
🌀	Category 1 hurricane
🌀	Category 2 hurricane
🌀	Category 3 hurricane
🌀	Category 4 hurricane
🌀	Category 5 hurricane

Aug. 29, 2005, 7:10 A.M.

Aug. 25, 2005, 6:30 P.M.

Gulf of Mexico

ATLANTIC OCEAN

Fla.

0   200 kilometers
0   200 miles
Albers Equal-Area projection

Think About It

1. **Regions** Where did Katrina strike? How much damage did it cause?

2. **Place** Why was the threat of flooding especially dangerous for New Orleans?

Climate Regions

Content Vocabulary

- drought *(p. 126)*
- tornado *(p. 127)*
- hurricane *(p. 127)*
- blizzard *(p. 128)*

Academic Vocabulary

- diverse *(p. 125)*
- adapt *(p. 125)*
- restore *(p. 126)*

Reading Strategy

Organizing Information Use a chart like the one below to organize key facts about at least three different climate zones in the region.

Climate Zones	Location	Description
1.		
2.		
3.		

Picture This This sea of red is actually a sea of cranberries. The small, red fruit—also known as bounce berries, crane berries, and rubies of the pines—grows on ground-hugging vines in wetlands and bogs. To harvest the cranberries, farmers flood the bogs. Small air pockets in the cranberries cause them to rise to the surface, where they can be gathered by harvesting machines. Read this section to learn more about the climates of the United States and Canada and how they influence farming and other human activities.

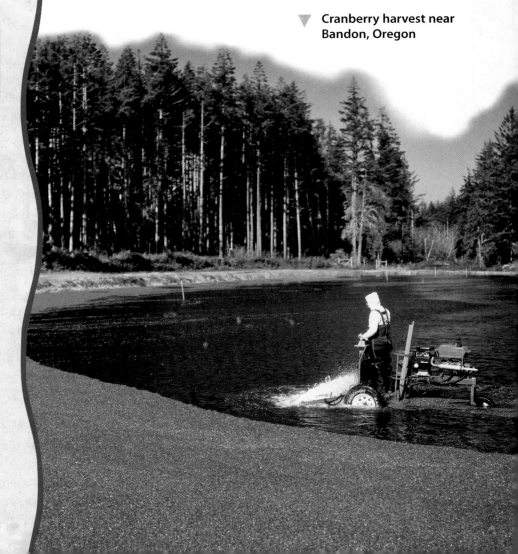

▼ **Cranberry harvest near Bandon, Oregon**

A Varied Region

Main Idea Most people in the United States and Canada live in temperate climate regions.

Geography and You What is the climate like in your area? Read to learn about the different climate regions of the United States and Canada.

The region of the United States and Canada stretches from cold Arctic wastelands in the far north to warm, sunny vacation areas near the Tropic of Cancer. This vast territory is **diverse** in both climate and vegetation. Most people in the United States and Canada, however, avoid the extremes of tropical and Arctic climates.

They live in the middle latitudes where climates are more moderate. **Figure 2** shows all of the region's climates.

The Far North

Tundra and subarctic climates are found in the northern parts of Alaska and Canada. Winters are long and cold, while summers are brief and cool. As a result, few people live in this harsh environment.

Along the Arctic Ocean's coastline, the extremely cold tundra prevents the growth of trees and most plants. In the subarctic region farther south, dense forests of evergreen trees are specially **adapted,** or adjusted, to the climate. The waxy coating of evergreen needles keeps in moisture during the bitterly cold winters.

NATIONAL GEOGRAPHIC **Maps In Motion** See StudentWorks™ Plus or glencoe.com.

Figure 2 **United States and Canada: Climate Zones**

Tropical
- Tropical wet
- Tropical dry

Dry
- Steppe
- Desert

Midlatitude
- Mediterranean
- Humid subtropical
- Marine west coast
- Humid continental

High latitude
- Subarctic
- Tundra
- Ice cap

- Highland (climate varies with elevation)

Map Skills

1 **Regions** What climate zones are found in the United States but not in Canada?

2 **Location** Which part of the region has a Mediterranean climate?

Snow Day

Heavy snowfall is common during the winter in Iowa, as well as in other states across the Great Plains. *Human-Environment Interaction* **How might a drought affect a farmer or rancher?**

The Pacific Coast

The region's Pacific coast is affected by moist ocean winds. The area from southern Alaska to northern California has a marine west coast climate of year-round mild temperatures and abundant rainfall. It is common to see evergreen forests, ferns, and mosses. By contrast, southern California has a Mediterranean climate of warm, dry summers and mild, wet winters. There is much less rainfall here than in northern areas.

The West

The inland West has a desert climate of hot summers and mild winters. Here, Pacific coastal mountains block humid ocean winds. Hot, dry air gets trapped between the Pacific ranges and the Rockies. As a result, the inland West receives little rainfall. Plants there have adapted to survive on little rain.

Areas on the eastern side of the Rockies have a partly dry steppe climate. **Droughts,** or long periods without rainfall, are a serious challenge, especially to farmers and ranchers who can lose crops and animals. In some areas, a growing population also strains water resources.

The Great Plains

The Great Plains area benefits from moisture-bearing winds from the Gulf of Mexico and from the Arctic. As a result, much of this area has a humid continental climate with cold, snowy winters and hot, humid summers. Enough precipitation falls to support prairie grasses and grains. Dry weather, however, sometimes affects the area. In the 1930s, winds eroded loose topsoil and turned the area into a wasteland called the Dust Bowl. Economic hardship forced many farmers to leave the Great Plains. Since the 1930s, better farming methods have **restored,** or renewed, this area's soil.

The East

The eastern United States and Canada have humid climate regions that receive plenty of year-round precipitation. The northeastern United States and some areas of eastern Canada have a humid continental climate. The southeastern United States has a humid subtropical climate. Both climate areas have a variety of forests. Wetlands and swamps cover some of the southeast.

Temperatures in the two humid climate regions are similar in the summer but can be very different in the winter. In summer, warm air from the south blocks cold Arctic air from reaching the eastern areas. In winter, however, the northeast receives strong blasts of icy Arctic air. For example, in Boston, Massachusetts, January temperatures can drop to an average low of 22°F (–6 °C).

Areas in the southeast still receive some warmth from the south. As a result, the average January temperature in Atlanta, Georgia, is 41°F (5°C).

Tropical Areas

Tropical climates are found in two areas of the United States. Southern Florida has a tropical dry climate. Temperatures are hot in summer and warm in winter. Rainfall occurs mainly during the summer. Hawaii, the other tropical area, has year-round temperatures that average above 70°F (21°C). The mild climate draws many visitors throughout the year. Rainfall, which varies throughout the state, supports tropical rain forests.

✔ **Reading Check** **Explaining** What factors affect climate in the Great Plains?

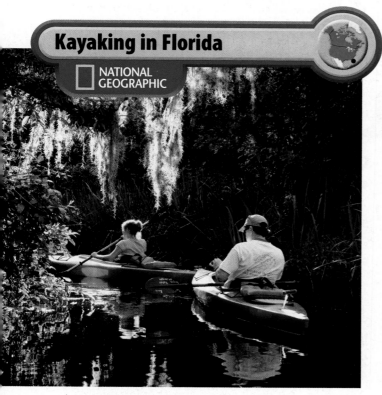

Kayaking in Florida

NATIONAL GEOGRAPHIC

▲ In the large wetlands area known as the Everglades, south Florida's tropical climate produces lush vegetation. *Location* Besides Florida, what other state has a tropical climate?

Natural Hazards

Main Idea **Hurricanes, tornadoes, and earthquakes can threaten parts of the region.**

Geography and You Does the area where you live experience severe storms? Read to learn about the environmental challenges that affect the United States and Canada.

The landforms and climate of this region provide people with many benefits. They also pose challenges in the form of severe storms and other natural hazards.

Severe Weather

One hazard related to severe weather is a tornado. A **tornado** is a windstorm in the form of a funnel-shaped cloud that often touches the ground. The high winds of a tornado, which can reach more than 300 miles per hour (482 km per hour), can level houses, knock down trees, and hurl cars from one place to another. These storms can occur anywhere in the region and at any time of the year. The central United States sees more tornadoes each year than any other place in the world. As a result, this area has been nicknamed "Tornado Alley."

Another severe storm is a hurricane. **Hurricanes** are wind systems that form over the ocean in tropical areas and bring violent storms with heavy rains. As with tornadoes, high winds can do serious damage. In addition, hurricanes can create a storm surge, or high levels of seawater. The high waters can flood low-lying coastal areas. Hurricanes generally develop from June to September. They most often strike along the southeastern Atlantic coast and the Gulf of Mexico. However, northeastern states can also be affected by hurricanes.

One of the most damaging hurricanes in history, Hurricane Katrina, struck the coast of the Gulf of Mexico in August of 2005. It damaged a wide area from Mobile, Alabama, to New Orleans, Louisiana. More than 1,800 people died, and hundreds of thousands lost their homes. Most of New Orleans and many nearby towns were completely flooded. In Mississippi, entire towns were destroyed.

Winter weather can also be hazardous. **Blizzards** are severe winter storms that last several hours and combine high winds with heavy snow. The blowing snow limits how far people can see. "White-out" conditions, or snow that falls so heavily that a person cannot see very far, make driving dangerous. Also, the wind and snow can knock down electric power lines and trees and create icy road conditions. Blizzards can halt activity in a busy city for days as city workers attempt to clear the streets.

Earthquakes and Volcanoes

While earthquakes can occur anywhere in the region, most take place along the Pacific coast. This area lies along various fault lines, or areas of weakness in the Earth where two tectonic plates meet. A 1906 earthquake heavily damaged buildings in San Francisco. Many of the buildings that remained standing were destroyed by fires triggered by broken natural gas lines. Today, buildings in the region are often built using special techniques to protect them from damage.

The area where tectonic plates meet can also be the site of volcanoes. Volcanoes are found in the Pacific coast mountains, southern Alaska, and Hawaii. Most are now dormant, or unlikely to erupt soon. Several of Hawaii's volcanoes are still active.

Reading Check   **Describing** Describe the types of damage that hurricanes can cause.

Section 2 Review

Vocabulary

1. **Describe** each of these weather conditions and where they are likely to occur: *drought, tornado, hurricane,* and *blizzard.*

Main Ideas

2. **Summarizing** Use a diagram like the one below to summarize information about one of the region's climate zones. Write the name of a climate zone in the large oval and details about it in the small ovals.

3. **Comparing and Contrasting** Compare and contrast tornadoes and hurricanes.

Critical Thinking

4. **Determining Cause and Effect** How do mountains in the region influence climate?

5. **BIG Idea** What were some of the effects of Hurricane Katrina?

6. **Challenge** Based on climate and the occurrence of natural hazards, which areas of the region do you think are most populated? Explain your answer.

Writing About Geography

7. **Personal Writing** Write a paragraph identifying which of the climates described in this section you think sounds most enjoyable to live in, and explain why.

Major Landforms

- The East has low coastal plains and heavily eroded highlands.

- Lowland areas with minerals and rich soil make up the region's interior.

- The West has several parallel mountain ranges. Plateaus, basins, and valleys lie between the mountains.

Lowland marsh, Virginia

Major Bodies of Water

- The Great Lakes and the St. Lawrence Seaway support trade between the region's interior areas and other parts of the world.

- The Mississippi River is the most important waterway in the central part of the United States.

Riverboat, Mississippi River

Farming in Manitoba, Canada

Natural Resources

- The region's energy resources include oil, natural gas, and coal.

- Abundant mineral resources are found in the eastern highlands, the Canadian Shield, and the western mountains.

- Rich soils support farming in the Central Lowlands, the Great Plains, and western valleys.

Climate Regions

- Most Americans and Canadians live in moderate, middle-latitude climate areas.

- The inland West has dry and semidry climates because mountains block moist air.

- Pacific coastal areas generally have mild, wet climates.

Natural Hazards

- Tornadoes occur primarily in the central area of the region.

- Hurricanes can bring heavy winds and rain to the Atlantic and Gulf coasts.

- Earthquakes are a destructive threat along coastal fault lines in the West.

- Volcanoes are found in western coastal areas, Alaska, and Hawaii. Most are dormant.

Tornado, Kansas

STUDY TO GO Study anywhere, anytime! Download quizzes and flash cards to your PDA from **glencoe.com**.

STANDARDIZED TEST PRACTICE

TEST-TAKING TIP

Do not wait until the last minute to study for an exam. Beginning about one week before the test, set aside some time each day for review.

Reviewing Vocabulary

Directions: Choose the word(s) that best completes the sentence.

1. Atlantic coastal cities and their suburbs form an almost continuous line of settlement called a _____.
   - **A** Piedmont
   - **B** megalopolis
   - **C** coastal plain
   - **D** coastal lowland

2. Much of the Great Plains is a _____, or rolling grassland.
   - **A** prairie
   - **B** canyon
   - **C** glacier
   - **D** cordillera

3. Ranchers in the dry steppe region east of the Rockies sometimes lose crops and animals due to _____.
   - **A** droughts
   - **B** blizzards
   - **C** hurricanes
   - **D** earthquakes

4. _____ most often strike along the southeastern Atlantic coast and the Gulf of Mexico.
   - **A** Droughts
   - **B** Tornadoes
   - **C** Hurricanes
   - **D** Earthquakes

Reviewing Main Ideas

Directions: Choose the best answer for each question.

Section 1 (pp. 116–122)

5. Which of the following areas of the United States has the highest elevation?
   - **A** Gulf coastal plain
   - **B** eastern Great Plains
   - **C** western Great Plains
   - **D** Atlantic coastal plain

6. _____ depend on the Mississippi River for shipping products on their way to foreign ports.
   - **A** Chicago and Detroit
   - **B** Quebec and Montreal
   - **C** Toronto and Cleveland
   - **D** St. Louis and Memphis

Section 2 (pp. 124–128)

7. The area from southern Alaska to northern California has a _____ climate with year-round mild temperatures and abundant rainfall.
   - **A** subtropical
   - **B** Mediterranean
   - **C** marine west coast
   - **D** humid continental

8. _____ has more tornadoes each year than any other place in the world.
   - **A** Eastern Canada
   - **B** Northern Canada
   - **C** The northeastern United States
   - **D** The central United States

GO ON

Critical Thinking

Directions: Choose the best answers to the following questions. Base your answers to questions 9 and 10 on the map below and your knowledge of Chapter 4.

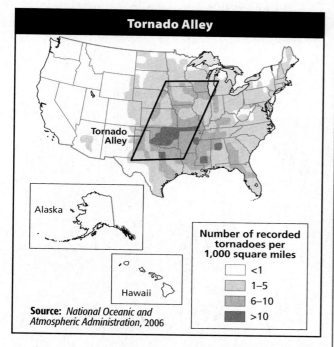

Tornado Alley

Tornado Alley

Alaska

Hawaii

Number of recorded tornadoes per 1,000 square miles
- <1
- 1–5
- 6–10
- >10

Source: *National Oceanic and Atmospheric Administration,* 2006

9. According to the map, which states have the most tornado activity?

 A Texas and Oklahoma

 B Texas and Louisiana

 C Oklahoma and Kansas

 D Missouri and Arkansas

10. According to the information in the map, which generalization is most accurate?

 A The western United States never experiences tornadoes.

 B Most tornadoes occur in the southeastern United States.

 C "Tornado Alley" is an area of moderate tornado activity.

 D The central United States has more tornadoes than the rest of the country.

Document-Based Questions

Directions: Analyze the following document and answer the short-answer questions that follow.

The news story below sums up findings in a 2005 study on recent hurricanes:

The number of Category 4 and 5 hurricanes worldwide has nearly doubled over the past 35 years, even though the total number of hurricanes has dropped since the 1990s. . . . The shift occurred as global sea surface temperatures have increased over the same period. . . .

"What we found was rather astonishing," said [Peter Webster, professor at Georgia Tech's School of Earth and Atmospheric Sciences]. "In the 1970s, there was an average of about 10 Category 4 and 5 hurricanes per year globally. Since 1990, the number of Category 4 and 5 hurricanes has almost doubled, averaging 18 per year globally."

Category 4 hurricanes have sustained winds from 131 to 155 miles per hour; Category 5 systems, such as Hurricane Katrina at its peak over the Gulf of Mexico, feature winds of 156 mph or more.

—The National Center for Atmospheric Research, 2005

11. How have hurricanes changed in the past 35 years?

12. What might be causing this hurricane intensity?

Extended Response

13. Suppose you are a foreign visitor to North America. Describe one region of the United States or Canada and write a letter to a friend, persuading him or her to visit.

Social Studies ONLINE

For additional test practice, use Self-Check Quizzes— Chapter 4 at glencoe.com.

Need Extra Help?

If you missed question...	1	2	3	4	5	6	7	8	9	10	11	12	13
Go to page...	117	118	126	127	118	120	126	127	26	26	127	127	116–128

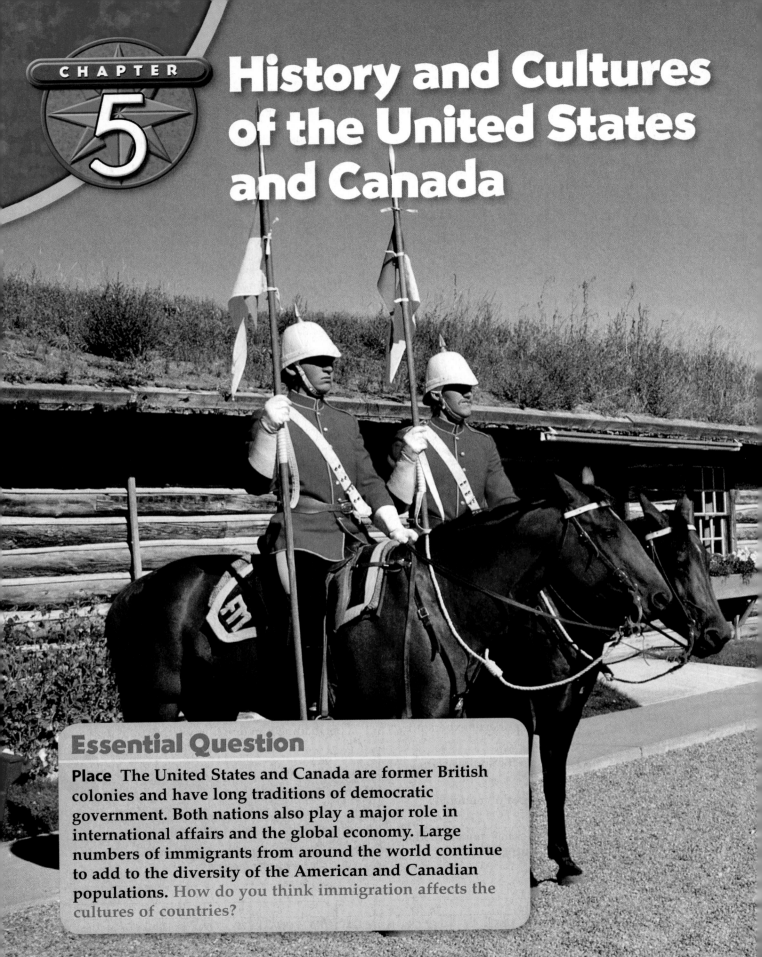

History and Cultures of the United States and Canada

Essential Question

Place The United States and Canada are former British colonies and have long traditions of democratic government. Both nations also play a major role in international affairs and the global economy. Large numbers of immigrants from around the world continue to add to the diversity of the American and Canadian populations. How do you think immigration affects the cultures of countries?

BIG Ideas

Section 1: History and Governments

BIG IDEA **The characteristics and movement of people impact physical and human systems.** England established several colonies in North America during the 1600s and 1700s. These colonies later formed two large, independent democracies: the United States and Canada. Today they have become home to millions of people from around the world who moved to these lands to start new lives.

Section 2: Cultures and Lifestyles

BIG IDEA **Culture influences people's perceptions about places and regions.** The cultures of the United States and Canada reflect the influence of many different ethnic groups. These groups range from the Native Americans who first lived in the area to the most recent arrivals from all parts of the world.

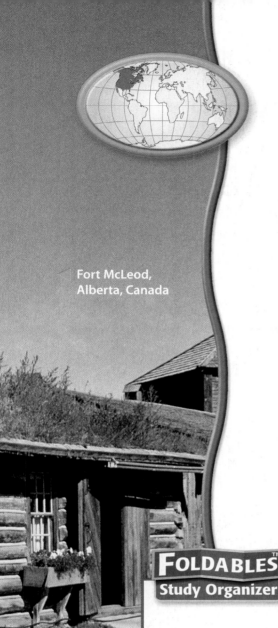

Fort McLeod, Alberta, Canada

FOLDABLES™ Study Organizer

Categorizing Information Make this four-tab Foldable to help you learn about the history, governments, and cultures of the United States and Canada.

Step 1 Fold the top and bottom of a piece of paper into the middle.

Step 2 Cut each flap at the midpoint to form 4 tabs.

Step 3 Label the tabs as shown.

Reading and Writing As you read the chapter, take notes about each section under the appropriate head. Use your Foldable to help you write a summary for each section.

Social Studies ONLINE

To preview Chapter 5, go to <u>glencoe.com</u>.

Guide to Reading

BIG Idea

The characteristics and movement of people impact physical and human systems.

Content Vocabulary

- colony (p. 136)
- annex (p. 136)
- terrorism (p. 137)
- dominion (p. 139)
- representative democracy (p. 140)
- federalism (p. 140)
- amendment (p. 141)
- parliamentary democracy (p. 141)

Academic Vocabulary

- economy (p. 136)
- regime (p. 137)
- principle (p. 140)
- core (p. 141)

Reading Strategy

Making a Time Line Use a diagram like the one below to list and compare key events and dates in the history of the United States and Canada.

History and Governments

Picture This This is not just any rock. It is the famous Plymouth Rock. Plymouth Rock, in the American state of Massachusetts, is believed to have been at the site where the Pilgrims first landed in 1620. The 10-ton rock is only about one-third of its original size. This is because, over the years, many souvenir hunters have broken off pieces to take home. To learn how people can affect the development of a nation, read Section 1.

▼ **Plymouth Rock, Massachusetts**

History of the United States

Main Idea **The United States emerged as a world power in the 1900s.**

Geography and You Do you like to make your own decisions without someone else telling you what to do? Read to find out why the Americans wanted to make their own decisions without British interference.

For thousands of years, people have been living in what is now the United States. They have come from many different parts of the world to settle a vast territory that stretches across much of North America. In the past few hundred years, Americans have made their country the most powerful nation in the world.

The First Americans

About 15,000 years ago, hunters in Asia followed herds of animals across a land bridge between eastern Siberia and Alaska. They are believed to be among the first people to settle the Americas. Eventually groups of people spread across the entire landmass. Their descendants today are called Native Americans. Over many centuries, Native American groups developed different ways of life using local resources.

The Colonial Era

Europeans were not aware of the Americas until 1492. That year, explorer Christopher Columbus sailed west from Europe in hopes of reaching Asia. Instead, he reached islands in the Caribbean Sea. His tales of these new lands excited many Europeans.

NATIONAL GEOGRAPHIC Maps In Motion See StudentWorks™ Plus or glencoe.com.

Figure 1 United States Expansion

Map Skills

1. **Regions** Describe the area that made up the United States in 1783.

2. **Place** When did the United States obtain Alaska? From what country was it obtained?

Quickly, many other people began making their own trips. Spain soon set up **colonies**, which are overseas settlements tied to a parent country. The Spanish gained great wealth from gold and silver mines in Mexico and South America. They also had colonies in what is now the southern United States, but they focused primarily on the lands farther south.

France and Great Britain also established colonies in North America. The French controlled eastern Canada, the Great Lakes area, and the Mississippi River valley. The British settled along the Atlantic coast. In 1763 Great Britain defeated France in a war and won France's North American colonies.

Soon after, the people in Great Britain's 13 coastal colonies grew resentful of British taxes and trade policies. Discontent boiled over, and fighting broke out between the colonists and British forces. In 1776 the colonists declared their independence. In 1783, after several years of fighting, Britain recognized American independence, and a new nation called the United States was born. George Washington became the first president of the United States.

Expansion and Growth

When the United States won independence, the country controlled only the eastern coast from Maine to Georgia. During the 1800s, however, it expanded all the way to the Pacific Ocean, as seen in **Figure 1** on the previous page. Some of this growth came through treaties with other countries. Some came when the United States **annexed** lands, or declared ownership of a particular area. This expansion brought suffering, however, including loss of land, culture, and often life, to Native Americans who had lived in the region for centuries.

Throughout the 1800s, the United States grew in population as well. High birthrates, advances in public health, and the arrival of millions of European immigrants helped the population grow.

The American **economy,** or way of producing goods, also changed. New machines made planting and harvesting crops faster and easier. Manufacturers developed the factory system to produce many goods. Roads, canals, steamboats, and railroads allowed manufacturers to move their goods to markets more quickly.

Social and economic differences, however, came to deeply divide the country. The southern states built their economy on agriculture and the labor of hundreds of thousands of enslaved Africans. By the mid-1800s, the practice of slavery was increasingly criticized by people in the northern states.

History at a Glance

1750

1800

1850

1763
Britain gains France's North American colonies

Native American belt, c. 1700s

1787
U.S. Constitution is written

Abraham Lincoln

1867
Dominion of Canada is formed

Southerners worried that northerners would attempt to end slavery. In 1860 Abraham Lincoln, an opponent of slavery, was elected president. By early 1861, several southern states had withdrawn from the United States to set up a new country. This action led to a civil war. After four years of fighting, northern forces won. The country was reunited, and slavery ended. Racial tensions, however, continued.

The late 1800s saw the spread of industry in the United States. Waves of new immigrants provided workers for the growing economy. By 1900, the United States was one of the world's major industrial powers.

A World Leader

During the 1900s, the United States became a world leader. Its armies fought in World War I and World War II. During these conflicts, United States leaders urged the world's people to fight for freedom against oppressive **regimes,** or governments. American factories produced tanks and airplanes, while American soldiers helped win the wars.

After World War II, the United States and the Soviet Union became the world's two major powers. They competed for world leadership in a rivalry known as the Cold War. This rivalry was called the Cold War because the conflict never became "hot," with actual combat between the two powers. Nevertheless, tensions remained high as the countries competed politically and economically. The Cold War ended with the breakup of the Soviet Union in 1991.

During this period, African Americans, Latino Americans, Native Americans, and women became more active in seeking equal rights in the United States. Leaders such as Martin Luther King, Jr.; Rosa Parks; and César Chávez used peaceful methods that led to social changes for these groups.

Since 2000, the United States has faced challenges from the growth of terrorism both at home and throughout the world. **Terrorism** refers to the use of violence against civilians, by individuals or groups, to reach political goals. On September 11, 2001, terrorists seized four passenger planes. Two planes were crashed into the World Trade Center in New York City. A third aircraft damaged the Pentagon, the headquarters of the U.S. military, in Washington, D.C. A fourth plane crashed in rural Pennsylvania after what is believed to have been a passenger uprising against the terrorists. About 3,000 people died in the attacks.

Soon after, the United States sent troops to the southwest Asian country of Afghanistan.

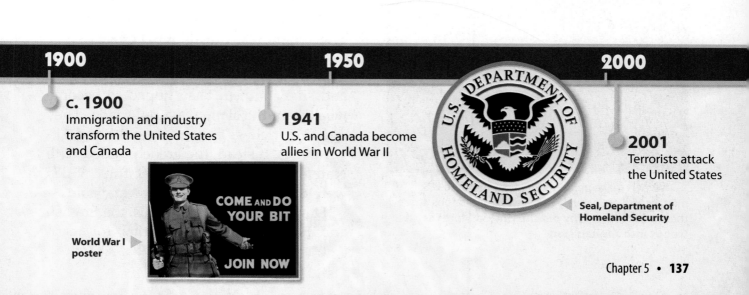

1900

1950

2000

c. 1900
Immigration and industry transform the United States and Canada

1941
U.S. and Canada become allies in World War II

2001
Terrorists attack the United States

Seal, Department of Homeland Security

COME AND DO YOUR BIT

JOIN NOW

World War I poster

Afghanistan's rulers, the Taliban, had protected the Muslim terrorist group al-Qaeda, which carried out the September 11 attacks. The Taliban were overthrown, although many terrorists escaped.

In 2003 U.S. troops overthrew Iraq's dictator, Saddam Hussein, who was accused of hiding illegal weapons and helping terrorists. In the years that followed, the United States worked with Afghanistan and Iraq to set up democratic governments. Continued fighting within both countries, though, made these efforts difficult.

Reading Check **Explaining** What role did the United States play in global affairs after 1900?

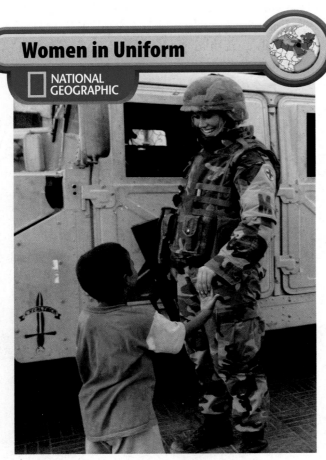

Women in Uniform

NATIONAL GEOGRAPHIC

▲ Women make up about 20 percent of the U.S. military and are actively involved in operations around the world. *Place* **Why did the United States send troops into Afghanistan?**

History of Canada

Main Idea **Canada gradually won independence from British rule during the late 1800s and early 1900s.**

Geography and You What similarities do you share with your neighbors? In what ways are you different? Read to find out how Canada's history is similar to and different from that of the United States.

Canada and the United States share similar backgrounds. Nonetheless, the two countries traveled different paths to becoming nations.

Early Settlement

Like the United States, Canada was originally settled by Native American groups. The first Europeans to arrive in the area that is today Canada were Viking explorers from Scandinavia. They landed in about A.D. 1000. The Vikings briefly lived on the Newfoundland coast, but they did not stay in their settlements very long. Eventually they left the Americas.

In the 1500s and 1600s, both England and France claimed areas of Canada. French explorers, settlers, and missionaries founded several cities. The most important were Quebec and Montreal. For almost 230 years, France ruled the area around the St. Lawrence River and the Great Lakes. This region was called New France.

The French knew that the Spanish had gained riches in South America from gold and silver mines. They hoped to become wealthy in the same way in Canada. They did find riches, but not in gold and silver mines. Instead, the French traded with Native Americans for beaver furs, which were then sent back to Europe and sold.

During the 1600s and 1700s, the English and French fought each other for territory around the globe. In 1707 England and Scotland united to form Great Britain. This union laid the foundation for the British Empire. By the 1760s, the British had won control of most of France's Canadian colony.

Beginning in the late 1700s, British and American settlers began moving to Canada in greater numbers. They set up farms along the Atlantic coast and in what is now Ontario. French-speaking Canadians lived mostly in present-day Quebec. Tragically, European warfare and diseases had nearly destroyed many Native American cultures by this time.

An Independent Nation

For the next 75 years, Great Britain held various colonies in eastern Canada. These colonies constantly quarreled with one another over colonial government policies. Fears of a United States takeover, however, forced them together. In 1867 most of the colonies became one nation known as the Dominion of Canada. As a **dominion**, Canada had its own central government to run local affairs. Great Britain, though, still controlled Canada's relations with other countries.

Under Canada's central government, the colonies became provinces, much like states in the United States. At first, there were four provinces—Quebec, Ontario, Nova Scotia, and New Brunswick. Neighboring British-ruled areas—Manitoba, British Columbia, Saskatchewan (suh·SKA·chuh·wuhn), and Alberta in the west and Prince Edward Island and Newfoundland along the Atlantic coast—became provinces of Canada during the next 100 years. Today Canada is made up of 10 provinces and 3 additional territories—the Yukon Territory, the Northwest Territories, and Nunavut (NOO·nah·VOOT).

NATIONAL GEOGRAPHIC

Trade in Canada

As Europeans explored Canada, they made treaties and traded with the Native Americans who lived there. *Place* **What two European nations colonized Canada?**

At Canada's founding, the government promised to protect the French language and culture in Quebec. However, the English-speaking minority there was far wealthier and ran the economy. This led to tensions between the two groups. French speakers claimed that they were treated unfairly because of their heritage.

During the early 1900s, many immigrants arrived, and Canada's population and economy grew. Meanwhile, Canadians fought alongside the British and Americans in the two World Wars. Canada's support in these wars led to its full independence. In 1982 Canadians won the right to change their constitution without British approval. Today Canada still faces the possibility that Quebec will separate and become independent.

Reading Check **Summarizing** How did Canada's government change over time?

Governments of the United States and Canada

Main Idea **The United States and Canada are democracies, but their governments are organized differently.**

Geography and You Do you think democracy is a good government system? Why? Read to discover the similarities and differences between the democracies of the United States and Canada.

The United States and Canada are both **representative democracies,** in which voters choose leaders who make and enforce the laws. However, the two government systems have some important differences.

U.S. Democracy

The United States Constitution is the basic plan that explains how our national, or central, government is set up and how it works. The document was written in the late 1780s by leaders who wanted to create a government strong enough to guide the country. Those leaders also wanted a government with limited powers so that people's rights would be protected from government interference.

To achieve these goals, the writers of the Constitution applied the **principle,** or rule, of separation of powers. This means they divided the power of the national government among three branches: executive, legislative, and judicial. In addition, they gave each branch unique powers as a way to prevent the other branches from abusing their power. This idea is called checks and balances. With it, the Founders aimed to prevent one branch from becoming too powerful.

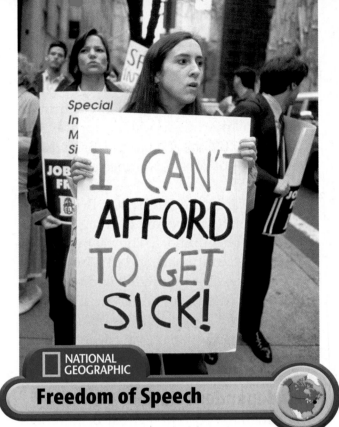

NATIONAL GEOGRAPHIC

Freedom of Speech

Political freedoms are stated in the U.S. Constitution. The First Amendment allows citizens to disagree with the U.S. government. *Place* **What is the purpose of the Bill of Rights?**

The U.S. Constitution created a strong central government, but state governments were given certain responsibilities. This structure reflects the idea called federalism. In **federalism,** power is divided between the federal, or national, government and state governments. The national government makes treaties with other countries, coins money, and has the power to make laws about trade between states. State governments handle such issues as the health and education of their citizens.

In the U.S. federal system, people are citizens of both the nation and their state. As a result, citizens have the right to vote for both national and state leaders. The U.S. Constitution and state constitutions provide for that right. Citizens have the duty to make informed decisions when they vote. Citizens also have the responsibility to obey national and state laws.

In 1791 ten **amendments,** or additions, known as the Bill of Rights were added to the U.S. Constitution. Their purpose was to prevent the government from taking away people's freedoms. For example, the Bill of Rights ensures that the government cannot limit Americans' freedom of speech or religion.

Throughout its history, the Constitution has had other amendments added to it. Individual freedom is a **core,** or basic, value of the United States. Another is equality. The Constitution's Fourteenth Amendment requires the states to provide equal protection under the law to all persons within their boundaries.

Still, all Americans have not always enjoyed equal rights. Some groups suffered unfair treatment. For several decades after independence, only white males could vote. African American males gained the right to vote only when the Constitution was changed in 1870. All women were given the right to vote in 1920.

Canadian Democracy

Canada has a **parliamentary democracy** in which voters elect representatives to a lawmaking body called Parliament. These representatives then choose an official called the prime minister to head the government. The British monarch serves as king or queen of Canada.

Like the United States, Canada has a federal system. Power is divided between the central government and the provinces and territories. Canada's Charter of Rights and Freedoms is similar to the U.S. Bill of Rights. It protects the liberties of Canadian citizens.

✔ Reading Check **Identifying** What powers do U.S. national and state governments have?

Section I Review

Social Studies ONLINE
Study Central™ To review this section, go to glencoe.com.

Vocabulary

1. **Explain** the significance of:
   a. colony
   b. annex
   c. terrorism
   d. dominion
   e. representative democracy
   f. federalism
   g. amendment
   h. parliamentary democracy

Main Ideas

2. **Describing** What was the Cold War, and what brought it to an end?

3. **Categorizing** Use a chart like the one below to list five major events in American and Canadian history. Categorize each event as social, economic, or political, and explain why each is significant.

Event	Category	Significance

4. **Comparing and Contrasting** How are the governments of the United States and Canada similar? How are they different?

Critical Thinking

5. **BIG Idea** How did the French and British colonies in Canada differ from the Spanish colonies in Mexico and South America?

6. **Challenge** Why do you think it is important in a democracy for people to make informed decisions?

Writing About Geography

7. **Using Your FOLDABLES** Use your Foldable to write a paragraph explaining how the core American values of freedom and equality are evident in America's government and laws.

The Electoral College: Should It Be Changed?

When people vote for the president and vice president of the United States, they are really voting for electors who will vote for these people. These electors make up the Electoral College. The number of electors each state has is based on the total number of its U.S. senators and representatives. Electors cast votes for the candidate who wins the popular vote in their state. In every state except Maine and Nebraska, the winner of the popular vote will get all of that state's electoral votes.

For Change

[The Electoral College] gives more weight to votes cast in small states. . . . Second, . . . people who disagree with the majority in their state are not represented. Finally, the system allows the election of a President who does not have the support of a majority of voters. Without the Electoral College, candidates would campaign to get as many individual votes as possible in every state, instead of focusing on states that provide key electoral votes. Each vote would make a difference . . . which could lead to increased voting across the country.

—Kay Maxwell
President,
League of Women Voters

Against Change

[The Electoral College] has worked well in practice. . . . This system usually produces a decisive result, even when the popular vote is very close. Second, if America were to vote for President by direct popular vote, the campaigns might ignore smaller states and rural areas and concentrate only on the big metropolitan areas. Third, the Electoral College reinforces our two-party system. Because candidates are required to win elections in states in different parts of the country, the candidates' parties must have a broad base, not a regional one.

—John Fortier
American Enterprise Institute

You Be the Geographer

1. **Analyzing** How might presidential candidates change their campaign plans if the Electoral College were done away with?

2. **Critical Thinking** Do you think that candidates would change where they campaign if elections were based on the popular vote? Why or why not?

3. **Read to Write** Write a paragraph that explains whether you think the current process of electing a president and vice president is effective. You might want to give examples from what you know about American history and government.

Guide to Reading

BIG Idea

Culture influences people's perceptions about places and regions.

Content Vocabulary

- ban *(p. 145)*
- suburb *(p. 147)*
- indigenous *(p. 149)*
- bilingual *(p. 149)*

Academic Vocabulary

- evolve *(p. 147)*
- generate *(p. 147)*
- participate *(p. 147)*

Reading Strategy

Organizing Information Use a chart like the one below to organize key facts about the languages, cultures, and lifestyles of the United States and Canada.

	Key Facts
Language	
Art and Literature	
Daily Life	

SECTION 2 Cultures and Lifestyles

Picture This Cadillacs, instead of cattle, populate this dusty wheat field near Amarillo, Texas. In 1974 a Texas millionaire had this unusual display of cars created to honor the Cadillac. Layers of graffiti have been added to the Cadillacs over the years, and new guests are invited to add their own messages. Read Section 2 to learn more about the unique cultures in the United States and Canada.

▼ **Cadillac Ranch near Amarillo, Texas**

Cultures and Lifestyles of the United States

Main Idea The culture of the United States has been shaped by immigrants from around the world.

Geography and You Have you ever decorated a Christmas tree or seen one at a store? This tradition actually comes from Germany. Read on to discover how immigration has transformed culture in the United States.

About 300 million people live in the United States, making it the third-most-populous country. The population of the United States includes people of many different ethnic backgrounds.

Diverse Traditions

The United States has been called "a nation of immigrants." Throughout its history, the United States has attracted vast numbers of immigrants from around the globe. Yet the pattern of immigration has changed over time. During the late 1700s and early 1800s, the largest number of immigrants came from Great Britain, Ireland, western and central Africa, and the Caribbean. From the late 1800s to the 1920s, most immigrants came from southern, central, and eastern Europe. Many Chinese, Japanese, Mexican, and Canadian immigrants also arrived during this period.

The diverse backgrounds of so many late-1800s immigrants caused some Americans to become concerned about cultural change. As a result, they passed laws limiting immigration. In 1882 Congress passed a law that **banned**, or legally blocked, almost all immigration from China. In 1924 another law limited the numbers of immi-

Becoming U.S. Citizens

Many immigrants eventually decide to become U.S. citizens. Once they meet the requirements and pass the citizenship test, they are officially sworn in as citizens and recite the Pledge of Allegiance. **Movement** How have immigration trends changed since the late 1900s?

grants from many countries. For many years, immigration to the United States slowed.

By the 1960s, opinions in the country had changed, in part due to growing support for civil rights. As a result, the country changed its immigration laws. A new law passed in 1965 based entry into the United States on a person's work skills and links to relatives already living in the United States. Changes in U.S. laws and in economic and political conditions worldwide led to increased immigration during the late 1900s. By 2000, nearly half of all the country's immigrants came from Latin America and Canada, and another third came from Asia. Less than 15 percent came from Europe.

Social Studies ONLINE

Student Web Activity Visit <u>glencoe.com</u> and complete the Chapter 5 Web Activity on the history of U.S. immigration.

Current immigration trends are changing the makeup of the American population. People of European descent still make up about two-thirds of the population, but the percentage of people from other areas is growing. Latinos, or Hispanics—who trace their heritages to the countries of Latin America and Spain—make up 15 percent of Americans. They are the fastest-growing ethnic group. African Americans, at 12 percent, are the next-largest ethnic group. Asian Americans make up 4 percent of the population, and Native Americans make up 1 percent.

The languages spoken in the United States reflect the diversity of its people. English is the primary language, but for one person in six, English is not their most familiar language. Spanish is the most widely spoken language after English. More than 1 million people speak one or more of the following: Chinese, French, Vietnamese, Tagalog, German, and Italian.

Diversity also extends to religion, which has long been an important factor in American life. Most Americans follow some form of Christianity. The largest number of Christians in the United States belongs to one of the many Protestant churches. These groups vary widely in their beliefs and practices. Roman Catholics make up the next-largest group of American Christians, followed by members of Eastern Orthodox churches. Judaism and Islam each have about 5 million followers in the United States. About 2 to 3 million Americans practice Buddhism, and another 2.5 million are followers of Hinduism.

Literature and the Arts

American artists, writers, and musicians have developed distinctly American styles. The earliest American artists used materials from their environments to create works of art. For centuries, Native Americans have carved wooden masks or created beautiful designs on pottery made from clay found in their areas. Later artists were attracted to the beauty of the landscape. For example, Winslow Homer painted the stormy waters of the North Atlantic. Georgia O'Keeffe painted the colorful deserts of the Southwest. In contrast, Thomas Eakins and John Sloan often painted the gritty, or rough, side of city life.

Two themes are common in American literature. One theme focuses on the rich diversity of the people in the United States. The poetry of Langston Hughes and the novels of Toni Morrison portray the triumphs and sorrows of African Americans. The novels of Amy Tan examine the lives of Chinese Americans. Oscar Hijuelos and Sandra Cisneros write about the country's Latinos.

Georgia O'Keeffe

NATIONAL GEOGRAPHIC

▲ Originally from Wisconsin, O'Keeffe began her career as an art teacher. She moved to New Mexico in 1946, and lived and worked there until her death at the age of 98. *Regions* **What themes or subjects have attracted American artists?**

A second theme in American literature focuses on the landscape and history of particular regions. Mark Twain's books tell about life along the Mississippi River in the mid-1800s. Nathaniel Hawthorne wrote about the people of New England. Willa Cather and Laura Ingalls Wilder portrayed the struggles people faced in settling the Great Plains. William Faulkner wrote about life in the South.

Americans have created several new musical styles. Country music grew out of folk music from the rural South in the 1920s. The style gained many fans as it **evolved,** or developed, over the following decades. In the early 1900s, African Americans developed blues and jazz. Blues later inspired rock and roll in the 1950s. More recently, rap and hip-hop have gained popularity.

In the early 1900s, movies started attracting large audiences. Today, the movie industry **generates,** or makes, enormous profits and continues to entertain audiences around the world. In addition to movies, after 1950, television became an important part of American culture.

Life in the United States

At one time, most Americans lived in rural areas. Today the United States is a land of urban dwellers. Many people, however, have moved from cities to **suburbs,** or smaller communities surrounding a larger city. They also have moved from one region to another. Since the 1970s, the fastest-growing regions have been the South and Southwest, often called the Sunbelt because of their sunny, mild climates.

Lifestyles vary across the United States. Americans live in different types of homes, from one-story houses in the suburbs to high-rise apartments in cities. About two-thirds of American families own their own

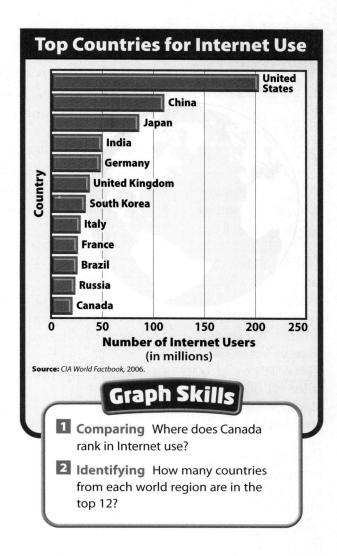

Top Countries for Internet Use

Country (vertical axis)

United States
China
Japan
India
Germany
United Kingdom
South Korea
Italy
France
Brazil
Russia
Canada

Number of Internet Users (in millions): 0, 50, 100, 150, 200, 250

Source: *CIA World Factbook,* 2006.

Graph Skills

1 **Comparing** Where does Canada rank in Internet use?

2 **Identifying** How many countries from each world region are in the top 12?

homes. This is one of the highest home ownership rates in the world. Because of their economic well-being, Americans also lead the world in the ownership of cars and personal computers and in Internet use.

Many Americans watch movies and television, but they also exercise and play sports. Millions of young Americans **participate** in sports leagues devoted to games such as baseball and soccer. Important U.S. holidays include Thanksgiving, the Fourth of July, and other celebrations based on religious and ethnic traditions.

✓ **Reading Check** **Summarizing** How has the United States controlled immigration?

I, Too

By Langston Hughes

I, too, sing America.

I am the darker brother.
They send me to eat in the kitchen
When company comes,
But I laugh,
And eat well,
And grow strong.

Tomorrow,
I'll be at the table
When **company** comes.
Nobody'll dare
Say to me,
"Eat in the kitchen,"
Then.

Besides,
They'll see how beautiful I am
And be **ashamed**—

I, too, am America.

"I, Too" from *Collected Poems* by Langston Hughes.
Copyright © 1994 by the Estate of Langston Hughes.
Reprinted by permission of Alfred A. Knopf, a division
of Random House, Inc.

Langston Hughes
(1902–1967)

Langston Hughes was one of the first African Americans to earn a living as a writer. He wrote plays, novels, essays, and children's stories, but he became best known for his poetry. Hughes's works celebrated the energy of life in New York City's Harlem, a largely African American neighborhood.

Background Information

Hughes was active in the Harlem Renaissance, an African American artistic movement of the 1920s. Inspired by jazz and blues, Hughes wove the rhythms of these forms of music into his poems. He urged African Americans to take pride in their culture and to stand up for their rights.

Reader's Dictionary

company: guests

ashamed: feel sorry or guilty for having done something wrong

Analyzing Literature

1. **Making Inferences** How does Hughes view the role of African Americans in society at the time he wrote this poem?

2. **Read to Write** Write a poem or paragraph that responds to Hughes's feelings in "I, Too."

Cultures and Lifestyles of Canada

Main Idea Canadians of many different backgrounds live in towns and cities close to the U.S. border.

Geography and You Have you played hockey or seen a hockey game? Hockey is a Canadian sport. Read to find out how Canadians have developed unique cultures.

Like the United States, Canada is a nation formed by immigrants with many different cultures. Unlike the United States, Canada has had difficulty achieving a strong sense of national identity. Canada's vast distances and separate cultures cause some Canadians to feel more closely attached to their own region than to Canada as a country.

A Mix of Cultures

About one-fourth of Canadians are of French ancestry. Most of these people live in Quebec, where they make up 80 percent of that province's population. People of British ancestry form another fourth of Canada's population, and they live mainly in Ontario, the Atlantic Provinces, and British Columbia. People of other European backgrounds form about 15 percent of Canada's population.

Canada also is home to people of Asian, African, and Latin American backgrounds. Indigenous Canadians, similar to Native Americans, number more than a million. **Indigenous** refers to people who are descended from an area's first inhabitants. Many people in Canada call these indigenous groups the "First Nations."

Canada is a **bilingual** country, which means it has two official languages. In Canada, the languages are English and French.

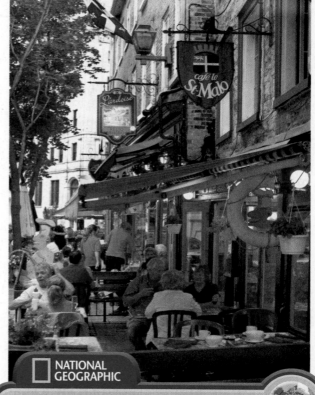

NATIONAL GEOGRAPHIC

Quebec's French Culture

The French-speaking city of Quebec, founded in 1608, is one of Canada's oldest settlements. *Regions* What percentage of Canadians are of French ancestry?

Despite promises of protection, many French speakers in Quebec do not believe that their language and culture can survive in largely English-speaking Canada. They would like Quebec to separate from Canada and become independent. So far, they have been defeated in two important votes on this issue. Canada's future as a united country, however, is still uncertain.

One cultural issue the country has been able to solve concerns the Inuit (IH·nu·wuht). The Inuit are a northern indigenous people who have wanted self-rule while remaining part of Canada. In 1999 the Canadian government created the territory of Nunavut for them. The name means "Our Land" in the Inuit language. There, the Inuit govern themselves, although they still rely on the national government for some services.

Art and Literature

The first Canadian artists were indigenous peoples who carved figures from stone and wood, made pottery, or were weavers. Today, Canadian art reflects both European and indigenous influences. The beauty of Canada's landscape has long been a favorite subject for many artists. Nature and history have been popular subjects for Canadian writers.

Centuries ago, indigenous peoples used song and dance as part of their religious rituals. European music, such as Irish and Scottish ballads, gained popularity after the 1700s. In recent decades, pop and rock have become as popular in Canada as in the United States.

Movies are also a major part of Canadian culture. The nation's film industry earns $5 billion each year. Theater is popular in Canada as well. Ontario's Stratford Festival is world famous for its productions of William Shakespeare's plays. The festival runs for a number of months each year and attracts over half a million fans.

Life in Canada

Like Americans, Canadians are a mobile people. Millions of them use cars to commute to work every day.

Certain foods are regional favorites. Seafood dishes are popular in the Atlantic Provinces, while French cuisine is preferred in Quebec. Ontario features Italian or Eastern European foods, reflecting the immigrant traditions there. British Columbia is known for salmon and Asian foods.

Canadians are enthusiastic about hockey—a sport that began in Canada—as well as lacrosse, which began as a Native American game. Many Canadians also enjoy hunting and fishing.

Canadians celebrate the founding of their country on July 1 and the fall Thanksgiving holiday in October. As in the United States, different ethnic groups celebrate their heritage at different times of the year.

✔ Reading Check **Explaining** Why was the territory of Nunavut created?

Section 2 Review

Social Studies ONLINE
Study Central™ To review this section, go to glencoe.com.

Vocabulary

1. **Explain** the meaning of *ban, suburb, indigenous,* and *bilingual* by using each word in a sentence.

Main Ideas

2. **Identifying** Which styles of music did Americans invent?

3. **Summarizing** Use a diagram like the one below to show three ways immigration has shaped Canada.

```
        Immigration
       /    |    \
     ( )   ( )   ( )
```

Critical Thinking

4. **Analyzing Information** How are immigration trends changing in the United States?

5. **BIG Idea** Explain why many people in Quebec have wanted to form a separate nation.

6. **Challenge** Why do you think the lifestyles of Americans and Canadians are similar?

Writing About Geography

7. **Expository Writing** Write a paragraph summarizing the styles of American art and literature.

Visual Summary

_ American History _

- Native Americans, or indigenous peoples, are North America's earliest inhabitants.

- The 13 British colonies declared independence in 1776.

- During the 1800s, the United States grew in population and had a prosperous economy.

- The United States became a global power during the 1900s.

Map of original 13 colonies

_ Canadian History _

- France and then Britain acquired control of the area that today is Canada.

- In 1867 the Dominion of Canada was founded.

- Canada grew through immigration and developed a modern economy.

___ American and ___ Canadian Governments

- The United States and Canada are democracies based on federal systems.

- The U.S. government has three branches, each with special powers to check the power of the others.

- Canada has a parliamentary system. Legislative members choose a prime minister to head the government.

_ American Culture _

- Immigration has created a diversity of groups, languages, and religions.

- American art and literature have focused on nature and freedom. American music includes country and jazz.

- American lifestyles reflect the economic well-being of the people.

Elvis Presley

Toronto, Canada

_ Canadian Culture _

- Canadian culture reflects the diversity of the many peoples who settled the country.

- Canadian art and literature draw on nature and the history of the country.

- Foods and pastimes in Canada reflect regional life and the contributions of immigrants.

Hockey, Canada

STUDY TO GO Study anywhere, anytime! Download quizzes and flash cards to your PDA from **glencoe.com**.

STANDARDIZED TEST PRACTICE

TEST-TAKING **TIP**

Outline information from your textbook to study for an exam. Use bold type, questions, and summary paragraphs for headings and details in your outline.

Reviewing Vocabulary

Directions: Choose the word(s) that best completes the sentence.

1. Overseas settlements tied to a parent country are called _____.

  A suburbs

  B colonies

  C dominions

  D provinces

2. Both the United States and Canada have _____.

  A monarchs

  B colonial governments

  C representative democracies

  D parliamentary democracies

3. Smaller communities surrounding a larger city are known as _____.

  A suburbs

  B colonies

  C dominions

  D provinces

4. The term _____ is used to describe people who are descended from an area's first inhabitants.

  A terrorist

  B indigenous

  C bilingual

  D federalist

Reviewing Main Ideas

Directions: Choose the best answer for each question.

Section 1 *(pp. 134–141)*

5. How did the United States become a world leader during the 1900s?

  A by developing the factory system

  B by building an economy based on agriculture

  C by enslaving hundreds of thousands of Africans

  D by helping to win World War I and World War II

6. What accomplishment marked Canada's full independence?

  A Canada's colonies became provinces.

  B Canada established its own central government.

  C Canadians fought in World War I and World War II.

  D Canadians won the right to change their constitution.

Section 2 *(pp. 144–150)*

7. By 2000 where did most immigrants in the United States come from?

  A Latin America, Canada, and Asia

  B Ireland and Great Britain

  C western and central Africa

  D southern and eastern Europe

8. What percentage of Canadians has a European background?

  A 15 percent

  B 25 percent

  C 50 percent

  D 65 percent

GO ON

Critical Thinking

Directions: Base your answers to questions 9 and 10 on the circle graph below and your knowledge of Chapter 5. Choose the best answer for each question.

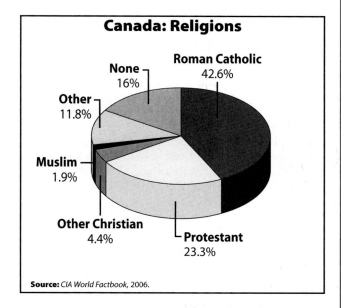

Canada: Religions

Roman Catholic 42.6%
None 16%
Other 11.8%
Muslim 1.9%
Other Christian 4.4%
Protestant 23.3%

Source: *CIA World Factbook, 2006.*

9. Which of the following generalizations is based on the circle graph?

A No Buddhists live in Canada.

B All Canadians are deeply religious.

C A majority of Canadians are Christian.

D Canadians are very tolerant of religious differences.

10. According to the graph, which of the following statements is correct?

A More Protestants than Catholics live in Canada.

B Muslims and other Christians (not including Catholics) outnumber Protestants.

C Islam has almost as many followers as Christianity.

D There are more Protestants than people who claim no religion.

Document-Based Questions

Directions: Analyze the following document and answer the short-answer questions that follow.

The following passage is from the *Canadian Charter of Rights and Freedoms* enacted in 1982.

Guarantee of Rights and Freedoms
1. The Canadian Charter of Rights and Freedoms guarantees the rights and freedoms set out in it subject only to such reasonable limits prescribed by law as can be demonstrably justified in a free and democratic society.

Fundamental Freedoms
2. Everyone has the following fundamental freedoms:
a) freedom of conscience and religion;
b) freedom of thought, belief, opinion and expression, including freedom of the press and other media of communication;
c) freedom of peaceful assembly; and
d) freedom of association.

Democratic Rights
3. Every citizen of Canada has the right to vote in an election of members of the House of Commons or of a legislative assembly and to be qualified for membership therein.

11. Do only Canadian citizens enjoy freedom of expression in Canada? Explain.

12. What qualification for membership in the Canadian House of Commons is mentioned?

Extended Response

13. Explain why Canada's future as a united country is uncertain.

Social Studies ONLINE
For additional test practice, use Self-Check Quizzes—Chapter 5 at glencoe.com.

Need Extra Help?													
If you missed question. . .	1	2	3	4	5	6	7	8	9	10	11	12	13
Go to page. . .	136	140	147	149	137	139	145	149	149	149	141	141	149

"Hello! My name is Taylor.

I'm 13 years old and live in Ashcroft, British Columbia. British Columbia is one of Canada's 10 provinces. My family runs a horse ranch and lodge there. Here's how I spend my day."

7:15 a.m. I wake up to the sound of my alarm clock. I shower and put on jeans, a T-shirt, and my tan cowboy boots. Then I head to the kitchen and say good morning to my parents and older brother, Daniel.

7:45 a.m. My mom has made pancakes and bacon for breakfast, and it smells great. I dig in. A hot breakfast is a nice treat. On most days, I just have cereal and toast.

8:25 a.m. Everyone goes their separate ways. My dad leaves for work in town. My brother goes off to high school, and my mom gets ready to work in the ranch office. I walk down our rural road and wait for the school bus.

9:00 a.m. My school day begins with math class. It's okay, but I am happy when the bell rings because I have English next. I love reading and writing and would like to become an author.

10:30 a.m. I stop at my locker, then go to French class. French is the official language in Quebec, Canada's biggest province. We speak English throughout the rest of Canada, but many kids study French as a second language.

 11:40 a.m. It's time for lunch. Sometimes I walk to my friend's house for lunch (she lives near the school). Today, I stay at school and buy a grilled cheese sandwich and an apple.

12:20 p.m. In physical education class, we play basketball. In Canada, kids take "phys. ed." until tenth grade. We learn everything from softball to gymnastics.

1:20 p.m. I head to the school wood shop for woodworking class. I put on my safety goggles and use a power tool to carve a wooden sign. In a few weeks, woodworking will be over and I will start a new class—health.

3:00 p.m. I take the bus back home. There, I feed the horses and tackle some other ranch chores. In the summer, when the ranch is full of guests, I will be much busier! Then I will have to set up for meals and wash dishes.

4:45 p.m. I have some free time before dinner, so I grab my helmet, get my horse from the stable, and go riding.

6:15 p.m. Tonight, my grandfather and two uncles join us for dinner. They live in a separate house here on the ranch, so we see them all the time. We eat thick steaks and salad.

7:30 p.m. I help clear the table then do my homework. For one assignment, I have to use the family computer to log on to the Internet.

10:00 p.m. I read in my room for a while then get ready for bed. I'm tired!

ILLUSTRATIONS BY BOOKMAPMAN

SCHOOL TIME Taylor and her classmates share a laugh. Each semester Taylor studies four or five subjects. She gets three minutes between classes to get to her next lesson.

HORSING AROUND Ranching and tourism are big business in Taylor's village. Taylor's family owns a guest ranch. One of Taylor's chores is to feed the horses.

GREAT OUTDOORS Hiking is a popular pastime around Ashcroft. Here, Taylor and her dog take a break at a scenic spot overlooking the Thompson River.

ON THE RANCH Taylor Nichols spends her time going to school, riding horses, and helping out on her family's ranch. Taylor lives in Canada's westernmost province.

ARON HUEY / POLARIS (4)

What's Popular in Canada

Ice hockey Canadians are passionate about this national sport. At the professional level, there are intense team rivalries, like the one between the Toronto Maple Leafs and the Montreal Canadiens.

AP PHOTO/RYAN REMIORZ

Doughnuts Canada has more doughnut shops per person than any other country in the world! Apple fritters are a big favorite.

MELANIE ACEVEDO

Maple syrup Canada produces 85 percent of the world's maple syrup. Syrup makers tap the maple trees in early March. In one season, a single tree can make one liter of syrup.

ROY MORSCH/ AGE FOTOSTOCK

Say It in Canadian Slang

English and French are the national languages of Canada. In fact, all official signs, including road signs across the country, are printed in both languages. But Canada also has its share of unusual slang expressions. Try these examples.

How are you doing?
Whadda'yat? (This expression is from eastern Canada.)

A Canadian dollar
Loonie (The nickname comes from the picture of a loon that appears on the coin.)

Very good
Skookum (SKOO·kum)

PURESTOCK / ALAMY

The United States and Canada Today

Essential Question

Regions The United States and Canada both have large land areas. Each has unique landforms and resources. Americans and Canadians have used their rich resources and technological skills to become leading economic powers. How might a region's economy influence the world economy?

BIG Ideas

San Francisco, California

Section 1: Living in the United States and Canada Today

BIG IDEA Places reflect the relationship between humans and the physical environment. Both the United States and Canada are often divided into economic regions. These regions are based on similar resources and climates. People in each region have developed distinctive ways of life based on the different physical characteristics of their area.

Section 2: Issues and Challenges

BIG IDEA Cooperation and conflict among people have an effect on the Earth's surface. The United States and Canada are peaceful neighbors, sharing the longest undefended border in the world. Landforms and weather patterns do not stop at the border, however, and environmental actions by one country can affect the other.

FOLDABLES™
Study Organizer

Organizing Information Make this Foldable to help you organize information about the economic regions and issues related to the United States and Canada.

Step 1 Fold an 11x17 piece of paper lengthwise to create 3 equal sections.

Step 2 Then fold it to form 3 columns.

Step 3 Label your Foldable as shown.

Country	Regions/ Economies	Global/ Environmental Issues
United States		
Canada		

Reading and Writing As you read the chapter, take notes in the correct area of your Foldable. Use your notes to write the script of a short newscast describing the economies of the United States and Canada today.

Social Studies ONLINE

To preview Chapter 6, go to glencoe.com.

Guide to Reading

BIG Idea

Places reflect the relationship between humans and the physical environment.

Content Vocabulary

- free market *(p. 159)*
- profit *(p. 159)*
- stock *(p. 159)*
- biotechnology *(p. 159)*
- newsprint *(p. 162)*

Academic Vocabulary

- guarantee *(p. 159)*
- media *(p. 159)*
- reluctant *(p. 162)*

Reading Strategy

Categorizing Information Use a diagram like the one below to list the economic regions in the United States and provide several key facts about each.

U.S. Regions

Living in the United States and Canada Today

Picture This "The doctor will see you now." Well, almost. This doctor of the future is actually a robot. It allows doctors who may be miles away to talk to patients, inspect wounds, and read charts through the use of a video camera and screen. A computer and a joystick allow the doctor to move through the hospital and visit patients. The robots have been developed for hospitals that are looking for ways to reduce expenses. Read Section 1 to find out more about other industries that shape the United States and Canada.

▼ **A new type of doctor**

Economic Regions

Main Idea **The United States can be organized into economic regions.**

Geography and You Do you live in an area with many office buildings, factories, or farms? Read to discover why economic regions have developed.

Geographers group states together into five economic regions. These regions, and those of Canada, are shown in **Figure 1** on the next page. All of these regions are linked by the country's free market economy.

The Free Market Economy

In a **free market** economy, people are free to buy, sell, and produce whatever they want, with limited government involvement. They also can work wherever they want. A free market economy has two key groups: business owners and consumers. Business owners produce the products they think will make the most **profits,** or the most money after business expenses are paid. Consumers shop for the best products at the lowest prices.

People also take part in a free market economy by investing in businesses. People can buy **stock,** which represents part ownership in a company. When a company succeeds, it often pays some of its profits to the people who own its stock. Investing in stock involves risk, however. If the business fails, the stock becomes worthless. Consumers can also save their money in a bank, which is safer than buying stock. Because of government **guarantees,** or promises, savers have some of their money protected should a bank fail or go out of business. Although savings accounts are better protected, stocks provide a greater chance for high financial payoff.

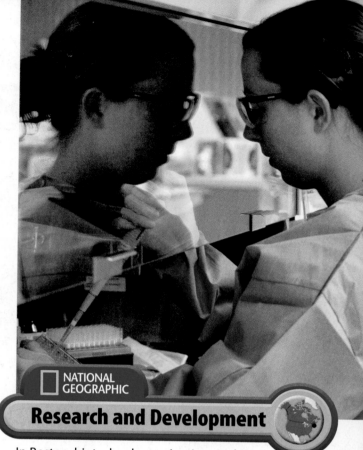

NATIONAL GEOGRAPHIC

Research and Development

In Boston, biotechnology scientists study cells and how they respond to treatment. *Regions* **Why has the Northeast focused on business?**

A free market economy allows people to produce what they want. Resources are needed to produce a good or service, but some resources in a region are more available than others. As a result, economic regions have developed that specialize in producing products using their available resources.

The Northeast

The Northeast is made up of several large urban areas. Among them are New York City, the country's most populous city, and Boston, Massachusetts. With few mineral resources and poor soil for farming in many areas, the economic focus of the Northeast has been on business and trade. New York City has many financial and **media,** or communications, companies. Boston is an important center for **biotechnology** research. Biotechnology is the study of cells to find ways of improving health.

Figure 1   United States and Canada: Regions

Canada
- Atlantic Provinces
- Central and Eastern
- West
- North

United States
- Northeast
- South
- Midwest
- Interior West
- Pacific

0   600 kilometers
0   600 miles
Azimuthal Equal-Area projection

160°W   155°W
PACIFIC OCEAN
20°N
0   200 kilometers
0   200 miles
Azimuthal Equal-Area projection

PACIFIC OCEAN

ATLANTIC OCEAN

Map Skills

1 Regions Which states make up the Pacific region?

2 Regions Which of Canada's regions includes the least territory?

The Midwest

The Midwest's rich soil enables farmers to grow crops such as corn, wheat, and soybeans. Mineral resources found here include iron ore, coal, lead, and zinc. Beginning in the 1800s, manufacturing developed in the Midwest. Towns like Cleveland and Detroit made steel and automobiles. Over time, however, the area's factories grew outdated. Many closed down, and thousands lost their jobs.

The South

With its rich soils, the South relied on agriculture. In recent decades the South has changed rapidly. The area now has expanding cities, growing industries, and diverse populations. Workers in cities such as Houston, Dallas, and Atlanta make tex-tiles, electrical equipment, computers, and airplane parts. Texas, Louisiana, and Alabama produce oil and related products. In Florida, tourism and trade are major activities.

The Interior West

The Interior West has magnificent scenery and outdoor recreation that attracts many people. Although the region is dry, irrigation allows for some agriculture. For many decades, mining, ranching, and lumbering were the Interior West's main economic activities. In recent years, other parts of the economy have grown rapidly. The cities of Denver and Salt Lake City have growing information technology industries. Tourism and service industries are important to Albuquerque and Phoenix.

The Pacific

Fruits and vegetables are important crops in the fertile valleys of California, Oregon, and Washington. Sugarcane, pineapples, and coffee grow in the rich volcanic soil of Hawaii. Fish, timber, and mineral resources are important in the Pacific area as well. California has gold, lead, and copper, and Alaska has vast reserves of oil.

Many industries thrive in the Pacific area. Workers in California and Washington build airplanes and develop computer software. The city of Los Angeles is the world center of the movie industry. The area's booming economy draws many newcomers. California, the nation's most populous state, has wide ethnic diversity. Nearly half of its people are Latino or Asian American.

✔**Reading Check** **Summarizing** How has the south's economy changed?

Ethnic Pride
NATIONAL GEOGRAPHIC

▲ This parade in Los Angeles, California, celebrates the participants' Latino heritage. **Movement** Why are people drawn to the Pacific region?

Regions of Canada

Main Idea **With a few exceptions, Canada's economic regions are similar to those in the United States.**

Geography and You Have you worked hard to build or make something? Did you feel a sense of accomplishment when you finished? Read to learn how Canadians have worked to build their economy despite geographic obstacles.

Like the United States, Canada consists of different economic regions. It also has a free market economy with limited government involvement. Canada's government, however, plays a more direct role in providing services. Unlike the United States, Canada's national and provincial governments provide health care for citizens. The government also regulates broadcasting, transport, and power companies.

Atlantic Provinces

Fishing was for many years a major industry in the Atlantic Provinces of Newfoundland and Labrador, Nova Scotia, Prince Edward Island, and New Brunswick. Overfishing, however, has weakened the industry. Today most people in the area hold jobs in manufacturing, mining, and tourism. The city of Halifax, in Nova Scotia, is a major shipping center in the region.

Central and Eastern Region

Canada's Central and Eastern Region includes the large provinces of Quebec and Ontario. The paper industry is important in Quebec, as is the creation of hydroelectric power. Montreal, on the St. Lawrence River, is a major port and leading financial and industrial center. Many in Quebec's largely French-speaking population would like the province to separate from Canada.

Because of the political and economic uncertainty this creates, many outside businesses have been **reluctant,** or hesitant, to invest in Quebec's economy.

Ontario has the largest population and greatest wealth of Canada's provinces. It is a major agricultural, manufacturing, forestry, and mining center. Ontario's capital, Toronto, is Canada's largest city and a major center of finance and business. Because of recent immigration, Toronto is now home to people from about 170 countries.

The West

Farming and ranching are major economic activities in the provinces of Manitoba, Saskatchewan, and Alberta. This area produces large amounts of wheat for export and contains some of the world's largest reserves of oil and natural gas.

The province of British Columbia has extensive forests. The forests help make Canada the world's largest producer of **newsprint,** the type of paper used for printing newspapers. Mining, fishing, and tourism also support British Columbia's economy. The city of Vancouver, its capital, is Canada's main Pacific port.

The North

Canada's vast north covers about one-third of the country. This area includes the Yukon Territory, the Northwest Territories, and Nunavut. Many of the 25,000 people in this area are indigenous (ihn·DIH·juh·nuhs) peoples. The main resources in the North are minerals such as gold and diamonds.

✔ **Reading Check** **Explaining** How has political uncertainty affected Quebec's economy?

Section Review

Social Studies ONLINE
Study Central™ To review this section, go to glencoe.com.

Vocabulary

1. **Explain** the significance of:
   a. free market
   b. profit
   c. stock
   d. biotechnology
   e. newsprint

Main Ideas

2. **Analyzing** Describe the basic principles of a free market economy.

3. **Summarizing** Use a chart like the one below to list important facts about the economies of three regions of Canada, and identify a physical characteristic of the region that relates to that fact.

Economic Fact	Physical Characteristic
1.	1.
2.	2.
3.	3.

Critical Thinking

4. **BIG Idea** What economic activities in the Interior West of the United States are related to the area's natural resources?

5. **Comparing and Contrasting** Compare and contrast the Northeast region of the United States and the Atlantic Provinces of Canada.

6. **Challenge** Which region of the United States do you think has undergone the greatest economic change? Why?

Writing About Geography

7. **Descriptive Writing** Create a map that shows the economic regions of either the United States or Canada. Write a paragraph for each region describing the economy and people of that region.

PROTECTING AMERICA FROM DISASTER

From terrorist attacks to hurricanes, the United States has faced a variety of deadly disasters. Will it be ready for the next crisis?

A victim of Hurricane Katrina is evacuated by helicopter.

Four years after the terrorist attacks of September 11, 2001, the United States was struck by three powerful hurricanes—Katrina, Rita, and Wilma. The massive storms brought a flood of despair as they tore through the U.S. Gulf Coast region. The hurricanes' strong winds and storm surges left death, destruction, and economic ruin in their paths.

As the government struggled to respond, thousands of survivors were left stranded. Many Americans wondered if the country had been too focused on preventing terrorist attacks and questioned whether officials had failed to plan for other types of disasters. People were also worried that the U.S. would be unprepared when the next catastrophe struck.

TIME PERSPECTIVES

EXPLORING
WORLD
ISSUES

BETH DIXSON

Smoke poured from the
World Trade Center's two
towers after terrorists
flew airplanes into them.

DISASTER STRIKES AMERICA

In recent years, the United States has been deeply affected by both human-made and natural disasters. On September 11, 2001, or "**9/11**," as the terrible events of that day are called, terrorists hijacked a jet airliner and crashed it into the north tower of the World Trade Center in New York City at 8:46 A.M. A second hijacked plane hit the south tower at 9:03 A.M. About an hour later, the south tower collapsed, crumbling to the ground.

At 9:43 A.M. outside Washington, D.C., a third hijacked plane crashed into the Pentagon, the headquarters of the U.S. military. About 20 minutes later, a fourth airliner went down in a field near Shanksville, Pennsylvania. Its target, which it never reached, might have been the White House or the U.S. Capitol. Back in New York City, the north tower of the World Trade Center collapsed at 10:28 A.M.

In less than two hours, 19 terrorists had murdered thousands of people.

Crisis Along the Coast

The 9/11 attacks stunned the country. Nearly four years later, a series of monster hurricanes would do the same. On August 29, 2005, Hurricane Katrina slammed into the Gulf Coast. The storm packed 145-mile-per-hour winds that pushed powerful storm surges, or walls of water, inland from the Gulf of Mexico.

Katrina hit southern Florida first. Then, after strengthening while over the warm waters of the Gulf of Mexico, the hurricane struck Biloxi and Gulf-port in Mississippi with deadly force. Homes, businesses, and entire towns were destroyed. The strong winds knocked down electrical lines. Power was lost across the Southeast, leaving millions without electricity.

A City Surrounded

Average annual high water (14 feet)

Levees

Normal lake level

30
20
10
0

Sea level

Mississippi River

Lake Pontchartrain

CHART NOT TO SCALE

AP PHOTO

INTERPRETING DIAGRAMS

Making Inferences What does this diagram tell you about the need to maintain the New Orleans levee system?

Large portions of New Orleans are below sea level. Canals and 22 huge pumps are used to drain New Orleans when heavy rains cause flooding. Hurricane Katrina's powerful winds and waves, though, overwhelmed the city's flood prevention defenses.

Survivors of Hurricane Katrina climbed to rooftops waiting to be rescued.

Young and old survivors of Hurricane Katrina hoped relief would come.

A roof was thrown onto the sidewalk by Hurricane Wilma's powerful winds.

Turmoil in New Orleans

Although New Orleans avoided a direct hit from Katrina, the storm punched four holes into the **levees**, or flood walls, that protect New Orleans from the sea. Soon, 80 percent of the city was under water.

Chaos followed. Officials called for all residents to leave the city. Across the city, thousands waited to be taken to safety. More than 20,000 people took shelter from the storm in New Orleans's Superdome. Conditions inside the stadium, however, had become unbearable as supplies of food and water ran out. People soon had to be evacuated.

The government was slow to respond with help. Evacuation plans were confusing, and coordination between local and national officials was poor. New Orleans would be a disaster area for months.

Soon after Katrina struck, another powerful storm, Hurricane Rita, ripped along the Gulf Coast with winds that reached 120 miles (193 km) per hour. More than 3 million people evacuated their homes. Then, in late October, Hurricane Wilma slammed into southwest Florida, leaving 6 million people without electricity.

A Stormy Economy

The devastation created by these deadly hurricanes affected Americans everywhere. Much of the country's oil and natural gas comes from the Gulf Coast. Oil platforms, refineries, and pipelines were damaged or shut down by Katrina. President George W. Bush authorized the release of oil from the nation's emergency reserve to help meet the country's energy demand.

Exports, or products sold outside the country, were affected too. Hundreds of barges that carried crops and products through the port of New Orleans to other countries sat backed up on the Mississippi River. Restoring the region would be costly. Experts estimated that the total price tag to rebuild the Gulf Coast would reach $200 billion.

Planning for the Future

Many Americans thought all levels of government—city, state, and federal—were unprepared to protect Gulf Coast residents. President Bush said, "Americans have every right to expect a more effective response in a time of emergency." Determining how to keep citizens safe will take time and hard work, but it is vital to the country's well-being.

EXPLORING THE ISSUE

1. Understanding Cause and Effect How did the 2005 hurricane season affect the broader U.S. economy?

2. Interpreting Points of View Do Americans have a right to expect the government to provide an "effective response" to emergencies? Why or why not?

AMERICA REACTS TO CATASTROPHES

The 2001 terrorist attacks and the 2005 hurricane season shocked many Americans. The tragic events also forced government leaders to take action. Finding new ways to protect the United States became a top priority.

Following 9/11, President George W. Bush signed a bill that created the **Department of Homeland Security**. The new department combined the duties and responsibilities of 22 different agencies. This included the Coast Guard and the **Federal Emergency Management Agency** (FEMA), the agency that responds to the nation's emergencies.

Lawmakers hoped the reorganization would improve communication between government agencies and help prevent future attacks. While some people thought the government changes were an effective response to terrorism, they were not useful for dealing with other types of disasters.

A Massive Cleanup

The aftermath of Hurricane Katrina made it clear that better coordination between local and national officials was required for disaster relief. The government was harshly criticized for its slow first response to Hurricane Katrina.

Congress approved $62 billion for relief work. These funds were used to find housing and provide health care for survivors. In the months after the hurricanes struck, local leaders and federal agencies began to reconstruct the Gulf Coast. By December 2005, the president pledged another $3.1 billion to repair New Orleans's levee system.

The task of rebuilding New Orleans and other areas of the Gulf Coast will take many years. As the government examines the results of these catastrophes, it hopes to make America safe from future disasters.

A relief worker carries young survivors to safety.

AP PHOTO

HEED 502

EXPLORING THE ISSUE

1. Making Inferences How might the Department of Homeland Security help officials fight terrorism? In what ways might the large department be ineffective in fighting natural disasters?

2. Problem Solving What steps do you think the government should take to fight terrorism and other types of catastrophes?

REVIEW AND ASSESS

UNDERSTANDING THE ISSUE

1 **Making Connections** How did Hurricane Katrina affect the country's oil supply?

2 **Writing to Inform** In a brief essay, explain how the nation is preparing for natural and human-made disasters.

3 **Writing to Persuade** Write a letter to the editor of a newspaper expressing your views about the government's response to Hurricane Katrina and its readiness for future disasters.

INTERNET RESEARCH ACTIVITIES

4 With your teacher's help, go to www.ready.gov. Explore one of the three main items on the Web site's home page. Write a short essay that explains what you learned about preparing for a terrorist attack.

5 Navigate to www.fema.gov/kids. Click through some of the Web site's links to learn more about FEMA, how it is organized, and what its responsibilities are. Summarize your findings in a short written report.

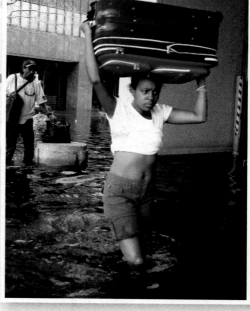

A survivor carries her belongings as she wades through water in New Orleans.

BEYOND THE CLASSROOM

6 **Research the impact of terrorism on nations such as Sri Lanka and Ireland.** How have these nations tried to prevent terrorist attacks? Describe these ways, and discuss as a class whether they would be effective in preventing terrorist attacks in the United States.

7 **Work in Groups.** Create and display posters that explain how to prepare for any disaster, including hurricanes and terrorist attacks.

After Hurricane Katrina, the Costly Recovery Plan

Congress approved $62.3 billion in Gulf Coast aid for FEMA (though the final relief tab could well top $200 billion). Here is how FEMA distributed some of the funds.

■ **$23 billion** for temporary housing, health care, clothing, household costs

■ **$8 billion** for search-and-rescue missions, road and bridge safety, and adequate water

■ **$3 billion** to the Defense Department for emergency repairs and evacuation

■ **$5 billion** for FEMA to set up support and recovery work

■ **$15 billion** for the Department of Homeland Security to monitor how relief aid was spent and distributed

Source: TIME research, 2005.

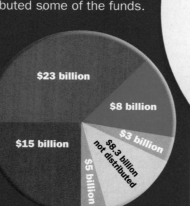

$23 billion
$8 billion
$3 billion
$8.3 billion not distributed
$5 billion
$15 billion

Building Graph Reading Skills

1. **Analyzing Data** How much money did FEMA give to search-and-rescue work and to keeping roads and bridges safe?

2. **Explaining** Why do you think most of the government relief funds were used to help Katrina survivors find housing, clothing, and health care?

Guide to Reading

BIG Idea

Cooperation and conflict among people have an effect on the Earth's surface.

Content Vocabulary

- trade deficit *(p. 169)*
- tariff *(p. 170)*
- trade surplus *(p. 170)*
- acid rain *(p. 171)*
- brownfield *(p. 172)*
- urban sprawl *(p. 172)*

Academic Vocabulary

- restrict *(p. 169)*
- community *(p. 172)*

Reading Strategy

Outlining Use a format like the one below to make an outline of the section. Write each main heading on a line with a Roman numeral, and list important facts below it.

I. **First Main Heading**
A. **Key Fact 1**
B. **Key Fact 2**
II. **Second Main Heading**
A. **Key Fact 1**
B. **Key Fact 2**

Issues and Challenges

Picture This Long ago, ice canoeing was a way to deliver supplies across the icy Saint Lawrence River during winter. Ice canoes were small enough to dodge floating ice and light enough to carry over solid ice. Traveling between the river's islands was dangerous, difficult work, but it was necessary to carry vital items such as medicine and mail. Today, ice canoes are used for sport. Many Canadian teams compete in ice races at winter festivals. Learn more about Canada today in Section 2.

▼ Ice canoe racing in Toronto, Canada

The Region and the World

Main Idea The United States and Canada trade with countries throughout the world.

Geography and You Think about all the trucks or trains you have seen carrying products to stores or to ports. Read to learn about our region's economic ties to the world.

Because of their large economies, the United States and Canada trade with many countries. In addition, the United States is one of the world's leading political and military powers.

Economic Ties

The free market system has helped the United States and Canada build productive economies. In fact, the United States has the world's largest economy and is a leader in world trade. The United States exports chemicals, farm products, and manufactured goods, as well as raw materials such as metals and cotton fiber. Canada sends many of the same goods overseas, as well as large amounts of seafood and timber products. Both countries also import many items from all around the world.

In recent years, the United States and Canada have supported free trade. This means the removal of trade **restrictions,** or barriers, so that goods flow freely among countries. In 1994 the United States, Canada, and Mexico joined together in the North American Free Trade Agreement

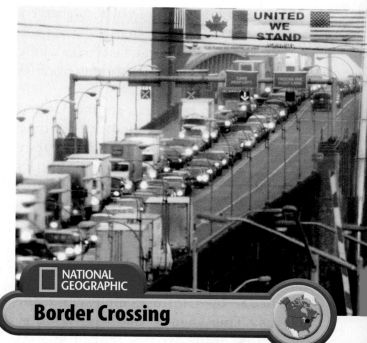

NATIONAL GEOGRAPHIC

Border Crossing

The Ambassador Bridge is the busiest international border crossing in North America. More than 10,000 trucks cross the bridge daily between Detroit, Michigan, and Windsor, Canada. **Regions** What did NAFTA establish?

(NAFTA). They promised to take away most barriers to trade among the three countries. Canada now sends more than 80 percent of its exports to the United States and buys nearly 60 percent of its imports from it. Canada is the largest trading partner of the United States, and Mexico is the second largest.

The United States depends on trade to supply most of its energy resources. As you may recall, the country uses nearly three times the amount of oil it produces. The United States must import additional oil from major suppliers such as Canada, Mexico, Venezuela, Saudi Arabia, Nigeria, and Angola.

Americans buy many additional products from other countries. In fact, the United States spends hundreds of billions of dollars more on imports than it earns from exports. The result is a massive **trade deficit.**

A trade deficit occurs when a country spends more on imports than it earns from exports. A trade deficit that lasts over a long period can cause serious economic troubles for a country.

To sell their products in the United States, some nations set the prices of their goods very low. Also, some countries place high **tariffs,** or taxes, on imports in order to protect their own industries from foreign competition. These tariffs then raise the price of U.S. products and thus reduce the sale of the products abroad. Such practices hurt American companies and cost American workers their jobs.

Canada, by contrast, enjoys a **trade surplus.** This means that the country earns more from exports than it spends for imports. Canada's smaller population makes its energy needs less costly. Also, Canada's export earnings have been growing.

Global Terrorism

Since the beginning of the 2000s, the United States and Canada have joined other nations to deal with increasing terrorism and violence around the world. As you may recall, the world changed dramatically on September 11, 2001, when terrorists attacked sites in New York City and Washington, D.C. To prevent further terrorist attacks, the United States and Canada have worked to increase security along their long border. They have also participated in international efforts to stop terrorism.

TIME GLOBAL CITIZENS

NAMES: BILL AND MELINDA GATES

HOME COUNTRY: United States

ACHIEVEMENT: In 2005 the Bill and Melinda Gates Foundation gave more money away faster than anyone ever has. Bill Gates, the head of Microsoft, and his wife, Melinda, created the foundation that is now the world's largest charitable organization. About 60 percent of the foundation's grants go toward global efforts—such as fighting disease—in more than 100 countries. The rest is dedicated to improving people's lives in the U.S. The foundation is committed to giving away more than $9 billion, including more than $1 billion to U.S. high schools and libraries. Another $1 billion is used for college scholarships for African Americans.

QUOTE: ❝I felt I had a role to give some voice to the voiceless.❞—Melinda Gates, referring to grants to developing countries

Melinda and Bill Gates visit a health research center in Mozambique.

CITIZENS IN ACTION Who are the "voiceless" that Melinda Gates refers to? Do they need champions such as the Gateses? Why or why not?

Guarding Against Terrorism

Since the 2001 terrorist attacks against New York City and Washington, D.C., new safeguards are in place to protect Americans. **Place** How did the U.S. and Canada disagree over Iraq policy?

Despite their generally close relations, the United States and Canada sometimes differ in their policies. In 2003 Canada opposed the U.S. decision to invade Iraq. Instead, it wanted the American government to continue seeking a peaceful solution through the United Nations (UN). The United Nations is the world organization that promotes cooperation among nations in settling disputes.

The United States and Canada both have strong roles in the United Nations. They provide much of the money that funds the organization. They also take part in UN agencies that provide aid to people in areas affected by war or natural disasters. The United States and especially Canada have sent soldiers to serve in UN forces that act as peacekeepers in troubled areas of the world.

Reading Check **Explaining** Why does the United States have a large trade deficit?

Environmental Issues

Main Idea The United States and Canada face similar environmental issues.

Geography and You Have you witnessed instances of air or water pollution in your area? Read to learn about challenges for the region's environment.

The United States and Canada face several environmental challenges. Because they are neighbors, some concerns are shared. Both countries have made progress in cleaning up their air and water. Still, pollution remains a problem.

Acid Rain and Climate Change

Americans and Canadians burn coal, oil, and natural gas to power their factories and run their cars. Burning these fossil fuels pollutes the air. The pollution also mixes with water vapor in the air to make **acid rain,** or rain containing high amounts of chemical pollutants. Acid rain damages trees and harms rivers, lakes, and the stone used in buildings. The United States and Canada have acted to reduce the amount of chemicals that are released into the air. They are particularly concerned about damage to some areas in the eastern parts of the region.

Many people in the United States and Canada also worry about global warming. Some scientists believe that global warming will lead to changing weather patterns. For example, a warmer climate could lead to drought conditions in some areas, or it could melt the polar ice caps. Melting would raise sea levels, which would be a problem for low-lying areas like Florida.

To address the issue of global warming, Canada has passed laws to reduce the amount of fossil fuels that are burned.

The United States has funded research to find new energy sources that are less harmful to the environment.

Pollution Issues

Changing climatic conditions and a rising demand for water have lowered water levels of the Great Lakes. Loss of water can cause a variety of problems. Lower lake levels decrease the amount of goods that can be shipped. Ships cannot carry extremely heavy loads into river channels or they might run aground. In addition, lower lake levels can harm fish populations. Tourism is also affected as water pulls back from the area's beaches. Government leaders of both countries have urged people to conserve water.

Brownfields are another challenge. **Brownfields** are places, such as old factories and gas stations, that have been abandoned and contain dangerous chem-icals. These chemicals hinder any new development. Governments in the United States and Canada have given money to **communities,** or neighborhoods, for cleanup.

Urban sprawl, or the spread of human settlement into natural areas, also has created difficulties. Urban growth leads to the loss of farmland and wilderness areas. The building of homes and roadways can also produce traffic jams and increase air pollution. Growing populations put strains on water and other resources as well. People in some areas that are growing rapidly want to slow the rate of growth. They fear that having too many people will destroy the wide-open spaces and magnificent scenery that attracted them.

✔ **Reading Check** **Explaining** How have the United States and Canada dealt with the issue of global warming?

Social Studies ONLINE
Study Central™ To review this section, go to glencoe.com.

Section 2 Review

Vocabulary

1. **Explain** the significance of:
   a. trade deficit
   b. tariff
   c. trade surplus
   d. acid rain
   e. brownfield
   f. urban sprawl

Main Ideas

2. **Describing** Describe the trade relationship between the United States and Canada.

3. **Determining Cause and Effect** Use a diagram like the one below to list the effects of falling water levels in the Great Lakes.

Falling Water Levels in Great Lakes	→	Effect
	→	Effect
	→	Effect

Critical Thinking

4. **Making Generalizations** Why is the U.S. economy important to the rest of the world?

5. **BIG Idea** Should the United States and Canada cooperate to try to reduce the problem of acid rain? Explain.

6. **Challenge** How would you describe overall relations between the United States and Canada? Why?

Writing About Geography

7. **Using Your FOLDABLES** Use the notes in your Foldable to write a letter to a member of Congress explaining what you think should be done about the U.S. trade deficit.

CHAPTER 6

Visual Summary

____ Free Market ____ Economies

- The United States and Canada have free market economies that allow people to own businesses and earn profits.

- Producers and consumers decide what to produce, how much to produce, and for whom to produce.

- Governments play a limited role in free market economies.

Small business owner, Los Angeles, California

____ U.S. Regions ____

- The five economic regions of the United States are the Northeast, the Midwest, the South, the Interior West, and the Pacific.

- The South and the Interior West are growing rapidly in population and economic strength.

- The Northeast focuses on business. The Midwest is rebuilding its industries.

- The Pacific area has diverse economies and populations.

Canadian wheelchair athlete

_____ Canadian _____ Regions

- Canada's main economic regions are the Atlantic Provinces, the Central and Eastern Region, the West, and the North.

- The Atlantic Provinces suffer from the decline of the fishing industry.

- Many people in French-speaking Quebec want their province to be independent.

- Ontario is Canada's most populous and economically prosperous province.

- The West includes the grain-producing areas and the Pacific coastal province of British Columbia.

Port at Seattle, Washington

_____ Global Ties _____

- The United States and Canada have joined Mexico in promoting free trade among their countries.

- The United States is a major global trading power. Its trade deficits, however, could cause future economic problems.

- The United States and other countries are working to prevent terrorist attacks.

_____ The _____ Environment

- The United States and Canada are reducing the amount of chemicals released into the air to reduce acid rain.

- Declining water levels and rising demand for water are affecting the Great Lakes.

- The United States and Canada face the loss of farmland and wilderness areas as urban sprawl increases.

New home construction, Florida

STUDY TO GO ▸ Study anywhere, anytime! Download quizzes and flash cards to your PDA from **glencoe.com**.

STANDARDIZED TEST PRACTICE

TEST-TAKING **TIP**

During an exam, answer the questions you know first. Then go back to those that need more thought.

Reviewing Vocabulary

Directions: Choose the word(s) that best completes the sentence.

1. Business owners produce products they think will be most _____.

  A beautiful

  B affordable

  C useful

  D profitable

2. British Columbia's forests help make Canada the world's largest producer of _____.

  A stocks

  B newsprint

  C acid rain

  D biotechnology

3. A _____ occurs when a country spends more on its imports than it earns from its exports.

  A trade deficit

  B import tariff

  C free market

  D trade surplus

4. A country sometimes places _____ on imports to protect industries from foreign competition.

  A trade deficits

  B tariffs

  C free markets

  D trade surpluses

Reviewing Main Ideas

Directions: Choose the best answer for each question.

Section 1 (pp. 158–162)

5. Because it has abundant oil, the _____ economic region of the United States produces petroleum-based products.

  A South

  B Pacific

  C Midwest

  D Interior West

6. Most people in Canada's Atlantic provinces make a living through the _____ industries.

  A fishing, farming, and forestry

  B oil, natural gas, and exporting

  C manufacturing, mining, and tourism

  D finance, hydroelectricity, and ranching

Section 2 (pp. 168–172)

7. The largest trading partner of the United States is _____.

  A Mexico

  B Canada

  C Nigeria

  D Venezuela

8. To address the issue of _____, Canada passed laws to lower the amount of fossil fuels that are burned.

  A low water levels

  B urban sprawl

  C global warming

  D brownfields

GO ON ➡

Critical Thinking

Directions: Base your answers to questions 9 and 10 on the graph below and your knowledge of Chapter 6.

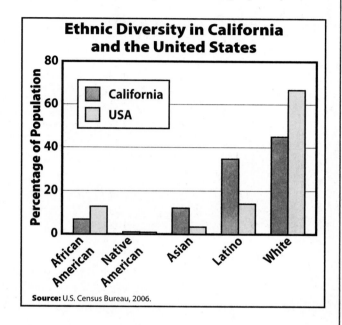

Ethnic Diversity in California and the United States

Percentage of Population

California
USA

African American · Native American · Asian · Latino · White

Source: U.S. Census Bureau, 2006.

9. What conclusion can you make from the data?

A More Latinos live in California than in the rest of the United States.

B California's population is about one-tenth of the nation's total population.

C California has a larger percentage of Japanese Americans than the country has as a whole.

D The U.S. population has a larger percentage of African Americans than does California's.

10. Which of these generalizations is accurate?

A Latinos are the fastest growing U.S. group.

B African Americans outnumber Asians 3 to 1 in California.

C Latinos and whites make up most of the nation's population.

D Whites outnumber the combined members of all other ethnic groups in the state.

Document-Based Questions

Directions: Analyze the following document and answer the short-answer questions that follow.

The following news story was broadcast in Canada on October 30, 2005.

> *Quebec Premier Jean Charest called federalism the "best choice for the future of Quebec" as provincial separatists vowed to continue to seek independence on Sunday—the 10th anniversary of the province's second referendum on sovereignty.*
>
> *On Oct. 30, 1995, more than 93 per cent of the province's 5.1 million registered voters cast a ballot. A razor-thin majority kept the province from heading towards independence, with 50.58 per cent voting No to 49.42 per cent voting Yes.*
>
> *Charest, in a closing speech to about 800 Liberals at the provincial party's general meeting on Sunday said his most fervent [strong] desire was to avoid the holding of another sovereignty referendum [independence vote] so Quebecers don't once again "inflict such wounds upon themselves."*
>
> —Debate still rages on 10th anniversary of Quebec's sovereignty referendum, *CBC News.*

11. What statement indicates that Charest believes Quebec should remain part of Canada?

12. Did most Quebecois in 1995 have strong feelings about Quebec's independence? How do you know?

Extended Response

13. If you lived in Quebec, would you like to see it become independent or remain part of Canada? Explain your answer.

STOP

Social Studies ONLINE

For additional test practice, use Self-Check Quizzes—Chapter 6 at glencoe.com.

Need Extra Help?													
If you missed question...	1	2	3	4	5	6	7	8	9	10	11	12	13
Go to page...	159	162	169	170	160	161	169	171	161	161	161	161	161–162

UNIT 3

Latin America

Rio de Janeiro, Brazil ▶

**NATIONAL
GEOGRAPHIC**

NGS ONLINE For more information about the region,
see www.nationalgeographic.com/education.

Latin America

Where Is It?

A It is about 2,086 miles (3,357 km) from New York City to Mexico City.

B It is about 5,125 miles (8,248 km) from New York City to Santiago.

How Big Is It?

The region of Latin America is about two-and-a-half times the size of the continental United States. Its land area is about 7.9 million square miles (20.5 million sq. km). Latin America has about 558 million people, almost twice as many as the United States.

Comparing Population

United States and Selected Countries of Latin America

United States	👤👤👤👤👤👤👤👤👤👤ᵗ
Brazil	👤👤👤👤👤👤
Mexico	👤👤👤ᵗ
Argentina	👤
Peru	👤
Honduras	ᵗ

👤 = 30,000,000

Source: *World Population Data Sheet, 2005.*

GEO Fast Facts

Largest Lake

▲ Lake Maracaibo (Venezuela) 5,217 sq. mi. (13,512 sq. km)

Highest Waterfall

▲ Angel Falls (Venezuela) 3,212 ft. (979 m) high

Longest River

▲ Amazon River (Peru, Brazil) 4,000 mi. (6,436 km) long

▼ Aconcagua (Argentina) 22,834 ft. (6,960 m) high

Highest Point

South Georgia Island (U.K.)

Latin America
POPULATION DENSITY

NORTH AMERICA

Tijuana
Ciudad Juárez
Torreón
Monterrey
Gulf of Mexico
Havana
León
Guadalajara
Mexico City
Toluca de Lerdo
Puebla
San Salvador
Managua
San José
Panama
San Juan
Port-au-Prince
Santo Domingo
Maracaibo
Barranquilla
Valencia
Caracas
Barquisimeto
Maracay
Bucaramanga
Medellín
Bogotá
Cali
Quito
Guayaquil
Manaus
Belém
Fortaleza
Natal
Recife
Maceió
Salvador
Lima
Lake Titicaca
La Paz
Santa Cruz
Brasília
Goiânia
Belo Horizonte
Campinas
Grande Vitória
Asunción
Curitiba
Rio de Janeiro
São Paulo
Córdoba
Pôrto Alegre
Santiago
Rosario
Buenos Aires
Montevideo

ATLANTIC OCEAN
PACIFIC OCEAN
ATLANTIC OCEAN

TROPIC OF CANCER
EQUATOR
TROPIC OF CAPRICORN

100°W   80°W   60°W   40°W
20°N
0°
20°S
40°S

N
W   E
S

Cities
(Statistics reflect metropolitan areas)
■ Over 10,000,000
□ 5,000,000–10,000,000
◉ 3,000,000–5,000,000
● 2,000,000–3,000,000
○ Under 2,000,000

POPULATION

Per sq. mi.	Per sq. km
1,250 and over	500 and over
250–1,249	100–499
62–249	25–99
25–61	10–24
2.5–24	1–9
Less than 2.5	Less than 1
Uninhabited	Uninhabited

Map Skills

1 **Place** What part of Mexico has the highest population density?

2 **Regions** What cities in the region have more than 10 million people?

0   600 kilometers
0   600 miles
Lambert Azimuthal Equal-Area projection

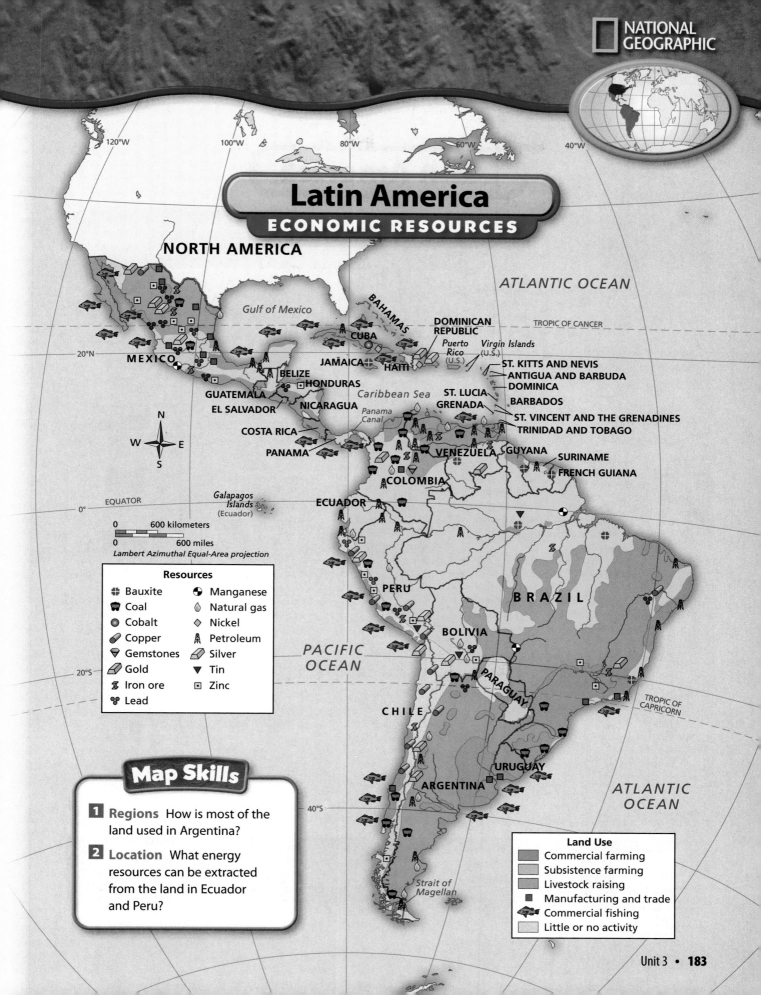

Latin America
ECONOMIC RESOURCES

NORTH AMERICA

ATLANTIC OCEAN

Gulf of Mexico

TROPIC OF CANCER

BAHAMAS

DOMINICAN
REPUBLIC

CUBA

*Puerto
Rico
(U.S.)*

*Virgin Islands
(U.S.)*

ST. KITTS AND NEVIS

JAMAICA

HAITI

ANTIGUA AND BARBUDA

DOMINICA

BELIZE

HONDURAS

Caribbean Sea

ST. LUCIA

BARBADOS

MEXICO

GUATEMALA

GRENADA

*Panama
Canal*

ST. VINCENT AND THE GRENADINES

EL SALVADOR

NICARAGUA

TRINIDAD AND TOBAGO

COSTA RICA

VENEZUELA

GUYANA

SURINAME

PANAMA

COLOMBIA

FRENCH GUIANA

20°N

N

W   E

S

EQUATOR

*Galapagos
Islands
(Ecuador)*

ECUADOR

0°

0   600 kilometers

0   600 miles

Lambert Azimuthal Equal-Area projection

BRAZIL

PERU

Resources

⊞	Bauxite	◗	Manganese
⛏	Coal	⬤	Natural gas
⬤	Cobalt	◆	Nickel
✎	Copper	⚒	Petroleum
▽	Gemstones	▨	Silver
▰	Gold	▼	Tin
𖤐	Iron ore	⊡	Zinc
❦	Lead		

BOLIVIA

PACIFIC
OCEAN

20°S

PARAGUAY

CHILE

TROPIC OF
CAPRICORN

URUGUAY

Map Skills

1 **Regions** How is most of the
land used in Argentina?

2 **Location** What energy
resources can be extracted
from the land in Ecuador
and Peru?

ARGENTINA

40°S

ATLANTIC
OCEAN

*Strait of
Magellan*

Land Use

▨	Commercial farming
▨	Subsistence farming
▨	Livestock raising
▪	Manufacturing and trade
🐟	Commercial fishing
☐	Little or no activity

Regional Atlas

Latin America

Country and Capital	Literacy Rate	Population and Density	Land Area	Life Expectancy (Years)	GDP* Per Capita (U.S. dollars)	Television Sets (per 1,000 people)	Flag and Language
ANTIGUA AND BARBUDA St. John's	89%	100,000 588 per sq. mi. 227 per sq. km	170 sq. mi. 440 sq. km	71	$11,000	493	English
ARGENTINA Buenos Aires	97.1%	38,600,000 36 per sq. mi. 14 per sq. km	1,073,514 sq. mi. 2,780,388 sq. km	74	$12,400	293	Spanish
Nassau **BAHAMAS**	95.6%	300,000 60 per sq. mi. 22 per sq. km	5,359 sq. mi. 13,880 sq. km	70	$17,700	243	English
BARBADOS Bridgetown	97.4%	300,000 1,807 per sq. mi. 698 per sq. km	166 sq. mi. 430 sq. km	72	$16,400	290	English
Belmopan **BELIZE**	94.1%	300,000 34 per sq. mi. 13 per sq. km	8,865 sq. mi. 22,960 sq. km	70	$6,500	183	English
La Paz **BOLIVIA** Sucre	87.2%	8,900,000 21 per sq. mi. 8 per sq. km	424,162 sq. mi. 1,098,574 sq. km	64	$2,600	118	Spanish, Quechua, Aymara
BRAZIL Brasília	86.4%	184,200,000 56 per sq. mi. 22 per sq. km	3,300,154 sq. mi. 8,547,359 sq. km	71	$8,100	333	Portuguese
CHILE Santiago	96.2%	16,100,000 55 per sq. mi. 21 per sq. km	292,135 sq. mi. 756,626 sq. km	76	$10,700	240	Spanish
Bogotá **COLOMBIA**	92.5%	46,000,000 105 per sq. mi. 40 per sq. km	439,734 sq. mi. 1,138,906 sq. km	72	$6,600	279	Spanish
UNITED STATES Washington, D.C.	97%	296,500,000 80 per sq. mi. 31 per sq. km	3,717,796 sq. mi. 9,629,047 sq. km	78	$40,100	844	English

*Gross Domestic Product

Countries and flags not drawn to scale

Latin America

Country and Capital	Literacy Rate	Population and Density	Land Area	Life Expectancy (Years)	GDP* Per Capita (U.S. dollars)	Television Sets (per 1,000 people)	Flag and Language
San José **COSTA RICA**	96%	4,300,000 218 per sq. mi. 84 per sq. km	19,730 sq. mi. 51,100 sq. km	79	$9,600	229	Spanish
Havana **CUBA**	97%	11,300,000 264 per sq. mi. 102 per sq. km	42,803 sq. mi. 110,859 sq. km	77	$3,000	248	Spanish
DOMINICA Roseau	94%	100,000 345 per sq. mi. 133 per sq. km	290 sq. mi. 751 sq. km	74	$5,500	232	English
DOMINICAN REPUBLIC Santo Domingo	84%	8,900,000 471 per sq. mi. 168 per sq. km	18,815 sq. mi. 48,731 sq. km	68	$6,300	96	Spanish
Quito **ECUADOR**	92.5%	13,000,000 119 per sq. mi. 46 per sq. km	109,483 sq. mi. 283,560 sq. km	74	$3,700	213	Spanish
San Salvador **EL SALVADOR**	80.2%	6,900,000 849 per sq. mi. 328 per sq. km	8,124 sq. mi. 21,041 sq. km	70	$4,900	191	Spanish
Cayenne **FRENCH GUIANA**	83%	200,000 6 per sq. mi. 2 per sq. km	34,749 sq. mi. 89,999 sq. km	75	$8,300	information not available	French
GRENADA St. George's	98%	100,000 769 per sq. mi. 295 per sq. km	131 sq. mi. 339 sq. km	71	$5,000	376	English
GUATEMALA Guatemala	70.6%	12,700,000 302 per sq. mi. 117 per sq. km	42,042 sq. mi. 108,888 sq. km	66	$4,200	61	Spanish
UNITED STATES Washington, D.C.	97%	296,500,000 80 per sq. mi. 31 per sq. km	3,717,796 sq. mi. 9,629,047 sq. km	78	$40,100	844	English

Sources: *CIA World Factbook,* 2005; Population Reference Bureau, *World Population Data Sheet,* 2005.

For more country facts, go to the **Nations of the World Databank** at glencoe.com.

Regional Atlas

Latin America

Country and Capital	Literacy Rate	Population and Density	Land Area	Life Expectancy (Years)	GDP* Per Capita (U.S. dollars)	Television Sets (per 1,000 people)	Flag and Language
Georgetown **GUYANA**	98.8%	800,000 10 per sq. mi. 4 per sq. km	83,000 sq. mi. 214,969 sq. km	63	$3,800	70	English
HAITI Port-au-Prince	52.9%	8,300,000 775 per sq. mi. 299 per sq. km	10,714 sq. mi. 27,749 sq. km	52	$1,500	5	French, Creole
HONDURAS Tegucigalpa	76.2%	7,200,000 166 per sq. mi. 64 per sq. km	43,278 sq. mi. 112,090 sq. km	71	$2,800	95	Spanish
JAMAICA Kingston	87.9%	2,700,000 636 per sq. mi. 246 per sq. km	4,243 sq. mi. 10,989 sq. km	73	$4,100	191	English
MEXICO Mexico City	92.2%	107,000,000 142 per sq. mi. 55 per sq. km	756,082 sq. mi. 1,958,243 sq. km	75	$9,600	272	Spanish
NICARAGUA Managua	67.5%	5,800,000 116 per sq. mi. 45 per sq. km	50,193 sq. mi. 129,999 sq. km	69	$2,300	69	Spanish
Panama **PANAMA**	92.6%	3,200,000 110 per sq. mi. 42 per sq. km	29,158 sq. mi. 75,519 sq. km	75	$6,900	192	Spanish
PARAGUAY Asunción	94%	6,200,000 39 per sq. mi. 15 per sq. km	157,046 sq. mi. 406,747 sq. km	71	$4,800	205	Spanish, Guarani
PERU Lima	87.7%	27,900,000 56 per sq. mi. 22 per sq. km	496,224 sq. mi. 1,285,214 sq. km	70	$5,600	147	Spanish, Quechua
UNITED STATES Washington, D.C.	97%	296,500,000 80 per sq. mi. 31 per sq. km	3,717,796 sq. mi. 9,629,047 sq. km	78	$40,100	844	English

*Gross Domestic Product

Countries and flags not drawn to scale

Latin America

Country and Capital	Literacy Rate	Population and Density	Land Area	Life Expectancy (Years)	GDP* Per Capita (U.S. dollars)	Television Sets (per 1,000 people)	Flag and Language
San Juan **PUERTO RICO**	94.1%	3,900,000 1,128 per sq. mi. 436 per sq. km	3,456 sq. mi. 8,951 sq. km	77	$17,700	information not available	Spanish
ST. KITTS-NEVIS Basseterre	97%	50,000 360 per sq. mi. 139 per sq. km	139 sq. mi. 360 sq. km	70	$8,800	256	English
Castries **ST. LUCIA**	67%	200,000 837 per sq. mi. 323 per sq. km	239 sq. mi. 619 sq. km	74	$5,400	368	English
Kingstown **ST. VINCENT AND THE GRENADINES**	96%	100,000 737 per sq. mi. 256 per sq. km	151 sq. mi. 391 sq. km	72	$2,900	230	English
Paramaribo **SURINAME**	93%	438,000 7 per sq. mi. 3 per sq. km	62,344 sq. mi. 161,470 sq. km	69	$4,300	241	Dutch
Port-of-Spain **TRINIDAD AND TOBAGO**	98.6%	1,300,000 656 per sq. mi. 253 per sq. km	1,981 sq. mi. 5,131 sq. km	71	$10,500	337	English
URUGUAY Montevideo	98%	3,400,000 50 per sq. mi. 19 per sq. km	68,498 sq. mi. 177,409 sq. km	75	$14,500	531	Spanish
Caracas **VENEZUELA**	93.4%	26,700,000 76 per sq. mi. 29 per sq. km	352,143 sq. mi. 912,046 sq. km	73	$5,800	185	Spanish
Charlotte Amalie **VIRGIN ISLANDS** (U.S.)	information not available	108,708 799 per sq. mi. 309 per sq. km	136 sq. mi. 352 sq. km	79	$17,200	information not available	English
UNITED STATES Washington, D.C.	97%	296,500,000 80 per sq. mi. 31 per sq. km	3,717,796 sq. mi. 9,629,047 sq. km	78	$40,100	844	English

Sources: *CIA World Factbook*, 2005; Population Reference Bureau, *World Population Data Sheet*, 2005.

For more country facts, go to the **Nations of the World Databank** at glencoe.com.

Reading Social Studies

Summarizing Information

Reading Skill ① **Learn It!**

Summarizing helps you focus on main ideas. By restating the important facts in a short summary, you can reduce the amount of information to remember. A summary can be a short paragraph that includes the main ideas.

Use these steps to help you summarize:
- Be brief—do not include many supporting details.
- Restate the text in a way that makes sense to you.

Read the text below. Then review the graphic organizer to see how you could summarize the information.

A people called the Maya lived in Mexico's Yucatán Peninsula and surrounding areas between A.D. 300 and A.D. 900. The Maya built huge stone temples in the shape of pyramids with steps. They were skilled at astronomy and used their knowledge of the stars, moon, and planets to develop a calendar. They also had a number system based on 20. Using hieroglyphics, which is a form of writing that uses signs and symbols, the Maya recorded the history of their kings.

—from page 209

Reading Tip

As you read and summarize in your own words, try not to change the author's original meanings or ideas.

Fact: The Maya used their knowledge of the stars, moon, and planets to develop a calendar.

Fact: The Maya had a number system based on 20.

Fact: The Maya recorded the history of their kings using hieroglyphics.

Summary:
The Maya developed a calendar, created a number system, and recorded their history using hieroglyphics.

Read to Write Activity

After you read each chapter in this unit, summarize its information. Then, use the chapter's Visual Summary to check to see if you identified the main ideas.

② Practice It!

Read the following paragraph from this unit.
- Draw an organizer like the one shown below.
- Write the main facts from the paragraph in the top boxes.
- Write a summary of the paragraph in the bottom box.

Family life is important in Latin America. Often several generations live together, and adults are expected to care for their aged parents. Adult brothers and sisters often live near each other, and their children—who are cousins—can form close relationships. Traditionally, the father is the family leader and the chief decision maker. In some parts of the Caribbean, however, the mother is the leader of the family.

—from page 223

▲ **Latin American teenagers**

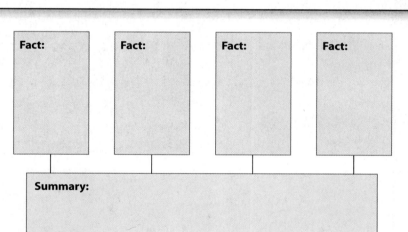

| Fact: | Fact: | Fact: | Fact: |

Summary:

③ Apply It!

With a partner, choose a section to summarize. After each of you summarizes the section on your own, exchange your papers and check to see if the summaries are complete. Note whether any important ideas are missing. Return your summaries to each other and make the changes. Use your summaries to help you study for assessment.

CHAPTER 7

Physical Geography of Latin America

Essential Question

Movement Latin America stretches from Mexico in North America to the southernmost tip of South America. The region has a great variety of physical contrasts. Steamy tropical forests, thundering waterfalls, cold mountain peaks, and peaceful island beaches make up Latin America. How might a wide variety of physical features affect transportation and communications within a region?

Quechuan
Indian woman
outside of
Cuzco, Peru

BIG Ideas

Section 1: Physical Features

BIG IDEA Geographic factors influence where people settle. In Latin America, vast river systems provide transportation and support fishing. The region's rugged mountains and thick forests, however, have been obstacles to transportation and trade.

Section 2: Climate Regions

BIG IDEA The physical environment affects how people live. Latin America's vast expanse of rain forest is the largest in the world and contains valuable resources. In mountainous areas, climate and vegetation are affected more by altitude than by latitude.

FOLDABLES™
Study Organizer

Summarizing Information Make this Foldable to help you summarize information about the landforms, waterways, resources, and climates of Latin America.

Step 1 Fold the top of an 11 x 17 sheet of paper down about 2 inches.

Step 2 Then fold the paper to create 3 equal columns.

Step 3 Label each column of your Foldable as shown.

Reading and Writing Use the notes from your Foldable to write a travel pamphlet highlighting one of the subregions of Latin America. In your pamphlet, explain why the landforms, waterways, and climates of your chosen area are attractive to tourists.

Social Studies ONLINE

To preview Chapter 7, go to glencoe.com.

Guide to Reading

BIG Idea

Geographic factors influence where people settle.

Content Vocabulary

- subregion *(p. 193)*
- isthmus *(p. 193)*
- archipelago *(p. 193)*
- escarpment *(p. 194)*
- Llanos *(p. 194)*
- Pampas *(p. 194)*
- tributary *(p. 194)*
- estuary *(p. 194)*
- gasohol *(p. 195)*

Academic Vocabulary

- transport *(p. 193)*
- reside *(p. 194)*

Reading Strategy

Identifying Central Issues Use a diagram like the one below to identify and briefly describe six key landforms in the region.

Landforms of Latin America

SECTION 1

Physical Features

Picture This How do you farm when there is no flat land? The Inca, an advanced civilization that existed hundreds of years ago in Peru, used a method called terracing. They carved layered fields, like wide steps, into the mountainsides. Today, descendants of the Inca still use this method to raise crops at high altitudes. To learn how the physical landscape has affected other human activities, read Section 1.

▼ **A terraced hillside near Pisac, Peru**

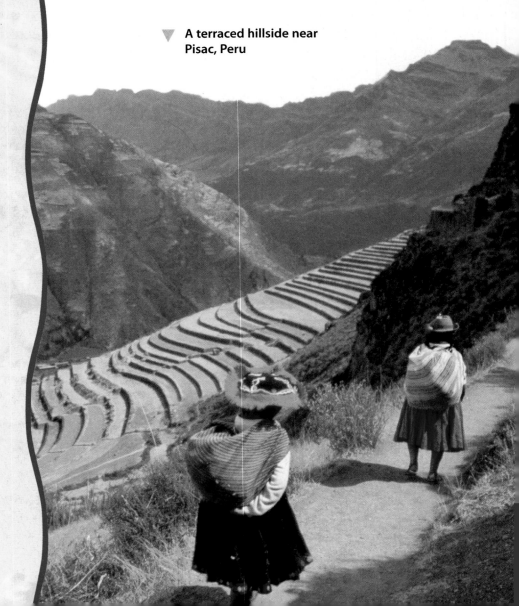

Landforms

Main Idea Mountains are prominent features in many parts of Latin America.

Geography and You If you traveled across your state, what geographic features would you see? Read on to learn about the landforms that Latin Americans would encounter if they crossed their region.

Geographers divide the region of Latin America into three **subregions,** or smaller areas. These subregions are Middle America, the Caribbean, and South America.

Middle America

Middle America is made up of Mexico and Central America. Central America is an **isthmus** (IHS·muhs), or a narrow piece of land that links two larger areas of land—North America and South America. Middle America lies where four tectonic plates meet. As a result, it has active volcanoes and frequent earthquakes. Deposits of ash and lava make the soil fertile.

Mexico has mountain ranges along its eastern and western coasts with a high plateau between. Farther south, mountains rise like a backbone through Central America. Lowlands along the coasts are often narrow. Thick forests, rugged mountains, and coastal marshes make it difficult to **transport** goods in Central America.

The Caribbean

The islands of the Caribbean Sea, also known as the West Indies, can be divided into three groups: the Greater Antilles, the Lesser Antilles, and the Bahamas. The Greater Antilles include the largest islands—Cuba, Hispaniola, Puerto Rico, and Jamaica. The Lesser Antilles is an **archipelago** (AHR·kuh·PEH·luh·GOH), or group of islands. It curves from the Virgin

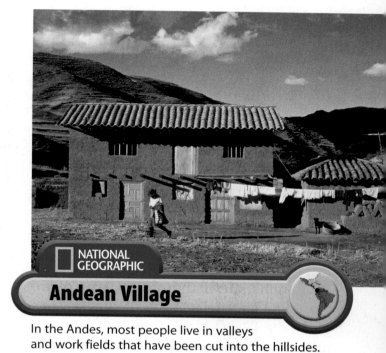

NATIONAL GEOGRAPHIC

Andean Village

In the Andes, most people live in valleys and work fields that have been cut into the hillsides.
Regions Besides the Andes, what is South America's other major landform?

Islands to Trinidad. The third group is the Bahamas, another archipelago.

Except for the largest islands, most Caribbean islands are small. Cuba alone has about half of the Caribbean's land area. Some islands are very low-lying. Others, formed by volcanoes, have rugged mountains. Some of the volcanoes are still active and can cause great damage. Farmers use the fertile volcanic soil here to grow crops such as sugarcane and tobacco.

South America

The Andes mountain ranges and the vast Amazon Basin are South America's major landforms. The Andes, the world's longest mountain system, are a cordillera (KAWR·duhl·YEHR·uh). They stretch along the Pacific coast of South America for about 5,500 miles (8,851 km). The high Andes ranges have many peaks that soar over 20,000 feet (6,096 m). Between the mountain chains lie plateaus and valleys.

That is where most people **reside,** or live, and the land can be farmed.

East of the Andes is the huge Amazon Basin. This low area contains the Amazon River and covers 2.7 million square miles (7.0 million sq. km). Highlands to the north and south border the basin. The Brazilian Highlands are so vast that they cross several climate zones. They end in an **escarpment,** a series of steep cliffs that drop down to the Atlantic coastal plain.

Other lowland plains are found north and south of the Amazon Basin. Tropical grasslands known as the **Llanos** (LAH·nohs) stretch through eastern Colombia and Venezuela. Another well-known plain, the **Pampas,** covers much of Argentina and Uruguay. Like North America's Great Plains, the Pampas is used for cattle herding and grain farming.

✔ **Reading Check** **Identifying** What areas make up Middle America?

The Pampas

NATIONAL GEOGRAPHIC

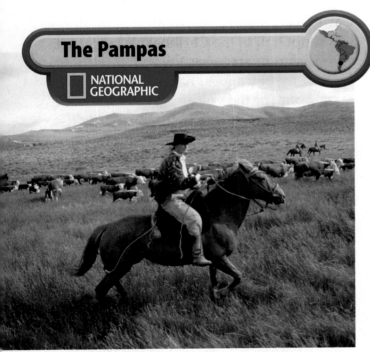

▲ Herding cattle is a major economic activity on the Pampas of Argentina and Uruguay. **Place** What are the Llanos?

Waterways

Main Idea Latin America's waterways provide important transportation routes.

Geography and You What major rivers flow through your part of the country? How are they important to your area? Read on to find out about the amazing Amazon, one of the world's longest rivers.

Latin America has many natural rivers and lakes, most of which are in South America. The people of the region have used these waterways for transportation and water resources for ages.

Rivers

Latin America's longest river is the Amazon, which starts in the Andes and flows east about 4,000 miles (6,437 km) to the Atlantic Ocean. Heavy rains and many tributaries feed the Amazon. A **tributary** is a small river that flows into a larger river. Some ships can follow the Amazon as far west as Peru, more than 2,500 miles (4,023 km) inland. People also rely on the river for its fish.

Three rivers—the Paraná (PAH·rah·NAH), Paraguay (PAH·rah·GWY), and Uruguay (oo·roo·GWY)—form Latin America's second-largest river system. Together, they drain the rainy eastern half of South America. After winding through inland areas, the three rivers flow into a broad estuary. An **estuary** is an area where river currents and ocean tides meet. This estuary, the Río de la Plata, or "River of Silver," meets the Atlantic Ocean.

Social Studies ONLINE
Student Web Activity Visit glencoe.com and complete the Chapter 7 Web Activity about the Amazon River.

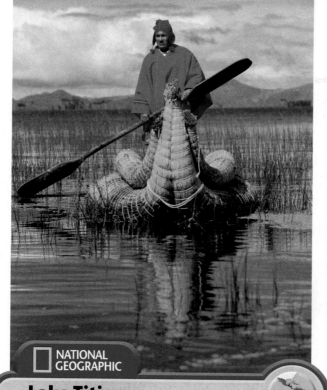

NATIONAL GEOGRAPHIC

Lake Titicaca

For hundreds of years, the native peoples around Lake Titicaca have traveled its waters using boats made from reeds. *Place* **What is unique about Lake Titicaca?**

The Orinoco is another important river. It flows through Venezuela to the Caribbean Sea. This river carries fertile soil into the Llanos region.

Other Waterways

Latin America has few large lakes. Lake Maracaibo, in Venezuela, is South America's largest lake. It contains some of Venezuela's oil fields. Lake Titicaca lies between Bolivia and Peru. About 12,500 feet (3,810 m) above sea level, it is the world's highest lake that can be used by large ships. The Panama Canal, a human-made waterway, stretches across the narrow Isthmus of Panama. Ships use the canal to shorten travel time between the Atlantic and Pacific Oceans.

✓ **Reading Check** **Identifying** Why is Lake Maracaibo important to Venezuela?

A Wealth of Natural Resources

Main Idea **Latin America has vast natural resources, but political and economic troubles have kept some countries from fully using them.**

Geography and You Do you use aluminum foil to wrap dinner leftovers? Bauxite, a mineral used to make aluminum, is an important resource on the Caribbean island of Jamaica. Read to find out about the kinds of mineral wealth in Latin America.

Latin America has many natural resources. These include minerals, forests, farmland, and water. Not all of Latin America's countries, however, share equally in this wealth. Remote locations, lack of money for development, and the wide gap between rich and poor have kept many of the region's natural resources from being fully developed.

Brazil's Abundant Resources

Brazil, the largest country in Latin America, possesses a great wealth of natural resources. More than 55 percent of Brazil is covered in forests, including a large area of tropical rain forests. The rain forests provide timber and a range of products such as rubber, palm oil, and Brazil nuts.

Brazil also has great mineral wealth. It has large amounts of bauxite, gold, and tin. Its deposits of iron ore and manganese help support one of the world's largest iron and steel industries. Brazil's oil and natural gas reserves, however, are limited. They provide only some of the energy this huge country needs. To reduce its dependence on oil imports, Brazil uses alcohol produced from sugarcane and gasoline to produce a fuel for cars called **gasohol.**

Energy Resources

In addition to Brazil, other countries of Latin America have energy resources. Venezuela has the region's largest oil and natural gas reserves. Mexico has large amounts of oil and natural gas along the coast of the Gulf of Mexico. Both Mexico and Venezuela use the supplies for their own energy needs as well as for exports.

Bolivia and Ecuador also have valuable oil and natural gas deposits. In Bolivia, however, foreign companies have attempted to control the country's energy resources. Bolivia's government has struggled to prevent this. As a result, production has slowed, and Bolivia has not been able to fully benefit from exports.

Other Resources

Other mineral resources found in Latin America include silver mined in Mexico and Peru. Venezuela has rich iron ore deposits and is a major exporter of the mineral. Colombian mines produce the world's finest emeralds. Chile is the world's largest exporter of copper.

By contrast, the Caribbean islands have relatively few mineral resources, with a few important exceptions. Jamaica has large deposits of bauxite, a mineral used to make aluminum. In addition, Cuba mines nickel, and the Dominican Republic mines gold and silver.

Certain Central American countries, such as Nicaragua and Guatemala, have rich gold deposits. However, political conflicts and transportation difficulties make mining these deposits difficult.

✔ **Reading Check** **Analyzing** Why are some Latin American countries unable to make full use of their natural resources?

Social Studies ONLINE
Study Central™ To review this section, go to glencoe.com.

Section Review

Vocabulary

1. **Explain** the significance of:
   - **a.** subregion
   - **b.** isthmus
   - **c.** archipelago
   - **d.** escarpment
   - **e.** Llanos
   - **f.** Pampas
   - **g.** tributary
   - **h.** estuary
   - **i.** gasohol

Main Ideas

2. **Describing** Describe the various mountains found throughout Middle America, the Caribbean, and South America.

3. **Explaining** Use a chart like the one below to note the significance of the listed waterways.

Waterway	Significance
Amazon River	
Paraguay, Paraná, Uruguay system	
Orinoco River	

4. **Identifying** Which Latin American country has the greatest resources? What are they?

Critical Thinking

5. **BIG Idea** What effects can volcanoes have on the peoples and economies of a region?

6. **Challenge** Based on Latin America's natural resources and physical geography, do you think the region will become more important economically in the future? Explain your answer.

Writing About Geography

7. **Using Your FOLDABLES** Use your Foldable to write a paragraph giving examples of how physical geography has affected the lives of people in the region.

The Columbian Exchange

What do corn, beans, and potatoes have in common? All of these foods were first grown in the Americas.

Separate Worlds For thousands of years, people living in the Eastern Hemisphere had no contact with those living in the Western Hemisphere. This changed in 1492 when European explorer Christopher Columbus arrived in the Americas. Columbus's voyages began what became known as "the Columbian Exchange"—a transfer of people, animals, plants, and even diseases between the two hemispheres.

For Better and for Worse The Europeans brought many new things to the Americas. They brought horses, which helped the Native Americans with labor, hunting, and transportation. European farm animals, such as sheep, pigs, and cattle, created new sources of income for people in the Americas. Europeans also brought crops— oats, wheat, rye, and barley. The sugarcane brought by Europeans grew well on plantations in the tropical Americas.

▲ **Tomato sauce on Italian pasta**

Some parts of the Exchange were disastrous, however. Europeans brought diseases that killed millions of Native Americans. Plantation owners put enslaved Africans to work in their fields.

From the Americas, explorers returned home with a wide variety of plants. Spanish sailors carried potatoes to Europe. Nutritious and easy to grow, the potato became one of Europe's most important foods. Corn from the Americas fed European cattle and pigs. Peanuts, tomatoes, hot peppers, and chocolate changed the diets of people in Europe, Asia, and Africa.

▼ **Mexican Indian making chocolate**

Think About It

1. **Place** What foods were unknown in Europe before 1492?

2. **Human-Environment Interaction** Why were some foods adopted from the Americas so important in other parts of the world?

Climate Regions

Guide to Reading

BIG Idea

The physical environment affects how people live.

Content Vocabulary

- Tropics *(p. 199)*
- rain forest *(p. 199)*
- canopy *(p. 200)*
- altitude *(p. 201)*

Academic Vocabulary

- facilitate *(p. 199)*
- considerable *(p. 200)*

Reading Strategy

Comparing and Contrasting Use a Venn diagram like the one below to compare and contrast the tropical rain forest and tropical savanna climate zones.

Picture This These huge, 6-foot-wide water lilies are found deep in Brazilian rain forests near the mighty Amazon River. They are so strong that an average-sized adult could rest his or her full weight on them! The warm temperatures and heavy rains of the rain forest create an ideal growing environment for many exotic plants. To learn more about how climate affects the people, vegetation, and wildlife of Latin America, read Section 2.

▼ **Rain forest water lilies**

Hot to Mild Climates

Main Idea Much of Latin America is located in the Tropics and has year-round high temperatures and heavy rainfall.

Geography and You What might the view be like at the top of a rain forest tree 130 feet up? Read to find out why rain forests thrive in Latin America's tropical areas.

Most of Latin America lies within the **Tropics**—the area between the Tropic of Cancer and the Tropic of Capricorn. This area has generally warm temperatures because it receives the direct rays of the sun for much of the year. Yet even within the Tropics, mountain ranges and wind patterns create a variety of climates in the region. **Figure 1** shows Latin America's different climate zones.

Tropical Climates

A tropical wet climate is found in some Caribbean islands and much of Central America and South America. This climate is marked by year-round hot temperatures and heavy rainfall. Vast areas of rain forest cover much of this climate zone. A **rain forest** is a dense stand of trees and other plants that receive high amounts of precipitation. Warm temperatures and heavy rains **facilitate,** or make possible, the growth of rain forests.

South America's Amazon Basin is home to the world's largest rain forest.

NATIONAL GEOGRAPHIC Maps In Motion See StudentWorks™ Plus or glencoe.com.

Figure 1 Latin America: Climate Zones

Tropical
- Tropical wet
- Tropical dry

Dry
- Steppe
- Desert

Midlatitude
- Mediterranean
- Humid subtropical
- Marine west coast
- Highland (climate varies with elevation)

✛ National capital

0 1,000 kilometers
0 1,000 miles
Lambert Azimuthal Equal-Area projection

Map Skills

1. **Location** What is the main climate zone found along the Equator in this region?

2. **Place** Why is there a long band of highland climate zone found in western South America?

It shelters more species of plants and animals per square mile than anywhere else on Earth. Trees there grow so close together that their tops form a dense **canopy,** an umbrella-like covering of leaves. The canopy may soar to 130 feet (40 m) above the ground. It is so dense that sunlight seldom reaches the forest floor.

A tropical dry climate zone extends over parts of Middle America, most Caribbean islands, and north central South America. This savanna area has hot temperatures and abundant rainfall but also experiences a long dry season.

From June to November, powerful hurricanes often strike the Caribbean islands. The heavy winds and rain of these storms can cause **considerable,** or much, damage. Still, many Caribbean islands have used their warm climate and beautiful beaches to build a strong tourist industry.

Temperate Climates

Temperate climates are found in the parts of South America that lie south of the Tropic of Capricorn. A humid subtropical climate dominates much of southeastern South America from southern Brazil to the Pampas of Argentina and Uruguay. This means that winters are short and mild, and summers are long, hot, and humid.

Temperate climates also are found in parts of southwestern South America. Central Chile has a Mediterranean climate that features dry summers and rainy winters. Farmers there grow large amounts of fruit in summer and export it to North America during that area's winter season. Farther south is a marine coastal climate zone. In this area, rainfall is heavier and falls throughout the year.

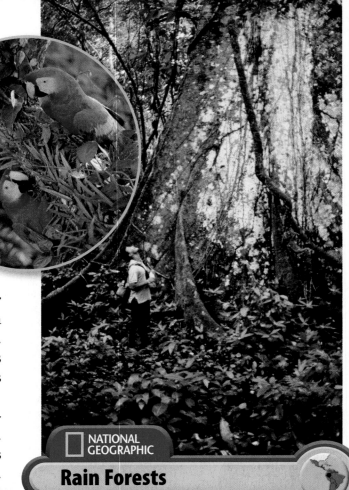

NATIONAL GEOGRAPHIC

Rain Forests

Vegetation can be dense on the rain forest floor. Many species of birds, including colorful macaws (inset), live in the rain forest canopy. **Location** Where is the world's largest rain forest found?

Dry Climates

Some parts of Latin America—northern Mexico, coastal Peru and Chile, northeastern Brazil, and southeastern Argentina—have dry climates. Grasses cover partly dry steppe lands, and cacti and hardy shrubs have adapted to harsher desert areas.

Along the Pacific coast of northern Chile lies the Atacama (AH·tah·KAH·mah) Desert. It is one of driest places on Earth. The Atacama Desert is located in the rain shadow of the Andes. Winds from the Atlantic Ocean bring rainfall to the regions east of the Andes, but they carry no moisture past them. In addition, the cold Peru Current in the Pacific Ocean does not evaporate as much moisture as a warm current does. As a result, only dry air hits the coast.

El Niño

As you may recall, weather in South America is strongly influenced by the El Niño effect. This is a set of changes in air pressure, temperature, and rainfall that begins in the Pacific Ocean.

When El Niño takes place, the Pacific waters off Peru's coast are unusually warm. As a result, winds blowing toward land carry heavy rains that lead to severe flooding along Peru's coast. El Niño can also bring a long dry season to northeastern Brazil, causing crop failures.

✔️ **Reading Check** **Summarizing** Why do the Tropics tend to have warm temperatures?

Elevation and Climate

Main Idea In tropical Latin America, altitude causes great changes in climate and vegetation.

Geography and You Have you ever traveled in the mountains and felt it getting cooler as you went higher? Read to find out how mountains affect climate in tropical areas of Latin America.

As you have read, mountains and highlands cover much of Latin America. **Altitude,** a place's height above sea level, affects climate in these rugged areas. The higher the altitude is, the cooler the temperatures are—even within the warm areas of the Tropics. The Andes, for example, have four altitude zones of climate.

NATIONAL GEOGRAPHIC

Figure 2 **Altitude Climate Zones**

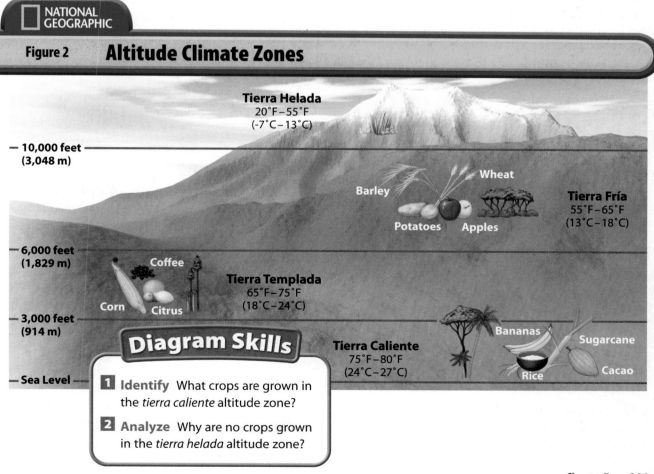

Tierra Helada
20°F–55°F
(-7°C–13°C)

— 10,000 feet
(3,048 m)

Wheat

Barley

Potatoes   Apples

Tierra Fría
55°F–65°F
(13°C–18°C)

— 6,000 feet
(1,829 m)

Coffee

Corn   Citrus

Tierra Templada
65°F–75°F
(18°C–24°C)

— 3,000 feet
(914 m)

Bananas   Sugarcane

Tierra Caliente
75°F–80°F
(24°C–27°C)

Rice   Cacao

— Sea Level

Diagram Skills

1 Identify What crops are grown in the *tierra caliente* altitude zone?

2 Analyze Why are no crops grown in the *tierra helada* altitude zone?

As **Figure 2** on the previous page shows, terms in the Spanish language are used to label the different zones.

The *tierra caliente,* or "hot land," refers to the hot and humid elevations near sea level. The average temperature range is between 75°F to 80°F (24°C to 27°C). There is little change from one month to another. In the *tierra caliente,* farmers grow a number of different tropical crops, including bananas, sugarcane, and rice.

Higher up the mountains—from 3,000 feet to 6,000 feet (914 m to 1,829 m), the air becomes cooler. Abundant rainfall encourages the growth of forests. This zone of moist, pleasant climates is called the *tierra templada,* or "temperate land." The mild temperatures—between 65°F and 75°F (18°C and 24°C)—make the *tierra templada* the most densely populated of the climate zones. Here, people grow corn and citrus fruits. Coffee, an important export crop in the region, is grown at this level.

The next zone is the *tierra fría,* or "cold land." It begins at 6,000 feet (1,829 m) and stretches up to 10,000 feet (3,048 m). Average yearly temperatures here can be as low as 55°F (13°C). The *tierra fría* has forested and grassy areas. Farming can take place in this zone in the warmer summers. The crops, however, are those that thrive in cooler, more difficult conditions. Potatoes, barley, and wheat are some of the major crops in this zone.

The *tierra helada,* or "frozen land," is the zone of highest elevation. It lies above 10,000 to 12,000 feet (3,048 m to 3,658 m). Conditions here can be harsh. The climate is cold, and the temperature can be as low as 20°F (–7°C). Vegetation throughout this zone is sparse. Relatively few people live at these heights.

Reading Check **Making Generalizations** Why do people grow different crops at different altitudes?

Section 2 Review

Social Studies ONLINE
Study Central™ To review this section, go to glencoe.com.

Vocabulary

1. **Explain** the significance of *Tropics, rain forest, canopy,* and *altitude* by using each word in a sentence.

Main Ideas

2. **Identifying** Use a diagram like the one below to list the effects of El Niño.

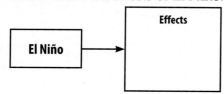

3. **Explaining** Why is the *tierra templada* the most populated altitude zone in the Latin American highlands?

Critical Thinking

4. **BIG Idea** How do some Caribbean countries benefit economically from their environment?

5. **Determining Cause and Effect** Why is the Pacific coast of northern Chile one of the driest places on Earth?

6. **Challenge** Why do parts of Latin America have mild temperatures even though they are located in the Tropics?

Writing About Geography

7. **Expository Writing** Create a chart that lists the climate zones of Latin America, explains where each zone is located, and describes the conditions and vegetation found in each zone.

Visual Summary

Tortola, British Virgin Islands

Waterways

- Latin America's waterways provide food and transportation.

- The Panama Canal, a human-made waterway, links the Atlantic and Pacific Oceans.

- Large reserves of oil are found near Venezuela's Lake Maracaibo.

Fishing on the Amazon River

An emerald from Colombia

Landforms

- Geographers divide Latin America into three subregions—Middle America, the Caribbean, and South America.

- Middle America, which joins North America and South America, has central mountains and narrow coastal plains.

- Caribbean islands can be low-lying or mountainous. Many have volcanoes.

- The towering Andes and the vast Amazon Basin are South America's major landforms.

- Highlands border the Amazon Basin. Lowland plains cross parts of Colombia, Venezuela, Uruguay, and Argentina.

Resources of Latin America

- Venezuela, Mexico, and Bolivia export oil and natural gas.

- Mineral resources from Latin America include iron ore, copper, tin, silver, and emeralds.

- Political conflicts and transportation difficulties keep some countries from fully using their resources.

Climate Regions

- Latin America's tropical rain forest and savanna climates have warm temperatures.

- Rain forests, such as those in the Amazon Basin, have a great variety of plant and animal life.

- The El Niño effect brings heavy rain or drought to parts of South America.

- Climates tend to be drier and cooler at higher elevations, even within the Tropics.

Andes, Argentina

STUDY TO GO Study anywhere, anytime! Download quizzes and flash cards to your PDA from **glencoe.com**.

STANDARDIZED TEST PRACTICE

TEST-TAKING

Look for words such as *usually, never, most,* and other qualifying words in exam questions. They indicate under what circumstances an answer is correct.

Reviewing Vocabulary

Directions: Choose the word(s) that best completes the sentence.

1. A group of islands is called a(n) _____.

A isthmus

B archipelago

C Pampas

D subregion

2. The Brazilian Highlands end with a(n) _____, or a steep cliff that drops down to the Atlantic coastal plain.

A Llanos

B estuary

C tributary

D escarpment

3. South American _____ have high temperatures and heavy rainfall year round.

A savannas

B rain forests

C steppes

D mountains

4. Cooler temperatures are found at higher _____.

A winds

B Tropics

C altitudes

D canopies

Reviewing Main Ideas

Directions: Choose the best answer for each question.

Section 1 *(pp. 192–196)*

5. The dominant landform along the Pacific coast of South America is _____.

A the Andes

B coastal marshes

C the Amazon Basin

D the Brazilian Highlands

6. _____, in South America, is the world's largest exporter of copper.

A Chile

B Brazil

C Bolivia

D Venezuela

Section 2 *(pp. 198–202)*

7. The Tropics have generally warm temperatures because

A hurricanes often strike the Tropics.

B the Tropics have a long dry season.

C they receive the direct rays of the sun.

D more plants grow there than anywhere else.

8. Vegetation is sparse in the _____ climate zone.

A *tierra fría*

B *tierra helada*

C *tierra caliente*

D *tierra templada*

GO ON

Critical Thinking

Directions: Base your answers to questions 9 and 10 on the chart below and your knowledge of Chapter 7.

Average Monthly Rainfall in Latin America		
	Manaus, Brazil	**Lima, Peru**
January	9.8 in. (24.9 cm)	0.1 in. (0.3 cm)
February	9.0 in. (23.1 cm)	0.0 in. (0.0 cm)
March	10.3 in. (26.2 cm)	0.0 in. (0.0 cm)
April	8.7 in. (22.1 cm)	0.0 in. (0.0 cm)
May	6.7 in. (17.0 cm)	0.2 in. (0.5 cm)
June	3.3 in. (8.4 cm)	0.2 in. (0.5 cm)
July	2.3 in. (5.8 cm)	0.3 in. (0.8 cm)
August	1.5 in. (3.8 cm)	0.3 in. (0.8 cm)
September	1.8 in. (4.6 cm)	0.3 in. (0.8 cm)
October	4.2 in. (10.7 cm)	0.1 in. (0.3 cm)
November	5.6 in. (14.2 cm)	0.1 in. (0.3 cm)
December	8.0 in. (20.3 cm)	0.0 in. (0.0 cm)
Source: BBC Weather Center, 2006.		

9. In which month does the average rainfall differ the least in Manaus and Lima?

    A January

    B May

    C August

    D December

10. Based on the chart, which of the following statements is accurate?

    A Lima has a much dryer climate than Manaus.

    B March is in the rainy season in both cities.

    C During Lima's rainy season, it gets more rainfall than Manaus.

    D Over the year, rainfall averages for both cities are about equal.

Document-Based Questions

Directions: Analyze the following document and answer the short-answer questions that follow.

The following passage is from an analysis by the Council on Foreign Relations of the struggle over control of Bolivia's natural gas.

> *[Bolivian President] Morales, a former coca farmer and union leader, won a resounding victory in the December 2005 elections. As the Movement to Socialism (MAS) candidate, he campaigned in favor of nationalizing, among other sectors of the economy, the gas and oil industries with the cooperation of foreign investors. Experts say that, given such promises, the nationalization was no surprise. But Peter DeShazo, director of the Center for Strategic and International Studies' Americas Program, says the move to occupy the gas fields with military forces lent a dramatic effect. "The confrontational nature of his move was certainly intended to get people's attention," he says, adding that Morales may be looking to garner [gain] votes in July elections for a[n] . . . assembly that will redraft Bolivia's constitution.*
>
> —Carin Zissis, "Bolivia's Nationalization of Oil and Gas"

11. What does it mean to "nationalize" the gas and oil industries?

12. What ideas expressed in the passage indicate that nationalization is popular among Bolivians?

Extended Response

13. Explain how El Niño affects the weather in South America.

STOP

Social Studies ONLINE

For additional test practice, use Self-Check Quizzes—Chapter 7 at <u>glencoe.com</u>.

Need Extra Help?													
If you missed question. . .	1	2	3	4	5	6	7	8	9	10	11	12	13
Go to page. . .	193	194	199	201	193	196	199	202	199	199	196	196	201

History and Cultures of Latin America

Essential Question

Regions Common threads of language and religion unite Latin America. Once claimed as European colonies, Latin American countries today are primarily Roman Catholic, and most still use either Spanish or Portuguese as the official language. These two languages are based on Latin, which is how the region gets its name. In what ways can language and religion both unite and divide a region?

BIG Ideas

Section 1: History and Governments

BIG IDEA All living things are dependent upon one another and their surroundings for survival. Native American civilizations of Latin America developed ways of living that used the resources of their environment. People who lived in different areas depended on trade to obtain the goods they wanted. In colonial times, the people of Latin America exchanged goods with Europeans.

Section 2: Cultures and Lifestyles

BIG IDEA The characteristics and movement of people impact physical and human systems. The different groups who have settled Latin America include Native Americans, Europeans, Africans, and Asians. These groups have influenced the cultures and lifestyles of the region.

FOLDABLES™ Study Organizer

Organizing Information Make this Foldable to help you organize information about the history, peoples, cultures, and daily life of Latin America.

Step 1 Fold a sheet of paper in half lengthwise. Leave a ½-inch tab along the left edge.

Step 2 Cut the top layer only to make four equal tabs.

Step 3 Label the tabs as shown.

Early History

New Nations

The People

Daily Life

Reading and Writing Use the notes in your Foldable to write a short essay that describes the development of the countries and peoples of Latin America.

◀ Murals by Diego Rivera, Mexico City, Mexico

Social Studies ONLINE
To preview Chapter 8, go to glencoe.com.

Guide to Reading

BIG Idea

All living things are dependent upon one another and their surroundings for survival.

Content Vocabulary

- maize *(p. 209)*
- jade *(p. 209)*
- obsidian *(p. 209)*
- hieroglyphics *(p. 209)*
- empire *(p. 210)*
- cash crop *(p. 211)*
- caudillo *(p. 213)*
- communist state *(p. 215)*

Academic Vocabulary

- complex *(p. 210)*
- transform *(p. 211)*
- stable *(p. 213)*
- revolution *(p. 215)*

Reading Strategy

Identifying Central Issues Use a chart like the one below to organize key facts about the Native American civilizations of the region.

	Key Facts
Olmec	
Maya	
Toltec	
Aztec	
Inca	

History and Governments

Picture This A Mayan village in Guatemala remembers its dead in a spectacular way. For their Day of the Dead celebration—when people remember relatives and friends who have died—villagers create enormous kites of tissue paper, bamboo, and wire. Finished kites can reach 40 feet across! Sailing above local cemeteries, the kites create a symbolic link between the living and the dead. Read this section to learn more about the historical traditions that have shaped Latin America.

▼ **Ready to fly in Guatemala**

Early History

Main Idea Some Native Americans developed advanced civilizations in the region. Europeans later conquered much of the region and set up colonies.

Geography and You What sorts of things do you like to read? History books, novels, comics? Read to find out what kinds of things the Maya wrote down.

The first people to arrive in Latin America were the ancestors of today's Native Americans. They came many thousands of years ago. Some settled and farmed. Eventually, some groups developed advanced civilizations. **Figure 1** on the next page shows these Native American civilizations.

Early Native American Civilizations

The Olmec of southern Mexico built Latin America's first civilization, which lasted from 1500 B.C. to 300 B.C. Each Olmec city focused on a certain activity, and they all depended on one another. Some cities were located near farming areas that grew **maize,** or corn, as well as squash and beans. Others controlled important mineral resources such as **jade,** a shiny green semiprecious stone; and **obsidian,** a hard, black, volcanic glass useful in making weapons. Some cities were religious centers with pyramid-shaped stone temples.

A people called the Maya lived in Mexico's Yucatán Peninsula and surrounding areas between A.D. 300 and A.D. 900. The Maya built huge stone temples in the shape of pyramids with steps. They were skilled at astronomy and used their knowledge of the stars, moon, and planets to develop a calendar. They also had a number system based on 20. Using **hieroglyphics** (HY·ruh·GLIH·fihks), which is a form of writing that uses signs and symbols, the

NATIONAL GEOGRAPHIC

Maya Architecture

A steep stairway leads to a temple at the top of the Pyramid of the Magician. The Maya built the pyramid about A.D. 800. **Place** How did the Maya record their history?

Maya recorded the history of their kings. About A.D. 900, the Maya civilization mysteriously collapsed. Despite intensive research, historians have not yet been able to determine what happened to the Maya.

Toltec, Aztec, and Inca

As the Maya civilization declined, a people called the Toltec seized what is now northern Mexico. These warriors built the city of Tula, northwest of present-day Mexico City. From Tula, they conquered lands all the way to the Yucatán (YOO·kah·TAHN) Peninsula.

Toltec rulers tightly controlled trade. They held a monopoly (muh·NAH·puh·lee), or sole right, to the trade in obsidian. As a result, the Toltec had the most powerful weapons in the surrounding areas. For many years this weaponry gave them the advantage they needed to maintain their rule.

Around A.D. 1200, the Aztec people from the north moved into central Mexico and captured Tula. They adopted Toltec culture, conquered neighboring peoples, and took control of the region's trade.

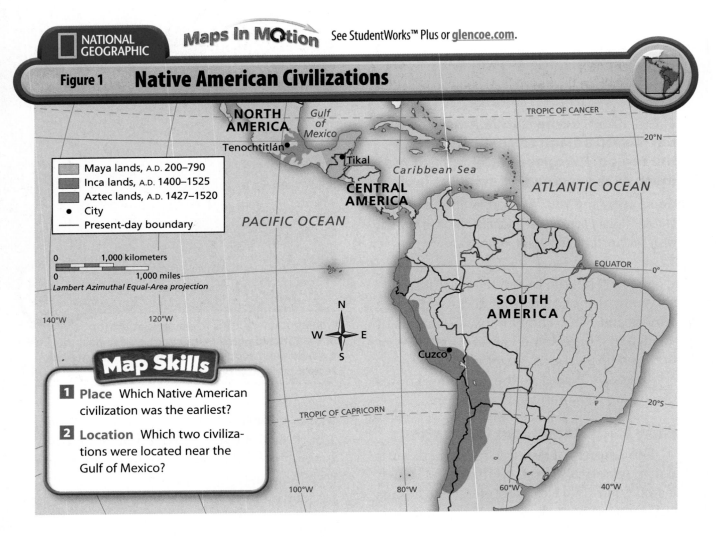

Figure 1 **Native American Civilizations**

Maya lands, A.D. 200–790
Inca lands, A.D. 1400–1525
Aztec lands, A.D. 1427–1520
● City
— Present-day boundary

0   1,000 kilometers
0   1,000 miles
Lambert Azimuthal Equal-Area projection

Map Skills

1 **Place** Which Native American civilization was the earliest?

2 **Location** Which two civilizations were located near the Gulf of Mexico?

Tenochtitlán (tay·NAWCH·teet·LAHN), the Aztec capital, was a beautiful city built on an island in a lake. It held about 250,000 people, which was a large population at that time. Tenochtitlán had huge temples, including one that was more than 100 feet (30 m) tall. Roads and bridges joined the city to the mainland, allowing the Aztec to bring food and other goods to their busy markets. Aztec farmers grew their crops on "floating gardens," or rafts filled with mud. The rafts eventually sank to the lake bottom and piled up. Over time, many of these rafts formed fertile islands.

During the 1400s, the Inca had a powerful civilization in South America in what is now Peru. Their empire stretched more than 2,500 miles (4,023 km) along the Andes. An **empire** is a large territory with many different peoples under one ruler. The Inca ruler founded military posts and put in place a **complex,** or highly developed, system of record keeping. Work crews built irrigation systems, roads, and suspension bridges that linked regions of the empire to Cuzco, the capital. You can still see the remains of magnificent fortresses and buildings erected centuries ago by the skilled Inca builders.

European Conquests

In the late 1400s and early 1500s, Spanish explorers arrived in the Americas. They were greatly impressed by the magnificent cities and the great riches of the Native Americans.

In 1519 a Spanish army led by Hernán Cortés landed on Mexico's Gulf coast.

He and about 600 soldiers marched to Tenochtitlán, which they had heard was filled with gold. Some Native Americans who opposed the harsh rule of the Aztec joined forces with the Spanish. The Aztec's simple weapons were no match for the guns, cannons, and horses of the Spanish. The Spanish also had the help of unknown allies—germs that carried diseases, such as measles and smallpox. These diseases killed more Aztec than did the Spanish weapons. Within two years, Cortés's conquest of the Aztec was complete.

Another Spanish explorer named Francisco Pizarro desired the Inca's gold and silver. In 1532 Pizarro took a small group of Spanish soldiers to South America. The Spanish attacked the Inca with cannons and swords. Pizarro captured the Inca ruler and had him killed. The Inca had already been weakened by smallpox and other European diseases. After the death of their ruler, the Inca soldiers collapsed into disorder. Pizarro then quickly conquered the Inca Empire.

Colonial Latin America

The Aztec and Inca conquests provided Spain with enormous wealth and control over vast territories. Spain then built an empire that included much of South America, the Caribbean, Middle America, and parts of the present-day United States. Other European countries wanted the same power and influence that Spain had achieved. So, these countries seized different parts of the Americas. Portugal became the colonial ruler of what is today Brazil. France, Britain, and the Netherlands took control of some Caribbean areas and parts of North America.

European rule **transformed,** or greatly changed, the populations of these lands. Europeans settled the land, set up colonial governments, and spread Christianity among the Native Americans. They also used Native Americans as workers to grow **cash crops,** or farm products grown for export.

When hardship and disease greatly reduced the numbers of Native Americans, Europeans brought enslaved Africans to meet the labor shortage. A busy trade eventually resulted. Ships carried enslaved people from Africa and manufactured goods from Europe to the Americas. On the return trip, products including sugar, cotton, tobacco, gold, and silver went from the Americas to Europe. Despite European control, many Native American and African ways survived, leading to a blending of cultures.

Reading Check **Explaining** Why did the Spanish conquer Native American empires?

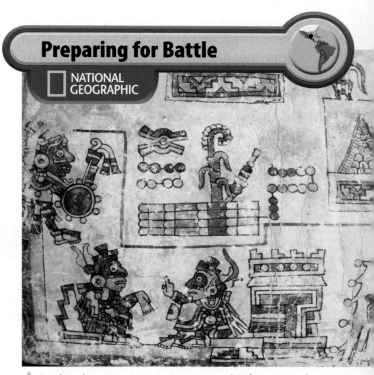

Preparing for Battle

NATIONAL GEOGRAPHIC

▲ In this drawing, Native American chiefs opposed to the Aztec discuss whether to join with Cortés's forces. **Regions** **Why did some Native Americans support the Spanish?**

Forming New Nations

Main Idea Most of Latin America gained independence in the 1800s, but hardships followed for many of the new nations.

Geography and You Suppose you have just been elected class president. What challenges would you face? Read to find out what challenges faced new governments in Latin America.

In the late 1700s, revolutions in North America and France stirred the people of Latin America to action. Colonists tried to take charge of their own affairs. While European colonists called for self-rule, Native Americans and enslaved Africans wanted freedom from mistreatment and slavery.

Independence

Latin America's first successful revolt against European rule took place in Haiti, a territory located on the Caribbean island of Hispaniola. There, enslaved Africans under François-Dominique Toussaint-Louverture began a revolt that threw off French rule in 1804. Haiti, which was established as a republic, became the only nation ever created as a result of a successful revolt by enslaved people.

In Spanish and Portuguese Latin America, the fight for freedom increased in the next decade. In Mexico, two Catholic priests, Miguel Hidalgo and José María Morelos, urged poorer Mexicans to fight for freedom from Spanish rule. Both men were defeated and executed.

Despite many battles, Mexicans did not gain their independence until 1821. After a short period of rule under an emperor, Mexico became a republic in 1823. That same year, the countries of Central America won their freedom from Spain.

In northern South America, a wealthy military leader named Simón Bolívar (see·MOHN buh·LEE·vAHR) led the fight for independence. In 1819 Bolívar defeated the Spanish and won freedom for the present-day countries of Venezuela, Colombia, Ecuador, and Bolivia.

While Bolívar fought for self-rule in the north, a soldier named José de San Martín (hoh·SAY day SAN MAHR·TEEN) was fighting for freedom in the south. In 1817 San Martín led his army from Argentina across the Andes Mountains and into Chile. Although the crossing was difficult, San Martín was able to take Spanish forces by surprise, and

History at a Glance

1250   **1400**   **1550**

c. 1200
Aztec settle in central Mexico

c. 1400
Inca Empire expands in South America

1521
Cortés conquers the Aztec

c. 1400s, Aztec mask

Atahuallpa, last Inca ruler

he began winning battles. A few years later, the armies of San Martín and Bolívar jointly defeated Spanish forces in Peru.

Political and Economic Challenges

By the end of 1824, all of Spain's colonies in Latin America had won their independence. The 1820s also saw Brazil break away from Portugal without bloodshed. Brazil was the only independent monarchy in Latin America before becoming a republic in 1889.

After winning independence, many of the new Latin American countries passed laws that ended slavery. Some people of African descent made economic and political gains. However, they generally did not have the advantages of Latin Americans of European background. On the other hand, African Latin Americans were better off than Native Americans, most of whom lived in poverty.

Although independent, many Latin American nations hoped their countries would become **stable,** or secure, democracies with prosperous economies. Because of a variety of problems, these goals proved hard to reach.

One major problem was frequent political conflict. Latin Americans quarreled over the role of religion in their society. Individual countries fought over boundary lines, and tensions developed between the rich and poor.

Meanwhile, strong leaders made it difficult for democracy and prosperity to develop. These leaders were known as caudillos (kow·THEE·yohs). **Caudillos** were usually high-ranking military officers or rich men supported by the upper class. They often ruled as dictators. Some built roads, schools, and new cities.

Many caudillos, however, favored the wealthy over the poor. Wealthy Latin Americans owned almost all of the land. The caudillos did nothing to help workers in the countryside. The workers remained landless and struggled to make a living.

Exporting Products

During the late 1800s, Latin America's economy depended on agriculture and mining. At this time, the United States and other industrial countries in Europe began to demand more of Latin America's food products and mineral resources. Businesspeople from these outside countries set up companies throughout Latin America. The companies exported Latin American products such as bananas, sugar, coffee, copper, and oil.

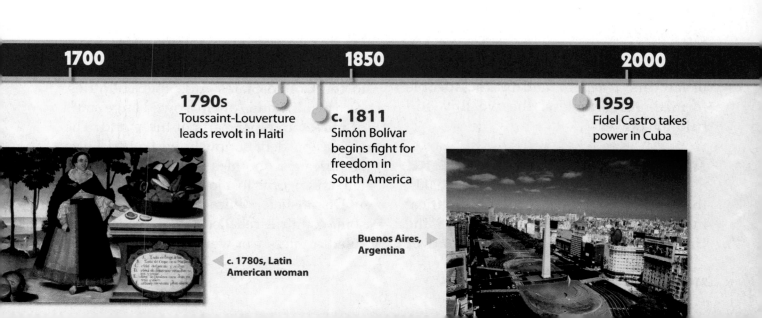

1700

1850

2000

1790s
Toussaint-Louverture leads revolt in Haiti

c. 1811
Simón Bolívar begins fight for freedom in South America

1959
Fidel Castro takes power in Cuba

Buenos Aires, Argentina

c. 1780s, Latin American woman

NATIONAL GEOGRAPHIC

Panama Canal

The Panama Canal was built between 1904 and 1914. Today about 14,000 ships go through the canal each year (inset). **Place** **How did the Panama Canal affect the U.S. role in Latin America?**

As the number of exports rose, some Latin American countries chose to grow only one or two key products. Prices and profits increased as a result, but a decline in demand had serious effects. Prices dropped, and people lost income and jobs.

Despite the problems it caused, Latin America's dependence on exports also brought benefits. Foreign investors built ports, roads, and railroads. Cities grew in size and population, and a middle class of lawyers, teachers, and businesspeople formed. Nevertheless, the wealthy still held the power.

The United States and Latin America

During the late 1800s and early 1900s, the United States increased its political influence in Latin America. In 1898 the United States and Spain fought a war over Spanish-ruled Cuba. Spain was defeated, and Cuba became a republic under U.S. protection. The United States also gained control of the Caribbean island of Puerto Rico.

In 1903 the United States helped Panama win its freedom from Colombia. In return, Panama allowed the United States to build the Panama Canal. Over the next 25 years, American troops landed in Haiti, Nicaragua, and the Dominican Republic to protect U.S. political and economic interests.

Many Latin Americans distrusted the United States because of its great wealth and power. They thought the United States might try to control them as their former rulers had. To improve relations, the United States announced the Good Neighbor Policy toward Latin America in the 1930s. Under this policy, the United States promised not to send military forces to Latin America. It also pledged a greater respect for the rights of Latin American countries.

Modern Times

In the mid-1900s, agriculture was still important in Latin America, but many industries had developed there as well. To encourage economic growth, Latin American leaders borrowed heavily from banks in the United States and other countries. As a result, Latin America owed large sums of money to other parts of the world. The increasing debt seriously weakened Latin American economies. Prices rose, wages fell, and people lost jobs.

Dissatisfied political and social groups in some countries rebelled against leaders who ruled ruthlessly or were in power too long.

For example, in 1959 a young lawyer named Fidel Castro carried out a **revolution,** or a sudden, violent change of government, in Cuba. Instead of favoring democracy, Castro set up a communist state, in which the government controlled the economy and society.

At the same time, other countries were divided by civil wars among political, ethnic, or social groups. In El Salvador, fighters supported by Castro battled government troops armed by the United States. Thousands of people died before a settlement ended the fighting.

Difficult economic and political reforms made during the 1980s helped strengthen many Latin American countries. These changes were often very harsh, which turned many Latin Americans against dictators. During the 1990s, democratic movements succeeded in several countries.

Today's Latin American governments face many challenges. Population is growing rapidly, but resources are limited. Growing trade in illegal drugs has increased crime and corruption. Differences between rich and poor still create social tensions. In the early 2000s, angry voters in Venezuela, Bolivia, Peru, Mexico, and Chile elected new leaders. These leaders promised significant changes that would weaken the power of the wealthy and benefit the poor.

✔Reading Check **Analyzing Information**
Why were economies in Latin America hurt by focusing on one or two products?

Section ✦ Review

Social Studies ONLINE
Study Central™ To review this section, go to glencoe.com.

Vocabulary

1. **Explain** the significance of:
   a. maize   e. empire
   b. jade   f. cash crop
   c. obsidian   g. caudillo
   d. hieroglyphics h. communist state

Main Ideas

2. **Comparing and Contrasting** Use a Venn diagram like the one below to show similarities and differences between the Aztec and Inca civilizations.

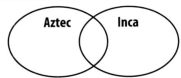

Aztec   Inca

3. **Explaining** What was the social status of African Americans and Native Americans in the newly independent countries of Latin America?

Critical Thinking

4. **Drawing Conclusions** How did European colonial rule change the populations of the region?

5. **BIG Idea** How were the economies of Latin American colonies and European countries connected by trade?

6. **Challenge** Write a paragraph explaining whether you think U.S. involvement in Latin America has helped or hurt the region.

Writing About Geography

7. **Using Your** **FOLDABLES** Use your Foldable to write a paragraph that explains how political unrest in much of Latin America can be tied to social and economic challenges in the region.

YOU Decide

The Darien Gap: Should a Highway Be Built?

The Pan-American Highway extends from Alaska to the tip of South America. The road stops short in Panama, at Darien National Park. In Colombia, the road starts again, where it continues for the length of South America. Roads have not been built through the Darien Gap because of its unique environment. Supporters of a road believe that it will help the region's economy and that the rain forest can still be preserved. Others, however, think that the forest could be lost forever.

 For Construction

I cannot understand why, having [come] to the end of the twentieth century and beginning of the twenty-first, we still have no Pan-American Highway. . . . We are behind in identifying the point in the Darien where the highways should interconnect. And they must first be built. The ecological issue must be confronted realistically. It is easier to safeguard our ecology by opening up the avenues so that we can watch over it than to keep that ecology hidden, just to wake up and suddenly find that it has been destroyed.

—Alvaro Uribe Vélez
President of the
Republic of Colombia

Against Construction

I get very angry, seeing how the Panamanian economy . . . places value on felled trees and does not recognize the terrible damage to an area suffering constant deforestation. . . . One of the most comforting and encouraging sights that you can see today in the Darien is the presence of eco-tourists. . . . The worst enemy of a rain forest is the road. . . .

We should look at the Darien rain forest as a highly productive mine of eco-dollars. That is really the value of it. . . . If the Darien were to be lost, Panama would lose its soul, because nature is the base of everything.

—Hernan Arauz
Panamanian naturalist guide

You Be the Geographer

1. **Analyzing** What argument does Vélez make for building the highway?

2. **Critical Thinking** What does Arauz claim is an encouraging sight in the Darien Gap? Why do you think he feels that way?

3. **Read to Write** Write a paragraph describing how a road might benefit trade between North America and South America.

Guide to Reading

BIG Idea

The characteristics and movement of people impact physical and human systems.

Content Vocabulary

- migration *(p. 219)*
- mestizo *(p. 221)*
- pidgin language *(p. 221)*
- carnival *(p. 224)*
- mural *(p. 224)*

Academic Vocabulary

- element *(p. 219)*
- comment *(p. 224)*
- style *(p. 224)*

Reading Strategy

Summarizing Use a diagram like the one below to summarize the cultures of Latin America by adding one or more facts to each of the outer boxes.

SECTION 2 Cultures and Lifestyles

Picture This Teenage girls celebrate their African heritage during Trinidad's Children's Carnival Competition. Carnival is celebrated in the days before Lent begins. Lent is a time of prayer and fasting in the Roman Catholic Church. During Carnival, both young people and adults dress in costumes. Costumes include characters from nursery rhymes and movie superheroes. As you read this section, you will learn about the different cultures of the people of Latin America.

▼ **Celebration in Port-of-Spain, Trinidad**

The People

Main Idea Latin Americans come from a variety of cultures, but many share common characteristics.

Geography and You Does anyone in your neighborhood speak a foreign language? Read to discover the mix of languages and cultures in Latin America.

Latin Americans come from many different backgrounds. Native Americans, Europeans, Africans, and others all have left their mark. Most Latin Americans today practice the Roman Catholic faith and speak either Spanish or Portuguese.

Population Patterns

Latin America has a high population growth rate. The region's highest birthrates are in Central America, except for Costa Rica, whose birthrate is relatively low. As a result, the Central American countries are growing most quickly in population. In fact, Guatemala and Honduras are expected to double in population by 2050.

Latin America's varied climates and landscapes affect where people live. Temperature extremes, rain forests, deserts, and mountains are common in many parts of Latin America. In these areas, harsh living conditions and poor soil limit where people live. As a result, most Latin Americans live in more favorable climates along the coasts of South America or in an area reaching from Mexico into Central America. These areas provide fertile land and easy access to transportation.

Migration

Migration, or the movement of people, has greatly shaped Latin America's population. In the past, Europeans, Africans, and Asians came to Latin America in

NATIONAL GEOGRAPHIC

A Young Population

About 30 percent of people in Latin America are age 15 and younger. In the United States, 21 percent are 15 and younger. **Regions** Which area of Latin America has the highest birthrate?

large numbers, either willingly or by force. Today, people from places as far away as Korea and Syria come to Latin America looking for jobs or personal freedom.

In addition to people immigrating into the region, some leave Latin America for other parts of the world. Many Latin Americans move north to the United States to escape political unrest or to find a better way of life. Some go through the process of legally entering the United States, while others enter illegally. All of these new arrivals bring **elements,** or parts, of their culture with them. Most stay in close contact with family and friends in their home countries. Many also plan to return when economic conditions in their home countries improve.

Social Studies ONLINE

Student Web Activity Visit glencoe.com and complete the Chapter 8 Web Activity about Latin American populations.

Latin Americans also move within their country or the region. As in many parts of the world, Latin America's rural areas have increased greatly in population. In certain areas, this growth has resulted in a shortage of fertile land. Smaller farms cannot always support large families. People often leave to find jobs elsewhere, usually in cities. The result is urbanization, or the movement of people from the countryside to the cities.

Growth of Cities

In the past, most Latin Americans lived in the countryside and worked the land. Today most of them live in rapidly growing cities. Some of the largest urban areas in the world are in Latin America, including Mexico City, Mexico; São Paulo (sow POW·loo) and Rio de Janeiro (REE·oo dee zhah·NAY·roo) in Brazil; and Buenos Aires, Argentina.

The number of urban dwellers, however, varies throughout the region. In South America, about 80 percent of people live in cities—about the same as in the United States. In Central America and the Caribbean, only about 65 percent of people are urban dwellers.

Most Latin Americans leave villages for the cities to find better jobs, schools, housing, and health care. In many cases, people do not find what they seek. As city populations grow, jobs and housing become scarce. At the same time, rural dwellers often lack the education and skills to find good jobs. There have been too few schools and health care centers to serve the growing number of city dwellers. Unable to return to the countryside, many people have been forced by poverty to live in crowded neighborhoods with poor housing, lack of sanitation, and rising crime.

Ethnic Groups and Languages

Latin America's people include Native Americans, Europeans, Africans, Asians, and mixtures of these groups. The blend of ethnic groups varies from area to area.

Most of Latin America's Native Americans live in Mexico, Central America, and the Andes countries of Ecuador, Peru, and Bolivia. Great Native American empires thrived in these places before Europeans arrived there. Today, Native Americans work to keep their languages and traditions alive while adopting features of other cultures.

Since the 1400s, millions of Europeans have settled in Latin America. Most settlers have been Spanish or Portuguese. Over the

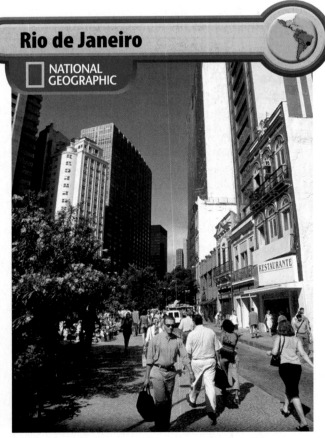

Rio de Janeiro

NATIONAL GEOGRAPHIC

▲ Once the capital city of Brazil, Rio de Janeiro remains an important center for trade and industry. *Place* **What percentage of South Americans live in cities?**

years, other Europeans—Italians, British, French, and Germans—have come as well. In the 1800s, many Spanish and Italian immigrants settled in Argentina, Uruguay, and Chile. As a result, these three nations today are mainly populated by people of European descent.

African Latin Americans form a high percentage of the populations in the Caribbean islands and northeastern Brazil. They are descended from enslaved Africans whom Europeans brought as laborers during colonial days. Over the years, Africans have added their rich cultural influences to the food, music, and arts of Latin America.

Large Asian populations live in the Caribbean islands and some countries of South America. Most Asians came during the 1800s to work as temporary laborers. They remained and formed ethnic communities. In Guyana about one-half of the population is of South Asian or Southeast Asian ancestry. Many people of Chinese descent make their homes in Peru, Mexico, and Cuba. About 1 million people of Japanese descent live in Brazil, making Brazil home to the largest number of Japanese in one place outside of Japan.

Over the centuries, there has been a blending of the different ethnic groups throughout Latin America. In countries such as Mexico, Honduras, El Salvador, and Colombia, **mestizos,** or people of mixed Native American and European descent, make up the largest part of the population. In Cuba, the Dominican Republic, and Brazil, people of mixed African and European descent form a large percentage of the population.

Because Spain once ruled most of Latin America, Spanish is the most widely spoken language in the region. In Brazil,

NATIONAL GEOGRAPHIC

Ethnic Diversity

São Paulo, Brazil, has a large Japanese community. Drummers in Barbados (inset) celebrate their African heritage. *Place* **What Latin American nations have populations that are mainly of European background?**

which was once a colony of Portugal, most people speak Portuguese. Native American languages are still spoken in many countries. For example, Quechua (KEH·chuh·wuh), spoken centuries ago by the Inca, is an official language of Peru and Bolivia. In the Caribbean, where the British and French once ruled many islands, English and French are widely spoken. In some countries, people have developed a **pidgin language** by combining parts of different languages. An example is Creole, spoken in Haiti. Most Creole words are from French, but sentence structure, or organization, reflects African languages.

Reading Check **Analyzing** What challenges do Latin America's growing cities face?

Mexican Folktale

Folktales are stories that have no known author. They are the literature of the common people of a country or region. They express the views these people have about life, what is important to society, and how individuals are expected to behave.

Background Information

The folktales of Mexico reflect Mexican society. Like that society, they include a mix of Spanish and Native American cultures. Some tales point out the tensions between different social and ethnic groups. This folktale reflects basic Mexican values, including the respect that children owe to their parents.

Reader's Dictionary

crystal: expensive, high-quality glass

weevil: a kind of beetle

The Hard-Hearted Son

Mexican Folktale

There was an old couple who had a married son. They were very poor, and one day they went to visit their son to see if he would give them some corn and ask them to dinner. His corn bins were full, and his table was laid out with many good things. For dessert there was candy in a large dish made of **crystal.**

When he saw his parents coming, he told his wife, "There come those old people! Put the cover on the candy dish and hide the food, so we won't have to ask them to dinner."

The wife did so, and when his parents came in and saw it all, they asked their son for a few handfuls of corn. But he told them he didn't have anything, that he hadn't harvested his crop yet. "It's all right," his parents said. "God bless you and give you more." And they left.

When [the son and his wife] sat down to dinner, they found the food had spoiled. The man went to his corn bins and found it all eaten by **weevils.** He came back, and when he was going to eat the candy, a serpent came out and wound itself about his neck and strangled him.

It [wasn't] his parents' curse; rather, [it was] a punishment for his greed and hard-heartedness.

From: *Folktales of Mexico,* ed. and trans. by Américo Paredes. Chicago: The University of Chicago Press, 1970.

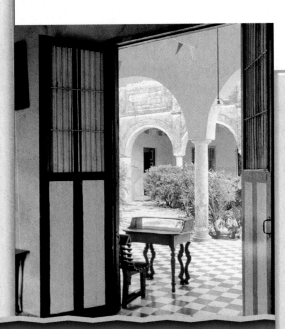

Analyzing Literature

1. **Making Inferences** What message does this tale give about how children should behave?

2. **Read to Write** Think about a kind of behavior or attitude that you think is important for people to have. Write a brief story like this one to illustrate why people should behave that way or have that attitude.

Daily Life

Main Idea Many aspects of daily life in Latin America reflect the region's blend of cultures.

Geography and You Do you enjoy eating tomatoes, potatoes, and chocolate? These foods were first eaten in Latin America. Read to find out about other features of Latin American daily life.

Religion and family play an important role in Latin American life. The region's history and politics are reflected in celebrations and art.

Religion

Religion has long played an important role in Latin American cultures. During colonial times, most Latin Americans became Christians, and Christianity still has the most followers. Roman Catholics form the largest Christian group. In recent years, however, Protestant missionaries have encouraged many people to convert, or to change their beliefs, to Protestant forms of Christianity.

Other faiths are also practiced in the region. For example, many traditional Native American and African religions thrive, often mixed with Christianity and other faiths. Islam, Hinduism, and Buddhism, brought by Asian immigrants, are practiced in the Caribbean region and coastal areas of South America. Judaism has followers in the largest Latin American cities.

Family

Family life is important in Latin America. Often several generations live together, and adults are expected to care for their aged parents. Adult brothers and sisters often live near each other, and their children—

NATIONAL GEOGRAPHIC

Colonial Church, Brazil

In Brazil, many churches—such as this one in the town of Tiradentes—were built during the 1700s under Portuguese rule. **Regions** How is Christianity changing in Latin America?

who are cousins—can form close relationships. Traditionally, the father is the family leader and the chief decision maker. In some parts of the Caribbean, however, the mother is the leader of the family.

Recreation and Celebrations

Most Latin Americans are devoted sports fans. Soccer is popular throughout the region, and Brazil and Argentina have produced outstanding players and world championship teams. Cuba was the second country in the world—after the United States—to play baseball. This sport has taken hold throughout the Caribbean, Central America, and northern South America. Several countries have their own leagues, and many skilled players have gone to play in the United States. In Caribbean countries that were once ruled by the British, cricket is a favorite sport.

Religious and patriotic holidays are celebrated throughout Latin America. Each spring, many countries hold a large festival called **carnival** on the last day before the Christian holy period called Lent. The celebration is marked by singing, dancing, and parades. The Carnival held in Rio de Janeiro, Brazil, is famous for its color and excitement. On the Mexican holiday known as the Day of the Dead, people honor family members who have died.

Feasting is an important part of Latin American celebrations. The foods of Latin America blend the traditions of the region's many peoples. Corn and beans—crops grown by Native Americans since ancient times—are important in Mexico and Central America. Beans and rice are a standard meal in the islands of the Caribbean and in Brazil. Fresh fish from the sea is also popular in those areas. Beef is the national dish in Argentina, Uruguay, and Chile.

The Arts

Culture in Latin America shows the influence of its ethnic mix. Cuban music is famous for its use of African rhythms. During the 1930s, Mexican artists, such as Diego Rivera, painted **murals,** or large paintings on walls, that recall the artistic traditions of the ancient Maya and Aztec. In Latin America, many writers have used their work to **comment** on, or talk about, social and political conflicts.

Latin American artists have influenced those in other countries. The music of Cuba and Brazil has shaped American jazz. Latin American writers of the late 1900s invented a **style,** or form, of writing called magic realism that combined fantastic events with the ordinary. This style was adopted by European and Asian writers.

✔ **Reading Check**   **Identifying** What sports are popular in Latin America?

Social Studies ONLINE
Study Central™ To review this section, go to glencoe.com.

Section 2 Review

Vocabulary

1. **Explain** the significance of:
   a. migration   d. carnival
   b. mestizo   e. mural
   c. pidgin language

Main Ideas

2. **Describing** Describe patterns of migration in Latin America in the past and today.

3. **Summarizing** Use a diagram like the one below to summarize key facts about religion in Latin America.

Religion

Critical Thinking

4. **BIG Idea** How do pidgin languages show the blending of different cultures in Latin America?

5. **Identifying Central Issues** In what parts of the region do most Latin Americans live? Why?

6. **Challenge** How has the region been influenced by other regions of the world?

Writing About Geography

7. **Expository Writing** Make a map of Latin America. Add labels that highlight facts about the population patterns, religions, and cultures of different countries and areas within the region. Then write a short paragraph describing the patterns you see.

Visual Summary

Native American Civilizations

- The Olmec built the first civilization in Latin America.
- The Maya created a calendar and a complex number system.
- The Aztec set up a large empire in central Mexico.
- The Inca developed a network of roads to unite their territories.

Aztec stone calendar

Colonial Rule

- Spanish explorers conquered the Aztec and Inca Empires.
- Spain and Portugal ruled most of Latin America from the 1500s to the early 1800s.
- Colonial rule brought a mixing of different cultures.

Hernán Cortés

Forming New Nations

- Most Latin American countries achieved independence during the 1800s.
- Dictators, the military, or wealthy groups ruled Latin American countries, while most people remained poor and powerless.
- Many Latin American countries developed more democratic systems in the 1900s.

People

- About 80 percent of South Americans live in urban areas.
- Most people in Latin America are of European, Native American, or African background.
- Most Latin Americans speak Spanish or Portuguese, and most practice the Roman Catholic faith.

Culture

- Family life is important to most Latin Americans.
- Soccer and baseball are major sports in Latin America.
- Food, arts, and music reflect the diverse ethnic mixture of the region.
- Religious and patriotic holidays are important throughout Latin America.

Baseball players, Dominican Republic

Bus rider in Brasília, Brazil

STUDY TO GO Study anywhere, anytime! Download quizzes and flash cards to your PDA from **glencoe.com**.

STANDARDIZED TEST PRACTICE

TEST-TAKING

On answer sheets for standardized tests, neatly print information, such as your name, and carefully fill in ovals.

Reviewing Vocabulary

Directions: Choose the word(s) that best completes the sentence.

1. The Olmec made weapons with a volcanic glass called _____.

  A jade

  B obsidian

  C maize

  D copper

2. The Inca of Peru established a(n) _____ in the Andes.

  A empire

  B caudillo

  C communist state

  D Good Neighbor Policy

3. Creole is an example of a _____.

  A mestizo

  B cash crop

  C hieroglyphic

  D pidgin language

4. In Mexico, some artists painted _____, or large paintings on walls, recalling the artistic traditions of the Maya and Aztec.

  A mestizos

  B carnivals

  C murals

  D caudillos

Reviewing Main Ideas

Directions: Choose the best answer for each question.

Section 1 *(pp. 208–215)*

5. The Maya built their civilization in an area that is known today as _____.

  A Brazil

  B the Caribbean

  C central Mexico

  D the Yucatán Peninsula

6. What happened because Latin American leaders borrowed heavily from United States banks in the mid-1900s?

  A Wages fell and people lost jobs.

  B Prices in their countries dropped.

  C Latin economies became stronger.

  D American troops landed in Nicaragua.

Section 2 *(pp. 218–224)*

7. _____ is populated mainly by people of European descent.

  A Bolivia

  B Ecuador

  C Guatemala

  D Argentina

8. In _____, Quechua is an official language.

  A Peru

  B Brazil

  C Honduras

  D El Salvador

GO ON ➡

Critical Thinking

Directions: Base your answers to questions 9 and 10 on the table below and your knowledge of Chapter 8. Choose the best answer for each question.

Internet and Cell Phone Users in Central America			
	Population	**Internet Users**	**Cell Phone Users**
Belize	287,730	35,000	93,100
Honduras	7,326,496	223,000	1,282,000
Guatemala	12,293,545	756,000	3,168,300
Costa Rica	4,075,261	1,000,000	1,101,000

Source: *CIA World Factbook.*

9. Divide the population by the number of cell phone users to find out the number of people per cell phone in each country. Which country has the fewest cell phones in proportion to its population?

   A Belize

   B Honduras

   C Guatemala

   D Costa Rica

10. Divide the number of Internet users by the population. Which country has the most Internet users in proportion to its population?

    A Belize

    B Honduras

    C Guatemala

    D Costa Rica

Document-Based Questions

Directions: Analyze the following document and answer the short-answer questions that follow.

The following passage is by a Catholic priest who came to the Yucatán Peninsula in the 1560s.

> *Before the Spaniards subdued [overcame] the country the Indians lived together in well ordered communities; they kept the ground in excellent condition, free from noxious [harmful] vegetation and planted with fine trees. The habitation was as follows: in the center of the town were the temples, with beautiful plazas, and around the temples stood the houses of the chiefs and the priests, and next those of the leading men. Closest to these came the houses of those who were wealthiest and most [respected], and at the borders of the town were the houses of the common people. The wells, where they were few, were near the houses of the chiefs; their plantations were set out in the trees for making wine, and sown with cotton, pepper and maize. They lived in these communities for fear of their enemies, lest [for fear that] they be taken in captivity; but after the wars with the Spaniards they dispersed [scattered] through the forests.*

> *—Friar Diego de Landa,*
> *Yucatán Before and After the Conquest*

11. How did the friar feel about the Indian communities? Explain your answer.

12. How did conquest by the Spaniards affect communities in the Yucatán Peninsula?

Extended Response

13. Describe challenges and successes for Latin Americans in the 1990s and 2000s.

STOP

Social Studies ONLINE

For additional test practice, use Self-Check Quizzes—Chapter 8 at glencoe.com.

Need Extra Help?													
If you missed question...	1	2	3	4	5	6	7	8	9	10	11	12	13
Go to page...	209	210	221	224	209	214	221	221	219	219	210	210	213–224

"Hello! My name is Miguel.

I'm 14 years old and I live in San Cristóbal Ecatepec, a town near Mexico City, the capital of Mexico. I live in a small house with my mother, sister, and grandmother. Read about my day."

6:15 a.m. I wake up and get dressed then have breakfast with my family. This morning, my two young cousins come over to eat with us. We have quesadillas, which are corn tortillas with melted cheese. My grandmother also puts out a plate of bananas and papayas.

6:45 a.m. I comb my hair, brush my teeth, and put my books in my backpack. It's time to leave for school, even though it's still pretty dark outside. I walk to school with my sister, Areli (ah•ray•LEE).

7:00 a.m. The sun is starting to come up as we arrive at José María Morelos y Pavón Middle School. The school is named for a famous leader in Mexico's struggle for independence from Spain. (We have learned about him in history class!)

7:10 a.m. English is my first class of the day. Our teacher, Mr. Aranda, encourages us to speak mostly English during class.

7:45 a.m. It is time for my least favorite class—math. Today, though, I get a break. The local police visit our school to lead an assembly on crime prevention. They talk to us about staying safe and drug-free.

8:45 a.m. In physical education class, we play *fútbol*, or soccer. Then I move on to music, where I practice my skills on the recorder. I am learning to play a song from a musical.

10:30 a.m. During a short recess, I sit outside and talk with my friends Alejandra, Ismael, and José.

10:45 a.m. I go to history class, then to Spanish. I am working hard for a good grade in both classes. In Mexico, we are graded on a 10-point scale. A passing grade is a 6 or higher.

12:45 p.m. It is time for my elective class—family values. It's about respecting family and friends, and doing community volunteer work.

1:00 p.m. The school day is over. While I walk home, I chat with my dad on my cell phone. He and my mother are separated, so he does not live with us. I see him often though.

1:10 p.m. I change clothes and feed my dogs. Then I help my grandmother with lunch. I squeeze oranges for juice while she makes chicken and rice. My mom comes home for lunch from her job as a secretary.

2:30 p.m. I ride my bike to the hardware store that my family owns. My grandmother and uncles work there. In the back of the store, my Uncle Ricardo raises roosters. I help my uncle by feeding the birds and cleaning their cages.

4:30 p.m. I go back home and play soccer outside with my cousins. Then I start my homework.

6:30 p.m. For dinner, we have *pollo con mole*. It is chicken in a delicious black sauce made with chocolate and spices. Later, I watch some TV (I like to watch reality shows).

10:00 p.m. I am tired, so I go to bed.

WHAT'S THE WORD? Miguel works on a team project in Spanish class.

MAKING MUSIC Miguel plays the recorder in music class. He also knows how to play the flute.

AT HOME Miguel, his sister, cousins, and grandmother spend time together.

ALL SMILES In his spare time, Miguel Rodriguez (mee·GELL rod·REE·guez) helps care for his uncle's roosters.

What's Popular in Mexico

Murals Mexico's early inhabitants, the ancient Maya, painted scenes from their daily lives on rock walls. Today, large murals or wall paintings are still a popular art form.

DANITA DELIMONT/ALAMY

Turning 15 In Mexican tradition, a girl's fifteenth birthday calls for a special celebration. The event is called *quince años*, or "fifteen years."

Mariachi music Lively mariachi bands often play at Mexican festivals and weddings. The musicians play violins, guitars, and trumpets and often dress like traditional Mexican cowboys called *charros*.

KEN WELSH/AGE FOTOSTOCK

Say It in Spanish

There are still several native Indian languages spoken in Mexico, but the national language is Spanish. It was brought to Mexico in the sixteenth century by Spanish settlers. Try these everyday Spanish expressions.

Hello
Hola (OH·lah)

Good-bye
Adios (ah·dee·OHS)

My name is _____.
Me llamo (may YAH·moh) _____.

RIANA ZEHBRAUSKAS / POLARIS (4)

LUC NOVOVITCH/ALAMY

289

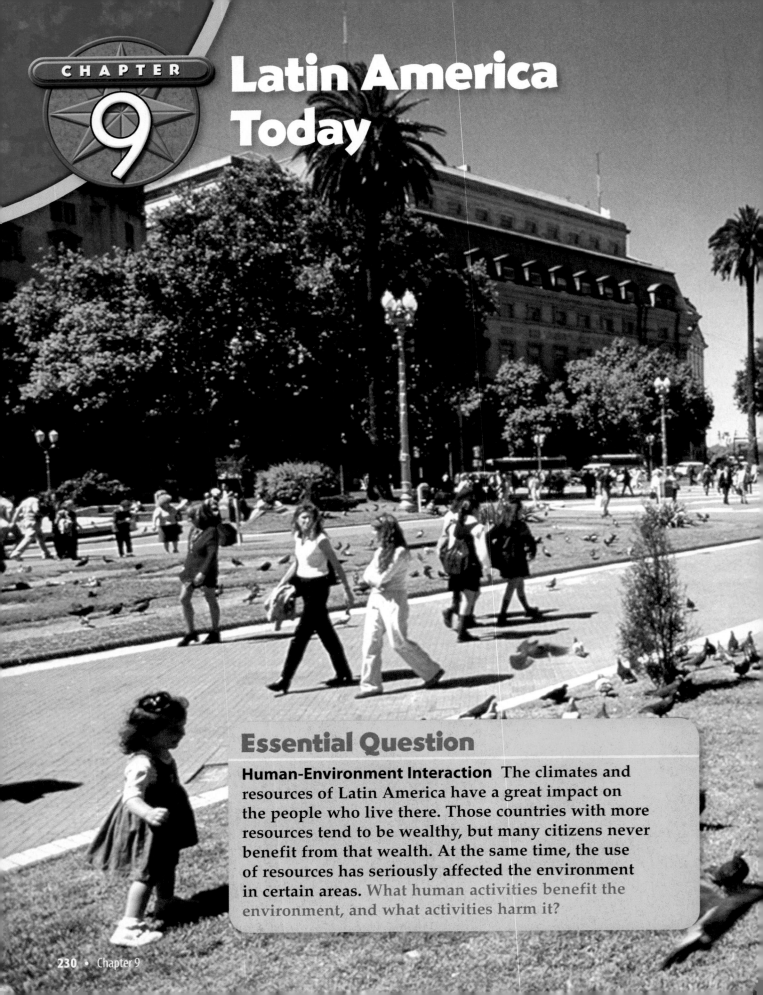

Latin America Today

Essential Question

Human-Environment Interaction The climates and resources of Latin America have a great impact on the people who live there. Those countries with more resources tend to be wealthy, but many citizens never benefit from that wealth. At the same time, the use of resources has seriously affected the environment in certain areas. What human activities benefit the environment, and what activities harm it?

BIG Ideas

Section 1: Mexico

BIG IDEA **Patterns of economic activities result in global interdependence.** Many Mexicans now depend on factory jobs. Those who cannot find work at home migrate to the United States in search of work.

Section 2: Central America and the Caribbean

BIG IDEA **The physical environment affects how people live.** Many Caribbean islands have limited resources. Their warm climate and beautiful beaches, however, make tourism an important industry.

Section 3: South America

BIG IDEA **People's actions can change the physical environment.** The Amazon basin holds the world's largest rain forest. People are now using the rain forest's resources to boost economic growth. Their actions greatly affect the Amazon basin's fragile environment.

FOLDABLES™
Study Organizer

Organizing Information Make this Foldable to help you organize information about the countries of Latin America today.

Step 1 Place two 11x17 pieces of paper together.

Step 2 Fold the papers in half to form a booklet.

Step 3 Label your booklet as shown.

Latin America Today

Reading and Writing As you read the chapter, take notes about each Latin American country. Use your notes to write five quiz questions for each section of the chapter.

Plaza de Mayo, Buenos Aires, Argentina

Social Studies ONLINE
To preview Chapter 9, go to <u>glencoe.com</u>.

Mexico

Guide to Reading

BIG Idea

Patterns of economic activities result in global interdependence.

Content Vocabulary

- plaza (p. 233)
- vaquero (p. 234)
- maquiladora (p. 235)
- subsistence farm (p. 235)
- plantation (p. 235)
- migrant worker (p. 236)

Academic Vocabulary

- reveal (p. 234)
- assemble (p. 235)

Reading Strategy

Summarizing Use a chart like the one below to organize key facts about Mexico's economic regions.

Region	Key Facts
North	
Central	
South	

Picture This They may not look like soccer balls, but these piles of plastic panels will be stitched together by workers in San Miguelito, Mexico, to create thousands of balls for the popular sport. The soccer balls are then sold to large companies that export them. Read this section to learn about Mexico's economy today and how it is connected to other regions of the world.

Soccer ball beginnings in San Miguelito, Mexico

Mexico's People, Government, and Culture

Main Idea Mexico's culture reflects its Native American and Spanish past as well as modern influences.

Geography and You Do you like tacos or enchiladas? These are tasty Mexican dishes. Read to learn about Mexico's people and culture.

Mexico is the United States's nearest southern neighbor. It is the third-largest country in area in Latin America, after Brazil and Argentina. Mexico also ranks second in population.

Mexico's People

Mexico's people reflect the blending of Spanish and Native American populations over the centuries. About two-thirds of Mexicans are mestizos. A quarter of Mexico's people are mostly or completely Native American.

In Mexico, rural traditions remain strong, but about 75 percent of Mexicans now live in cities. The largest city by far is Mexico City, the country's capital. With nearly 22 million people, Mexico City is one of the world's largest and most crowded urban areas.

Mexican cities show the influence of Spanish culture. Many of them are organized around large **plazas,** or public squares. City plazas serve as centers of public life. The main government buildings and the largest church are located alongside each city's plaza. Newer sections of the cities have glass office buildings and modern houses. In poorer sections, homes are built of boards, sheet metal, or even cardboard.

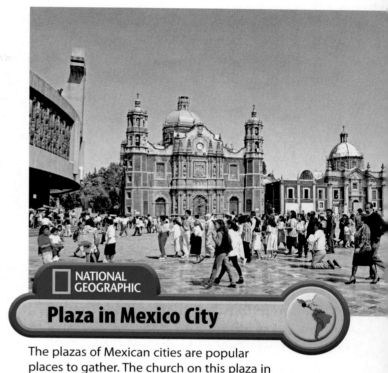

NATIONAL GEOGRAPHIC

Plaza in Mexico City

The plazas of Mexican cities are popular places to gather. The church on this plaza in Mexico City was built in 1536. ***Place*** About what percentage of Mexico's people live in cities today?

Mexico's Government

Mexico, like the United States, is a federal republic, where power is divided between national and state governments. A strong president leads the national government. He or she can serve only one six-year term but has more power than the legislative and judicial branches.

After a revolution in the early 1900s, one political party ruled Mexico for many decades. Then, in the 1990s, economic troubles and the people's lack of political power led to calls for change. In 2000 Mexican voters elected a president from a different political party for the first time in more than 70 years. In the next presidential election six years later, the vote count was too close to call. An election court finally ruled Felipe Calderón president of Mexico, despite bitter protests from supporters of the opposing candidate.

Mexican Culture

Mexican culture **reveals** both European and Native American influences. Folk arts, such as wood carving, are deeply rooted in Native American traditions. Favorite sports, such as soccer, were brought from Europe. Carved and painted religious statues display the mixing of the two cultures.

Mexican artists and writers have created many national treasures. In the early 1900s, Diego Rivera and his wife, Frida Kahlo, became well-known for their paintings. Carlos Fuentes and Octavio Paz have written works about the values of Mexico's people.

Mexicans enjoy celebrations called fiestas (fee·EHS·tuhs) that include parades, fireworks, music, and dancing. Food is an important part of Mexican fiestas. Tacos and enchiladas are now as popular in the United States as they are in Mexico.

Reading Check **Identifying** What are the sources of Mexico's culture?

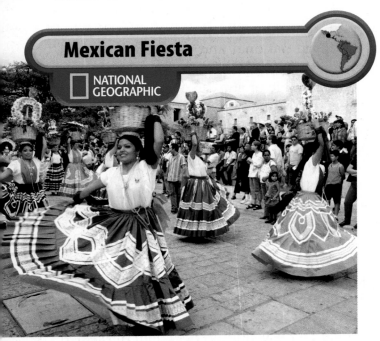

Mexican Fiesta

NATIONAL GEOGRAPHIC

▲ Women wearing traditional clothes dance in a parade at a fiesta in Oaxaca, Mexico. **Place** In what other ways do Mexicans celebrate at a fiesta?

Mexico's Economy and Society

Main Idea While Mexico's economy is improving, the country still faces significant challenges from poverty, overcrowded cities, and environmental issues.

Geography and You Have you seen the brown haze of smog? Read to find out how economic growth in Mexico City has contributed to the increase of smog there.

With many resources and workers, Mexico has a growing economy. Mexico has tried to use its resources to improve the lives of its people. Although these efforts have brought some gains for Mexicans, they have also created some challenges for the future.

Economic Regions

Mexico's physical geography and climate together give the country three distinct economic regions. These regions are the North, Central Mexico, and the South.

Mexico's North has large stretches of land that are too dry and rocky to farm without irrigation. So farmers have built canals to carry water to their fields. As a result, they are able to grow cotton, grains, fruits, and vegetables for export. Areas in the North have grasslands that support cattle ranches. Mexican cowhands called **vaqueros** (vah·KEHR·ohs) developed tools and methods for raising cattle during Spanish colonial times. Their skills were later passed on to American cowhands. Vaqueros still carry on this work today.

In addition to farming and ranching, the North profits from rich deposits of copper, zinc, iron, lead, and silver. Manufacturing is located in cities near or along the Mexico–United States border. These cities include Monterrey, Tijuana (tee·HWAH·nah), and Ciudad Juárez (syoo·THAHTH HWAHR·ehs). In the North, many companies from the United States and elsewhere have built **maquiladoras** (muh·KEE·luh·DOHR·uhs). These are factories in which workers **assemble** parts made in other countries. The finished products are then exported to the United States and other countries.

Central Mexico holds more than half of Mexico's people. Although it is situated in the Tropics, this area has a high elevation that keeps it from being hot and humid. Temperatures are mild, and the climate is pleasant year-round. Fertile soil created by volcanic eruptions over the centuries allows for productive farming.

Large industrial cities, such as Mexico City and Guadalajara (GWAH·thuh·lah·HAH·rah), prosper in central Mexico. Workers in these cities make cars, clothing, household items, and electronic goods. The coastal area along the Gulf of Mexico is a center of Mexico's energy industry. This is because of the major oil and gas deposits that lie offshore.

Mexico's South is the poorest economic region. The mountains towering in the center of this region have poor soil. **Subsistence farms,** or small plots where farmers grow only enough food to feed their families, are common here. In contrast, coastal lowlands have good soil and abundant rain. Wealthy farmers grow sugarcane or bananas on **plantations,** large farms that raise a single crop for sale. Both coasts in the South have beautiful beaches and a warm climate. Tourists from all over the world flock to resort cities, such as Acapulco on the Pacific coast and Cancun on the Caribbean coast's Yucatán (YOO·kah·TAHN) Peninsula.

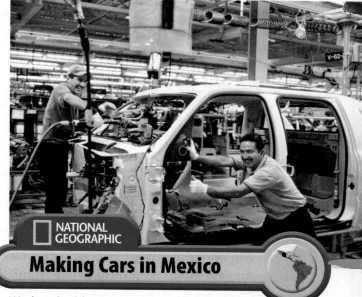

NATIONAL GEOGRAPHIC

Making Cars in Mexico

Workers build a new car at an assembly plant in central Mexico. American and Japanese companies have located hundreds of plants in Mexico. **Regions** **What agreement has helped Mexico's economy?**

Economic and Social Changes

For years Mexico's economy relied on agriculture. Today, Mexico still exports food products, but it relies less on farming and more on manufacturing. Much of the change has come about because of Mexico's closer ties with its northern neighbors: the United States and Canada. As you recall, Mexico, the United States, and Canada entered into the North American Free Trade Agreement (NAFTA) in 1994. Under NAFTA, the three countries decided to end barriers to trade among themselves.

Mexico's growing industries now provide a wide range of goods, such as steel, cars, and consumer goods. Many service industries, such as banking and tourism, also contribute to Mexico's economy.

Social Studies ONLINE

Student Web Activity Visit glencoe.com and complete the Chapter 9 Web Activity about economic changes in Mexico.

Economic advances have raised the standard of living, especially in the North. The speed of growth also has brought concerns about damage to the environment, as well as dangers to workers' health and safety.

As Mexico's economy has grown, pollution has increased. For example, the mountains that surround Mexico City trap car fumes and factory smoke. As a result, the city is often covered by unhealthy smog, a thick haze of fog and chemicals.

Population and Ethnic Challenges

Like the economy, Mexico's population has grown rapidly in recent decades. Many people have moved to the cities to find jobs. Because many jobs pay low wages, people have had to live crowded together in slums, or poor sections of the cities.

Many Mexicans who cannot find work become **migrant workers**. These are people who travel to find work when extra help is needed to plant or harvest crops. They legally and sometimes illegally cross Mexico's long border to work in the United States. Despite low pay, migrant workers can earn more in the United States than in Mexico. To reduce illegal immigration, the United States has tightened controls along the border. This has increased tensions with Mexico. Poorer Mexicans depend on money sent from relatives in the United States.

Many of Mexico's Native Americans are poor and live in rural areas. In the 1990s, Native Americans in southern Mexico rose up against the Mexican government. They demanded changes that would improve their lives. By the early 2000s, the struggle between Native Americans and the government had not been resolved.

 Reading Check **Determining Cause and Effect** Why have many Mexicans migrated to the United States?

Section Review

Social Studies ONLINE
Study Central™ To review this section, go to glencoe.com.

Vocabulary

1. **Explain** the significance of:
   a. plaza
   b. vaquero
   c. maquiladora
   d. subsistence farm
   e. plantation
   f. migrant worker

Main Ideas

2. **Describing** Describe Mexico's form of government and recent events concerning the government.

3. **Identifying** Use a diagram like the one below to explain the challenges facing Mexico.

Mexico's Challenges

Critical Thinking

4. **Determining Cause and Effect** Why is irrigation needed to farm parts of the northern region?

5. **BIG Idea** Compare Mexico's three economic regions.

6. **Challenge** What problems might people in northern Mexico face if maquiladoras are closed, even if they do not work in the maquiladoras?

Writing About Geography

7. **Persuasive Writing** Choose one of the challenges facing Mexico. Write a newspaper editorial in which you suggest steps Mexico's government could take to improve the situation.

Guide to Reading

BIG Idea

The physical environment affects how people live.

Content Vocabulary

- literacy rate (p. 239)
- command economy (p. 240)
- remittance (p. 240)
- commonwealth (p. 240)

Academic Vocabulary

- shift (p. 239)
- fee (p. 239)

Reading Strategy

Comparing and Contrasting Use a Venn diagram like the one below to compare and contrast Guatemala and Costa Rica.

Guatemala   Costa Rica

Central America and the Caribbean

Picture This What is it like to glide along a cable 230 feet (70 m) above a lagoon? Tourists can use this method to enjoy the spectacular views of Tiscapa Lagoon and the surrounding forest in Nicaragua. Opportunities like this show why ecotourism is fast replacing coffee, meat, and seafood as Nicaragua's primary source of income. Read this section to learn more about Central America and the Caribbean today.

▼ "Flying" over Tiscapa Lagoon in Nicaragua

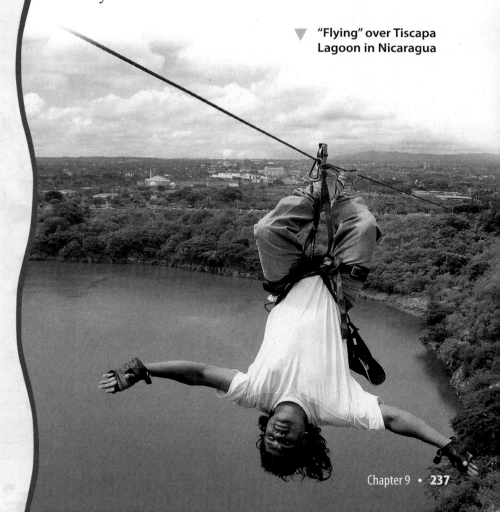

Countries of Central America

Main Idea **Farming is the main way of life in Central America, where many people are poor.**

Geography and You Do you enjoy eating bananas at breakfast? They might have come from Central America. Read to find out about other ways in which Central Americans use their land and resources.

Central America is made up of seven countries: Belize, Guatemala, El Salvador, Honduras, Nicaragua, Costa Rica, and Panama. Most people in Central America depend on farming. For many decades, they have produced crops, such as bananas, sugarcane, and coffee, for export. In some Central American countries, conflict between ethnic or political groups has held back their economies.

Guatemala

Guatemala is a country of rugged mountains, thick forests, and blue lakes. About half of its people are descended from the ancient Maya. Many Guatemalans are also of mixed Maya and Spanish origin. Maya languages and Spanish are spoken.

Guatemala has fertile volcanic soil. Most of the land is owned by a small group of people who hold most of the wealth and power. During the late 1990s, rebel groups fought the government for control of the land.

TIME GLOBAL CITIZENS

NAME: MARIE CLAIRE PAIZ   **HOME COUNTRY:** Guatemala

ACHIEVEMENT: Biologist Marie Claire Paiz directs a major preservation project for The Nature Conservancy in the Maya Forest, one of the world's largest rain forests. Here, for more than 1,000 years, ancient Maya flourished on both sides of the Usumacinta River, which divides Guatemala and Mexico. Maya ruins and writings that date back to 2300 B.C. attract tourists and scientists. Today, however, the forest is being destroyed by farmers clearing the land. And the possible construction of a hydroelectric dam threatens to flood the area. Paiz works to educate Latin Americans about the importance of the site's cultural heritage and what they can do to protect it.

QUOTE: ❝I hope that through conservation work, the wonders shared by Guatemala and Mexico can endure.❞

Paiz at work in Mexico's Calakmul Biosphere Reserve near the border of Guatemala.

CITIZENS IN ACTION Paiz believes that it is important for human-made structures and nature to exist in harmony. How would that benefit both nature and humans?

COURTESY MARIE CLAIRE PAIZ; (INSET) MARK GODFREY © 2004 THE NATURE CONSERVANCY

When the conflict ended, more than 200,000 people had been killed or were missing.

Guatemala has shown recent signs of economic change. In the past, many farmers produced only bananas and coffee. Today they are **shifting** production to other crops that have higher values, such as fruits, flowers, and spices. In the early 2000s, Guatemala and its Central American neighbors agreed to free trade with the United States. This will remove trade barriers among these countries. Central Americans hope they can then sell more of their goods to the United States.

Costa Rica

Costa Rica has long stood out from its war-torn neighbors. A stable democracy is in place, and no wars have been fought within or outside the country since the 1800s. As a result, Costa Rica has no army—only a police force to keep law and order.

Costa Rica also has fewer poor people than other Central American countries. One reason is that Costa Rica has a higher literacy rate. **Literacy rate** is the percentage of people who can read and write. Workers with reading skills can be more productive and earn higher incomes.

Panama

Panama lies on the narrowest part of Central America. It is best known for the Panama Canal. The canal shortens distance and travel time between the Atlantic and Pacific Oceans. In 1999 the United States gave Panama control of the canal. Today, Panama profits from **fees,** or set charges, that ships pay to use the canal. Because of the commerce brought by the canal, Panama is an important banking center.

✔ **Reading Check** **Determining Cause and Effect** How does literacy rate affect income?

Countries of the Caribbean

Main Idea **Although most Caribbean island countries are poor, several are turning to tourism to help their economies grow.**

Geography and You Do many tourists visit the community where you live? Read to find out how several countries in the Caribbean are turning to tourism to boost their economies.

Many of the island countries of the Caribbean face political and economic challenges. For example, the people of Cuba and Haiti endure great poverty. Puerto Rico, which has connections to the United States, is more stable economically.

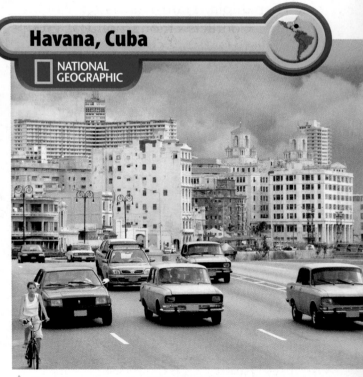

Havana, Cuba

NATIONAL GEOGRAPHIC

▲ Cars zoom down the Malecón, a famous avenue that runs along the coastline in Havana. *Regions* What major economic challenge do Cuba and other Caribbean nations face?

Cuba

Cuba lies about 90 miles (145 km) south of Florida. It has a **command economy**, in which the communist government decides how resources are used and what goods and services are produced. Many Cubans have not prospered under this system.

For years Cuba relied on selling its chief crop, sugar. To end that dependence, Cuba's government is developing tourism and other industries. These efforts, however, have not yet succeeded. Meanwhile, Cuba's longtime dictator, Fidel Castro, tightly controls society. People who criticize the government are often arrested and jailed. The United States condemns Cuba's government for these actions. Because Fidel Castro is aging, Cuba's future is uncertain.

Haiti

Located on the western half of the island of Hispaniola, Haiti has had a troubled history. Conflicts among political groups have made for an unstable government. In addition, most of Haiti's people are poor. A major source of income is **remittances,** or money sent back home by Haitians who work in other countries.

Puerto Rico

Since 1952, Puerto Rico has been a **commonwealth,** or a self-governing territory, of the United States. Puerto Ricans are American citizens. They can come and go as they wish between Puerto Rico and the United States mainland.

Puerto Rico has a high standard of living compared to most other Caribbean islands. It has industries that produce medicines, machinery, and clothes. Farmers there grow sugarcane and coffee. Puerto Rico makes more money from tourism than any other Caribbean island.

✔ **Reading Check** **Drawing Conclusions** Is Cuba's command economy effective?

Section 2 Review

Social Studies ONLINE
Study Central™ To review this section, go to glencoe.com.

Vocabulary

1. **Explain** the meaning of *literacy rate, command economy, remittance,* and *commonwealth* by using each term in a sentence.

Main Ideas

2. **Analyzing** How is Costa Rica different from its Central American neighbors?

3. **Comparing** Use a chart like the one below to examine the economies of Cuba, Haiti, and Puerto Rico.

Country	Economy
Cuba	
Haiti	
Puerto Rico	

Critical Thinking

4. **Contrasting** How does Cuba's government contrast with Costa Rica's?

5. **BIG Idea** Why are many people on the Caribbean islands poor?

6. **Challenge** Do you think farmers in Guatemala will earn more money by growing different crops? Why?

Writing About Geography

7. **Expository Writing** Write a paragraph explaining how specific countries in this region have achieved some economic success and how they have done it.

PROTECTING NATURAL RESOURCES

People are learning how to profit from the land without harming it.

Activists camp out in an Ecuadorian forest to protest an oil pipeline being built through it.

For decades many natural environments and wildlife species have been damaged by human activity. Farmers and loggers in Brazil and Ecuador have cut down or set fire to countless trees in order to acquire the land for farming and other economic activities. Miners in Bolivia have also cleared land in search of minerals. As a result, thousands of miles of forests have disappeared and wildlife populations have suffered.

Human activities have also hurt other environments. In Chile, fish farms that raise salmon in large tanks have harmed marine ecosystems.

In recent years, however, people have been working to protect but still profit from natural resources. Governments and citizens are working to limit the damage to forests and wildlife. Industries are developing alternative energy sources that are less harmful to natural environments. But is it too late?

Colorful macaws live in
the Amazon rain forest.

ENVIRONMENT-FRIENDLY SOLUTIONS

South America has some of the world's largest and most beautiful forests. From the Amazon rain forest to the woodlands of the Andes mountain ranges, the region's green lush forests are home to many species of wildlife.

In recent decades, however, this fragile environment has changed. Since the 1960s, loggers, miners, and farmers have been clearing the trees from this region's forests. Some people cut down trees to produce wood and paper. Others burn the trees to clear land for mining, farming, and industry. The process of clearing an area of forest is called **deforestation**.

Deforestation is a major challenge for South America and the world. Developing countries in this region need the land for industries that will help their economies grow. But deforestation destroys ecosystems and wildlife habitats. Deforestation also contributes to global warming. The burning of wooded areas sends large amounts of carbon dioxide into the atmosphere and speeds up the rate of global warming.

There is much work to be done to protect these lush forests. After years of neglect, the region's governments and citizens are beginning to realize how much is at stake. In recent years, people have been working to reverse decades of damage.

Amazon Alert!

The Amazon rain forest covers about 2.7 million square miles (7 million sq. km) of land in South America—mostly in Brazil. Parrots, jaguars, and piranhas are just some of the thousands of animals that make their home in the Amazon and the many rivers that run through it.

For decades, this tropical environment has been shrinking. In addition to farmers, cattle ranchers, and others clearing the land, the rain forest has also been cut down to make way for roads and highways that crisscross through the center of it. By 2004, nearly 204,000 square miles (528,358 sq. km) of the rain forest had been destroyed.

The Destruction of the Amazon Rain Forest

By 2004, nearly 204,000 square miles (528,358 square km) of the Amazon rain forest had been cleared. Here is a look at the amount of deforestation in recent years.

Square miles cleared (in thousands)

Source: National Institute of Space Research.

INTERPRETING GRAPHS

Analyzing Information During which two years did the largest amount of deforestation occur? About how many total square miles were cleared during those two years?

At a Brazilian ranch, cattle graze on cleared land.

This land was deforested by Brazilian farmers in order to grow soybeans.

The beauty and ecological diversity of the rain forest are at risk.

Stopping the Damage

Brazil's government has been working to preserve the Amazon rain forest. In order to slow the rate of deforestation, Brazil is studying ways to make land that has been cleared more productive. If deforested land can grow more crops or feed more cattle, it will lessen the need for more deforestation.

Legal limits on the amount of land that can be cleared have also been created. However, these laws have not always been enforced. In recent years, though, Brazilian officials are doing a better job at imposing and enforcing laws that protect the Amazon rain forest. Now companies and individuals who ignore the limits are punished with large fines.

Saving Wildlife Populations

Citizens throughout South America are also taking action to protect wildlife. In Chile, fish are often raised on fish farms in giant tanks, called cages. Breeding fish in captivity raises production. Chile is one of the world's biggest exporters of cage-bred salmon. In 2004 the country exported 782 million pounds of fish (355 million kg).

But success has created its share of problems. Fish raised in crowded cages pollute the ocean floor and are prone to illness. Critics of the farms say that the fish are given large amounts of antibiotics and other chemicals to keep them from getting sick. When people eat the fish, the drugs may be passed on to them, which can be unhealthy.

Juan Carlos Cárdenas is the director of Centro Ecocéanos, an organization that works to protect marine life. For years, the center has been working to improve the production methods of Chile's fishing industry. The center teaches local fisheries how to catch more fish using traditional methods. It also conducts research and educates the public about how fish farms affect ecosystems.

Cárdenas says there is still much work to do. He is encouraged that consumers are learning about the health risks associated with eating cage-bred fish. Cárdenas hopes that if people buy fewer farmed fish, the lower sales will force the fish industry to make changes in how it operates.

EXPLORING THE ISSUE

1. Identifying Cause and Effect How does deforestation speed up the process of global warming?

2. Finding Solutions Human activity can threaten the environment. What can you do in your community to help protect your natural environment?

A Chilean worker observes tanks full of farmed salmon.

A SWEET RIDE IN BRAZIL

Brazil's "Flex car" has a sweet tooth. *Flex* is short for "flexible," which describes the kinds of fuel the car uses. The Flex car looks and works like a regular vehicle, but it can run on gasoline or ethanol. Many Brazilians are filling up their gas tanks with ethanol—a fuel that is produced from sugarcane. The alternative fuel is pressed from sugarcane and then blended with gasoline. This "gasohol" mixture could eventually take the place of fossil fuels to keep cars running.

Ethanol-powered cars are not new in Brazil. The country developed them—and the fuel they operate on—in the 1980s, when the cost of buying oil from foreign nations began to soar. Over time, ethanol-powered cars zoomed onto the fast track. By 1988, more than 88 percent of cars sold each year in Brazil were running on a combination of ethanol and gasoline. Throughout Brazil there are now about 29,000 ethanol stations.

Today, Brazil is the world's largest producer of ethanol, and Flex cars are seen everywhere. In 2006 sales of Flex vehicles were higher than sales of cars that ran only on gasoline. Flex car technology is also spreading to other Brazilian industries. Small planes, such as crop dusters, are using ethanol because it is more widely available than conventional aviation fuel.

Added Mileage

Flex cars are also good for the environment and the economy. The ethanol they run on is cleaner than gasoline, so Flex cars create less air pollution. And ethanol is less expensive. Its price is almost half that of gasoline.

As gasoline prices continue to skyrocket, the nations of the world are expected to follow Brazil's example. In 2006 President George W. Bush called for the United States to develop more ethanol. "There is an enormous demand from abroad to know more," said the president of Brazil's carmakers' association. "This is an opportunity for Brazil." Perhaps it will be an opportunity for the rest of the world to have a sweet ride, too.

EXPLORING THE ISSUE

1. Explaining Why did Brazil develop ethanol as an alternative fuel?

2. Identifying Cause and Effect How might Brazil's success with ethanol inspire other nations to develop and use alternative fuels?

REUTERS/JAMIL BITTAR

A Flex car

REVIEW AND ASSESS

This ethanol distillery produces fuel from sugarcane.

UNDERSTANDING THE ISSUE

1 **Making Connections** How does deforestation affect wildlife?

2 **Writing to Inform** In a short article, explain some of the ways governments are working to preserve the natural environments in their countries.

3 **Writing to Persuade** In a letter to an editor of a newspaper, discuss your beliefs about driving vehicles that use alternative fuels.

INTERNET RESEARCH ACTIVITIES

4 Go to www.savethehighseas.org, the Web site of the Deep Sea Conservation Coalition. Click the "About Us" link and scroll down to the "Coalition Steering Group Members." Read about some of the organizations and how they work to protect marine ecosytems. Write a short essay describing one of these activities.

5 With your teacher's help, do an online search on alternative fuel sources, such as ethanol or solar power. Read about how the nations of the world are developing these energy sources. Write a brief article that explains your findings.

BEYOND THE CLASSROOM

6 **Work in groups** to create and display an ecological mural on paper that illustrates how people can protect natural environments in your community.

7 **At your school or local library,** research what other countries are doing to decrease their dependency on foreign oil imports. Do you think their strategies will succeed? Why or why not?

Major Producers of Ethanol

Ethanol can be made from sugarcane and corn. As oil prices soar, the nations of the world are expected to produce more ethanol. Here is a look at major producers in 2006.

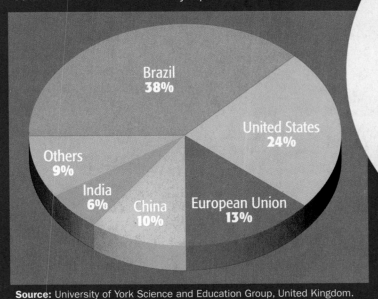

Brazil 38%

United States 24%

Others 9%

India 6%

China 10%

European Union 13%

Source: University of York Science and Education Group, United Kingdom.

Building Graph Reading Skills

1. **Analyzing Data** What percentage of the world's ethanol is produced by the United States and the European Union?

2. **Identifying Cause and Effect** Brazil is the world's largest producer of ethanol. As the world searches for less expensive energy sources, how might Brazil's top ranking help its economy grow?

Guide to Reading

BIG Idea

People's actions can change the physical environment.

Content Vocabulary

- selva *(p. 247)*
- favela *(p. 247)*
- gaucho *(p. 249)*
- national debt *(p. 250)*
- default *(p. 250)*
- sodium nitrate *(p. 252)*

Academic Vocabulary

- maintain *(p. 248)*
- issue *(p. 248)*

Reading Strategy

Identifying Central Issues Use a diagram like the one below to describe Brazil's economy. Write the main idea on the line to the left and supporting details on the lines to the right. You can add as many additional lines as you have details.

South America

Picture This This giant dish is like an "eye" studying the universe. The Swedish ESO (European Southern Observatory) Sub-millimeter Telescope, or SEST, is not like some telescopes that use light from stars or planets to "see" them. SEST is able to study distant objects by gathering radio waves that radiate from them. The telescope is located in the southern Atacama Desert in Chile, where the clear sky conditions are ideal for this type of research. To learn more about South America today, read Section 3.

▼ **Learning about the universe in Chile**

Brazil

Main Idea Brazil is a leading economic power, but concerns have grown about its use of the Amazon rain forest.

Geography and You Did you know that some of the best farmland in the United States was once forestland? The forests were cleared by farmers. Read to find out how Brazil's forests are being cut down for mining, logging, and farming.

Brazil is the fifth-largest country in the world and the largest in South America. The country is known for its Amazon rain forest, which Brazilians call the **selva**. This resource is threatened by Brazil's economic growth.

Brazil's People

With 187 million people, Brazil has the largest population of all Latin American countries. Brazil's culture is largely Portuguese because they were the first and largest European group to settle Brazil. Today Brazilians are of European, African, Native American, Asian, or mixed ancestry. Almost all of them speak a Brazilian form of Portuguese, which includes many words from Native American and African languages.

Most of Brazil's people live in cities along the Atlantic coast. São Paulo and Rio de Janeiro are among the largest cities in the world. In recent years, millions of Brazilians have moved from rural areas to coastal cities to find better jobs. Many of these migrants have settled in favelas. **Favelas** are overcrowded slum areas that surround many Brazilian cities. To reduce city crowding, the government now encourages people to move back to less-populated, inland areas. In 1960 Brazil moved its capital from Rio de Janeiro to the newly built city of Brasília 600 miles (966 km) inland.

NATIONAL GEOGRAPHIC

Harvesting Sugarcane

A truck is loaded with sugarcane at a farm in southeastern Brazil. *Human-Environment Interaction* In what unique way does Brazil make use of its sugarcane?

With more than 2 million people, Brasília is a modern and rapidly growing city.

Brazil's Economy

Brazil is one of the world's leading producers of food crops. It grows more coffee, oranges, and cassava than any other country. Brazil's agricultural output has grown greatly in recent years. This is partly because Brazilian farmers have cleared more land in rain forest areas to grow crops. They also now use machinery to perform many tasks. Finally, farmers have planted crops that have been scientifically changed to produce more and to prevent disease.

In addition to productive farms, Brazil has valuable mineral resources, such as iron ore, bauxite, tin, manganese, gold, silver, and diamonds. Offshore deposits of oil, as well as hydroelectric power from rivers, supply the country with energy. Brazil also uses sugarcane to produce a substitute for gasoline.

Figure 1   **Deforestation in Brazil**

Map legend:
- Forest vegetation
- Nonforest vegetation
- Deforested
- Roads
- National capital
- City

Map Skills

1 **Location** Where has most of the Amazon's deforestation taken place?

2 **Human-Environment Interaction** In some areas, how do patterns of deforestation relate to roads?

Brazil has successful industries too. Most manufacturing takes place in São Paulo and other southeastern cities. Factory workers produce heavy industrial goods, such as machinery, airplanes, and cars. They also make food products, medicines, paper, and clothing.

The Rain Forest

Brazil's greatest natural resource is the Amazon rain forest. It is the world's largest rain forest area, yet it also has the highest rate of deforestation. Each year, the land deforested in the Amazon rain forest is equal in size to Ohio. **Figure 1** shows how much of the rain forest has been lost.

Why is the rain forest shrinking? To increase jobs and make products for export, Brazil's government has encouraged mining, logging, and farming in the rain for-

est. These activities lead to soil erosion and harm the rain forest's ecosystem and biodiversity.

As deforestation takes place, roads are built, bringing companies, farmers, and change. Native Americans who live in the rain forest find it difficult to follow their traditional cultures as this occurs.

In addition, tropical forests give off huge amounts of oxygen and play a role in **maintaining,** or keeping up, the Earth's climate patterns. They also provide shelter to many wildlife species that may not survive if deforestation continues. Thus, although the rain forest belongs to Brazil, the effects of deforestation are felt worldwide. Because deforestation is a global **issue,** or problem, other nations have convinced Brazil to protect at least part of the rain forest from economic development.

Brazil's Government

Brazil declared independence from Portugal in 1822. During most of the 1800s, emperors ruled the country. Today Brazil is a democratic federal republic, in which people elect a president and other leaders. Brazil has many political parties, not just two main ones, as does the United States.

The national government of Brazil is much stronger than its 26 state governments. Like the United States, Brazil's national government has three branches. The president heads the executive branch, which carries out the laws. The National Congress, which is similar to the U.S. Congress, makes the laws. A Supreme Federal Tribunal, or court, heads a judicial system that interprets the laws.

✔ Reading Check **Analyzing Information** Why has Brazil's agricultural output greatly increased?

NATIONAL GEOGRAPHIC

Brazil's Government

▲ Brazil's President Luiz Inacio Lula da Silva (left) talks with Governor Rosinha Garotinho of the state of Rio de Janeiro. **Place** How is Brazil's government like that of the United States?

Argentina

Main Idea **Argentina has experienced harsh military rule but now has a democratic government.**

Geography and You How would you feel if the government seized a member of your family and you never saw him or her again? Read to find out how Argentina went through a period of violent rule in recent decades.

Argentina is South America's second-largest country after Brazil. It is about the size of the United States east of the Mississippi River. The Andes tower over western Argentina. South and east of the Andes lies a dry, windswept plateau called Patagonia. The center of Argentina has vast treeless plains known as the Pampas. More than two-thirds of Argentina's people live in this central area.

Argentina's People

About 85 percent of Argentina's people are of European ancestry, especially Spanish and Italian. European cultural traditions are stronger in Argentina than in most other Latin American countries.

The majority of people in Argentina are city dwellers. In fact, more than one-third of the country's population lives in the capital, Buenos Aires. This bustling city is a seat of government, a busy port, and a center of culture. Buenos Aires resembles a European city with its parks, beautiful buildings, wide streets, and cafés. It has been nicknamed "the Paris of the South."

Argentina's Economy

Argentina's economy depends heavily on farming and ranching. Huge ranches cover the Pampas. There, **gauchos** (GOW·chohs), or cowhands, raise livestock. Gauchos are Argentina's national symbol.

Beef Cattle in Argentina

Beef plays an important role in Argentina's foreign trade. Earnings from exports of animal products were about 1.9 billion dollars a year in the early 2000s. **Location** Where are most of Argentina's livestock raised?

They are admired for their independence and horse-riding skills. The livestock that the gauchos herd and tend are a vital part of the economy. Beef and beef products are Argentina's chief exports.

Argentina is one of the most industrialized countries in South America. Most factories are in or near Buenos Aires. They produce food products, cars, chemicals, and textiles. Zinc, iron ore, and copper are mined in the Andes. Oil fields also lie in the Andes as well as in Patagonia.

Despite these resources, Argentina's economy has struggled. To help its economy grow, Argentina borrowed money from foreign banks during the late 1900s. However, this led to a high **national debt,** or money owed by the government. A few years ago, Argentina had to default on its debts to the foreign banks. To **default** is to miss a debt payment to the company or person who lent the money. People in other countries stopped investing money in Argentina's businesses. This caused a severe economic

slowdown in Argentina. Recently the economy has recovered, and the government has paid off part of the debt.

Argentina's Government

After independence in the early 1800s, Argentina was torn apart by civil war. By the mid-1850s, a strong national government had emerged, and Argentina prospered. During the early 1900s, though, the economy suffered, and the military took over. One of the military leaders, Juan Perón, became a dictator in the late 1940s. Perón tried to improve the economy and to help the workers. At the same time, he restricted freedom of speech and the press. These actions made people unhappy. In 1955 a revolt drove Perón from power and restored democracy.

Military officers again took control of Argentina in the 1970s. They ruled harshly and secretly seized and killed thousands of people they believed opposed their policies. The families of these people did not know what had happened to them. It was a time of fear.

In 1982 Argentina suffered defeat in a war with the United Kingdom over control of the Falkland Islands. The Falklands, known to Argentinians as the Malvinas, lie in the Atlantic Ocean. After this loss, military leaders gave up power, and elected leaders gained control of the government.

Today, Argentina is a democratic federal republic. It consists of a national government and 23 provincial, or state, governments. The nation is led by a powerful president who is elected every four years. A legislature with two houses makes the laws. A Supreme Court heads a system of judges.

Reading Check **Explaining** Why are food products among the leading manufactured items in Argentina?

Other Countries of South America

Main Idea Economic growth for other countries of South America has been hindered by political and social troubles.

Geography and You Can you recall hard times and good times in your life? Read on to learn which nations in South America are experiencing hard times and which are experiencing good times.

Many countries in South America face the same challenges as Brazil and Argentina. Some, such as Venezuela, Colombia, and Chile, have relatively strong economies. Others, however, face more difficult economic hardships.

Venezuela

Venezuela lies along the Caribbean Sea in northern South America. It is one of the world's leading producers of oil and natural gas. Although it relies mainly on oil production, Venezuela also benefits from mining bauxite, gold, diamonds, and emeralds. The country's factories make steel, chemicals, and food products. Farmers grow sugarcane and bananas or raise cattle. Most Venezuelans are poor, and some live in slums that sprawl over the hills around the capital, Caracas.

In 1998 Venezuelans elected a former military leader, Hugo Chávez, as president. Chávez promised to use oil money to better the lives of Venezuela's poor. His strong rule, however, split the country into opposing groups. Chávez also tried to spread his influence overseas. He became friendly with Cuba's leader, Fidel Castro, and frequently criticized the United States.

Colombia

Venezuela's neighbor, Colombia, has coasts on both the Caribbean Sea and the Pacific Ocean. The Andes rise in the western part of Colombia. Nearly 80 percent of Colombia's people live in the valleys and highland plateaus of the Andes. Bogotá (ᴠᴏʜ·goh·TAH), the capital and largest city, lies on one of these plateaus.

Colombia has many natural resources, such as coal, oil, and copper. It is the world's leading supplier of emeralds. Colombian coffee, a major export, is famous for its rich flavor. Colombia also exports bananas, sugarcane, rice, and cotton.

Despite these economic strengths, Colombia has much political unrest. Wealth remains in the hands of a few, and many people are poor. Since the 1970s, rebel forces have fought the government and now control parts of the country.

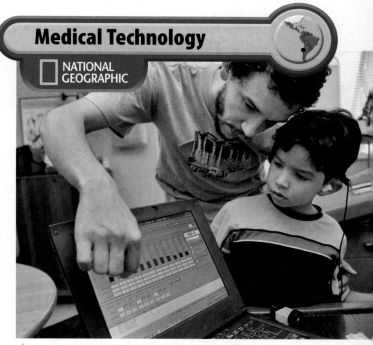

Medical Technology

NATIONAL GEOGRAPHIC

▲ A six-year-old boy hears for the first time as a result of new medical equipment provided by Chile's government. **Regions** In addition to Chile, what other South American countries have relatively strong economies?

Drug dealers are a major problem in Colombia. The dealers pay farmers to grow coca leaves, which are used to make the illegal drug cocaine. Much of the cocaine is smuggled into the United States and Europe. Drug dealers have used their profits to build private armies. The United States has lent Colombia support in an effort to break the power of the drug dealers.

Chile

Chile lies along the southern Pacific coast of South America. It has an unusual ribbonlike shape that is 2,652 miles long (4,268 km) and an average of 110 miles (177 km) wide. Chile's landscapes range from extremely dry desert in the north to ice formations in the south.

In recent years, Chile has had strong economic growth. Mining forms the backbone of Chile's economy. Chile is a major

world producer of copper. It also mines and exports gold, silver, iron ore, and **sodium nitrate,** a mineral used in fertilizer and explosives.

Agriculture is also a major economic activity. Farmers produce wheat, corn, beans, sugarcane, and potatoes. The grapes and apples you eat in winter may come from Chile's summer harvest. Many people also raise cattle, sheep, and other livestock. Northern Chile's fishing industry is the largest in South America.

Like Argentina, Chile has emerged from a long period of military rule. During that time, the government treated its opponents harshly. Today, Chile is a democracy. In 2006 Michelle Bachelet was elected the country's first woman president.

 Reading Check **Identifying** What resource is especially important to Venezuela?

Social Studies ONLINE
Study Central™ To review this section, go to glencoe.com.

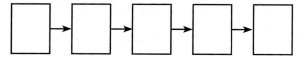

Section 3 Review

Vocabulary

1. **Explain** the significance of:
   a. selva   c. gaucho   e. default
   b. favela   d. national debt   f. sodium nitrate

Main Ideas

2. **Explaining** In what ways has Brazil improved its economy?

3. **Sequencing** Use a diagram like the one below to show changes in Argentina's government following independence.

☐ → ☐ → ☐ → ☐ → ☐

4. **Describing** Describe the problem of illegal drugs in Colombia.

Critical Thinking

5. **BIG Idea** How are Brazilians changing the rain forest, and why does that matter to people in other areas of the world?

6. **Challenge** Do you think Venezuela is likely to suffer from focusing on one major product? Why or why not?

Writing About Geography

7. **Using Your FOLDABLES** Use your Foldable to write a paragraph comparing the roles that two governments of South America play in economic affairs. Be sure to analyze how effective you think their governments are.

Mexico

- Mexico City is one of the world's largest cities.

- Mexico's culture reflects both European and Native American influences.

- Industry and farming dominate Mexico's North; agriculture leads in the South.

- Many Mexicans have migrated to cities and to the United States to find jobs.

Subsistence farming, Mexico

Central America and the Caribbean

- Civil wars have held back economic growth in parts of Central America.

- Costa Rica's citizens have a high literacy rate and enjoy a stable government.

- The Panama Canal enables ships to pass between the Atlantic and Pacific Oceans.

- Many Caribbean islands' economies rely on tourism.

Logs from Amazon forest, Brazil

Brazil

- Brazil is the biggest and most populous country in South America.

- Brazil's people, who speak Portuguese, are a mix of many different ethnic backgrounds.

- Brazil has many resources and a productive economy.

- Economic development threatens the Amazon rain forest.

Cruise ship docked in the British Virgin Islands

Argentina

- A large grassland called the Pampas covers much of Argentina.

- Argentina's economy depends on farming and ranching.

- More than a third of Argentina's people live in the capital, Buenos Aires.

- After years of military rule, Argentina is today a democracy.

Oil rig in Venezuela

Other Countries of South America

- Venezuela has relied on oil wealth to build a stronger economy.

- Colombia has been weakened by political unrest and illegal drug trade.

- Chile's economy depends on the export of copper and agricultural products.

STANDARDIZED TEST PRACTICE

TEST-TAKING

> Before answering essay questions, jot down a list of things you want to discuss.

Reviewing Vocabulary

Directions: Choose the word(s) that best completes the sentence.

1. Main government buildings in Mexican cities are located around central squares called _____.

A plazas

B murals

C selvas

D favelas

2. _____ are small plots where farmers grow only enough food for their families.

A Plantations

B Maquiladoras

C Commonwealths

D Subsistence farms

3. An important source of income in Haiti is _____.

A canal-use fees

B the literacy rate

C remittances

D the command economy

4. _____ take care of the livestock on ranches in Argentina.

A Gauchos

B Vaqueros

C Farmers

D Migrant workers

Reviewing Main Ideas

Directions: Choose the best answer for each question.

Section 1 *(pp. 232–236)*

5. Which expression of Mexican culture is rooted in Native American traditions?

A soccer

B bullfighting

C wood carving

D public squares

6. What helped change the Mexican economy in recent years?

A farmers' small plots

B foreign-built factories

C large sugarcane farms

D resort cities along the coast

Section 2 *(pp. 237–240)*

7. What country makes more money in tourism than any other country in the Caribbean?

A Cuba

B Haiti

C Puerto Rico

D El Salvador

Section 3 *(pp. 246–252)*

8. Why is deforestation in Brazil felt worldwide?

A Farmers grow crops in the rain forest.

B Native Americans live in the rain forest.

C The rain forest has large deposits of oil.

D The rain forest helps maintain climate patterns.

GO ON

Critical Thinking

Directions: Base your answers to questions 9 and 10 on the graph below and your knowledge of Chapter 9. Choose the best answer for each question.

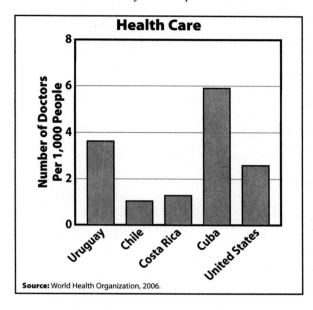

Health Care

Number of Doctors Per 1,000 People

Uruguay | Chile | Costa Rica | Cuba | United States

Source: World Health Organization, 2006.

9. Which of the following countries has the fewest doctors per thousand population?

A Cuba

B Chile

C Uruguay

D Costa Rica

10. Which of the following generalizations does the graph support?

A Chile has more disease than the other countries.

B Chile is healthier than the other countries.

C Cuba has more doctors per 1,000 people than either the United States or Uruguay.

D The United States has more doctors per 1,000 people than all Latin American countries.

Document-Based Questions

Directions: Analyze the following document and answer the short-answer questions that follow.

The following passage discusses a movement that has helped strengthen Argentina's economy.

> *Since 1972 the Mil Hojas pasta factory [in Argentina] has churned out delicacies like ravioli and Italian desserts. But Mil Hojas' fortunes—along with those of the national economy—began to decline with the late 1990s as deep recession set in.*
>
> *The factory owners decided to abandon it amid a national epidemic of bankruptcies. Mil Hojas, like many other factories in Argentina, was to permanently close its doors.*
>
> *That was when its workers decided to act. They took back, or "recovered" Mil Hojas, transforming it into what today is a thriving cooperative, as Argentina emerges from one of the worst economic crises in its history.*
>
> *Today, thousands of workers are reactivating previously closed factories on their own terms and . . . breathing life into the national economy.*
>
> —Eduardo Stanley, "Argentina's Recovered Factories: A Story of Economic Success"

11. What happened to factories during economic hard times in Argentina?

12. Were the workers' actions consistent with a command economy or with free enterprise? Explain.

Extended Response

13. Compare and contrast the political systems of Brazil and the United States.

STOP

Social Studies ONLINE

For additional test practice, use Self-Check Quizzes—Chapter 9 at <u>glencoe.com</u>.

If you missed question. . .	1	2	3	4	5	6	7	8	9	10	11	12	13
Need Extra Help? Go to page. . .	233	235	240	249	234	235	240	248	239	239	249	249	249

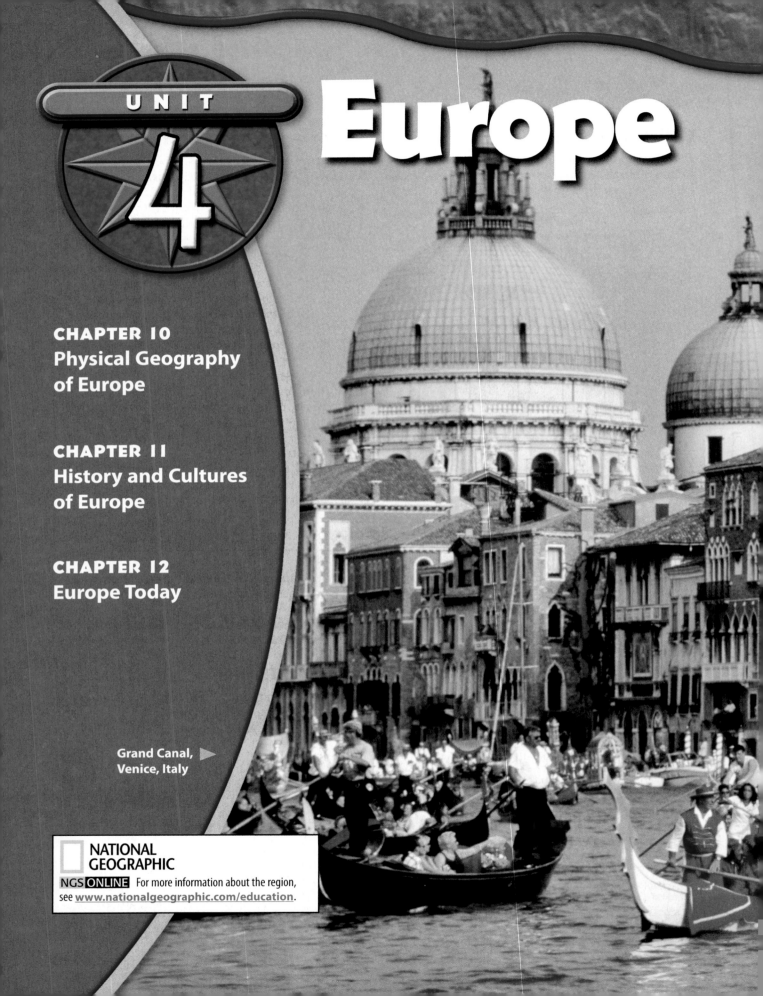

UNIT 4

Europe

Grand Canal, ▶
Venice, Italy

**NATIONAL
GEOGRAPHIC**

NGS ONLINE For more information about the region,
see www.nationalgeographic.com/education.

UNIT 4

Regional Atlas

Europe

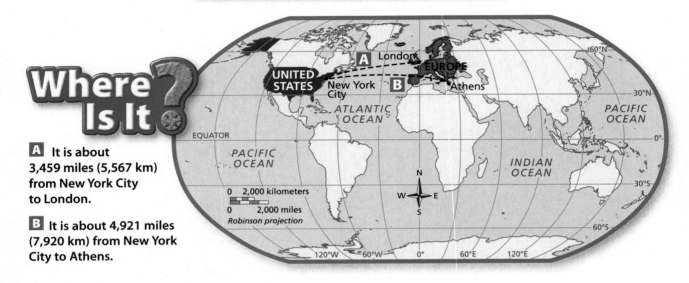

Where Is It?

A It is about 3,459 miles (5,567 km) from New York City to London.

B It is about 4,921 miles (7,920 km) from New York City to Athens.

How Big Is It?

At about 2.3 million square miles (5.9 million sq. km), Europe is about three-fourths the size of the United States. More than 580 million people—almost twice the population of the United States—live in this area, which is one of the most densely populated regions on Earth.

Comparing Population

United States and Selected Countries of Europe	
United States	🧍🧍🧍🧍🧍🧍🧍🧍🧍🧍
Germany	🧍🧍🧍
France	🧍🧍
United Kingdom	🧍🧍
Italy	🧍🧍
Ukraine	🧍🧍
Czech Republic	🧍

🧍 = 30,000,000

Source: *World Population Data Sheet*, 2005.

GEO Fast Facts

Largest Island

Great Britain
80,823 sq. mi.
(209,331 sq. km)

Largest Lake

Lake Vänern (Sweden)
2,156 sq. mi.
(5,584 sq. km) ▶

Highest Point

◀ **Mont Blanc (France/Italy)**
15,771 ft. (4,807 m) high

Longest River

Danube River
1,771 mi.
(2,850 km) long ▶

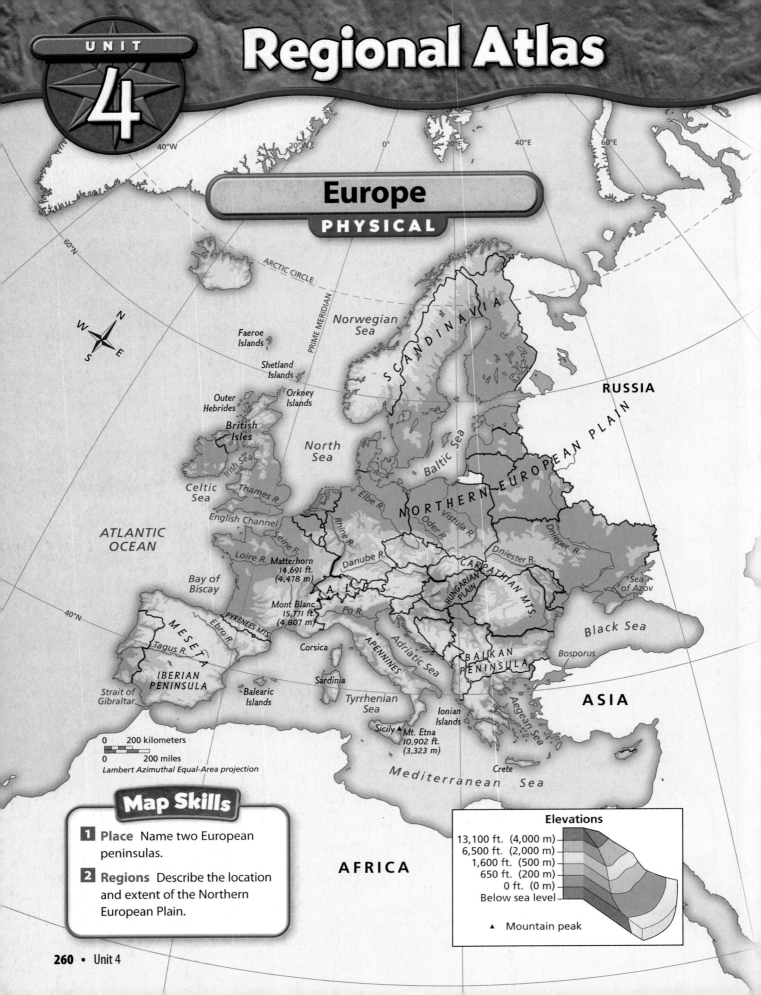
Europe
PHYSICAL

40°W   20°W   0°   20°E   40°E   60°E

ARCTIC CIRCLE

PRIME MERIDIAN

60°N

Norwegian
Sea

Faeroe
Islands

Shetland
Islands

Outer
Hebrides

Orkney
Islands

British
Isles

North
Sea

S C A N D I N A V I A

Baltic Sea

RUSSIA

N O R T H E R N   E U R O P E A N   P L A I N

ATLANTIC
OCEAN

Celtic
Sea

Irish Sea

Thames R.

English Channel

Elbe R.

Rhine R.

Seine R.

Oder R.

Vistula R.

Dniester R.

Dnieper R.

Sea
of Azov

Bay of
Biscay

Loire R.

Matterhorn
14,691 ft.
(4,478 m)

Danube R.

C A R P A T H I A N   M T S.

A L P S

Mont Blanc
15,771 ft.
(4,807 m)

Po R.

HUNGARIAN
PLAIN

Black Sea

40°N

M E S E T A

Ebro R.

PYRENEES MTS.

Corsica

APENNINES

Adriatic Sea

B A L K A N
P E N I N S U L A

Bosporus

ASIA

Tagus R.

IBERIAN
PENINSULA

Strait of
Gibraltar

Balearic
Islands

Sardinia

Tyrrhenian
Sea

Ionian
Islands

Aegean
Sea

Sicily ▲ Mt. Etna
10,902 ft.
(3,323 m)

Crete

Mediterranean   Sea

0   200 kilometers
0   200 miles
Lambert Azimuthal Equal-Area projection

Map Skills

1 **Place** Name two European peninsulas.

2 **Regions** Describe the location and extent of the Northern European Plain.

AFRICA

Elevations

13,100 ft. (4,000 m)
6,500 ft. (2,000 m)
1,600 ft. (500 m)
650 ft. (200 m)
0 ft. (0 m)
Below sea level

▲   Mountain peak

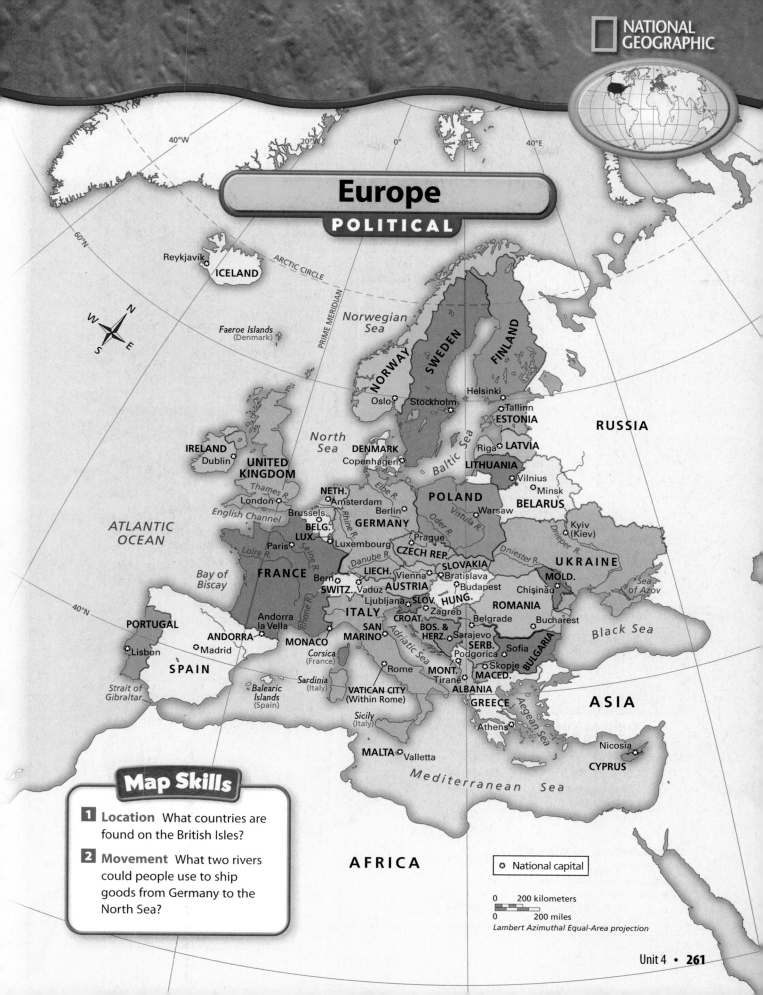

Europe
POLITICAL

Reykjavik ✪
ICELAND

ARCTIC CIRCLE

PRIME MERIDIAN

Faeroe Islands
(Denmark)

Norwegian Sea

NORWAY

SWEDEN

FINLAND

Helsinki ✪

Oslo ✪   Stockholm ✪   ✪ Tallinn

ESTONIA

RUSSIA

North Sea

IRELAND
Dublin ✪

UNITED KINGDOM

DENMARK
Copenhagen ✪

Riga ✪ **LATVIA**

Baltic Sea

LITHUANIA

Vilnius ✪

✪ Minsk

BELARUS

Thames R.

London ✪

English Channel

Brussels ✪

NETH.
✪ Amsterdam

Elbe R.

Berlin ✪

POLAND

Warsaw ✪

Vistula R.

Oder R.

Kyiv ✪
(Kiev)

BELG.
LUX.

Rhine R.

GERMANY

Prague ✪

Dnieper R.

Paris ✪

Seine R.

✪ Luxembourg

CZECH REP.

UKRAINE

Loire R.

Danube R.

Dniester R.

SLOVAKIA

Bratislava ✪

MOLD.

ATLANTIC OCEAN

FRANCE

Rhone R.

Bern ✪

LIECH.

Vaduz ✪

SWITZ.

AUSTRIA

Vienna ✪

✪ Budapest

Chișinău ✪

Sea of Azov

Bay of Biscay

Ljubljana ✪

SLOV.

HUNG.

ROMANIA

Zagreb ✪

Belgrade ✪

✪ Bucharest

Black Sea

ITALY

CROAT.

Andorra la Vella ✪

SAN MARINO

BOS. & HERZ.

Sarajevo ✪

SERB.

PORTUGAL

ANDORRA ✪

MONACO

Corsica (France)

Podgorica ✪

Sofia ✪

BULGARIA

Lisbon ✪

✪ Madrid

Rome ✪

Adriatic Sea

MONT.

✪ Skopje

MACED.

SPAIN

Sardinia (Italy)

VATICAN CITY
(Within Rome)

Tirane ✪

ALBANIA

Strait of Gibraltar

Balearic Islands (Spain)

Aegean Sea

GREECE

ASIA

Nicosia ✪

CYPRUS

Sicily (Italy)

Athens ✪

MALTA ✪ Valletta

Mediterranean Sea

AFRICA

Map Skills

1 **Location** What countries are found on the British Isles?

2 **Movement** What two rivers could people use to ship goods from Germany to the North Sea?

✪ National capital

0   200 kilometers
0   200 miles
Lambert Azimuthal Equal-Area projection

Europe
POPULATION DENSITY

40°W · 20°W · 0° · 20°E · 40°E · 60°E

60°N

ARCTIC CIRCLE

PRIME MERIDIAN

Norwegian Sea

RUSSIA

Helsinki

Stockholm

Glasgow

North Sea

Copenhagen

Baltic Sea

Minsk

Dublin

Manchester

Birmingham

London

Amsterdam

Rotterdam

Hamburg

Berlin

Warsaw

ATLANTIC OCEAN

Lille

Brussels

Prague

Kyiv (Kiev)

Kharkiv

Paris

Dnipropetrovs'k

Bay of Biscay

Munich

Vienna

Budapest

Odesa

Lyon

Zurich

Milan

Turin

Belgrade

Bucharest

Black Sea

Porto

40°N

Madrid

Marseille

Sofia

Barcelona

Rome

ASIA

Lisbon

Naples

Strait of Gibraltar

Athens

Aegean Sea

Mediterranean Sea

AFRICA

POPULATION

Per sq. mi.	Per sq. km
1,300 and over	500 and over
260–1,299	100–499
65–259	25–99
25–64	10–24
1–24	1–9
Less than 1	Less than 1
Uninhabited	Uninhabited

Cities
(Statistics reflect metropolitan areas.)

■ Over 5,000,000

□ 2,000,000–5,000,000

⊙ 1,250,000–2,000,000

0   200 kilometers

0   200 miles

Lambert Azimuthal Equal-Area projection

Map Skills

1 Regions Which areas are the most densely populated?

2 Location Why do you think Scandinavia is less densely populated than the rest of northern Europe?

Europe
ECONOMIC RESOURCES

Land Use
- Commercial farming
- Subsistence farming
- Manufacturing and trade
- Nomadic herding
- Livestock raising
- Commercial fishing
- Little or no activity

ICELAND
ARCTIC CIRCLE
Norwegian Sea
NORWAY
SWEDEN
FINLAND
RUSSIA
North Sea
UNITED KINGDOM
IRELAND
DENMARK
ESTONIA
LATVIA
LITHUANIA
Baltic Sea
ATLANTIC OCEAN
English Channel
NETH.
BELG.
GERMANY
POLAND
BELARUS
LUX.
CZECH REP.
UKRAINE
FRANCE
LIECH.
SWITZ.
AUSTRIA
SLOVAKIA
HUNGARY
MOLD.
Bay of Biscay
MONACO
SLOV.
ROMANIA
PORTUGAL
ANDORRA
SAN MARINO
CROAT.
BOS. & HERZ.
SERB.
BULGARIA
Black Sea
SPAIN
ITALY
MONT.
MACED.
ALBANIA
ASIA
Strait of Gibraltar
GREECE
Aegean Sea
MALTA
CYPRUS
Mediterranean Sea
AFRICA

0   200 kilometers
0   200 miles
Lambert Azimuthal Equal-Area projection

Map Skills

1 Regions What natural resources are found in the North Sea?

2 Place How is most of the land in Spain used?

Resources
- Bauxite
- Chrome
- Coal
- Cobalt
- Copper
- Iron ore
- Lead
- Manganese
- Natural gas
- Petroleum
- Silver
- Tin
- Zinc

Regional Atlas

Europe

Country and Capital	Literacy Rate	Population and Density	Land Area	Life Expectancy (Years)	GDP* Per Capita (U.S. dollars)	Television Sets (per 1,000 people)	Flag and Language
Tiranë **ALBANIA**	86.5%	3,200,000 286 per sq. mi. 111 per sq. km	11,100 sq. mi. 28,749 sq. km	74	$4,900	146	Albanian
ANDORRA Andorra la Vella	100%	100,000 426 per sq. mi. 222 per sq. km	174 sq. mi. 451 sq. km	—	$26,800	440	Catalan
Vienna **AUSTRIA**	98%	8,200,000 252 per sq. mi. 98 per sq. km	32,378 sq. mi. 83,859 sq. km	79	$31,300	526	German
Minsk **BELARUS**	99.6%	9,800,000 122 per sq. mi. 47 per sq. km	80,154 sq. mi. 207,598 sq. km	69	$6,800	331	Belarusian
Brussels **BELGIUM**	98%	10,500,000 887 per sq. mi. 344 per sq. km	11,787 sq. mi. 30,528 sq. km	79	$30,600	532	Dutch, French, German
BOSNIA AND HERZEGOVINA Sarajevo	—	3,800,000 195 per sq. mi. 74 per sq. km	19,741 sq. mi. 51,129 sq. km	74	$6,500	112	Bosnian
BULGARIA Sofia	98.6%	7,700,000 181 per sq. mi. 69 per sq. km	42,822 sq. mi. 110,908 sq. km	72	$8,200	429	Bulgarian
Zagreb **CROATIA**	98.5%	4,400,000 203 per sq. mi. 78 per sq. km	21,830 sq. mi. 56,539 sq. km	75	$11,200	286	Croatian
UNITED STATES Washington, D.C.	97%	296,500,000 80 per sq. mi. 31 per sq. km	3,717,796 sq. mi. 9,629,047 sq. km	78	$40,100	844	English

*Gross Domestic Product

Countries and flags not drawn to scale

Europe

Country and Capital	Literacy Rate	Population and Density	Land Area	Life Expectancy (Years)	GDP* Per Capita (U.S. dollars)	Television Sets (per 1,000 people)	Flag and Language
CYPRUS Nicosia	97.6%	1,000,000 270 per sq. mi. 108 per sq. km	3,571 sq. mi. 9,249 sq. km	77	$20,300	154	Greek
Prague **CZECH REPUBLIC**	99.9%	10,200,000 335 per sq. mi. 129 per sq. km	30,448 sq. mi. 78,860 sq. km	75	$16,800	487	Czech
DENMARK Copenhagen	100%	5,400,000 326 per sq. mi. 125 per sq. km	16,637 sq. mi. 43,090 sq. km	77	$32,200	776	Danish
Tallinn **ESTONIA**	99.8%	1,300,000 77 per sq. mi. 29 per sq. km	17,413 sq. mi. 45,099 sq. km	72	$14,300	567	Estonian
FINLAND Helsinki	100%	5,200,000 40 per sq. mi. 15 per sq. km	130,560 sq. mi. 338,149 sq. km	79	$29,000	643	Finnish, Swedish
Paris **FRANCE**	99%	60,700,000 285 per sq. mi. 110 per sq. km	212,934 sq. mi. 551,497 sq. km	80	$28,700	620	French
Berlin **GERMANY**	99%	82,500,000 598 per sq. mi. 231 per sq. km	137,830 sq. mi. 356,978 sq. km	79	$28,700	581	German
GREECE Athens	97.5%	11,100,000 218 per sq. mi. 84 per sq. km	50,950 sq. mi. 131,960 sq. km	76	$21,300	480	Greek
UNITED STATES Washington, D.C.	97%	296,500,000 80 per sq. mi. 31 per sq. km	3,717,796 sq. mi. 9,629,047 sq. km	78	$40,100	844	English

Sources: *CIA World Factbook,* 2005; Population Reference Bureau, *World Population Data Sheet,* 2005.

For more country facts, go to the **Nations of the World Databank** at <u>glencoe.com</u>.

Regional Atlas

Europe

Country and Capital	Literacy Rate	Population and Density	Land Area	Life Expectancy (Years)	GDP* Per Capita (U.S. dollars)	Television Sets (per 1,000 people)	Flag and Language
Budapest **HUNGARY**	99.4%	10,100,000 281 per sq. mi. 109 per sq. km	35,919 sq. mi. 93,030 sq. km	68	$14,900	447	Hungarian
ICELAND Reykjavík	99.9%	300,000 8 per sq. mi. 3 per sq. km	39,768 sq. mi. 102,999 sq. km	81	$31,900	505	Icelandic
Dublin **IRELAND**	98%	4,100,000 151 per sq. mi. 58 per sq. km	27,135 sq. mi. 70,279 sq. km	78	$31,900	406	English, Irish
ITALY Rome	98.6%	58,700,000 505 per sq. mi. 195 per sq. km	116,320 sq. mi. 301,267 sq. km	77	$27,700	492	Italian
Riga **LATVIA**	99.8%	2,300,000 92 per sq. mi. 36 per sq. km	24,942 sq. mi. 64,599 sq. km	72	$11,500	757	Latvian
LIECHTENSTEIN Vaduz	100%	40,000 645 per sq. mi. 248 per sq. km	62 sq. mi. 161 sq. km	80	$25,000	469	German
LITHUANIA Vilnius	99.6%	3,400,000 135 per sq. mi. 52 per sq. km	25,174 sq. mi. 65,200 sq. km	72	$12,500	422	Lithuanian
LUXEMBOURG Luxembourg	100%	500,000 501 per sq. mi. 193 per sq. km	999 sq. mi. 2,587 sq. km	78	$58,900	599	Luxembourgish, German, French
UNITED STATES Washington, D.C.	97%	296,500,000 80 per sq. mi. 31 per sq. km	3,717,796 sq. mi. 9,629,047 sq. km	78	$40,100	844	English

*Gross Domestic Product

Countries and flags not drawn to scale

Europe

Country and Capital	Literacy Rate	Population and Density	Land Area	Life Expectancy (Years)	GDP* Per Capita (U.S. dollars)	Television Sets (per 1,000 people)	Flag and Language
Skopje **MACEDONIA**	—	2,000,000 201 per sq. mi. 78 per sq. km	9,927 sq. mi. 25,711 sq. km	71	$7,100	273	Macedonian
MALTA Valletta	92.8%	400,000 3,278 per sq. mi. 1,246 per sq. km	124 sq. mi. 321 sq. km	79	$18,200	549	Maltese, English
MOLDOVA Chișinău	99.1%	4,200,000 323 per sq. mi. 125 per sq. km	13,012 sq. mi. 33,701 sq. km	65	$1,900	297	Moldovan
MONACO Monaco	99%	30,000 30,000 per sq. mi. 11,538 per sq. km	1 sq. mi. 2.6 sq. km	—	$27,000	758	French
MONTENEGRO Podgorica	97%	650,000 122 per sq. mi. 47 per sq. km	5,333 sq. mi. 13,812 sq. km	73	$2,200	277	Montenegrin, Serbian, Albanian
Amsterdam **NETHERLANDS**	99%	16,400,000 1,023 per sq. mi. 395 per sq. km	13,082 sq. mi. 33,883 sq. km	79	$29,500	540	Dutch
NORWAY Oslo	100%	4,600,000 37 per sq. mi. 14 per sq. km	125,050 sq. mi. 323,878 sq. km	80	$40,000	653	Norwegian
Warsaw **POLAND**	99.8%	38,200,000 306 per sq. mi. 118 per sq. km	124,807 sq. mi. 323,249 sq. km	71	$12,000	387	Polish
UNITED STATES Washington, D.C.	97%	296,500,000 80 per sq. mi. 31 per sq. km	3,717,796 sq. mi. 9,629,047 sq. km	78	$40,100	844	English

Sources: *CIA World Factbook,* 2005; Population Reference Bureau, *World Population Data Sheet,* 2005.

For more country facts, go to the **Nations of the World Databank** at glencoe.com.

Regional Atlas

Europe

Country and Capital	Literacy Rate	Population and Density	Land Area	Life Expectancy (Years)	GDP* Per Capita (U.S. dollars)	Television Sets (per 1,000 people)	Flag and Language
PORTUGAL Lisbon	93%	10,600,000 298 per sq. mi. 115 per sq. km	35,502 sq. mi. 91,951 sq. km	78	$17,900	567	Portuguese
ROMANIA Bucharest	98.4%	21,600,000 235 per sq. mi. 91 per sq. km	92,042 sq. mi. 238,388 sq. km	68	$7,700	312	Romanian
San Marino **SAN MARINO**	96%	30,000 1,304 per sq. mi. 500 per sq. km	23 sq. mi. 60 sq. km	81	$34,600	875	Italian
Belgrade **SERBIA**	96%	10,100,000 272 per sq. mi. 114 per sq. km	34,107 sq. mi. 88,337 sq. km	74	$2,200	277	Serbian
SLOVAKIA Bratislava	—	5,400,000 285 per sq. mi. 110 per sq. km	18,923 sq. mi. 49,010 sq. km	70	$14,500	418	Slovak
SLOVENIA Ljubljana	99.7%	2,000,000 256 per sq. mi. 99 per sq. km	7,819 sq. mi. 20,251 sq. km	77	$19,600	362	Slovenian
Madrid **SPAIN**	97.9%	43,500,000 225 per sq. mi. 87 per sq. km	193,363 sq. mi. 500,808 sq. km	80	$23,300	555	Spanish
SWEDEN Stockholm	99%	9,000,000 52 per sq. mi. 20 per sq. km	173,730 sq. mi. 449,959 sq. km	81	$28,400	551	Swedish
UNITED STATES Washington, D.C.	97%	296,500,000 80 per sq. mi. 31 per sq. km	3,717,796 sq. mi. 9,629,047 sq. km	78	$40,100	844	English

*Gross Domestic Product

Countries and flags not drawn to scale

Europe

Country and Capital	Literacy Rate	Population and Density	Land Area	Life Expectancy (Years)	GDP* Per Capita (U.S. dollars)	Television Sets (per 1,000 people)	Flag and Language
Bern **SWITZERLAND**	96%	7,400,000 464 per sq. mi. 179 per sq. km	15,942 sq. mi. 41,290 sq. km	80	$33,800	457	German, French, Italian
Kyiv (Kiev) **UKRAINE**	93%	47,100,000 202 per sq. mi. 70 per sq. km	233,089 sq. mi. 603,698 sq. km	63	$6,300	433	Ukrainian
UNITED KINGDOM London	—	60,100,000 636 per sq. mi. 245 per sq. km	94,548 sq. mi. 244,878 sq. km	78	$29,600	661	English
VATICAN CITY	99.7%	1,000 1,000 per sq. mi. 385 per sq. km	1 sq. mi. 2.6 sq. km	—	—	—	Italian, Latin
UNITED STATES Washington, D.C.	97%	296,500,000 80 per sq. mi. 31 per sq. km	3,717,796 sq. mi. 9,629,047 sq. km	78	$40,100	844	English

Sources: *CIA World Factbook,* 2005; Population Reference Bureau, *World Population Data Sheet,* 2005.

For more country facts, go to the **Nations of the World Databank** at glencoe.com.

▼ L'Arc de Triomphe, Paris, France

Making Inferences

① Learn It!

It is impossible for authors to write every detail about a topic in a textbook. Because of this, good readers must make inferences to help them understand what they are reading. To infer means to evaluate information and form a conclusion.

- Read the paragraph below.
- Think about what you already know about the topic.
- Then, look for clues that might explain what is happening in the passage even though it might not be stated.
- What inference can you make about Napoleon's skill as a military leader?

Clues

> A brilliant military leader named Napoleon Bonaparte gained power and made himself emperor. Napoleon was a small man with big ambitions. His armies conquered much of Europe, until several countries united to defeat him in 1815.
>
> —*from page 301*

Use the diagram below to help you make an inference about Napoleon's skill as a military leader.

What you already know:
What traits must brilliant military leaders have?

Clues in the text:
• Napoleon was able to gain power and lead armies to conquer much of Europe.
• The word *several* hints that it took many European countries to defeat him.

Inference:
Napoleon must have been a skillful military leader.

Reading Tip

Making inferences is an everyday part of life. For example, if you look at the sky and see dark clouds, you may infer that it is going to rain. As you read, use the facts in the text to make inferences by thinking beyond the words on the page.

2 Practice It!

Read the following paragraph from this unit.
- Draw a diagram like the one shown below.
- Write what you know about the United Kingdom's constitutional monarchy, along with facts from the text.
- Make an inference about the power of the king or queen in the United Kingdom.

Read to Write Activity

In Chapter 11, Section 1, read the paragraphs titled "Industry and Conflict." Then take notes about the Industrial Revolution. Write a statement in which you make an inference about what life was like for a teenager during the Industrial Revolution.

The government of the United Kingdom is a constitutional monarchy. A king or queen serves as head of state and takes part in ceremonies, but elected officials actively run the government.

—*from page 322*

What you already know:

Inference:

Clues in the text:

▲ Queen Elizabeth II of the United Kingdom and members of the royal family

3 Apply It!

For each chapter in this unit choose a topic, and create a diagram like the one above. Write related information that you already know, along with facts from the text, in the diagrams. Make inferences using this information. Read your facts to a partner, and ask your partner to make inferences from them. Are your inferences the same?

Physical Geography of Europe

Essential Question

Regions Europe's landforms include high, snowcapped mountains and broad, fertile plains that are good for farming. Europe might be most influenced, however, by its nearness to water. A number of oceans and seas border Europe's countries. Europe also has many important rivers. How do people use waterways?

BIG Ideas

◄ Bridges span the Vltava River in Prague, Czech Republic.

Section 1: Physical Features

BIG IDEA Geographic factors influence where people settle. Europe has a variety of landforms and plentiful natural resources that have attracted a large population. Most people live on Europe's plains, where industry and agriculture flourish. Such successes, however, have contributed to environmental problems in the region.

Section 2: Climate Regions

BIG IDEA The physical environment affects how people live. Although Europe is located relatively far north, much of the region has a mild climate that is ideal for farming and development. However, many Europeans are concerned that the climate is warming, which may have dangerous consequences.

FOLDABLES™
Study Organizer

Summarizing Information Make this Foldable to help you gather notes and summarize information about Europe's physical features, climate, and environmental issues.

Step 1 Mark the midpoint of the side edge of a sheet of paper.

Step 2 Fold the top and bottom of the paper into the middle to make a shutter fold.

Step 3 Fold the paper in half from side to side.

Step 4 Open and cut along the inside fold lines to form four tabs.

Step 5 Label the tabs as shown.

Reading and Writing As you read the chapter, fill in the Foldable. When you have finished the chapter, use your Foldable to write a list of the 10 most important facts about Europe's physical geography.

Social Studies ONLINE

To preview Chapter 10, go to **glencoe.com**.

Guide to Reading

BIG Idea
Geographic factors influence where people settle.

Content Vocabulary
- landlocked *(p. 275)*
- pass *(p. 277)*
- navigable *(p. 277)*

Academic Vocabulary
- access *(p. 275)*
- affect *(p. 275)*
- impact *(p. 279)*

Reading Strategy

Organizing Information Use a diagram like the one below to organize key facts about each of Europe's major landforms (Islands and Peninsulas, Plains, Mountains and Highlands).

Europe's Landforms

Physical Features

Picture This Snowdrifts? No, these snow-like mounds were formed about 1,500 years ago during a volcanic eruption on the island of Lipari, off the coast of Sicily, in Italy. The mounds are made of pumice, a stone formed from the cooling of lava, which rained down on the island during the eruption. Today the volcano is quiet, but Lipari hums with the sounds of open-pit pumice mines. Pumice is used to polish smooth surfaces. The stone is often used to give "stonewashed" jeans their worn look. In Section 1, you will learn about the different European landforms and the effect they have had on people living in the region.

▼ **Walking on the island of Lipari**

Landforms and Waterways

Main Idea Europe's landforms and waterways have greatly influenced where and how Europeans live.

Geography and You What landforms can you find near your community? In Europe you would find impressive mountains, shimmering seas, and rolling farmland. Read to learn more about the variety of landscapes on this small continent.

When you look at a map of Europe, one of the first things you notice is that the continent is not a separate landmass. Instead, Europe and Asia share a common landmass called Eurasia. Europe extends to the west, from Asia to the Atlantic Ocean.

Europe's long coastline is framed by the Atlantic and by several seas. These include the Baltic, North, Mediterranean, and Black Seas. Most land in Europe lies within 300 miles (483 km) of a coast. Only a few countries are **landlocked,** meaning they do not border an ocean or a sea. Relatively long rivers, however, do give these inland countries **access** to coastal ports.

This nearness to water has shaped the lives and history of Europe's people. Europeans developed skills in sailing and fishing, which encouraged trade and helped Europe's economy grow. The closeness to the sea also allowed people to move easily between Europe and other continents. As a result, European culture has both influenced and been influenced by the cultures of Asia, Africa, and the Americas.

Peninsulas and Islands

Look at the physical map in this unit's Regional Atlas. You can see that Europe is a huge peninsula, with many smaller peninsulas branching out from it. Europe also includes many islands. Some of the major islands are Great Britain, Ireland, and Iceland in the Atlantic Ocean. Other large islands, such as Sicily, Crete, and Cyprus, are located in the Mediterranean Sea.

The large number of peninsulas and islands has **affected** Europe's history. Groups of people were separated by Europe's many seas, rivers, and mountains. As a result, many different cultures developed. Today, Europe is home to more than 40 independent countries. That is a remarkable number of neighbors squeezed together on a relatively small continent.

Plains

Europe's major landform is the Northern European Plain. This large lowland area stretches like a rumpled blanket across the northern half of mainland Europe.

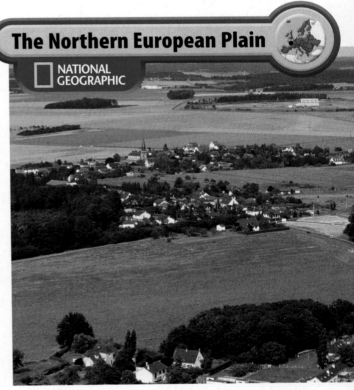

The Northern European Plain

NATIONAL GEOGRAPHIC

▲ Rich farmland in the region of Normandy in France is part of the Northern European Plain. **Regions Describe the Northern European Plain.**

It has rolling land with isolated hills. The Northern European Plain reaches from Belarus and Ukraine westward to France and also extends to the British Isles.

The plain's rich soil makes its farms highly productive. Farmers grow a great variety of grains, fruits, and vegetables. Some farmers raise dairy cattle to produce milk used in making cheese and other dairy products.

The Northern European Plain also has important energy and mineral resources. Deposits of coal, iron ore, and other minerals lie underground. These resources aided Europe's industrial growth.

Because the plain is so rich agriculturally and industrially, it is densely populated. Today, most of Europe's people live in this area. The landscape is dotted with villages, towns, and cities, including the busy capital cities of Warsaw, Berlin, Paris, and London.

Europe has other lowlands in addition to the Northern European Plain. For example, narrow plains rim the coasts of southern Europe. Two larger lowlands in the east—the Hungarian Plain, east of the Alps, and the Ukrainian Steppe, a broad, grassy plain north of the Black Sea—have rich soil that supports farming.

Mountains and Highlands

Highlands mark the northern border of the Northern European Plain. Steeper mountains lie south of the plain. Europe's highest mountain ranges form the Alpine Mountain System, which stretches from Spain to the Balkan Peninsula. The system takes its name from the Alps of south-central Europe. It also includes the Pyrenees, which lie between France and Spain, and the Carpathians, in east-central Europe.

The region's highest peak is Mont Blanc in the Alps of France. It rises to 15,771 feet (4,807 m). Most of Europe's mountains, however, are not very tall compared to those of Asia.

NATIONAL GEOGRAPHIC

The Alps

▲ Rugged beauty and good skiing conditions make the Alps a popular tourist destination. *Place* **What mountain ranges form the Alpine Mountain System?**

Like some of Europe's other landforms, mountains have helped isolate certain countries and peoples. Switzerland, for example, is located high in the Alps. While European wars have raged around it, the country has remained free from conflict and invasion for many centuries. Europe's mountains have never completely blocked movement though. **Passes,** or low areas between mountains, allow the movement of people and goods.

Less dramatic than Europe's mountains are three older highland areas that have eroded over time. Uplands in the northwest extend from Sweden through northern Great Britain to Iceland. Stripped of soil by glaciers, the land here is poor for farming, so many people raise sheep. A second highland area, the Central Uplands, contains much of Europe's coal. The area reaches from southern Poland to France. The third highland, the Meseta in Spain, is a plateau on which people grow grains and raise livestock.

Waterways

In addition to plains and mountains, Europe has an abundance of rivers, lakes, and other waterways. Europe's major rivers flow from inland highlands and mountains into the oceans and seas surrounding the region.

Many European rivers are **navigable,** or wide and deep enough for ships to use. People and goods can sail easily from inland areas to the open sea and, from there, around the world. The Danube and the Rhine, two of Europe's longest rivers, are important for transporting goods. Canals link these rivers, further improving Europe's water transportation network.

Rivers carry rich soil downstream, creating productive farmland along their banks

NATIONAL GEOGRAPHIC

Hydroelectric Power

This hydroelectric power plant is located on the Danube River between Austria and Germany. **Human-Environment Interaction** How do Europeans use their rivers?

and at their mouths. For this reason, river valleys have long been home to large numbers of people. Today, fast-flowing rivers are also used to generate electricity to support these large populations.

Lakes cover only a small fraction of Europe. They are valuable for recreation, though, and for tourism. Most lakes are located on the Northern European Plain and in Scandinavia. The highland lakes in northern Great Britain and the Alps, however, are among the most beautiful and frequently visited. People flock to these lakes to boat, fish, swim, and appreciate nature.

Reading Check **Explaining** How have Europeans improved their water transportation network?

Social Studies ONLINE
Student Web Activity Visit glencoe.com and complete the Chapter 10 Web Activity about the Northern European Plain.

Europe's Resources

Main Idea **Europe has valuable resources that strengthen its economy.**

Geography and You Think of the products that you use every day. What are these products made of? As you read, think about how Europe's natural resources benefit people around the world.

Europe is a leader in the world economy. Part of this success comes from Europe's rich supply of natural resources.

Energy Resources

Coal has been a major energy source in Europe for many decades. By burning coal, Europeans fueled the development of modern industry in the 1800s. Today, almost half of the world's coal comes from Europe. Coal mining provides jobs for people from the United Kingdom in the west to Ukraine, Poland, and the Czech Republic in the east.

Petroleum and natural gas are other important energy resources found in Europe. The region's most productive oil fields lie beneath the North Sea, in areas controlled by the United Kingdom and Norway. To discourage dependence on oil, though, European governments tax gasoline heavily. Drivers in Europe pay some of the highest gasoline prices in the world.

Europe also relies on several "clean" energy sources that cause less pollution than burning coal or oil. In the highlands and mountains, swift-flowing rivers are used to create hydroelectric power. Europeans also make use of the wind's power. Germany, Spain, and Denmark are leaders in building wind farms, which use large turbines to create electricity from the wind.

Other Natural Resources

Besides energy resources, Europe has many other important natural resources. European mines produce about one-third of the world's iron ore, which is used in making steel. Ukraine has deposits of manganese, another important ingredient of steel. The United Kingdom exports a special clay used to make fine china dishes. Marble from Italy and granite from Norway and Sweden provide fine building materials. Of course, stone has always been used for building. Many European towns have narrow cobblestone streets and quaint stone houses that are centuries old.

Forests once covered a large part of Europe. Long ago, however, people cleared the land for farms and used much of the wood for building and for fuel. Today, only small pockets of forest remain. Sweden and Finland have the most forestland and produce the most lumber.

Wind Farm in Spain

NATIONAL GEOGRAPHIC

▲ Europe produces more electricity from wind turbines than any other world region. *Human-Environment Interaction* Why is wind power considered a "clean" energy source?

Environmental Issues

Main Idea Europe's plentiful resources have helped its economy, but environmental problems are a growing concern.

Geography and You Do you recycle at home and try to use energy wisely? As you read, see how Europeans are taking similar steps to protect their resources.

NATIONAL GEOGRAPHIC
Air Pollution

Air pollution from industrial plants, such as this one in Wales, can destroy forests in Poland (inset). *Human-Environment Interaction* What is acid rain, and why is it harmful?

By taking advantage of its natural resources, Europe has become an economic powerhouse. The **impact** on the environment, however, has sometimes been harmful. For instance, in deforested areas of Southern Europe, tree roots no longer hold the soil in place. Valuable topsoil can be washed away.

Air Pollution and Acid Rain

Industrial growth in Europe has also hurt the environment—and created health risks. For example, car exhaust and smoke from burning oil and coal create air pollution. This pollution causes breathing problems, eye irritation, and lung disease.

Air pollution has another serious effect. When pollutant particles mix with precipitation, acid rain falls to Earth. Acid rain can make trees vulnerable to attack from insects and disease. Forests in eastern Europe are especially threatened. In that region, lignite coal is a major fuel source because it is cheap. It burns poorly, however, and pollutes heavily. The resulting acid rain has destroyed many forest areas in Hungary, Poland, the Czech Republic, and Slovakia.

Acid rain falls on Europe's waterways as well as its forests. As acids build up in lakes, rivers, and streams, fish and other wildlife are poisoned and die.

Fertile soil is another valuable resource, providing Europe with some of the best farmland on the planet. European farmers grow large amounts of grains, including nearly all of the world's rye, most of its oats, and nearly half of its wheat. Europe also produces more potatoes than any other region in the world.

The waters around Europe contain yet another resource—fish. From the Mediterranean Sea to the North Atlantic, Europeans catch salmon, cod, and other varieties of fish. Fishing is important to the economy, but many Europeans also eat a lot of fish and value its health benefits.

✓ **Reading Check** **Describing** Where are Europe's most productive oil fields?

Acid rain is also a problem for Europe's historic buildings. The famous Tower of London, Germany's Cologne Cathedral, and ancient buildings and monuments dating from Greek and Roman times all show damage from acid deposits.

Water Pollution

Water pollution is another challenge for Europe. Sewage, garbage, and industrial waste have all been dumped into the region's seas, lakes, and rivers. As populations and tourism have increased, the problem has worsened.

Runoff from farms is also a problem for Europe's waters. Runoff is precipitation that flows over the ground, often picking up pesticides and fertilizers along the way. When chemicals from runoff enter a river, they encourage the growth of algae. Algae rob the river of so much oxygen that fish cannot survive. Runoff spilling into the Danube River, for example, has killed much of its marine life.

Finding Solutions

European leaders are trying to solve environmental problems in a number of ways. Many are working to prevent air pollution and acid rain by limiting the amount of chemicals that factories and cars can release into the air. Norway and Sweden are adding lime to their lakes. This substance stops the damage caused by acid rain and allows fish to multiply again.

Europeans are also making their lakes and rivers cleaner by treating waste and sewage. In addition, some countries encourage farmers to use less fertilizer to reduce damaging runoff.

Recycling is another strategy for protecting the environment. Europeans now recycle more paper, plastics, and glass than in the past. This saves energy that would otherwise be needed to produce these goods and cuts down on wastes.

✔ **Reading Check** **Explaining** How does runoff contribute to water pollution?

Section ✦ Review

Social Studies ONLINE
Study Central™ To review this section, go to glencoe.com.

Vocabulary

1. **Explain** the significance of:
   a. landlocked   **c.** navigable
   b. pass

Main Ideas

2. **Organizing Information** Use a diagram like the one below to explain the importance of rivers in Europe.

Europe's Rivers

3. **Analyzing** Why are Europe's clean energy sources important to the region?

4. **Explaining** Why and where is acid rain especially a problem?

Critical Thinking

5. **BIG Idea** Which resources helped industry and farming develop in Europe?

6. **Challenge** Describe how Europe's landforms and bodies of water influenced where people settled.

Writing About Geography

7. **Expository Writing** Write a paragraph explaining which physical feature you think has most helped Europe's economy to prosper.

Disaster at Chernobyl

In the modern world, we depend on technology to survive. What happens when technology goes wrong?

The Accident On April 26, 1986, the world saw its worst nuclear disaster. That day, a reactor at the Chernobyl nuclear power plant in Ukraine exploded. Dangerous radioactive material shot into the sky. The explosion also caused a fire that raged for 10 days, pouring out more radioactive dust and ash. During that time, radioactive material—called fallout—fell to the Earth over large parts of Ukraine and Belarus, as well as other parts of Europe.

The Impact Fewer than a hundred people died from the high levels of radiation that resulted from the explosion and fire. About 4,000 more, however, are expected to die from cancers caused by the accident. Fortunately, these numbers are far below what had originally been feared.

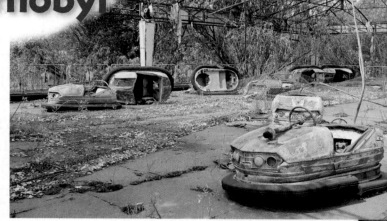

▲ **Abandoned amusement park, Pripyat', Russia**

Nevertheless, more than 20 years after the accident, its effects are ongoing. Around the area contaminated by fallout, officials created an exclusion zone of about 1,545 square miles (4,002 sq. km). People are prohibited from living within this zone. More than 350,000 people were forced to leave their homes following the accident. The disaster scarred the land as well. More than 1.8 million acres (728,435 hectares) of farmland and 1.7 million acres (687,966 hectares) of forest were abandoned because of contamination from fallout.

Meanwhile, a threat remains at Chernobyl. A protective concrete shell, built around the reactor to contain the contamination, could collapse. Also, rainwater leaks into the shell. When the water seeps back into the ground, it carries radioactive material with it, further poisoning the land.

NATIONAL GEOGRAPHIC
Chernobyl Area

29°E   30°E   31°E   32°E

52°N

BELARUS

Pripyat'

Chernobyl Nuclear Power Plant

51°N

U K R A I N E

0   60 kilometers
0   60 miles
Lambert Azimuthal Equal-Area projection

- –·– Present-day exclusion zone
- — Original evacuation zone
- — National border

Think About It

1. **Movement** How many people were forced to leave the contaminated area?
2. **Human-Environment Interaction** What effect did the accident have on the environment?

Guide to Reading

BIG Idea

The physical environment affects how people live.

Content Vocabulary

• deciduous *(p. 285)*
• coniferous *(p. 285)*
• mistral *(p. 287)*
• sirocco *(p. 287)*

Academic Vocabulary

• major *(p. 283)*
• feature *(p. 284)*

Reading Strategy

Categorizing Information Use a chart like the one below to describe Europe's climate zones.

Climate Zone	Characteristics
1.	1.
2.	2.
3.	3.
4.	4.

Climate Regions

Picture This These carefully balanced baskets will carry grapes that are handpicked in the Côte d'Or ("Golden Hill") region of Burgundy, France. The region has been producing wine since A.D. 900, and the grape harvest is vital to the local economy. Because of this, and because grapes are highly sensitive to the climate, big changes in temperature are always cause for concern. Read this section to find out about climate conditions in Europe and the concern over the warming trend.

▼ **Carrying grape baskets in Burgundy, France**

Wind and Water

Main Idea Wind patterns and water currents shape Europe's climate.

Geography and You Doesn't a cool breeze feel great on a hot day? Read to learn how winds are helpful to Europe too.

Look at the physical map of the world in the Reference Atlas. Because Europe is farther north than the United States, you might expect Europe's climate to be colder than ours. In fact, much of Europe enjoys a milder climate. Why?

As **Figure 1** shows, the North Atlantic Current carries warm waters from the Gulf of Mexico toward Europe. Winds from the west pass over this water and carry more warmth to Europe. These prevailing winds, known as westerlies, are a **major** influence on warming the European climate.

Other wind patterns also affect the climate in parts of Europe. For example, warm winds from Africa contribute to the high temperatures in southern Europe. Blustery winter winds from Asia lower temperatures throughout much of eastern Europe.

The water surrounding Europe also affects the region's climate. Winds blowing off the water cool the hot land in the summer and warm the cold land in the winter. For this reason, coastal areas tend to have a more moderate climate than inland areas.

✓ **Reading Check** **Explaining** Why does northwestern Europe have a mild climate?

NATIONAL GEOGRAPHIC **Maps In Motion** See StudentWorks™ Plus or <u>glencoe.com</u>.

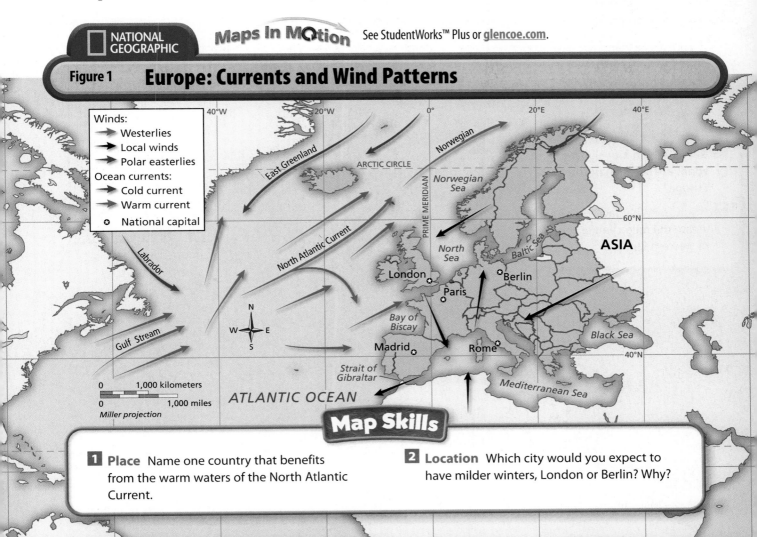

Figure 1 **Europe: Currents and Wind Patterns**

Map Skills

1 **Place** Name one country that benefits from the warm waters of the North Atlantic Current.

2 **Location** Which city would you expect to have milder winters, London or Berlin? Why?

Climate Zones

Main Idea Europe has eight climate zones, each with different vegetation.

Geography and You What is your ideal climate? Chances are, you can find it in Europe! Read to learn how Europe's climate varies from area to area.

Most of Europe falls into three main climate zones—marine west coast, humid continental, and Mediterranean. **Figure 2** also shows five other climate zones that appear in smaller areas—subarctic, tundra, highland, steppe, and humid subtropical.

Marine West Coast

Much of northwestern and central Europe has a marine west coast climate. This climate has two **features,** one of which is mild temperatures. The North Atlantic Current carries so much warmth that southern Iceland has mild temperatures, even though it is near the Arctic Circle. Because of the mild temperatures, this climate zone has surprisingly long growing seasons. In the United Kingdom, for example, farmers have a window of 250 or more days for planting and harvesting—nearly 60 more days than in eastern Canada—which is located at the same latitude.

NATIONAL GEOGRAPHIC

Figure 2   Europe: Climate Zones

Map Skills

1 Place Which four climate zones are found in northern Europe?

2 Regions What factors help create the mild climate zones of western Europe?

Dry
Steppe

Midlatitude
Mediterranean
Humid subtropical
Marine west coast
Humid continental

High latitude
Subarctic
Tundra
Highland (climate varies with elevation)
✪ National capital

Although temperatures stay mild, differences do exist across the region. In the north, summers are shorter and cooler. Also, the farther away you get from water, the wider the range of temperatures will be. For example, in the coastal city of Brest, France, a December day might be only 20 degrees cooler than a July day. However, in Strasbourg, France, which is more than 400 miles (644 km) from the Atlantic Ocean, the temperature can differ by 40 degrees between summer and winter.

The second feature of the marine west coast climate, besides mild temperatures, is abundant precipitation. This typically falls in autumn and early winter. Although the zone as a whole gets plenty of rain, certain mountainous areas stay dry because of the rain shadow effect. For example, the coastal area of Norway, on the western edge of highlands, receives a yearly average of 90 inches (229 cm) of precipitation. The eastern slopes of those same highlands receive only one-third that amount.

Forests thrive in much of Europe's marine west coast climate zone. Some forests consist of **deciduous** trees, which lose their leaves in the fall. **Coniferous** trees, also called evergreens, grow in cooler areas of the marine west coast climate zone.

NATIONAL GEOGRAPHIC

Figure 3   Europe: Natural Vegetation

Map Skills

1. **Location** What type of vegetation is found in the United Kingdom?

2. **Regions** How does Europe's climate affect the type of vegetation found there?

Legend:
- Temperate grassland
- Mediterranean scrub
- Deciduous forest
- Coniferous forest
- Mixed forest (deciduous and coniferous)
- Tundra
- Highland (vegetation varies with elevation)
- Ice cap
- National capital

They dominate the landscape in southern Norway, Sweden, and parts of eastern Europe.

Although forests no longer blanket the continent, many people still earn their living from forest-related industries. They cut timber and produce a huge array of products, from lumber and paper to charcoal and turpentine.

Humid Continental

Eastern Europe and some areas of northern Europe have a humid continental climate. Cool, dry winds from the Arctic and Asia give this zone cooler summers and colder winters than the marine west coast zone. The city of Minsk in Belarus does not get much warmer than 70°F (21°C) in July. By January, however, you would definitely need a warm jacket—the high temperature averages only 22°F (–6°C)!

Poland's Forests

NATIONAL GEOGRAPHIC

▲ Bialowieza National Park in eastern Poland contains deciduous and coniferous trees. The park is home to animals such as wolves, lynx, and bison. *Place* **What type of climate does Poland have?**

Because of drier winds, the humid continental zone gets less rain and snow than the marine west coast zone. Nonetheless, some low-lying areas are wet and marshy. This is because the precipitation that does fall can be slow to evaporate in the cool climate. The humid continental zone supports mixed forests of deciduous and evergreen trees. However, only evergreens grow farther north and in higher elevations.

Mediterranean

Europe's third major climate zone, the Mediterranean zone, includes much of southern Europe. With average high temperatures in July ranging from 83°F to 98°F (28°C to 37°C), Mediterranean summers are hot. They are also very dry. Many Mediterranean areas receive just a trace of rainfall during the summer.

Because of the heat, the pace of life seems to slow down in the summer. Many people take August vacations. Others take long midday lunches and relax at outdoor cafes for hours in the evening.

Winters in the Mediterranean zone are mild and wet. With temperatures in the 50s Fahrenheit (low teens Celsius), nobody worries about snow. Rainfall, however, averages 3 to 4 inches (7.6 to 10.2 cm) per month, so an umbrella comes in handy.

The mountains of southern Europe affect the Mediterranean climate zone. The Pyrenees and Alps block chilly northern winds from reaching Spain and Italy. Some mountains also create rain shadows. Winds coming over the mountains from the west bring more rain to the western slopes. The eastern side stays drier. The effect is dramatic in Spain, where the northwest region is cool, wet, and green. Inland Spain, on the other hand, is hot, dry, and brown.

In southern France, the lack of a mountain barrier allows a cold, dry wind to blow

Greek Herder

Herding goats and sheep is a common economic activity in areas with a Mediterranean climate. *Regions* **What types of vegetation grow in Europe's Mediterranean climate zone?**

northern reaches of these countries and in Iceland. The tundra is an area of vast tree-less plains near the North Pole. With cool summers that reach only about 40°F (4°C) and frigid winter temperatures that plunge as low as –25°F (–32°C), only low shrubs and mosses can grow in this region.

Because of Earth's tilt, the sun shines on the far north for up to 20 hours per day in late spring and early summer. As a result, the nights are extremely short. In the deep of winter, however, conditions are reversed. The days are short, and nights can last as long as 20 hours. Some people are so affected by the scarce light in winter that they lose energy and feel depressed.

Highland

The highland zone is found in the higher altitudes of the Alps and Carpathians where the climate is generally cool to cold. However, temperatures and precipitation vary greatly from place to place, depending on three factors—wind direction, orientation to the sun, and altitude. As an example, consider two peaks in the Swiss Alps—Säntis and Saint Gall. Säntis receives more than twice the precipitation of Saint Gall even though the two mountains are only 12 miles (19 km) apart. The difference is due to altitude—Säntis is about three times higher than Saint Gall.

Sturdy trees add color to the highland zone, but they grow only so far up the mountainsides. The point at which they stop growing is called the timberline. Above the timberline, where the sun barely warms the ground, only scrubby bushes and low-lying plants can survive.

Other Climate Zones

Europe's last two climate zones cover a relatively small part of the region. The steppe zone includes the southern part of Ukraine.

in from the north. This wind, the **mistral** (MIHS·truhl), occurs in winter and spring. It also creates waves, making southern France a popular site for windsurfing.

Countries in the Mediterranean climate zone are also affected by hot, dry winds from Africa to the south. In Italy, these winds are called **siroccos** (suh·RAH·kohs). They pick up moisture as they cross the Mediterranean, bringing uncomfortably humid conditions to southern Europe.

Because of the Mediterranean zone's low rainfall, plants that grow there must be drought resistant. Vegetation includes low-lying shrubs and grasses, as well as the olive trees and grapevines that the region is known for. Forests are rare, and stands of trees appear only on rainy mountainsides or along rivers.

Subarctic and Tundra

Farther north, Europe has two zones of extreme cold. The subarctic zone covers parts of Norway, Sweden, and Finland. Evergreens grow in this region at low altitudes. The tundra zone is found in the

Steppes are dry, treeless grasslands, much like prairies but with shorter grass. Here the climate is not dry enough to be classified as desert, but not wet enough for forests to flourish.

A small sliver of land north of the Adriatic Sea falls into the humid subtropical zone. This zone has hot, wet summers and mild, wet winters.

Climate Change

Most scientists agree that the world's climate is growing warmer. Average temperatures have been inching upward for several decades. Measurements and photos show that glaciers are steadily eroding. In 2003 western Europe suffered its worst heat wave since the Middle Ages.

People debate whether this global warming is just part of nature's cycle or is instead related to human activities. Many scientists, though, believe that burning fossil fuels, such as coal and oil, contributes to the greenhouse effect. Gases build up in the atmosphere and trap large amounts of warm air near Earth's surface.

People also debate what this warming means for the planet. Many European leaders are worried. They fear that melting glaciers will produce higher ocean levels that will flood low-lying areas, such as the Netherlands and coastal cities like Venice, Italy. Such flooding would affect millions of people.

As a result, European officials are taking action. They are trying to slow global warming by encouraging changes in energy use. Most European governments have signed the Kyoto Treaty. This is an international agreement to limit the output of greenhouse gases, but its terms are not yet fully in effect.

Reading Check **Explaining** How do mountains affect southern Europe's Mediterranean climate zone?

Section 2 Review

Social Studies ONLINE
Study Central™ To review this section, go to glencoe.com.

Vocabulary

1. **Explain** the meaning of *deciduous*, *coniferous*, *mistral*, and *sirocco* by using each term in a sentence.

Main Ideas

2. **Identifying** What factors affect Europe's climates?

3. **Summarizing** Using a diagram like the one below, identify each of Europe's climate zones and the vegetation found in each zone.

Europe's Climate Zones and Vegetation

Critical Thinking

4. **Comparing and Contrasting** How are Norway and Spain similar in climate? How are they different?

5. **BIG Idea** How does the North Atlantic Current affect farming in the marine west coast climate zone?

6. **Challenge** Describe how latitude and altitude affect climate and vegetation in Europe.

Writing About Geography

7. **Using Your FOLDABLES** Use your Foldable to write a paragraph comparing and contrasting two of Europe's climate zones.

Visual Summary

Landforms

- The Northern European Plain is a rich farming region and has a high population density.

- Mountains separate much of northern and southern Europe.

- Uplands regions are found in northwest and central Europe and in Spain.

Berlin, Germany, on the Northern European Plain

Waterways

- Waterways have had a major impact on Europe's population and ways of life.

- Rivers provide transportation, good soil for farming, and hydroelectric power.

European Resources

- Europe's energy resources include coal, petroleum, natural gas, and hydroelectric and wind power.

- In some areas, good soil promotes farming and dairy farming.

- Fishing is important to coastal Europe.

Fishers in Spain

Environmental Issues

- The European environment has been damaged by deforestation, pollution, and acid rain.

- Europeans are working to protect and improve their environment through recycling and limiting forms of chemical pollution.

Tulip harvest in the Netherlands

Climate Regions

- Europe's nearness to water and its wind patterns greatly affect its climates.

- Europe has eight main climate zones: marine west coast, humid continental, Mediterranean, subarctic, tundra, highland, steppe, and humid subtropical.

- Europeans are concerned about the negative effects of global warming.

Reindeer on Norwegian tundra

STANDARDIZED TEST PRACTICE

TEST-TAKING

> Eliminate answers that you know for certain are incorrect. Then choose the most likely answer from those remaining.

Reviewing Vocabulary

Directions: Choose the word(s) that best completes the sentence.

1. Europe has many _____ rivers—rivers that are deep and wide enough for ships to travel.

  A polluted

  B passable

  C navigable

  D deciduous

2. In Europe, _____, or low areas between mountains, have allowed the movement of people and goods.

  A ports

  B siroccos

  C runoffs

  D passes

3. Hot, dry winds that pick up moisture as they cross the Mediterranean Sea and bring uncomfortable humidity to southern Europe are called _____.

  A siroccos

  B the mistral

  C currents

  D El Niño

4. Evergreens, or _____ trees, grow in cooler areas of Europe's marine west coast climate zone.

  A palm

  B coniferous

  C deciduous

  D banyan

Reviewing Main Ideas

Directions: Choose the best answer for each question.

Section 1 *(pp. 274–280)*

5. Europeans developed skills in fishing, sailing, and trading because

  A much of Europe is landlocked.

  B most Europeans live close to a coast or a navigable river.

  C Europeans were more adventurous than other people.

  D Europeans did not like farming or manufacturing.

6. One of Europe's most important resources has been _____, which helped modern industry grow there in the 1800s.

  A clay

  B granite

  C soil

  D coal

Section 2 *(pp. 282–288)*

7. The _____ has a major warming effect on Europe's climate.

  A North Atlantic Current

  B Asian landmass

  C polar easterly

  D region's position on the Equator

8. Much of northwest and central Europe has a(n) _____ climate.

  A tundra

  B highland

  C marine west coast

  D equatorial

GO ON ➡

Critical Thinking

Directions: Choose the best answer for each question.

Base your answers to questions 9 and 10 on the bar graph below and your knowledge of Chapter 10.

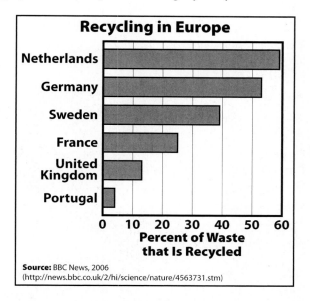

Recycling in Europe

Netherlands
Germany
Sweden
France
United Kingdom
Portugal

0 10 20 30 40 50 60
Percent of Waste that Is Recycled

Source: BBC News, 2006
(http://news.bbc.co.uk/2/hi/science/nature/4563731.stm)

9. Which two European countries recycle more than 50 percent of their waste?

A Sweden and Portugal

B Netherlands and Germany

C Sweden and the United Kingdom

D France and Germany

10. Based on the graph, which of the following statements is accurate?

A Most European countries recycle more than half their waste.

B The seven countries represented in the graph pollute more than any other European nations.

C The Netherlands relies more on recycling to handle waste than does France.

D The Netherlands produces more waste than the other six countries represented on the graph.

Document-Based Questions

Directions: Analyze the document and answer the short-answer questions that follow.

Eyewitness Account of Natalia Ivanovna Ivanova, Deputy Director, Vesnova Orphanage, Mogilev Oblast, Belarus:

> *It was terrible having to knock on the door or window in the middle of the night to tell the parents that their children should be evacuated the next morning. We said it was because of the radioactivity, which could have bad consequences for all of them. We arranged a place for everyone to gather to be put on buses. It was a dreadful sight.*
>
> —Natalia Ivanovna Ivanova,
> "Return to Chernobyl: 20 Years 20 Lives"

11. What did Natalia Ivanova have to do following the accident?

12. Describe Ivanova's reaction to the Chernobyl accident. How did she feel about the situation?

Extended Response

13. Write a short essay describing how Europe's successful use of its many resources has led to environmental problems in the region. Also describe what is being done to solve those problems.

STOP

Social Studies ONLINE

For additional test practice, use Self-Check Quizzes—Chapter 10 at **glencoe.com**.

Need Extra Help?													
If you missed question...	1	2	3	4	5	6	7	8	9	10	11	12	13
Go to page...	277	277	287	285	275	278	283	284	280	280	281	281	279

CHAPTER 11

History and Cultures of Europe

Essential Question

Regions Europe is rich in history and culture. Like the United States, most countries in Europe are industrialized and have high standards of living. Unlike the United States, however, the people of Europe do not share a common language and government. What forces have helped unify Europeans at different times?

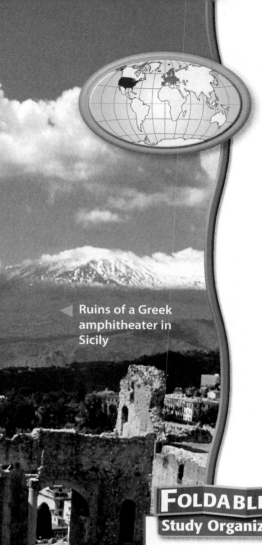

Ruins of a Greek amphitheater in Sicily

BIG Ideas

Section 1: History and Governments

BIG IDEA **The characteristics and movement of people impact physical and human systems.** Over the centuries, migrations and wars have brought different groups to power in Europe. As modern nations have taken the place of empires and kingdoms, ways of living and thinking have also changed.

Section 2: Cultures and Lifestyles

BIG IDEA **Culture groups shape human systems.** Europe is a region of many peoples with different ethnic backgrounds, languages, religions, and traditions. Despite their differences, Europeans lead similar lifestyles and share a rich cultural heritage.

FOLDABLES™
Study Organizer

Organizing Information Make this Foldable to help you organize information about Europe's history, population, and cultures.

Step 1 Place three sheets of paper on top of one another about 1 inch apart.

Step 2 Fold the papers to form six equal tabs.

Step 3 Staple the sheets, and label each tab as shown.

Europe's History and Cultures
Greece and Rome
Middle Ages
Modern Times
Europe's Population
Europe's Culture

Reading and Writing As you read, use your Foldable to write down facts related to each period of European history, Europe's population, and European cultures. Then use the facts to write brief summaries for each of the tabs on the Foldable.

Social Studies ONLINE
To preview Chapter 11, go to glencoe.com.

Guide to Reading

The characteristics and movement of people impact physical and human systems.

Content Vocabulary

- classical *(p. 295)*
- city-state *(p. 295)*
- democracy *(p. 295)*
- republic *(p. 296)*
- emperor *(p. 297)*
- pope *(p. 298)*
- feudalism *(p. 298)*
- nation-state *(p. 299)*
- revolution *(p. 301)*
- Holocaust *(p. 302)*
- communism *(p. 303)*

Academic Vocabulary

- dominant *(p. 296)*
- authority *(p. 300)*
- currency *(p. 303)*

Reading Strategy

Making a Time Line Use a time line like the one below to list at least five key events and dates in Europe's history.

History and Governments

Picture This Who is that giant? Is it a warrior? A farmer? A king? One thing is certain—at almost 230 feet (70 m) high, the Long Man of Wilmington, in England, is one of the world's largest carved figures. Originally a chalk outline that became overgrown by grass, the Long Man was restored in 1969 with 770 concrete blocks. As scientists study the earth around the giant, they will be better able to judge when it was made—and maybe even why it was made! Read this section to learn more about the history of Europe.

▼ **Ancient Long Man in hills of southern England**

Ancient Europe

Main Idea Ancient Greece and Rome laid the foundations of European civilization.

Geography and You Do you get to vote on family decisions or elect leaders to your student government? Read to find out how voting rights arose with the ancient Greeks and Romans.

The story of European civilization begins with the ancient Greeks and Romans. More than 2,500 years ago, these peoples settled near the Mediterranean Sea. Eventually their cultures spread throughout Europe and beyond. Even today, the influence of the **classical** world—meaning ancient Greece and Rome—lingers.

Ancient Greece

Physical geography naturally shaped the development of ancient Greece. The people felt deep ties to the land, which is ruggedly beautiful. At the same time, Greece's many mountains, islands, and the surrounding seas isolated early communities and kept them fiercely independent.

The earliest Greek civilizations began among farming and fishing peoples who lived near the Aegean Sea. These civilizations became wealthy through trade. After warfare led to their decline, independent territories called **city-states** developed throughout Greece. Each city-state was made up of a city and its surrounding area. Although separated by geography, the Greek city-states shared the same language and culture.

One of the most prosperous and powerful city-states was Athens. The people of Athens introduced the world's first **democracy,** a political system in which all

NATIONAL GEOGRAPHIC

Socrates and Plato

Socrates, on the left, taught by asking students pointed questions. His most famous student was Plato, another great Greek thinker. *Place* In which Greek city-state did democracy develop?

citizens share in running the government. Although women and enslaved persons could not vote because they were not citizens, Athenian democracy set an example for later civilizations. Learning and the arts also thrived in Athens. Among the city-state's great thinkers were Socrates, Plato, and Aristotle. Their ideas about the world and humankind had a major influence on Europe.

During the mid-300s B.C., warfare weakened the Greek city-states. Soon an invader from the north, Philip II of Macedonia, conquered Greece. Philip's son earned the name Alexander the Great by making even more conquests. As shown in **Figure 1** on the next page, his empire included Egypt and Persia and stretched eastward into India. Trade boomed, Greek culture mixed with Egyptian and Persian cultures, and scientific advances spread. Alexander died young, however, and his empire quickly broke into several smaller kingdoms. By about 130 B.C., the Romans had conquered most of the Greek kingdoms.

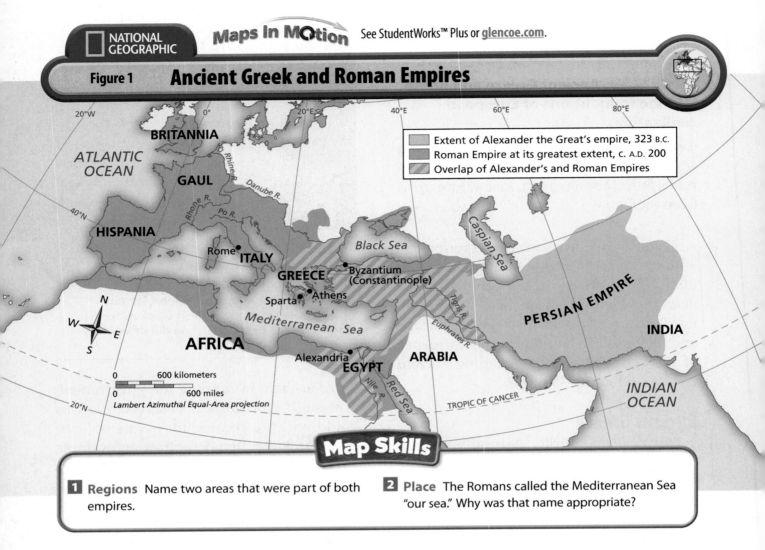

Figure 1 **Ancient Greek and Roman Empires**

Extent of Alexander the Great's empire, 323 B.C.
Roman Empire at its greatest extent, C. A.D. 200
Overlap of Alexander's and Roman Empires

BRITANNIA

ATLANTIC OCEAN

GAUL

40°N

HISPANIA

Rhine R.
Danube R.
Rhone R.
Po R.

Rome ITALY

GREECE

Sparta Athens

AFRICA

Black Sea

Byzantium (Constantinople)

Mediterranean Sea

Alexandria
EGYPT

ARABIA

Caspian Sea

Tigris R.
Euphrates R.

PERSIAN EMPIRE

INDIA

Nile R.
Red Sea

TROPIC OF CANCER

INDIAN OCEAN

0 600 kilometers
0 600 miles
Lambert Azimuthal Equal-Area projection

N W E S

20°N

Map Skills

1 Regions Name two areas that were part of both empires.

2 Place The Romans called the Mediterranean Sea "our sea." Why was that name appropriate?

The Roman Empire

While Greece ruled the eastern Mediterranean, Rome became a **dominant** power on the Italian Peninsula. Rome began as a monarchy but changed to a republic in 509 B.C. In a **republic,** people choose their leaders. Rome was led by two consuls who were elected by the citizens. The consuls reported to and were advised by the Senate, an assembly of rich landowners who served for life. One of the government's great achievements was the development of a code of laws. Written on bronze tablets known as the Twelve Tables, the laws stated that all free citizens had the right to be treated equally. Roman law led to standards of justice still used today. For example, a person was regarded as innocent until proven guilty. Also, judges were expected to examine evidence in a case.

About 200 B.C., Roman armies began seizing territory throughout the Mediterranean region. Instead of ruling only by force, though, the Romans allowed many of the people they conquered to become Roman citizens. By granting people citizenship, the Romans were able to build a strong state with loyal members.

Social Studies ONLINE
Student Web Activity Visit glencoe.com and complete the Chapter 11 Web Activity on ancient Rome.

As the Roman Republic expanded, it evolved into the massive Roman Empire. The first **emperor**, or all-powerful ruler, was Augustus, who gained that position in 27 B.C. His rule brought order to Rome's vast lands. This period, called the *Pax Romana*, was a time of peace, artistic growth, and expanding trade that lasted about 200 years.

Christianity

During the *Pax Romana*, Christianity was developing in Palestine in the eastern part of the Roman Empire. There, a Jewish teacher, Jesus of Nazareth, preached a message of love and forgiveness. Jesus soon attracted followers as well as enemies. Fearing public unrest, the Roman authorities had Jesus executed. Yet within days, Jesus' followers, known as Christians, reported that he had risen from the dead. They took this as proof that Jesus was the son of God.

Eager to spread Jesus' teachings, two early Christian leaders, Peter and Paul, established the Christian Church in Rome. Roman officials at first persecuted, or mistreated, Christians. Despite this abuse, the new religion grew in popularity. In A.D. 392, Christianity became Rome's official religion.

Rome's Decline

By the late A.D. 300s, the Roman Empire was in decline. Rivals struggled to become emperor, and Germanic groups attacked from the north. About A.D. 395, the empire was divided into eastern and western parts. The eastern part remained strong and prosperous. Known as the Byzantine Empire, it lasted another thousand years. The western part was occupied by Germanic groups. In A.D. 476, Germanic leaders overthrew the last emperor in Rome and brought the Western Roman Empire to an end.

Despite its fall, Rome had great influence on Europe and the West. It helped spread classical culture and Christianity. Roman law shaped the legal systems in many countries. The Roman idea of a republic later influenced the founders of the United States. The Latin language of Rome became the basis for many modern European languages known as the Romance languages, such as Italian, French, and Spanish. Ancient Rome also influenced architectural styles in the Western world. For example, the U.S. Capitol and many other buildings have domes and arches inspired by Roman architecture.

Reading Check **Analyzing** Describe ancient Rome's influences on the modern world.

Roman Influences

NATIONAL GEOGRAPHIC

▲ The style of the U.S. Capitol was influenced by Roman architecture. Barbara Mikulski (inset) is a member of the U.S. Senate, which has powers similar to the ancient Roman Senate. *Place Who made up the Roman Senate?*

Expansion of Europe

Main Idea During the Middle Ages, European society, religion, and government underwent great changes.

Geography and You Are there still parts of the world left to explore? Read to learn about changes in Europe, including how Europeans began to explore the far reaches of the world in the 1400s.

After Rome's fall, Europe entered the Middle Ages, a 1,000-year period between ancient and modern times. Christianity strongly influenced society during this period. In the 1300s, though, interest in education, art, and science exploded. Questions began to arise about earlier beliefs and practices. By the 1500s, Europe was experiencing changes that gave birth to the modern period.

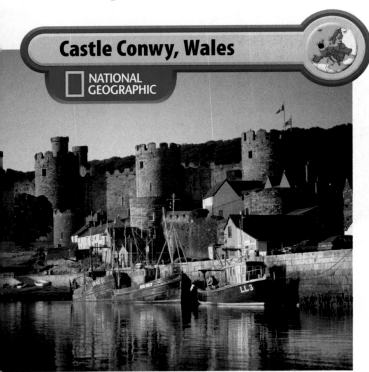

Castle Conwy, Wales

NATIONAL GEOGRAPHIC

▲ During the Middle Ages, nobles were forced to build thick-walled castles for protection against invaders. **Place** How can you tell that this castle was built for defense?

A Christian Europe

During the Middle Ages, Christianity held a central place in people's lives. Two separate branches of the religion had formed, though. The Roman Catholic Church, based in Rome, was headed by a powerful **pope**. The Eastern Orthodox Church was centered in the Byzantine Empire. The Roman Catholic Church spread Roman culture and law to the Germanic groups living in western and central Europe. In eastern Europe, the Byzantine Empire passed on Eastern Orthodoxy and Greek and Roman culture to Slavic groups.

The Middle Ages

About A.D. 800, a Germanic king named Charlemagne united much of western Europe. After his death, this empire broke up. At that point, no strong governments existed to help western Europeans withstand invaders. To bring order, a new political and social system arose by the 1000s. Under this system, called **feudalism**, kings gave land to nobles. The nobles in turn provided military service, becoming knights, or warriors, for the king. As romantic as this may sound, life was hard for the masses. Most western Europeans were poor peasants. They farmed the lands of kings, nobles, and church leaders, who housed and protected them but who also limited their freedom.

The Crusades

In feudal times, the Christian faith united Europeans. Yet the religion of Islam, founded in the A.D. 600s by an Arab named Muhammad, was on the rise. Followers of Islam, called Muslims, spread through Southwest Asia to North Africa and parts of Europe. They also gained control of Palestine, alarming Christians who considered this the Holy Land. Beginning in the

1000s, nobles from western Europe gathered volunteers into large armies to win back the Holy Land. These religious wars, called the Crusades, were only partly successful. Muslims eventually recaptured much of the region.

The Crusades, however, had a major impact on Europeans. Goods began to flow more steadily between Europe and the Muslim lands. This trade benefited European kings, who taxed the goods that crossed their borders. Kings also took over land from nobles who left to fight in the Crusades. As a result, feudalism gradually withered, and Europe's kingdoms grew stronger and larger. Many of them later became modern Europe's **nation-states.** A nation-state is a country made up of people who share a common culture or history.

Muslim-Christian conflict arose again in Spain in the late 1400s. Since the A.D. 700s, Muslim groups had controlled parts of Spain. In what came to be known as the Reconquest, Spanish rulers forced out Muslims and united the country in 1492.

Meanwhile, in the 1300s, people all across Europe were battling a frightful disease. The bubonic plague, or Black Death, spread rapidly and killed perhaps a third of Europe's population. One consequence was a shortage of labor. Although the shortage hurt the economy, it helped workers earn higher wages and gain more freedom. In this way, the Black Death became another force that weakened feudalism.

The Renaissance

As parts of Europe recovered from the Black Death, interest in art and learning revived. Ways of thinking changed so much between about 1350 and 1550 that this period is called the Renaissance, from the French word for "rebirth."

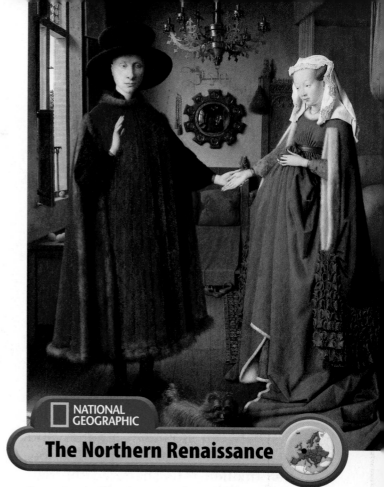

NATIONAL GEOGRAPHIC

The Northern Renaissance

Several great Renaissance artists were from northern Europe, including Jan van Eyck, who painted this portrait of a married couple. **Location** Why did the Renaissance begin in Italian city states?

The Renaissance thrived in Italian city-states, such as Florence, Rome, and Venice. Merchants in these city-states had gained great wealth through trade with Asia and the Mediterranean world. They then used this wealth to support scholars and artists. Poets, sculptors, and painters, such as Michelangelo and Leonardo da Vinci, created stunning masterpieces. People also took an interest in the cultures of ancient Greece and Rome. Another important element of the Renaissance was humanism, a way of thinking that gave importance to the individual and human society. Humanism held that reason, as well as faith, was a path to knowledge. Over time, Renaissance ideas and practices spread from Italy to other parts of Europe.

The Reformation

During the 1500s, the Renaissance idea of humanism led people to think about religion in a new way. Some people felt there were problems in the Roman Catholic Church that needed to be corrected.

In 1517 Martin Luther, a German religious leader, set out to reform, or correct, certain church practices. The pope in Rome, however, did not accept Luther's ideas, and Luther broke away from the Roman Catholic Church. Luther's ideas sparked a religious movement called the Reformation, which led to a new form of Christianity called Protestantism. By the mid-1500s, different Protestant groups dominated northern Europe, while the Roman Catholic Church remained strong in southern Europe.

Wars between Roman Catholics and Protestants soon swept through Europe. The Reformation thus shattered the religious unity of Europeans. It also strengthened the power of monarchs. As the **authority** of church leaders was challenged, kings and queens claimed more authority for themselves.

European Explorations

As Europe's kingdoms grew stronger, European seafarers began a series of ocean voyages that led to a great age of exploration and discovery. During the 1400s, Portugal wanted an easier way to get exotic spices from India and other parts of East Asia. Portuguese navigators developed new trade routes by sailing south around the continent of Africa to Asia. Sailing for Spain in 1492, the Italian-born explorer Christopher Columbus tried to find a different route to Asia. Instead of sailing south around the coast of Africa, Columbus attempted to sail west, across the Atlantic Ocean. Columbus's voyage took him to the Americas, continents unknown in Europe at the time.

In the Americas, Spain found gold and other resources and grew wealthy as a result of its overseas expeditions. Its success made other European countries, such as England, France, and the Netherlands, eager to send forth their own explorers. Conquests followed these voyages. Europeans began founding colonies, or overseas settlements, in the Americas, Asia, and Africa. Trade with the colonies brought Europe great wealth and power. Sadly, though, the Europeans often destroyed the local cultures in the lands they claimed.

✓ **Reading Check** **Determining Cause and Effect** What changes did the Black Death bring to Europe?

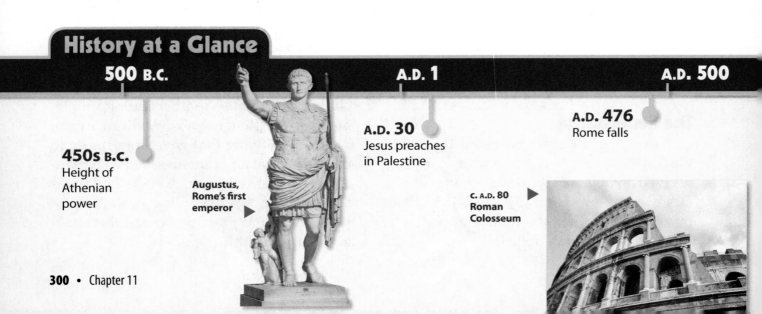

History at a Glance

| 500 B.C. | A.D. 1 | A.D. 500 |

450s B.C.
Height of Athenian power

Augustus, Rome's first emperor ▶

A.D. 30
Jesus preaches in Palestine

C. A.D. 80 Roman Colosseum ▶

A.D. 476
Rome falls

Modern Europe

Main Idea From the 1600s to the 1800s and beyond, new ideas and discoveries helped Europe become a global power.

Geography and You How would your life be different without computers, cell phones, or other modern technologies? Read on to discover how new technology changed Europe after 1600.

From the 1600s to the 2000s, Europe experienced rapid change. New machines helped economies grow. Powerful new weapons, however, made for deadly wars.

The Enlightenment

After the Renaissance, educated Europeans turned to science as a way to explain the world. Nicolaus Copernicus, a Polish mathematician, concluded that the sun, not the Earth, is the center of the universe. An Italian scientist named Galileo Galilei believed that new knowledge could come from carefully observing and measuring the natural world. These and other ideas sparked a **revolution**, or sweeping change, in the way people thought. During this Scientific Revolution, many Europeans relied on reason, rather than faith or tradition, to guide them. Reason, they believed, could bring both truth and error to light. As a result, the 1700s became known as the Age of Enlightenment.

Englishman John Locke was an important Enlightenment thinker. He said that all people have natural rights, including the rights to life, liberty, and property. He also said that when a government does not protect these rights, citizens can overthrow it. The American colonists later used Locke's ideas to support their war for independence from Britain in 1776.

Inspired by the American example, the people of France carried out their own political revolution in 1789. They overthrew their king, executed him three years later, and set up a republic. The French republic did not last long, however. A brilliant military leader named Napoleon Bonaparte gained power and made himself emperor. Napoleon was a small man with big ambitions. His armies conquered much of Europe, until several countries united to defeat him in 1815.

Political revolutions continued to erupt in Europe in the 1800s. By 1900, most countries had responded by limiting the powers of rulers and guaranteeing at least some political rights to citizens.

A.D. 1000

A.D. 1500

A.D. 2000

A.D. 1095
First Crusade begins

A.D. 1350
Renaissance begins in Italy

1993
European Union forms

◀ **Coin from the Crusades**

◀ **c. 1503**
Renaissance artist Da Vinci's *Mona Lisa*

Figure 2 The European Union

Original members, 1993
Members joining in 1995
Members joining in 2004
Members joining in 2007
Nations expected to join
€ Nations using the euro as currency
● EU headquarters

Map Skills

1 **Location** In which city is the headquarters of the European Union located?

2 **Regions** Why have many countries replaced their national currencies with the euro?

Industry and Conflict

Meanwhile, an economic revolution was also transforming Europe. The Industrial Revolution began in Britain. As it spread, it changed the way that people across Europe lived and worked.

Instead of making goods by hand, people began using machines and building factories. Machines could produce goods faster and at lower cost. People could now afford more things, such as comfortable cotton clothes. Travel improved, too, thanks to new inventions such as the railroad. Machines also helped farmers grow more food, which led to population growth. Additionally, farms required less labor.

Many people left farms to find work in cities. Cities became crowded, industries spewed out pollution, and diseases spread. Urban life remained grim for many Europeans until the mid-1800s. In the long run, though, the achievements of the Industrial Revolution benefited most people.

Industrial advances also helped European countries grow more powerful. They developed new weapons and competed aggressively for colonies. Tensions soon led to World War I (1914–1918) and World War II (1939–1945). These devastating conflicts left much of Europe in ruins, with millions of people dead or homeless. A major horror of World War II was the **Holocaust,** the mass killing of 6 million European Jews by Germany's Nazi rulers.

After World War II, the United States and the Soviet Union became rivals in the Cold War. This was not a war of bullets and bombs, but a struggle for world power. Much of Western Europe allied with the United States. Most lands in Eastern Europe allied with the Communist Soviet Union. **Communism** is a system in which the government controls the ways of producing goods.

A New Era for Europe

In 1989 people in Eastern Europe forced several Communist governments from power and set up new democracies. A year later, East and West Germany merged to become one democratic state. Then in 1991, the Soviet Union broke apart.

In 1993 several democracies in Western Europe formed the European Union (EU). The goal of the organization, which now also includes eastern European countries, is a united Europe. The EU allows goods, services, and workers to move freely among member countries. It has also created a common EU **currency** called the euro. Member countries, shown in **Figure 2,** can now trade more easily among themselves because there is no need to exchange, for example, French francs for German marks.

✔ **Reading Check** **Describing** What was the Age of Enlightenment?

Social Studies ONLINE
Study Central™ To review this section, go to glencoe.com.

Section 1 Review

Vocabulary

1. **Explain** the significance of:
   a. classical
   b. city-state
   c. democracy
   d. republic
   e. emperor
   f. pope
   g. feudalism
   h. nation-state
   i. revolution
   j. Holocaust
   k. communism

Main Ideas

2. **Describing** Describe the political system of ancient Athens.

3. **Explaining** How did the Crusades help lead to the creation of modern Europe's nation-states?

4. **Summarizing** Use a diagram like the one below to summarize the changes brought about by the Industrial Revolution.

Industrial Revolution

Critical Thinking

5. **Analyzing** How did Rome build a large, strong empire?

6. **Challenge** Which of Europe's revolutions do you think was most important for the creation of modern Europe? Explain your answer.

7. **BIG Idea** Provide an example of how political or social ideas, such as democracy or Christianity, spread in Europe.

Writing About Geography

8. **Using Your FOLDABLES** Use your Foldable to write a summary describing how governments in Europe have changed over time.

YOU Decide

Learning in School: Should All Students Speak the Same Language?

In Europe, migration between countries is common. As a result, many students do not speak the local language where they live. Some educators believe that all students should speak the nation's official language in school. For example, in Berlin, Germany, several schools allow only the German language to be spoken during class, on school property, and on school trips. However, others disagree, arguing that students should be allowed to learn in their own languages.

For Speaking the Same Language

I believe that knowledge of the German language is the key to integration [becoming part of society] and to success both at school and in a future profession. . . . The pupils themselves are very satisfied with [this rule], because they know that speaking correct German increases their opportunities. . . .

When children start school and don't speak the language correctly, they . . . receive worse grades. That continues throughout their schooling and in the end they aren't able to get a vocational [job] training place. That's why we are in favour of introducing language tests starting from the age of four and thereby promoting language skills from kindergarten on.

—Armin Laschet
Minister for Generations, Family, Women, and Integration
North Rhine-Westphalia, Germany

Against | # Speaking the Same Language

Banning pupils from speaking their [traditional] languages in the schoolyard is not the answer, even if it were workable, which it is not. Other means of developing their linguistic [language] skills, such as pre-school instruction in German, are much more likely to be effective and should be fully supported.

. . . It is perfectly acceptable to ban other languages within the classroom. But outside the classroom pupils should be free to speak whichever language they like. Banning pupils' [traditional] languages sends a message that they are somehow "second class" citizens, which is likely to promote resentment rather than integration. . . .

Many children of immigrants choose to communicate in German in any case. . . .

There also appears to be a fallacy [mistaken belief] that speaking another language somehow [takes away] from pupils' ability with German. This is not the case. Humans have an almost unlimited ability to learn languages and in general there is no reason why the average person cannot master two or more languages.

—David Gordon Smith
Editor, Expatica: Germany

You Be the Geographer

1. **Identifying** What reasons do Laschet and Smith give to support their opinions?

2. **Critical Thinking** What might be some challenges for a student who speaks a different language than that of the other students in his or her class?

3. **Read to Write** Write a paragraph that explains your own opinion about students speaking only one language at school.

BIG Idea

Culture groups shape human systems.

Content Vocabulary

- ethnic group *(p. 307)*
- welfare state *(p. 307)*
- fertility rate *(p. 307)*
- urbanization *(p. 308)*
- secular *(p. 310)*

Academic Vocabulary

- bond *(p. 307)*
- attitude *(p. 310)*

Reading Strategy

Organizing Information Use a diagram like the one below to list key facts about Europe's population patterns.

Cultures and Lifestyles

Picture This Bog snorkeling? For more than twenty years, competitors wearing snorkels and flippers have met in the small town of Powys, Wales, to swim in its slimy bog. The challenge is to swim the fastest without using any standard swimming strokes. The just-for-fun event has attracted swimmers from as far away as South Africa and Australia. Read Section 2 to learn more about the cultures and lifestyles of Europeans.

▼ **Decorated in blue paint, this swimmer hopes to win first place.**

Population Patterns

NATIONAL GEOGRAPHIC

A Changing Population

These schoolgirls in London demonstrate Europe's growing immigrant population and ethnic diversity. **Movement** From where have people immigrated to Europe?

Main Idea **Ethnic differences and population changes pose challenges for Europe.**

Geography and You How do you treat a new person who joins your class? What kind of challenges does he or she face? Read to discover how Europe is responding to its new immigrant populations.

Europe's people are crowded into a relatively small space. The population is not distributed evenly, however, and it continues to undergo change.

A Rich Ethnic Mix

Today Europe is home to many ethnic groups. An **ethnic group** is a group of people with shared ancestry, language, and customs. Europe's ethnic mix has resulted from migrations, wars, and changing boundaries over the centuries.

Many Europeans identify strongly with their particular country or ethnic group. Having a common heritage or culture creates **bonds** among people. National and ethnic loyalties, however, have also led to conflict. In the 1990s, disputes among ethnic groups split Yugoslavia into five separate countries. In some of these new countries, ethnic hatred sparked the worst fighting in Europe since World War II.

Despite divisions, Europeans have a growing sense of unity. They realize that because their countries are linked by geography, cooperation can help bring peace and prosperity. In addition, the people share many values that go beyond ethnic or national loyalties. For example, Europeans value democracy and human rights. They also believe that a government must care for its citizens. Many European countries are **welfare states** in which the gov-ernment is the main provider of support for the sick, the needy, and the retired.

Population Changes

Because of recent immigration, Europe's population is still undergoing change. Since World War II, many people from Asia, Africa, and Latin America have settled in Europe. Tensions have risen as immigrants and local residents compete for jobs, housing, and social services. As a result, immigrants have not always felt welcome in many places in Europe.

European countries deal with immigrants in various ways. Some want immigrants to adapt quickly, so they require newcomers to learn the national language. Other countries pass laws to keep immigrants from settling within their borders. Still others try to improve educational and job opportunities for newcomers.

You might be surprised to learn that although the number of immigrants is increasing, the region's overall population is decreasing. Europe has a low **fertility rate,** which is the average number of children born to each woman.

As a result, Europe is expected to have 10 percent fewer people by 2050. This is worrisome, because there will be fewer workers to keep Europe's economy growing. Meanwhile, Europeans are living longer because of better health care. As older people increasingly account for a greater share of the population, young workers will face higher taxes to support them.

Reading Check **Making Generalizations**
How do national and ethnic loyalties benefit and harm Europeans?

NATIONAL GEOGRAPHIC

European Fashion

▲ With their generally high incomes, many Europeans can afford the latest fashions, like the one worn by this model at a fashion show in Paris. *Regions* **How might a shrinking population affect Europe's economy?**

Life in Europe

Main Idea **European lifestyles today reflect the region's urban society and level of wealth.**

Geography and You Does the idea of living in a city appeal to you? Read to discover how cities play an important part in the lives of Europeans.

Customs, languages, and religions have always differed among Europeans. In recent decades, however, differences in lifestyles among Europe's peoples have lessened as a result of industrial and economic growth, urban growth, and improved standards of living. Today, most Europeans are well-educated city dwellers with comfortable incomes.

Cities

Beginning in the late 1700s, the Industrial Revolution changed Europe from a rural, farming society to an urban, industrial society. Rural villagers moved in large numbers to urban areas. This concentration of people in towns and cities is known as **urbanization.** Many of Europe's cities grew quickly and became some of the world's largest.

Today, three of every four Europeans live in cities. Paris and London rank among the largest urban areas on the globe. The next biggest cities are Milan, Italy; Madrid, Spain; and Berlin, Germany.

Many European cities blend the old and the new. Ancient landmarks often stand near modern highways and skyscrapers. European cities are also crisscrossed by public transportation systems that bring people to jobs and urban attractions. In recent decades, however, more Europeans have bought cars and have chosen to live in suburbs outside the cities.

Transportation

Most of Europe's transportation systems are government owned. Standards differ from country to country, but overall, Europe boasts one of the world's most advanced transportation networks. The rail system links cities and towns across the continent. Trains travel underwater between England and France via a 31-mile (50-km) tunnel under the English Channel, known as the Chunnel. France developed the use of high-speed trains, which cause less damage to the environment than most other forms of transportation. High-speed rail lines now operate in many European countries.

Highways also allow high-speed, long-distance travel. Cars can zip along Germany's autobahns at more than 80 miles (129 km) per hour. Trucks use the roadways to carry the great majority of freight within Europe.

Canals and rivers are also used to transport goods. The Main-Danube Canal in Germany links hundreds of inland ports between the North Sea and the Black Sea. Europe's long coastline is dotted with other important ports, such as Rotterdam, in the Netherlands. This is one of the busiest ports in the world.

Airports connect European cities too. Planes fly both people and goods to their destinations all around Europe.

Education and Income

Europeans take schooling seriously. They tend to be well educated and have some of the highest literacy rates in the world. More than three-quarters of young people complete high school.

Because of their high levels of education, Europeans earn more money than people in many other parts of the world. There are differences, however, from place to place. Incomes are higher in northern and west-

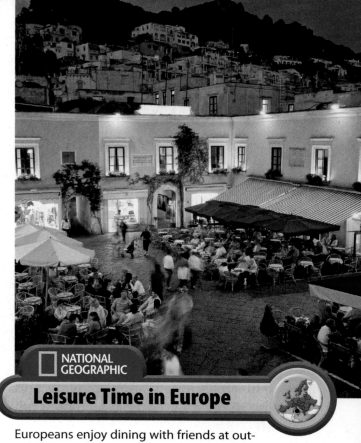

NATIONAL GEOGRAPHIC

Leisure Time in Europe

Europeans enjoy dining with friends at outdoor cafés, such as this one on the island of Capri, Italy. **Regions** What other leisure activities are popular with Europeans?

ern Europe than in southern and eastern Europe. Many eastern European countries are still struggling to rebuild economies that were damaged by conflicts or slowed by years of Communist rule. Throughout Europe, service industries, such as banking, provide more jobs than any other economic activity.

Income can also vary greatly within a country. For example, unemployment and poverty are common in southern Italy. Mountains and a lack of natural resources in the area have slowed the development of industry. Workers are better off in northern and central Italy, where rich farmland and modern industries provide many jobs.

Leisure

Their relatively high incomes allow many Europeans to enjoy their leisure time. They have a generous amount of it too!

In a number of European countries, workers receive four weeks of paid vacation each year. Many Europeans use this vacation time to travel. France and Italy are popular vacation spots because of their lively cities, beautiful countryside, mild climate, and fine food.

Europeans also take full advantage of their natural surroundings. The region's mountains, seas, lakes, and rivers provide great opportunities for recreation. Winter sports such as ice skating and skiing had their beginnings in Scandinavia about 5,000 years ago. In summer, Europeans lace up their hiking boots, hop on their bikes, or take to the water. Many Europeans are also passionate about playing and watching rugby and soccer, which they call football.

✓ **Reading Check** **Making Connections** What type of industry provides the most jobs in Europe?

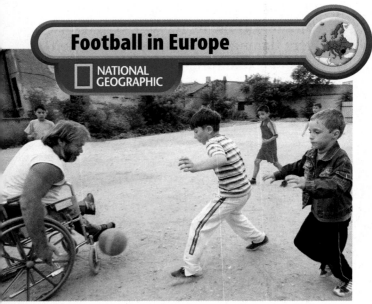

Football in Europe

NATIONAL GEOGRAPHIC

▲ Many Europeans, like these Romanians, enjoy playing soccer. Rules for the game were first established in England in the 1800s. *Regions* **What winter sports developed in Europe?**

Religion and the Arts

Main Idea **Religion, especially Christianity, has had an important effect on European society and arts.**

Geography and You If you enjoy creative writing or making art or music, what ideas inspire you? Read on to find out how religion, nature, and other influences shaped the arts in Europe.

As in other parts of the world, religion has shaped European culture, including its arts. Today, though, European art reflects a variety of influences.

Religion

For centuries, Christianity was a major influence in European life. Since the 1700s, however, European **attitudes** have become more **secular,** or nonreligious. Today many Europeans do not belong to a particular religious group. Still, Christian moral teachings, such as respect for human life and compassion for others, remain core values throughout the region.

Most of Europe's Christians are Roman Catholic. As you can see in **Figure 3,** Roman Catholics are heavily concentrated in the southern part of western Europe and in some eastern European countries. Protestants are dominant in northern Europe. Eastern Orthodox churches are strongest in the southern part of eastern Europe.

Judaism and Islam have also influenced European culture. Judaism, like Christianity, reached Europe during Roman times. Despite eras of persecution, Jews have made major contributions to European life. Today, Jewish communities thrive in all major European cities. Thousands of Muslim immigrants are also settling in the region.

For the most part, Europeans of different faiths live together peacefully. In some cases, though, Europe's religious differences have led to violence. For years, hostility between Catholics and Protestants created conflict in Northern Ireland, a part of the United Kingdom. Since 1998, both sides have agreed to share political power, but the situation remains unstable. Religious and ethnic differences were also at the heart of troubles on the Balkan Peninsula. There, Roman Catholic, Eastern Orthodox, and Muslim groups fought over land and political power during the 1990s.

Arts

The arts have flourished in Europe for centuries. In ancient times, the Greeks and Romans constructed stately temples and public buildings with huge, graceful columns. During the Middle Ages, a new style known as Gothic architecture arose. Europeans built majestic churches called cathedrals, designing them with pointed arches and large, stained-glass windows.

Religion also inspired European art, literature, and music. From ancient times to the Middle Ages, artists and writers focused on holy or heroic subjects.

NATIONAL GEOGRAPHIC

Figure 3   Europe's Religions

Legend:
- Roman Catholicism
- Eastern Orthodox
- Protestantism
- ☪ Islam
- ✡ Judaism

Map Skills

1. **Place** Which religions are found in France?

2. **Regions** Why do you think most Christians in southern Europe are Catholic?

0 500 kilometers
0 500 miles
Lambert Azimuthal Equal-Area projection

Composers wrote pieces to accompany religious services. In eastern Europe, Christian art included icons, or symbolic religious images painted on wood.

During the 1500s and 1600s, Renaissance artists continued to create religious art, but their art also portrayed life in the everyday world. Renaissance artists tried to make their works more realistic. When you study a painting by Leonardo da Vinci or a statue by Michelangelo, you will see lifelike figures. In the writings of England's William Shakespeare or Spain's Miguel de Cervantes, you will encounter believable characters with timeless problems.

Artistic creativity continued to soar in Europe. In the 1600s and 1700s, new types of music, such as opera and symphony, emerged. In the 1800s, musicians, writers, and artists developed a style known as Romanticism, which aimed to stir strong emotions. This style drew inspiration not from religion but from nature and historical events. Later in the 1800s, the Impressionist movement began. Impressionist painters used bold colors and brushstrokes to create "impressions" of the natural world.

In the 1900s, European artists moved away from portraying the world as it appeared to the human eye. They turned to abstract painting to express feelings and ideas. Architects began to create sleek, modern buildings using materials such as glass and concrete. New kinds of music, such as rock and roll, caught on. Today Europe's artists remain creative and influential.

✔ **Reading Check** **Analyzing** How has religion influenced the arts in Europe?

Section 2 Review

Social Studies ONLINE
Study Central™ To review this section, go to glencoe.com.

Vocabulary

1. **Explain** how the terms *ethnic group, welfare state, fertility rate, urbanization,* and *secular* relate to Europe's population by writing a sentence containing each word.

Main Ideas

2. **Explaining** How do individual European countries deal with immigration?

3. **Describing** How does Europe's generally high level of education affect life there?

4. **Identifying** Use a chart like the one below to identify Europe's major religions, including the major forms of Christianity, and where each religion is generally located in Europe.

Major Religion	Where Found

Critical Thinking

5. **Challenge** Will immigration benefit Europe in the future? Explain your answer.

6. **Drawing Conclusions** What factors have slowed economic development in certain areas of Europe?

7. **BIG Idea** What factors help unify Europe's different ethnic groups today?

Writing About Geography

8. **Expository Writing** Write a paragraph comparing European and American cultures.

Visual Summary

__Ancient Europe__

- The Greek city-state of Athens introduced the world's first democracy.

- Rome influenced later civilizations through its legal system, its language, and its role in the spread of Christianity.

- Invasions by Germanic peoples led to the Roman Empire's decline.

Map of the world, c. 1620

Caesar Augustus

__Modern Europe__

- Through revolutions people challenged the power of kings and demanded certain rights for citizens.

- As industries grew, many people left rural areas to find work in city factories.

- Two costly world wars led European countries to seek peace and greater unity.

__Europe's Expansion__

- Christianity shaped Europe's society and culture during the Middle Ages.

- The Renaissance, which began in Italy, brought about a new interest in learning.

- European countries controlled various parts of the world as a result of overseas explorations.

Eurostar train, London

__Population Patterns__

- Europe is densely populated in many areas.

- Europe's population is aging, and the total population is declining.

- Many people have immigrated to Europe from Asia, Africa, and Latin America.

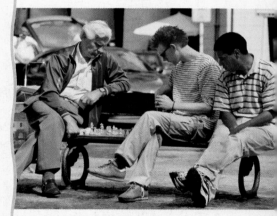

Playing chess in Prague, Czech Republic

__Life and Culture__

- Europeans tend to live in urban areas and have relatively high levels of education and income.

- With more leisure time, Europeans enjoy sports such as soccer.

- European society and culture have become more secular.

STUDY TO GO Study anywhere, anytime! Download quizzes and flash cards to your PDA from **glencoe.com**.

STANDARDIZED TEST PRACTICE

TEST-TAKING **TIP**

Eliminate answers that do not make sense. For instance, if an answer refers to a region of the world other than Europe, you know it cannot be correct.

Reviewing Vocabulary

Directions: Choose the word(s) that best completes the sentence.

1. In the system known as _____, nobles provided service to a king in exchange for land.

   A communism

   B feudalism

   C a republic

   D a city-state

2. The head of the Catholic Church is called the _____.

   A emperor

   B king

   C pope

   D archbishop

3. The _____ world refers to ancient Greece and Rome.

   A classical

   B Hellenistic

   C democratic

   D dominant

4. In a(n) _____, the government is the main provider of support for the sick, needy, and retired.

   A democracy

   B corporate donor

   C urbanized center

   D welfare state

5. Because Europe has a low _____, it is expected to have 10 percent fewer people by 2050.

   A urbanization rate

   B fertility rate

   C ethnic group

   D secular group

Reviewing Main Ideas

Directions: Choose the best answer for each question.

Section 1 *(pp. 294–303)*

6. The prosperous Greek city-state of Athens introduced the world's first _____.

   A democracy

   B artistic thinkers

   C free society

   D army

7. The _____ resulted in the rise of a new form of Christianity called Protestantism.

   A Crusades

   B Reformation

   C Enlightenment

   D Renaissance

Section 2 *(pp. 306–312)*

8. Europe's population shifts may pose challenges because

   A few jobs exist for the growing population.

   B few people immigrate into the region.

   C Europeans are no longer living as long.

   D there will be fewer workers to keep Europe's economy growing.

9. Which of the following most clearly explains how European lifestyles reflect the region's level of wealth?

   A Europeans are able to enjoy their leisure time.

   B Transportation standards vary from country to country.

   C More than three-quarters of Europeans complete high school.

   D Many eastern Europeans are still struggling from years of Communist rule.

GO ON ➡

Critical Thinking

Directions: Choose the best answer for each question.

10. Which of the following was a result of the Renaissance?

   A A revival in art and literature began.

   B Workers gained higher wages and more freedoms.

   C A new form of Christianity developed.

   D Many European countries began to send out explorers.

Base your answer to question 11 on the map below and your knowledge of Chapter 11.

The Black Death

11. Which city was first affected by the Black Death?

   A Constantinople

   B Paris

   C Lübeck

   D Barcelona

Document-Based Questions

Directions: Analyze the document and answer the short-answer questions that follow.

In 1215 nobles in England forced King John to sign the Magna Carta. This document gave common people some freedoms and limited the power of the king. It was an important influence in the rise of democratic governments.

> *TO ALL FREE MEN OF OUR KINGDOM*
>
> *we have also granted, for us and our heirs for ever, all the liberties written out below . . .*
>
> *(20) For a trivial offence, a free man shall be fined only in proportion to the degree of his offence. . . .*
>
> *(30) No sheriff, royal official, or other person shall take horses or carts for transport from any free man, without his consent. . . .*
>
> *(40) To no one will we sell, to no one deny or delay right or justice.*
>
> —Magna Carta

12. What does article 20 of the Magna Carta mean? Rephrase it in your own words.

13. What complaints do you think the Magna Carta attempted to fix?

Extended Response

14. Take the role of a citizen of a European country that is not in the European Union but is debating whether to apply for membership. Write a short speech explaining why you think your country should or should not join the EU.

STOP

Social Studies ONLINE

For additional test practice, use Self-Check Quizzes—Chapter 11 at glencoe.com.

Need Extra Help?													
If you missed question. . .	1	2	3	4	5	6	7	8	9	10	11	12	13	14
Go to page. . .	298	298	295	307	307	295	300	308	309	299	299	299	299	303

"Hello! My name is Kade.

I am 13 years old and live in Paris, the capital of France. My family moved here from Guinea, a country in Africa. Like other immigrant families, we blend some of our own traditions with France's rich culture. Here's how I spend my day."

8:45 a.m. My mom wakes me up. I sleep late today because school does not start until 10 o'clock on Mondays! (On other days, it begins at 8 o'clock.) I shower and get dressed.

9:15 a.m. I eat breakfast with my parents and little brother and sister. We have warm chocolate milk, which we drink out of bowls. We also have flaky rolls called croissants. Croissants are delicious. I like them best when they are filled with chocolate.

9:40 a.m. I meet my friends and walk to school. We can see the Eiffel Tower from our building.

10:00 a.m. It's the start of a long day—and a long week. Like many French kids, I go to school six days a week. Wednesdays and Saturdays are half days, though. I look forward to them!

10:15 a.m. In history, my first class, we are learning about ancient Greece. Then I study geography. Our geography classroom is decorated with flags from all over the world.

12:00 p.m. In music class, I take an exam on the flute. I hope I did well!

1:00 p.m. It's time for *déjeuner* (day•zhuh•NAY), or lunch. Many students go home for lunch, but I buy my meal in the cafeteria. Today I choose a grapefruit, chicken nuggets, and pasta.

2:00 p.m. I go to the computer lab for technology class. After that, we have a short recess period. My friends and I play dodgeball. I enjoy sports. I think I would like to be a handball instructor one day.

3:00 p.m. In English class, we practice saying sentences that begin with the phrase, "Do you like…?" My English is already strong because we often speak it at home, but this lesson is fun.

4:00 p.m. School is over. I walk back home with my friends. Today, some of them come to my apartment. We watch music videos and listen to CDs. I like most kinds of music, including rock and reggae.

6:00 p.m. My dad will be home from work soon. He designs and sells clothing. My mom is starting to prepare dinner. I help her out by picking up my brother from school.

6:30 p.m. I do my homework.

7:30 p.m. Dinner is ready. We are having rice with fish and vegetables in a spicy sauce. It is a dish that is popular in Guinea. Now my family has brought it to France!

8:30 p.m. I play and watch cartoons with my little brother and sister.

9:30 p.m. I brush my teeth and go to bed. I listen to music until I get sleepy. I use earphones so I do not wake my sister.

ILLUSTRATIONS BY BOOKMAPMAN

BEFORE CLASS Kade meets up with her friends. French students go to school six days a week.

DODGEBALL At Kade's school, this sport is popular at recess. Soccer is still the number one sport in France, as it is in most of Europe.

MAP TIME Kade's teacher checks her work. Geography is a required subject in France, a nation that borders several countries.

BACKPACKED Kade Diallo (kahd dee•AH•low) passes the Eiffel Tower on her way to school. The teen moved to France with her parents and brother and sister in search of better economic opportunities.

RICHARD HARBUS / POLARIS (4)

PATRICK SHEANDELL O'CARROLL/GETTY IMAGES

What's Popular in France

Cheese France produces hundreds of varieties. The average French person eats about 50 pounds of cheese each year.

STEVEN MARK NEEDHAM/ PICTUREARTS/NEWSCOM

Cycling Every July, France hosts a three-week, 2,000-mile bicycle race called the Tour de France. More people come to watch the race than any other sporting event in the world.

FRANCK FIFE/AFP/NEWSCOM

Fashion France is home to some of the world's top clothing designers. Styles that start in workrooms here end up in stores all over the world.

Say It in French

France's 60 million people are united by a common language, French. Like English and many other languages, the French language has roots in Latin. Try these simple French phrases.

Hello
Bonjour (bohn·ZHOOR)

Good-bye
Au revoir (oh reh·VWAH)

My name is _____.
Je m'appelle (zhuh mah·PELL) _____.

317

Europe Today

Essential Question

Human-Environment Interaction Europe is one of the economic powerhouses of the world, home to many large companies that sell goods in the United States. Europe is also an important market for goods and services produced in North America, such as movies and computer programs. What factors help make a region an important world economic center?

Trafalgar Square, London

BIG Ideas

Section 1: Northern Europe

BIG IDEA **Geographers organize the Earth into regions that share common characteristics.** The countries of northern Europe have developed diverse economies and high standards of living.

Section 2: Europe's Heartland

BIG IDEA **People's actions can change the physical environment.** Today the countries of Europe's heartland are agricultural and manufacturing centers.

Section 3: Southern Europe

BIG IDEA **Places reflect the relationship between humans and the physical environment.** Seas and mountains have influenced where people live and how they work in southern Europe.

Section 4: Eastern Europe

BIG IDEA **Geography is used to interpret the past, understand the present, and plan for the future.** After changes in government, eastern Europe's economies are struggling to recover.

FOLDABLES™
Study Organizer

Summarizing Information Make this Foldable to help you collect information about Europe's people, politics, and economies.

Step 1 Fold the sides of a piece of paper into the middle to make a shutter fold.

Step 2 Cut each flap at the midpoint to form four tabs.

Step 3 Label the tabs as shown.

Reading and Writing Use the notes in your Foldable to write a short essay comparing the economies of Europe's four subregions.

Social Studies ONLINE

To preview Chapter 12, go to glencoe.com.

Guide to Reading

BIG Idea

Geographers organize the Earth into regions that share common characteristics.

Content Vocabulary

- constitutional monarchy *(p. 322)*
- parliamentary democracy *(p. 323)*
- peat *(p. 325)*
- bog *(p. 325)*
- productivity *(p. 325)*
- geyser *(p. 327)*
- fjord *(p. 327)*
- geothermal energy *(p. 327)*

Academic Vocabulary

- differentiate *(p. 321)*
- document *(p. 322)*
- vary *(p. 326)*

Reading Strategy

Organizing Information Use a graphic organizer like the one below to organize key facts about the people and cultures of northern Europe.

People and Cultures
→ United Kingdom
→ Ireland
→ Scandinavia

Northern Europe

Picture This Iceland's huge chunks of moving ice are centuries old. Iceland, however, is not a bitter cold wasteland. It has a relatively mild climate even though it is near the Arctic Circle. The people of Iceland have adjusted to living in this climate and have made efficient use of the country's resources. Learn more about Iceland and other countries of northern Europe by reading Section 1.

▼ A glacial wall in Iceland

The United Kingdom

Main Idea Once the center of a world-wide empire, the United Kingdom has had a great impact on the rest of the world.

Geography and You Have you ever seen a picture of Big Ben, the large clock tower located in London? Big Ben is a symbol of the United Kingdom. Read to find out more about this country in the North Atlantic.

It is easy to be confused by the different names for the island nation off the northwest coast of mainland Europe. People sometimes call it Great Britain, the British Isles, or simply England. The true name, though, is the *United Kingdom of Great Britain and Northern Ireland,* or the *United Kingdom.*

The country includes four separate regions, which you can see in **Figure 1.** Three of them—England, Scotland, and Wales—make up the island of Great Britain. The fourth region, Northern Ireland, occupies a corner of the nearby island of Ireland. (The rest of that island is a completely independent country known as the Republic of Ireland.)

All the people of the United Kingdom can be described as British. Sometimes, though, people **differentiate** among them by referring to the English, the Scots, the Welsh, or the Irish.

The Land

Great Britain is separated from the rest of Europe by the English Channel. Historically, this body of water both connected and protected the British. They were close enough to the mainland to share in European culture. At the same time, they were far enough away to be largely safe from foreign invasions and free to develop their own government and economy.

NATIONAL GEOGRAPHIC

Figure 1 **The United Kingdom and Ireland**

Map Skills

1 Regions Which four regions make up the United Kingdom?

2 Place Which region probably has a larger percentage of people in rural areas, England or Scotland? Why do you think so?

Rolling fertile plains cover the southern and eastern areas of England. These plains support productive farms. Rough highlands and mountains are found to the north and west in Scotland and Wales. Poor soil and a cold climate make farming difficult in these areas, but many people herd sheep.

Government in the United Kingdom

The Palace of Westminster, with the clock tower known as Big Ben, lies in the heart of London. It is home to Parliament, the lawmaking body of the United Kingdom.
Place How did the United Kingdom become a parliamentary democracy?

In southeastern England, the Thames (TEHMZ) River helped make London a center for world trade. Today, shipping is much less important than it once was, and the Thames riverbanks in London are lined with apartment buildings rather than warehouses. London, however, remains a world center of finance and business.

The Economy

More than 250 years ago, British inventors and scientists sparked the Industrial Revolution. Today, the United Kingdom is still a major industrial and trading country. Manufactured goods and machinery are its leading exports. New computer and electronics industries, however, are gradually replacing these older industries. Service industries, such as banking and health care, are now a major part of the economy.

Coal once powered the British economy, but oil and natural gas are now the lead-ing energy sources. These fossil fuels come from fields beneath the North Sea. These oil and gas fields meet most of the United Kingdom's energy needs. They also provide fuel exports that give the country a valuable source of income.

Government

The government of the United Kingdom is a **constitutional monarchy**. A king or queen serves as head of state and takes part in ceremonies, but elected officials actively run the government.

The British trace the roots of this form of government to the early 1200s. At that time, nobles forced King John of England to sign the Magna Carta, a **document** that took away some of the king's powers. For example, the king could no longer collect taxes unless a group of nobles agreed. Also, people accused of crimes had a right to fair trials by their peers, or equals.

Gradually, a lawmaking body called Parliament arose. In 1628 Parliament decided that King Charles I had misused his power. It forced him to sign the Petition of Right, which said that taxes could be enacted only if Parliament approved. In addition, the king could not imprison people unless they were convicted of a crime. As time passed, more limits were placed on the ruler's authority. The English Bill of Rights, passed in 1689, gave Parliament the power to tax and stated that monarchs could not suspend the laws or form their own armies. That document later helped shape the thinking of the men who wrote the U.S. Constitution.

Today, the United Kingdom is a **parliamentary democracy** as well as a constitutional monarchy. Voters elect members of Parliament, and the leader of the party with the most elected officials becomes prime minister, or head of the government. The prime minister can propose new laws, but only Parliament can put them into action. The prime minister must appear in Parliament regularly to explain and defend his or her decisions. Parliament also has the power to force the prime minister out of office and require new elections. This is a power the U.S. Congress does not have over the U.S. president.

Scotland, Wales, and Northern Ireland have regional legislatures that have control over matters such as health care and education. The Scottish Parliament even has the power to raise or lower taxes in Scotland.

The People

With more than 60 million people, the United Kingdom is the third-most-populous country in Europe. Nearly 9 of every 10 people live in cities. London is by far the largest city, with some 7.6 million residents.

The British people speak English, although Welsh and Scottish Gaelic (GAY·lihk) are spoken in some areas. Most people in the United Kingdom are Protestant Christians. Immigrants from South Asia, Africa, and the Caribbean area, however, practice religions such as Islam, Sikhism, and Hinduism.

In the 1700s and 1800s, when the United Kingdom had a powerful empire, British culture spread to many lands. As a result, the British sport of cricket is now played in Australia, South Asia, and the Caribbean. The English language is spoken in the United States, Canada, South Africa, and a number of other countries. Britain's rich literature of poems, plays, and novels is enjoyed worldwide, too.

✔ Reading Check **Determining Cause and Effect** How has the location of the United Kingdom shaped its history?

Cricket: A British Sport

NATIONAL GEOGRAPHIC

▲ A batsman, or player, hits the ball in a cricket match between England and the South Asian country of Bangladesh. *Movement* **How did British sports and culture spread to other lands?**

Charles Dickens
(1812–1870)

One of Britain's most famous novelists, Charles Dickens, had a difficult childhood because of family financial problems. As a result, Dickens developed a deep sympathy for the lower classes and for the young children who sometimes suffered from society's strict rules. These feelings are evident in many of his books.

Background Information

In *Hard Times*, Charles Dickens explores the problems raised by the Industrial Revolution. His book harshly criticizes the people who promoted this new way of working and the effects it had on the environment. In this passage, Dickens describes an industrial city, which he names Coketown.

Reader's Dictionary

interminable: unending

melancholy: sad

workful: useful

infirmary: hospital

dearest: for the highest price

HARD TIMES

By Charles Dickens

It was a town of red brick, or of brick that would have been red if the smoke and ashes had allowed it; but as matters stood it was a town of unnatural red and black. . . .

It was a town of machinery and tall chimneys, out of which **interminable** serpents of smoke trailed themselves for ever and ever, and never got uncoiled.

It had a black canal in it, and a river that ran purple with ill-smelling dye, and vast piles of buildings full of windows where there was a rattling and a trembling all day long, and where the piston of the steam-engine worked monotonously up and down, like the head of an elephant in a state of **melancholy** madness. It contained several large streets all very like one another, and many small streets still more like one another inhabited by people equally like one another, who all went in and out at the same hours, with the same sound upon the same pavements, to do the same work, and to whom every day was the same as yesterday and to-morrow, and every year the counterpart [duplicate] of the last and the next. . . .

You saw nothing in Coketown but what was severely **workful**. . . . All the public inscriptions in the town were

painted alike, in severe characters of black and white. The jail might have been the **infirmary,** the infirmary might have been the jail, the townhall might have been either, or both, or anything else. . . . What you couldn't state in figures, or show to be purchasable in the cheapest market and salable in the **dearest,** was not [to be found there], and never should be. . . .

From: *Hard Times,* Charles Dickens, New York Books, Inc., n.d.

Analyzing Literature

1. **Making Inferences** How would you describe Coketown?

2. **Read to Write** Suppose you were a person who moved from a farm to work in a factory in Coketown. Write a letter to a family member that contrasts life on the farm with life in the city.

The Republic of Ireland

Main Idea Ireland is growing economically, but a territorial dispute remains unsettled.

Geography and You Why do you think Ireland is called the Emerald Isle? Read to find out about Ireland and its resources.

When people speak of Ireland, they usually mean the Republic of Ireland. This is the Catholic country that occupies the southern five-sixths of the island of Ireland. The country won its independence from the United Kingdom in 1922. The British, meanwhile, keep control of Northern Ireland, where most people are Protestants.

The Land

Ireland has the shape of a shallow bowl. The interior is a lowland plain with gently rolling hills. The coastal areas are rocky highlands and towering cliffs.

Ireland's regular rainfall produces lush, green fields. The landscape stays so green year-round that the country is nicknamed the Emerald Isle. Low-lying areas are rich in **peat,** or plants that have partly decayed in water. Peat is dug from **bogs,** or low swampy lands. It is then dried and can be burned for fuel.

The Economy

Irish farmers raise sheep and cattle and grow vegetables such as sugar beets and potatoes. Potatoes were Ireland's chief food in the 1800s. When disease destroyed the potato crop in the 1840s, more than one million people died. Another million left for the United States and other countries.

Today, manufacturing employs more of Ireland's people than farming does.

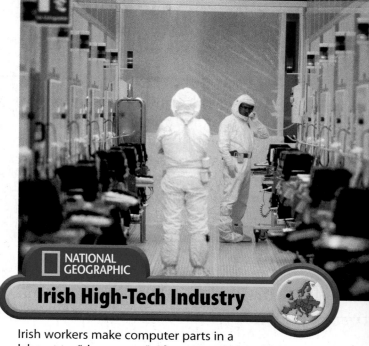

Irish High-Tech Industry

Irish workers make computer parts in a laboratory "clean room." *Place* **How has Ireland's economy changed in recent years?**

The Irish work in industries that produce clothing, pharmaceuticals, and computer equipment. In recent years, the increased productivity of Irish workers has helped Ireland's economy. **Productivity** is a measure of how much work a person does in a specific amount of time. When workers produce more goods, companies earn higher profits and the workers earn higher incomes.

The People

The Irish trace their ancestry to the Celts, who settled the island hundreds of years ago. Irish Gaelic, a Celtic language, and English are Ireland's two languages. About 60 percent of the Irish live in cities or towns. Nearly one-third live in Dublin, the capital.

The Irish are very proud of their culture. Irish music and folk dancing are performed around the world. Of all the arts, however, the Irish have had their greatest influence on literature. Playwright George Bernard Shaw, poet William Butler Yeats, and novelist James Joyce are some of Ireland's best-known writers.

Conflict Over Northern Ireland

The Irish are also strong Catholics, and many of their Catholic neighbors in Northern Ireland would like to unite with them. However, most Protestants in Northern Ireland—who are the dominant group there—wish to remain part of the United Kingdom. This dispute over Northern Ireland has led to violence, especially from the 1960s to the 1990s. In 1998 leaders of the United Kingdom and the Republic of Ireland met with leaders of both sides in Northern Ireland. They signed an agreement to end the violence, but disputes have since erupted. The future of Northern Ireland remains uncertain.

Reading Check **Identifying Cause and Effect** What happened as a result of the potato crop failure in the 1840s?

Irish Folk Dance

NATIONAL GEOGRAPHIC

▲ The féis (FESH) is a celebration of Irish culture that includes dances such as the jig, reel, and hornpipe. *Place* **To whom do the Irish trace their ancestry?**

Scandinavia

Main Idea **The Scandinavian countries have similar cultures and high standards of living.**

Geography and You How would you like to live in a place where the sun never sets in midsummer? The Land of the Midnight Sun lies in the far north of Europe. Read on to see how the people there, known as Scandinavians, adapt to their environment.

Scandinavia, the northernmost part of Europe, is made up of five nations: Norway, Sweden, Finland, Denmark, and Iceland. These countries have related histories and, except for Finland, share similar cultures. They also have standards of living that are among the world's highest.

The Land

Although Scandinavia lies north, warm winds from the North Atlantic Current give its southern and western areas a relatively mild climate. Central Scandinavia has long, cold winters and short, warm summers. The northernmost part of Scandinavia near the Arctic Circle, however, has a very cold climate. Because this rugged area is so far north, there are summer days when the sun never sets. Many people have to darken their windows to sleep. In midwinter, though, these same people may battle depression, because there are days when the sun never rises.

Scandinavia's physical landscape is quite **varied** because of its large size. Many islands dot the jagged coastlines. Lowland plains stretch over Denmark and the southern part of Sweden and Finland. Mountains form a backbone along the border of Norway and Sweden. Forests and lakes cover much of Sweden and Finland. In the far north, above the Arctic Circle, the land is barren tundra that remains frozen for most of the year.

Two countries—Iceland and Norway—have special features. The island of Iceland sits in an area of the North Atlantic Ocean where two of Earth's tectonic plates meet. The two plates are pulling away from each other, allowing hot magma to rise to the surface. This creates hot springs and **geysers** (GY·zuhrs), which are springs that shoot hot water and steam into the air. Iceland also has about 200 volcanoes, though many are not active.

Norway, meanwhile, is known for its many beautiful **fjords** (fee·AWRDS), or narrow inlets of the sea. Steep cliffs or slopes surround the fjords, which were carved by glaciers long ago. Fjords provide inland waterways that supply fish for food and export.

The Economies

The countries of Scandinavia are wealthy and prosperous. Their economies are based on a mix of agriculture, manufacturing, and service industries. Although farmland is limited, most Scandinavian countries produce most of the food they need. Fishing is an important industry, especially in Norway and Iceland.

For energy, Norway relies on its own oil and natural gas, taken from fields under the North Sea. Iceland taps the molten rock beneath its surface to make **geothermal energy.** This is electricity produced by natural underground sources of steam. Iceland also uses hydroelectric power. Finland takes advantage of its fast-running rivers to generate hydroelectric power as well. Sweden uses a combination of nuclear power and oil.

Some Scandinavian countries have abundant mineral and forest resources that support various industries. Sweden has

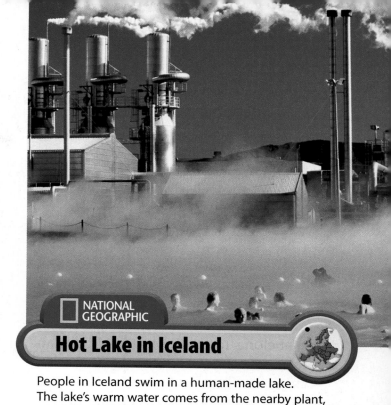

NATIONAL GEOGRAPHIC

Hot Lake in Iceland

People in Iceland swim in a human-made lake. The lake's warm water comes from the nearby plant, which produces energy from hot springs. **Place Why are hot springs numerous in Iceland?**

reserves of iron ore that it uses to produce steel for a variety of products, including cars such as Saabs and Volvos. Shipbuilding is important in Finland and Denmark, as are wood and wood product industries in Finland and Sweden.

Denmark plays an important role in world trade. Copenhagen, its capital, sits at the entrance to the Baltic Sea. The largest ships cannot enter that sea because it is not deep enough for them. As a result, many ships stop in Copenhagen, where workers transfer cargoes to other vessels.

People and Culture

Most of the Scandinavian countries are less densely settled than other European countries. Large parts of Scandinavia are located in the cold north or are too mountainous to attract many people. Only Denmark, the smallest of the five countries, has a high population density. Denmark has a mild climate and relatively flat land that supports much agriculture.

The peoples of Norway, Sweden, Denmark, and Iceland share ethnic ties and speak related languages. They mostly descend from Germanic peoples who settled Scandinavia thousands of years ago. The ancestors of Finland's people, however, probably came from what is now Siberia in Russia. As a result, the Finnish language and culture differ from those of the other Scandinavian countries. Still, Finland shares close historic and religious links to the rest of Scandinavia. For example, most Finns—like most other Scandinavians—belong to the Protestant Lutheran Church.

During the Middle Ages, Scandinavian sailors and traders known as Vikings raided areas of western Europe and explored the North Atlantic Ocean, even reaching America. They also laid the foundation of the modern nations of Denmark, Norway, Sweden, and Iceland. For several hundred years, Sweden ruled its neighbor, Finland. Finland later was controlled by Russia for many years before gaining independence.

Today, Denmark, Norway, and Sweden are constitutional monarchies with governments similar to that of the United Kingdom. Finland and Iceland are republics with elected presidents. Iceland's parliament, the Althing, first met in A.D. 930, making it one of the oldest surviving legislatures in the world.

The Scandinavian countries take pride in providing extensive services to their citizens. As welfare states, they not only help the needy, but they also offer health care, child care, elder care, and retirement benefits to all. In return for these services, the people pay some of the highest taxes in the world.

 Reading Check **Identifying** What energy resources are found in Scandinavia?

Section Review

Social Studies ONLINE
Study Central™ To review this section, go to glencoe.com.

Vocabulary

1. **Explain** the meaning of:
   a. constitutional monarchy
   b. parliamentary democracy
   c. peat
   d. bog
   e. productivity
   f. geyser
   g. fjord
   h. geothermal energy

Main Ideas

2. **Summarizing** Use a graphic organizer like the one below to summarize important details about the United Kingdom's government, its history, and how it has influenced governments around the world.

   Government of the United Kingdom
   → □ → □ → □

3. **Explaining** Why is the island of Ireland divided, and how has that led to conflict?

4. **Making Generalizations** What do the Scandinavian countries have in common?

Critical Thinking

5. **BIG Idea** Why are the United Kingdom, Ireland, and the countries of Scandinavia considered a subregion of Europe?

6. **Challenge** How are the constitutional monarchies of northern Europe similar to the government of the United States? How are they different?

Writing About Geography

7. **Expository Writing** Write a paragraph comparing the economies of the countries of northern Europe.

Europe's Heartland

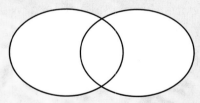
Picture This Mont Blanc, near the French-Italian border, is the highest point in Europe. Glacial hazards and frequent avalanches make hiking and skiing in this area dangerous. Torchlight parades are held to honor those who have lost their lives on the mountain. Mountains in Europe influence how and where people live. Read this section to learn how major landforms affect people living in the heartland of Europe.

▼ **Skiers carrying torches descend Mont Blanc**

France and the Benelux Countries

Main Idea France and the Benelux countries are important cultural, agricultural, and manufacturing centers of Europe.

Geography and You When you think of France, perhaps you picture the Eiffel Tower in Paris. There is, of course, much more to the country, as you will read.

France is in the heart of western Europe. Its three small neighbors to the northeast are known as the Benelux countries. The group name comes from the first syllables of the individual country names—*Bel*gium, the *Net*herlands, and *Lux*embourg.

France's Land and Economy

France is the second-largest country in Europe. It is slightly smaller than the state of Texas. The landscape in France varies widely. Most of northern France is part of the vast Northern European Plain. In the south, high mountain ranges separate the country from Spain, Italy, and Switzerland. Rivers, such the Seine (SAYN) and the Loire (LWAHR), link France's different regions.

Most of France has a mild or warm climate and rich soil that is ideal for farming. France's agriculture is characterized by **specialization**. This means focusing efforts on certain activities to make the best use of resources. One area of specialization for the French is growing grapes and making wines. Farmers also use the milk of dairy cattle and sheep to produce about 250 kinds of world-famous cheese. France sells these cheeses and other food products to countries that cannot produce them on their own. In turn, France imports goods that it cannot easily make.

Louvre Museum, Paris

NATIONAL GEOGRAPHIC

The Louvre, in Paris, houses some of the world's most famous paintings and sculptures. *Place* **What other attractions in France draw tourists?**

France **relies** on industry as well as agriculture. Workers in traditional industries make cars and trucks, chemicals, textiles, and processed foods. France also has new **high-technology industries,** which include making computers and other products that require sophisticated engineering. Tourism is an important industry in France. It provides jobs to about 1 in 12 French workers. Millions of people come each year to visit Paris, France's vibrant capital. Other tourists vacation on sunny Mediterranean beaches, ski in the snowy Alps, and tour historic castles called châteaux (sha·TOHZ).

France's People and Culture

Most French trace their ancestry to the Celts, Romans, and Germanic peoples of early Europe. The majority speak French and consider themselves to be Roman Catholic. Islam is France's second religion, because so many people have migrated from Muslim countries in Africa.

Most of France's 60.7 million people live in urban areas. Almost 10 million make their homes in Paris, one of Europe's largest cities.

There, people can enjoy museums, universities, fine restaurants, and charming cafes. The Seine River and landmarks like the Eiffel Tower and Notre Dame Cathedral add to the city's beauty.

The French take great pride in their culture, which has greatly influenced the Western world. French cooking and French fashion are admired far and wide. France also boasts famous philosophers, writers, artists, composers, and film directors.

The French Revolution of the late 1700s also influenced the Western world. It brought about the decline of powerful monarchies and the rise of democracies. Today France is a democratic republic with both a president, elected by the people, and a prime minister, appointed by the president. The president has a great deal of power and can even dismiss the legislature, forcing new elections to be held.

The Benelux Countries

The small Benelux countries—Belgium, the Netherlands, and Luxembourg—have much in common. Their lands are low, flat, and densely populated. Most people live in cities, work in businesses or factories, and enjoy a high standard of living. All three nations are also parliamentary democracies with monarchs as heads of state.

Belgium has long been a trade and manufacturing center. With relatively few natural resources of its own, the country imports the raw materials to make and export vehicles, chemicals, and textiles.

TIME GLOBAL CITIZENS

NAME: THIERRY HENRY   **HOME COUNTRY:** France

ACHIEVEMENT: This soccer player helped power the French national team to years of success. Now Henry is using his hero status on the soccer field to fight racism in European society. Henry has been the target of racist slurs and has witnessed racial abuse by players and fans at European sporting events. So in January 2005, Henry launched the Stand Up Speak Up campaign to fight racism. In one year, Henry raised nearly $6 million to be distributed to groups in Europe dedicated to fighting racism. The funds also support teen athletic groups that emphasize sportsmanship and respect for others.

QUOTE: ❝I want to be able to watch football [soccer] on TV or attend a match and not hear a single racist insult. That's what I'd like to do for future generations of players.❞

Henry speaks out against racism at sporting events.

CITIZENS IN ACTION Why might some people respect the views of athletes and celebrities more than those of other citizens? How should athletes handle this "power"?

Most Belgians live in crowded urban areas. Antwerp is a busy port and the center of the world diamond industry. Brussels is the capital and headquarters of the European Union (EU).

Belgium is made up of three regions—Flanders, Wallonia, and Brussels. In Flanders, to the north and west of Brussels, most people speak Dutch and are known as Flemings. In Wallonia, the areas south and east of Brussels, most people speak French and are known as Walloons. The population of the Brussels region comes from both language groups. As a result, the Brussels region is officially **bilingual,** using two languages. While each region practices self-rule, tensions sometimes arise between Flemings and Walloons.

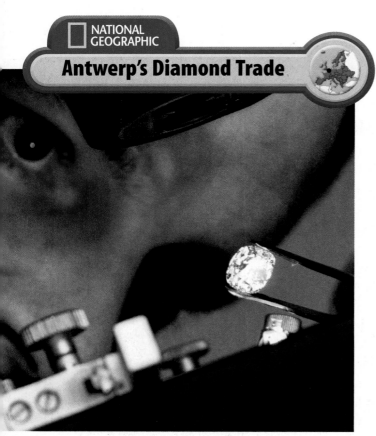

NATIONAL GEOGRAPHIC
Antwerp's Diamond Trade

▲ Antwerp has been a center of the world's diamond trade for more than 500 years. Some $20 billion in diamond sales occur there annually. ***Movement*** **What goods does Belgium export?**

To the north of Belgium is the Netherlands, whose people are known as the Dutch. About 25 percent of the Netherlands lies below sea level. Without defenses against the sea, high tides would flood much of the country. The Dutch have built dikes, or banks of soil, to control and confine the sea as seen in **Figure 2.** They drain and pump the wetlands dry. Once run by windmills, pumps are now driven by steam or electricity. The drained lands, called **polders,** have rich farming soil.

About 90 percent of the Dutch live in cities and towns. Amsterdam is the capital and largest city. Living in a densely populated country, the Dutch make good use of their space. Houses are narrow but tall, and apartments are often built on canals and over highways. The Dutch work in service industries, manufacturing, and trade. The major exports of the Netherlands are cheese, vegetables, and flowers. Acres and acres of tulip fields bloom in the spring, and each year the Dutch export about two million tulip bulbs.

Southeast of Belgium lies Luxembourg, one of Europe's smallest countries. Centrally located in Europe, Luxembourg thrives as a center of trade and finance. Many **multinational companies,** or firms that do business in several countries, have their headquarters here. The people of Luxembourg have a mixed French and German background.

Challenges

France and the Benelux countries are challenged by population changes. First, their populations are aging. An aging population puts pressure on workers who must pay taxes to provide retirement and health care benefits for older people. Second, France and the Benelux countries have fairly large African and Asian minority

Figure 2 **Areas of the Netherlands Reclaimed From the Sea**

Windmills in the Netherlands

Land Reclamation
- 1200–1600
- 1600–1900
- 1900–present
- — Dike

North Sea

Wunseradiel

Stavoren

Andijk

Alkmaar

Amsterdam ✛

Rotterdam

Rhine R.

Meuse R.

GERMANY

Rhine R.

BELGIUM

0   40 kilometers
0   40 miles
Lambert Conformal Conic projection

Map Skills

1 **Location** Where did most of the land reclamation take place before 1900?

2 **Human-Environment Interaction** Why did the Dutch reclaim land from the sea?

populations. Some people in the majority culture fear that many in these groups appear unwilling to accept European culture and customs. However, many members of minority groups live in crowded neighborhoods with poor schools, high unemployment, and little contact with the majority culture. In 2005 frustration among North Africans in France boiled over into almost three weeks of rioting. French government leaders have vowed to fight discrimination and improve conditions in ethnic communities.

✓ Reading Check **Explaining** How does France's physical geography contribute to its agriculture?

Germany and the Alpine Countries

Main Idea Germany, Switzerland, and Austria are known for their mountain scenery and prosperous economies.

Geography and You Have you ever found yourself working alongside someone you used to compete against? Germans are in that position now that the two halves of their country are reunited. Read to learn more.

Germany and the Alpine countries—Switzerland, Austria, and Liechtenstein—lie in Central Europe. They all have strong economies and a high standard of living.

German Clock Maker

NATIONAL GEOGRAPHIC

▲ Germany's Black Forest region is famous for its finely crafted clocks, including cuckoo clocks. **Place** Describe Germany's industry and agriculture today.

Germany's Land

A large country encircled by nine other nations, Germany sits snugly in the heart of Europe. The flat Northern European Plain extends across northern Germany. Rocky highlands, some of which contain rich coal deposits, cover the central part of the country. The majestic Alps rise in the far south. The Alps are famous for their beauty, but many forests on the lower slopes of these mountains are threatened by acid rain.

Rivers have been vital to Germany's economic growth. They are used to transport raw materials to factories and to carry manufactured goods to market. The Danube River, one of Europe's most important waterways, begins in the Black Forest and winds eastward across southern Germany. Another river, the Elbe, flows from the central highlands to the North Sea. Hamburg, Germany's largest port city, is located on the Elbe River.

The most important of Germany's rivers—the Rhine—actually begins in the Swiss Alps. It then passes through Germany and the Netherlands before spilling into the North Sea. The Rhine is long and deep, allowing oceangoing ships to travel far inland.

History and Government

Germany's central location in Europe has long made it a crossroads for peoples, ideas, and armies. For centuries, Germany was a collection of states that were deeply involved in Europe's wars and religious struggles. In 1871 these states joined together to form the modern nation of Germany.

During the 1900s, Germany's efforts to dominate Europe helped spark two world wars. Allied countries—the United States, the Soviet Union, the United Kingdom, and France—defeated Germany in World War II.

In 1945 the Allies divided Germany into four zones of occupation. The Soviet zone later became Communist-ruled East Germany. The three other zones, controlled by the United States, the United Kingdom, and France, became democratic West Germany. After the collapse of communism, the two parts of Germany were reunited in 1990.

Today, Germany—like the United States—is a federal republic. This means that the national government and state governments share power. An elected president serves as Germany's head of state, but he or she performs only ceremonial duties. The country's chancellor, chosen by parliament, is the real head of government.

Germany's People

Germany has the largest population of the European countries—82.5 million. Nearly 90 percent of the people live in urban areas. The largest city, and the nation's capital, is Berlin. With many museums, concert halls, and theaters, Berlin is a cultural center as well as the seat of government. Germans are proud to have produced many brilliant thinkers and writers, as well as composers such as Johann Sebastian Bach and Ludwig van Beethoven.

About 90 percent of the country's people are native Germans, and German is the main language. Most of the rest of the population has immigrated from eastern Europe and Turkey. These immigrants came to Germany to find work or to escape political troubles in their homelands. The newcomers include many Muslims and Jews, but most Germans are Protestant or Catholic.

The Economy

Today, Germany is a global economic power and a leader in the European Union. This is due in part to Germany's highly

NATIONAL GEOGRAPHIC

Germany's Auto Industry

New cars are placed in a huge storage tower near an automobile plant in Wolfsburg, Germany.
Place What role does Germany have in the global economy?

productive agriculture. In the river valleys and plains areas, the fertile land and mild climate are well suited for farming. Germany produces enough food to feed its people and export its surplus.

It is industry, though, that is most responsible for Germany's strong economy. The country is a leading producer of steel, chemicals, cars, and electrical equipment. During the late 1900s, many Western industrialized countries experienced a decline in manufacturing. In Germany, however, the decrease was not dramatic. German firms had **invested** money to research and develop desirable, competitive products.

One of Germany's economic challenges has come as a result of **reunification,** when East and West Germany united under one government in 1990. At the time, workers in East Germany had less experience and less training in modern technology than workers in West Germany. Old and inefficient factories in the east could not compete with the more advanced industries in the west. Many businesses closed, and economic activities in the eastern part of Germany continue to lag behind those in the prosperous west.

The Alpine Countries

The Alpine countries take their name from the Alps of central Europe. These mountainous countries include Switzerland, Austria, and Liechtenstein. Liechtenstein is a tiny country of only 62 square miles (161 sq. km)—smaller than Washington, D.C. The whole population—about 40,000 people—would not even fill a major league baseball stadium.

Switzerland is also a small country, but it is much bigger than Liechtenstein and far more important internationally. The few travel routes that cut through the Alps lie in Switzerland. So for centuries, the Swiss have been "gatekeepers" between northern and southern Europe. That role helped Switzerland decide long ago to practice **neutrality,** or refusal to take sides in wars. As a result, for more than 700 years the Swiss have enjoyed a stable democratic government, even when fighting has raged around them. Today many international organizations, such as the International Red Cross, are based in the Swiss city of Geneva.

Switzerland's geography also affected the growth of individual communities. The rugged mountains isolated groups of peo-

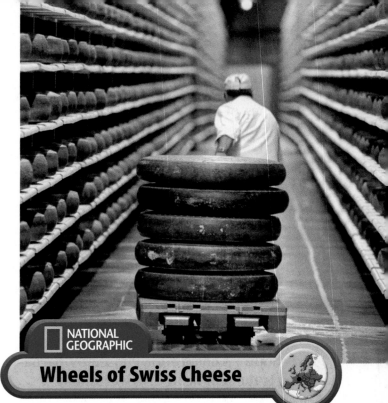

NATIONAL GEOGRAPHIC

Wheels of Swiss Cheese

Fine cheeses may be aged for years before they are ready to eat. Switzerland exports more than 50,000 tons of cheese each year. *Place* How did Switzerland's geography affect its communities?

ple from one another. As a result, each town and city treasures its unique traditions and independence. Today the people of Switzerland represent many different ethnic groups and religions. The country also has not one but four national languages: German, French, and Italian—which are the native tongues of Switzerland's neighbors—and Romansch. Most Swiss speak German, and many speak more than one language.

Although it has few natural resources, Switzerland is a thriving industrial nation. Dams on Switzerland's rivers produce great amounts of hydroelectric power for industries and homes. Using imported materials, Swiss workers make high-quality electronic equipment, chemicals, and other goods. The country is also known for its fine clocks and watches, excellent chocolate and cheeses, and its multipurpose Swiss army knives. A large part of the Swiss economy is dependent upon its banking and other financial services. Because Switzerland's neutrality is honored by other countries, people from around the world consider Swiss banks to be safe and secure.

East of Switzerland is landlocked Austria. The Alps cover the western three-quarters of Austria, so there is little good farmland. The beautiful mountain scenery does, however, attract many skiers and tourists. The mountains also provide valuable timber and iron ore and, as in Switzerland, fast-moving rivers generate hydroelectric power. With these resources, Austria's factories produce machinery, chemicals, metals, and vehicles. Austria also has strong banking and insurance industries.

The people of Austria mainly speak German and are Roman Catholic. Most Austrians live in cities and towns. Vienna, on the Danube River, is the capital and largest city, and about one-fifth of Austrians live there. Before World War I, Vienna was the heart of the vast Austro-Hungarian Empire that covered much of central and southeastern Europe. Vienna was also a center of culture and learning. Some of the world's greatest composers, including Wolfgang Amadeus Mozart, lived or performed in Vienna. The city's concert halls, historic palaces, and churches continue to draw music lovers and other visitors today.

✓ **Reading Check** **Contrasting** How do the economies of the western and eastern parts of Germany differ?

Social Studies ONLINE
Study Central™ To review this section, go to glencoe.com.

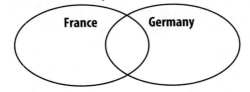

Section 2 Review

Vocabulary

1. **Explain** the significance of the following terms:
   a. specialization
   b. high-technology industry
   c. bilingual
   d. polder
   e. multinational company
   f. reunification
   g. neutrality

Main Ideas

2. **Explaining** How has French culture influenced the world?

3. **Analyzing** Draw a Venn diagram to analyze how agriculture is similar and different in France and Germany.

France   Germany

Critical Thinking

4. **Making Generalizations** How does specialization in French agriculture and food production lead to interdependence with other countries?

5. **BIG Idea** Give three examples of how people in this part of Europe have changed the environment. Explain if you think those changes are positive or negative.

6. **Challenge** Do you think the economic successes of the countries of Europe's heartland can continue in the future? Explain your answer fully.

Writing About Geography

7. **Persuasive Writing** Write a letter to a friend trying to persuade him or her to visit a specific country in Europe's heartland with you. Describe why that country interests you.

Guide to Reading

BIG Idea

Places reflect the relationship between humans and the physical environment.

Content Vocabulary

- dry farming (p. 339)
- autonomy (p. 339)
- subsidy (p. 340)

Academic Vocabulary

- similar (p. 339)
- militant (p. 340)

Reading Strategy

Making Generalizations Use a diagram like the one below to write three characteristics shared by the countries in this region.

Southern Europe

Picture This Lunchtime lineup! Visit Antiparos, Greece, and you are likely to see octopuses draped over fishing lines to dry in preparation for a later meal. The boneless octopus has a parrot-like beak, a doughnut-shaped brain, eight arms, three hearts, and—it can change colors. Octopuses thrive in the clear, blue waters of the Mediterranean Sea. The sea and the lands surrounding it have supported numerous cultures. Read this section to learn about today's cultures of southern, or Mediterranean, Europe.

▼ **Octopuses drying on line, Antiparos, Greece**

Spain and Portugal

Main Idea Spain and Portugal are young democracies with growing economies.

Geography and You Can you imagine chasing bulls down the main streets of your hometown? People in Pamplona, Spain, do this every year as part of a summer festival. Keep reading to discover more about colorful Spain and its neighbor, Portugal.

Spain and Portugal occupy the Iberian Peninsula in southwestern Europe. They share it with the tiny nation of Andorra, nestled in the Pyrenees Mountains.

Spain

Most of Spain is covered by the Meseta, a dry plateau surrounded by mountain ranges. The reddish-yellow soil there tends to be poor, and rain is scarce. However, crops such as wheat and vegetables are grown by **dry farming**. This technique does not depend on irrigation. Instead the land is left unplanted every few years so that it can store moisture.

Farming is easier in other parts of the country. Northwestern Spain, which borders the Atlantic Ocean, has mild temperatures and plenty of rain. Southern Spain, which borders the Mediterranean Sea, has wet winters and dry summers. In this area, farmers use irrigation to grow citrus fruits, olives, and grapes—Spain's leading agricultural products.

In the late 1900s, Spain's manufacturing and service industries grew rapidly. Today they dominate the economy. Spanish workers produce processed foods, clothing, footwear, steel, and cars. Spain also benefits greatly from tourism. The country's attractions include castles, cathedrals, and

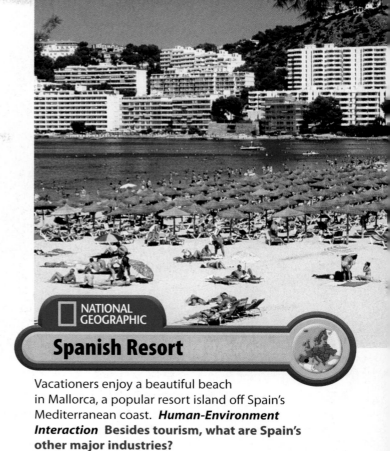

NATIONAL GEOGRAPHIC

Spanish Resort

Vacationers enjoy a beautiful beach in Mallorca, a popular resort island off Spain's Mediterranean coast. **Human-Environment Interaction** Besides tourism, what are Spain's other major industries?

sunny Mediterranean beaches. Tourists also enjoy Spain's cultural traditions, such as bullfighting and flamenco dancing.

Most of Spain's people speak Castilian Spanish, the country's official language. Some regions of Spain, however, are home to distinct groups with their own languages. The people of Catalonia, in the northeast, speak Catalan, which is **similar** to an old language of southern France. In the Pyrenees, the Basques speak Euskera, a language unrelated to any other in the world.

After years of rule by a dictator, Spain became a democracy in the late 1970s. In recent times, Spain's democratic government has given the different regions of Spain greater **autonomy,** or self-rule. In the Basque region, though, many people want to be completely separate from Spain. Some Basque separatists have used terrorism to try to achieve this goal.

NATIONAL GEOGRAPHIC

Harvesting Cork

The bark of a cork oak is stripped and then cut and shaped into corks for bottles (inset). The trees will grow new bark within 10 years. **Place** How have subsidies from the European Union impacted agriculture in Portugal?

Most of Spain's 43.5 million people live in urban areas. The main cities are Madrid, the capital, and Barcelona, the leading seaport and industrial center. The cities of Seville, Granada, and Córdoba, in the south, show the influence of the Muslims who ruled Spain for much of the Middle Ages.

Most people in Spain today are Roman Catholic. A large number of Muslims from North Africa have migrated to Spain in recent years. Tensions have sometimes developed between the Spanish population and Muslim immigrants. Spain was shaken in 2004 when terrorist attacks by suspected Muslim **militants** killed 191 people on Madrid trains.

Portugal

Spain's smaller neighbor to the west is Portugal. Most of Portugal's land is a low coastal plain split in half by the Tagus River. In both the north and the south, people grow a variety of crops. The most impor-

tant are grapes used for wine making and oak trees that provide cork. Most Portuguese live in small villages on the coast, near the cities of Lisbon and Porto. Many people earn a living there by fishing in the Atlantic Ocean.

Closeness to the ocean helped Portugal become a sea power during the 1500s. The Portuguese built an empire that included Brazil and parts of Asia and Africa. Today Portugal has a democratic government, and its shaky economy is growing stronger with the help of subsidies from the European Union. **Subsidies** are special payments a government makes to support a group or industry. With this help, manufacturing and service industries have become more important than agriculture to Portugal's economy.

Reading Check **Identifying** What languages are spoken in Spain?

Italy

Main Idea Italy's north and south form two distinct economic regions.

Geography and You Do you have a favorite Italian food? When people think of Italy, they often think of delicious pasta. Read to learn what else the country produces.

Italy juts out from Europe into the Mediterranean Sea. The mainland looks like a boot about to kick a triangular football. The "football" is Sicily (SIH·suh·lee), an island that is also part of the country.

In Italy's north, the Alps tower over the broad Lombardy plain. In central and southern areas, the Apennine Mountains form a backbone that stretches into Sicily. Volcanoes also dot the landscape. Throughout history, southern Italy has experienced volcanic eruptions and earthquakes.

The Economy

Since the mid-1900s, Italy has changed from a mainly agricultural country into a leading industrial economy. Most of this growth has taken place in northern Italy. Workers in northern manufacturing cities, such as Milan, Turin, and Genoa, produce cars, technical instruments, appliances, clothing, and high-quality goods. The north's fertile Po River valley is also the country's richest farming region. Farmers there raise livestock and grow grapes, olives, and other crops.

Southern Italy is poorer and less industrialized than northern Italy. Much of the terrain is mountainous, with limited mineral deposits, poor land for farming and grazing, and few navigable rivers. As a result, unemployment is high. Unemployment has led many southern Italians to seek a better life in northern Italy or other parts of Europe.

The People

About 90 percent of Italy's 58.7 million people live in urban areas. In the cities, modern life is mingled with the past. Rome, Italy's largest city, was once the center of the Roman Empire. Today, Rome is Italy's capital and home to the country's democratic republic form of government.

The people of Italy speak Italian, and nearly all are Roman Catholic. In fact, the Roman Catholic Church is based in Rome. The Church rules tiny Vatican City, where the pope and other Church leaders live and work. Although Vatican City is within Rome's boundaries, it is an independent country—the smallest in the world.

Reading Check **Explaining** How do the economies of northern and southern Italy differ?

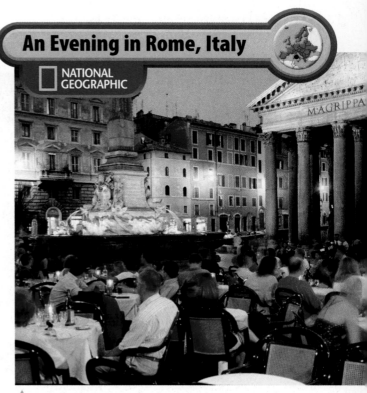

An Evening in Rome, Italy

NATIONAL GEOGRAPHIC

▲ People dine at an outdoor restaurant near the Pantheon, a public building built by the ancient Romans. **Place** **What percentage of Italy's people live in urban areas?**

Greece

Main Idea Mountains, seas, and islands have shaped Greece's people and economy.

Geography and You Do you ever go boating or fishing? You will understand why these are popular activities for the Greeks when you read about Greece's geography.

East of Italy, Greece extends from the Balkan Peninsula into the Mediterranean Sea. The country includes not only a mainland, but about 2,000 islands. Like other Mediterranean areas, Greece is often shaken by earthquakes.

Because of mountains and poor, stony soil, agriculture plays a declining role in the Greek economy. In the highlands, people raise sheep and goats. On farms in plains and valleys, farmers grow wheat, olives, and other crops. In recent decades, Greece has developed new industries, such as textiles, footwear, and chemicals. Shipping is a major business. Greece has one of the world's largest shipping fleets, including oil tankers, cargo ships, and passenger vessels. Tourism is another key industry. Each year millions of tourists come to visit historic sites such as the Parthenon, an ancient temple in the city of Athens.

About 60 percent of Greeks are urban dwellers. Nearly a third live in or around Athens, the capital. The Greeks speak a form of Greek similar to that spoken in ancient times. Most of them are Greek Orthodox Christian. Today, Greece is a democratic republic and a member of the European Union.

Reading Check **Explaining** How has geography affected the way Greeks earn a living?

Section 3 Review

Social Studies ONLINE
Study Central™ To review this section, go to glencoe.com.

Vocabulary

1. **Define** *dry farming, autonomy,* and *subsidy,* and use each word in a sentence.

Main Ideas

2. **Explaining** How did Portugal benefit from joining the EU?

3. **Identifying** Create a graphic organizer like the one below to identify Italy's agricultural and industrial products.

Products of Italy

4. **Comparing and Contrasting** How is Greece similar to and different from the other countries of southern Europe?

Critical Thinking

5. **BIG Idea** Write two generalizations describing the connection between the physical geography of southern Europe and the lives of the region's people.

6. **Challenge** Write a paragraph explaining how countries in southern Europe have worked to improve their economies.

Writing About Geography

7. **Descriptive Writing** Write the text for a travel brochure that encourages visitors to take a cruise that stops in the countries of southern Europe. Describe the landscapes, cities, and activities that visitors could see in those countries.

TIME
PERSPECTIVES

WHOSE EUROPE IS IT?

As millions of immigrants relocate to Europe, the region's democracies struggle to redefine themselves.

Muslim immigrants gather on Westminster Bridge in London.

People in the United States, a nation formed by immigrants from around the world, understand the concept "out of many, one." Today, the countries of Europe are struggling to comprehend the idea too. For more than 60 years, millions of immigrants—many of them Muslims—have emigrated to some of Europe's oldest democracies.

It has not been easy to get so many different people to respect each other and live together in harmony. In recent years, cultural and religious clashes have developed as immigrants and Europeans struggle to understand each other. As that work continues, there is no doubt that the struggle will have an enormous impact on Europe's future.

In a restaurant in Paris, a Muslim immigrant and a woman born in France work together.

THE NEW MULTICULTURAL EUROPE

From Paris to Amsterdam and Brussels to Berlin, Europe is changing. Not long ago, most citizens of European countries shared certain characteristics. They were mostly all born in Europe, and the majority of them were white and Christian. These similarities helped create a **national identity** for countries like France, Great Britain, and Germany.

After World War II, many of Europe's immigrants were from countries that had been European colonies, like Algeria, India, and Pakistan. Friendly immigration policies following World War II welcomed the newcomers. Governments also established favorable labor policies in the 1960s that were designed to bring much-needed foreign workers to Europe.

But in recent years, the population of Europe has become more diverse. Millions of immigrants, many of them Muslims from North Africa, Turkey, and Southwest Asia, have left their homelands to start new lives in European nations.

Creating a New Identity

The number of immigrants living in Europe has greatly increased. In 2006, for example, there were about 7 million non-Germans living in Germany. Many of these immigrants are from Turkey. The large population of immigrants and their offspring have transformed and challenged traditional European beliefs.

Europe's immigrant **populations**, or groups of people, often view the world differently from people who were born in Europe. Many of the differences deal with culture, religious freedom, and the rights of women. At times, these different perceptions have caused conflict and bad feelings between Europe's older populations and its new ones. "We feel unwelcome," said a Muslim immigrant in Denmark. Some of the conflicts have been violent and have had a global impact.

Muslim Populations in European Countries

Muslim populations
- Less than 5%
- 5% - 10%
- 10% - 50%
- More than 50%
- Not available

United Kingdom
Sweden
Atlantic Ocean
Denmark
Netherlands
Belgium
Germany
Austria
Bosnia-Herzegovina
Serbia
Montenegro
Macedonia
France
Black Sea
Spain
Italy
Switzerland
Albania
Turkey
Mediterranean Sea
500 miles

Source: BBC News.

INTERPRETING MAPS

Categorizing Which countries in Europe have the largest Muslim populations?

Many Turks support their country's proposed admission to the European Union.

Muslims stage a rally to protest the printing of cartoons of the prophet Muhammad.

Danish Prime Minister Fogh Rasmussen, center, discusses the cartoons with a Pakistani diplomat.

AP PHOTO

When Cultures Collide

Early in 2006, Muslims around the world protested cartoons that were published in Europe. The cartoons showed the Muslim religion's prophet Muhammad in a negative way. They were first published in a newspaper in Denmark and later reprinted in various papers throughout Europe.

Muslims across Europe and the world were angry. They thought the cartoons were disrespectful of their religion, **Islam**. This is because Islam does not allow the publication of any images of Muhammad.

Religion and a Free Press

Anger over the cartoons led thousands of Muslims to protest worldwide. Angry protestors marched in several European cities, including London and Copenhagen. Demonstrations were also held throughout Southwest Asia. Many of the protests turned violent as demonstrators burned Danish flags and set fire to Denmark's embassy in Beirut, Lebanon. The riots killed at least 11 people in Afghanistan.

Denmark's prime minister, Anders Fogh Rasmussen, called the protests a global crisis and called for "calm and steadiness." But Fogh Rasmussen would not apologize for what the newspapers did. Like many European leaders and citizens, Fogh Rasmussen believed in the right of a free press. He defended the newspaper's right to print the cartoons of Muhammad even if their publication caused controversy and protest.

A Search for Common Ground

Learning to live with—and absorb—new ethnic groups is one of the greatest challenges facing Europe. Some experts believe that Turkey's proposed admission to the European Union, or the EU, may help bridge the gap between Muslims and traditional Europeans. Turkey would be the first Muslim country in the EU, a group of European nations that have joined together to solve common problems and create economic opportunities.

Experts believe that the European nations will have to learn to compromise and be tolerant of the cultural and religious differences of all of their citizens. Learning how to do that will be a challenge in a multiethnic Europe.

EXPLORING THE ISSUE

1. Comparing How were the opinions of Muslim immigrants and European-born citizens different concerning publishing the cartoons of Muhammad?

2. Making Inferences How might Turkey's admission into the EU change the way citizens born in Europe view Muslim immigrants?

FRANCE'S CLASH OVER SYMBOLS

In January 2004, thousands of Muslim women and men in France took to the streets of Paris to send a message to the French government. Marching hand in hand, many of the women wore head scarves. Some covered their hair with the French flag.

The protesters were angry over a proposed French law. If passed, the law would stop students from wearing head scarves and other noticeable religious symbols in public schools. French president Jacques Chirac (ZHAHK shee•RAHK) proposed the ban on the head scarves, called *hijab* (HEH•JAB), worn by Muslim women and girls. Chirac said the ban was created to make sure French children are not exposed to differences that will "drive people apart." Some Jewish and Christian religious symbols were also included in the proposed ban.

A Heated Debate

Despite the protests, the French government voted the bill into law in 2005. The law continued to be contro- versial. There are about 5 million Muslims in France, nearly 8 percent of the country's population. Critics of the law say wearing a head scarf in school is a personal choice and a basic right. "The government should not be in the business of telling a woman how to dress," said Salam Al-Marayati, of the Muslim Public Affairs Council.

French officials say the law is not directed against any religion. "The idea is to keep the influence of religion away from public schools," said one French diplomat. "A teacher does not have to know whether students are Muslim, Christian, Jewish, or whatever."

Soon after the ban went into effect, some French Muslims who arrived at school wearing scarves pushed them off their heads when they entered the school grounds. Will cultural differences continue to divide Europe's people? That question remains to be answered by European nations as their populations become more diverse.

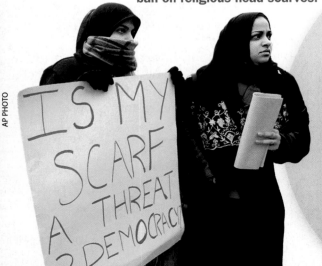

Muslim women protest France's ban on religious head scarves.

AP PHOTO

IS MY SCARF A THREAT 2 DEMOCRACY

EXPLORING THE ISSUE

1. **Predicting** How might the ban on head scarves impact the French government's relations with Muslim countries around the world?

2. **Making Inferences** Why do you think France's law banning *hijab* also forbids the wearing of other religious symbols?

The EU flag

REVIEW AND ASSESS

UNDERSTANDING THE ISSUE

1 **Making Connections** What might be some reasons that people leave their homeland to live in another country?

2 **Writing to Inform** Write a short article describing the protests of cartoons about Muhammad. Include information about demonstrations around the world.

3 **Writing to Persuade** Write a letter to a friend in Denmark. Convince your friend that newspapers did or did not have the right to publish the cartoons of Muhammad.

INTERNET RESEARCH ACTIVITIES

4 Use Internet resources to find information about the European Union. Read about the EU's three main governing organizations. Choose one and write a brief description of it in your own words.

5 With your teacher's help, use Internet resources to find information about a former European colony such as India, Algeria, or Hong Kong. Read about how the colony was formed and the relationship it had with the colonizing country. Why do you think immigrants from former colonies might want to live in Europe? Write your answer in a 250-word essay.

BEYOND THE CLASSROOM

6 **Research the history of immigration in the United States during the early 1900s.** What were some of the challenges immigrants faced as they settled in the U.S.? Write your answer in an article appropriate for a school newspaper.

7 **Debate the issue.** Debate this resolution: "Wearing a religious head scarf in school is a personal choice and a basic right." A panel of student judges should decide which team has the most compelling arguments.

How the European Union Grew

For nearly 60 years, European nations have been forming an ever-closer economic and political union. Here's a look at the steps they have taken along the way.

The Council of Europe is established, creating a forum for Europe's leaders to discuss ways to work together.

France, Germany, Italy, the Netherlands, Belgium, and Luxembourg unite their coal and steel industries.

The European Economic Community is formed. The EEC is the first step toward a common economic market.

EEC merges with other European organizations to form the European Community (EC).

The United Kingdom, Denmark, and Ireland join the EC.

The Maastricht Treaty creates plans for a common currency and for cooperation in foreign affairs.

Greece becomes the EC's tenth member.

Most EU members agree to use a common currency, the euro. Britain, Sweden, and Denmark refuse.

The EU admits ten new member nations. EU leaders sign a new constitution for Europe. A year later, voters in France and the Netherlands reject it.

1948 1951   1957   1967   1973   1981   1991   2002 2004

Building Time Line Reading Skills

1. Analyzing Information How many years does this time line cover? When did Greece join the EC?

2. Making Inferences Why do you think European nations cooperated economically before they worked together politically?

Whose Europe Is It? **347**

Guide to Reading

BIG Idea

Geography is used to interpret the past, understand the present, and plan for the future.

Content Vocabulary

- command economy *(p. 349)*
- market economy *(p. 350)*
- potash *(p. 350)*
- ethnic cleansing *(p. 356)*

Academic Vocabulary

- income *(p. 350)*
- medical *(p. 356)*

Reading Strategy

Summarizing Use a chart like the one below to summarize key facts about each group of countries.

Country Groups	Key Facts
Poland, Belarus, Baltic Republics	
Czech Republic, Slovakia, Hungary	
Countries of Southeastern Europe	

SECTION 4 Eastern Europe

Picture This Show your colors! A young person in Kyiv (Kiev), Ukraine, shows his support for the new government of the Orange Revolution. The Orange Revolution took place during the 2004 presidential elections. Orange was the color of the victorious political party. The party chose orange to represent the change in Ukraine's government. Orange represents the changing color of the leaves in autumn—a process that is peaceful and unstoppable. Read this section to learn more about life in eastern Europe today.

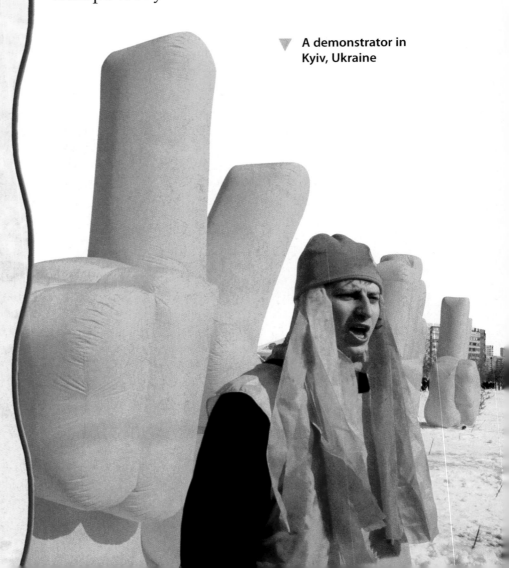

▼ A demonstrator in Kyiv, Ukraine

Poland, Belarus, and the Baltic Republics

Main Idea Poland and the Baltic Republics have become democratic, while Belarus is still influenced by its Communist past.

Geography and You How do you feel when someone orders you to do something? The people of Poland, Belarus, and the Baltic states were all under foreign control at one time. Read what happened to these countries.

Poland, Belarus, and the three Baltic Republics—Lithuania, Latvia, and Estonia—are located in northeastern Europe on or near the Baltic Sea. Although they are neighboring countries, they have distinct histories and cultures.

Poland's Land and History

The sizable country of Poland lies east of Germany. The Carpathian Mountains and other highlands rise on its southern and western edges. Most of Poland, however, is a fertile lowland plain, and the majority of its people live there.

Throughout Poland's history, the largely flat landscape made the country an easy target for invading armies. By the 1800s, Poland had fallen victim to stronger neighbors—Germany, Russia, and Austria.

Poland established its independence again after World War I. But in 1939, German troops once more attacked the country, starting World War II. Poles suffered greatly during the war. Warsaw, the capital, was bombed to ashes.

Struggle for Freedom

After World War II, a Communist government came to power in Poland. Its leaders set up a **command economy,** in which

NATIONAL GEOGRAPHIC

Auschwitz Memorial

Auschwitz was a World War II German prison camp located in Poland. At the camp's entrance was a sign in German that read "Work Sets You Free." Today the camp is a memorial to those who suffered there. **Movement** Why was it easy for armies to invade Poland?

the government decided what, how, and for whom goods would be produced. Poland's postwar government wanted heavy industry and military goods, so few products were made for consumers. This led to food shortages, causing Poland's people to become dissatisfied and demand huge changes.

The Poles wanted a better life, complete with political liberties and religious freedom. Deeply Roman Catholic, most Poles rejoiced when a Polish church leader was chosen to be the head of the Roman Catholic Church in 1978. Pope John Paul II not only stirred national pride in Poland, but he also encouraged the Poles to resist Communist rule.

In the 1980s, Polish workers and farmers formed Solidarity, a labor group that supported peaceful democratic change. Communist leaders finally allowed free elections in 1989 that brought about a democracy.

Social Studies ONLINE

Student Web Activity Visit glencoe.com and complete the Chapter 12 Web Activity about Poland.

This event helped bring about the fall of Communist governments that had long ruled in eastern Europe.

Poland Today

Poland's democratic leaders quickly moved Poland toward a **market economy**. In this system, individuals and businesses make the decisions about how they will use resources and what goods and services to make.

Economic change caused great hardship at first, and many people lost their jobs. Within a few years, however, the economy began to improve. Agriculture remains important, with Poland among the world's top producers of rye and potatoes. Industries, however, are growing. As Poland's economy changes, more people are moving from rural areas to cities, such as Warsaw and Kraków.

Belarus

East of Poland is Belarus, which also is covered by a lowland plain. Belarus was once part of the Soviet Union, and it still has close ties to Russia. Its leaders favor strong government and a command economy.

Belarus has few resources other than **potash,** a mineral used in making fertilizer. Industries include processing fertilizer and manufacturing trucks, radios, televisions, and bicycles. Government-controlled farms produce vegetables, grain, and other crops.

Most people in Belarus are Eastern Orthodox Slavs. Two-thirds live in cities, such as Minsk, the capital.

The Baltic Republics

The small countries of Lithuania, Latvia, and Estonia lie on the shores of the Baltic Sea. Until 1991, the Baltic Republics were part of the Soviet Union. Today, all three countries have large Russian minority populations. Most people in Estonia and Latvia are Protestant, while Roman Catholics make up the majority in Lithuania.

All three Baltic Republics have seen strong economic growth since the mid-1990s. Their economies are based on dairy farming, beef production, fishing, and shipbuilding. Estonia has done especially well, and its people have the Baltic group's highest average **incomes.** Estonia's major export is telecommunications equipment.

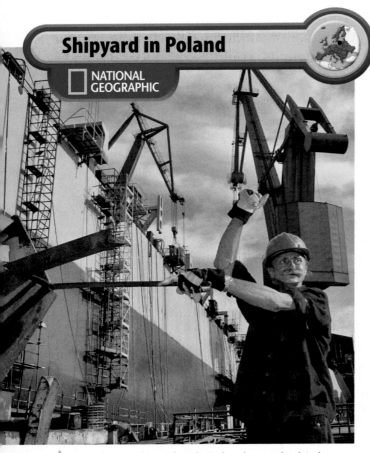

Shipyard in Poland

NATIONAL GEOGRAPHIC

▲ This shipyard in Gdansk, Poland, was the birthplace of the labor group Solidarity in the 1980s. Shipbuilding is still an important industry in Poland today. *Place* **What was Solidarity? What was its goal?**

✓ **Reading Check** Comparing and Contrasting
What do the Baltic Republics, Belarus, and Poland have in common? How are they different?

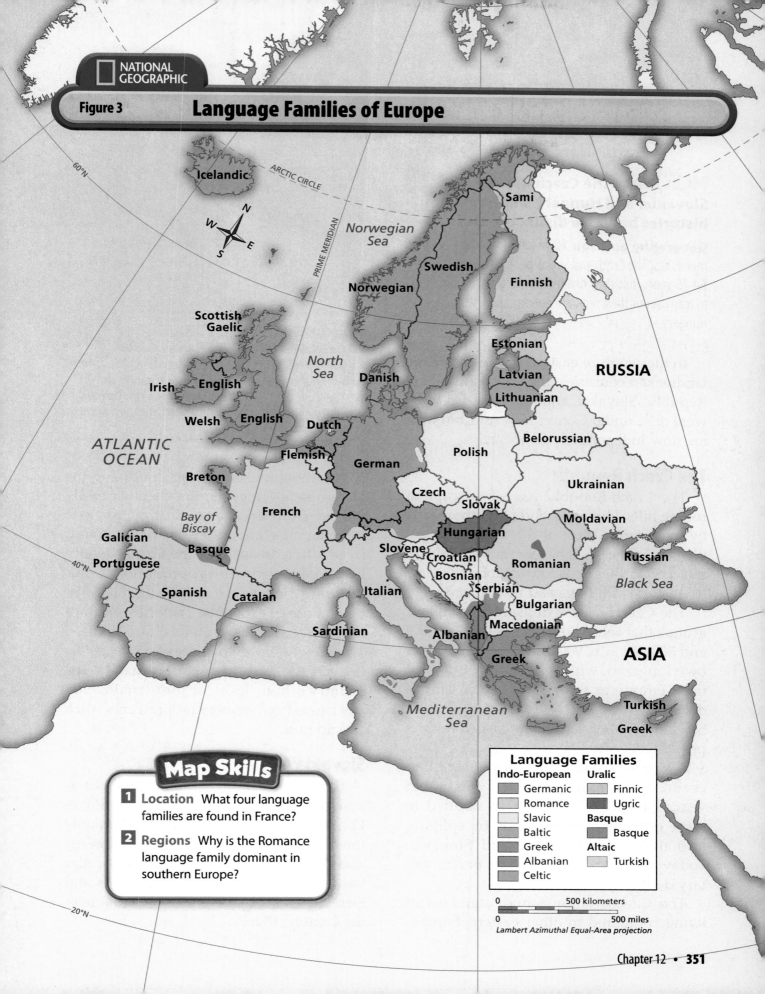

Figure 3 · **Language Families of Europe**

Icelandic

ARCTIC CIRCLE

60°N

Sami

Norwegian Sea

PRIME MERIDIAN

Swedish

Norwegian

Finnish

Scottish Gaelic

Estonian

RUSSIA

North Sea

Latvian

Danish

Lithuanian

Irish · English

Belorussian

Welsh · English

Dutch

ATLANTIC OCEAN

Flemish

German

Polish

Ukrainian

Breton

Czech

French

Slovak

Moldavian

Bay of Biscay

Hungarian

Galician

Slovene

Russian

Basque

Croatian

Romanian

40°N

Portuguese

Bosnian

Black Sea

Spanish

Catalan

Italian

Serbian

Bulgarian

Sardinian

Macedonian

Albanian

ASIA

Greek

Turkish

Mediterranean Sea

Greek

Map Skills

1 **Location** What four language families are found in France?

2 **Regions** Why is the Romance language family dominant in southern Europe?

Language Families

Indo-European
- Germanic
- Romance
- Slavic
- Baltic
- Greek
- Albanian
- Celtic

Uralic
- Finnic
- Ugric

Basque
- Basque

Altaic
- Turkish

0   500 kilometers
0   500 miles
Lambert Azimuthal Equal-Area projection

20°N

The Czech Republic, Slovakia, and Hungary

Main Idea The Czech Republic, Slovakia, and Hungary share common histories but have distinct cultures.

Geography and You Have you ever ended a close friendship? The Czech and Slovak people shared a country for 75 years, but they divided it into two in 1993. Read to learn about their separate nations and their neighbor, Hungary.

In the center of eastern Europe are three landlocked countries: the Czech (CHEHK) Republic, Slovakia, and Hungary. All three were once under Communist rule, but they are now independent democracies.

The Czech Republic

The Czech Republic has a landscape of rolling hills, lowlands, and plains bordered by mountains. Most of the country's people live in cities, such as Prague (PRAHG), the capital. Prague is known for its beautiful historic buildings and monuments.

The Czech people descend from Slavic groups that settled the area in the A.D. 400s and 500s. By A.D. 900, the Czechs had their own kingdom, which became part of Austria's empire in the 1500s. After Austria's defeat in World War I, the Czechs and their Slovak neighbors united to create an independent country.

Czechoslovakia (CHEHK·uh·sloh·VAHK·ee·uh) lasted from 1918 until 1993. In that year, the Czechs and Slovaks decided to settle ongoing disagreements by splitting into the Czech Republic and Slovakia. Today the Czech Republic is a parliamentary democracy.

The Czechs enjoy a high standard of living compared to other eastern Europe-

Old and New in Prague

A teenager in Prague, the Czech Republic, talks on her cell phone as she strolls through the city's historic area. **Regions** How does the Czech standard of living compare to that in other eastern European countries?

ans. Although Communists controlled the government for years, the Czechs rapidly moved from a command economy to a free market economy in the 1990s. Today, large fertile areas make the Czech Republic a major agricultural producer. Manufacturing, however, forms the backbone of the country's economy. Factories produce machinery, vehicles, metals, and textiles. The Czech Republic is also known for its fine crystal and beer. Unfortunately, the country's high level of industrialization has caused environmental problems, such as acid rain.

Slovakia

East of the Czech Republic lies its former partner, Slovakia. In northern Slovakia, the Carpathian Mountains dominate the landscape. Rugged peaks, thick forests, and blue lakes make this area a popular vacation spot. In the south, vineyards and farms spread across fertile lowlands near the Danube River.

Independent since 1993, Slovakia is a democracy today. The Slovaks, however, have moved more slowly to a free market economy than the Czechs have. Slovakia has fewer factories than the Czech Republic, and the country is much less industrialized.

The Slovaks also have a language and culture different from the Czechs. While most Czechs are nonpracticing Catholics or are not religious at all, most Slovaks are devout Catholics. Nearly 60 percent of Slovaks live in towns and cities. Bratislava, on the Danube River, is Slovakia's capital.

Hungary

Hungary is located on a large lowland area south of Slovakia and east of Austria. The capital city, Budapest, straddles Hungary's most important waterway, the Danube River.

The Hungarians are not related to the Slavic and Germanic peoples who live in most of eastern Europe, and the language spoken in Hungary is unique (see **Figure 3**). Their ancestors are the Magyars, who moved into the area from Central Asia about a thousand years ago. Like the Czechs and Slovaks, though, the Hungarians were once part of the Austro-Hungarian Empire. Later, after becoming an independent nation, Hungary too was led by Communists. Today it is a democracy headed by a president.

Hungary has few natural resources besides its fertile land, which is valuable for farming. By importing the necessary raw materials, though, the country began to industrialize after World War II. Today Hungary is an exporter of chemicals, food products, and other goods.

Reading Check **Explaining** Why did Czechoslovakia split into two countries?

Countries of Southeastern Europe

Main Idea **Because of limited natural resources, political upheaval, and ethnic conflict, many countries in southeastern Europe face challenges.**

Geography and You Do you adapt easily to change? The countries of southeastern Europe have been through major political and economic changes in recent times. Read to find out how they have responded.

A dozen or so countries are clustered in southeastern Europe. Ukraine, the largest, lies north of the Black Sea. Romania, Moldova, and Bulgaria are also on or close to the shores of the Black Sea. Their neighbors on the Balkan Peninsula include Albania, Slovenia, Croatia, Bosnia and Herzegovina, Serbia, Montenegro, and Macedonia.

Europe's Breadbasket

NATIONAL GEOGRAPHIC

▲ Workers harvest hay on a farm in western Ukraine, an area known for its productive agriculture.
Human-Environment Interaction **What food crops are harvested in Ukraine?**

With the exception of Albania, these are young countries with newly drawn borders. It is not surprising, then, that many of them are struggling for stability and economic success.

Ukraine

Slightly smaller than Texas, Ukraine is the largest country in all of Europe. It lies on a lowland plain with the Carpathian Mountains rising along its southwestern border. The most important waterway, the Dnieper (NEE·puhr) River, has been made navigable to allow the shipping of goods.

The Dnieper River divides Ukraine into two regions. To the west, the lowland steppes have rich, black soil that is ideal for farming. Farmers in this "breadbasket of Europe" grow grains, fruits, and vegetables and raise cattle and sheep. The people living here are of Ukrainian descent. To the east of the Dnieper lies a plains area that has coal and iron ore deposits. Heavily industrialized, this eastern area produces cars, ships, locomotives, and airplanes. Many of the people in eastern Ukraine are of Russian descent.

Ukraine was one of the original republics in the Soviet Union, but it became an independent nation after the Soviet Union dissolved in 1991. Since then, ethnic divisions have grown sharper. Ethnic Ukrainians in the west want to link the country to western Europe and join the European Union. Ethnic Russians in the east want closer ties to Russia.

NATIONAL GEOGRAPHIC

Figure 4 **Percentage of Workforce in Agriculture**

Map Skills

1 Location Which three countries have the greatest percentage of farmworkers?

2 Regions How do you think the percentage of workers in agriculture affects national income?

Percentage of workers employed in agriculture

- 0–5%
- 6–10%
- 11–20%
- 21–40%
- Over 40%
- No information available

0   500 kilometers

0   500 miles

Lambert Azimuthal Equal-Area projection

Romania and Moldova

Unlike other eastern European countries, which ended Communist rule peacefully, Romania drove out the Communists in a bloody revolt in 1989. Soon after, the country fell into a deep economic slump. Romania has a wealth of natural resources, however, and the country is now rebounding. Thanks to deposits of coal, petroleum, and natural gas, industry output is growing. Bucharest (BOO·kuh·REHST), the capital, is the major economic and commercial center in the country. Farming also contributes to the economy, and many Romanians are employed in agriculture, as shown in **Figure 4.** Farmers here grow grains, grapes, and other crops.

As the name *Romania* suggests, the Romans once ruled this region and influenced its culture. The Romanian language, for example, is based on the Latin spoken in ancient Rome. In religion, though, Romanians take after their Slavic neighbors. Many are Eastern Orthodox Christian.

Moldova is a small, landlocked country sandwiched between Ukraine on the east and Romania on the west. Moldova's people are mainly Romanian, but Ukrainians and Russians also make up part of the population. Moldova's farms are productive as a result of its fertile soil. Because there are few mineral resources and limited industry, however, Moldova ranks as Europe's poorest country.

Bulgaria

Bulgaria lies south of Romania. It is a mountainous country, but people farm in the fertile river valleys between the peaks. Manufacturing employs many people in Sofia, the capital, and other cities. Tourism is growing as visitors seek out Bulgaria's scenic resorts on the Black Sea.

Most of Bulgaria's 7.7 million people trace their ancestry to the Slavs, Turks, and

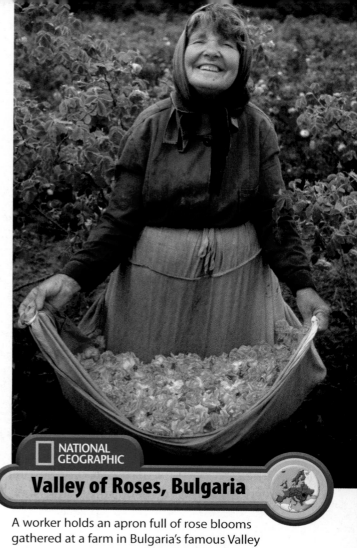

NATIONAL GEOGRAPHIC

Valley of Roses, Bulgaria

A worker holds an apron full of rose blooms gathered at a farm in Bulgaria's famous Valley of Roses. *Place* **What are Bulgaria's major economic activities?**

other groups from Central Asia. Most Bulgarians are Eastern Orthodox Christian. A sizable minority are Muslim.

Other Balkan States

To the south and west of Bulgaria, a number of other countries crowd the Balkan Peninsula. Albania, on the Adriatic Sea, is the only country in Europe with a majority Muslim population. It is also unique because farmers outnumber factory workers. With its economy still heavily agricultural, Albania is one of the poorest countries in Europe.

Other Balkan countries include Slovenia, Croatia, Bosnia and Herzegovina, Macedonia, Serbia, and Montenegro.

None of these nations were even on the map until the 1990s. Before then, they were all part of a Communist country called Yugoslavia.

When communism collapsed in Eastern Europe, the different ethnic groups of Yugoslavia struggled for power. In the early 1990s, four parts of the country—Slovenia, Croatia, Bosnia and Herzegovina, and Macedonia—declared their independence. Meanwhile, another strong part, Serbia, wanted to keep Yugoslavia together under Serbian rule. Serbia's leader used force to try to build power.

The heaviest fighting took place in Bosnia and Herzegovina. There, Serbs carried out **ethnic cleansing**—removing or killing an entire ethnic group—against the Bosnian population. Many people died or became refugees. This and other conflicts left the region badly scarred. Today Serbia has given up hope of reclaiming Yugoslav lands. Montenegro split away from Serbia in 2006, and where Yugoslavia once was, there are now six separate nations.

These Balkan countries were relatively poor during Communist rule, and they continue to be among the poorest in Europe. The mountainous landscape of the Balkan Peninsula makes farming difficult, and there are few natural resources to support economic growth. Ethnic conflict has added to these problems.

Despite these challenges, some countries are moving forward. Slovenia has experienced steady economic growth since it gained independence. Slovenian industries produce machinery, appliances, vehicles, and **medical** supplies. Croatia's economy has also improved, although not as much as Slovenia's.

✓ **Reading Check** **Explaining** Why have conflicts been fought in the Balkan Peninsula?

Section 4 Review

Social Studies ONLINE
Study Central™ To review this section, go to glencoe.com.

Vocabulary

1. **Explain** the differences between *command economy* and *market economy*. Define *potash* and *ethnic cleansing*.

Main Ideas

2. **Sequencing** List the events that led to democracy in Poland.

3. **Comparing** Create a Venn diagram like the one below to compare the Czech Republic and Slovakia.

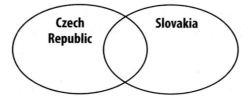

Czech Republic | Slovakia

4. **Explaining** Why are many of the countries of southeastern Europe struggling for economic success?

Critical Thinking

5. **BIG Idea** How have eastern Europe's history and physical geography led to differences between that region and other parts of Europe today?

6. **Challenge** Based on what you have read, what do you think will happen politically in Ukraine over the next few years? Why?

Writing About Geography

7. **Using Your FOLDABLES** Use your Foldable to write a paragraph comparing and contrasting conditions in two countries in eastern Europe.

Northern Europe

- The United Kingdom is a major industrial and trading country.

- The Republic of Ireland's economy is becoming more industrial.

- Fishing is an important industry in the Scandinavian countries.

Schoolgirls in France

Members of the British royal family

Germany and the _Alpine Countries_

- Rivers have been vital to Germany's economic growth.

- The Alps dominate Switzerland, Austria, and Liechtenstein.

Southern Europe

- Spain's historic sites and sunny beaches attract many tourists.

- Most of Italy's industry lies in the northern part of the country.

- Greece consists of a mountainous mainland and more than 2,000 islands.

__ France and the __ Benelux Countries

- France is a world center of art, learning, and culture.

- The Benelux countries are low, flat, and densely populated.

Europe at night

Eastern Europe

- Poland is a large country with northern plains and southern highlands.

- The Danube River flows through Budapest, Hungary's historic capital.

- Ukrainians disagree on whether to strengthen ties to western Europe or to Russia.

- Ethnic conflict has torn apart Balkan countries in recent years.

Industry in eastern Europe

Fisher in Malta

STUDY TO GO Study anywhere, anytime! Download quizzes and flash cards to your PDA from **glencoe.com**.

STANDARDIZED TEST PRACTICE

TEST-TAKING **TIP**

> Consider carefully before changing your answer to a multiple-answer test question. Unless you misread the question, your first answer choice is often correct.

Reviewing Vocabulary

Directions: Choose the word(s) that best completes the sentence.

1. In a _____, a king or queen serves as a ceremonial head of state but elected officials actively run the government.

  A constitutional dictatorship

  B constitutional monarchy

  C multinational organization

  D parliamentary democracy

2. Focusing on certain economic activities in order to make the most advantageous use of a nation's resources is called _____.

  A reunification

  B neutrality

  C specialization

  D productivity

3. A country allowing a region within its borders a certain amount of self-rule is known as _____.

  A autonomy

  B neutrality

  C specialization

  D subsidy

4. In a _____, the government decides what, how, and for whom goods will be produced.

  A market economy

  B parliamentary democracy

  C constitutional monarchy

  D command economy

Reviewing Main Ideas

Directions: Choose the best answer for each question.

Section 1 *(pp. 320–328)*

5. _____ has been troubled by a history of violence between Catholics and Protestants.

  A Finland

  B Northern Ireland

  C Sweden

  D Iceland

Section 2 *(pp. 329–337)*

6. In the Netherlands, wetlands that have been drained, called _____, have rich farming soil.

  A Benelux

  B chateaus

  C polders

  D Walloons

Section 3 *(pp. 338–342)*

7. In _____, the southern part of the country is poorer and less industrialized than the northern part.

  A Portugal

  B Ireland

  C Greece

  D Italy

Section 4 *(pp. 348–356)*

8. In Eastern Europe, Poland and the Baltic Republics have moved toward democracy and market economies, but _____ maintains a command economy and strong central government.

  A Belarus

  B Lithuania

  C Hungary

  D Bosnia

GO ON ➡

Critical Thinking

Directions: Choose the best answer for each question.

Base your answers to questions 9 and 10 on your knowledge of Chapter 12 and the map below.

Internet Use in Europe

ATLANTIC OCEAN

Mediterranean Sea

Percentage of country's population online

- 1–10%
- 11–25%
- 26–40%
- 41–60%
- >60%

0   400 kilometers
0   400 miles
Lambert Azimuthal
Equal-Area projection

Source: *CIA World Factbook*, 2006.

9. Which of the following countries has the lowest percentage of residents online?

- **A** Ukraine
- **B** Czech Republic
- **C** Bulgaria
- **D** Poland

10. In general, which subregion of Europe has the highest percentage of people online?

- **A** Southern Europe
- **B** Northern Europe
- **C** Eastern Europe
- **D** the Balkan countries

Document-Based Questions

Directions: Analyze the document and answer the short-answer questions that follow.

The EU [European Union] views enlargement as a historic opportunity to help in the transformation of the countries involved, extending peace, stability, prosperity, democracy, human rights and the rule of law throughout Europe. The carefully managed process of enlargement is one of the EU's most powerful policy tools that has helped to transform the countries of Central and Eastern Europe into more modern, functioning democracies.

—from "European Union Enlargement," CRS Report for Congress, Congressional Research Service, 2006

11. According to this report, how does the European Union view its own enlargement? What effects does the EU's enlargement have on Europe?

12. How do you think the EU's carefully managed process of enlargement can be a powerful policy tool?

Extended Response

13. Imagine you have been invited to be on a panel that is going to pick "Europe's Most Promising Economy of the Future." Prepare a speech in which you nominate a European country for this award. Explain why you believe this country's economy will either grow or remain strong in the future. Be sure to use geographical, population, and economic factors to support your position.

STOP

Social Studies ONLINE

For additional test practice, use Self-Check Quizzes—Chapter 12 at **glencoe.com**.

Need Extra Help?													
If you missed question...	1	2	3	4	5	6	7	8	9	10	11	12	13
Go to page...	322	330	339	349	326	332	341	350	26	26	355	355	321

St. Basil's Cathedral, ▶
Moscow, Russia

Regional Atlas

Russia

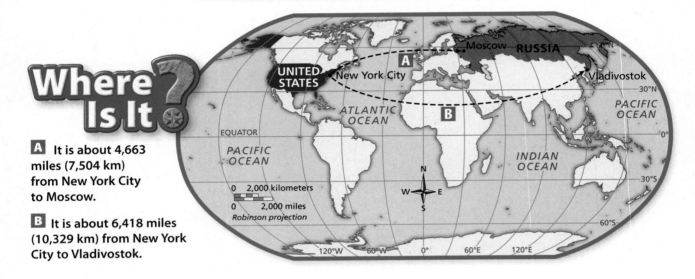

Where Is It?

A It is about 4,663 miles (7,504 km) from New York City to Moscow.

B It is about 6,418 miles (10,329 km) from New York City to Vladivostok.

How Big Is It?

The region of Russia is more than twice the size of the continental United States. Its land area is about 6,592,819 square miles (17,075,322 sq. km). Russia is the third-largest culture region and the largest single country in the world.

Comparing Population

United States and Russia	
United States	🧍🧍🧍🧍🧍🧍🧍🧍🧍
Russia	🧍🧍🧍🧍 🧍 = 30,000,000

Source: *World Population Data Sheet, 2005.*

NATIONAL GEOGRAPHIC

GEO Fast Facts

Longest River

Deepest Lake

Ob-Irtysh River
3,461 mi.
(5,569 km) long

Lake Baikal
5,715 ft. (1,742 m) deep

Lowest Point

Caspian Sea
92 ft. (28 m)
below sea level

Highest Point

Mount Elbrus
18,510 ft. (5,642 m) high

Russia

PHYSICAL

+ NORTH POLE

ARCTIC OCEAN

Wrangel Island

CHUKCHI PENINSULA

60°N

ARCTIC CIRCLE

0°

80°N

20°E

40°E

60°E

80°E

120°E

140°E

160°E

180°

East Siberian Sea

New Siberian Islands

Franz Josef Land

Severnaya Zemlya

Bering Sea

EUROPE

Barents Sea

Kara Sea

Laptev Sea

KOLA PENINSULA

Novaya Zemlya

Klyuchevskaya Sopka 15,584 ft. (4,750 m)

60°N

Baltic Sea

KOLYMA MTS.

KAMCHATKA PENINSULA

NORTHERN EUROPEAN PLAIN

N. Dvina R.

Yenisey R.

CENTRAL SIBERIAN PLATEAU

VERKHOYANSKI MTS.

Lena R.

Sea of Okhotsk

Don R.

URAL MOUNTAINS

Ob R.

WEST SIBERIAN PLAIN

Sakhalin Island

Volga R.

Irtysh R.

STANOVOY RANGE

Ural R.

Mt. Elbrus 18,510 ft. (5,642 m)

Lake Baikal

YABLONOVYY RANGE

40°N

CAUCASUS MTS.

SAYAN MTS.

N

Black Sea

Caspian Sea

W — E

S

Sea of Japan (East Sea)

ASIA

20°N

---

0   400 kilometers

0   400 miles

Two-Point Equidistant projection

Elevations

13,100 ft. (4,000 m)
6,500 ft. (2,000 m)
1,600 ft. (500 m)
650 ft. (200 m)
0 ft. (0 m)
Below sea level

▲ Mountain peak

Map Skills

1 Location What mountain range separates the Northern European Plain and West Siberian Plain?

2 Regions How does the terrain of eastern Russia compare with that of western Russia?

3 Regions Describe the general location of many of Russia's cities.

Russia

POLITICAL

NATIONAL GEOGRAPHIC

NORTH POLE

ARCTIC OCEAN

EUROPE

Baltic Sea
Murmansk
Kaliningrad
St. Petersburg
Moscow
Nizhniy Novgorod
Kazan'
Don R.
Volga R.
Samara
Ural R.
Volgograd
Astrakhan
Black Sea
Caspian Sea

Barents Sea
Kara Sea
Yenisey R.
Yekaterinburg
Irtysh R.
Ob R.
Omsk
Novosibirsk

RUSSIA

East Siberian Sea
Laptev Sea
Lena R.
Verkhoyansk
Yakutsk
Sea of Okhotsk
Bering Sea

Lake Baikal
Irkutsk
Vladivostok
Sea of Japan (East Sea)

ASIA

ARCTIC CIRCLE

N
W   E
S

| | National capital |
| | City |

0   400 kilometers
0   400 miles
Two-Point Equidistant projection

Country and Capital	Literacy Rate	Population and Density	Land Area	Life Expectancy (Years)	GDP* Per Capita (U.S. dollars)	Television Sets (per 1,000 people)	Flag and Language
RUSSIA Moscow	99.6%	143,000,000 22 per sq. mi. 8 per sq. km	6,592,819 sq. mi. 17,075,322 sq. km	66	$9,800	421	Russian
UNITED STATES Washington, D.C.	97%	296,500,000 80 per sq. mi. 31 per sq. km	3,717,796 sq. mi. 9,629,047 sq. km	78	$40,100	844	English

Sources: CIA World Factbook, 2005; Population Reference Bureau, World Population Data Sheet, 2005.
For more country facts, go to the **Nations of the World Databank** at glencoe.com.

Countries and flags not drawn to scale
*Gross Domestic Product

Russia

POPULATION DENSITY

NORTH POLE

ARCTIC OCEAN

60°N

ARCTIC CIRCLE

0°

80°N

180°

20°E

40°E

160°E

East Siberian Sea

Bering Sea

60°N

EUROPE

Barents Sea

60°E

80°E

120°E

140°E

80°N

Baltic Sea

Kara Sea

Laptev Sea

St. Petersburg

Moscow

Nizhniy Novgorod

Voronezh

Kazan'

Perm

Yekaterinburg

Saratov

Samara

Ufa

Rostov-na-Donu

Volgograd

Chelyabinsk

Omsk

Novosibirsk

Krasnoyarsk

Irkutsk

Grozny

Black Sea

Caspian Sea

Sea of Okhotsk

Khabarovsk

Vladivostok

40°N

Sea of Japan (East Sea)

ASIA

N
W   E
S

POPULATION

Per sq. mi.	Per sq. km
1,250 and over	500 and over
250–1,249	100–499
63–249	25–99
25–62	10–24
2.5–24	1–9
Less than 2.5	Less than 1

Cities
(Statistics reflect metropolitan areas.)

■ Over 5,000,000
□ 1,000,000–5,000,000
⊙ Less than 1,000,000

0   400 kilometers
0   400 miles
Two-Point Equidistant projection

20°N

Map Skills

1 Place Describe the population density pattern in European Russia.

2 Regions How does population density change from north to south?

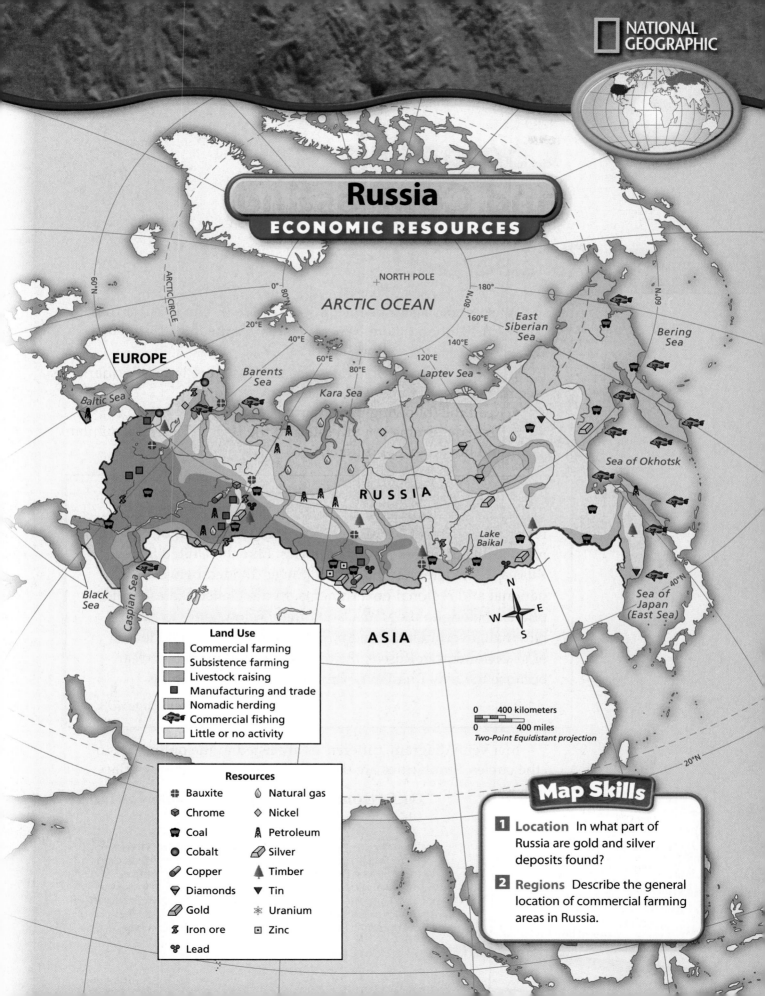

Russia
ECONOMIC RESOURCES

NATIONAL GEOGRAPHIC

NORTH POLE

ARCTIC OCEAN

ARCTIC CIRCLE

EUROPE

Baltic Sea

Barents Sea

Kara Sea

East Siberian Sea

Bering Sea

Laptev Sea

Sea of Okhotsk

RUSSIA

Black Sea

Caspian Sea

Lake Baikal

Sea of Japan (East Sea)

ASIA

Land Use
- Commercial farming
- Subsistence farming
- Livestock raising
- Manufacturing and trade
- Nomadic herding
- Commercial fishing
- Little or no activity

0   400 kilometers
0   400 miles
Two-Point Equidistant projection

Resources

Bauxite	Natural gas
Chrome	Nickel
Coal	Petroleum
Cobalt	Silver
Copper	Timber
Diamonds	Tin
Gold	Uranium
Iron ore	Zinc
Lead	

Map Skills

1 Location In what part of Russia are gold and silver deposits found?

2 Regions Describe the general location of commercial farming areas in Russia.

Comparing and Contrasting

1 Learn It!

When you *compare* people, things, or ideas, you look for the similarities among them. When you *contrast* people, things, or ideas, you identify their differences.

Textbook authors sometimes use this structure to help readers see the similarities and differences between topics.

- Read the following paragraph.
- Then determine how Russia and the United States are similar and how they are different.

Russia's official name is the Russian Federation. This name reflects the fact that Russia comprises, or is made up of, many different regions and territories. Like the United States, Russia is a federal republic, with power divided between national and regional governments. In the United States, some powers belong to the states, and others belong only to the national government. Some powers are shared by both levels of government. In Russia, the division of powers is less clear because the new Russian government is still developing.

—*from page 409*

In a Venn diagram, differences are listed in the outer parts of the circles. Similarities are described where the circles overlap.

Reading Tip

As you read, look for signal words that show comparisons, such as *similarly, at the same time,* and *likewise.* Contrast signal words include *however, rather,* and *on the other hand.*

The Governments of Russia and the United States

Russia
The division of powers between regional governments and the national government is not clear.

Similarities
- Both countries are federal republics.
- Both countries divide power between national and regional governments.

United States
Some powers are given solely to states and solely to the national government, while some powers are shared by both governments.

② Practice It!

Read the following sentences from this unit that describe Russian leaders Ivan IV and Joseph Stalin.
- Draw a Venn diagram like the one shown below.
- List the differences and similarities between the two leaders.

Read to Write Activity

Read and take notes about Russia's physical geography in Chapter 13. Then find similar information about another region in your book. Write an essay that describes the similarities and differences between the two regions.

In 1547 Ivan IV declared himself czar, or emperor. He ruled harshly, using secret police to carry out his will, and earned the name "Ivan the Terrible." By conquering neighboring territories, Ivan expanded his empire south to the Caspian Sea and east past the Ural Mountains.

—from page 390

Lenin's policies were later continued by Joseph Stalin, who ruled the Soviet Union after Lenin's death in 1924. A harsh dictator, Stalin prevented the Soviet people from practicing their religions and had religious property seized. His secret police killed or imprisoned anyone who disagreed with his policies.

—from page 392

▲ Ivan the Terrible

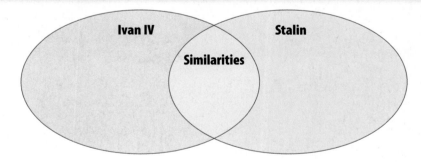

Ivan IV   Stalin

Similarities

③ Apply It!

As you read Chapters 13, 14, and 15, look for people, things, or ideas that you can compare and contrast. As you read, put notes in a Venn diagram like the one above to help you compare and contrast.

Physical Geography of Russia

Essential Question

Human-Environment Interaction Russia's vast, cold landscapes include mountain ranges, plains, and evergreen forests. The country is also rich in natural resources, especially those used to create energy. To take advantage of these resources, however, Russia's people must overcome problems created by the country's landforms and climate. How do Russia's location and landforms affect its population and its use of resources?

Reindeer in Siberia

BIG Ideas

Section 1: Physical Features

BIG IDEA Changes occur in the use and importance of natural resources. Russians have used their soil, water, and timber for their own needs. As global demand for energy rises, Russia's rich supply of energy resources will be increasingly important.

Section 2: Climate and the Environment

BIG IDEA People's actions change the physical environment. Because much of Russia has a harsh climate, most Russians live where the climate is milder. The Russian people have adapted to their surroundings, but some of their actions have damaged the environment. Planning is necessary to take advantage of the country's great resources while preserving the environment.

FOLDABLES™
Study Organizer

Organizing Information Make this Foldable to help you organize facts about Russia's physical features, climate, and environment.

Step 1 Fold a piece of 11x17 paper in half.

Step 2 Fold the bottom edge up two inches. Glue the outer edges of the tab to create two pockets.

Step 3 Label each pocket as shown. Use these pockets to hold notes taken on index cards or quarter sheets of paper.

Physical Features | Climate & Environment

Reading and Writing As you read the chapter, write down facts on separate cards or sheets of paper and place them in the correct pocket. Use your cards to write quiz questions for each section topic.

Social Studies ONLINE

To preview Chapter 13, go to glencoe.com.

Guide to Reading

BIG Idea

Changes occur in the use and importance of natural resources.

Content Vocabulary

- fossil fuel *(p. 375)*
- softwood *(p. 375)*
- infrastructure *(p. 375)*

Academic Vocabulary

- benefit *(p. 373)*
- inhibit *(p. 375)*

Reading Strategy

Identifying Use a diagram like the one below to list six of Russia's major landforms.

Russia's Landforms

Physical Features

Picture This The bubbling goo in this volcanic pool is like a pot of boiling soup. Here in far eastern Russia, a huge volcano exploded tens of thousands of years ago. The area now contains cold, rushing rivers, hot springs, and pools filled with steaming, toxic mud. As volcanic gases push their way up through the thick ooze, they create bubbles. The bubbles are evidence that forces under Earth's crust are always in motion. Read this section to learn more about the different types of physical features found in Russia.

▼ Volcanic crater on Kamchatka Peninsula in eastern Russia

Landforms of Russia

Main Idea Russia is a huge country with a location and landforms that greatly affect how people live.

Geography and You If you have ever traveled across the United States, you know that it takes a long time. It would take twice as long to travel across Russia. Read to learn about the landforms of Russia's vast terrain.

Russia is the world's largest country. From east to west, it measures some 6,200 miles (9,980 km). Nearly twice as large as the United States, Russia straddles both Europe and Asia. The Ural Mountains serve as a dividing line between the European and Asian parts of Russia.

A Vast Northern Land

Because of its enormous size, Russia has a long coastline. Russia does not **benefit** from its closeness to the sea, though, because of its northern location. Most of its coast lies along waters that are frozen for much of the year. As a result, Russia has few seaports that are free of ice year-round. Through the Black Sea in the southwest, though, Russian ships have a warm-water route to the Mediterranean Sea.

Russia contains a variety of landforms. Rugged mountains and plateaus lie in the south and east. In the north and west, vast lowland plains reach to the horizon.

European Russia

Most of European Russia lies on the Northern European Plain. This fertile area has Russia's mildest climate, and about 75 percent of Russians live here. Moscow, the capital, and St. Petersburg, a large port city near the Baltic Sea, are located in this region. Much of Russia's agriculture and industry are found on the Northern European Plain.

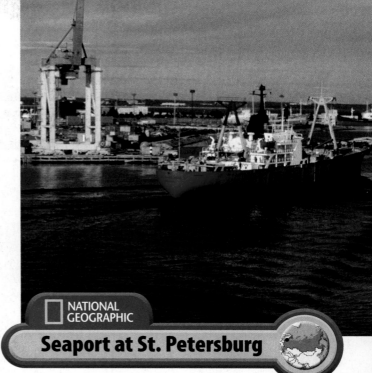

NATIONAL GEOGRAPHIC

Seaport at St. Petersburg

The port at St. Petersburg is one of the busiest in Russia, even though it is frozen three to four months every year. *Location* Which sea provides a warm water outlet for Russian ships?

Good farmland also lies farther south, along the Volga and other rivers. This area consists of a nearly treeless grassy plain. To the far south of European Russia are the rugged Caucasus Mountains. Located near a fault line, the Caucasus area is prone to destructive earthquakes. Other mountains—the Urals—divide European and Asian Russia. Worn down by erosion, the Urals are not very tall.

Asian Russia

East of the Urals is Asian Russia, which includes Siberia. Northern Siberia has one of the coldest climates in the world. It is a vast treeless plain that remains frozen much of the year. The few people who live here make their living fishing, hunting seals and walruses, or herding reindeer.

Social Studies ONLINE
Student Web Activity Visit glencoe.com and complete the Chapter 13 Web Activity about Siberia.

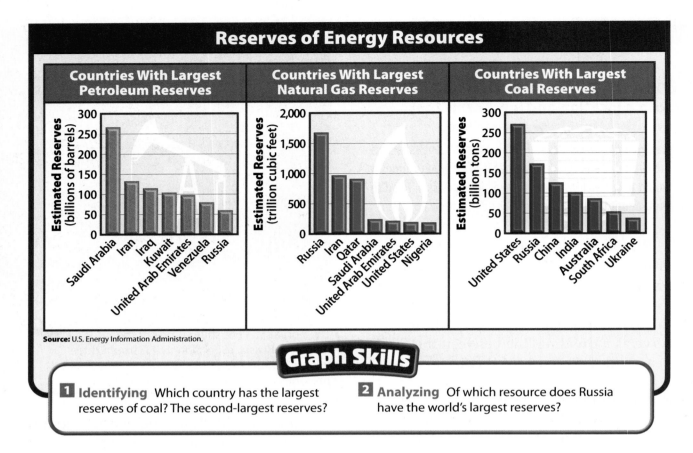

Reserves of Energy Resources

Countries With Largest Petroleum Reserves

Estimated Reserves (billions of barrels)

Saudi Arabia, Iran, Iraq, Kuwait, United Arab Emirates, Venezuela, Russia

Countries With Largest Natural Gas Reserves

Estimated Reserves (trillion cubic feet)

Russia, Iran, Qatar, Saudi Arabia, United Arab Emirates, United States, Nigeria

Countries With Largest Coal Reserves

Estimated Reserves (billion tons)

United States, Russia, China, India, Australia, South Africa, Ukraine

Source: U.S. Energy Information Administration.

Graph Skills

1 Identifying Which country has the largest reserves of coal? The second-largest reserves?

2 Analyzing Of which resource does Russia have the world's largest reserves?

To the south of the northern plains area is a region of dense forests where people make their living by lumbering or hunting. Plains, plateaus, and mountain ranges cover the southern part of Siberia.

Mountains also rise on the far eastern Kamchatka (kam·CHAHT·kuh) Peninsula. These mountains are part of the Ring of Fire. This is a region along the rim of the Pacific Ocean where tectonic plates meet and cause Earth's crust to be unstable. As a result, Kamchatka has many volcanoes.

Inland Waters

Russia has many rivers. The Volga is European Russia's major river. Russians have long relied on the Volga for transportation. In Siberia, many rivers begin in mountains in the south and flow north across marshy lowlands, emptying into the frigid Arctic Ocean. The Lena (LEE·nuh),

the Yenisey (YIH·nih·SAY), and the Ob' (AWB) are among the longest rivers in the world.

Russia includes or borders many inland bodies of water. Almost the size of California, the Caspian Sea in southwestern Russia is the largest inland body of water in the world. It is actually a saltwater lake that is an important resource for fishing. Major oil and gas deposits are found near or under the Caspian Sea.

In southern Siberia lies Lake Baikal—the world's deepest freshwater lake. The lake holds one-fifth of the world's supply of unfrozen freshwater. Baikal is home to many kinds of aquatic life, including Baikal seals, or nerpa, the only seals that live in freshwater.

Reading Check **Describing** Describe the landforms of the Kamchatka Peninsula.

Natural Resources

Main Idea Although Russia has plentiful resources, many of them are in remote Siberia and are difficult to obtain.

Geography and You Have you ever worked or played outside in the extreme cold of winter? Read to find out how a cold climate affects Russians' use of resources.

Russia is rich in natural resources. As the graphs on the previous page show, Russia is a leader in reserves of the **fossil fuels**—oil, natural gas, and coal. The country also has major deposits of iron ore, which the Russians have used to develop a large steel industry. Other important metals mined in Russia include copper and gold.

Russia's other great resource is timber. Trees cover much of Siberia, and Russia pro-duces about a fifth of the world's **softwood**. This wood from evergreen trees is used in buildings and for making furniture.

Russia's large size and cold climate **inhibit,** or limit, humans' ability to use its many resources. Siberia is vast and remote, and its resources are difficult to use because of the area's lack of **infrastructure.** Infrastructure is the system of roads and railroads for transporting materials.

In addition to transportation difficulties, Siberia's cold climate brings other challenges. Besides trying to stay warm, workers must keep their equipment from freezing. Some advances in technology have made it easier to collect Siberia's resources. For example, a pipeline now carries natural gas from Siberia to Europe.

✔ **Reading Check** **Explaining** Why are Russia's natural resources difficult to gather?

Section 1 Review

Social Studies ONLINE
Study Central™ To review this section, go to glencoe.com.

Vocabulary

1. **Explain** the meaning of *fossil fuel, softwood,* and *infrastructure* by using each term in a sentence.

Main Ideas

2. **Comparing and Contrasting** Use a Venn diagram like the one below to compare and contrast physical features in European Russia and Siberia.

European Russia   Siberia

3. **Explaining** Why are Siberia's resources valuable?

Critical Thinking

4. **Analyzing Information** In what part of the country does most of Russia's population live? Why?

5. **BIG Idea** Name some natural resources found in Russia. How do these resources contribute to the Russian and world economies?

6. **Challenge** How might a country's far-north location affect its people and economy? Consider factors such as agriculture and transportation.

Writing About Geography

7. **Expository Writing** Write a paragraph describing what you believe is Russia's most prominent physical feature. Be sure to explain your choice.

Russia's Forests: Should They Be Used for Economic Development?

The boreal forests are located south of the Arctic Circle. They are found in northern Canada, Europe, and Russia. The forests contain most of the world's unfrozen freshwater. Many species of birds and animals live there or migrate through the forests. The forests are also home to various indigenous peoples.

The Russian boreal forest, also known as the taiga, extends about 4,000 miles (6,436 km) across northern Russia. Some Russians want to develop the resources of the forest, such as lumber, oil, and natural gas. Many environmentalists, though, would like to preserve the forest and its biodiversity.

For Development

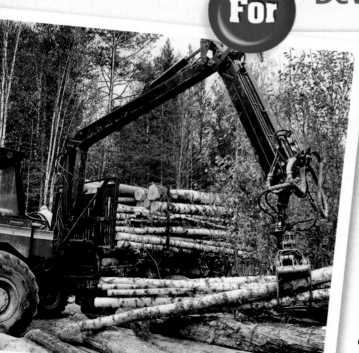

These environmentalists . . . who criticize me have no idea what's really happening in the forest. . . . I was shocked by the extent of destruction I saw here 30 years ago. . . . But I've been surprised by the way nature has reacted and how well the trees have grown back. The law of the north woods is, the more you destroy them, the stronger they recover. . . . The world's environmentalists say don't touch the boreal forest—leave it alone, leave it natural. . . . But my philosophy with the forests is to use them. You want to watch TV, drive a car, live well, right? And how do you do that if you don't touch nature?

—Vladimir Sedykh
Chief Scientist
Sukachev Forest Institute, Novosibirsk

Against Development

The current economic model of forest use is oriented [directed] mainly towards the export of raw materials and cannot provide long-term economic growth for the region. This model . . . destroys the last old-growth forests in Russia, which have now become the most threatened natural ecosystems. If the current situation does not change, we will lose the most valuable old-growth areas in [the] next 5–10 years. Logging the last European old-growth forests will not solve any social or economical problem in Russia. In its best light it will only postpone the social and economic crash in the forest industry and logging settlements by a matter of several years.

—from *The Last of the Last: The Old-growth Forests of Boreal Europe*
Dmitry Aksenov, Mikhail Karpachevskiy,
Sarah Lloyd, and Alexei Yaroshenko

You Be the Geographer

1. **Summarizing** In your own words, summarize the opinion of each writer about how the forest should be used.

2. **Critical Thinking** What argument does Sedykh make to appeal to people who want to live a modern lifestyle?

3. **Read to Write** Do you think developers and environmentalists can work together to use and preserve the boreal forest? Explain your opinion in a one-page essay.

Climate and the Environment

BIG Idea

People's actions change the physical environment.

Content Vocabulary

- permafrost *(p. 380)*
- taiga *(p. 380)*
- smog *(p. 380)*
- pollutant *(p. 380)*

Academic Vocabulary

- period *(p. 379)*
- decline *(p. 382)*

Reading Strategy

Analyzing Information Use a diagram like the one below to list factors that lead to Russia's cold climate, especially those related to location and landforms.

Russia's Climate

Picture This For many Russians, ice fishing is a favorite pastime. In this photo, an ice fisher is shielded from the cold winds blowing along the Tom River in Siberia. The fisher must often reach into the icy water and remove slush from the hole to keep it from freezing over. Read this section to learn how Russia's many climate zones have influenced its people.

▼ **Ice fishing on the Tom River near Kemerovo in central Siberia**

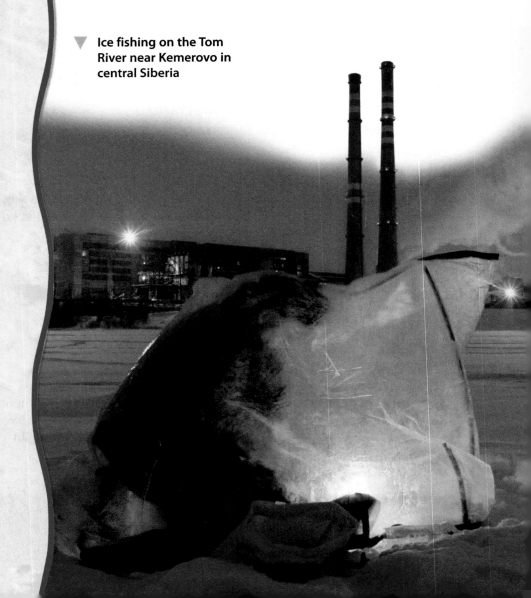

A Cold Climate

Main Idea Russia has a generally cool to cold climate because of its northern location.

Geography and You Have you ever experienced a winter that was extremely cold and snowy and seemed to go on too long? Read to find out why much of Russia has long, cold winters and short summers.

As **Figure 1** shows, most of Russia lies in the high latitudes. As a result, Russia receives very little of the sun's heat even during summer. In addition, much of Russia lies inland, far from the moist, warm currents of the Atlantic and Pacific Oceans that help moderate temperature in other parts of the world. In Russia's far north, elevations are generally too low to prevent the southerly flow of icy Arctic air. In the country's south and east, tall mountains stop the warm air coming from the lower latitudes. Consequently, Russia has a generally cool to cold climate. Large areas of the country experience only winter- and summerlike conditions. Spring and autumn are simply brief **periods** of changing weather.

NATIONAL GEOGRAPHIC

Maps In Motion See StudentWorks™ Plus or glencoe.com.

Figure 1 **Russia: Climate Zones**

Dry
- Steppe

Midlatitude
- Humid continental

High latitude
- Subarctic
- Tundra
- ⊙ National capital
- • City

Map Skills

1 **Regions** What four climate zones does Russia have?

2 **Location** Which Russian city is in the tundra climate zone?

Most of western Russia has a humid continental climate. Summers are warm and rainy, and winters are cold and snowy. Moscow's average July temperature is just 66°F (19°C), while its average January temperature can plunge as low as 16°F (–9°C). The cold winters have played an important role in Russia's history. During World War II, bitter cold halted the German army's advance into Russia. Better-prepared Russian troops soon forced the Germans to retreat.

In contrast, the northern and eastern areas of Russia have short, cool summers and long, snowy winters. The northern tundra climate zone is so cold that moisture in the soil cannot evaporate. Cold temperatures and lack of precipitation result in **permafrost**, a permanently frozen layer of soil beneath the surface. Only mosses, lichens, and small shrubs can survive in the tundra.

South of the tundra lies the subarctic zone, Russia's largest climate area. Warmer temperatures support a greater variety of vegetation than the tundra does. The **taiga**, the world's largest coniferous forest, stretches about 4,000 miles (6,436 km) across the subarctic zone. This forest is roughly the size of the United States.

✔ **Reading Check** **Determining Cause and Effect** How do Russia's landforms affect the country's climate?

Russia's Environment

Main Idea As Russia's economy expanded, the country's environment was poorly cared for.

Geography and You What might happen if the garbage in your neighborhood was not disposed of properly? Read to learn about Russia's efforts to clean up its environment.

For most of the 1900s, Russia's leaders stressed economic growth. They ignored the damage this growth caused to the environment. Today, **smog**—a thick haze of fog and chemicals—blankets many of Russia's cities. Factories pour **pollutants**, which are chemicals and smoke particles that cause pollution, into the air. Many Russians suffer from lung diseases and cancer.

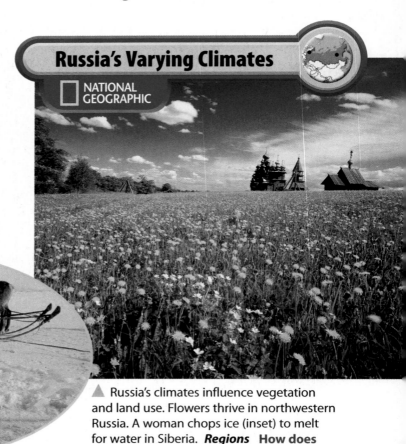

Russia's Varying Climates

NATIONAL GEOGRAPHIC

▲ Russia's climates influence vegetation and land use. Flowers thrive in northwestern Russia. A woman chops ice (inset) to melt for water in Siberia. **Regions** How does Russia's latitude affect its climate?

Farewell to Matyora

By Valentin Rasputin

And so the village had lived on in its lean and simple way, clinging to its spot on the bluff by the left bank [of the Angara River], greeting and seeing off the years, like the water that joined [the villagers] to other settlements and that had helped feed them since time **immemorial.** And just as the flowing water seemed to have no end or limit, the village seemed ageless: some went off to their Maker, others were born, old buildings collapsed, new ones were built. And the village lived on, through hard times and troubles, for three hundred and more years ... until the rumor thundered down on them that the village would be no more. A dam was being built downriver on the Angara for a hydroelectric power station, and the waters would rise in the rivers and streams, flooding much land, including, first and foremost, Matyora. Even if you were to pile five islands like Matyora one on top of the other, they would still be flooded and you wouldn't be able to show the spot where people once lived. They would have to move. It wasn't easy to believe that it really would come to pass. ... A year after the first rumors an evaluating **commission** came by [boat] and began assessing the **depreciation** of the buildings and determining how much money they were worth. There was no more doubt about the fate of Matyora, it was living out its last years. Somewhere on the right bank they were building a new settlement for the ... state-owned farm, into which they were bringing all the neighboring **kolkhozes,** and some that were not so neighboring, and it was decided, so as not to have to deal with rubbish, to set fire to the old villages.

From: *Farewell to Matyora*, by Valentin Rasputin, translated by Antonina W. Bouis, Evanston, Ill.: Northwestern University Press, 1991.

Analyzing Literature

1. **Identifying Central Issues** What attitude do you think the government has toward the village?

2. **Read to Write** Take the role of a local government official and write an editorial explaining why you either support or oppose the building of the dam.

Valentin Rasputin
(1937–)

Born in Siberia, Valentin Rasputin often celebrates the region in his writing. The short novel *Farewell to Matyora* expresses his fear that modern life can erase the traditions of the villagers there.

Background Information

In Soviet times, huge power plants and hydroelectric projects were built to provide energy for heavy industry. Decisions to build factories and power plants were made by the Communist government without consulting the local communities that would be affected by such actions. The government's attempts at modernization often had serious effects on Russia's people.

Reader's Dictionary

immemorial: before memory

commission: official government body

depreciation: lowered value

kolkhozes: government-owned farming villages

Water Pollution

Water pollution is also a problem. Chemicals used in agriculture and industry often end up in rivers and lakes. Pollution entering Lake Baikal may be causing a **decline** in the populations of some animal species in the area. Another source of water pollution is poor sewer systems. Because of these problems, more than half of Russia's people do not have safe drinking water.

Cleaning Up

Steps have been taken to solve Russia's pollution problems. Other countries are providing Russia with aid to improve sewage systems and clean up heavily polluted sites. Cities are building more efficient power plants that use less energy and burn fuel more cleanly. Still, it will be a long time before Russia has a healthy environment.

✓ Reading Check **Explaining** What government ment policies harmed Russia's environment?

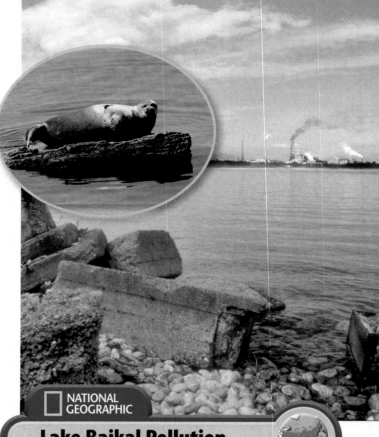

NATIONAL GEOGRAPHIC

Lake Baikal Pollution

Russian industries have polluted their environments, threatening species like the Baikal seal (inset), or nerpa. *Human-Environment Interaction* What **are sources of water pollution in Russia?**

Section 2 Review

Social Studies ONLINE
Study Central™ To review this section, go to glencoe.com.

Vocabulary

1. **Explain** the significance of:
   a. permafrost   **c.** smog
   b. taiga   **d.** pollutant

Main Ideas

2. **Summarizing** Use a chart like the one below to describe characteristics of three major climate zones in Russia.

Climate Zone	Characteristics
Humid Continental	
Tundra	
Subarctic	

3. **Explaining** What steps are being taken to solve Russia's pollution problems?

Critical Thinking

4. **Determining Cause and Effect** How did Russia's climate lead to the defeat of the German army's invasion during World War II?

5. **BIG Idea** How might Russia's vast size, climate, and pollution problems be related?

6. **Challenge** Why do you think the vast wooded areas of the Russian taiga still exist?

Writing About Geography

7. **Use Your FOLDABLES** Use your Foldable to write a letter to a Russian government official explaining why you think improving Russia's environment should be a priority.

Visual Summary

A Vast Northern Land

- Straddling Europe and Asia, Russia is the world's largest country.

- Most of Russia's long coast lies along waters that are frozen for many months of the year.

Russian icebreaker in the Arctic Ocean

Russia's Landforms

- Northern and western parts of Russia are mostly plains. Eastern and southern areas of the country are covered with mountains and plateaus.

- Inland waterways are important for moving goods through Russia. Many long rivers flow north, however, into the cold Arctic Ocean and freeze in winter.

- Russia has many inland bodies of water, including the Caspian Sea and Lake Baikal.

Natural Resources

- Russia is rich in natural resources, including fossil fuels, metals, and timber.

- Russia's large size and generally cold climate make it difficult for Russians to use their resources.

Climate

- Most of western Russia has a humid continental climate of warm, rainy summers and cold, snowy winters.

- Northern and eastern parts of Russia have cold high latitude climates. The far north of Russia is so cold that moisture in the soil cannot evaporate.

- The country's cold winters helped the Russians defeat German forces during World War II.

Russian coal miner

Environment

- Communist leaders paid little attention to the damage that economic growth was causing to Russia's environment.

- Other countries are providing Russia with aid to clean up heavily polluted areas.

Mount Elbrus

 STUDY TO GO Study anywhere, anytime! Download quizzes and flash cards to your PDA from **glencoe.com**.

STANDARDIZED TEST PRACTICE

TEST-TAKING

When an answer contains multiple items, such as in question 10, make sure that all the items in the answer are correct.

Reviewing Vocabulary

Directions: Choose the word(s) that best complete the sentence.

1. Russia is among the world's leaders in reserves of _____, which include oil, natural gas, and coal.

   A pollutants

   B renewable resources

   C fossil fuels

   D ores

2. Siberia lacks a(n) _____, a system of roads and railroads for transporting materials.

   A infrastructure

   B trade barrier

   C tariff system

   D commercial sector

3. In Russia's northern tundra, cold temperatures and lack of precipitation result in a permanently frozen layer of soil beneath the surface called _____.

   A taiga

   B smog

   C steppes

   D permafrost

4. Russia has the world's largest coniferous forest called the _____.

   A tundra

   B taiga

   C Baikal

   D steppe

Reviewing Main Ideas

Directions: Choose the best answer for each question.

Section 1 *(pp. 372–375)*

5. The great majority of Russians live _____.

   A in Siberian Russia

   B in European Russia

   C east of the Urals

   D in Asian Russia

6. Many of Russia's plentiful resources are difficult to obtain because of their location _____.

   A in European Russia

   B west of the Urals

   C in Siberia

   D south of the Caucasus

Section 2 *(pp. 378–382)*

7. Russia has a generally _____ climate.

   A cool to cold

   B warm to hot

   C dry to desert

   D low latitude

8. Russia's largest climate zone is called the _____ zone.

   A tundra

   B taiga

   C arctic

   D subarctic

GO ON

Critical Thinking

Directions: Use the following results of a Russian public opinion survey on the environment to answer questions 9 and 10. Choose the best answer for each question.

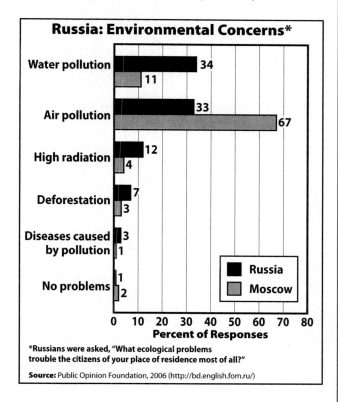

Russia: Environmental Concerns*

Water pollution: 34 (Russia), 11 (Moscow)
Air pollution: 33 (Russia), 67 (Moscow)
High radiation: 12 (Russia), 4 (Moscow)
Deforestation: 7 (Russia), 3 (Moscow)
Diseases caused by pollution: 3 (Russia), 1 (Moscow)
No problems: 1 (Russia), 2 (Moscow)

Percent of Responses (0, 10, 20, 30, 40, 50, 60, 70, 80)

■ Russia
▨ Moscow

*Russians were asked, "What ecological problems trouble the citizens of your place of residence most of all?"

Source: Public Opinion Foundation, 2006 (http://bd.english.fom.ru/)

9. Residents of Moscow, Russia's largest city, are more concerned than others about _____.

A high radiation

B water pollution

C air pollution

D ecologically caused diseases

10. Russian citizens living outside of Moscow are almost equally concerned about both _____.

A high radiation and disease

B water and air pollution

C air pollution and high radiation

D water pollution and high radiation

Document-Based Questions

Directions: Analyze the document and answer the short-answer questions that follow.

Mark Sergeev, a Russian poet from the Siberian city of Irkutsk close to Lake Baikal, wrote the following in an essay about the lake.

> [Native] Siberians have a mystical feeling for [Lake Baikal]. They believe that this is not simply 23 thousand cubic kilometers of water in some enormous stone bowl, but a wizard and healer who should neither be jested with nor enraged. This is why they never call Baikal a lake, only—the sea, or the Old Man, but more often than not they say—He!
>
> —Mark Sergeev, Irkutsk poet

11. How do native Siberians feel about Lake Baikal? How do they show their feelings?

12. Why might Lake Baikal produce such feelings in the local Siberians?

Extended Response

13. Write an essay describing Asian Russia, including its landforms, waters, climates, and resources. Explain why Asian Russia may play an important role in the country's future economic development in your essay.

STOP

Social Studies ONLINE

For additional test practice, use Self-Check Quizzes—Chapter 13 on glencoe.com.

Need Extra Help?													
If you missed question...	1	2	3	4	5	6	7	8	9	10	11	12	13
Go to page...	375	375	380	380	373	375	379	380	380	380	374	374	373

History and Cultures of Russia

Essential Question

Movement Today, Russia is the world's largest country. Early in its history, however, it was a small territory on the edge of Europe. Strong rulers gradually expanded Russia's borders. While Russia's government has undergone a number of changes, the country's culture and traditions have remained strong. Why do countries often wish to expand their territory?

BIG Ideas

Section 1: History and Governments

BIG IDEA The characteristics and movement of people impact physical and human systems. Russia grew from a small trading center into a large empire. Although Russia's leaders and a few citizens enjoyed great power, most Russians remained poor and had few rights. In time, these conditions led to great changes in Russia's government.

Section 2: Cultures and Lifestyles

BIG IDEA Culture groups shape human systems. The Russian people have created a rich culture that reflects strong national feelings. Cultural traditions have shaped many areas of daily life, such as housing, recreation, and celebrations.

FOLDABLES™
Study Organizer

Categorizing Information Make this Foldable to help you collect and organize information about Russia's history and cultures.

Step 1 Place three sheets of paper on top of one another about 1 inch apart.

Step 2 Fold the papers to form six equal tabs.

Step 3 Staple the sheets, and label each tab as shown.

Russian History and Culture
The Russian Empire
The Soviet Union
The Rise of Democracy
People and Culture
Life in Russia

Reading and Writing
Use the notes in your Foldable to write a short essay comparing population, culture, and everyday life in Russia and the United States.

Social Studies ONLINE
To preview Chapter 14, go to glencoe.com.

◄ State Historical Museum, Moscow, Russia

Guide to Reading

BIG Idea

The characteristics and movement of people impact physical and human systems.

Content Vocabulary

- missionary *(p. 389)*
- czar *(p. 390)*
- serf *(p. 390)*
- communist state *(p. 391)*
- collectivization *(p. 392)*
- Cold War *(p. 393)*
- glasnost *(p. 393)*
- perestroika *(p. 393)*
- coup *(p. 394)*

Academic Vocabulary

- convert *(p. 389)*
- release *(p. 391)*
- eliminate *(p. 392)*

Reading Strategy

Outlining Use the model below to make an outline of the section. Use Roman numerals to number the main headings. Use capital letters to list important facts below each main heading.

I. First Main Heading
    A. Key fact 1
    B. Key fact 2
II. Second Main Heading
    A. Key fact 1
    B. Key fact 2

History and Governments

Picture This A giant cat? No, it is actually a miniature city. The highest building in this model of the city of Königsberg stands only 3 feet (91 cm) high. *Königsberg* means "King's Mountain" and was once a German capital. In 1945, during the final days of World War II, German and Soviet armies fought a desperate four-day battle in the city. After the war, the Soviet Union took control of the city and renamed it Kaliningrad. Today, Kaliningrad is part of Russia, which became independent after the Soviet Union's fall in 1991. Read this section to find out more about Russia's history.

▼ **Roaming around Königsberg**

The Russian Empire

Main Idea
Strong leaders made Russia a vast empire, but widespread suffering eventually led to revolution.

Geography and You What causes people to rise up and overthrow their government? Read on to learn about Russia's history up to the time of the Russian Revolution.

Russia today is a vast country, covering millions of square miles and spreading across two continents. This world power, however, began as a small trade center.

Early Russia

Modern Russians descend from Slavic peoples who settled along the rivers of what are today Ukraine and Russia. During the A.D. 800s, these early Slavs built a civilization around the city of Kiev (Kyiv), today the capital of Ukraine. This civilization, called Kievan Rus (KEE·eh·vuhn ROOS), prospered from river trade between Scandinavia and the Byzantine Empire.

In A.D. 988 the people of Kievan Rus **converted** to Eastern Orthodox Christianity. **Missionaries,** or people who move to another area to spread their religion, brought this form of Christianity from the Byzantine Empire to Kievan Rus. The missionaries also brought a written language.

In the 1200s, Mongol warriors from Central Asia conquered Kievan Rus. Under Mongol rule, Kiev lost much of its power. Many Slavs moved northward and built settlements. One new settlement was the small trading post of Moscow.

NATIONAL GEOGRAPHIC **Maps In Motion** See StudentWorks™ Plus or glencoe.com.

Figure 1 **Expansion of Russia**

Kievan Territory
1360–1533
1533–1689
1689–1917
Boundary of the Soviet Union in 1945
Present-day Russian boundary

Map Skills

1 Location Which cities are located within the original Kievan territory?

2 Movement In which period did the Russian Empire expand beyond Europe and Asia? To what areas did it expand during this period?

It became the center of a new Slavic territory called Muscovy (muh·SKOH·vee). In 1480 Ivan III, a prince of Muscovy, rejected Mongol rule and declared independence. Because he was a strong ruler, Ivan became known as "Ivan the Great."

The Czars

Muscovy developed into the country known today as Russia. In 1547 Ivan IV declared himself **czar** (ZAHR), or emperor. He ruled harshly, using secret police to carry out his will, and earned the name "Ivan the Terrible." By conquering neighboring territories, Ivan expanded his empire south to the Caspian Sea and east past the Ural Mountains.

The expansion of Russian territory, shown in **Figure 1** on the preceding page, continued under later czars, such as Peter the Great and Catherine the Great. These czars wanted to obtain a warm-water port for trade. They also wanted to increase Russia's contact with Europe. In the early 1700s, Peter the Great built a new capital—St. Petersburg—close to Europe near the Baltic coast. By this time, the Russian Empire extended to the Pacific Ocean. Over the next hundred years, it came to include large parts of Central Asia. As a result, non-Russians, including many Muslims, became part of the Russian Empire.

Through the centuries, Russia remained largely rural and agricultural. The czars, large landowners, and wealthy merchants enjoyed comfortable lives. The majority of Russians, however, were poor peasants. Many were **serfs**, or farm laborers who could be bought and sold with the land. Serfs sometimes revolted, but the czars' armies put down their rebellions.

Revolution

Several times during Russia's history, the country's cold climate and huge size proved to be strong defenses against invasion. In 1812 a French army led by Napoleon Bonaparte invaded Russia. To conquer Russia, the French forces had to march hundreds of miles and capture Moscow. All along the French army's way, the Russian army burned villages and any supplies the French could use. The Russians then abandoned and burned Moscow, and the czar moved to St. Petersburg. Even though they had captured Moscow, French troops had few supplies and were forced to retreat during the brutal Russian winter. Thousands died from the harsh conditions and constant Russian attacks. Russia remained independent.

History at a Glance

A.D. **1000**   **1200**   **1400**

A.D. **988**
Kievan Rus accepts Christianity

Russian church, built c. 1050

1240s
Mongols conquer Kievan Rus

Prince's crown, c. 1400

1480
Ivan the Great ends Mongol ru...

In the late 1800s, Russia entered a period of great change. In 1861 Czar Alexander II freed the country's 40 million serfs. Freedom did not **release** them from poverty, however. Alexander began to modernize Russia's economy, building industries and expanding railroads. Despite these changes, most Russians remained poor, and unrest spread among workers and peasants.

In 1914 Russia joined France and Britain to fight Germany and Austria in World War I. Poorly prepared, Russia suffered military defeats, losing millions of men between 1914 and 1916. Many Russians blamed Czar Nicholas II for the country's poor performance in the war and for food shortages. In early 1917 the people staged a revolution that forced the czar to step down from the throne. Later that year, Vladimir Lenin led a second revolt that overthrew the temporary government. He set about establishing a **communist state** in which the government controlled the economy and society. Fearing invasion, Lenin also moved Russia's capital from coastal St. Petersburg inland to Moscow.

✔️ **Reading Check** **Summarizing** Briefly describe the founding of Kievan Rus and its development into Russia.

The Rise and Fall of Communism

Main Idea The Communist system controlled many aspects of people's lives, but democratic ideas eventually took hold.

Geography and You What would it be like if the government told you what job you had to do and also greatly limited the choices of products you could buy in stores? Read to learn about the changes that the Communist government brought to Russia.

Vladimir Lenin and his followers created a new nation called the Union of Soviet Socialist Republics (U.S.S.R.), or the Soviet Union. This nation included 15 republics made up of different ethnic groups. Russia was the largest republic, and the Russian ethnic group dominated the Soviet Union's government.

Lenin followed the ideas of a German political thinker named Karl Marx. Marx believed that industrialization created an unjust system in which factory owners held great power, while the workers held very little. Lenin said that he wanted to make everyone in Soviet society more equal.

1600

1800

2000

1703
Building of St. Petersburg begins

Russian peasants, c. 1900

1917
Revolution sweeps Russia

Medal commemorating Trans-Siberian Railroad

1991
Soviet Union falls

So he ended private ownership, bringing all farms and factories under the control of the Soviet government. Lenin's policies were later continued by Joseph Stalin, who ruled the Soviet Union after Lenin's death in 1924. A harsh dictator, Stalin prevented the Soviet people from practicing their religions and had religious property seized. His secret police killed or imprisoned anyone who disagreed with his policies.

Agriculture and Industry

Soviet leaders set up a command economy in which the government ran all areas of economic life. They decided what crops farmers should grow and what goods factories should produce.

Leaders also introduced collectivization— a system in which small farms were combined into large, factorylike farms run by the government. Government leaders hoped these farms would be more efficient and reduce the need for farmworkers. Thousands of former peasants could then be put to work in factories to increase industrialization.

The Soviet economic plans had mixed success. The new farms were inefficient and did not produce enough food for the Soviet people. Industrial production was more successful. Huge factories produced steel, machinery, and military equipment. Strict government control, however, had drawbacks. The government **eliminated,** or did away with, competition, allowing only certain factories to make certain goods. This led to a lack of efficiency and poor-quality goods.

TIME GLOBAL CITIZENS

NAMES: NIKOLAI AND TATYANA SHCHUR
HOME COUNTRY: RUSSIA

ACHIEVEMENT: As Russia becomes a democracy, this husband-and-wife team is trying to make sure that citizens' rights are protected. In 2002 the couple visited Karabolka, a village near the site of a nuclear plant accident 50 years ago. Many people moved after the accident—but some stayed. For decades, those who remained were not told why so many of them fell mysteriously ill. The Shchurs have forced the government to acknowledge the area's radioactive contamination and to take action. Their dream is to educate a new generation of journalists, teachers, and police with a respect for human rights, including the right to live in an area free of radiation.

QUOTE: Tatyana says, 66 Nothing will really change until a generation grows up in Russia that is completely free from fear. 99

The Shchurs stand by a Russian sign warning of high radiation levels.

CITIZENS IN ACTION Why do you think exposing past government cover-ups might be a difficult task?

Soviet Power

In 1941, during World War II, Germany invaded the Soviet Union. The Soviets joined Great Britain and the United States to defeat the Germans. About 20 to 30 million Russian soldiers and civilians died in the war. After the war, Stalin wanted to make sure the Soviet Union would not be invaded again. He kept Soviet troops in neighboring eastern European countries and established Communist governments in them.

The Soviet Union and the United States were allies during the war but became bitter rivals after it. From the late 1940s until about 1990, these superpowers, the two most powerful nations in the world, engaged in a struggle for world influence. Because the struggle never became "hot," with actual combat between the two opponents, the conflict became known as the **Cold War.**

Each superpower became the center of a group of nations. Members of each group pledged to come to one another's aid if a member country were attacked by a country from the other group. The United States was the chief member of the North Atlantic Treaty Organization, or NATO, which included most of western Europe's democracies. The Soviet Union led the Warsaw Pact, a group of Communist countries that included most of Eastern Europe.

The Soviet Union and the United States competed to produce military weapons and to explore outer space. With so many resources going to the military, the Soviet people had to endure shortages of basic goods, such as food and cars. By the 1980s, many Soviets were ready for change.

Social Studies ONLINE

Student Web Activity Visit glencoe.com and complete the Chapter 14 Web Activity about the Cold War.

NATIONAL GEOGRAPHIC

Woman in Space

In 1963 Valentina Tereshkova of the Soviet Union became the first woman to travel in space. *Place* With whom did the Soviet Union compete in space exploration?

Attempts at Reform

In 1985 Mikhail Gorbachev (mih·KAH·eel GAWR·buh·CHAWF) became the Soviet leader. He quickly began a number of reforms in the Soviet Union. Under the policy of **glasnost** (GLAZ·nohst), or "openness," Soviet citizens could say and write about what they thought without fear of being punished. Another policy, known as **perestroika** (PEHR·uh·STROY·kah), or "restructuring," aimed at boosting the Soviet economy. It gave factory managers more freedom to make economic decisions and encouraged the creation of small, privately owned businesses.

Instead of strengthening the country, Gorbachev's policies made the Soviet people doubt communism even more. Huge protests against Soviet control arose across Eastern Europe. By 1991 all of the region's Communist governments had fallen. Gorbachev hoped that giving some freedoms would win the people's support.

When Eastern Europeans rejected continued Communist rule, Gorbachev decided not to resort to force. He refused to send troops to Eastern Europe as other Soviet leaders had done in the past.

Collapse of the Soviet Union

As communism ended in Eastern Europe, the Soviet Union faced growing unrest among its ethnic groups. Gorbachev was criticized both by hard-liners who wished to maintain Communist rule as well as by reformers. The hard-liners wanted to stop changes. The reformers, on the other hand, felt that Gorbachev was not making changes fast enough. The reformers were led by a rising politician named Boris Yeltsin (BUHR·YEES YEHLT·suhn). He became the president of Russia, the largest of the Soviet republics.

In August 1991, hard-line Communists attempted a **coup** (KOO), an overthrow of the government by military force. Boris Yeltsin called on the people to resist. When many Russians stood firm, the hard-liners were forced to give up. The coup's failure was the beginning of the end of the Soviet Union. Within a few months, Russia and all of the other Soviet republics declared independence. By the end of 1991, the Soviet Union no longer existed as a nation.

In Russia, Yeltsin had some success in building democracy and a market economy. His successor, Vladimir Putin (vlah·DEE·meer POO·tuhn), however, increased government controls to deal with rising crime and violence. Challenges also came from some ethnic minorities. In the Chechnya (chehch·NYAH) region, a group trying to separate from Russia waged a bloody civil war.

✔ **Reading Check** **Explaining** What were Gorbachev's reforms? Why were they introduced?

Section 1 Review

Social Studies ONLINE
Study Central™ To review this section, go to glencoe.com.

Vocabulary

1. **Explain** the significance of:
   a. missionary   **f.** Cold War
   b. czar   **g.** glasnost
   c. serf   **h.** perestroika
   d. communist state **i.** coup
   e. collectivization

Main Ideas

2. **Identifying** What geographic goal drove the czars to expand their empire?

3. **Sequencing** Use a diagram like the one below to list events leading up to the collapse of the Soviet Union.

   ☐ → ☐ → ☐ → ☐ → **Soviet Union Collapses**

Critical Thinking

4. **Determining Cause and Effect** How did the Soviet Union's involvement in the Cold War affect the Soviet economy?

5. **BIG Idea** How did Russia become a society that included many different ethnic groups?

6. **Challenge** How did the economic systems of the Soviet Union and the United States differ?

Writing About Geography

7. **Using Your FOLDABLES** Use your Foldable to write a summary of how Russia's government changed after World War I.

The Longest Railroad

How long does it take to cross the world's largest country? Thanks to the world's longest railroad, you can make the trip in less than a week—barely.

Building the Railroad The Trans-Siberian Railroad starts in Moscow, in western Russia. Nearly 5,800 miles (9,334 km) later, it reaches Vladivostok, on the shores of the Pacific Ocean. Work to build the railroad began in 1891 and was completed in 1901.

The first route crossed Manchuria, a northern part of China. Russian leaders soon feared that Japan would seize Manchuria, however, which would threaten their rail line. As a result, they ordered work on a new route that went north of Manchuria and stayed entirely within Russian land. That route was finished in 1916.

Construction of the railroad was difficult. Track had to be laid across swamps and permafrost and through dense forests and mountains. In eastern Russia, where the railroad crosses many rivers, dozens of bridges had to be built. To keep the railroad running, wells for water and mines to obtain coal and iron were needed.

▲ **A train on the Trans-Siberian Railroad**

The Impact of the Railroad The railroad had a huge impact on Russia. Even today, no highway connects western and eastern Russia. As a result, the railroad is the only land-based route linking these halves of the country. The railroad serves as a vital lifeline for bringing supplies to eastern settlements. It also moves Siberia's timber and mineral resources to factories in the west.

During World War II, the railroad helped save Russia. When Germany invaded western Russia in 1941, the government used the railroad to move equipment from that area into Siberia. There it set up new factories to make the vehicles, weapons, and ammunition needed to continue fighting the war.

NATIONAL GEOGRAPHIC
The Trans-Siberian Railroad

— Trans-Siberian Railroad

Moscow

Irkutsk

Vladivostok

0   1,000 kilometers
0   1,000 miles
Two-Point Equidistant projection

Think About It

1. **Human-Environment Interaction** What obstacles did workers building the railroad have to overcome?

2. **Movement** Why was the railroad important during World War II?

Guide to Reading

BIG Idea

Culture groups shape human systems.

Content Vocabulary

- oral tradition *(p. 397)*
- nationalism *(p. 397)*
- autonomy *(p. 399)*

Academic Vocabulary

- promote *(p. 398)*
- primary *(p. 400)*
- exploit *(p. 400)*

Reading Strategy

Summarizing Use a diagram like the one below to list details about Russian music and dance.

Russian Music and Dance

SECTION 2

Cultures and Lifestyles

Picture This The model in this photograph is getting ready for Siberian Fashion Week in Krasnoyarsk, Russia. Once a fortress city that protected Siberia from invaders, the city is now home to a festival that highlights the world of beauty. Krasnoyarsk links the eastern and western regions of icy Siberia. In a similar way, Fashion Week combines the artistic traditions of the regions with the business of high fashion. Read Section 2 to learn more about the rich cultures of Russia.

▼ **Siberian Fashion Week in Krasnoyarsk, Russia**

Russia's Cultures

Main Idea Russia's many ethnic groups and a tradition of great achievements in the arts and sciences contribute to the country's cultures.

Geography and You Have you ever watched the graceful motions of a ballet dancer? Read to find out how ballet and other arts are an important part of Russia's culture.

Russia has many different ethnic groups and religions. As the Russian Empire expanded, different peoples came under its control. Today dozens of ethnic groups live in Russia. Many of these groups speak their own language and have their own culture. Most people, however, speak Russian, the country's official language.

Russians, or Slavs who descended from the people of Muscovy, are the largest ethnic group. They live throughout Russia, although most Russians live west of the Urals. The next-largest groups include Tatars, who are Muslim descendants of the Mongols, and Ukrainians, who are descendants of Slavs that settled the area around Kiev (Kyiv). Smaller ethnic groups include the Yakut, who herd reindeer and also raise horses and cattle in eastern Siberia.

Under communism, Russia's people were not allowed to practice religion. The Soviet government officially promoted the position in its schools that there is no god or other supreme being. By the late 1980s, however, the Soviets began to relax their ban on religions. Today, people enjoy religious freedom, and about half of the population practices a faith. Eastern Orthodox Christianity is the country's major religion. Russia also has many Muslims, who live mainly in the Caucasus region. Lesser

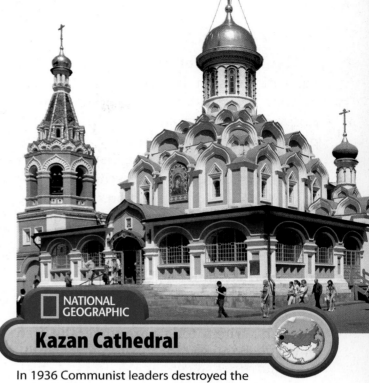

Kazan Cathedral

In 1936 Communist leaders destroyed the cathedral that stood on this site in Moscow. It was rebuilt in the 1980s. **Regions** What is Russia's major religion today?

numbers of Roman Catholics, Protestants, and Jews also live in Russia.

The Arts

Russia has a rich tradition of literature, art, and music. Early Russians developed a strong **oral tradition,** or passing stories by word of mouth from generation to generation. Later, many writers and musicians drew on these stories or on folk music for their works. The Russian people's strong sense of **nationalism,** or feelings of loyalty toward their country, is reflected in many artistic works.

Russia has long been a center of music and dance. In the late 1800s, Peter Ilich Tchaikovsky (chy·KAWF·skee) wrote some of the world's favorite ballets, including *Swan Lake* and *The Nutcracker*. In the early 1900s, Igor Stravinsky wrote *The Firebird Suite* and other works. Today, the Bolshoi of Moscow and the Kirov of St. Petersburg are among the world's famous ballet companies.

The 1800s are often called the "golden age" of Russian literature. During this period, Leo Tolstoy, one of the greatest Russian writers, wrote *War and Peace*. This patriotic novel describes the Russians' defense against the French invasion in 1812.

During the Soviet era, writers did not enjoy freedom of expression. They were required to **promote** government policies in their works. Alexander Solzhenitsyn (SOHL·zhuh·NEET·suhn), who wrote about the harsh conditions of Communist society, spent time in Russian prison camps before he was forced to leave the country. Russian writers today are generally free to write about any idea or topic. Recently, however, the government placed new limits on freedom of speech.

The visual arts are also an important part of Russian culture. The Hermitage Museum in St. Petersburg has one of the most famous art collections in the world. Among its treasures are the jewel-encrusted Easter eggs crafted by jeweler Peter Carl Fabergé for the czars.

Scientific Advances

For decades, the Soviet Union emphasized education in the sciences. As a result, Russia has many scientists, mathematicians, and doctors. During the Cold War, Russian scientists helped the Soviet Union compete with the United States in space exploration. In 1961 Russian Yuri Gagarin was the first person to fly in space. Since 1998 the Russians have joined with Americans and people from other countries in building the International Space Station.

Reading Check **Explaining** How have religious practices in Russia changed since the fall of communism?

NATIONAL GEOGRAPHIC

Russian Treasures

▲ The State Russian Museum in St. Petersburg holds more than 400,000 exhibits of Russian art from the last 1,000 years. Ornate Fabergé eggs (inset) were handcrafted for the czar's family and others. *Regions* **For what other arts is Russia known?**

Life in Russia

Main Idea Russian lifestyles are influenced by the region's cold climate and vast area, as well as the country's changing economic system.

Geography and You Do you like to celebrate the arrival of spring after a long, cold winter? Read on to find out about Russia's spring festival and other aspects of Russian life.

While Russia continues to modernize after shedding Soviet control, it faces several challenges. Housing is still in short supply, and transportation and communication networks need updating.

Everyday Life

Most Russians live in cities located west of the Ural Mountains. City residents generally live in large apartment buildings rather than in single-family houses. Housing is scarce and often expensive. For this reason, grandparents, parents, and children frequently share the same apartment or house. Since many Russian mothers work outside of the home, grandparents often help take care of the household. Grandparents may cook, clean, shop, and care for young children in the family.

Middle-class and wealthy Russians may own country homes called dachas (DAH·chuhs). At their country homes, people often tend gardens, growing vegetables that they can either eat or sell in the cities. In rural areas, dachas and other homes are usually built of wood.

In the coldest areas of Russia, people take extra steps to keep their homes warm. For example, some homes in Siberia have three doors at each entrance. This prevents a cold blast of air from rushing in when the outside doors are opened.

NATIONAL GEOGRAPHIC

Family Life in Russia

In Russia it is common for several generations of one family to share a home. *Location* Where do most Russians live?

Sports and Holidays

It is not surprising that the country's most popular sports are associated with winter or are played indoors. During the Communist era, the Soviet Union placed great emphasis on training world-class athletes. Today, Russian hockey players, figure skaters, and gymnasts are strong competitors in international events.

Russians celebrate several holidays. The newest holiday, Independence Day, falls on June 12 and marks Russia's declaration of **autonomy**, or independence from the Soviet Union. New Year's Eve is one of the most festive holidays. Russian children decorate a fir tree and exchange presents with others in their families. In the spring, Russians celebrate *Maslenitsa*. This week-long holiday marks the end of winter and includes organized snowball fights, sleigh rides, and parties. Straw dolls that represent winter are burned to signal the beginning of spring.

Transportation and Communications

Russia is so large that people and goods must often be transported over great distances. Railroads were the **primary** means of transportation during the Soviet era and are still important today. The heavily populated area west of the Urals is covered by an extensive railroad network.

This railroad system is linked to the famed Trans-Siberian Railroad, which runs from Moscow in the west to Vladivostok in the east. Completed in the early 1900s, it is the longest rail line in the world. The railroad made it possible for Russians to **exploit,** or use, Siberia's natural resources.

Russia still lacks an effective highway system. No multilane highway system links major cities, and the roads that do exist are in poor condition. There are few gas stations or restaurants along the roads. The government is currently building a 6,600-mile (10,622-km) highway across the country. When completed, it will be the longest national highway in the world.

One reason that highway improvements are needed is because Russian car ownership is rising. In Soviet times, few families had cars. Now about half of Russian families own a car.

Russia's communications systems also need improvement. For years, telephones were less common in Russia than in most European countries. Since the early 1990s, major improvements have been made that will benefit Russian citizens and the country's economy. New phone lines allow for the rapid transfer of information, making it easier to use the Internet in Russia. Rural areas, however, still have poor phone service.

Reading Check **Making Connections** How does the *Maslenitsa* celebration reflect Russia's culture and environment?

Section 2 Review

Social Studies ONLINE
Study Central™ To review this section, go to glencoe.com.

Vocabulary

1. **Explain** the meaning of *oral tradition, nationalism,* and *autonomy* by using each term in a sentence.

Main Ideas

2. **Identifying** Name and describe four of Russia's ethnic groups.

3. **Organizing** Use a diagram like the one below to list details about Russia's transportation system.

Critical Thinking

4. **Determining Cause and Effect** Why do many grandparents, parents, and children in Russia share the same apartment or house?

5. **BIG Idea** How are Russia's nationalist feelings represented in the country's arts?

6. **Challenge** Why do you think the Soviet Union competed with the United States in the area of space exploration?

Writing About Geography

7. **Expository Writing** Write a paragraph explaining how Russia's cold climate affects Russians' daily lives.

Visual Summary

____ The Russian ____ Empire

- Russia had its beginnings in small trading centers built by Slavic peoples.

- Rulers known as czars governed the Russian Empire from 1547 to 1917.

- The czars expanded Russian territory to reach from Europe to the Pacific Ocean.

- Revolutions in 1917 overthrew the czar and brought the Communists to power.

Joseph Stalin

____ The Rise of ____ Democracy

- In 1991 the Soviet Union broke up into Russia and other independent republics.

- Russia has struggled to build a democracy and a market economy.

Medieval Moscow

____ The Soviet ____ Union

- Under the Communist Party, the government ran all areas of economic life.

- After World War II, the Soviet Union and the United States became bitter rivals.

Cold War parade with missiles

____ People and ____ Culture

- Russia has many different ethnic groups.

- Russians practice a number of different religions, but most of the population is Eastern Orthodox Christian.

- Russian artists, musicians, and writers often used themes based on Russian history.

Dacha outside of Moscow

____ Life in Russia ____

- Most Russians live in apartments in large cities rather than in single-family homes.

- Railroads link heavily populated European Russia with sparsely settled Siberia.

- Russia is working to improve its highway and communications systems.

STUDY TO GO Study anywhere, anytime! Download quizzes and flash cards to your PDA from **glencoe.com**.

STANDARDIZED TEST PRACTICE

TEST-TAKING

Read all the choices before choosing your answer. You may overlook the correct answer if you are hasty!

Reviewing Vocabulary

Directions: Choose the word(s) that best completes the sentence.

1. The emperors of Russia were called _____.

   A serfs

   B converts

   C czars

   D missionaries

2. Mikhail Gorbachev introduced _____, which was aimed at boosting the Soviet economy.

   A perestroika

   B collectivization

   C Cold War

   D glasnost

3. _____ were farm laborers who could be bought and sold with the land.

   A Serfs

   B Converts

   C Missionaries

   D Guilds

4. Early Russians developed a strong _____, which means passing stories by word of mouth from generation to generation.

   A nationalism

   B oral tradition

   C autonomy

   D glasnost

5. Russia's newest holiday, Independence Day, marks its declaration of _____ the Soviet Union.

   A collectivization of

   B dependence on

   C alliance with

   D autonomy from

Reviewing Main Ideas

Directions: Choose the best answer for each question.

Section 1 *(pp. 388–394)*

6. The Russian Empire eventually fell to a revolution due mostly to _____.

   A threats from invaders

   B widespread hunger and suffering

   C outside agitators

   D a decline in the military

7. When Communist leaders took control of Russia and renamed it the Soviet Union, they established a _____.

   A free market economy

   B democratic government

   C government controlled economy

   D new government controlled by a czar

Section 2 *(pp. 396–400)*

8. The Russian people's sense of nationalism _____.

   A has little impact on Russia's arts

   B has caused them to avoid foreign art

   C is reflected in many artistic works

   D is the only topic used in Russian literature

9. Russia's many good hockey players and gymnasts are partly a result of the country's _____.

   A high mountains

   B many factories and industries

   C many professional sports teams

   D cold climate

GO ON

Critical Thinking

Directions: Choose the best answer for each question.

10. Which of the following was a result of perestroika?

  A The Soviet economy was weakening.

  B The people were ready for change.

  C Factory managers gained more freedoms.

  D Citizens could say what they thought without punishment.

Base your answer to question 11 on the chart below.

Infant Mortality Rates per 1,000 Live Births		
Years	Soviet Union/Russia	United States
1950–1955	97	28
1955–1960	57	26
1960–1965	40	25
1965–1970	32	22
1970–1975	28	18
1975–1980	30	14
1980–1985	26	11
1985–1990	24	10
1990–1995*	21	9
1995–2000	17	8
*After 1991 the Soviet Union collapsed.		
Source: http://world.britannica.com/analyst/chrono/table		

11. Which of the following statements seems most likely?

  A Between 1950 and 2000, medical care decreased in the United States.

  B Between 1950 and 2000, infants in the Soviet Union had greater access to hospitals than in the United States.

  C Between 1950 and 2000, infants in the Soviet Union had a better chance of surviving than in the United States.

  D Between 1950 and 2000, medical care improved in the Soviet Union.

Document-Based Questions

Directions: Analyze the document and answer the short-answer questions that follow.

After it was first adopted in 1918, the constitution of the Soviet Union was rewritten several times. The following is part of the preamble from the 1977 version.

> The supreme goal of the Soviet state is the building of a classless communist society in which there will be public, communist self-government. The main aims of the people's socialist state are: to lay the material and technical foundation of communism, to perfect socialist social relations and transform them into communist relations, to mould the citizen of communist society, to raise the people's living and cultural standards, to safeguard the country's security, and to further the consolidation of peace and development of international cooperation.

12. How do you think the Soviet state will "lay the material and technical foundation of communism"?

13. Which parts of the preamble deal directly with Soviet citizens?

Extended Response

14. Citizens of the Soviet Union faced many problems during the period the Communist government was in control. Write an essay in which you explain what you think were the most difficult problems people had to face. Make sure to explain why these problems were worse than others.

STOP

Social Studies ONLINE

For additional test practice, use Self-Check Quizzes—Chapter 14 at glencoe.com.

Need Extra Help?													
If you missed question...	1	2	3	4	5	6	7	8	9	10	11	12	13	14
Go to page...	390	393	390	397	399	391	392	397	399	393	398	391	391	391

"Hello! My name is Irina.

I am 13 years old and I live in Moscow, the capital of Russia, with my parents and little brother, Misha. I go to Moscow School No. 429. This is how I spend a typical day."

7:30 a.m. I wake up and dress quickly in jeans and a sweater. Then I join my parents and Misha in the kitchen and have yogurt for breakfast. (On weekends, I like fried eggs, but today there is not enough time!)

8:00 a.m. My father drives me to school and Misha to kindergarten. In Russia, public schools do not provide buses. After dropping us off, my father will go to his job as a manager at a paper supply company.

8:10 a.m. I arrive at school. School No. 429 is a modern building, but Moscow is a very old city. Some of its buildings are more than 500 years old!

8:30 a.m. Classes begin. One of my first classes of the day is "work study," in which we learn different trades. Right now we are learning to sew clothes. It's interesting, but I don't think it's the right job for me. I would like to be a makeup artist one day.

9:30 a.m. It is time for geography class. I raise my hand to respond to a question, and I answer correctly.

This makes me happy because I would like to get a grade of 4 or 5 in this class. A *4* means "very good." A *5* means "excellent."

11:30 a.m. I'm hungry! During a break between classes, I stop in at the canteen (cafeteria) for a small piece of pizza. Later, I will have a bigger lunch at home.

12:30 p.m. In computer class, we log on to the Internet. This is one of my favorite classes.

2:00 p.m. The school day is over, and I take the tram home. The tram is a street car that runs on electricity. Moscow's tramway is more than 100 years old.

3:00 p.m. My mother is home from her job at a print house and Misha is home from school. I help make a lunch of chicken and cold borscht. Borscht is a soup made of beets and other vegetables. It can be served cold or hot.

3:30 p.m. My mother, Misha, and I walk to a large park near our flat, or apartment. There I meet up with my friend Yulia. We roller skate and play with Misha.

5:30 p.m. Back at home, I help do the laundry and dust the flat. When I am done with my chores, I go to my bedroom and start my homework.

7:30 p.m. My father is home, and it is time for a light dinner. Tonight we have a salad made of eggs, cabbage, mayonnaise, and beets. Another dinner I enjoy is pelmeni. It is pieces of meat that are covered in dough and boiled in salty water.

8:00 p.m. I finish my homework and listen to music. I like Russian bands, but I also enjoy American pop music. I listen to it on the radio and on music videos.

10:30 p.m. I go to bed. Tomorrow is Friday, my last day of school for the week. I am looking forward to the weekend! We will spend it at our dacha, or country cottage. It is in the village of Istra, where my grandparents live. I enjoy spending time with them.

ILLUSTRATIONS BY BOOKMAPMAN

GLOBETROTTING Irina is tested on her geography skills. She got an "excellent"!

COME AND GET IT! Irina helps her mom make dinner. Russians often eat a big lunch and a light supper.

SOAP STORY Blowing bubbles in the park is fun for Irina and her friend Yulia.

GOING SKATING After school, Irina Timoshenko (uh•REE•nah teem•oh•SHENK•oh) loves to roller skate with her friends. Irina lives in Moscow, Russia's capital, which is filled with parks that are perfect for skating.

JEREMY NICHOLL / POLARIS (4)

What's Popular in Russia

Tea Time Many Russian families drink weak black tea all day long. It is brewed in a pot called a samovar.

BILL ARON / PHOTO EDIT

Steam baths This hot trend is actually an old Russian tradition. At a *banya,* or bath house, a visitor sits in a steam room, then takes an icy cold dip, and finally, receives a gentle massage.

Dachas Many Russian city dwellers—both rich and poor— own cottages, or dachas, in the country. They go on weekends and in summers to relax.

Ballet Russia is home to some of the world's most famous dancers. Moscow's Bolshoi Ballet brought the world *Swan Lake.*

ANATOLY RUKHADZE / ITAR-TASS PHOTOS / NEWSCOM

Say It in Russian

Most of Russia's 140 million people speak the official national language, Russian. Russian is also spoken in Belarus, Kazakhstan, and other nations that were once republics of the Soviet Union. Try saying these phrases in Russian.

Hello
Zdravstvuite (ZDRAHST•vet•yah)

Good-bye
Do svidanja (doh svee•DAH•nee•yah)

My name is
_____.
Menya zavut (mee•NYAH zah•VOOT)

CREATAS / PUNCHSTOCK

Russia Today

Essential Question

Regions Since the fall of the Soviet Union, Russia has been struggling to build a democracy and a free market economy. It also has sought to regain its influence in world affairs. Such major changes are difficult, however, and the world will watch with great interest as Russia works to become a successful democratic nation. Why is the success of democracy in Russia important to the rest of the world?

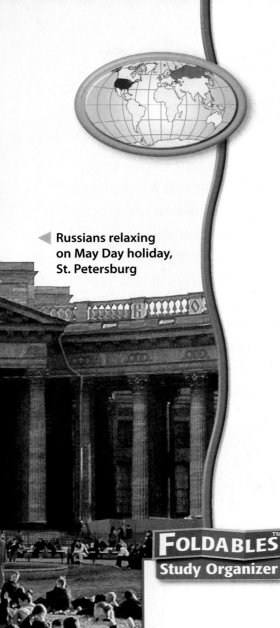

◀ Russians relaxing on May Day holiday, St. Petersburg

BIG Ideas

Section 1: A Changing Russia

BIG IDEA Geographers organize the Earth into regions that share common characteristics.
New democratic institutions and a free market economy link the different parts of Russia. These positive changes, however, are threatened by the government's abuse of power, the spread of corruption in business, and a decline in population.

Section 2: Issues and Challenges

BIG IDEA Geography is used to interpret the past, understand the present, and plan for the future.
The change to democracy and a market economy has been difficult for Russia because of its long history of all-powerful governments. The country also faces challenges from ethnic groups that want independence.

FOLDABLES™
Study Organizer

Organizing Information Make this Foldable to organize information about political and social changes in Russia and other issues in Russia today.

Step 1 Fold a sheet of paper in half from side to side so that the left edge lies about ½ inch from the right edge.

Step 2 Cut the top layer only to make five tabs.

Step 3 Label the Foldable as shown.

Reading and Writing Use the notes in your Foldable to create an outline showing the major issues facing Russia today.

Social Studies ONLINE
To preview Chapter 15, go to <u>glencoe.com</u>.

Guide to Reading

BIG Idea

Geographers organize the Earth into regions that share common characteristics.

Content Vocabulary

- privatization *(p. 409)*
- middle class *(p. 410)*
- underemployment *(p. 410)*
- pensioner *(p. 410)*
- heavy industry *(p. 411)*
- light industry *(p. 411)*

Academic Vocabulary

- comprise *(p. 409)*
- invest *(p. 410)*
- volume *(p. 411)*

Reading Strategy

Identifying Central Issues Use a diagram like the one below to show three major effects of the fall of communism on Russia.

Fall of Communism

SECTION 1

A Changing Russia

Picture This The figures below are toys, art, and a history lesson all in one! *Matryoshka* dolls, which fit one inside the other, are popular toys and have been hand painted in Russia since the late 1800s. The traditional version of the *Matryoshka* shows a Russian woman wearing a babushka (scarf) and an apron. Here, art becomes history, as the colorful dolls represent Soviet and Russian leaders (from left to right) Mikhail Gorbachev, Boris Yeltsin, and Vladimir Putin. To learn more about recent changes in Russia, read Section 1.

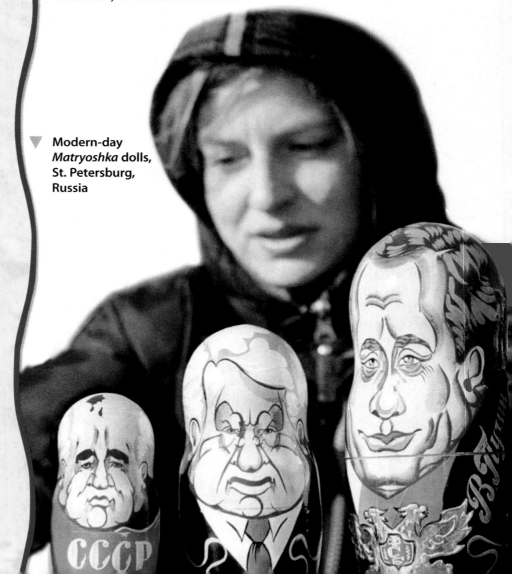

▼ **Modern-day *Matryoshka* dolls, St. Petersburg, Russia**

Changing Politics and Society

Main Idea The fall of communism led to great changes in Russia's government, economy, and society.

Geography and You Can you imagine having to completely change your way of life? Read to learn how Russians faced that situation in the early 1990s.

Russia is still adjusting to the changes that occurred in the 1990s. When communism fell in 1991, Russia was forced to build a new government and economy. These ongoing changes continue to greatly affect the everyday lives of the Russian people.

A New Form of Government

The Communist Party ruled Russia when it was part of the Soviet Union. The Communists did not allow people to challenge their power, and everyday citizens had no voice in choosing their leaders. After the fall of communism, however, Russia became more democratic.

In a 1993 election, Russian voters approved a new constitution and elected members of a legislature to represent them. This new legislature included candidates from many different political parties. Boris Yeltsin, who was Russia's leader when it was a Soviet republic, was elected the first president of Russia.

Russia's official name is the Russian Federation. This name reflects the fact that Russia **comprises,** or is made up of, many different regions and territories. Like the United States, Russia is a federal republic, with power divided between national and regional governments. In the United States, some powers belong to the states, and others belong only to the national gov-

NATIONAL GEOGRAPHIC

Voting in Russia

Voters in Russia today can choose from many political parties and groups. *Regions* What role did most citizens have in their government when Russia was part of the Soviet Union?

ernment. Some powers are shared by both levels of government. In Russia, the division of powers is less clear because the new Russian government is still developing.

A New Economic System

As part of the Soviet Union, Russia had a command economy. In a command economy, the central government makes all the economic decisions. Since the fall of communism, Russia has attempted to shift to a market economy.

To create a market economy, the government introduced **privatization** (PRY·vuh·tuh·ZAY·shuhn). This is the transfer of ownership of businesses from the government to individuals. In the new system, businesses have to compete with one another. As a result, Russian companies have begun to advertise to attract customers. The government has also dropped price controls, which were official prices set for different goods and services. In a market economy, prices result from competition among companies and from what Russian consumers need, want, and are willing to pay.

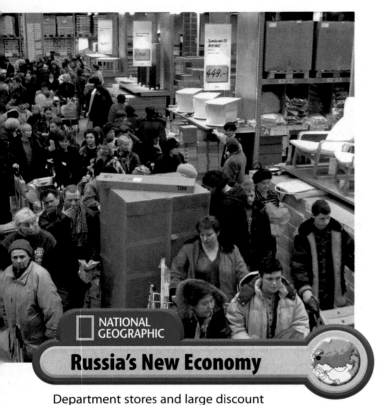

Russia's New Economy

Department stores and large discount stores are opening in Russia as the economy grows and people have more money to spend on consumer goods. **Place** What is the middle class?

Changes in Society

With the end of Communist rule, the government loosened its control on Russian society. Many different political parties were able to organize. Russians were allowed to criticize leaders and their policies. Additionally, the government no longer controlled the content of news reports or books.

Along with political freedom, Russians began to have more contact with other cultures. American and European books, television shows, and CDs became more readily available to Russians. Many people embraced the new ideas, music, and fashions that became available.

Russia's new economy led to the spread of consumerism—the desire to buy goods. Russians eagerly sought goods they had not been able to buy for years. Businesses

prospered, and a Russian **middle class** emerged. This term refers to a social group that is neither very rich nor poor, but has enough money to buy cars, new clothing, electronics, and other luxury items.

The new economic system gave workers freedom to quit their jobs and seek employment elsewhere. Russians who were willing to take risks could open their own businesses. People also could **invest,** or put money into businesses run by others, in the hope of making even more money. This new economic freedom, however, did not guarantee success. Both new businesses and old businesses, which were no longer supported by the government, failed. Some tried to stay open by firing workers to cut costs. Other businesses simply could not compete and closed, putting more Russians out of work. Some skilled Russian workers still face **underemployment,** which means they are forced to take jobs that require lesser skills than they have. Many people must work second jobs to survive.

The unsettled economy is also difficult for **pensioners** (PEHN·shuh·nuhrs). Pensioners are people who receive regular payments from the government because they are too old or too sick to work. The amount of these payments is usually fixed, or remains the same. When prices rise but the amount of the payments does not increase, it becomes difficult for pensioners to buy goods. These problems caused many Russians to oppose privatization.

Population Changes

Russia's population also has experienced change. During Soviet times, many ethnic Russians moved to other parts of the Soviet Union. When these republics became independent, the ethnic Russians often were no longer welcome. About 3 million of them decided to return to Russia. People of other ethnic groups also left for Russia to escape hardships in the new republics.

Despite this arrival of immigrants, Russia's population declined from 150 million people in 1991 to 143 million in 2006. This decline is the result of a combination of low birthrates and rising death rates. The life expectancy of men has decreased to 60 years, compared with 74 years for women. These rates are well below those of other developed countries.

The sharp decline in life expectancy is a result of poor nutrition, alcoholism, and drug abuse. Also, pollution has led to more lung diseases. Meanwhile, government spending on health care has dropped.

Reading Check **Comparing** How is Russia's government similar to that of the United States?

Life Expectancies: Russia and Europe

Country	Average Life Expectancy	
	Men	Women
Sweden	78	83
Italy	77	83
France	76	84
Germany	76	82
Poland	71	79
Russia	60	74

Source: *CIA World Factbook,* 2006.

Chart Skills

1 **Identifying** Which country has the highest average life expectancy for women?

2 **Explaining** Why are life expectancies in Russia lower than those in most of Europe?

Russia's Economic Regions

Main Idea **Russia's four economic regions differ in the resources and products they supply.**

Geography and You How does your community contribute to your state's or the nation's economy? Read to learn how Russia's different regions contribute to the Russian economy.

The Moscow Region

Moscow is the political, economic, and transportation center of Russia. A large amount of manufacturing takes place in or near Moscow. Under Soviet rule, most of Russia's factories focused on **heavy industry,** or the production of goods such as machinery, mining equipment, and steel. After communism's fall, more factories shifted to **light industry,** or the production of consumer goods, such as clothing and household products. High technology and electronics industries have also developed in Moscow.

St. Petersburg and the Baltic Region

St. Petersburg and the Baltic region are located in northwestern Russia. St. Petersburg, once Russia's capital, is a major port and cultural center. Well-known for its palaces and churches, St. Petersburg attracts thousands of tourists from around the world each year.

Located near the Baltic Sea, St. Petersburg is an important trading center. A high **volume,** or amount, of goods passes through its port. The city is also a major industrial center. Factories here make machinery, ships, automobiles, and other items. St. Petersburg relies on other regions for food, fuel, and other resources.

Kaliningrad is another major Russian port along the Baltic Sea. It lies in a small piece of Russian land, about the size of the state of Connecticut, between Poland and Lithuania. This small area of Russia is isolated from the country's main area. Goods shipped to Kaliningrad must cross other countries to reach the nearest inland part of Russia. Kaliningrad is Russia's only port on the Baltic Sea that stays ice-free all year.

The Volga and Urals Region

The Volga and Urals region lies south and east of Moscow. It is a major center of manufacturing and farming. The Volga River is vital to these economic activities. This 2,300-mile (3,701-km) waterway carries nearly half of Russia's river traffic. The Volga River also supplies water for hydroelectric power and for irrigation. Farmers in the region grow large amounts of wheat, sugar beets, and other crops.

The area of the Ural Mountains is a major source for Russian resources. The mountains contain important minerals, including copper, gold, lead, nickel, and bauxite, as well as energy resources.

Siberia

Siberia's cold Arctic winds, rugged landscapes, and frozen ground make it difficult to take advantage of the region's many resources. The lands of Siberia hold valuable deposits of iron ore, uranium, gold, and coal. Timber from the sprawling taiga is also an important resource for Russia. Since resources in other parts of the world are being used up, Russia's economic future may depend on its ability to make use of Siberia's resources.

✓ Reading Check **Categorizing** Which of Russia's economic regions are important for manufacturing? For agriculture?

Section 1 Review

Social Studies ONLINE
Study Central™ To review this section, go to glencoe.com.

Vocabulary

1. **Explain** the significance of:
   - **a.** privatization
   - **b.** middle class
   - **c.** underemployment
   - **d.** pensioner
   - **e.** heavy industry
   - **f.** light industry

Main Ideas

2. **Describing** Describe some of the freedoms the Russian people gained after the fall of communism.

3. **Explaining** Create a chart like the one below to list at least two ways each economic region contributes to the Russian economy.

Region	Contributions

Critical Thinking

4. **Analyzing Information** Why have some Russians opposed the privatization of industries and businesses?

5. **BIG Idea** Compare and contrast the cities of Moscow and St. Petersburg in terms of location and economic activity.

6. **Challenge** What might happen to a country if it cannot obtain and make use of its own available resources?

Writing About Geography

7. **Persuasive Writing** Write an editorial to support or oppose the changes that the new democratic Russian government made after the fall of communism.

TIME PERSPECTIVES

RUSSIA'S CHALLENGING ROAD TO DEMOCRACY

Russians are enjoying new freedoms under democracy. But are their freedoms threatened?

Russians attend a political rally.

Since the collapse of the Soviet Union in 1991, Russians have worked hard to turn their country into a democracy with a free market system. Today, many Russians have more freedom than ever. As a result of recent reforms, citizens can now own private businesses and elect their leaders.

The new freedoms, however, have also brought new challenges. Corruption has risen among government and private workers. A minority group in Chechnya has carried out terrorist acts that have killed hundreds. As Russia's government combats these challenges, experts wonder if Russia's new freedoms could be lost.

Increased housing construction is a sign of Russia's growing economy.

WHERE WILL REFORMS LEAD?

With territory that extends from Europe to Asia, Russia is the largest country in the world. Throughout its history, Russia has faced many great challenges. For centuries Russia was ruled by **czars**, or absolute rulers. In 1922, following a violent revolution, Russia became part of a group of republics called the Union of Soviet Socialist Republics (U.S.S.R.).

The U.S.S.R. had a Communist government that was very powerful and controlling. The U.S.S.R.'s Communist rulers often kept information about the country secret from the outside world. British prime minister Winston Churchill once called the U.S.S.R. "a riddle wrapped in a mystery."

The government controlled nearly every part of Soviet society. It owned all property and businesses and told citizens what they could do for a living and where they would live. Those suspected of disagreeing with the government were sent to labor camps in Siberia, a brutally cold area in eastern Russia. During the Soviet era, millions of people were imprisoned, executed, or tortured.

A New Chapter

Over time, the Soviet Union began to decline under its harsh system. Many citizens were assigned jobs they did not like. Many of those people were uninspired and did not work very hard. As a result, production suffered, and there were all types of shortages, including food and energy.

In the mid-1980s, the Soviet Union's leaders tried to reform the nation's Communist system. They introduced the policies of glasnost and perestroika. *Glasnost* is a Russian word that means "openness." *Perestroika* means "restructuring." Under glasnost, people were allowed to speak their opinions freely for the first time ever. Perestroika gave some of the government's decision-making power to private individuals and businesses.

Who Russia Trades With

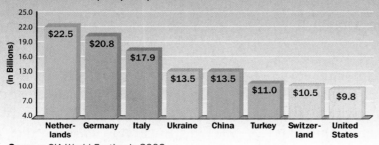

In 2005, Russia exported $245 billion worth of goods. These are its top export partners.

	Value (in Billions)
Netherlands	$22.5
Germany	$20.8
Italy	$17.9
Ukraine	$13.5
China	$13.5
Turkey	$11.0
Switzerland	$10.5
United States	$9.8

Source: *CIA World Factbook*, 2006.

INTERPRETING GRAPHS

Analyzing Information On what continent are Russia's three top export partners located?

U.S. president George W. Bush meets with Russian president Vladimir Putin.

Oil wells such as this one dot the Siberian landscape.

A Russian family shops at a modern mall in Moscow.

Not everyone, however, agreed with these reforms. Conservatives who supported the Communist Party and the military tried to take control of the Soviet government. Their attempt failed and eventually led to the Soviet Union's collapse in 1991. Since then, the Russian government and people have been working to change their country into a democracy.

Some of these changes have been successful. Russians now elect their leaders in free and open elections. Under the Soviet system, only members of the Communist Party could vote. Economic reforms have also been introduced to create a free market economy. Russians can now own their own factories, shops, and other businesses. Companies are buying materials to help them grow in the future. As a result of the reforms, the economy has grown.

A Long Road to Democracy

As successful as the economic reforms have been, many experts believe Russia has a long way to go before it has a stable democracy. The reforms have brought freedom, but they have also created new challenges. Criminal gangs and corruption thrive in Russia's open market. Many people must secretly pay officials to get drivers' licenses and permits to build houses and businesses.

Other challenges threaten Russia's security. In Chechnya, an area in southern Russia, rebels have been at war with the government since 1994. The rebels want Chechnya to be an independent nation. They have carried out terrorist attacks against Russia. Hundreds of innocent people, including children, have died.

An Uncertain Future

Some experts think that the challenges Russia faces could weaken the nation's young democracy. They worry that the new freedoms are in danger of being lost as the government works to stop corruption and improve security. Critics of Russia's president Vladimir Putin have complained that, under his leadership, the government has abused **civil liberties**, or individual freedoms, and attacked democratic institutions like the free media.

Is a lasting democracy possible in Russia? The Russian people have a long history of dealing with difficult times and challenges. The future will tell whether history's lessons will be enough to establish democracy in the world's largest country.

EXPLORING THE ISSUE

1. **Making Inferences** How might widespread government corruption threaten democracy in Russia?

2. **Identifying Cause and Effect** How do you think glasnost and perestroika contributed to the collapse of the Soviet Union?

TERROR IN RUSSIA

In recent years, Russia has suffered a series of deadly terrorist attacks by Chechen rebels. In 2004 terrorists took control of a school and killed more than 300 people, including many children. Other bombings took place at bus and train stations. Altogether, more than 500 people were killed in 2004 as a result of terrorist attacks.

The attacks have shocked and angered the people of Russia. In September 2004, Russians filled the streets of St. Petersburg and Moscow to protest terrorism against their country. Many carried signs with antiterrorism slogans. Some read, "We won't give Russia to terrorists."

The demonstrators believed rebels from Chechnya were responsible for the attacks in 2004. In 2005, however, the violence continued as Chechen rebels set off another bomb in a village in the Caucasus region. The explosion killed 14 people.

Russians protested the terrorist attacks.

A Bitter History

The people of Chechnya want to form their own country. Most Chechens are Muslims, which sets them apart from Russians, who tend to be Christians. Russia first **conquered** Chechnya in 1858, but Chechens never accepted Russian rule. In 1991 Chechnya declared independence, but Russia would not allow it. Russians believe the territory belongs to them. In 1994 Russia went to war against the Chechen rebels. Hundreds of thousands of Chechens died in the fighting.

In 1996 Chechnya won the right to elect its own government, but it remained part of Russia. When Chechen attacks continued, Russian president Vladimir Putin sent troops back into the region in 1999.

Will there be peace? Putin said he would not make deals with terrorists. He said the violence was a "full-scale war." Still, the ongoing hostility puts pressure on Russian and Chechen leaders to find a way to end this deadly conflict.

EXPLORING THE ISSUE

1. **Explaining** Why does Vladimir Putin call the violence a "full scale war"?

2. **Making Inferences** Why might the Chechen rebels feel that Chechnya should be free?

REVIEW AND ASSESS

A Russian worker produces steel at a metallurgy plant in the Ural Mountains.

UNDERSTANDING THE ISSUE

1 Making Connections How might glasnost and perestroika have contributed to the creation of new ideas and ways of doing business?

2 Writing to Inform Suppose you are a Russian student. Write a letter to an American friend explaining some of the new freedoms that Russian citizens enjoy.

3 Writing to Persuade Russia has large amounts of natural resources, like oil and timber, and a well-educated population. Write a brief essay about how these strengths might help Russia build a strong democracy.

INTERNET RESEARCH ACTIVITIES

4 Like today's Russia, the United States had a weak banking system when it was first founded. With your teacher's help, browse the Internet to learn how the U.S. strengthened its early banking system. List ways Russia might learn from the U.S. experience.

5 Important industries in Russia, like steel and manufacturing, need to be modernized. Browse the Internet for information about how Russia plans to update one of these industries. Share your findings with the class.

BEYOND THE CLASSROOM

6 Visit your school or local library to learn more about the Soviet Union's labor camps in Siberia. Work in a group to find out what it was like to live in a camp. What hardships did those living in the camps have to endure? Present your findings to your classmates.

7 Research other nations, such as Great Britain and Spain, that have had to fight terrorism. What might Russia learn from those nations in dealing with Chechnya? Put your findings in a report.

Russia's Natural Resources

Russia is a vast country that holds many of the world's natural resources. The map shows where some of Russia's resources are located.

Building Map Reading Skills

1. Analyzing Information Based on the map's key, what type of work might prisoners in Siberian labor camps have done?

2. Drawing Conclusions Why might Russia want to protect its interests in its southwest?

KEY		
Oil	Mining	Grain
Furs	Timber	Corn
Fishing	Natural Gas	

Issues and Challenges

BIG Idea

Geography is used to interpret the past, understand the present, and plan for the future.

Content Vocabulary

- decree *(p. 419)*
- oligarch *(p. 420)*
- deposit insurance *(p. 421)*
- separatist movement *(p. 421)*

Academic Vocabulary

- prior *(p. 419)*
- unify *(p. 421)*
- conduct *(p. 421)*

Reading Strategy

Analyzing Information Use a diagram like the one below to identify the changes, both positive and negative, that have resulted from Russia's switch to a free market economy.

Russia's Changing Economy

Picture This What do you think is the most popular possession in Russia? A car? A computer? No, it is most likely a cell phone. The popularity of cell phones has skyrocketed in Russia. Russia has a growing middle class with money to spend. Young business-savvy Russians are starting companies that provide trendy and modern products—like cell phones—to this middle class. As the number of cell phone businesses has increased, so has cell phone use. It is estimated that in 1996, only 10,000 people in Moscow owned cell phones, which cost about $2,000 each! Now 80 million Russians, or about 60 percent of the population, own cell phones, which cost about $100 each. The economy is just one part of Russia that is changing. Read on to learn more about modern Russia's challenges.

▼ **Most popular possession in Russia**

Борется с

ст

Political and Economic Challenges

Main Idea **Russians face many challenges as they try to build a democracy and a market economy.**

Geography and You Do you think a country needs strong leaders to solve serious problems? Can leaders become too strong? Read to learn about growing challenges to Russia's democracy and free market economy.

Even with its many resources and industrial power, Russia is finding it difficult to make its new government and economy successful. **Prior** to 1991, Russians had little experience with democratic government. Now many political parties compete in free elections. Also, after communism's fall, Russians began to make their own economic decisions.

Roadblocks to Democracy

Becoming truly democratic has not been easy for Russia. Confusion over governmental powers is one problem. For example, the Russian president's power to issue **decrees**—rulings that have the force of law but do not need the approval of the legislature—might make that office too strong.

Since becoming president in 1999, Vladimir Putin has strengthened presidential powers. When people began to criticize government policies, Putin shut down all independent television news networks. Newspapers still remain free, but television news in Russia is subject to government control.

Russia is a federal republic. Power is shared among national, regional, and local governments. To ensure that regional leaders would obey his wishes, Putin organ-

NATIONAL GEOGRAPHIC

Freedom in Russia

Russians gather in central Moscow to watch a televised news conference given by Russian President Vladimir Putin. *Regions* **How has Putin responded to criticisms of his rule?**

ized the country into seven large districts and appointed governors who would support his policies.

Throughout Russian government, many politicians disregard democratic ways. The courts and the legal system often favor rich, powerful citizens. In addition, many Russians still understand little about their government and, therefore, do not know how to make changes in the way it works.

Social Studies ONLINE

Student Web Activity Visit <u>glencoe.com</u> and complete the Chapter 15 Web Activity about Russia's government.

Shifting to a Market Economy

Russia's shift to a free market economy has brought many positive changes. New companies have been started, and some personal incomes have risen. Higher prices for Russia's oil and natural gas exports have brought the country more income.

Economic success, however, has brought an increase in crime and business corruption. A small group of people, often referred to as oligarchs, control various parts of the economy. An **oligarch** (AH·luh·gahrk) is a member of a small group of rulers that holds great power. In Russia, oligarchs are often corrupt business leaders. Putin has limited the power of some of these oligarchs, but to do so, he has had to strengthen government authority.

Another problem is that the benefits of economic change have not reached all of Russia's people. A few Russians have grown wealthy, but some have become even poorer. There are also strong regional differences in economic success. **Figure 1** shows the average income per capita—or per person—in Russia's seven districts.

NATIONAL GEOGRAPHIC

Maps In Motion See StudentWorks™ Plus or glencoe.com.

Figure 1 **Russia's Per Capita Income**

Monthly per capita income in U.S. dollars, May 2005
⊙ National capital
• City

Map Skills

1 Place How does the per capita income in the central region compare to incomes in the southern region?

2 Regions Why do you think the Urals and far eastern regions have higher per capita incomes?

Monthly incomes in Moscow are much higher compared to other cities and areas of the country.

Russia's banking system also has not been able to fully contribute to economic growth. Banks play a vital role in an economy by collecting people's deposits and lending some of that money to other people. These people borrow the money to buy houses and cars or to start new businesses. All of these actions help create jobs within a region's economy. Greater savings means there is more money to loan, which in turn helps strengthen the economy. If people do not have enough money to deposit into savings, though, banks have fewer funds to lend and the economy suffers.

Many Russians, however, do not trust the country's banks. To encourage people to save their money, the government created a **deposit insurance** system, which will repay people who deposit their money in a bank if the bank goes out of business. Officials hope this system will make people feel safer and more willing to use the banking system.

Challenges to National Unity

While dealing with economic issues, Russians have had to face challenges to their country's political unity. Regional rivalries have increased in recent years. Such resentments have made it difficult to **unify,** or bring together, the country. An even larger challenge is the desire of many ethnic groups to form their own independent countries.

When the Soviet Union fell, several ethnic groups in Russia saw a chance for independence. They launched **separatist movements,** campaigns to break away from the national government and form independent countries. One of the most violent separatist movements began

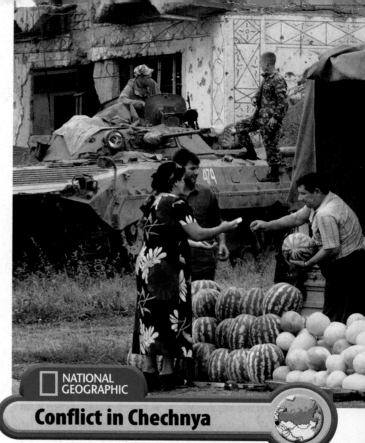

NATIONAL GEOGRAPHIC

Conflict in Chechnya

Chechens buy watermelons as Russian soldiers guard a shopping area in Grozny, Chechnya's capital. *Place* **Why did conflict break out in Chechnya?**

in Chechnya, a Muslim region near the Caucasus Mountains in southern Russia.

In the early 1990s, Russia's President Boris Yeltsin gave Chechnya more self-rule, but many Chechens (CHEH·chehnz) wanted complete independence from Russia. Yeltsin did not want to allow Chechen separatists to succeed, believing that other regions would also demand independence. In 1994 he sent a large Russian army into Chechnya to crush Chechen forces. Both sides suffered heavy losses.

The Chechen separatists continued to **conduct,** or carry out, terrorist attacks against the Russian government. Truces and agreements between the two sides have failed, and the situation remains unresolved.

✓ Reading Check **Describing** Identify and describe a major challenge to Russian unity.

Russia and the World

Main Idea Although Russia remains a world power, other nations have questioned some of its actions.

Geography and You How do good relations among neighbors build a stronger community? Read to learn about Russia's relations with the rest of the world.

As a major world power, Russia plays an important role in world affairs. In recent years, it has worked to strengthen ties with other countries. Russia sees the war in Chechnya, for example, as a struggle against terrorism. As a result, it agreed in 2002 to support the United States and other NATO (North Atlantic Treaty Organization) countries in fighting global terrorist activities.

Still, the United States and other countries are concerned about President Vladimir Putin's growing power and his declining support for democracy. Meanwhile, Russia has uneasy relations with some of the countries that were once part of the Soviet Union. Some Russian leaders have said they would like to see Russian influence increase, which worries people in these former Soviet countries. In 2004 Putin supported a pro-Russian candidate in Ukraine's presidential election—a position many Ukrainians protested. While other neighboring countries are sometimes unhappy with Russia's actions, they also know they depend on Russia for certain resources, such as oil and natural gas.

Reading Check **Analyzing Information** Why has Russia supported the global war against terrorism?

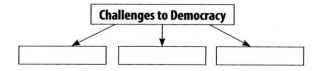

Section 2 Review

Social Studies ONLINE
Study Central™ To review this section, go to glencoe.com.

Vocabulary

1. **Explain** the meaning of the following terms by using each in a sentence.
   a. decree
   b. oligarch
   c. deposit insurance
   d. separatist movement

Main Ideas

2. **Identifying** Use a diagram like the one below to identify challenges to the growth of democracy in Russia.

   Challenges to Democracy

3. **Explaining** Why are some of Russia's neighbors concerned with recent Russian actions?

Critical Thinking

4. **Identifying Cause and Effect** How has the rapid change to a democratic government affected the Russian people's involvement in government? What drawback has this swift change created?

5. **BIG Idea** What factors create challenges to Russian unity?

6. **Challenge** Describe the influence of banking on a country's economy.

Writing About Geography

7. **Using Your FOLDABLES** Use your Foldable to write a paragraph predicting how successful Russia's change to a democracy and free market economy will be. Be sure to support your prediction with facts.

Visual Summary

Communism to Democracy

- After communism's fall, Russia became more democratic.
- Russia is a federal republic, with power divided among national, regional, and local governments.
- Russia has been moving from a command economy to a market economy.

Cargo ship on Volga River

Russia's duma, or parliament, in session

Changes in Society

- Russians now can vote freely and have increased contact with the cultures of other countries.
- The switch to a market economy has benefited some Russians while bringing hardships to others.
- Low birthrates and rising death rates have led to a decline in Russia's population.

Economic Regions

- Moscow, with its many industries, is the economic center of Russia.
- Ports in the St. Petersburg and Baltic region carry on trade between Russia and other countries.
- The Volga and Urals region is a center of manufacturing, mining, and farming.
- Siberia's resources are difficult to tap because of the area's remoteness and harsh climate.

Young Russians playing chess

Challenges

- The increasing power of Russia's president has placed limits on democracy.
- Crime and business corruption have grown in Russia.
- Some ethnic groups want to separate from Russia and form their own countries.

Russia and the World

- Russian leaders have worked to strengthen Russia's ties with the West.
- Russia has uneasy relations with some of the countries that were once part of the Soviet Union.

Vladimir Putin (right) meets with a South African leader

STUDY TO GO — Study anywhere, anytime! Download quizzes and flash cards to your PDA from **glencoe.com**.

STANDARDIZED TEST PRACTICE

TEST-TAKING **TIP**

Do not pick an answer choice just because it sounds good. Sometimes a choice is meant to sound correct but is not. Read all of the answer choices very carefully before you select the best one.

Reviewing Vocabulary

Directions: Choose the word(s) that best completes the sentence.

1. In order to create a market economy, the Russian government legalized _____ .

  A underemployment

  B privatization

  C heavy industry

  D light industry

2. Due to changes in Russia's new economy, many people are _____ , which means they have to take jobs requiring lesser skills than they have.

  A unemployed

  B privatized

  C underemployed

  D invested

3. A(n) _____ is a member of a small ruling group that controls great power.

  A decree

  B pensioner

  C separatist

  D oligarch

4. When the Soviet Union fell, several ethnic groups in Russia launched _____ .

  A separatist movements

  B privatization efforts

  C light industries

  D oligarchies

5. A Russian president may issue _____ , or rulings that have the force of law and do not need the approval of the legislature.

  A vetos

  B decrees

  C opinions

  D considerations

Reviewing Main Ideas

Directions: Choose the best answer for each question.

Section 1 *(pp. 408–412)*

6. A new market economy took root in Russia after

  A World War II.

  B the fall of communism.

  C separatist movements.

  D a middle class emerged.

7. After the fall of communism, there was a manufacturing shift toward more

  A heavy industry.

  B oligarchy.

  C light industry.

  D separatist movements.

Section 2 *(pp. 418–422)*

8. A problem that has accompanied Russia's shift to a free market economy is

  A starting up new companies.

  B higher prices for gas and oil exports.

  C the deposit insurance system.

  D the rise of business oligarchs.

9. Other nations in the world have questioned some of Russia's actions, including the

  A growing power of the Russian president.

  B establishment of free elections.

  C creation of a market economy.

  D creation of a deposit insurance program.

GO ON ➡

Critical Thinking

Directions: Base your answers to questions 10 and 11 on the chart below. Choose the best answer for each question.

GNP Per Capita in U.S. Dollars				
Year(s)	Russia	United States	France	Germany
1991	$3,470	$22,340	$20,460	$20,510
1992	2,820	23,830	22,300	23,360
1993	2,350	24,750	22,360	23,560
1994	2,650	25,860	23,470	25,580
1995	2,240	26,980	24,990	27,510
1996	2,410	28,020	26,270	28,870
1997	2,680	29,080	26,300	28,280
1998	2,260	29,240	24,210	26,570
1999	2,250	31,910	24,170	26,620
2000	1,660	34,100	24,090	25,120
2001	1,750	34,280	22,730	23,560

GNP per capita is the dollar value of a country's final output of goods and services in a year (its GNP), divided by its population. It reflects the average income of a country's citizens.

Source: http://world.britannica.com/analyst/chrono/table

10. What happened to Russia's GNP per capita during the period shown?

A It jumped rapidly between 1999 and 2000.

B It rose gradually.

C It declined drastically.

D It grew following 1997.

11. Which nation's GNP per capita increased the most between 1991 and 2001?

A United States

B Germany

C Russia

D France

Document-Based Questions

Directions: Analyze the document and answer the short-answer questions that follow.

"Things Fall Apart–Russia After the Fall of Communism"

The break-up of the USSR and the failures of economic reform have hurt primarily the elderly and the children. In addition, the systems of social services, education, and health care also fell apart. The fabric of society changed with the disappearance of values and morals. Secrecy and [control] were quickly replaced by the power of money.... In the past there was a common expression–"Without papers you are a bug, but with papers, you are a man"–which meant that you were constantly required to ask permission from a countless army of [government officials].... Now you cannot expect to be treated with respect unless your pocket is full of a wad of "greens."... It doesn't matter if you earned this money by [illegal activities or] selling drugs.... Your social status will be much higher than that of an engineer, a professor, or a doctor.

—by Nikolai Zlobin
World Affairs, Winter, 1996

12. According to the writer, who has been most seriously affected by the "new" Russia after the fall of communism? Why?

13. How does the writer feel that Russian society has changed since the breakup of the USSR?

Extended Response

14. Do you believe Russia's transition to a market economy has been good for the country or caused more harm than good? Write a short essay in which you choose one side of the argument. Defend your position by using examples.

STOP

Social Studies ONLINE

For additional test practice, use Self-Check Quizzes—Chapter 15 at glencoe.com.

Need Extra Help?														
If you missed question...	1	2	3	4	5	6	7	8	9	10	11	12	13	14
Go to page...	409	410	420	421	419	409	411	420	422	420	420	419	419	420

Appendix

Contents

What Is an Appendix?

What Is an Appendix?

An appendix is the additional material you often find at the end of books. The following information will help you learn how to use the Appendix in *Exploring Our World: People, Places, and Cultures.*

Skills Handbook

The Skills Handbook offers you information and practice using critical thinking and social studies skills. Mastering these skills will help you in all your courses.

Gazetteer

The Gazetteer (GA•zuh•TIHR) is a geographical dictionary. It lists many of the world's largest countries, cities, and important geographic features. Each entry also includes a page number telling where the place is shown on a map in the textbook.

English-Spanish Glossary

A glossary is a list of important or difficult terms found in a textbook. The glossary gives a definition of each term as it is used in the textbook. The glossary also includes page numbers telling you where in the textbook the term is used. Since words may have additional meanings, you may wish to use a dictionary to find other uses for them.

In *Exploring Our World: People, Places, and Cultures*, the Spanish glossary is included with the English glossary. The Spanish term is located directly across from the English term. A Spanish glossary is especially important to bilingual students, or those Spanish-speaking students who are learning the English language.

Index

The Index is an alphabetical listing that includes the subjects of the book and the page numbers where those subjects can be found. The index in this book also lets you know that certain pages contain maps, graphs, photos, or paintings about the subject.

Acknowledgments

This section lists photo credits and literary credits for the book. You can look at this section to find out where the publisher obtained the permission to use a photograph or to use excerpts from other books.

Test Yourself

Find the answers to these questions by using the Appendix on the following pages.

1. What does *famine* mean?
2. Where did you find what the word *famine* means?
3. What is the Spanish word for *availability*?
4. What skill is discussed on page 498?
5. What are the latitude and longitude of Moscow?
6. On what pages can you find information about the government of the United Kingdom?

Exploring the Eastern Hemisphere

Use this handbook to explore other regions of the world.

I n *Exploring Our World: People, Places, and Cultures—Western Hemisphere, Europe, and Russia,* you studied several western world regions. Read this special handbook to learn about eastern world regions.

As you read the information, remember what you have already learned about the physical geography, history, culture, and current-day issues of western world regions. Think about how the western world regions are similar to and different from these eastern world regions.

Contents

① Canoeing near Kongou Falls in Gabon
② Strolling in a Japanese garden
③ Harvesting tea in Sri Lanka
④ Traveling across the Nam Song River in Laos

North Africa, Southwest Asia, and Central Asia

Bicycle race, Doha, Qatar ▶

NATIONAL GEOGRAPHIC

NGS ONLINE For more information about the region, see www.nationalgeographic.com/education.

Regional Atlas

North Africa, Southwest Asia, and Central Asia

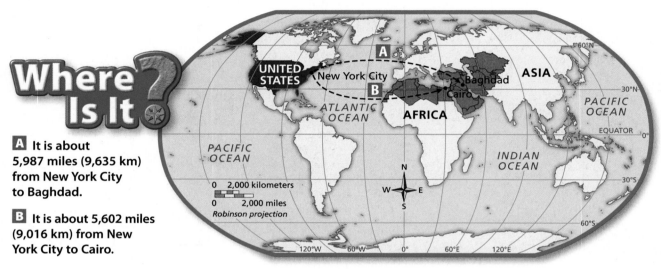

A It is about 5,987 miles (9,635 km) from New York City to Baghdad.

B It is about 5,602 miles (9,016 km) from New York City to Cairo.

How Big Is It?

Together, North Africa, Southwest Asia, and Central Asia occupy almost 6.6 million square miles (17 million sq. km), more than twice the area of the continental United States. At almost 530 million, the population of North Africa, Southwest Asia, and Central Asia is more than one and a half times that of the United States.

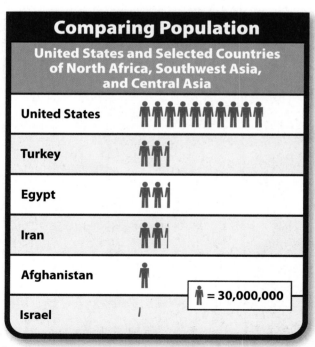

Comparing Population

United States and Selected Countries of North Africa, Southwest Asia, and Central Asia

United States	
Turkey	
Egypt	
Iran	
Afghanistan	
	= 30,000,000
Israel	

Source: *World Population Data Sheet,* 2005.

GEO Fast Facts

Largest Lake

Caspian Sea
143,550 sq. mi.
(371,795 sq. km)

Lowest Point

Dead Sea (Israel and Jordan)
1,312 ft. (400 m)
below sea level

Highest Point

Ismoili Somoni Peak
(Tajikistan)
24,590 ft.
(7,495 m) high

Largest Desert

Sahara (northern Africa)
3,500,000 sq. mi.
(9,065,000 sq. km)

North Africa, Southwest Asia, and Central Asia
PHYSICAL

EUROPE

ATLANTIC OCEAN

Strait of Gibraltar

Canary Islands

Atlas Mountains

TROPIC OF CANCER

20°N

Ahaggar Mountains

S A H A R A

0   600 kilometers
0   600 miles
Lambert Azimuthal Equal-Area projection

AFRICA

40°N

Bosporus
Sea of Marmara

Black Sea

Anatolian Peninsula

Dardanelles

Taurus Mts.

Mt. Ararat
16,945 ft.
(5,165 m)

Caucasus Mts.

Caspian Sea

The Steppes

Ertis R.

Lake Balkash

Aral Sea

Syr Darya R.

Ismoili Somoni Peak
24,590 ft.
(7,495 m)

Kyzyl Kum

Amu Darya R.

Tian Shan

Pamirs

Kara-Kum

Hindu Kush Mts.

Khyber Pass

Damavand
18,606 ft.
(5,671 m)

Elburz Mts.

Plateau of Iran

ASIA

Mediterranean Sea

Akhdar Mts.

Qattara Depression

Suez Canal

Nile R.

Aswān High Dam

Syrian Desert

Dead Sea

Euphrates R.

Tigris R.

Mesopotamian Plain

Zagros Mts.

Persian Gulf
(Arabian Gulf)

Strait of Hormuz

Gulf of Oman

Sinai Peninsula

Hejaz

Arabian Peninsula

Rub' al-Khali

Asir

Red Sea

Boundary claimed by Sudan

White Nile R.

Blue Nile R.

Gulf of Aden

Arabian Sea

INDIAN OCEAN

0° EQUATOR

N
W   E
S

0°   20°E   40°E   60°E

Map Skills

1 Place What physical feature covers much of North Africa?

2 Regions Would you describe this region as mostly lowlands or highlands? Explain.

Elevations

13,100 ft. (4,000 m)
6,500 ft. (2,000 m)
1,600 ft. (500 m)
650 ft. (200 m)
0 ft. (0 m)
Below sea level

▲ Mountain peak
⋈ Pass
⊢ Dam

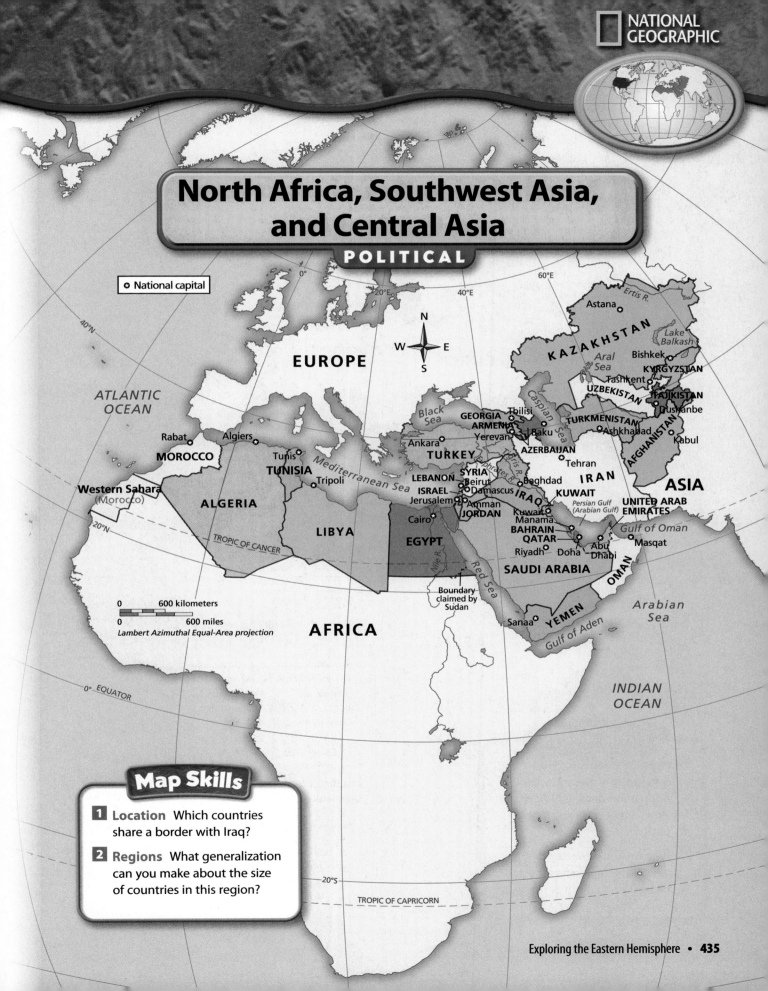

North Africa, Southwest Asia, and Central Asia

POLITICAL

○ National capital

EUROPE

N
W · E
S

ATLANTIC OCEAN

Black Sea

KAZAKHSTAN

Astana

Ertis R.

Lake Balkash

Aral Sea

Bishkek

KYRGYZSTAN

Tashkent

UZBEKISTAN

TAJIKISTAN

Dushanbe

TURKMENISTAN

Ashkhabad

AFGHANISTAN

Kabul

Caspian Sea

Tbilisi

GEORGIA

ARMENIA

Yerevan

Baku

AZERBAIJAN

Tehran

IRAN

ASIA

Rabat

Algiers

Tunis

MOROCCO

TUNISIA

Tripoli

Mediterranean Sea

Ankara

TURKEY

Euphrates R.

Tigris R.

LEBANON

Beirut

SYRIA

Damascus

Baghdad

IRAQ

KUWAIT

Kuwait

Persian Gulf (Arabian Gulf)

UNITED ARAB EMIRATES

Western Sahara (Morocco)

ALGERIA

ISRAEL

Jerusalem

Amman

JORDAN

Manama

BAHRAIN

QATAR

Riyadh

Doha

Abu Dhabi

Masqat

Gulf of Oman

20°N

TROPIC OF CANCER

LIBYA

Cairo

EGYPT

Nile R.

Red Sea

SAUDI ARABIA

OMAN

0   600 kilometers
0   600 miles
Lambert Azimuthal Equal-Area projection

Boundary claimed by Sudan

AFRICA

Sanaa

YEMEN

Gulf of Aden

Arabian Sea

40°N

20°E   0°   40°E   60°E

0°   EQUATOR

INDIAN OCEAN

20°S

TROPIC OF CAPRICORN

Map Skills

1 **Location** Which countries share a border with Iraq?

2 **Regions** What generalization can you make about the size of countries in this region?

Regional Atlas

North Africa, Southwest Asia, and Central Asia
POPULATION DENSITY

EUROPE

ATLANTIC OCEAN

Algiers

Tripoli

Benghazi

Mediterranean Sea

Black Sea

Istanbul
Bursa
İzmir
Ankara
Adana
Aleppo
Beirut
Tel Aviv-Jaffa
Damascus
Amman
Alexandria
Cairo

Tbilisi
Yerevan
Tabriz
Mosul
Karaj
Qom
Baghdad
Kuwait

Baku
Caspian Sea
Tehran
Eşfahān
Shīrāz

Mashhad

Kabul

ASIA

Ertis R.
Lake Balkash
Aral Sea
Almaty
Tashkent

Persian Gulf (Arabian Gulf)

Gulf of Oman

Dubai
Riyadh

Jidda
Makkah (Mecca)

Nile R.
Red Sea

Boundary claimed by Sudan

Arabian Sea

Sanaa
Gulf of Aden

AFRICA

TROPIC OF CANCER

20°N

0° EQUATOR

20°S

TROPIC OF CAPRICORN

INDIAN OCEAN

0   600 kilometers
0   600 miles
Lambert Azimuthal Equal-Area projection

N
W   E
S

0°   20°E   40°E   60°E

40°N

20°N

40°N

POPULATION

Per sq. mi.	Per sq. km
1,250 and over	500 and over
250–1,249	100–499
62.5–249	25–99
25–62.4	10–24
2.5–24	1–9
Less than 2.5	Less than 1
Uninhabited	Uninhabited

Cities
(Statistics reflect metropolitan areas.)
- ■ Over 5,000,000
- ▫ 2,000,000–5,000,000
- ◉ 1,000,000–2,000,000

Map Skills

1 Human-Environment Interaction Describe the population density of Egypt. How would you explain this pattern?

2 Regions In general, what area of the region has the highest population densities?

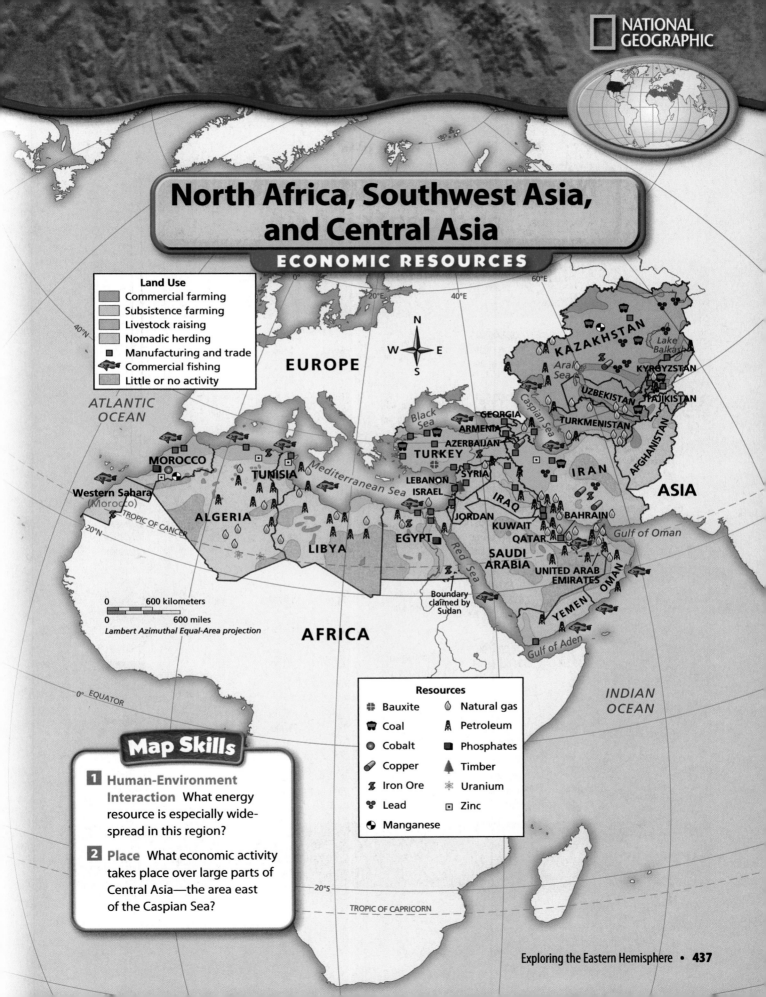

North Africa, Southwest Asia, and Central Asia

ECONOMIC RESOURCES

Land Use
- Commercial farming
- Subsistence farming
- Livestock raising
- Nomadic herding
- Manufacturing and trade
- Commercial fishing
- Little or no activity

Resources
- Bauxite
- Coal
- Cobalt
- Copper
- Iron Ore
- Lead
- Manganese
- Natural gas
- Petroleum
- Phosphates
- Timber
- Uranium
- Zinc

Map Skills

1 **Human-Environment Interaction** What energy resource is especially widespread in this region?

2 **Place** What economic activity takes place over large parts of Central Asia—the area east of the Caspian Sea?

Regional Atlas

North Africa, Southwest Asia, and Central Asia

Country and Capital	Literacy Rate	Population and Density	Land Area	Life Expectancy (Years)	GDP* Per Capita (U.S. dollars)	Television Sets (per 1,000 people)	Flag and Language
AFGHANISTAN Kabul	36%	29,900,000 119 per sq. mi. 46 per sq. km	251,772 sq. mi. 652,086 sq. km	42	$800	14	Dari, Pashto
Algiers ALGERIA	70%	32,800,000 36 per sq. mi. 14 per sq. km	919,591 sq. mi. 2,381,730 sq. km	73	$6,600	107	Arabic
ARMENIA Yerevan	98.6%	3,000,000 261 per sq. mi. 101 per sq. km	11,506 sq. mi. 29,800 sq. km	71	$4,600	241	Armenian
AZERBAIJAN Baku	97%	8,400,000 251 per sq. mi. 97 per sq. km	33,436 sq. mi. 86,599 sq. km	72	$3,800	257	Azerbaijan
Manama BAHRAIN	89.1%	700,000 2,632 per sq. mi. 1,016 per sq. km	266 sq. mi. 689 sq. km	74	$19,200	446	Arabic
Cairo EGYPT	57.5%	74,000,000 191 per sq. mi. 74 per sq. km	386,660 sq. mi. 1,001,445 sq. km	70	$4,200	170	Arabic
GEORGIA Tbilisi	99%	4,500,000 167 per sq. mi. 65 per sq. km	26,911 sq. mi. 69,699 sq. km	72	$3,100	516	Georgian
Tehran IRAN	79.4%	69,500,000 110 per sq. mi. 43 per sq. km	630,575 sq. mi. 1,633,182 sq. km	70	$7,700	154	Persian
UNITED STATES Washington, D.C.	97%	296,500,000 80 per sq. mi. 31 per sq. km	3,717,796 sq. mi. 9,629,047 sq. km	78	$40,100	844	English

*Gross Domestic Product

Countries and flags not drawn to scale

North Africa, Southwest Asia, and Central Asia

Country and Capital	Literacy Rate	Population and Density	Land Area	Life Expectancy (Years)	GDP* Per Capita (U.S. dollars)	Television Sets (per 1,000 people)	Flag and Language
IRAQ Baghdad	40.4%	28,800,000 170 per sq. mi. 66 per sq. km	169,236 sq. mi. 438,319 sq. km	59	$2,100	82	Arabic
ISRAEL† Jerusalem	95.4%	7,100,000 873 per sq. mi. 337 per sq. km	8,131 sq. mi. 21,059 sq. km	80	$20,800	328	Hebrew
Amman **JORDAN**	91.3%	5,800,000 184 per sq. mi. 71 per sq. km	31,444 sq. mi. 81,440 sq. km	72	$4,500	83	Arabic
Astana **KAZAKHSTAN**	98.4%	15,100,000 14 per sq. mi. 6 per sq. km	1,049,151 sq. mi. 2,717,289 sq. km	66	$7,800	240	Kazakh, Russian
KUWAIT Kuwait	83.5%	2,600,000 378 per sq. mi. 146 per sq. km	6,880 sq. mi. 17,819 sq. km	78	$21,300	480	Arabic
Bishkek **KYRGYZSTAN**	97%	5,200,000 68 per sq. mi. 26 per sq. km	76,641 sq. mi. 198,499 sq. km	68	$1,700	49	Kyrgyz, Russian
LEBANON Beirut	87.4%	3,800,000 947 per sq. mi. 365 per sq. km	4,015 sq. mi. 10,399 sq. km	74	$5,000	355	Arabic
Tripoli **LIBYA**	82.6%	5,800,000 9 per sq. mi. 3 per sq. km	679,359 sq. mi. 1,759,532 sq. km	76	$6,700	139	Arabic
UNITED STATES Washington, D.C.	97%	296,500,000 80 per sq. mi. 31 per sq. km	3,717,796 sq. mi. 9,629,047 sq. km	78	$40,100	844	English

† Israel has proclaimed Jerusalem as its capital, but many countries' embassies are in Tel Aviv. The Palestinian Authority has assumed all governmental duties in non-Israeli-occupied areas of the West Bank and Gaza Strip.

Sources: *CIA World Factbook,* 2005; Population Reference Bureau, *World Population Data Sheet,* 2005.

For more country facts, go to the **Nations of the World Databank** at glencoe.com.

Regional Atlas

North Africa, Southwest Asia, and Central Asia

Country and Capital	Literacy Rate	Population and Density	Land Area	Life Expectancy (Years)	GDP* Per Capita (U.S. dollars)	Television Sets (per 1,000 people)	Flag and Language
Rabat MOROCCO†	51.7%	30,700,000 178 per sq. mi. 69 per sq. km	172,413 sq. mi. 446,548 sq. km	70	$4,200	165	Arabic
Masqat OMAN	75.8%	2,400,000 29 per sq. mi. 11 per sq. km	82,031 sq. mi. 212,459 sq. km	74	$13,100	575	Arabic
QATAR Doha	82.5%	800,000 188 per sq. mi. 73 per sq. km	4,247 sq. mi. 11,000 sq. km	70	$23,200	866	Arabic
SAUDI ARABIA Riyadh	78.8%	24,600,000 30 per. sq. mi. 11 per sq. km	829,996 sq. mi. 2,149,680 sq. km	72	$12,000	263	Arabic
SYRIA Damascus	76.9%	18,400,000 257 per sq. mi. 99 per sq. km	71,498 sq. mi. 185,179 sq. km	72	$3,400	68	Arabic
Dushanbe TAJIKISTAN	99.4%	6,800,000 123 per sq. mi. 48 per sq. km	55,251 sq. mi. 143,099 sq. km	63	$1,100	328	Tajik
Tunis TUNISIA	74.2%	10,000,000 158 per sq. mi. 61 per sq. km	63,170 sq. mi. 163,610 sq. km	73	$7,100	190	Arabic, French
Ankara TURKEY	86.5%	72,900,000 244 per sq. mi. 94 per sq. km	299,158 sq. mi. 774,816 sq. km	69	$7,400	328	Turkish
UNITED STATES Washington, D.C.	97%	296,500,000 80 per sq. mi. 31 per sq. km	3,717,796 sq. mi. 9,629,047 sq. km	78	$40,100	844	English

*Gross Domestic Product

Countries and flags not drawn to scale

† Morocco claims the Western Sahara area, but other countries do not accept this claim.

North Africa, Southwest Asia, and Central Asia

Country and Capital	Literacy Rate	Population and Density	Land Area	Life Expectancy (Years)	GDP* Per Capita (U.S. dollars)	Television Sets (per 1,000 people)	Flag and Language
TURKMENISTAN Ashkhabad	98%	5,200,000 28 per sq. mi. 11 per sq. km	188,456 sq. mi. 488,099 sq. km	63	$5,700	198	Turkmen
Abu Dhabi UNITED ARAB EMIRATES	77.9%	4,600,000 143 per sq. mi. 55 per sq. km	32,278 sq. mi. 83,600 sq. km	77	$25,200	309	Arabic
UZBEKISTAN Tashkent	99.3%	26,400,000 153 per sq. mi. 59 per sq. km	172,741 sq. mi. 447,397 sq. km	67	$1,800	280	Uzbek
YEMEN Sanaa	50.2%	20,700,000 102 per sq. mi. 39 per sq. km	203,849 sq. mi. 527,966 sq. km	61	$800	286	Arabic
UNITED STATES Washington, D.C.	97%	296,500,000 80 per sq. mi. 31 per sq. km	3,717,796 sq. mi. 9,629,047 sq. km	78	$40,100	844	English

Sources: *CIA World Factbook,* 2005; Population Reference Bureau, *World Population Data Sheet,* 2005.

For more country facts, go to the **Nations of the World Databank** at glencoe.com.

Africa South of the Sahara

Waterfront in ▶
Cape Town,
South Africa

Regional Atlas

Africa South of the Sahara

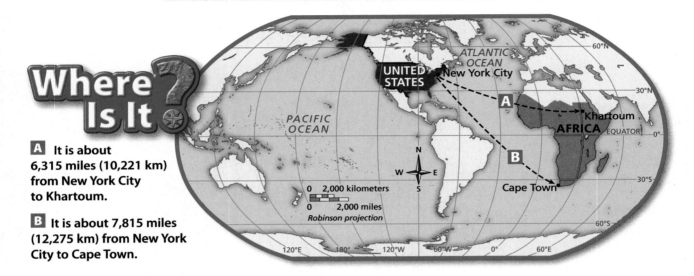

Where Is It?

A It is about 6,315 miles (10,221 km) from New York City to Khartoum.

B It is about 7,815 miles (12,275 km) from New York City to Cape Town.

How Big Is It?

At about 10.3 million square miles (26.8 million sq. km), Africa south of the Sahara accounts for about one-fifth of all the land in the world. The region is about three times larger than the United States.

Comparing Population

United States and Selected Countries of Africa South of the Sahara	
United States	👤👤👤👤👤👤👤👤👤👤
Nigeria	👤👤👤👤
Democratic Republic of the Congo	👤👤
South Africa	👤
Kenya	👤
Senegal	👤

👤 = 30,000,000

Source: *World Population Data Sheet, 2005.*

GEO Fast Facts

Longest River

Nile River
4,160 mi.
(6,693 km) long

Lowest Point

Lake Assal
(Djibouti)
500 ft. (152 m)
below sea level

Largest Lake

Lake Victoria (Tanzania, Kenya,
and Uganda) 26,828 sq. mi.
(69,485 sq. km)

Highest Point

Kilimanjaro (Tanzania)
19,341 ft. (5,895 m) high

Regional Atlas

Africa South of the Sahara
PHYSICAL

ATLANTIC OCEAN

Mediterranean Sea

SOUTHWEST ASIA

NORTH AFRICA

40°N

20°W

20°E

40°E

60°E

TROPIC OF CANCER

20°N

El Djouf

S A H A R A

Air Mountains

Tibesti Mountains

Nubian Desert

Red Sea

Senegal

Niger R.

S A H E L

Lake Chad

Nile R.

Gulf of Aden

Benue R.

Darfur

White Nile R.

Blue Nile R.

Lake Tana

ETHIOPIAN HIGHLANDS

Lake Volta

Gulf of Guinea

Great Rift Valley

Lake Turkana

Mt. Kenya 17,058 ft. (5,199 m)

EQUATOR

0°

Congo R.

Congo Basin

Lake Victoria

Serengeti Plain

Kilimanjaro 19,341 ft. (5,895 m)

INDIAN OCEAN

Lake Tanganyika

Lake Malawi

Bie Plateau

Okavango R.

Zambezi R.

Victoria Falls

Limpopo R.

Mozambique Channel

Namib Desert

20°S

TROPIC OF CAPRICORN

Kalahari Desert

Drakensberg Range

Orange R.

Cape of Good Hope

40°S

Elevations

13,100 ft. (4,000 m)
6,500 ft. (2,000 m)
1,600 ft. (500 m)
650 ft. (200 m)
0 ft. (0 m)
Below sea level

▲ Mountain peak

Map Skills

1 Location Which two rivers join to form the Nile River?

2 Regions Name three countries located in the Sahel region.

N
W   E
S

0   500 kilometers
0   500 miles
Lambert Azimuthal Equal-Area projection

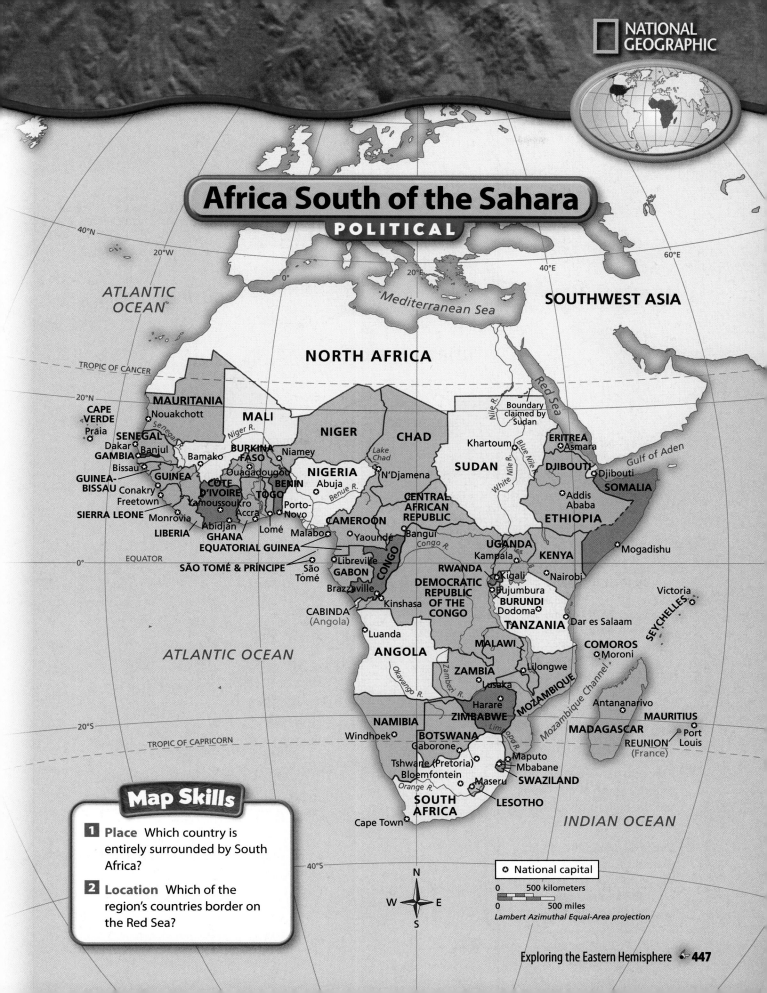

Africa South of the Sahara
POLITICAL

ATLANTIC OCEAN

NORTH AFRICA

SOUTHWEST ASIA

Mediterranean Sea

TROPIC OF CANCER

40°N
20°W
0°
20°E
40°E
60°E
20°N
EQUATOR
0°
20°S
TROPIC OF CAPRICORN
40°S

CAPE VERDE
Nouakchott
Práia
MAURITANIA
MALI
SENEGAL
Dakar
Banjul
GAMBIA
Bissau
BURKINA FASO
Niamey
NIGER
CHAD
Lake Chad
Khartoum
ERITREA
Asmara
Red Sea
Boundary claimed by Sudan
GUINEA-BISSAU
GUINEA
Conakry
Freetown
SIERRA LEONE
Monrovia
LIBERIA
Bamako
Ouagadougou
CÔTE D'IVOIRE
Yamoussoukro
Accra
Abidjan
GHANA
BENIN
TOGO
Lomé
Porto-Novo
Malabo
EQUATORIAL GUINEA
NIGERIA
Abuja
Benue R.
CAMEROON
Yaoundé
N'Djamena
CENTRAL AFRICAN REPUBLIC
Bangui
SUDAN
White Nile R.
Blue Nile R.
Nile R.
DJIBOUTI
Djibouti
Addis Ababa
SOMALIA
ETHIOPIA
Gulf of Aden
Mogadishu

SÃO TOMÉ & PRÍNCIPE
São Tomé
Libreville
GABON
CONGO
Brazzaville
Kinshasa
CABINDA (Angola)
Congo R.
DEMOCRATIC REPUBLIC OF THE CONGO
UGANDA
Kampala
RWANDA
Kigali
BURUNDI
Bujumbura
Dodoma
TANZANIA
Dar es Salaam
KENYA
Nairobi
Victoria
SEYCHELLES

Luanda
ANGOLA
Okavango R.
Zambezi R.
ZAMBIA
Lusaka
MALAWI
Lilongwe
COMOROS
Moroni
Mozambique Channel
Antananarivo
MADAGASCAR
MAURITIUS
Port Louis
REUNION (France)

NAMIBIA
Windhoek
BOTSWANA
Gaborone
Harare
ZIMBABWE
MOZAMBIQUE
Limpopo R.
Maputo
Mbabane
SWAZILAND
Tshwane (Pretoria)
Bloemfontein
Maseru
LESOTHO
Orange R.
SOUTH AFRICA
Cape Town
Senegal R.
Niger R.

ATLANTIC OCEAN

INDIAN OCEAN

Map Skills

1 **Place** Which country is entirely surrounded by South Africa?

2 **Location** Which of the region's countries border on the Red Sea?

⊕ National capital

0   500 kilometers
0   500 miles
Lambert Azimuthal Equal-Area projection

N
W   E
S

Regional Atlas

Africa South of the Sahara
POPULATION DENSITY

ATLANTIC OCEAN

SOUTHWEST ASIA

Mediterranean Sea

NORTH AFRICA

Red Sea

TROPIC OF CANCER

40°N
20°W
0°
20°E
40°E
60°E

20°N

Dakar

Khartoum

Kano

Ibadan

Addis Ababa

Accra
Abidjan
Lagos

Mogadishu

EQUATOR
0°

Nairobi

INDIAN OCEAN

Kinshasa-Brazzaville

Luanda

Dar es Salaam

Lusaka

20°S

Harare

TROPIC OF CAPRICORN

Tshwane (Pretoria)

Johannesburg

Durban

40°S

Cape Town

POPULATION

Per sq. mi.	Per sq. km
1,250 and over	500 and over
250–1,249	100–499
63–249	25–99
25–62	10–24
2.5–24	1–9
Less than 2.5	Less than 1

Cities
(Statistics reflect metropolitan areas.)

■ Over 10,000,000
□ 5,000,000–10,000,000
⊙ 2,000,000–5,000,000

Map Skills

1 Place In general, what part of Africa south of the Sahara has the highest population density?

2 Regions Using the physical map of the region, explain the population patterns in the northern and southwestern areas of the region.

N
W   E
S

0   500 kilometers
0   500 miles
Lambert Azimuthal Equal-Area projection

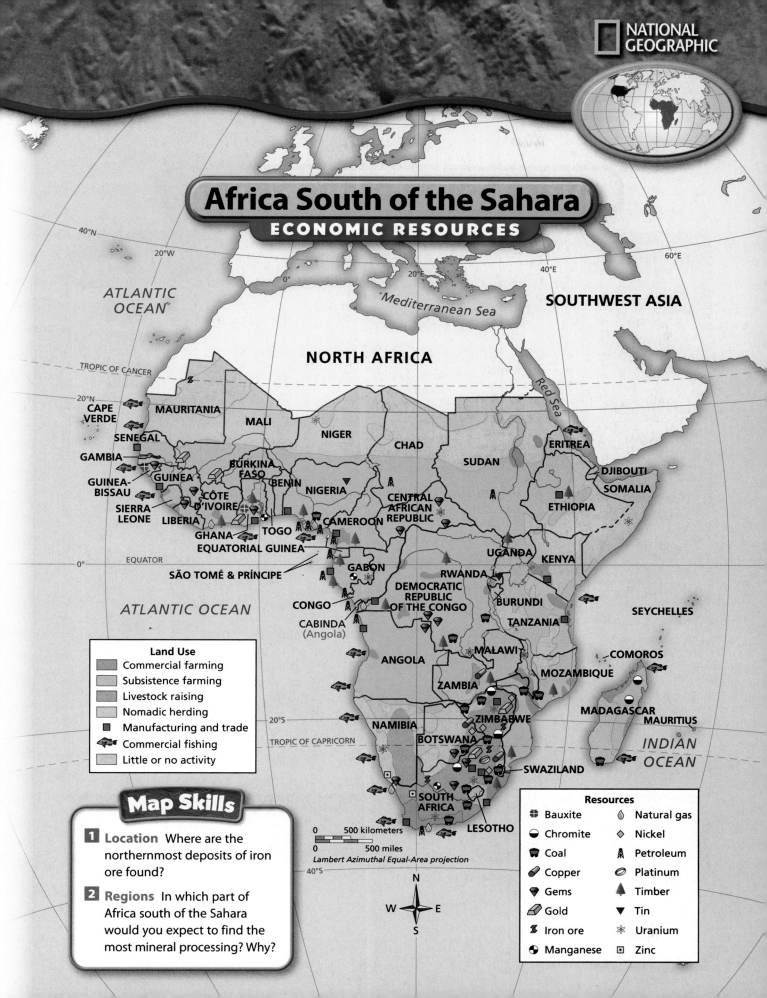

Africa South of the Sahara
ECONOMIC RESOURCES

NATIONAL GEOGRAPHIC

ATLANTIC OCEAN

Mediterranean Sea

SOUTHWEST ASIA

NORTH AFRICA

TROPIC OF CANCER

CAPE VERDE
MAURITANIA
MALI
NIGER
CHAD
SUDAN
ERITREA
SENEGAL
GAMBIA
GUINEA-BISSAU
GUINEA
BURKINA FASO
BENIN
NIGERIA
DJIBOUTI
SOMALIA
SIERRA LEONE
CÔTE D'IVOIRE
CENTRAL AFRICAN REPUBLIC
ETHIOPIA
LIBERIA
GHANA
TOGO
CAMEROON
EQUATORIAL GUINEA
UGANDA
KENYA

EQUATOR

SÃO TOMÉ & PRÍNCIPE
GABON
RWANDA
CONGO
DEMOCRATIC REPUBLIC OF THE CONGO
BURUNDI
CABINDA (Angola)
TANZANIA
SEYCHELLES

ATLANTIC OCEAN

Red Sea

MALAWI
ANGOLA
COMOROS
MOZAMBIQUE
ZAMBIA
MADAGASCAR
MAURITIUS
NAMIBIA
ZIMBABWE
BOTSWANA
SWAZILAND
INDIAN OCEAN
SOUTH AFRICA
LESOTHO

TROPIC OF CAPRICORN

Land Use

■	Commercial farming
■	Subsistence farming
■	Livestock raising
■	Nomadic herding
■	Manufacturing and trade
🐟	Commercial fishing
■	Little or no activity

0   500 kilometers
0   500 miles
Lambert Azimuthal Equal-Area projection

Resources

✦	Bauxite	◐	Natural gas
◖	Chromite	◆	Nickel
◗	Coal	♠	Petroleum
✎	Copper	⬭	Platinum
▼	Gems	▲	Timber
◢	Gold	▼	Tin
🗡	Iron ore	✳	Uranium
◓	Manganese	⊡	Zinc

Map Skills

1 Location Where are the northernmost deposits of iron ore found?

2 Regions In which part of Africa south of the Sahara would you expect to find the most mineral processing? Why?

N
W   E
S

Regional Atlas

Africa South of the Sahara

Country and Capital	Literacy Rate	Population and Density	Land Area	Life Expectancy (Years)	GDP* Per Capita (U.S. dollars)	Television Sets (per 1,000 people)	Flag and Language
Luanda ANGOLA	42%	15,400,000 32 per sq. mi. 12 per sq. km	481,351 sq. mi. 1,246,693 sq. km	40	$2,100	15	Portuguese
BENIN Porto-Novo	40.9%	8,400,000 193 per sq. mi. 75 per sq. km	43,483 sq. mi. 112,620 sq. km	54	$1,200	44	French
BOTSWANA Gaborone	79.8%	1,600,000 7 per sq. mi. 3 per sq. km	224,606 sq. mi. 581,727 sq. km	35	$9,200	21	English, Setswana
BURKINA FASO Ouagadougou	26.6%	13,900,000 131 per sq. mi. 51 per sq. km	105,792 sq. mi. 274,000 sq. km	44	$1,200	11	French
Bujumbura BURUNDI	51.6%	7,800,000 726 per sq. mi. 280 per sq. km	10,745 sq. mi. 27,829 sq. km	49	$600	15	Kirundi, French
CAMEROON Yaounde	79%	16,400,000 89 per sq. mi. 34 per sq. km	183,568 sq. mi. 475,439 sq. km	48	$1,900	34	English, French
CAPE VERDE Praia	76.6%	500,000 321 per sq. mi. 124 per sq. km	1,556 sq. mi. 4,030 sq. km	69	$1,400	5	Portuguese
CENTRAL AFRICAN REPUBLIC Bangui	51%	4,200,000 17 per sq. mi. 8 per sq. km	240,533 sq. mi. 622,978 sq. km	44	$1,100	6	French
UNITED STATES Washington, D.C.	97%	296,500,000 80 per sq. mi. 31 per sq. km	3,717,796 sq. mi. 9,629,047 sq. km	78	$40,100	844	English

*Gross Domestic Product

Countries and flags not drawn to scale

Africa South of the Sahara

Country and Capital	Literacy Rate	Population and Density	Land Area	Life Expectancy (Years)	GDP* Per Capita (U.S. dollars)	Television Sets (per 1,000 people)	Flag and Language
CHAD N'Djamena	47.5%	9,700,000 20 per sq. mi. 8 per sq. km	495,753 sq. mi. 1,283,994 sq. km	47	$1,600	1	French, Arabic
Moroni **COMOROS**	56.5%	700,000 813 per sq. mi. 314 per sq. km	861 sq. mi. 2,230 sq. km	60	$700	4	Arabic, French
DEMOCRATIC REPUBLIC OF THE CONGO Kinshasa	65.5%	60,800,000 67 per sq. mi. 26 per sq. km	905,351 sq. mi. 2,344,848 sq. km	50	$700	2	French
REPUBLIC OF THE CONGO Brazzaville	83.8%	4,000,000 30 per sq. mi. 12 per sq. km	132,046 sq. mi. 341,998 sq. km	52	$800	13	French
CÔTE D'IVOIRE Yamoussoukro	50.9%	18,200,000 146 per sq. mi. 56 per sq. km	124,502 sq. mi. 322,459 sq. km	47	$1,500	65	French
DJIBOUTI Djibouti	67.9%	800,000 89 per sq. mi. 34 per sq. km	8,958 sq. mi. 23,201 sq. km	52	$1,300	48	French, Arabic
Malabo **EQUATORIAL GUINEA**	85.7%	500,000 46 per sq. mi. 18 per sq. km	10,830 sq. mi. 28,050 sq. km	45	$2,700	116	Spanish, French
ERITREA Asmara	58.6%	4,700,000 104 per sq. mi. 40 per sq. km	45,405 sq. mi. 117,598 sq. km	58	$900	16	Afar
UNITED STATES Washington, D.C.	97%	296,500,000 80 per sq. mi. 31 per sq. km	3,717,796 sq. mi. 9,629,047 sq. km	78	$40,100	844	English

Sources: *CIA World Factbook*, 2005; Population Reference Bureau, *World Population Data Sheet*, 2005.

For more country facts, go to the **Nations of the World Databank** at glencoe.com.

Regional Atlas

Africa South of the Sahara

Country and Capital	Literacy Rate	Population and Density	Land Area	Life Expectancy (Years)	GDP* Per Capita (U.S. dollars)	Television Sets (per 1,000 people)	Flag and Language
ETHIOPIA Addis Ababa	42.7%	77,400,000 182 per sq. mi. 70 per sq. km	426,371 sq. mi. 1,104,296 sq. km	48	$800	5	Amharic
Libreville **GABON**	63.2%	1,400,000 14 per sq. mi. 5 per sq. km	103,347 sq. mi. 267,667 sq. km	56	$5,900	251	French
Banjul **GAMBIA**	40.1%	1,600,000 367 per sq. mi. 142 per sq. km	4,363 sq. mi. 11,300 sq. km	53	$1,800	3	English
GHANA Accra	74.8%	22,000,000 239 per sq. mi. 92 per sq. km	92,100 sq. mi. 238,538 sq. km	58	$2,300	115	English
GUINEA Conakry	35.9%	1,600,000 17 per sq. mi. 7 per sq. km	94,927 sq. mi. 245,860 sq. km	49	$2,100	47	French
GUINEA-BISSAU Bissau	42.4%	1,600,000 115 per sq. mi. 44 per sq. km	13,946 sq. mi. 36,120 sq. km	44	$700	information not available	Portuguese
KENYA Nairobi	85.1%	33,800,000 151 per sq. mi. 58 per sq. km	224,081 sq. mi. 580,367 sq. km	47	$1,100	22	English, Kiswahili
Maseru **LESOTHO**	84.8%	1,800,000 154 per sq. mi. 59 per sq. km	11,718 sq. mi. 30,349 sq. km	35	$3,200	16	Sesotho, English
UNITED STATES Washington, D.C.	97%	296,500,000 80 per sq. mi. 31 per sq. km	3,717,796 sq. mi. 9,629,047 sq. km	78	$40,100	844	English

*Gross Domestic Product

Countries and flags not drawn to scale

Africa South of the Sahara

Country and Capital	Literacy Rate	Population and Density	Land Area	Life Expectancy (Years)	GDP* Per Capita (U.S. dollars)	Television Sets (per 1,000 people)	Flag and Language
LIBERIA Monrovia	57.5%	3,300,000 77 per sq. mi. 30 per sq. km	43,000 sq. mi. 111,369 sq. km	42	$900	26	English
MADAGASCAR Antananarivo	68.9%	17,300,000 76 per sq. mi. 29 per sq. km	226,656 sq. mi. 587,036 sq. km	55	$800	23	French, Malagasy
MALAWI Lilongwe	62.7%	12,300,000 269 per sq. mi. 104 per sq. km	45,745 sq. mi. 118,479 sq. km	45	$600	3	Chichewa
MALI Bamako	46.4%	13,500,000 28 per sq. mi. 11 per sq. km	478,838 sq. mi. 1,240,185 sq. km	48	$900	13	French
MAURITANIA Nouakchott	41.7%	3,100,000 8 per sq. mi. 3 per sq. km	395,954 sq. mi. 1,025,516 sq. km	52	$1,800	95	Arabic
Port Louis **MAURITIUS**	85.6%	1,200,000 1,523 per sq. mi. 588 per sq. km	788 sq. mi. 2,041 sq. km	72	$12,800	248	Creole, French
MOZAMBIQUE Maputo	47.8%	19,400,000 63 per sq. mi. 24 per sq. km	309,494 sq. mi. 801,586 sq. km	42	$1,200	5	Portuguese
NAMIBIA Windhoek	84%	2,000,000 6 per sq. mi. 2 per sq. km	318,259 sq. mi. 824,287 sq. km	46	$7,300	38	English
UNITED STATES Washington, D.C.	97%	296,500,000 80 per sq. mi. 31 per sq. km	3,717,796 sq. mi. 9,629,047 sq. km	78	$40,100	844	English

Sources: *CIA World Factbook,* 2005; Population Reference Bureau, *World Population Data Sheet,* 2005.

For more country facts, go to the **Nations of the World Databank** at glencoe.com.

Regional Atlas

Africa South of the Sahara

Country and Capital	Literacy Rate	Population and Density	Land Area	Life Expectancy (Years)	GDP* Per Capita (U.S. dollars)	Television Sets (per 1,000 people)	Flag and Language
NIGER Niamey	17.6%	14,000,000 29 per sq. mi. 11 per sq. km	489,189 sq. mi. 1,266,994 sq. km	43	$900	15	French
NIGERIA Abuja	68%	131,500,000 369 per sq. mi. 142 per sq. km	356,668 sq. mi. 923,766 sq. km	44	$1,000	69	English
Kigali **RWANDA**	70.4%	8,700,000 855 per sq. mi. 330 per sq. km	10,170 sq. mi. 26,340 sq. km	44	$1,300	0.09	Kinyarwanda, English, French
SÃO TOMÉ AND PRÍNCIPE São Tomé	79.3%	200,000 539 per sq. mi. 208 per sq. km	371 sq. mi. 961 sq. km	63	$1,200	229	Portuguese
Dakar **SENEGAL**	40.2%	11,700,000 154 per sq. mi. 59 per sq. km	75,954 sq. mi. 196,720 sq. km	56	$1,700	41	French
Victoria **SEYCHELLES**	58%	100,000 575 per sq. mi. 222 per sq. km	174 sq. mi. 451 sq. km	71	$7,800	214	Creole, English
SIERRA LEONE Freetown	31.4%	5,500,000 199 per sq. mi. 77 per sq. km	27,699 sq. mi. 71,740 sq. km	40	$600	13	English
SOMALIA Mogadishu	37.8%	8,600,000 35 per sq. mi. 13 per sq. km	246,201 sq. mi. 637,658 sq. km	47	$600	14	Somali
UNITED STATES Washington, D.C.	97%	296,500,000 80 per sq. mi. 31 per sq. km	3,717,796 sq. mi. 9,629,047 sq. km	78	$40,100	844	English

*Gross Domestic Product

Countries and flags not drawn to scale

Africa South of the Sahara

Country and Capital	Literacy Rate	Population and Density	Land Area	Life Expectancy (Years)	GDP* Per Capita (U.S. dollars)	Television Sets (per 1,000 people)	Flag and Language
Tshwane (Pretoria), Bloemfontein, Cape Town **SOUTH AFRICA**	86.4%	46,900,000 99 per sq. mi. 38 per sq. km	471,444 sq. mi. 1,221,034 sq. km	52	$11,100	138	Afrikaans, English, Zulu
SUDAN Khartoum	61.1%	40,200,000 42 per sq. mi. 16 per sq. km	967,494 sq. mi. 2,505,798 sq. km	57	$1,900	173	Arabic
Mbabane **SWAZILAND**	81.6%	1,138,000 170 per sq. mi. 66 per sq. km	6,642 sq. mi. 17,203 sq. km	33	$5,100	112	English, siSwati
TANZANIA Dodoma, Dar es Salaam	78.2%	36,500,000 100 per sq. mi. 39 per sq. km	364,900 sq. mi. 945,087 sq. km	44	$700	21	Kiswahili, English
TOGO Lomé	60.9%	6,100,000 278 per sq. mi. 107 per sq. km	21,927 sq. mi. 56,791 sq. km	54	$1,600	22	French
UGANDA Kampala	69.9%	26,900,000 289 per sq. mi. 112 per sq. km	93,066 sq. mi. 241,040 sq. km	48	$1,500	28	English
ZAMBIA Lusaka	80.6%	11,200,000 39 per sq. mi. 15 per sq. km	290,583 sq. mi. 752,606 sq. km	37	$900	145	English
Harare **ZIMBABWE**	90.7%	13,000,000 86 per sq. mi. 33 per sq. km	150,873 sq. mi. 390,759 sq. km	41	$1,900	35	English
UNITED STATES Washington, D.C.	97%	296,500,000 80 per sq. mi. 31 per sq. km	3,717,796 sq. mi. 9,629,047 sq. km	78	$40,100	844	English

Sources: *CIA World Factbook,* 2005; Population Reference Bureau, *World Population Data Sheet,* 2005.

For more country facts, go to the **Nations of the World Databank** at glencoe.com.

South Asia

Jaisalmer Fort, ▶
Rajasthan, India

Regional Atlas

South Asia

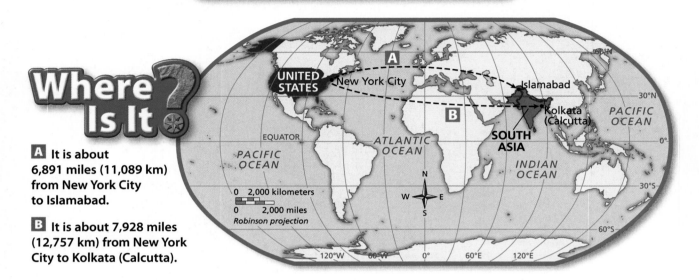

Where Is It?

A It is about 6,891 miles (11,089 km) from New York City to Islamabad.

B It is about 7,928 miles (12,757 km) from New York City to Kolkata (Calcutta).

How Big Is It?

The region of South Asia is more than half the size of the continental United States. Its land area is about 1.7 million square miles (4.5 million sq. km). Though smaller than the United States, South Asia has nearly five times the number of people as the United States and more than one-fifth of the people in the world.

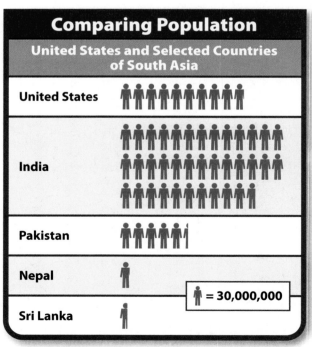

Comparing Population

United States and Selected Countries of South Asia

United States	
India	
Pakistan	
Nepal	
Sri Lanka	

= 30,000,000

Source: *World Population Data Sheet,* 2005.

GEO Fast Facts

Longest Rivers

Brahmaputra River (shown) *and* Indus River (tied) 1,800 mi. (2,896 km) long

Highest Point

▲ Mount Everest (Nepal) 29,028 ft. (8,848 m) high

Largest Island

◄ Sri Lanka 25,332 sq. mi. (65,610 sq. km)

Lowest Point

▲ Coast of Indian Ocean (Bangladesh) 0 ft. (0 m) high

Regional Atlas

South Asia
PHYSICAL

CENTRAL ASIA

EAST ASIA

HINDU KUSH

Khyber Pass

KARAKORAM RANGE

K2
28,250 ft.
(8,611 m)

Indus R.

THAR DESERT

HIMALAYA

Mt. Dhaulagiri
26,810 ft.
(8,172 m)

Mt. Everest
29,028 ft.
(8,848 m)

Kanchenjunga
28,169 ft.
(8,586 m)

Ganges R.

GANGES PLAIN

Brahmaputra R.

KATHMANDU VALLEY

Meghna R.

TROPIC OF CANCER

20°N

Narmada R.

SATPURA RANGE

Mahanadi R.

Sundarbans

Godavari R.

DECCAN PLATEAU

EASTERN GHATS

Krishna R.

Bay of Bengal

Arabian Sea

WESTERN GHATS

Andaman Islands

Lakshadweep

Nicobar Islands

N
W   E
S

0   400 kilometers
0   400 miles
Albers Equal-Area projection

0° EQUATOR

INDIAN OCEAN

60°E   80°E   100°E

40°N

20°S

Elevations

13,100 ft. (4,000 m)
6,500 ft. (2,000 m)
1,600 ft. (500 m)
650 ft. (200 m)
0 ft. (0 m)
Below sea level

⌤ Pass
▲ Mountain peak

Map Skills

1 Location Which country is located nearest the Equator?

2 Regions How does the far north of the region differ from the rest of the region?

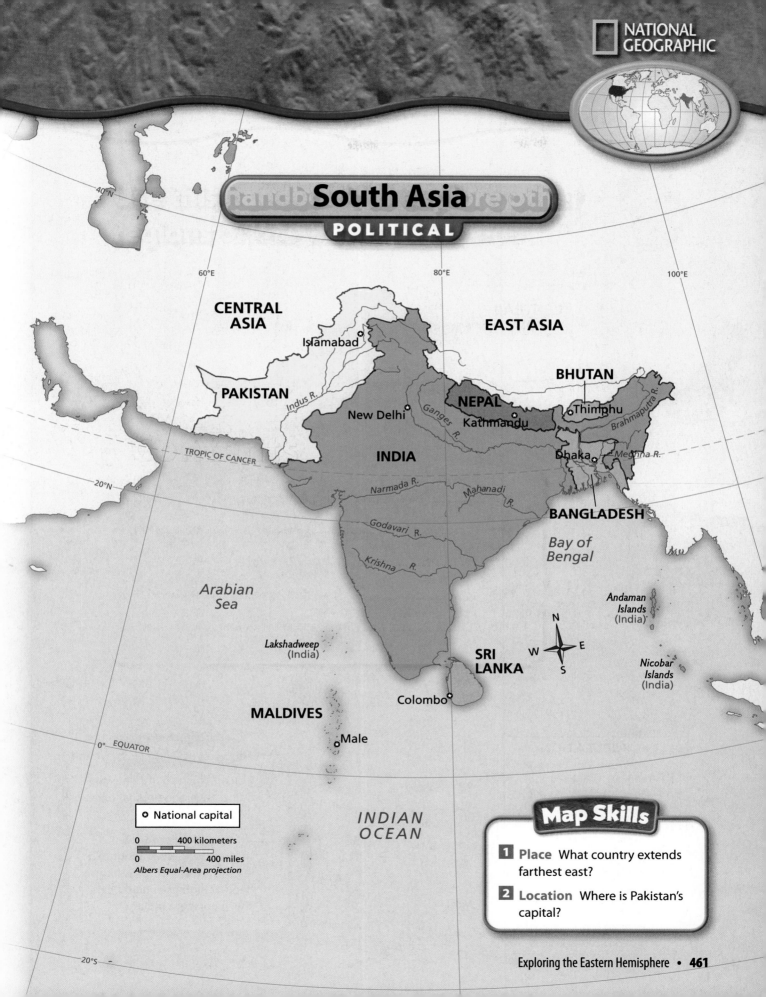

NATIONAL GEOGRAPHIC

South Asia
POLITICAL

40°N

60°E   80°E   100°E

CENTRAL
ASIA

EAST ASIA

Islamabad

PAKISTAN

Indus R.

BHUTAN

NEPAL   Thimphu

New Delhi   *Ganges R.*   *Brahmaputra R.*

Kathmandu

INDIA   Dhaka   *Meghna R.*

TROPIC OF CANCER

20°N   BANGLADESH

Narmada R.   *Mahanadi R.*

Godavari R.   Bay of
Bengal

Krishna R.

Arabian
Sea   Andaman
Islands
(India)

Lakshadweep
(India)   N   SRI
LANKA   W   E   *Nicobar
Islands
(India)*   S

Colombo

MALDIVES

0° EQUATOR   Male

INDIAN
OCEAN

⊙ National capital

0   400 kilometers
0   400 miles
Albers Equal-Area projection

Map Skills

1 **Place** What country extends
farthest east?

2 **Location** Where is Pakistan's
capital?

20°S

Regional Atlas

South Asia
POPULATION DENSITY

CENTRAL ASIA

EAST ASIA

Peshawar
Srinagar
Rawalpindi
Lahore
Faisalabad
Ludhiana
Multan
Meerut
Delhi
Faridabad
Jaipur
Agra
Lucknow
Hyderabad
Kanpur
Patna
Karachi
Varanasi
Dhaka
TROPIC OF CANCER
Asansol
Khulna
Chittagong
Ahmadabad
Bhopal
Jamshedpur
Rajkot
Indore
Jabalpur
Kolkata
(Calcutta)
Vadodara
Surat
Nagpur
Durg-Bhilai
Nasik
Bay of Bengal
Mumbai
(Bombay)
Pune
Sholapur
Hyderabad
Vishakhapatnam

Arabian Sea

Vijayawada

Bengaluru
(Bangalore)
Chennai (Madras)

Coimbatore

Cochin
Madurai

N
W   E
S

0   400 kilometers

0   400 miles
Albers Equal-Area projection

INDIAN OCEAN

EQUATOR

POPULATION

Per sq. mi.	Per sq. km
1,250 and over	500 and over
250–1,250	100–500
62.5–250	25–100
25–62.5	10–25
2.5–25	1–10
Less than 2.5	Less than 1
Uninhabited	Uninhabited

Cities
(Statistics reflect metropolitan areas.)

■ Over 5,000,000

□ 2,000,000–5,000,000

⊙ 1,000,000–2,000,000

Map Skills

1 Place Which country has the highest average population density?

2 Human-Environment Interaction What geographic feature is associated with the band of high population density in northern India?

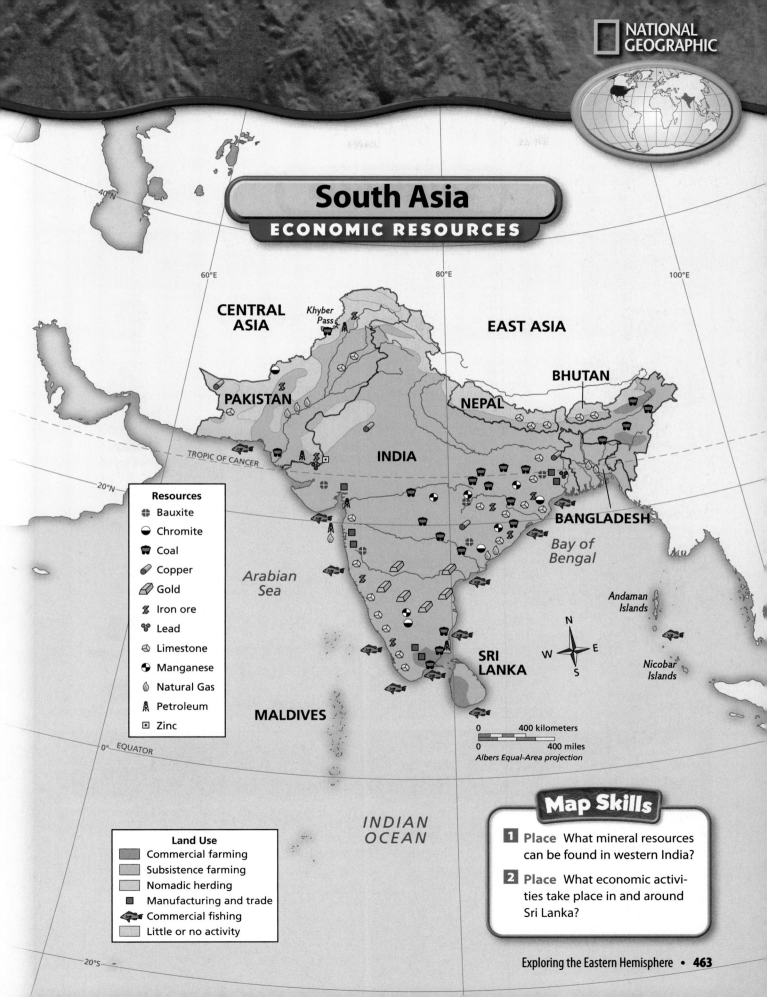

South Asia
ECONOMIC RESOURCES

CENTRAL ASIA

Khyber Pass

EAST ASIA

BHUTAN

PAKISTAN

NEPAL

INDIA

BANGLADESH

TROPIC OF CANCER

Bay of Bengal

Arabian Sea

Andaman Islands

SRI LANKA

Nicobar Islands

MALDIVES

Maldives

EQUATOR

Resources
- Bauxite
- Chromite
- Coal
- Copper
- Gold
- Iron ore
- Lead
- Limestone
- Manganese
- Natural Gas
- Petroleum
- Zinc

0 400 kilometers
0 400 miles
Albers Equal-Area projection

INDIAN OCEAN

Land Use
- Commercial farming
- Subsistence farming
- Nomadic herding
- Manufacturing and trade
- Commercial fishing
- Little or no activity

Map Skills

1 Place What mineral resources can be found in western India?

2 Place What economic activities take place in and around Sri Lanka?

Regional Atlas

South Asia

Country and Capital	Literacy Rate	Population and Density	Land Area	Life Expectancy (Years)	GDP* Per Capita (U.S. dollars)	Television Sets (per 1,000 people)	Flag and Language
BANGLADESH Dhaka	43.1%	144,200,000 2,594 per sq. mi. 1,001 per sq. km	55,598 sq. mi. 143,998 sq. km	61	$2,000	7	Bengali
Thimphu BHUTAN	42.2%	1,000,000 55 per sq. mi. 21 per sq. km	18,147 sq. mi. 47,001 sq. km	63	$1,400	6	Dzongkha
New Delhi INDIA	59.5%	1,103,600,000 869 per sq. mi. 336 per sq. km	1,269,340 sq. mi. 3,287,575 sq. km	62	$3,100	75	Hindi, English
Male MALDIVES	97.2%	300,000 2,586 per sq. mi. 1,000 per sq. km	116 sq. mi. 300 sq. km	72	$3,900	38	Maldivian Dhivehi, English
NEPAL Kathmandu	45.2%	25,400,000 447 per sq. mi. 173 per sq. km	56,826 sq. mi. 147,179 sq. km	62	$1,500	516	Nepali
Islamabad PAKISTAN	45.7%	162,400,000 528 per sq. mi. 204 per sq. km	307,375 sq. mi. 796,098 sq. km	62	$2,200	105	Punjabi, Urdu, English
SRI LANKA Colombo	92.3%	19,700,000 778 per sq. mi. 300 per sq. km	25,332 sq. mi. 65,610 sq. km	73	$4,000	102	Sinhala, Tamil, English
UNITED STATES Washington, D.C.	97%	296,500,000 80 per sq. mi. 31 per sq. km	3,717,796 sq. mi. 9,629,047 sq. km	78	$40,100	844	English

*Gross Domestic Product

Countries and flags not drawn to scale

Sources: *CIA World Factbook,* 2005; Population Reference Bureau, *World Population Data Sheet,* 2005.

For more country facts, go to the **Nations of the World Databank** at glencoe.com.

Braga, Nepal

East Asia and Southeast Asia

Lantern Festival, Singapore ▶

"CONTINUOUS FLOW" LANTERNS

Regional Atlas

East Asia and Southeast Asia

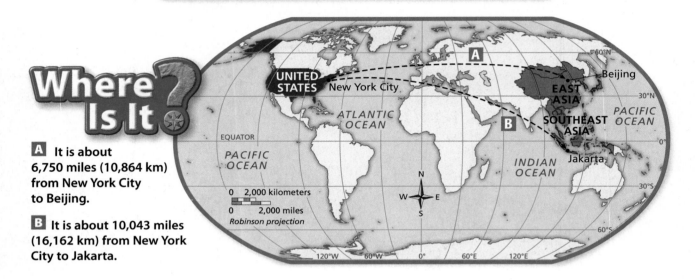

Where Is It?

A It is about 6,750 miles (10,864 km) from New York City to Beijing.

B It is about 10,043 miles (16,162 km) from New York City to Jakarta.

How Big Is It?

The region of East Asia and Southeast Asia is more than two times the size of the continental United States. Its land area is nearly 6.3 million square miles (16.3 million sq. km). With a population of more than two billion people, almost one-third of the people of the world live in the region.

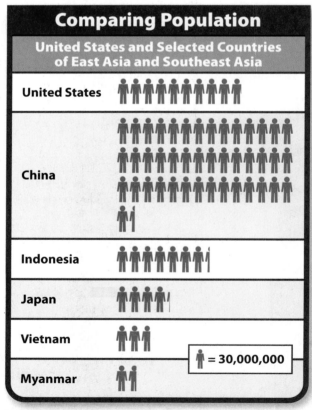

Comparing Population

United States and Selected Countries of East Asia and Southeast Asia

United States	
China	
Indonesia	
Japan	
Vietnam	
Myanmar	

= 30,000,000

Source: *World Population Data Sheet,* 2005.

GEO Fast Facts

Largest Desert

▶ Gobi (Mongolia and China)
500,000 sq. mi.
(1,295,000 sq. km)

Longest River

▲ Chang Jiang
(Yangtze River)
(China) 3,434 mi.
(5,525 km) long

Largest Lake

▲ Tonle Sap (Cambodia)
9,500 sq. mi. (24,605 sq. km)

Regional Atlas

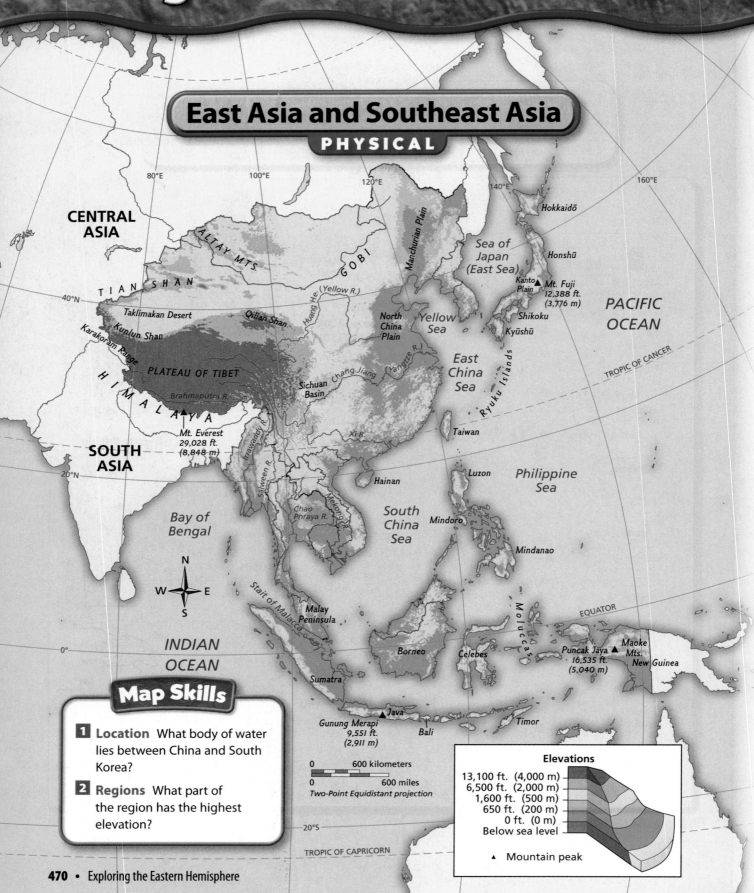

East Asia and Southeast Asia
PHYSICAL

CENTRAL ASIA

ALTAY MTS.

TIAN SHAN

Taklimakan Desert

Kunlun Shan

Karakoram Range

PLATEAU OF TIBET

Brahmaputra R.

HIMALAYA

Mt. Everest
29,028 ft.
(8,848 m)

SOUTH ASIA

Qilian Shan

Huang He (Yellow R.)

GOBI

Manchurian Plain

Sichuan Basin

Chang Jiang

Yangtze R.

North China Plain

Xi R.

Irrawaddy R.

Salween R.

Chao Phraya R.

Mekong R.

Yellow Sea

East China Sea

Taiwan

Hainan

South China Sea

Mindoro

Luzon

Mindanao

Sea of Japan (East Sea)

Hokkaidō

Honshū

Kanto Plain

Mt. Fuji
12,388 ft.
(3,776 m)

Shikoku

Kyūshū

Ryukyu Islands

PACIFIC OCEAN

TROPIC OF CANCER

Philippine Sea

Bay of Bengal

N
W E
S

Strait of Malacca

Malay Peninsula

INDIAN OCEAN

Sumatra

Borneo

Celebes

Moluccas

EQUATOR

Puncak Jaya
16,535 ft.
(5,040 m)

Maoke Mts.

New Guinea

Gunung Merapi
9,551 ft.
(2,911 m)

Java

Bali

Timor

Map Skills

1 Location What body of water lies between China and South Korea?

2 Regions What part of the region has the highest elevation?

0   600 kilometers

0   600 miles

Two-Point Equidistant projection

Elevations

13,100 ft. (4,000 m)
6,500 ft. (2,000 m)
1,600 ft. (500 m)
650 ft. (200 m)
0 ft. (0 m)
Below sea level

▲ Mountain peak

TROPIC OF CAPRICORN

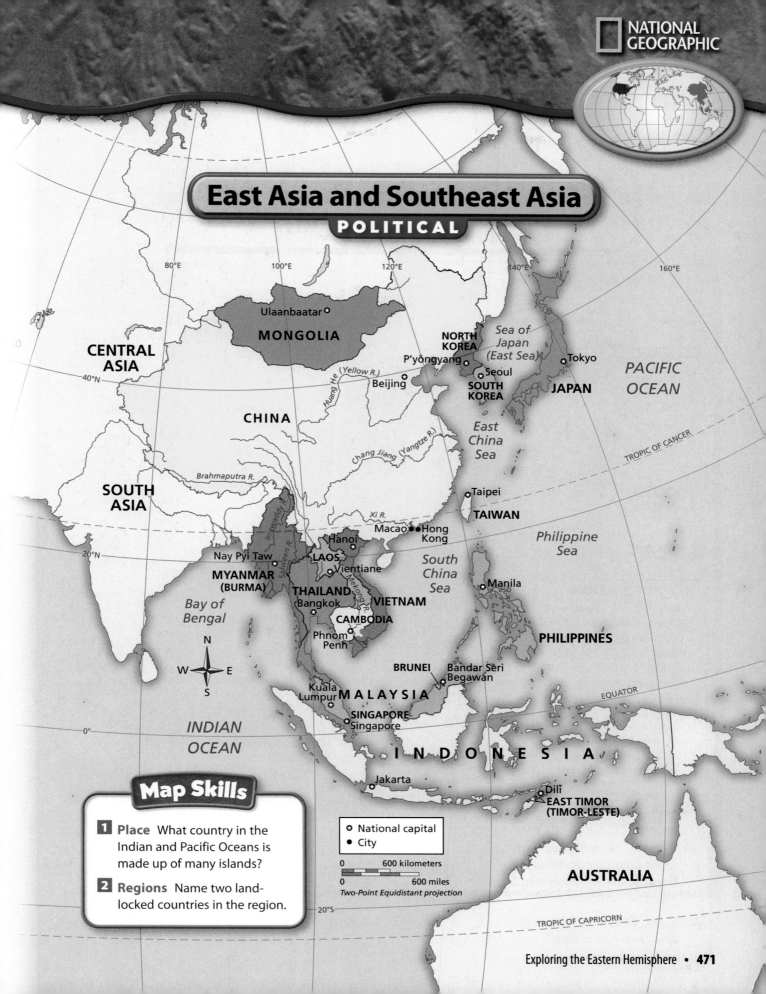

East Asia and Southeast Asia
POLITICAL

CENTRAL ASIA

Ulaanbaatar ☉

MONGOLIA

NORTH KOREA

Sea of Japan (East Sea)

P'yŏngyang ☉

Tokyo •

40°N

Beijing ●

Huang He (Yellow R.)

● Seoul ☉

SOUTH KOREA

JAPAN

PACIFIC OCEAN

CHINA

Chang Jiang (Yangtze R.)

East China Sea

Brahmaputra R.

SOUTH ASIA

Xi R.

Taipei •

TAIWAN

TROPIC OF CANCER

20°N

Macao ●●Hong Kong

Hanoi ●

Philippine Sea

Nay Pyi Taw ●

LAOS

Vientiane ☉

South China Sea

MYANMAR (BURMA)

THAILAND

Bangkok ●

VIETNAM

Manila •

Bay of Bengal

CAMBODIA

N

W E

S

Phnom Penh ●

PHILIPPINES

BRUNEI

Bandar Seri Begawan •

Kuala Lumpur ●

MALAYSIA

EQUATOR

INDIAN OCEAN

SINGAPORE

Singapore ☉

0°

I N D O N E S I A

Jakarta •

Dili ☉

EAST TIMOR (TIMOR-LESTE)

Map Skills

1 Place What country in the Indian and Pacific Oceans is made up of many islands?

2 Regions Name two land-locked countries in the region.

☉ National capital
● City

0   600 kilometers
0   600 miles
Two-Point Equidistant projection

AUSTRALIA

20°S

TROPIC OF CAPRICORN

Regional Atlas

East Asia and Southeast Asia
POPULATION DENSITY

CENTRAL ASIA

SOUTH ASIA

Ürümqi

Harbin
Changchun
Shenyang
Jinxi
Dalian
Beijing
Tianjin
Taiyuan
Lanzhou
Zhengzhou
Xi'an
Chengdu
Chongqing
Changsha
Guiyang
Kunming
Guangzhou
Shenzhen
Hong Kong
Hanoi
Yangon
Bangkok
Ho Chi Minh City
Medan
Singapore
Jakarta
Bandung
Surabaya

Jinan
Nanjing
Wuhan
Hangzhou
Shanghai
Qingdao
Zibo
Fuzhou
Xiamen
Dongguan
Taipei

P'yŏngyang
Seoul
Inch'ŏn
Taegu
Pusan
Fukuoka
Hiroshima
Ōsaka-Kōbe-Kyōto
Nagoya
Tokyo
Sendai
Sapporo

Sea of Japan (East Sea)

PACIFIC OCEAN

East China Sea

Philippine Sea

South China Sea

Manila

EQUATOR

AUSTRALIA

TROPIC OF CANCER

TROPIC OF CAPRICORN

80°E 100°E 120°E 140°E 160°E
40°N
20°N
0°
20°S

POPULATION

Per sq. mi.	Per sq. km
1,250 and over	500 and over
250-1,250	100–500
62.5-250	25–100
25-62.5	10–25
2.5-25	1–10
Less than 2.5	Less than 1

Cities
(Statistics reflect metropolitan areas.)
■ Over 6,000,000
□ 4,000,000–6,000,000
⊙ 2,000,000–4,000,000

0   600 kilometers
0   600 miles
Two-Point Equidistant projection

Map Skills

1 Regions Compare this map to the physical map. What are the most densely populated islands in Southeast Asia?

2 Place What is the least densely populated part of Japan?

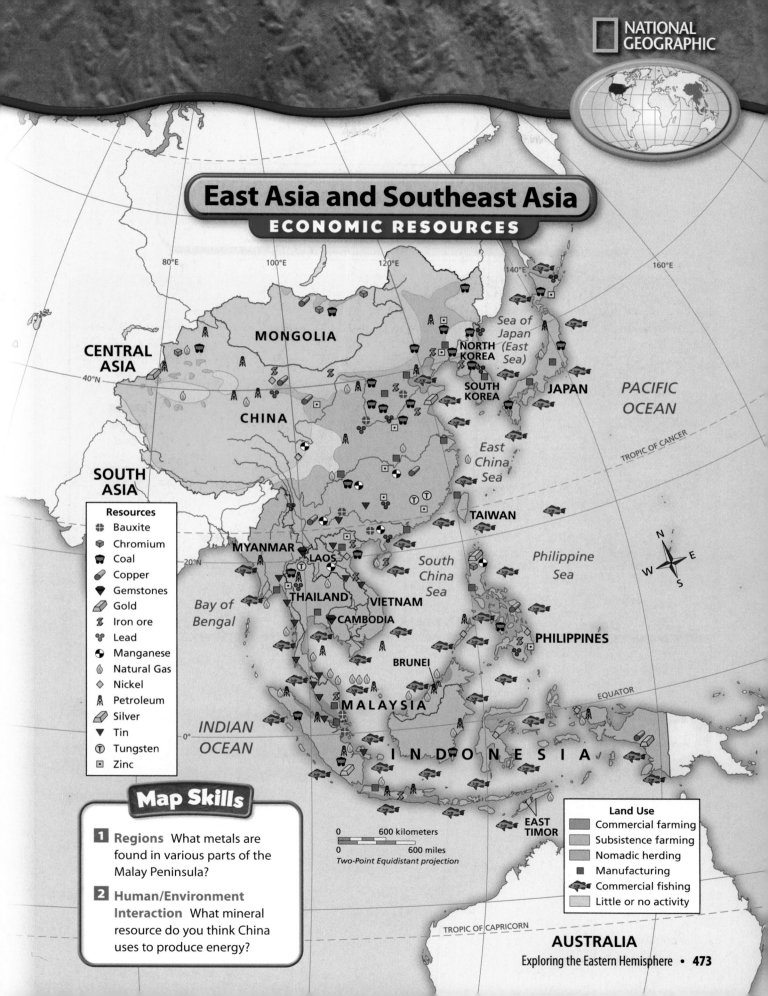

East Asia and Southeast Asia
ECONOMIC RESOURCES

Resources

⊕	Bauxite
◈	Chromium
⛏	Coal
▱	Copper
▼	Gemstones
▭	Gold
⚡	Iron ore
❧	Lead
◕	Manganese
◊	Natural Gas
◇	Nickel
⚘	Petroleum
▱	Silver
▼	Tin
Ⓣ	Tungsten
⊡	Zinc

Land Use

Commercial farming
Subsistence farming
Nomadic herding
■ Manufacturing
🐟 Commercial fishing
Little or no activity

CENTRAL ASIA
MONGOLIA
SOUTH ASIA
CHINA
NORTH KOREA
SOUTH KOREA
JAPAN
Sea of Japan (East Sea)
PACIFIC OCEAN
TROPIC OF CANCER
East China Sea
TAIWAN
MYANMAR
LAOS
THAILAND
VIETNAM
South China Sea
Philippine Sea
Bay of Bengal
CAMBODIA
PHILIPPINES
BRUNEI
INDIAN OCEAN
MALAYSIA
EQUATOR
I N D O N E S I A
EAST TIMOR
AUSTRALIA

80°E 100°E 120°E 140°E 160°E
40°N
20°N
0°

0   600 kilometers
0   600 miles
Two-Point Equidistant projection

Map Skills

1 Regions What metals are found in various parts of the Malay Peninsula?

2 Human/Environment Interaction What mineral resource do you think China uses to produce energy?

TROPIC OF CAPRICORN

AUSTRALIA
Exploring the Eastern Hemisphere • 473

Regional Atlas

East Asia and Southeast Asia

Country and Capital	Literacy Rate	Population and Density	Land Area	Life Expectancy (Years)	GDP* Per Capita (U.S. dollars)	Television Sets (per 1,000 people)	Flag and Language
Bandar Seri Begawan **BRUNEI**	93.9%	400,000 180 per sq. mi. 72 per sq. km	2,228 sq. mi. 5,570 sq. km	74	$23,600	637	Malay
CAMBODIA Phnom Penh	69.4%	13,300,000 190 per sq. mi. 73 per sq. km	69,900 sq. mi. 181,040 sq. km	56	$2,000	9	Khmer
Beijing **CHINA**	90.9%	1,303,700,000 353 per sq. mi. 136 per sq. km	3,696,100 sq. mi. 9,572,855 sq. km	72	$5,600	291	Mandarin Chinese
Dili **EAST TIMOR (TIMOR-LESTE)**	58.6%	900,000 157 per sq. mi. 61 per sq. km	5,741 sq. mi. 14,869 sq. km	55	$400	information not available	Tetum, Portuguese
INDONESIA Jakarta	87.9%	221,900,000 302 per sq. mi. 117 per sq. km	735,355 sq. mi. 1,904,561 sq. km	68	$3,500	143	Bahasa Indonesia
JAPAN Tokyo	99%	127,700,000 875 per sq. mi. 338 per sq. km	145,869 sq. mi. 377,799 sq. km	82	$29,400	719	Japanese
UNITED STATES Washington, D.C.	97%	296,500,000 80 per sq. mi. 31 per sq. km	3,717,796 sq. mi. 9,629,047 sq. km	78	$40,100	844	English

*Gross Domestic Product

Countries and flags not drawn to scale

East Asia and Southeast Asia

Country and Capital	Literacy Rate	Population and Density	Land Area	Life Expectancy (Years)	GDP* Per Capita (U.S. dollars)	Television Sets (per 1,000 people)	Flag and Language
LAOS Vientiane	66.4%	5,900,000 65 per sq. mi. 25 per sq. km	91,429 sq. mi. 236,800 sq. km	54	$1,900	10	Lao
MALAYSIA Kuala Lumpur	88.7%	26,100,000 205 per sq. mi. 79 per sq. km	127,317 sq. mi. 329,750 sq. km	73	$9,700	174	Bahasa Melayu
Ulaanbaatar **MONGOLIA**	97.8%	2,600,000 4 per sq. mi. 2 per sq. km	604,826 sq. mi. 1,566,492 sq. km	64	$1,900	58	Khalkha Mongol
MYANMAR Nay Pyi Taw	85.3%	50,500,000 193 per sq. mi. 75 per sq. km	261,228 sq. mi. 676,577 sq. km	60	$1,700	7	Burmese
NORTH KOREA P'yŏngyang	99%	22,900,000 492 per sq. mi. 190 per sq. km	46,541 sq. mi. 120,541 sq. km	71	$1,700	55	Korean
PHILIPPINES Manila	92.6%	84,800,000 732 per sq. mi. 283 per sq. km	115,830 sq. mi. 299,998 sq. km	70	$5,000	110	Filipino, English
UNITED STATES Washington, D.C.	97%	296,500,000 80 per sq. mi. 31 per sq. km	3,717,796 sq. mi. 9,629,047 sq. km	78	$40,100	844	English

Sources: *CIA World Factbook,* 2005; Population Reference Bureau, *World Population Data Sheet,* 2005.

For more country facts, go to the **Nations of the World Databank** at glencoe.com.

Regional Atlas

East Asia and Southeast Asia

Country and Capital	Literacy Rate	Population and Density	Land Area	Life Expectancy (Years)	GDP* Per Capita (U.S. dollars)	Television Sets (per 1,000 people)	Flag and Language
SINGAPORE Singapore	92.5%	4,300,000 17,992 per sq. mi. 6,947 per sq. km	239 sq. mi. 619 sq. km	79	$27,800	341	Mandarin
Seoul **SOUTH KOREA**	97.9%	48,300,000 1,260 per sq. mi. 487 per sq. km	38,324 sq. mi. 99,259 sq. km	77	$19,200	364	Korean
Taipei **TAIWAN†**	96.1	22,700,000 1,625 per sq. mi. 627 per sq. km	13,969 sq. mi. 36,180 sq. km	76	$25,300	327	Mandarin Chinese
THAILAND Bangkok	92.6%	65,000,000 328 per sq. mi. 127 per sq. km	198,116 sq. mi. 513,118 sq. km	71	$8,100	274	Thai
Hanoi **VIETNAM**	90.3%	83,300,000 650 per sq. mi. 251 per sq. km	128,066 sq. mi. 331,689 sq. km	72	$2,700	184	Vietnamese
UNITED STATES Washington, D.C.	97%	296,500,000 80 per sq. mi. 31 per sq. km	3,717,796 sq. mi. 9,629,047 sq. km	78	$40,100	844	English

*Gross Domestic Product

Countries and flags not drawn to scale

† The People's Republic of China claims Taiwan as its 23rd province.

Bicycle rickshaws outside
temple in George Town,
Malaysia

錢鐷哥

Australia, Oceania, and Antarctica

Sydney, Australia ▶

Regional Atlas

Australia, Oceania, and Antarctica

Where Is It?

A It is about 7,931 miles (12,764 km) from New York City to Suva.

B It is about 9,928 miles (15,978 km) from New York City to Sydney.

How Big Is It?

The land area of the region of Australia, Oceania, and Antarctica is about 8.8 million square miles (22.8 million sq. km), and it includes the continents of Australia and Antarctica. With an area of 3.0 million square miles (7.8 million sq. km), Australia is slightly smaller than the continental United States, whereas Antarctica is almost twice as large. The islands of Oceania make up a very small part of the region's land.

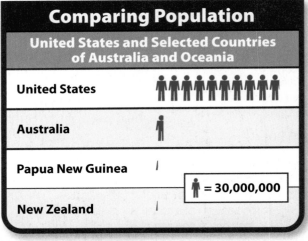

Comparing Population		
United States and Selected Countries of Australia and Oceania		
United States	🧍🧍🧍🧍🧍🧍🧍🧍🧍	
Australia	🧍	
Papua New Guinea	ı	🧍 = 30,000,000
New Zealand	ı	

Source: *World Population Data Sheet,* 2005.

GEO Fast Facts

Largest Coral Reef

Great Barrier Reef (Australia)
1,250 mi. (2,011 km) long

Longest River

Darling River (Australia)
1,702 mi. (2,739 km) long

Largest Lake

Lake Eyre (Australia)
3,600 sq. mi.
(9,324 sq. km)

Highest Point

Vinson Massif
(Antarctica)
16,066 ft.
(4,897 m) high

Regional Atlas

Australia, Oceania, and Antarctica
PHYSICAL

EAST ASIA

140°E 160°E 180° 160°W 140°W

TROPIC OF CANCER

20°N

Philippine Sea

South China Sea

PACIFIC OCEAN

Hawaiian Islands

INTERNATIONAL DATE LINE

MICRONESIA

Caroline Islands

EQUATOR 0°

MELANESIA

New Guinea

Gilbert Islands

▲ Mt. Wilhelm 14,762 ft. (4,500 m)

Cape York Peninsula

Coral Sea

POLYNESIA

Cook Islands

Society Islands

Marquesas Islands

20°S

Great Sandy Desert

Great Barrier Reef

AUSTRALIA

Macdonnell Ranges

Gibson Desert

▲ Ayers Rock 1,143 ft. (348 m)

Great Artesian Basin

Lake Eyre

Great Dividing Range

Great Victoria Desert

Murray R.

Darling R.

TROPIC OF CAPRICORN

Great Australian Bight

▲ Mt. Kosciuszko 7,310 ft. (2,228 m)

North Island

Mt. Ruapehu 9,175 ft. (2,797 m) ▲

Tasmania

Tasman Sea

Mt. Cook 12,349 ft. (3,764 m) ▲

Southern Alps

Cook Strait

South Island

INDIAN OCEAN

Elevations

13,100 ft. (4,000 m)
6,500 ft. (2,000 m)
1,600 ft. (500 m)
650 ft. (200 m)
0 ft. (0 m)
Below sea level

▲ Mountain peak

0   1,000 kilometers
0   1,000 miles
Mercator projection

40°W 20°W 0° 20°E 40°E

ATLANTIC OCEAN

ANTARCTIC CIRCLE

60°S

Queen Maud Land

Antarctic Peninsula

Ronne Ice Shelf

80°W

ANTARCTICA

80°E

Vinson Massif ▲ 16,066 ft. (4,897 m) WEST ANTARCTICA

South Pole

Transantarctic Mountains

EAST ANTARCTICA

100°W

Marie Byrd Land

Ross Ice Shelf

Wilkes Land

60°S

PACIFIC OCEAN

0   1,000 kilometers
0   1,000 miles
Lambert Azimuthal Equal-Area projection

160°E 140°E

INDIAN OCEAN

Map Skills

1 Location Where are the region's only major rivers located?

2 Place Outside of Antarctica, what is the region's highest mountain? Where is it located?

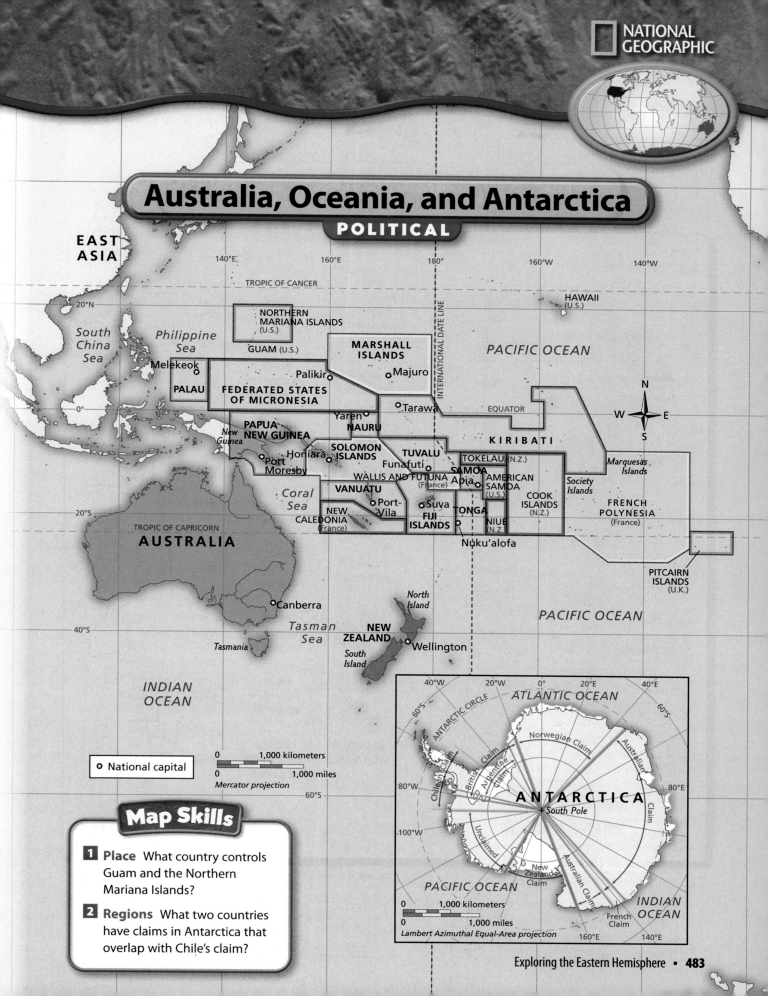

Australia, Oceania, and Antarctica
POLITICAL

NATIONAL GEOGRAPHIC

EAST ASIA

140°E 160°E 180° 160°W 140°W

TROPIC OF CANCER

20°N

HAWAII (U.S.)

South China Sea

Philippine Sea

NORTHERN MARIANA ISLANDS (U.S.)

GUAM (U.S.)

PACIFIC OCEAN

Melekeok

PALAU

Palikir

FEDERATED STATES OF MICRONESIA

MARSHALL ISLANDS

Majuro

0°

New Guinea

PAPUA NEW GUINEA

Yaren

NAURU

Tarawa

EQUATOR

KIRIBATI

N W E S

Port Moresby

Honiara

SOLOMON ISLANDS

TUVALU

Funafuti

Marquesas Islands

Society Islands

Coral Sea

WALLIS AND FUTUNA (France)

TOKELAU (N.Z.)

SAMOA Apia

AMERICAN SAMOA (U.S.)

COOK ISLANDS (N.Z.)

FRENCH POLYNESIA (France)

VANUATU

Port-Vila

Suva

FIJI ISLANDS

TONGA

NIUE (N.Z.)

20°S

NEW CALEDONIA (France)

Nuku'alofa

TROPIC OF CAPRICORN

AUSTRALIA

PITCAIRN ISLANDS (U.K.)

Canberra

North Island

PACIFIC OCEAN

Tasman Sea

NEW ZEALAND

Wellington

Tasmania

South Island

40°S

INDIAN OCEAN

⊕ National capital

0   1,000 kilometers
0   1,000 miles
Mercator projection

60°S

Antarctica inset
40°W 20°W 0° 20°E 40°E

ATLANTIC OCEAN

60°S

ANTARCTIC CIRCLE

60°S

80°W

Chilean Claim

British Claim

Argentine Claim

Norwegian Claim

Australian Claim

80°E

ANTARCTICA
•South Pole

100°W

Unclaimed

New Zealand Claim

Australian Claim

PACIFIC OCEAN

French Claim

INDIAN OCEAN

0   1,000 kilometers
0   1,000 miles
Lambert Azimuthal Equal-Area projection

160°E 140°E

Map Skills

1 Place What country controls Guam and the Northern Mariana Islands?

2 Regions What two countries have claims in Antarctica that overlap with Chile's claim?

Regional Atlas

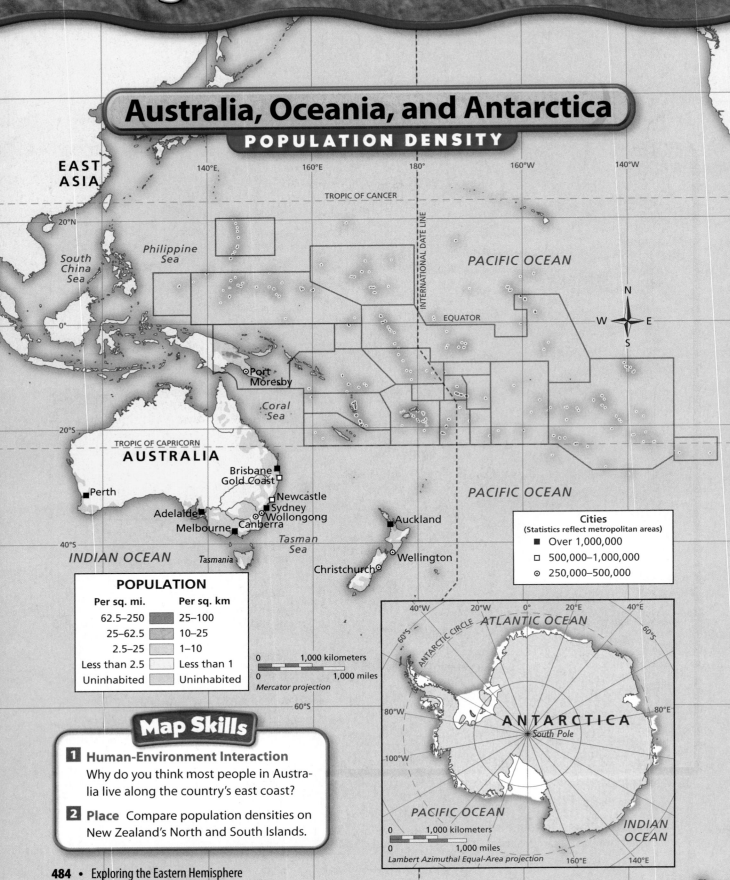

Australia, Oceania, and Antarctica
POPULATION DENSITY

EAST ASIA

140°E.   160°E   180°   160°W   140°W

TROPIC OF CANCER

20°N

South China Sea

Philippine Sea

PACIFIC OCEAN

INTERNATIONAL DATE LINE

0°

EQUATOR

N
W   E
S

⊙Port Moresby

Coral Sea

20°S

TROPIC OF CAPRICORN

AUSTRALIA

PACIFIC OCEAN

Brisbane
Gold Coast

■ Perth

Newcastle
Sydney
Adelaide   Wollongong
Melbourne   Canberra

Auckland

Tasman Sea

40°S

INDIAN OCEAN   Tasmania

Wellington

Christchurch

Cities
(Statistics reflect metropolitan areas)
■ Over 1,000,000
□ 500,000–1,000,000
⊙ 250,000–500,000

POPULATION

Per sq. mi.	Per sq. km
62.5–250	25–100
25–62.5	10–25
2.5–25	1–10
Less than 2.5	Less than 1
Uninhabited	Uninhabited

0   1,000 kilometers
0   1,000 miles
Mercator projection

40°W   20°W   0°   20°E   40°E

ANTARCTIC CIRCLE   ATLANTIC OCEAN

60°S   60°S

80°W   80°E

ANTARCTICA
• South Pole

100°W

PACIFIC OCEAN   INDIAN OCEAN

60°S

0   1,000 kilometers
0   1,000 miles
Lambert Azimuthal Equal-Area projection   160°E   140°E

Map Skills

1 **Human-Environment Interaction**
Why do you think most people in Australia live along the country's east coast?

2 **Place** Compare population densities on New Zealand's North and South Islands.

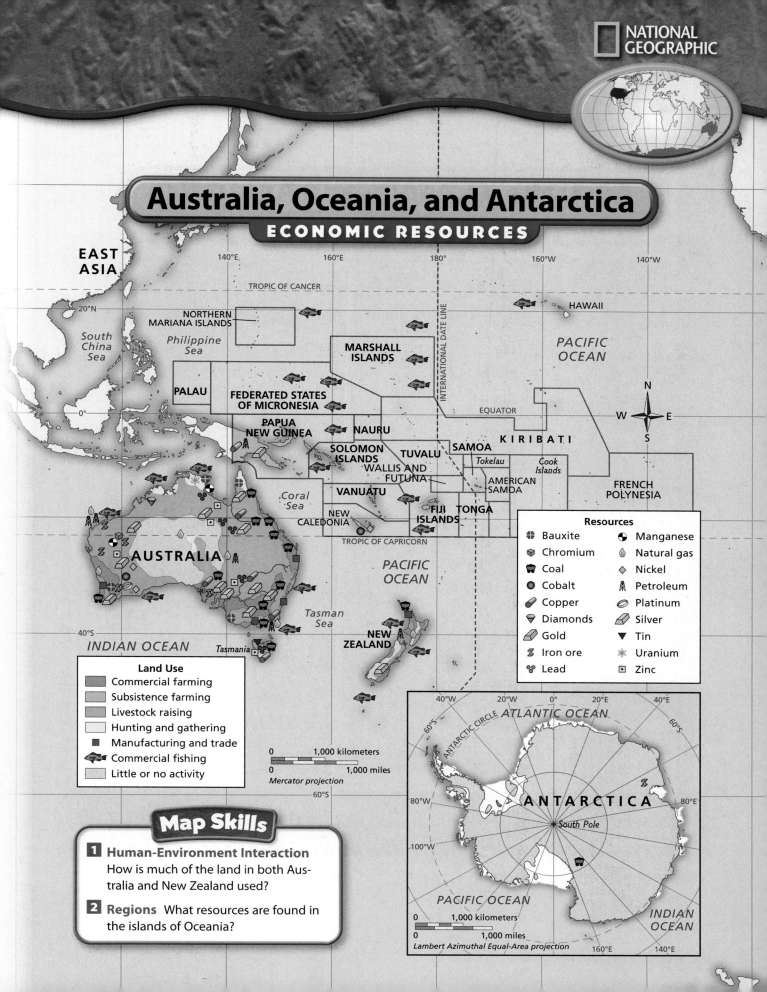

Australia, Oceania, and Antarctica
ECONOMIC RESOURCES

NATIONAL GEOGRAPHIC

EAST ASIA

TROPIC OF CANCER

20°N

NORTHERN MARIANA ISLANDS

Philippine Sea

South China Sea

PALAU

MARSHALL ISLANDS

PACIFIC OCEAN

HAWAII

FEDERATED STATES OF MICRONESIA

EQUATOR

0°S

PAPUA NEW GUINEA

NAURU

KIRIBATI

SOLOMON ISLANDS

TUVALU

SAMOA

Tokelau

Cook Islands

WALLIS AND FUTUNA

AMERICAN SAMOA

FRENCH POLYNESIA

Coral Sea

VANUATU

AUSTRALIA

NEW CALEDONIA

FIJI ISLANDS

TONGA

TROPIC OF CAPRICORN

PACIFIC OCEAN

N
W E
S

Resources

✤ Bauxite	◓ Manganese
⬙ Chromium	⬦ Natural gas
⬛ Coal	◆ Nickel
● Cobalt	⚒ Petroleum
⬠ Copper	⬭ Platinum
▽ Diamonds	▱ Silver
▬ Gold	▼ Tin
⬚ Iron ore	✳ Uranium
⬙ Lead	⊡ Zinc

INDIAN OCEAN

Tasman Sea

Tasmania

NEW ZEALAND

40°S

Land Use

- Commercial farming
- Subsistence farming
- Livestock raising
- Hunting and gathering
- ■ Manufacturing and trade
- 🐟 Commercial fishing
- Little or no activity

0   1,000 kilometers
0   1,000 miles

Mercator projection

60°S

ATLANTIC OCEAN

40°W   20°W   0°   20°E   40°E

60°S

ANTARCTIC CIRCLE

80°W

ANTARCTICA

South Pole

80°E

100°W

PACIFIC OCEAN

INDIAN OCEAN

0   1,000 kilometers
0   1,000 miles

Lambert Azimuthal Equal-Area projection

160°E   140°E

Map Skills

1 Human-Environment Interaction
How is much of the land in both Australia and New Zealand used?

2 Regions What resources are found in the islands of Oceania?

Regional Atlas

Australia, Oceania, and Antarctica

Country and Capital	Literacy Rate	Population and Density	Land Area	Life Expectancy (Years)	GDP* Per Capita (U.S. dollars)	Television Sets (per 1,000 people)	Flag and Language
AUSTRALIA Canberra	100%	20,400,000 7 per sq. mi. 3 per sq. km	2,988,888 sq. mi. 7,741,184 sq. km	80	$30,700	716	English
FEDERATED STATES OF MICRONESIA Palikir	89.1%	100,000 370 per sq. mi. 143 per sq. km	270 sq. mi. 699 sq. km	67	$2,000	20	English
FIJI Suva	93.7%	800,000 113 per sq. mi. 44 per sq. km	7,054 sq. mi. 18,270 sq. km	68	$5,900	110	English
Tarawa (Bairiki) KIRIBATI	NA	100,000 355 per sq. mi. 136 per sq. km	282 sq. mi. 730 sq. km	63	$800	23	I-Kiribati, English
MARSHALL ISLANDS Majuro	93.7%	100,000 1,449 per sq. mi. 559 per sq. km	69 sq. mi. 179 sq. km	68	$1,600	information not available	Marshallese, English
NAURU Yaren	NA	10,000 1,111 per sq. mi. 435 per sq. km	9 sq. mi. 23 sq. km	61	$5,000	1	Nauruan, English
Wellington NEW ZEALAND	99%	4,100,000 39 per sq. mi. 15 per sq. km	104,452 sq. mi. 270,529 sq. km	79	$23,200	516	English, Maori
Melekeok PALAU	92%	20,000 112 per sq. mi. 43 per sq. km	178 sq. mi. 461 sq. km	70	$9,000	98	Palauan, English
UNITED STATES Washington, D.C.	97%	296,500,000 80 per sq. mi. 31 per sq. km	3,717,796 sq. mi. 9,629,047 sq. km	78	$40,100	844	English

*Gross Domestic Product

Countries and flags not drawn to scale

Australia, Oceania, and Antarctica

Country and Capital	Literacy Rate	Population and Density	Land Area	Life Expectancy (Years)	GDP* Per Capita (U.S. dollars)	Television Sets (per 1,000 people)	Flag and Language
PAPUA NEW GUINEA Port Moresby	64.6%	5,900,000 33 per sq. mi. 13 per sq. km	178,703 sq. mi. 462,839 sq. km	55	$2,200	13	Melanesian Pidgin
SAMOA Apia	99.7%	200,000 182 per sq. mi. 70 per sq. km	1,097 sq. mi. 2,841 sq. km	73	$5,600	56	Samoan
SOLOMON ISLANDS Honiara	NA	500,000 45 per sq. mi. 17 per sq. km	11,158 sq. mi. 28,889 sq. km	62	$1,700	16	Melanesian Pidgin, English
TONGA Nuku'alofa	98.5%	100,000 345 per sq. mi. 133 per sq. km	290 sq. mi. 751 sq. km	71	$2,300	61	Tongan, English
TUVALU Funafuti	NA	10,000 1,000 per sq. mi. 385 per sq. km	10 sq. mi. 26 sq. km	64	$1,100	9	Tuvaluan
VANUATU Port-Vila	53%	200,000 42 per sq. mi. 16 per sq. km	4,707 sq. mi. 12,191 sq. km	67	$2,900	12	Local Languages, Bislama
UNITED STATES Washington, D.C.	97%	296,500,000 80 per sq. mi. 31 per sq. km	3,717,796 sq. mi. 9,629,047 sq. km	78	$40,100	844	English

Sources: *CIA World Factbook*, 2005; Population Reference Bureau, *World Population Data Sheet*, 2005.

For more country facts, go to the **Nations of the World Databank** at glencoe.com.

Skills Handbook

Contents

Interpreting Political Cartoons

Why Learn This Skill?

Political cartoons express opinions through art. The cartoons appear in newspapers, magazines, books, and on the Internet. Political cartoons usually focus on public figures, political events, or economic or social conditions. This type of art can give you a summary of an event or circumstance, along with the artist's opinion, in an entertaining way.

1 Learn It!

Follow these steps to interpret political cartoons:

- Read the title, caption, or conversation balloons. They help you identify the subject of the cartoon.

- Identify the characters or people in the cartoon. They may be caricatures, or unrealistic drawings that exaggerate the characters' physical features.

- Identify any symbols. Symbols are objects that stand for something else. An example is the American flag, which is a symbol of our country. Commonly recognized symbols may not be labeled. Unusual symbols might be labeled.

- Examine the actions in the cartoon—what is happening and why?

- Identify the cartoonist's purpose. What statement or idea is he or she trying to express? Decide if the cartoonist wants to persuade, criticize, or just make people think.

2 Practice It!

On a separate sheet of paper, answer these questions about the political cartoon below.

1. What is the subject of the cartoon?
2. What words give clues to the meaning of the cartoon?
3. What item seems out of place?
4. What message do you think the cartoonist is trying to send?

3 Apply It!

Bring a newsmagazine to class. With a partner, analyze the message in each political cartoon you find in the magazine.

Predicting

Why Learn This Skill?

You have probably read about people making difficult decisions based on something they think *might* happen. You will have a better understanding of why people make certain choices when you consider the factors that influenced their decisions.

1 Learn It!

As you read a paragraph or section in your book, think about what might happen next. What you think will happen is your *prediction*. A prediction does not have a correct or incorrect answer. A prediction is an educated guess of what might happen next based on facts.

To make a prediction, ask yourself:

- What happened in this paragraph or section?

- What prior knowledge do I have about the information in the text?

- What similar circumstances do I know of?

- What do I think might happen next?

- Test your prediction: read further to see if you were correct.

▲ **Aztec shield**

2 Practice It!

To practice the skill, read the following paragraphs about the Aztec Empire. Then answer the questions.

In the late 1400s and early 1500s, Spanish explorers arrived in the Americas. They were greatly impressed by the magnificent cities and the great riches of the Native Americans.

In 1519 a Spanish army led by Hernán Cortés landed on Mexico's Gulf coast. He and about 600 soldiers marched to Tenochtitlán, which they had heard was filled with gold.

1. Choose the outcome that is most likely to occur between the Native Americans and the Spaniards.

   a. The Spaniards will conquer the Native Americans.

   b. The Native Americans will conquer the Spaniards.

   c. The two groups will become friends.

2. What clues in the text help you make your prediction?

3 Apply It!

Watch a television show or a movie. Halfway through the show, write down your prediction of how it will end. At the end of the show, check your prediction. Were you correct? What clues did you use to make your prediction?

Analyzing Library and Research Resources

Why Learn This Skill?

Imagine that your teacher asked you to write a report about the physical geography of Australia using library or Internet resources. Knowing how to choose sources that contain accurate information will help you save time in the library or on the Internet. You will also be able to write a better report.

1 Learn It!

Not all sources will be useful for your report on Australia's physical geography. Even some sources that involve topics about Australia will not always provide the information you want. In analyzing sources for your research project, choose items that are nonfiction and that contain the most information about your topic.

When choosing research resources, ask these questions:

- Is the information up-to-date?
- Does a book's index have several page references listed for the topic?
- Is the research written in a way that is easy to understand?
- Are there helpful illustrations and photos?

2 Practice It!

Look at the following list of sources. Which would be most helpful in writing a report on the physical geography of Australia? Explain your choices.

(1) A current travel guide to Australia

(2) A book about Australia's landforms and climates

(3) A children's storybook about an Australian kangaroo

(4) A student's notes on the Internet about a family trip to Australia

(5) A study of the rise and fall of the British Empire

(6) A Web site with physical maps of Australia

(7) A book about Australian government

(8) A geographical dictionary

3 Apply It!

Go to your local library or use the Internet to create a bibliography of sources you might use to write a report on the physical geography of Australia. Explain why you chose each source.

▲ Uluru (Ayers Rock) in central Australia

Interpreting a Chart

Why Learn This Skill?

To make learning easier, you can organize information into groups of related facts and ideas. One way to organize information is with a chart. A chart presents written or numerical information in columns and rows. It helps you to remember and compare information more easily.

① Learn It!

To organize information in a chart, follow these steps:

- Decide what information you must organize.

- Identify several major categories of ideas or facts about the topic, and use these categories as column headings.

- Find information that fits into each category, and write those facts or ideas under the appropriate column heading.

② Practice It!

On a separate sheet of paper, answer the following questions using the chart at the bottom of this page.

1. What type of information does the chart contain?

2. What other related information appears in the chart?

3. Canada also exports clothing and beverages to the United States. Is it necessary to create a new chart to show this information?

③ Apply It!

Create a chart to track your school assignments. Work with five areas of information: Subject, Assignment, Description, Due Date, and Date Completed. Be sure to keep your chart up-to-date.

U.S. International Trade			
	Japan	**United Kingdom**	**Canada**
Exports to U.S.	Engines, rubber goods, cars, trucks, buses	Dairy products, beverages, petroleum products	Wheat, minerals, paper, mining machines
Value of Exports to U.S.	$138 billion	$51.1 billion	$287.9 billion
Imports from U.S.	Meat, fish, sugar, tobacco, coffee	Fruit, tobacco, electrical equipment	Fish, sugar, metals, clothing
Value of Imports from U.S.	$55.4 billion	$38.6 billion	$211.3 billion

Source: *CIA World Factbook, 2006; United States Census Bureau, Foreign Trade Statistics, 2005.*

Making Comparisons

Why Learn This Skill?

Suppose you want to buy a portable CD player, and you must choose among three models. To make this decision, you would probably compare various features of the three models, such as price, sound quality, size, and so on. After you compare the models, you will choose the one that is best for you. In your studies of world geography, you must often compare countries of the world to identify patterns, make predictions, or make generalizations about regions.

 Learn It!

When making comparisons, you identify and examine two or more places, peoples, economies, or forms of government. Then you identify any similarities between two topics, or ways the two topics are alike.

When making comparisons, apply the following steps:

- Decide what topics to compare. Clue words such as *also*, *as well as*, *like*, *same as*, and *similar to* can help you identify when topics are being compared.

- Read the information about each topic carefully.

- Identify what information is similar for both topics.

❷ Practice It!

To practice the skill, analyze the information in the chart at the bottom of this page. Then answer these questions.

1. What countries are being compared?

2. What categories for each country are being compared?

3. In what ways are the United States and the United Kingdom similar?

4. Suppose you wanted to compare the two countries in more detail. What other categories might you use?

❸ Apply It!

Think about two sports that are played at your school. Make a chart comparing categories such as where the games are played, who plays them, what equipment is used, and so on.

The United States and the United Kingdom		
	United States	**United Kingdom**
Location	North America	Europe
Language	English	English
Form of Government	Federal republic	Constitutional monarchy
Popular Sports	Baseball, football, basketball	Soccer, rugby, cricket
Popular Foods	Hamburgers, hot dogs	Fish and chips, roast beef

Analyzing Primary Sources

Why Learn This Skill?

People who study history examine pieces of evidence to reconstruct events. These types of evidence—both written and illustrated—are called *primary sources*. Examining primary sources can help you understand the history of a place.

① Learn It!

Primary sources are firsthand accounts that describe a historical event or time period. They can include letters, diaries, photographs and pictures, news articles, legal documents, stories, literature, and artwork.

Ask yourself the following questions when analyzing primary sources:

- What is the primary source?
- Who created it?
- Where is it from?
- When was it created?
- What does it reveal about the topic I am studying?

② Practice It!

The following primary source is from *The Log of Christopher Columbus*. Christopher Columbus reached the new world on October 12, 1492. Columbus's entry explains what occurred when he and his shipmates encountered Native Americans. Read the entry, and then answer the questions that follow.

October 12:

The people here called this island Guanahani in their language, and their speech is very fluent [easily flowing], although I do not understand any of it. They are friendly . . . people who [bear] no arms except for small spears, and they have no iron. I showed one my sword, and through ignorance he grabbed it by the blade and cut himself. . . .

. . . They traded and gave everything they had with good will, but it seems to me that they have very little and are poor in everything. . . .

This afternoon the people of San Salvador came swimming to our ships and in boats made from one log. They brought us parrots, balls of cotton thread, spears, and many other things. . . . For these items we swapped them little glass beads and hawks' bells.

—The Log of Christopher Columbus

---

1. Why did Columbus believe that the Native Americans had no knowledge about weapons?

2. Does Columbus fear the Native Americans? Explain.

3. What items did Columbus and his crew exchange with the Native Americans?

4. Why is this reading a primary source?

③ Apply It!

Find a primary source from your past, such as a photo, newspaper clipping, or diary entry. Explain to the class what it shows about that time in your life.

Recognizing Bias

Why Learn This Skill?

If you say, "Cats make better pets than dogs," you are stating a bias. A *bias* is an attitude that favors one way of thinking over another. It can prevent you from looking at a situation in a reasonable or truthful way.

① Learn It!

Most people have feelings and ideas that affect their point of view on a subject. Their viewpoint, or *bias*, influences the way they interpret events. For this reason, an idea that is stated as a fact may really be only an opinion. Recognizing bias will help you judge the accuracy of what you read.

To recognize bias, follow these steps:

- Identify the speaker or writer and examine his or her views. Why did he or she speak or write about a particular issue?

- Look for language that shows emotion or opinion. Look for words such as *all*, *never*, *best*, *worst*, *might*, or *should*.

- Examine the information for imbalances. Is it written from one point of view? Does it take into consideration other points of view?

- Identify statements of fact. Factual statements usually answer the *who*, *what*, *where*, and *when* questions.

- Does the writer use facts to support his or her point of view?

② Practice It!

Read the following statement about wildlife in Africa, and answer the questions below.

Mountain gorillas live in the misty mountain forests of East Africa. Logging and mining, however, are destroying the forests. Unless the forests are protected, the gorillas will lose their homes and disappear forever. As a concerned African naturalist, I must emphasize that this will be the worst event in Africa's history.

1. What problem is the speaker addressing?

2. What reasons does the speaker give for the loss of the forests?

3. What is the speaker's point of view, or bias?

4. What words give clues as to the speaker's bias?

③ Apply It!

Choose a letter from the editorial page of a newspaper. Summarize the issue being discussed and the writer's bias about the issue. Describe a possible opposing opinion and who might have it and why.

Mountain gorilla

Interpreting a Circle Graph

Why Learn This Skill?

Have you ever watched someone serve pieces of pie? When the pie is cut evenly, everyone's slice is the same size. If one slice is cut a little larger, however, someone else gets a smaller piece. A *circle graph* is like a sliced pie. In fact, a circle graph is also called a pie chart. In a circle graph, the complete circle represents a whole group—or 100 percent. The circle is divided into "slices," or wedge-shaped sections representing parts of the whole.

① Learn It!

To read and interpret a circle graph, follow these steps:

- Read the title of the circle graph to find the subject.

- Study the labels or the key to see what each "slice" represents.

- Compare the sizes of the circle slices.

② Practice It!

Study the circle graph on this page, and answer the following questions.

1. What is the subject of the circle graph?

2. On what do Americans spend most of their incomes?

3. On what do Americans spend the least portion of their incomes?

4. What is the total percentage of income spent on transportation and food?

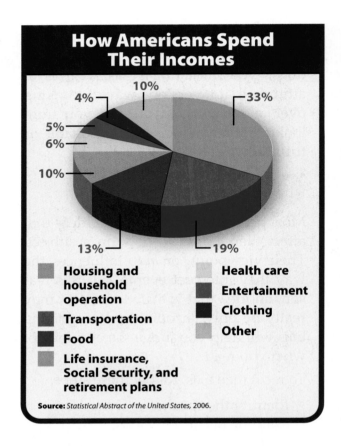

How Americans Spend Their Incomes

- 10%
- 4%
- 33%
- 5%
- 6%
- 10%
- 13%
- 19%

Key:
- Housing and household operation
- Transportation
- Food
- Life insurance, Social Security, and retirement plans
- Health care
- Entertainment
- Clothing
- Other

Source: *Statistical Abstract of the United States, 2006.*

③ Apply It!

Quiz 10 friends about the capitals of India, Pakistan, and Bangladesh. Create a circle graph showing what percentage knew (a) all three capitals; (b) two capitals; (c) one capital; or (d) no capitals.

Sequencing Events

Why Learn This Skill?

Have you ever had to remember events and their dates in the order in which they happened? *Sequencing* means listing facts in the correct order that they occurred. A time line helps you do this. A time line is a diagram that shows how dates and events relate to one another. The years are evenly spaced along most time lines. Events on time lines are described beside the date on which they occurred.

 Learn It!

To understand how to sequence events, follow these steps:

- As you read, look for dates or clue words that hint at chronological order, such as *in 2006, the late 1900s, first, then, finally,* and *after.*

- To read a time line, find the dates on the opposite ends of the time line. These dates show the range of time that is covered.

- Note the equal spacing between dates on the time line.

- Study the order of events.

- Look to see how the events relate to one another.

 Practice It!

Examine the time line on this page and answer the following questions.

1. When does the time line begin? When does it end?

2. What major event happened in the late 1700s?

3. Did the Civil War begin before or after the United States entered World War I?

4. During what decade did the Cold War end?

 Apply It!

List key events from one of the chapters in your textbook that covers the history of a region. Create a time line that lists these events in the order they occurred.

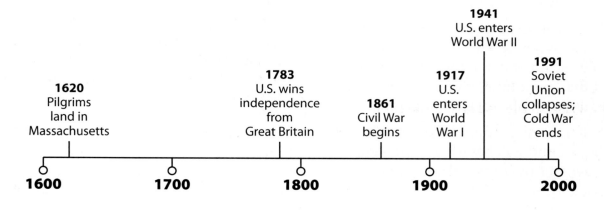

1620 Pilgrims land in Massachusetts

1783 U.S. wins independence from Great Britain

1861 Civil War begins

1917 U.S. enters World War I

1941 U.S. enters World War II

1991 Soviet Union collapses; Cold War ends

1600   1700   1800   1900   2000

Interpreting a Population Pyramid

Why Learn This Skill?

A population pyramid shows a country's population by age and gender. Geographers use population pyramids to plan for a country's future needs.

① Learn It!

A population pyramid is two bar graphs. These bar graphs show the number of males and females living in a region. The number of males and females is given as a percentage along the bottom of the graph. The age range for each group is listed along the left side of the graph.

To interpret population pyramids, follow these steps:

- Look at the bar graphs for the male and female groups.

- Identify, for each group, the bars that indicate the largest percentage and the smallest percentage.

- Find the age range for these groups.

- If a country's population is *growing*, the pyramid will be large at the bottom. This shows that the country's population has a large number of children and young people.

- If a country's population is *declining*, the pyramid will be narrow at the bottom and wider at the top. This means that the country's population has a large number of elderly people.

- If a country's population is *stable*, the pyramid will have bars with similar lengths over several age ranges.

② Practice It!

Study the 2007 population pyramid for Spain shown below, then answer the following questions.

1. Which age group makes up the largest portion of Spain's population?

2. Does it appear that Spanish men or Spanish women live longer? Explain.

3. What does the shape of the pyramid tell you about Spain's population?

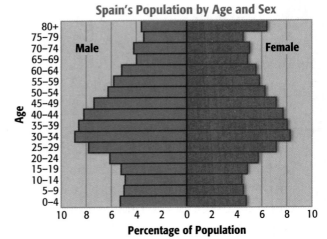

Spain's Population by Age and Sex

Source: *U.S. Census Bureau, International Data Base.*

③ Apply It!

Find the population pyramids for two countries at www.census.gov/ipc/www/idbpyr.html. Then write a paragraph to describe the similarities and differences between their populations.

Gazetteer

Gazetteer

A gazetteer (GA·zuh·TIHR) is a geographic index or dictionary. It shows latitude and longitude for cities and certain other places. Latitude and longitude are shown in this way: 48°N 2°E, or 48 degrees north latitude and two degrees east longitude. This Gazetteer lists many important geographic features and most of the world's largest independent countries and their capitals. The page numbers tell where each entry can be found on a map in this book. As an aid to pronunciation, most entries are spelled phonetically.

Abidjan [AH·bee·JAHN] Capital of Côte d'Ivoire. 5°N 4°W (p. RA22)

Abu Dhabi [AH·boo DAH·bee] Capital of the United Arab Emirates. 24°N 54°E (p. RA24)

Abuja [ah·BOO·jah] Capital of Nigeria. 8°N 9°E (p. RA22)

Accra [ah·KRUH] Capital of Ghana. 6°N 0° longitude (p. RA22)

Addis Ababa [AHD·dihs AH·bah·BAH] Capital of Ethiopia. 9°N 39°E (p. RA22)

Adriatic [AY·dree·A·tihk] **Sea** Arm of the Mediterranean Sea between the Balkan Peninsula and Italy. (p. RA20)

Afghanistan [af·GA·nuh·STAN] Central Asian country west of Pakistan. (p. RA25)

Albania [al·BAY·nee·uh] Country on the Adriatic Sea, south of Serbia. (p. RA18)

Algeria [al·JIHR·ee·uh] North African country east of Morocco. (p. RA22)

Algiers [al·JIHRZ] Capital of Algeria. 37°N 3°E (p. RA22)

Alps [ALPS] Mountain ranges extending through central Europe. (p. RA20)

Amazon [A·muh·ZAHN] **River** Largest river in the world by volume and second-largest in length. (p. RA17)

Amman [a·MAHN] Capital of Jordan. 32°N 36°E (p. RA24)

Amsterdam [AHM·stuhr·DAHM] Capital of the Netherlands. 52°N 5°E (p. RA18)

Andes [AN·DEEZ] Mountain system extending north and south along the western side of South America. (p. RA17)

Andorra [an·DAWR·uh] Small country in southern Europe between France and Spain. 43°N 2°E (p. RA18)

Angola [ang·GOH·luh] Southern African country north of Namibia. (p. RA22)

Ankara [AHNG·kuh·ruh] Capital of Turkey. 40°N 33°E (p. RA24)

Antananarivo [AHN·tah·NAH·nah·REE·voh] Capital of Madagascar. 19°S 48°E (p. RA22)

Arabian [uh·RAY·bee·uhn] **Peninsula** Large peninsula extending into the Arabian Sea. (p. RA25)

Argentina [AHR·juhn·TEE·nuh] South American country east of Chile. (p. RA16)

Armenia [ahr·MEE·nee·uh] European-Asian country between the Black and Caspian Seas. 40°N 45°E (p. RA26)

Ashkhabad [AHSH·gah·BAHD] Capital of Turkmenistan. 38°N 58°E (p. RA25)

Asmara [az·MAHR·uh] Capital of Eritrea. 16°N 39°E (p. RA22)

Astana Capital of Kazakhstan. 51°N 72°E (p. RA26)

Asunción [ah·SOON·see·OHN] Capital of Paraguay. 25°S 58°W (p. RA16)

Athens Capital of Greece. 38°N 24°E (p. RA19)

Atlas [AT·luhs] **Mountains** Mountain range on the northern edge of the Sahara. (p. RA23)

Australia [aw·STRAYL·yuh] Country and continent in Southern Hemisphere. (p. RA30)

Austria [AWS·tree·uh] Western European country east of Switzerland and south of Germany and the Czech Republic. (p. RA18)

Azerbaijan [A·zuhr·BY·JAHN] European-Asian country on the Caspian Sea. (p. RA25)

Baghdad Capital of Iraq. 33°N 44°E (p. RA25)

Bahamas [buh·HAH·muhz] Country made up of many islands between Cuba and the United States. (p. RA15)

Bahrain [bah·RAYN] Country located on the Persian Gulf. 26°N 51°E (p. RA25)

Baku [bah·KOO] Capital of Azerbaijan. 40°N 50°E (p. RA25)

Balkan [BAWL·kuhn] **Peninsula** Peninsula in southeastern Europe. (p. RA21)

Baltic [BAWL·tihk] **Sea** Sea in northern Europe that is connected to the North Sea. (p. RA20)

Bamako [BAH·mah·KOH] Capital of Mali. 13°N 8°W (p. RA22)

Bangkok [BANG·KAHK] Capital of Thailand. 14°N 100°E (p. RA27)

Bangladesh [BAHNG·gluh·DEHSH] South Asian country bordered by India and Myanmar. (p. RA27)

Bangui [BAHNG·GEE] Capital of the Central African Republic. 4°N 19°E (p. RA22)

Banjul [BAHN·JOOL] Capital of Gambia. 13°N 17°W (p. RA22)

Barbados [bahr•BAY•duhs] Island country between the Atlantic Ocean and the Caribbean Sea. 14°N 59°W (p. RA15)

Beijing [BAY•JIHNG] Capital of China. 40°N 116°E (p. RA27)

Beirut [bay•ROOT] Capital of Lebanon. 34°N 36°E (p. RA24)

Belarus [BEE•luh•ROOS] Eastern European country west of Russia. 54°N 28°E (p. RA19)

Belgium [BEHL•juhm] Western European country south of the Netherlands. (p. RA18)

Belgrade [BEHL•GRAYD] Capital of Serbia. 45°N 21°E (p. RA19)

Belize [buh•LEEZ] Central American country east of Guatemala. (p. RA14)

Belmopan [BEHL•moh•PAHN] Capital of Belize. 17°N 89°W (p. RA14)

Benin [buh•NEEN] West African country west of Nigeria. (p. RA22)

Berlin [behr•LEEN] Capital of Germany. 53°N 13°E (p. RA18)

Bern Capital of Switzerland. 47°N 7°E (p. RA18)

Bhutan [boo•TAHN] South Asian country northeast of India. (p. RA27)

Bishkek [bihsh•KEHK] Capital of Kyrgyzstan. 43°N 75°E (p. RA26)

Bissau [bihs•SOW] Capital of Guinea-Bissau. 12°N 16°W (p. RA22)

Black Sea Large sea between Europe and Asia. (p. RA21)

Bloemfontein [BLOOM•FAHN•TAYN] Judicial capital of South Africa. 26°E 29°S (p. RA22)

Bogotá [BOH•goh•TAH] Capital of Colombia. 5°N 74°W (p. RA16)

Bolivia [buh•LIHV•ee•uh] Country in the central part of South America, north of Argentina. (p. RA16)

Bosnia and Herzegovina [BAHZ•nee•uh HEHRT•seh•GAW•vee•nuh] Southeastern European country bordered by Croatia, Serbia, and Montenegro. (p. RA18)

Botswana [bawt•SWAH•nah] Southern African country north of the Republic of South Africa. (p. RA22)

Brasília [brah•ZEEL•yuh] Capital of Brazil. 16°S 48°W (p. RA16)

Bratislava [BRAH•tih•SLAH•vuh] Capital of Slovakia. 48°N 17°E (p. RA18)

Brazil [bruh•ZIHL] Largest country in South America. (p. RA16)

Brazzaville [BRAH•zuh•VEEL] Capital of Congo. 4°S 15°E (p. RA22)

Brunei [bru•NY] Southeast Asian country on northern coast of the island of Borneo. (p. RA27)

Brussels [BRUH•suhlz] Capital of Belgium. 51°N 4°E (p. RA18)

Bucharest [BOO•kuh•REHST] Capital of Romania. 44°N 26°E (p. RA19)

Budapest [BOO•duh•PEHST] Capital of Hungary. 48°N 19°E (p. RA18)

Buenos Aires [BWAY•nuhs AR•eez] Capital of Argentina. 34°S 58°W (p. RA16)

Bujumbura [BOO•juhm•BUR•uh] Capital of Burundi. 3°S 29°E (p. RA22)

Bulgaria [BUHL•GAR•ee•uh] Southeastern European country south of Romania. (p. RA19)

Burkina Faso [bur•KEE•nuh FAH•soh] West African country south of Mali. (p. RA22)

Burundi [bu•ROON•dee] East African country at the northern end of Lake Tanganyika. 3°S 30°E (p. RA22)

Cairo [KY•ROH] Capital of Egypt. 31°N 32°E (p. RA24)

Cambodia [kam•BOH•dee•uh] Southeast Asian country south of Thailand and Laos. (p. RA27)

Cameroon [KA•muh•ROON] Central African country on the northeast shore of the Gulf of Guinea. (p. RA22)

Canada [KA•nuh•duh] Northernmost country in North America. (p. RA6)

Canberra [KAN•BEHR•uh] Capital of Australia. 35°S 149°E (p. RA30)

Cape Town Legislative capital of the Republic of South Africa. 34°S 18°E (p. RA22)

Cape Verde [VUHRD] Island country off the coast of western Africa in the Atlantic Ocean. 15°N 24°W (p. RA22)

Caracas [kah•RAH•kahs] Capital of Venezuela. 11°N 67°W (p. RA16)

Caribbean [KAR•uh•BEE•uhn] **Islands** Islands in the Caribbean Sea between North America and South America, also known as West Indies. (p. RA15)

Caribbean Sea Part of the Atlantic Ocean bordered by the West Indies, South America, and Central America. (p. RA15)

Caspian [KAS•pee•uhn] **Sea** Salt lake between Europe and Asia that is the world's largest inland body of water. (p. RA21)

Caucasus [KAW•kuh•suhs] **Mountains** Mountain range between the Black and Caspian Seas. (p. RA21)

Central African Republic Central African country south of Chad. (p. RA22)

Chad [CHAD] Country west of Sudan in the African Sahel. (p. RA22)

Chang Jiang [CHAHNG jee•AHNG] Principal river of China that begins in Tibet and flows into the East China Sea near Shanghai; also known as the Yangtze River. (p. RA29)

Chile [CHEE•lay] South American country west of Argentina. (p. RA16)

China [CHY•nuh] Country in eastern and central Asia, known officially as the People's Republic of China. (p. RA27)

Chişinău [KEE•shee•NOW] Capital of Moldova. 47°N 29°E (p. RA19)

Colombia [kuh•LUHM•bee•uh] South American country west of Venezuela. (p. RA16)

Colombo [kuh•LUHM•boh] Capital of Sri
Lanka. 7°N 80°E (p. RA26)

Comoros [KAH•muh•ROHZ] Small island
country in Indian Ocean between the island of
Madagascar and the southeast African mainland.
13°S 43°E (p. RA22)

Conakry [KAH•nuh•kree] Capital of Guinea.
10°N 14°W (p. RA22)

Congo [KAHNG•goh] Central African country
east of the Democratic Republic of the Congo.
3°S 14°E (p. RA22)

Congo, Democratic Republic of the Central
African country north of Zambia and Angola. 1°S
22°E (p. RA22)

Copenhagen [KOH•puhn•HAY•guhn] Capital of
Denmark. 56°N 12°E (p. RA18)

Costa Rica [KAWS•tah REE•kah] Central
American country south of Nicaragua. (p. RA15)

Côte d'Ivoire [KOHT dee•VWAHR] West African
country south of Mali. (p. RA22)

Croatia [kroh•AY•shuh] Southeastern European
country on the Adriatic Sea. (p. RA18)

Cuba [KYOO•buh] Island country in the
Caribbean Sea. (p. RA15)

Cyprus [SY•pruhs] Island country in the eastern
Mediterranean Sea, south of Turkey. (p. RA19)

Czech [CHEHK] **Republic** Eastern European
country north of Austria. (p. RA18)

Dakar [dah•KAHR] Capital of Senegal. 15°N
17°W (p. RA22)

Damascus [duh•MAS•kuhs] Capital of Syria.
34°N 36°E (p. RA24)

Dar es Salaam [DAHR EHS sah•LAHM]
Commercial capital of Tanzania. 7°S 39°E (p. RA22)

Denmark Northern European country between
the Baltic and North Seas. (p. RA18)

Dhaka [DA•kuh] Capital of Bangladesh. 24°N
90°E (p. RA27)

Djibouti [jih•BOO•tee] East African country on
the Gulf of Aden. 12°N 43°E (p. RA22)

Dodoma [doh•DOH•mah] Political capital of
Tanzania. 6°S 36°E (p. RA22)

Doha [DOH•huh] Capital of Qatar. 25°N 51°E
(p. RA25)

Dominican [duh•MIH•nih•kuhn] **Republic**
Country in the Caribbean Sea on the eastern part
of the island of Hispaniola. (p. RA15)

Dublin [DUH•blihn] Capital of Ireland. 53°N
6°W (p. RA18)

Dushanbe [doo•SHAM•buh] Capital of
Tajikistan. 39°N 69°E (p. RA25)

East Timor [TEE•MOHR] Previous province of
Indonesia, now under UN administration. 10°S
127°E (p. RA27)

Ecuador [EH•kwuh•dawr] South American
country southwest of Colombia. (p. RA16)

Egypt [EE•jihpt] North African country on the
Mediterranean Sea. (p. RA24)

El Salvador [ehl SAL•vuh•dawr] Central
American country southwest of Honduras.
(p. RA14)

Equatorial Guinea [EE•kwuh•TOHR•ee•uhl
GIH•nee] Central African country south of
Cameroon. (p. RA22)

Eritrea [EHR•uh•TREE•uh] East African country
north of Ethiopia. (p. RA22)

Estonia [eh•STOH•nee•uh] Eastern European
country on the Baltic Sea. (p. RA19)

Ethiopia [EE•thee•OH•pee•uh] East African
country north of Somalia and Kenya. (p. RA22)

Euphrates [yu•FRAY•teez] **River** River in
southwestern Asia that flows through Syria and
Iraq and joins the Tigris River. (p. RA25)

Fiji [FEE•jee] **Islands** Country comprised of an
island group in the southwest Pacific Ocean. 19°S
175°E (p. RA30)

Finland [FIHN•luhnd] Northern European country east of Sweden. (p. RA19)

France [FRANS] Western European country
south of the United Kingdom. (p. RA18)

Freetown Capital of Sierra Leone. (p. RA22)

French Guiana [gee•A•nuh] French-owned territory in northern South America. (p. RA16)

Gabon [ga•BOHN] Central African country on
the Atlantic Ocean. (p. RA22)

Gaborone [GAH•boh•ROH•nay] Capital of
Botswana. (p. RA22)

Gambia [GAM•bee•uh] West African country
along the Gambia River. (p. RA22)

Georgetown [JAWRJ•TOWN] Capital of Guyana.
8°N 58°W (p. RA16)

Georgia [JAWR•juh] European-Asian country
bordering the Black Sea south of Russia. (p. RA26)

Germany [JUHR•muh•nee] Western European
country south of Denmark, officially called the
Federal Republic of Germany. (p. RA18)

Ghana [GAH•nuh] West African country on the
Gulf of Guinea. (p. RA22)

Great Plains The continental slope extending
through the United States and Canada. (p. RA7)

Greece [GREES] Southern European country on
the Balkan Peninsula. (p. RA19)

Greenland [GREEN•luhnd] Island in northwestern Atlantic Ocean and the largest island in the
world. (p. RA6)

Guatemala [GWAH•tay•MAH•lah] Central
American country south of Mexico. (p. RA14)

Gazetteer

Guatemala Capital of Guatemala. 15°N 91°W (p. RA14)

Guinea [GIH•nee] West African country on the Atlantic coast. (p. RA22)

Guinea-Bissau [GIH•nee bih•SOW] West African country on the Atlantic coast. (p. RA22)

Gulf of Mexico Gulf on part of the southern coast of North America. (p. RA7)

Guyana [gy•AH•nuh] South American country between Venezuela and Suriname. (p. RA16)

Haiti [HAY•tee] Country in the Caribbean Sea on the western part of the island of Hispaniola. (p. RA15)

Hanoi [ha•NOY] Capital of Vietnam. 21°N 106°E (p. RA27)

Harare [hah•RAH•RAY] Capital of Zimbabwe. 18°S 31°E (p. RA22)

Havana [huh•VA•nuh] Capital of Cuba. 23°N 82°W (p. RA15)

Helsinki [HEHL•SIHNG•kee] Capital of Finland. 60°N 24°E (p. RA19)

Himalaya [HI•muh•LAY•uh] Mountain ranges in southern Asia, bordering the Indian subcontinent on the north. (p. RA28)

Honduras [hahn•DUR•uhs] Central American country on the Caribbean Sea. (p. RA14)

Hong Kong Port and industrial center in southern China. 22°N 115°E (p. RA27)

Huang He [HWAHNG HUH] River in northern and eastern China, also known as the Yellow River. (p. RA29)

Hungary [HUHNG•guh•ree] Eastern European country south of Slovakia. (p. RA18)

Iberian [eye•BIHR•ee•uhn] **Peninsula** Peninsula in southwest Europe, occupied by Spain and Portugal. (p. RA20)

Iceland Island country between the North Atlantic and Arctic Oceans. (p. RA18)

India [IHN•dee•uh] South Asian country south of China and Nepal. (p. RA26)

Indonesia [IHN•duh•NEE•zhuh] Southeast Asian island country known as the Republic of Indonesia. (p. RA27)

Indus [IHN•duhs] **River** River in Asia that begins in Tibet and flows through Pakistan to the Arabian Sea. (p. RA28)

Iran [ih•RAN] Southwest Asian country that was formerly named Persia. (p. RA25)

Iraq [ih•RAHK] Southwest Asian country west of Iran. (p. RA25)

Ireland [EYER•luhnd] Island west of Great Britain occupied by the Republic of Ireland and Northern Ireland. (p. RA18)

Islamabad [ihs•LAH•muh•BAHD] Capital of Pakistan. 34°N 73°E (p. RA26)

Israel [IHZ•ree•uhl] Southwest Asian country south of Lebanon. (p. RA24)

Italy [IHT•uhl•ee] Southern European country south of Switzerland and east of France. (p. RA18)

Jakarta [juh•KAHR•tuh] Capital of Indonesia. 6°S 107°E (p. RA27)

Jamaica [juh•MAY•kuh] Island country in the Caribbean Sea. (p. RA15)

Japan [juh•PAN] East Asian country consisting of the four large islands of Hokkaido, Honshu, Shikoku, and Kyushu, plus thousands of small islands. (p. RA27)

Jerusalem [juh•ROO•suh•luhm] Capital of Israel and a holy city for Christians, Jews, and Muslims. 32°N 35°E (p. RA24)

Jordan [JAWRD•uhn] Southwest Asian country south of Syria. (p. RA24)

Kabul [KAH•buhl] Capital of Afghanistan. 35°N 69°E (p. RA25)

Kampala [kahm•PAH•lah] Capital of Uganda. 0° latitude 32°E (p. RA22)

Kathmandu [KAT•MAN•DOO] Capital of Nepal. 28°N 85°E (p. RA26)

Kazakhstan [kuh•ZAHK•STAHN] Large Asian country south of Russia and bordering the Caspian Sea. (p. RA26)

Kenya [KEHN•yuh] East African country south of Ethiopia. (p. RA22)

Khartoum [kahr•TOOM] Capital of Sudan. 16°N 33°E (p. RA22)

Kigali [kee•GAH•lee] Capital of Rwanda. 2°S 30°E (p. RA22)

Kingston [KIHNG•stuhn] Capital of Jamaica. 18°N 77°W (p. RA15)

Kinshasa [kihn•SHAH•suh] Capital of the Democratic Republic of the Congo. 4°S 15°E (p. RA22)

Kuala Lumpur [KWAH•luh LUM•PUR] Capital of Malaysia. 3°N 102°E (p. RA27)

Kuwait [ku•WAYT] Country on the Persian Gulf between Saudi Arabia and Iraq. (p. RA25)

Kyiv [KEE•ihf] Capital of Ukraine. 50°N 31°E (p. RA19)

Kyrgyzstan [KIHR•gih•STAN] Central Asian country on China's western border. (p. RA26)

Laos [LOWS] Southeast Asian country south of China and west of Vietnam. (p. RA27)

La Paz [lah PAHS] Administrative capital of Bolivia, and the highest capital in the world. 17°S 68°W (p. RA16)

Latvia [LAT•vee•uh] Eastern European country west of Russia on the Baltic Sea. (p. RA19)

Lebanon [LEH•buh•nuhn] Country south of Syria on the Mediterranean Sea. (p. RA24)

Lesotho [luh•SOH•TOH] Southern African country within the borders of the Republic of South Africa. (p. RA22)

Liberia [ly•BIHR•ee•uh] West African country south of Guinea. (p. RA22)

Libreville [LEE•bruh•VIHL] Capital of Gabon. 1°N 9°E (p. RA22)

Libya [LIH•bee•uh] North African country west of Egypt on the Mediterranean Sea. (p. RA22)

Liechtenstein [LIHKT•uhn•SHTYN] Small country in central Europe between Switzerland and Austria. 47°N 10°E (p. RA18)

Lilongwe [lih•LAWNG•GWAY] Capital of Malawi. 14°S 34°E (p. RA22)

Lima [LEE•mah] Capital of Peru. 12°S 77°W (p. RA16)

Lisbon [LIHZ•buhn] Capital of Portugal. 39°N 9°W (p. RA18)

Lithuania [LIH•thuh•WAY•nee•uh] Eastern European country northwest of Belarus on the Baltic Sea. (p. RA21)

Ljubljana [lee•oo•blee•AH•nuh] Capital of Slovenia. 46°N 14°E (p. RA18)

Lomé [loh•MAY] Capital of Togo. 6°N 1°E (p. RA22)

London Capital of the United Kingdom, on the Thames River. 52°N 0° longitude (p. RA18)

Luanda [lu•AHN•duh] Capital of Angola. 9°S 13°E (p. RA22)

Lusaka [loo•SAH•kah] Capital of Zambia. 15°S 28°E (p. RA22)

Luxembourg [LUHK•suhm•BUHRG] Small European country bordered by France, Belgium, and Germany. 50°N 7°E (p. RA18)

Macao [muh•KOW] Port in southern China. 22°N 113°E (p. RA27)

Macedonia [MA•suh•DOH•nee•uh] Southeastern European country north of Greece. (p. RA19). Macedonia also refers to a geographic region covering northern Greece, the country Macedonia, and part of Bulgaria.

Madagascar [MA•duh•GAS•kuhr] Island in the Indian Ocean off the southeastern coast of Africa. (p. RA22)

Madrid Capital of Spain. 41°N 4°W (p. RA18)

Malabo [mah•LAH•boh] Capital of Equatorial Guinea. 4°N 9°E (p. RA22)

Malawi [mah•LAH•wee] Southern African country south of Tanzania and east of Zambia. (p. RA22)

Malaysia [muh•LAY•zhuh] Southeast Asian country with land on the Malay Peninsula and on the island of Borneo. (p. RA27)

Maldives [MAWL•DEEVZ] Island country southwest of India in the Indian Ocean. (p. RA26)

Mali [MAH•lee] West African country east of Mauritania. (p. RA22)

Managua [mah•NAH•gwah] Capital of Nicaragua. (p. RA15)

Manila [muh•NIH•luh] Capital of the Philippines. 15°N 121°E (p. RA27)

Maputo [mah•POO•toh] Capital of Mozambique. 26°S 33°E (p. RA22)

Maseru [MA•zuh•ROO] Capital of Lesotho. 29°S 27°E (p. RA22)

Masqat [MUHS•KAHT] Capital of Oman. 23°N 59°E (p. RA25)

Mauritania [MAWR•uh•TAY•nee•uh] West African country north of Senegal. (p. RA22)

Mauritius [maw•RIH•shuhs] Island country in the Indian Ocean east of Madagascar. 21°S 58°E (p. RA3)

Mbabane [uhm•bah•BAH•nay] Capital of Swaziland. 26°S 31°E (p. RA22)

Mediterranean [MEH•duh•tuh•RAY•nee•uhn] **Sea** Large inland sea surrounded by Europe, Asia, and Africa. (p. RA20)

Mekong [MAY•KAWNG] **River** River in southeastern Asia that begins in Tibet and empties into the South China Sea. (p. RA29)

Mexico [MEHK•sih•KOH] North American country south of the United States. (p. RA14)

Mexico City Capital of Mexico. 19°N 99°W (p. RA14)

Minsk [MIHNSK] Capital of Belarus. 54°N 28°E (p. RA19)

Mississippi [MIH•suh•SIH•pee] **River** Large river system in the central United States that flows southward into the Gulf of Mexico. (p. RA11)

Mogadishu [MOH•guh•DEE•SHOO] Capital of Somalia. 2°N 45°E (p. RA22)

Moldova [mawl•DAW•vuh] Small European country between Ukraine and Romania. (p. RA19)

Monaco [MAH•nuh•KOH] Small country in southern Europe on the French Mediterranean coast. 44°N 8°E (p. RA18)

Mongolia [mahn•GOHL•yuh] Country in Asia between Russia and China. (p. RA23)

Monrovia [muhn•ROH•vee•uh] Capital of Liberia. 6°N 11°W (p. RA22)

Monetenegro [MAHN•tuh•NEE•groh] Eastern European country. (p. RA18)

Montevideo [MAHN•tuh•vuh•DAY•OH] Capital of Uruguay. 35°S 56°W (p. RA16)

Morocco [muh•RAH•KOH] North African country on the Mediterranean Sea and the Atlantic Ocean. (p. RA22)

Moscow [MAHS•KOW] Capital of Russia. 56°N 38°E (p. RA19)

Mount Everest [EHV•ruhst] Highest mountain in the world, in the Himalaya between Nepal and Tibet. (p. RA28)

Mozambique [MOH•zahm•BEEK] Southern African country south of Tanzania. (p. RA22)

Myanmar [MYAHN•MAHR] Southeast Asian country south of China and India, formerly called Burma. (p. RA27)

Nairobi [ny•ROH•bee] Capital of Kenya. 1°S 37°E (p. RA22)

Namibia [nuh•MIH•bee•uh] Southern African country south of Angola on the Atlantic Ocean. 20°S 16°E (p. RA22)

Nassau [NA•SAW] Capital of the Bahamas. 25°N 77°W (p. RA15)

N'Djamena [uhn•jah•MAY•nah] Capital of Chad. 12°N 15°E (p. RA22)

Nepal [NAY•PAHL] Mountain country between India and China. (p. RA26)

Netherlands [NEH•thuhr•lundz] Western European country north of Belgium. (p. RA18)

New Delhi [NOO DEH•lee] Capital of India. 29°N 77°E (p. RA26)

New Zealand [NOO ZEE•luhnd] Major island country southeast of Australia in the South Pacific. (p. RA30)

Niamey [nee•AHM•ay] Capital of Niger. 14°N 2°E (p. RA22)

Nicaragua [NIH•kuh•RAH•gwuh] Central American country south of Honduras. (p. RA15)

Nicosia [NIH•kuh•SEE•uh] Capital of Cyprus. 35°N 33°E (p. RA19)

Niger [NY•juhr] West African country north of Nigeria. (p. RA22)

Nigeria [ny•JIHR•ee•uh] West African country along the Gulf of Guinea. (p. RA22)

Nile [NYL] **River** Longest river in the world, flowing north through eastern Africa. (p. RA23)

North Korea [kuh•REE•uh] East Asian country in the northernmost part of the Korean Peninsula. (p. RA27)

Norway [NAWR•way] Northern European country on the Scandinavian peninsula. (p. RA18)

Nouakchott [nu•AHK•SHAHT] Capital of Mauritania. 18°N 16°W (p. RA22)

Oman [oh•MAHN] Country on the Arabian Sea and the Gulf of Oman. (p. RA25)

Oslo [AHZ•loh] Capital of Norway. 60°N 11°E (p. RA18)

Ottawa [AH•tuh•wuh] Capital of Canada. 45°N 76°W (p. RA13)

Ouagadougou [WAH•gah•DOO•goo] Capital of Burkina Faso. 12°N 2°W (p. RA22)

Pakistan [PA•kih•STAN] South Asian country northwest of India on the Arabian Sea. (p. RA26)

Palau [puh•LOW) Island country in the Pacific Ocean. 7°N 135°E (p. RA30)

Panama [PA•nuh•MAH] Central American country on the Isthmus of Panama. (p. RA15)

Panama Capital of Panama. 9°N 79°W (p. RA15)

Papua New Guinea [PA•pyu•wuh NOO GIH•nee] Island country in the Pacific Ocean north of Australia. 7°S 142°E (p. RA30)

Paraguay [PAR•uh•GWY] South American country northeast of Argentina. (p. RA16)

Paramaribo [PAH•rah•MAH•ree•boh] Capital of Suriname. 6°N 55°W (p. RA16)

Paris Capital of France. 49°N 2°E (p. RA18)

Persian [PUHR•zhuhn] **Gulf** Arm of the Arabian Sea between Iran and Saudi Arabia. (p. RA25)

Peru [puh•ROO] South American country south of Ecuador and Colombia. (p. RA16)

Philippines [FIH•luh•PEENZ] Island country in the Pacific Ocean southeast of China. (p. RA27)

Phnom Penh [puh•NAWM PEHN] Capital of Cambodia. 12°N 106°E (p. RA27)

Poland [POH•luhnd] Eastern European country on the Baltic Sea. (p. RA18)

Port-au-Prince [POHRT•oh•PRIHNS] Capital of Haiti. 19°N 72°W (p. RA15)

Port Moresby [MOHRZ•bee] Capital of Papua New Guinea. 10°S 147°E (p. RA30)

Port-of-Spain [SPAYN] Capital of Trinidad and Tobago. 11°N 62°W (p. RA15)

Porto-Novo [POHR•toh•NOH•voh] Capital of Benin. 7°N 3°E (p. RA22)

Portugal [POHR•chih•guhl] Country west of Spain on the Iberian Peninsula. (p. RA18)

Prague [PRAHG] Capital of the Czech Republic. 51°N 15°E (p. RA18)

Puerto Rico [PWEHR•toh REE•koh] Island in the Caribbean Sea; U.S. Commonwealth. (p. RA15)

P'yŏngyang [pee•AWNG•YAHNG] Capital of North Korea. 39°N 126°E (p. RA27)

Qatar [KAH•tuhr] Country on the southwestern shore of the Persian Gulf. (p. RA25)

Quito [KEE•toh] Capital of Ecuador. 0° latitude 79°W (p. RA16)

Rabat [ruh•BAHT] Capital of Morocco. 34°N 7°W (p. RA22)

Reykjavík [RAY•kyah•VEEK] Capital of Iceland. 64°N 22°W (p. RA18)

Rhine [RYN] **River** River in western Europe that flows into the North Sea. (p. RA20)

Riga [REE•guh] Capital of Latvia. 57°N 24°E (p. RA19)

Rio Grande [REE•oh GRAND] River that forms part of the boundary between the United States and Mexico. (p. RA10)

Riyadh [ree•YAHD] Capital of Saudi Arabia. 25°N 47°E (p. RA25)

Rocky Mountains Mountain system in western North America. (p. RA7)

Romania [ru•MAY•nee•uh] Eastern European country east of Hungary. (p. RA19)

Rome Capital of Italy. 42°N 13°E (p. RA18)

Russia [RUH•shuh] Largest country in the world, covering parts of Europe and Asia. (pp. RA19, RA27)

Rwanda [ruh•WAHN•duh] East African country south of Uganda. 2°S 30°E (p. RA22)

Sahara [suh•HAR•uh] Desert region in northern Africa that is the largest hot desert in the world. (p. RA23)

Saint Lawrence [LAWR•uhns] **River** River that flows from Lake Ontario to the Atlantic Ocean and forms part of the boundary between the United States and Canada. (p. RA13)

Sanaa [sahn•AH] Capital of Yemen. 15°N 44°E (p. RA25)

San José [SAN hoh•ZAY] Capital of Costa Rica. 10°N 84°W (p. RA15)

San Marino [SAN muh•REE•noh] Small European country located on the Italian Peninsula. 44°N 13°E (p. RA18)

San Salvador [SAN SAL•vuh•DAWR] Capital of El Salvador. 14°N 89°W (p. RA14)

Santiago [SAN•tee•AH•goh] Capital of Chile. 33°S 71°W (p. RA16)

Santo Domingo [SAN•toh duh•MIHNG•goh] Capital of the Dominican Republic. 19°N 70°W (p. RA15)

São Tomé and Príncipe [sow too•MAY PREEN•see•pee] Small island country in the Gulf of Guinea off the coast of central Africa. 1°N 7°E (p. RA22)

Sarajevo [SAR•uh•YAY•voh] Capital of Bosnia and Herzegovina. 43°N 18°E (p. RA18)

Saudi Arabia [SOW•dee uh•RAY•bee•uh] Country on the Arabian Peninsula. (p. RA25)

Senegal [SEH•nih•GAWL] West African country on the Atlantic coast. (p. RA22)

Seoul [SOHL] Capital of South Korea. 38°N 127°E (p. RA27)

Serbia [SUHR•bee•uh] Eastern European country south of Hungary. (p. RA18)

Seychelles [say•SHEHL] Small island country in the Indian Ocean off eastern Africa. 6°S 56°E (p. RA22)

Sierra Leone [see•EHR•uh lee•OHN] West African country south of Guinea. (p. RA22)

Singapore [SIHNG•uh•POHR] Southeast Asian island country near tip of the Malay Peninsula. (p. RA27)

Skopje [SKAW•PYAY] Capital of the country of Macedonia. 42°N 21°E (p. RA19)

Slovakia [sloh•VAH•kee•uh] Eastern European country south of Poland. (p. RA18)

Slovenia [sloh•VEE•nee•uh] Southeastern European country south of Austria on the Adriatic Sea. (p. RA18)

Sofia [SOH•fee•uh] Capital of Bulgaria. 43°N 23°E (p. RA19)

Solomon [SAH•luh•muhn] **Islands** Island country in the Pacific Ocean northeast of Australia. (p. RA30)

Somalia [soh•MAH•lee•uh] East African country on the Gulf of Aden and the Indian Ocean. (p. RA22)

South Africa [A•frih•kuh] Country at the southern tip of Africa, officially the Republic of South Africa. (p. RA22)

South Korea [kuh•REE•uh] East Asian country on the Korean Peninsula between the Yellow Sea and the Sea of Japan. (p. RA27)

Spain [SPAYN] Southern European country on the Iberian Peninsula. (p. RA18)

Sri Lanka [SREE LAHNG•kuh] Country in the Indian Ocean south of India, formerly called Ceylon. (p. RA26)

Stockholm [STAHK•HOHLM] Capital of Sweden. 59°N 18°E (p. RA18)

Sucre [SOO•kray] Constitutional capital of Bolivia. 19°S 65°W (p. RA16)

Sudan [soo•DAN] East African country south of Egypt. (p. RA22)

Suriname [SUR•uh•NAH•muh] South American country between Guyana and French Guiana. (p. RA16)

Suva [SOO•vah] Capital of the Fiji Islands. 18°S 177°E (p. RA30)

Swaziland [SWAH•zee•land] Southern African country west of Mozambique, almost entirely within the Republic of South Africa. (p. RA22)

Sweden Northern European country on the eastern side of the Scandinavian peninsula. (p. RA18)

Switzerland [SWIHT•suhr•luhnd] European country in the Alps south of Germany. (p. RA18)

Syria [SIHR•ee•uh] Southwest Asian country on the east side of the Mediterranean Sea. (p. RA24)

Taipei [TY•PAY] Capital of Taiwan. 25°N 122°E (p. RA27)

Taiwan [TY•WAHN] Island country off the southeast coast of China; the seat of the Chinese Nationalist government. (p. RA27)

Tajikistan [tah•JIH•kih•STAN] Central Asian country east of Turkmenistan. (p. RA26)

Tallinn [TA•luhn] Capital of Estonia. 59°N 25°E (p. RA19)

Tanzania [TAN•zuh•NEE•uh] East African country south of Kenya. (p. RA22)

Tashkent [tash•KEHNT] Capital of Uzbekistan. 41°N 69°E (p. RA26)

Tbilisi [tuh•bih•LEE•see] Capital of the Republic of Georgia. 42°N 45°E (p. RA26)

Tegucigalpa [tay•GOO•see•GAHL•pah] Capital of Honduras. 14°N 87°W (p. RA14)

Tehran [TAY•uh•RAN] Capital of Iran. 36°N 52°E (p. RA25)

Thailand [TY•LAND] Southeast Asian country east of Myanmar. 17°N 101°E (p. RA27)

Thimphu [thihm•POO] Capital of Bhutan. 28°N 90°E (p. RA27)

Tigris [TY•gruhs] **River** River in southeastern Turkey and Iraq that merges with the Euphrates River. (p. RA25)

Tiranë [tih•RAH•nuh] Capital of Albania. 42°N 20°E (p. RA18)

Togo [TOH•goh] West African country between Benin and Ghana on the Gulf of Guinea. (p. RA22)

Tokyo [TOH•kee•OH] Capital of Japan. 36°N 140°E (p. RA27)

Trinidad and Tobago [TRIH•nuh•DAD tuh•BAY•goh] Island country near Venezuela between the Atlantic Ocean and the Caribbean Sea. (p. RA15)

Tripoli [TRIH•puh•lee] Capital of Libya. 33°N 13°E (p. RA22)

Tshwane [ch•WAH•nay] Executive capital of South Africa. 26°S 28°E (p. RA22)

Tunis [TOO•nuhs] Capital of Tunisia. 37°N 10°E (p. RA22)

Tunisia [too•NEE•zhuh] North African country on the Mediterranean Sea between Libya and Algeria. (p. RA22)

Turkey [TUHR•kee] Country in southeastern Europe and western Asia. (p. RA24)

Turkmenistan [tuhrk•MEH•nuh•STAN] Central Asian country on the Caspian Sea. (p. RA25)

Uganda [yoo•GAHN•dah] East African country south of Sudan. (p. RA22)

Ukraine [yoo•KRAYN] Eastern European country west of Russia on the Black Sea. (p. RA25)

Ulaanbaatar [oo•LAHN•BAH•TAWR] Capital of Mongolia. 48°N 107°E (p. RA27)

United Arab Emirates [EH•muh•ruhts] Country made up of seven states on the eastern side of the Arabian Peninsula. (p. RA25)

United Kingdom Western European island country made up of England, Scotland, Wales, and Northern Ireland. (p. RA18)

United States of America Country in North America made up of 50 states, mostly between Canada and Mexico. (p. RA8)

Uruguay [YUR•uh•GWAY] South American country south of Brazil on the Atlantic Ocean. (p. RA16)

Uzbekistan [UZ•BEH•kih•STAN] Central Asian country south of Kazakhstan. (p. RA25)

Vanuatu [VAN•WAH•TOO] Country made up of islands in the Pacific Ocean east of Australia. (p. RA30)

Vatican [VA•tih•kuhn] **City** Headquarters of the Roman Catholic Church, located in the city of Rome in Italy. 42°N 13°E (p. RA18)

Venezuela [VEH•nuh•ZWAY•luh] South American country on the Caribbean Sea between Colombia and Guyana. (p. RA16)

Vienna [vee•EH•nuh] Capital of Austria. 48°N 16°E (p. RA18)

Vientiane [vyehn•TYAHN] Capital of Laos. 18°N 103°E (p. RA27)

Vietnam [vee•EHT•NAHM] Southeast Asian country east of Laos and Cambodia. (p. RA27)

Vilnius [VIL•nee•uhs] Capital of Lithuania. 55°N 25°E (p. RA19)

Warsaw Capital of Poland. 52°N 21°E (p. RA19)

Washington, D.C. Capital of the United States, in the District of Columbia. 39°N 77°W (p. RA8)

Wellington [WEH•lihng•tuhn] Capital of New Zealand. 41°S 175°E (p. RA30)

West Indies Caribbean islands between North America and South America. (p. RA15)

Windhoek [VIHNT•HUK] Capital of Namibia. 22°S 17°E (p. RA22)

Yamoussoukro [YAH•moo•SOO•kroh] Second capital of Côte d'Ivoire. 7°N 6°W (p. RA22)

Yangon [YAHNG•GOHN] City in Myanmar; formerly called Rangoon. 17°N 96°E (p. RA27)

Yaoundé [yown•DAY] Capital of Cameroon. 4°N 12°E (p. RA22)

Yemen [YEH•muhn] Country south of Saudi Arabia on the Arabian Peninsula. (p. RA25)

Yerevan [YEHR•uh•VAHN] Capital of Armenia. 40°N 44°E (p. RA25)

Zagreb [ZAH•GREHB] Capital of Croatia. 46°N 16°E (p. RA18)

Zambia [ZAM•bee•uh] Southern African country north of Zimbabwe. (p. RA22)

Zimbabwe [zihm•BAH•bway] Southern African country northeast of Botswana. (p. RA22)

Glossary/Glosario

- Content vocabulary are words that relate to geography content. They are **boldfaced** and highlighted yellow in your text.
- Words below that have an asterisk (*) are academic vocabulary. They help you understand your school subjects and are **boldfaced** in your text.

English

Español

absolute location exact spot where a place is found (p. 15)

*access a way or means of approach (p. 275)

*accumulate to increase in amount (p. 48)

acid rain chemicals from air pollution that combine with precipitation (pp. 64, 171)

*adapt change (p. 125)

*affect to influence, or produce an effect upon (p. 275)

*alter to change (p. 57)

altitude height above sea level (p. 201)

amendment an addition to a legal document or law (p. 141)

annex declare ownership of an area (p. 136)

aquifer underground layer of rock through which water flows (p. 52)

archipelago group of islands (p. 193)

*assemble put together (p. 235)

atmosphere layer of oxygen and other gases that surrounds Earth (p. 36)

*attitudes a particular feeling or way of thinking about something (p. 310)

*authority power or influence over others (p. 300)

autonomy having independence from another country (pp. 339, 399)

*availability state of being easy or possible to get or use (p. 52)

axis imaginary line that passes through the center of Earth from the North Pole to the South Pole (p. 36)

ubicación absoluta punto exacto donde se encuentra un lugar (pág. 15)

*acceso manera o medio de acercamiento (pág. 275)

*acumular aumentar en cantidad (pág. 48)

lluvia ácida sustancias químicas producto de la contaminación ambiental que se mezclan con las precipitaciones (págs. 64, 171)

*adaptar cambiar (pág. 125)

*afectar influir o producir un efecto en algo o alguien (pág. 275)

*alterar cambiar (pág. 57)

altitud altura sobre el nivel del mar (pág. 201)

enmienda adición a un documento legal o ley (pág. 141)

anexar declarar posesión de un área (pág. 136)

acuífero capa de roca subterránea a través de la que fluye agua (pág. 52)

archipiélago groupo de islas (pág. 193)

*reunir juntar (pág. 235)

atmósfera capa de oxígeno y otros gases que rodean la Tierra (pág. 36)

*actitudes sentimientos o maneras de pensar particulares respecto de algo (pág. 310)

*autoridad poder o influencia sobre los demás (pág. 300)

autonomía ser independiente de otro país (págs. 339, 399)

*disponibilidad fácil o posible de obtener o usar (pág. 52)

eje línea imaginaria que atraviesa el centro de la Tierra desde el Polo Norte al Polo Sur (pág. 36)

ban legally block (p. 145)

prohibir impedir legalmente (pág. 145)

Glossary/Glosario

*benefit something that does good to a person or thing (pp. 373)

bilingual accepting two official languages; able to speak two languages (pp. 149, 332)

biodiversity variety of plants and animals living on the planet (p. 66)

biome area that includes particular kinds of plants and animals adapted to conditions there (p. 60)

biotechnology study of cells to find ways of improving health (p. 159)

birthrate number of children born each year for every 1,000 people (p. 73)

blizzard severe winter storm that lasts several hours and combines high winds with heavy snow (p. 128)

bog low swampy area (p. 325)

*bonds a uniting or binding force or influence (p. 307)

brownfield sites that have been abandoned and may contain dangerous chemicals (p. 172)

*beneficio bien que se hace a una persona o cosa (pág. 373)

bilingüe que acepta dos idiomas oficiales, que puede hablar dos idiomas (págs. 149, 332)

biodiversidad variedad de plantas y animales que viven en el planeta (pág. 66)

bioma área que incluye clases particulares de plantas y animales adaptadas a las condiciones del área (pág. 60)

biotecnología estudio de las células para descubrir maneras de mejorar la salud (pág. 159)

índice de natalidad cantidad de niños nacidos por año cada 1,000 personas (pág. 73)

ventisca tormenta de invierno intensa que dura varias horas y combina vientos y nevadas fuertes (pág. 128)

ciénaga zona pantanosa y baja (pág. 325)

*lazos fuerza influyente que une o vincula (pág. 307)

zona industrial abandonada sitios abandonados que pueden contener sustancias químicas peligrosas (pág. 172)

canopy umbrella-like covering formed by the tops of trees in a rain forest (p. 200)

canyon deep valleys with steep sides (p. 119)

carnival large festival held each spring in countries in Latin America on the last day before the Christian holy period called Lent (p. 224)

cash crop farm product grown for export (p. 211)

caudillo Latin American ruler, often a military officer or wealthy individual ruling as a dictator (p. 213)

century a period of 100 years (p. 16)

city-state independent political unit that includes a city and the surrounding area (p. 295)

civilization highly developed culture (p. 86)

classical referring to the civilizations of ancient Greece and Rome (p. 295)

climate pattern of weather that takes place in an area over many years (p. 56)

climate zone areas that have similar patterns of temperature and rainfall, and may have similar vegetation (p. 59)

bóveda de follaje cubierta en forma de sombrilla, formada por las copas de los árboles en una selva tropical (pág. 200)

cañón valles profundos con laterales de pendientes agudas (pág. 119)

carnaval gran festival que se realiza cada primavera en países de América Latina el día antes del período sagrado cristiano llamado Cuaresma (pág. 224)

cultivo comercial producto agrícola cultivado para la exportación (pág. 211)

caudillo gobernante latinoamericano, a menudo un oficial militar o un hombre rico que gobierna como dictador (pág. 213)

siglo período de cien años (pág. 16)

ciudad-estado unidad política independiente que incluye una ciudad y el área circundante (pág. 295)

civilización cultura con un alto desarrollo (pág. 86)

clásico referente a las civilizaciones de la Grecia y Roma antiguas (pág. 295)

clima conjunto de condiciones atmosféricas que ocurren en una zona durante muchos años (pág. 56)

zona climática áreas que tienen patrones similares de temperatura y precipitaciones, y pueden tener vegetación similar (pág. 59)

Glossary/Glosario

Cold War period from about 1947 until 1991 when the United States and the Soviet Union engaged in a political struggle for world influence but did not fight each other (p. 393)

collection part of the water cycle; process by which streams and rivers carry water that has fallen to the earth back to the oceans (p. 54)

collectivization a system in which small farms were combined into huge state-run enterprises with work done by mechanized techniques in the hopes of making farming more efficient and reducing the need for farmworkers (p. 392)

colony overseas settlement tied to a parent country (p. 136)

command economy economic system in which the government decides how resources are used and what goods and services are produced (pp. 240, 349)

*comment talk about (p. 224)

commonwealth self-governing territory (p. 240)

communism system of government in which the government controls the ways of producing goods (p. 303)

communist state country whose government has strong control over the economy and society as a whole (pp. 215, 391)

community neighborhood (p. 172)

*complex highly developed (p. 210)

*comprise to be made up of (p. 409)

condensation part of the water cycle; process by which water changes from gas to liquid (p. 54)

*conduct carry out (p. 421)

coniferous referring to evergreen trees that have their seeds in cones (p. 285)

conservation careful use of resources to avoid wasting them (p. 66)

*considerable much (p. 200)

*constant happening a lot or all the time (p. 47)

constitutional monarchy form of government in which a monarch is the head of state but elected officials run the government (p. 322)

*constrain limit (p. 117)

contiguous joined together inside a common boundary (p. 117)

continent large landmass that rises above an ocean (p. 45)

Guerra Fría período desde 1947 hasta 1991, cuando los Estados Unidos y la Unión Soviética se involucraron en una lucha política para influir en el mundo pero sin combatir entre sí (pág. 393)

escurrimiento parte del ciclo del agua; proceso en el que los ríos y arroyos llevan el agua que cayó a la tierra, de regreso a los océanos (pág. 54)

colectivización sistema en el que pequeñas granjas se combinaron en grandes emprendimientos controlados por el estado; el trabajo se realizaba con técnicas mecanizadas con la esperanza de que la agricultura fuera más eficiente y que disminuyera la necesidad de empleados (pág. 392)

colonia asentamiento en el extranjero unido a un país madre (pág. 136)

economía de mando sistema económico en el que el gobierno decide cómo se usan los recursos y qué bienes y servicios se producen (págs. 240, 349)

*comentar hablar sobre algo (pág. 224)

mancomunidad territorio que se autogobierna (pág. 240)

comunismo sistema de gobierno en el que el estado controla los modos de producción de los bienes (pág. 303)

estado comunista país cuyo gobierno tiene un fuerte control de la economía y la sociedad como un todo (págs. 215, 391)

comunidad vecindario (pág. 172)

*complejo altamente desarrollado (pág. 210)

*componer estar compuesto de (pág. 409)

condensación parte del ciclo del agua; proceso en el que el agua cambia de la forma gaseosa a la forma líquida (pág. 54)

*conducir llevar a cabo (pág. 421)

coníferas referente a árboles perennes que guardan sus semillas en conos (pág. 285)

conservación uso cuidadoso de los recursos para evitar su derroche (pág. 66)

*considerable mucho (pág. 200)

*constante que sucede la mayor parte del o todo el tiempo (pág. 47)

monarquía constitucional forma de gobierno en la que un monarca es la cabeza del estado pero en el que funcionarios electos controlan el gobierno (pág. 322)

*obligar limitar (pág. 117)

contiguo unidos juntos dentro de una misma frontera (pág. 117)

continente gran masa continental que se alza por encima de un océano (pág. 45)

Glossary/Glosario

continental shelf plateau off of a continent that lies under the ocean and stretches for several miles (p. 50)

*convert change from one to another (p. 389)

cordillera region of parallel mountain chains (p. 118)

core area at the center of the Earth, which includes a solid inner core and a hot liquid outer core (p. 45)

*core basic or fundamental (p. 141)

coup action in which a group of individuals seizes control of a government (p. 394)

crop rotation changing what crops farmers plant in a field from year to year (p. 65)

crust uppermost layer of the Earth (p. 45)

cultural diffusion process of spreading ideas, languages, and customs from one culture to another (p. 87)

culture way of life of a group of people who share similar beliefs and customs (p. 83)

culture region area that includes different countries that share similar cultural traits (p. 88)

*currency money (p. 303)

current steadily flowing stream of water in the ocean (p. 57)

czar title given to the emperors of Russia's past (p. 390)

plataforma continental meseta saliente de un continente que se encuentra bajo el océano y se extiende por varias millas (pág. 50)

*convertir cambiar de una cosa a otra (pág. 389)

cordillera región de cadenas montañosas paralelas (pág. 118)

núcleo área del centro de la Tierra que incluye un núcleo interno sólido y un núcleo externo de líquido caliente (pág. 45)

*esencial básico o fundamental (pág. 141)

golpe acción en que un grupo de individuos toma el control de un gobierno (pág. 394)

rotación de cultivos cambio en los cultivos que los agricultores plantan en un campo entre un año y el siguiente (pág. 65)

corteza capa superior de la Tierra (pág. 45)

difusión cultural proceso de divulgación de ideas, idiomas y costumbres de una cultura a otra (pág. 87)

cultura estilo de vida de un grupo de personas que comparten creencias y costumbres similares (pág. 83)

región cultural zona que incluye diferentes países que comparten características culturales similares (pág. 88)

*moneda dinero (pág. 303)

corriente curso de agua que fluye constantemente en el océano (pág. 57)

zar título que recibían los emperadores de Rusia en el pasado (pág. 390)

D

death rate number of deaths per year out of every 1,000 people (p. 73)

decade a period of 10 years (p. 16)

deciduous trees that lose their leaves in the fall (p. 285)

*decline a change to a lower state or level (p. 382)

decree order issued by a leader that has the force of law (p. 419)

default failure to make debt payments that are due to a lender (p. 250)

*define to describe or establish (p. 50)

deforestation cutting down of forests without replanting new trees (p. 65)

democracy form of limited government in which power rests with the people, and all citizens share in running the government (pp. 85, 295)

índice de mortalidad número de muertes por año cada 1,000 personas (pág. 73)

década período de diez años (pág. 16)

caducifolios árboles que pierden sus hojas en otoño (pág. 285)

*descenso cambio a un nivel o estado inferior (pág. 382)

decreto orden emitida por un líder que tiene el poder de ley (pág. 419)

incumplimiento imposibilidad de realizar los pagos de deuda que se deben a un prestamista (pág. 250)

*definir describir o establecer (pág. 50)

deforestación destrucción de bosques sin plantar nuevos árboles (pág. 65)

democracia forma de gobierno limitado en el que el poder reside en la gente, y en el que todos los ciudadanos comparten la gestión del gobierno (págs. 85, 295)

Glossary/Glosario

deposit insurance government plan that promises to repay people who deposit their money in a bank if the bank should go out of business (p. 421)

developed country country with an economy that has a mix of agriculture, a great deal of manufacturing, and service industries and that is very productive and provides its people with a high standard of living (p. 94)

developing country country that has limited industry, where agriculture remains important, incomes are generally low (p. 94)

dialect local form of a language that may have a distinct vocabulary and pronunciation (p. 84)

dictatorship form of government in which a leader rules by force and typically limits citizens' freedoms (p. 86)

***differentiate** to make or become different in some way (p. 321)

***distribute** to spread out (p. 56)

***diverse** varied (p. 125)

divide the high point in a landmass that determines the direction rivers flow (p. 120)

***document** an important paper (p. 322)

***dominant** having controlling influence over others (p. 296)

dominion self-governing country in the British Empire (p. 139)

drought long period of time without rainfall (p. 126)

dry farming agriculture that conserves water and uses crops and growing methods suited to semiarid environments (p. 339)

seguros de depósito plan del gobierno que promete devolver el dinero a la gente que lo deposita en un banco si éste cierra sus puertas (pág. 421)

país desarrollado país con una economía que combina agricultura, manufacturas e industrias de servicio; es muy productivo y proporciona a sus habitantes un nivel de vida alto (pág. 94)

país en vías de desarrollo país que posee una industria limitada, en el que la agricultura sigue siendo importante y los ingresos son, en general, bajos (pág. 94)

dialecto forma local de un idioma que puede tener un vocabulario y una pronunciación diferentes (pág. 84)

dictadura forma de gobierno en el que un líder gobierna por la fuerza y, por lo general, limita las libertades de los ciudadanos (pág. 86)

***distinguir, diferenciar** hacer o volver diferente de algún modo (pág. 321)

***distribuir** dispersar (pág. 56)

***diverso** variado (pág. 125)

divisoria de aguas punto alto de una masa continental que determina la dirección en la que fluye un río (pág. 120)

***documento** papel importante (pág. 322)

***dominante** que posee influencia controladora sobre los demás (pág. 296)

dominio país con gobierno propio en el Imperio Británico (pág. 139)

sequía período de tiempo largo sin lluvia (pág. 126)

agricultura de secano agricultura que conserva el agua y usa cultivos y métodos de crecimiento apropiados para medios semiáridos (pág. 339)

E

earthquake sudden and violent movement of the Earth's crust that shakes the land, and can cause great damage (p. 47)

economic system system that sets rules for deciding what goods and services to produce, how to produce them, and who will receive them (p. 94)

***economy** way of producing goods (p. 136)

ecosystem place shared by plants and animals that depend on one another for survival (p. 66)

***element** part of something larger (p. 219)

***eliminate** to remove or get rid of (p. 392)

terremoto movimiento sorpresivo y violento de la corteza terrestre que sacude la tierra y puede ocasionar grandes daños (pág. 47)

sistema económico sistema que establece las reglas que deciden qué bienes y servicios se producen, cómo producirlos y quién los recibirá (pág. 94)

***economía** modo de producción de bienes (pág. 136)

ecosistema lugar compartido por plantas y animales que dependen unos de otros para sobrevivir (pág. 66)

***elemento** parte de algo más grande (pág. 219)

***eliminar** quitar o deshacerse de (pág. 392)

Glossary/Glosario

El Niño weather phenomenon marked by very heavy rains in western South America, often causing flooding; reduced rainfall in Southern Asia, Australia, and Africa; and severe storms in North America; opposite of **La Niña** (p. 58)

emigrate to leave a country and move to another (p. 75)

emperor all-powerful ruler (p. 297)

empire collection of different territories united under the rule of one government (p. 210)

environment natural surroundings of people (p. 15)

equinox either of the days in spring and fall in which the noon sun is overhead at the Equator and day and night are of equal length in both the Northern and Southern Hemispheres (p. 38)

erosion process by which weathered bits of rock are moved elsewhere by water, wind, or ice (p. 48)

escarpment steep cliff at the edge of a plateau with a lowland area below (p. 194)

estuary an area where river currents and ocean tide meet (p. 194)

ethnic cleansing forcing people from one ethnic or religious group to leave an area so that it can be used by another group (p. 356)

ethnic group people with a common language, history, religion, and some physical traits (pp. 84, 307)

evaporation part of the water cycle; process by which water changes from liquid to gas (p. 53)

*evolve develop (p. 147)

*exploit use (p. 400)

export to sell goods or resources to other countries (p. 95)

El Niño fenómeno meteorológico caracterizado por lluvias muy fuertes en la parte occidental de América del Sur, que suelen provocar inundaciones; lluvias reducidas en el sur de Asia, Australia y África, y grandes tormentas en América del Norte; opuesto de **La Niña** (pág. 58)

emigrar dejar un país y mudarse a otro (pág. 75)

emperador gobernante todopoderoso (pág. 297)

imperio conjunto de diferentes territorios unidos bajo el control de un gobierno (pág. 210)

medio ambiente entorno natural de las personas (pág. 15)

equinoccio cualquier de los días en primavera y otoño cuando el sol del mediodía está sobre el Ecuador y el día y la noche tienen igual duración en los hemisferios Sur y Norte (pág. 38)

erosión proceso por el que trozos de roca expuestos a la intemperie se mueven a otros sitios con el agua, el viento o el hielo (pág. 48)

escarpadura acantilado en gran pendiente en el borde de una meseta con una área de tierra baja debajo (pág. 194)

estuario área donde las corrientes del río y la marea del océano se encuentran (pág. 194)

limpieza étnica forzar a la gente de un grupo étnico o religioso a abandonar un área para que la use otro grupo (pág. 356)

grupo étnico personas con idioma, historia, religión y ciertas características físicas en común (págs. 84, 307)

evaporación parte del ciclo del agua; proceso en el que el agua cambia de la forma líquida a la forma gaseosa (pág. 53)

*evolucionar desarrollar (pág. 147)

*explotar usar (pág. 400)

exportar vender bienes o recursos a otros países (pág. 95)

*facilitate make possible (p. 199)

famine severe lack of food (p. 73)

fault crack in the Earth's crust where two tectonic plates meet; prone to earthquakes (p. 47)

favela an overcrowded city slum in Brazil (p. 247)

*feature a part or detail that stands out (p. 284)

federalism form of government in which power is divided between the federal, or national, government and the state governments (p. 140)

*facilitar hacer posible (pág. 199)

hambruna falta grave de alimentos (pág. 73)

falla fractura en la corteza terrestre donde se unen dos placas tectónicas, propensa a los terremotos (pág. 47)

favela barrio pobre y superpoblado de una ciudad en Brasil (pág. 247)

*característica parte o detalle que se destaca (pág. 284)

federalismo forma de gobierno en el que el poder está dividido entre el gobierno federal, o nacional, y los estados (pág. 140)

Glossary/Glosario

*fee payment (p. 239)

fertility rate average number of children born to each woman (p. 307)

feudalism political and social system in which kings gave land to nobles in exchange for the nobles' promise to serve them; those nobles provided military service as knights for the king (p. 298)

*finance provide funds or capital (p. 95)

*finite limited in supply (p. 93)

fjord narrow, U-shaped coastal valley with steep sides formed by the action of glaciers (p. 327)

fossil fuel oil, natural gas, or coal, which are an important part of the world's energy supply (p. 375)

free market type of economy in which people are free to buy, produce, and sell with limited government involvement (p. 159)

free trade removal of trade restrictions so that goods flow freely among countries (p. 96)

*cargo pagos (pág. 239)

tasa de fertilidad cantidad de niños nacidos de cada mujer (pág. 307)

feudalismo sistema político y social en el que los reyes entregaban tierras a los nobles a cambio de su promesa de servirlos; dichos nobles brindaban servicio militar como caballeros del rey (pág. 298)

*financiar proporcionar fondos o capital (pág. 95)

*finito limitado en el suministro (pág. 93)

fiordo valle costero angosto y en forma de U con laderas abruptas que se formó por la acción de los glaciares (pág. 327)

combustibles fósiles petróleo, gas natural o carbón, que son una parte importante del suministro de la energía del mundo (pág. 375)

mercado libre tipo de economía en el que las personas son libres para comprar, producir y vender con participación limitada del gobierno (pág. 159)

libre comercio eliminación de restricciones comerciales de modo que los bienes circulen libremente entre los países (pág. 96)

gaucho cowhand in Argentina (p. 249)

gasohol human-made fuel produced from mixing gasoline and alcohol made from sugarcane (p. 195)

*generate make (p. 147)

Geographic Information System (GIS) combination of computer hardware and software used to gather, store, and analyze geographic information and then display it on a screen (p. 17)

geography study of the Earth and its people (p. 15)

geothermal energy electricity produced by natural underground sources of steam (p. 327)

geyser spring of water heated by molten rock inside the Earth that, from time to time, shoots hot water into the air (p. 327)

glacier giant sheets of ice (p. 119)

glasnost policy of political openness in the Soviet Union that allowed people to speak freely about the country's problems (p. 393)

globalization development of a worldwide culture with an interdependent economy (p. 89)

gaucho vaqueros de Argentina (pág. 249)

gasohol combustible fabricado por el ser humano, producto de la mezcla de gasolina y alcohol hecho de caña de azúcar (pág. 195)

*generar hacer (pág. 147)

Sistema de Información Geográfica (GIS) combinación de hardware y software para obtener, almacenar y analizar información geográfica y luego exhibirla en una pantalla (pág. 17)

geografía estudio de la Tierra y sus habitantes (pág. 15)

energía geotérmica electricidad producida por fuentes de vapor subterráneas naturales (pág. 327)

géiser fuente de agua calentada por roca derretida dentro de la Tierra que de vez en cuando lanza agua caliente al aire (pág. 327)

glaciar capas gigantes de hielo (pág. 119)

glásnost plan de acción de apertura política en la Unión soviética, que permitió que las personas hablaran libremente sobre los problemas del país (pág. 393)

globalización desarrollo de una cultura amplia mundial con una economía interdependiente (pág. 89)

Glossary/Glosario

Global Positioning System (GPS) group of satellites that uses radio signals to determine the exact location of places on Earth (p. 17)

greenhouse effect buildup of certain gases in the Earth's atmosphere that, like a greenhouse, retain the sun's warmth (p. 64)

groundwater water that filters through the soil into the ground (p. 52)

*guarantee promise (p. 159)

Sistema de Posicionamiento Global (GPS) grupos de satélites que envían señales de radio que registran la ubicación exacta de cada lugar en la Tierra (pág. 17)

efecto invernadero acumulación de ciertos gases en la atmósfera de la Tierra que, al igual que un invernadero, retienen el calor del Sol (pág. 64)

agua subterránea agua que se filtra a través del suelo hacia las profundidades (pág. 52)

*garantizar prometer (pág. 159)

heavy industry manufacture of goods such as machinery, mining equipment, and steel (p. 411)

hieroglyphics system of writing that uses small pictures to represent sounds or words (p. 209)

high-technology industry areas of business that include making computers and other products with sophisticated engineering (p. 330)

Holocaust mass killing of 6 million European Jews by Germany's Nazi leaders during World War II (p. 302)

hurricane wind system that forms over the ocean in tropical areas and brings violent storms with heavy rains (p. 127)

industria pesada fabricación de bienes como maquinarias, equipo de minería y acero (pág. 411)

jeroglíficos sistema de escritura que usa pequeños dibujos para representar sonidos o palabras (pág. 209)

industria de alta tecnología áreas de negocios que incluyen la creación de computadoras y otros productos con ingeniería sofisticada (pág. 330)

Holocausto asesinato masivo de 6 millones de judíos europeos por parte de los líderes nazis de Alemania durante la Segunda Guerra Mundial (pág. 302)

huracán sistema de vientos que se forma sobre el océano en áreas tropicales y provoca tormentas violentas y fuertes lluvias (pág. 127)

*identical exactly the same (p. 38)

*impact effect (p. 279)

import to buy resources or goods from other countries (p. 95)

*income earned money (p. 350)

indigenous people descended from an area's first inhabitants (p. 149)

infrastructure system of roads and railroads that allows the transport of materials (pp. 375)

*inhibit limit (p. 375)

interdependence condition that exists when countries rely on each other for ideas, goods, services, and markets (p. 96)

*internal existing or taking place within (p. 75)

*invest to lay out money so as to return a profit (pp. 335, 410)

irrigation process of collecting water and distributing it to crops (p. 66)

*idéntico exactamente lo mismo (pág. 38)

*impacto efecto (pág. 279)

importar comprar bienes o recursos a otros países (pág. 95)

*ingreso dinero ganado (pág. 350)

indígenas pueblo descendiente de los primeros habitantes de un área (pág. 149)

infraestructura sistema de carreteras y vías férreas que permiten el transporte de materiales (pág. 375)

*inhibir limitar (pág. 375)

interdependencia condición que existe cuando los países dependen uno del otro para obtener ideas, bienes, servicios y mercados (pág. 96)

*interno que existe o sucede dentro de (pág. 75)

*invertir colocar dinero de manera de obtener una ganancia (págs. 335, 410)

irrigación proceso de recolección de agua y su distribución en los cultivos (pág. 66) *issue problem (p. 248)

isthmus narrow stretch of land connecting two larger land areas (p. 193)

*asunto problema (pág. 248)

istmo extensión estrecha de tierra que conecta dos masas de tierra más grandes (pág. 193)

jade shiny stone that comes in many shades of green (p. 209)

jade piedra brillante de varios tonos de verde (pág. 209)

landlocked having no border with ocean or sea (p. 275)

La Niña weather phenomenon marked by unusually cool waters in the eastern Pacific and low amounts of rainfall there and heavier rains—and a greater chance of typhoons—in the western Pacific; opposite of El Niño (p. 58)

*layer a thickness or fold (p. 64)

leap year year with 366 days, which happens every fourth year to make calendars match Earth's movement around the sun (p. 36)

light industry manufacture of consumer goods such as clothing, shoes, furniture, and household products (p. 411)

literacy rate percentage of people who can read and write (p. 239)

Llanos tropical grasslands that stretch through eastern Colombia and Venezuela (p. 194)

local wind wind pattern typical of a small area (p. 59)

sin salida al mar que no posee fronteras al mar o al océano (pág. 275)

La Niña fenómeno meteorológico caracterizado por aguas inusualmente frías y bajas cantidades de lluvia en el este del Pacífico, y fuertes lluvias (y una mayor posibilidad de tifones) en el oeste del Pacífico; opuesto de El Niño (pág. 58)

*capa grosor o doblez (pág. 64)

año bisiesto año con 366 días, que ocurre cada cuatro años para hacer que los calendarios coincidan con el movimiento de la Tierra alrededor del Sol (pág. 36)

industria liviana fabricación de bienes de consumo como ropas, calzado, muebles y productos para la casa (pág. 411)

tasa de alfabetización porcentaje de personas que saben leer y escribir (pág. 239)

llanos praderas tropicales que se extienden a través del este de Colombia y Venezuela (pág. 194)

viento local patrón de viento típico de un área pequeña (pág. 59)

magma hot melted rock inside the Earth that flows to the surface when a volcano erupts (p. 45)

*maintain keep up (p. 248)

maize corn (p. 209)

*major to be great in size or impact (p. 283)

mantle Earth's thickest layer, found between the core and the crust (p. 45)

maquiladora a foreign-owned factory in Mexico where workers assemble parts made in other countries (p. 235)

market economy economic system in which individuals make the decisions about how resources are used and what goods and services to provide (p. 350)

magma roca caliente y derretida dentro de la Tierra que fluye a la superficie durante la erupción de un volcán (pág. 45)

*mantener conservar (pág. 248)

maíz mazorca y grano (pág. 209)

*principal grande en tamaño o impacto (pág. 283)

manto capa más gruesa de la Tierra que se encuentra entre el núcleo y la corteza (pág. 45)

maquiladora fábrica de propiedad extranjera en México donde los trabajadores montan piezas hechas en otros países (pág. 235)

economía de mercado sistema económico en el que las personas toman las decisiones sobre cómo se usan los recursos y qué bienes y servicios se proveen (pág. 350)

Glossary/Glosario

*media types of communication such as the Internet, television, and radio (p. 159)

*medical relating to the science or practice of medicine (p. 356)

megalopolis huge urban area made up of several large cities and nearby communities (p. 117)

mestizo in Latin America, a person of mixed Native American and European heritage (p. 221)

middle class part of society that is neither very rich nor poor but has enough money to buy cars, new clothing, electronics, and luxury items (p. 410)

migrant worker person who earns a living by temporarily moving to a place separate from his or her home in order to work (p. 236)

migration movement of people (p. 219)

*militant person who uses war or violence to accomplish goals (p. 340)

millennium a period of 1,000 years (p. 16)

missionary person who moves to another area to spread his or her religion (p. 389)

mistral cold, dry winter wind from the north that strikes southern France (p. 287)

monarchy government led by king or queen who inherited power by being born into ruling family (p. 86)

mural large painting on a wall (p. 224)

multinational company company that has locations in more than one country (p. 332)

*medios de comunicación tipos de comunicación como Internet, la televisión y la radio (pág. 159)

*médico relativo a la ciencia o la práctica de la medicina (pág. 356)

megalópolis área urbanizada gigantesca compuesta por varias ciudades grandes y comunidades cercanas (pág. 117)

mestizo en América Latina, persona de herencia mixta de nativos americanos y europeos (pág. 221)

clase media parte de la sociedad que no es ni muy rica ni muy pobre, pero que posee suficiente dinero para comprar autos, ropas nuevas, y artículos electrónicos y de lujo (pág. 410)

trabajador migratorio persona que se gana la vida mudándose temporalmente a un sitio alejado de su hogar para poder trabajar (pág. 236)

migración movimiento de personas (pág. 219)

*militante persona que usa la guerra o la violencia para lograr objetivos (pág. 340)

milenio período de 1000 años (pág. 16)

misionero persona que se muda a otra zona para difundir su religión (pág. 389)

mistral viento invernal, frío y seco, que llega al sur de Francia desde el norte (pág. 287)

monarquía gobierno conducido por un rey o una reina que heredaron el poder al nacer dentro de la familia reinante (pág. 86)

mural pintura grande sobre una pared (pág. 224)

compañía multinacional empresa que tiene ubicaciones en más de un país (pág. 332)

national debt money owed by the government (p. 250)

nationalism feelings of affection and loyalty towards one's country (p. 397)

nation-state country formed of people who share a common culture and history (p. 299)

natural resource material from the Earth that people use to meet their needs (p. 93)

navigable referring to a body of water wide and deep enough for ships to use (pp. 119, 277)

neutrality refusal to take sides in a war between other countries (p. 336)

newly industrialized country country that is creating new manufacturing and business (p. 94)

deuda nacional dinero que el gobierno debe (pág. 250)

nacionalismo sentimiento de afecto y lealtad hacia el propio país (pág. 397)

estado-nación país formado por personas que comparten una historia y una cultura en común (pág. 299)

recurso natural material del planeta Tierra que la gente usa para cubrir sus necesidades (pág. 93)

navegable referente a un cuerpo de agua con anchura y profundidad suficientes para que lo usen barcos (págs. 119, 277)

neutralidad negativa a tomar posición en una guerra entre otros países (pág. 336)

país recientemente industrializado país que está creando nuevos negocios y manufacturas (pág. 94)

Glossary/Glosario

newsprint type of paper used for printing newspapers (p. 162)

nonrenewable resource natural resource such as a mineral that cannot be replaced (p. 93)

papel de periódico tipo de papel usado para imprimir periódicos (pág. 162)

recurso no renovable recurso natural, como un mineral, que no se puede reemplazar (pág. 93)

obsidian hard, black, volcanic glass useful for making weapons (p. 209)

*occur to be found in (p. 50)

oligarch member of a small ruling group that holds great power (p. 420)

oral tradition passing stories by word of mouth from generation to generation (p. 397)

orbit specific path each planet follows around the sun (p. 35)

obsidiana vidrio volcánico de color negro y resistente, útil para fabricar armas (pág. 209)

*ocurrir que se encuentra en algo (pág. 50)

oligarca miembro de un grupo pequeño de gobierno que posee gran poder (pág. 420)

tradición oral pasar historias de boca en boca de generación en generación (pág. 397)

órbita trayectoria específica que cada planeta sigue alrededor del Sol (pág. 35)

Pampas treeless grassland of Argentina and Uruguay (p. 194)

parliamentary democracy form of government in which voters elect representatives to a law-making body called Parliament, and members of Parliament vote for an official called the prime minister to head the government (pp. 141, 323)

*participate take part in (p. 147)

pass space people can use to travel through a mountain range (p. 277)

peat plants partly decayed in water which can be dried and burned for fuel (p. 325)

pensioner person who receives regular payments from the government because he or she is too old or sick to work (p. 410)

perestroika policy of economic restructuring in the Soviet Union that called for less government control of the economy (p. 393)

*period a portion of time (p. 379)

permafrost permanently frozen lower layers of soil found in the tundra and subarctic climate zones (p. 380)

pesticide powerful chemicals that kill crop-destroying insects (p. 66)

*physical related to natural science (p. 15)

pidgin language language formed by combining parts of several different languages (p. 221)

pampas pradera desprovista de árboles en Argentina y Uruguay (pág. 194)

democracia parlamentaria forma de gobierno en la que los votantes eligen representantes para un cuerpo que crea las leyes denominado Parlamento, sus miembros votan a un funcionario llamado primer ministro como jefe del gobierno (págs. 141, 323)

*participar tomar parte en (pág. 147)

paso lugar que la gente puede usar para viajar a través de una cordillera montañosa (pág. 277)

turba plantas parcialmente descompuestas en agua que pueden secarse y usarse como combustible (pág. 325)

pensionado persona que recibe pagos regulares del gobierno dado que está demasiado anciana o enferma para trabajar (pág. 410)

perestroika política de reestructuración económica en la Unión Soviética que exigía menos control gubernamental de la economía (pág. 393)

*período lapso de tiempo (pág. 379)

permafrost capas de suelo inferiores que están permanentemente congeladas en la tundra y en las zonas de clima ártico (pág. 380)

pesticidas fuertes sustancias químicas que matan los insectos que destruyen los cultivos (pág. 66)

*físico relativo a las sciencias naturales (pág. 15)

lengua mixta idioma formado por la combinación de partes de varios idiomas diferentes (pág. 221)

Glossary/Glosario

plantation large farm (p. 235)

plate tectonics scientific theory that explains how processes within the Earth form continents and cause their movement (p. 46)

plaza public square in Latin American city around which government buildings and major churches were built (p. 233)

polder reclaimed wetlands that use a system of dikes and pumps to keep out the sea's waters (p. 332)

pollutant chemical and smoke particles that cause pollution (p. 380)

pope head of the Roman Catholic Church (p. 298)

population density average number of people living in a square mile or square kilometer (p. 74)

potash mineral salt used in making fertilizer (p. 350)

prairie rolling inland grassland region with fertile soil (p. 118)

precipitation part of the water cycle; process by which water falls to the Earth as, for example, rain or snow (p. 54)

prevailing winds wind patterns that are similar over time (p. 57)

*****primary** main or most important (p. 400)

*****principle** rule or guideline (p. 140)

*****prior** earlier in time or order (p. 419)

privatization transfer of ownership of businesses from the government to individuals (p. 409)

productivity measure of how much work a person produces in a set amount of time (p. 325)

profit money a business earns after all its expenses are met (p. 159)

*****promote** to put forward (p. 398)

plantación granja grande (pág. 235)

tectónica de placas teoría científica que explica cómo los procesos dentro de la Tierra forman los continentes y causan su movimiento (pág. 46)

plaza lugar público en las ciudades de América Latina alrededor del que se construyeron las iglesias principales y los edificios gubernamentales (pág. 233)

pólder pantanos recuperados que usan un sistema de diques y bombas para mantener fuera a las aguas marinas (pág. 332)

contaminantes sustancias químicas y partículas de humo que provocan contaminación (pág. 380)

papa líder de la Iglesia Católica Romana (pág. 298)

densidad de población cantidad promedio de personas que viven en una milla cuadrada o un kilómetro cuadrado (pág. 74)

potasa sal mineral usada en la fabricación de fertilizantes (pág. 350)

pradera región interna de las llanuras, con pastizales ondulantes y tierras fértiles (pág. 118)

precipitación parte del ciclo del agua; proceso mediante el que el agua cae a la Tierra, por ejemplo, como lluvia o nieve (pág. 54)

vientos predominantes patrones de viento que se mantienen similares con el paso del tiempo (pág. 57)

*****primario** principal o más importante (pág. 400)

*****principio** regla o pauta (pág. 140)

*****precedente** anterior en tiempo u orden (pág. 419)

privatización transferencia de propiedad de los negocios del gobierno a particulares (pág. 409)

productividad medición de cuánto trabajo produce una persona en una cantidad fija de tiempo (pág. 325)

ganancia dinero que se gana en un negocio luego de cubrir todos los gastos (pág. 159)

*****promover** impulsar (pág. 398)

Q

quota number limit on how many items of a particular product can be imported from a certain nation (p. 95)

cupo límite de la cantidad de artículos de un producto determinado que puede importarse de cierto país (pág. 95)

R

rain forest dense stand of trees and other growth that receives high amounts of precipitation each year (p. 199)

selva tropical agrupación densa de árboles y otras plantas que reciben grandes cantidades de precipitación cada año (pág. 199)

rain shadow effect of mountains that blocks rain from reaching interior regions (p. 59)

refugee person who flees to another country to escape persecution or disaster (p. 76)

*regime government (p. 137)

relative location description of where a place is in relation to the features around it (p. 15)

*release to relieve pressure (p. 45); to set free (p. 391)

*reluctant hesitant (p. 162)

*rely to depend on (p. 330)

remittance money sent back home by workers who leave their home country to work in other nations (p. 240)

renewable resource natural resource that can be replaced naturally or grown again (p. 93)

republic government in which people choose their leaders (p. 296)

representative democracy form of government in which voters choose leaders who make and enforce the laws (p. 140)

*reside live (p. 194)

*restore return; to put or bring back into existence or use (p. 126)

*restrict to limit (p. 169)

reunification the act of being brought back together (p. 336)

*reveal make known (p. 234)

revolution one complete circuit around the sun (p. 36); sweeping change (pp. 215, 301)

*reverse opposite (p. 38)

rotate to spin on an axis (p. 36)

*route journey (p. 119)

sombra de lluvia efecto de las montañas que impiden que la lluvia alcance regiones interiores (pág. 59)

refugiado persona que huye a otro país para escapar de la persecución o el desastre (pág. 76)

*régimen gobierno (pág. 137)

ubicación relativa descripción de dónde está un lugar en relación con las características a su alrededor (pág. 15)

*liberar aliviar la presión (pág. 45); dar la libertad (pág. 391)

*reacio indeciso (pág. 162)

*confiar depender de (pág. 330)

remesa dinero que envían a su hogar los trabajadores que abandonan su país para trabajar en otras naciones (pág. 240)

recurso renovable recurso natural que puede reemplazarse o crecer nuevamente de manera natural (pág. 93)

república gobierno en el que las personas eligen a sus líderes (pág. 296)

democracia representativa forma de gobierno en el que los votantes eligen a sus líderes para que hagan cumplir las leyes (pág. 140)

*residir vivir (pág. 194)

*restituir devolver; restablecer al estado o uso (pág. 126)

*restringir limitar (pág. 169)

reunificación el acto de ser vuelto a reunir (pág. 336)

*revelar dar a conocer (pág. 234)

revolución giro completo alrededor del Sol (pág. 36); cambio radical (págs. 215, 301)

*reverso opuesto (pág. 38)

rotar girar sobre su eje (pág. 36)

*travesía viaje (pág. 119)

S

secular nonreligious (p. 310)

selva Brazilian name for the Amazonian rain forest (p. 247)

separatist movement campaign by members of an ethnic group to break away from the national government and form an independent state (p. 421)

serf farm laborer who could be bought and sold along with the land (p. 390)

secular no religioso (pág. 310)

selva nombre brasilero para los bosques tropicales del Amazonas (pág. 247)

movimiento separatista campaña realizada por los miembros de un grupo étnico para separarse del gobierno nacional y formar un estado independiente (pág. 421)

siervo labriego que podía comprarse y venderse junto con la tierra (pág. 390)

Glossary/Glosario

Glossary/Glosario

*shift to change from one to another (p. 239)

*significant important (p. 37)

*similar having qualities in common (p. 339)

sirocco hot winds from Africa that blow across southern Europe (p. 287)

smog thick haze of smoke and chemicals (pp. 64, 380)

sodium nitrate mineral used in fertilizer and explosives (p. 252)

softwood wood of evergreen trees, often used in buildings or making furniture (p. 375)

solar system planets, along with their moons, asteroids and other bodies, and the sun (p. 35)

specialization focusing on certain economic activities to make the best use of resources (p. 330)

*stable firmly established; not likely to change suddenly or greatly (p. 213)

stock part ownership in a company (p. 159)

*style form (p. 224)

subregion smaller area of a region (p. 193)

subsidy special payment made by a government to support a particular group or industry (p. 340)

subsistence farm small plot of land on which a farmer grows only enough food to feed his or her family (p. 235)

suburb smaller community just outside a large city (p. 147)

summer solstice day that has the most daylight hours and the fewest hours of darkness (p. 37)

*alternar cambiar de una cosa a otra (pág. 239)

*significativo importante (pág. 37)

*similar que posee cualidades en común (pág. 339)

siroco vientos calientes de África que soplan atravesando el sur de Europa (pág. 287)

smog neblina espesa, resultado de la combinación de humo y sustancias químicas (págs. 64, 380)

nitrato de sodio mineral que se usa en fertilizantes y explosivos (pág. 252)

madera blanda madera de árboles siempre verdes, que se utiliza comúnmente en edificios o muebles (pág. 375)

sistema solar los planetas y sus lunas, los asteroides y otros cuerpos celestes además del Sol (pág. 35)

especialización concentrarse en ciertas actividades económicas para hacer el mejor uso de recursos (pág. 330)

*estable establecido con firmeza; sin probabilidades de cambiar repentina o ampliamente (pág. 213)

acción parte propietaria en una empresa (pág. 159)

*estilo forma (pág. 224)

subregión zona más pequeña de una región (pág. 193)

subsidio pago especial hecho por un gobierno para apoyar a un grupo o industria particular (pág. 340)

agricultura de subsistencia parcela de tierra en la cual un granjero cultiva sólo los alimentos suficientes para alimentar a su familia (pág. 235)

suburbio comunidad justo en las afueras de una ciudad grande (pág. 147)

solsticio de verano día que tiene la mayor cantidad de horas de luz diurna y la menor cantidad de horas de oscuridad (pág. 37)

taiga large coniferous forests (p. 380)

tariff tax added to the price of goods that are imported (pp. 95, 170)

*technique a method of accomplishing something (p. 65)

*technology the application of scientific discoveries to practical use (p. 73)

terrorism violence used against the people or government in the hopes of winning political goals (p. 137)

*theme topic (p. 15)

taiga grandes bosques coníferos (pág. 380)

tarifa impuesto agregado al precio de los bienes que se importan (págs. 95, 170)

*técnica un método para lograr algo (pág. 65)

*tecnología la aplicación de los descubrimientos científicos a un uso práctico (pág. 73)

terrorismo violencia usada en contra del pueblo o del gobierno con la esperanza de alcanzar metas políticas (pág. 137)

*tema tópico (pág. 15)

tornado severe windstorm that takes the form of a funnel-shaped cloud and often touches the ground (p. 127)

trade deficit situation that occurs when the value of a country's imports is higher than the value of its exports (p. 169)

trade surplus situation that occurs when the value of a country's exports is higher than the value of its imports (p. 170)

*transform greatly change (p. 211)

*transport move (p. 193)

trench deep cut in the ocean floor (p. 50)

tributary small river that flows into a larger river (p. 194)

Tropics area between the Tropic of Cancer and the Tropic of Capricorn, which has generally warm temperatures because it receives the direct rays of the sun for much of the year (pp. 38, 199)

tornado intensa tormenta de viento que toma forma de embudo y suele tocar el suelo (pág. 127)

déficit comercial situación que ocurre cuando el valor de las importaciones de un país es mayor que el valor de sus exportaciones (pág. 169)

excedente comercial situación que ocurre cuando el valor de las exportaciones de un país es mayor que el valor de sus importaciones (pág. 170)

*transformar cambiar mucho (pág. 211)

*transportar mover (pág. 193)

fosa marina corte profundo en el suelo marino (pág. 50)

tributario río pequeño que fluye dentro de un río más grande (pág. 194)

trópicos área entre el Trópico de Cáncer y el Trópico de Capricornio con temperaturas generalmente cálidas, ya que recibe los rayos directos del Sol durante gran parte del año (págs. 38, 199)

underemployment situation that arises when a worker must take a job that requires lesser skills than he or she possesses (p. 410)

*unify to unite or bring together (p. 421)

*unique being the only one of its kind (p. 89)

urban climate weather patterns in cities, including higher temperatures and distinct wind patterns, as compared to nearby rural areas (p. 61)

urban sprawl spread of human settlement into natural areas (p. 172)

urbanization growth of cities (pp. 75, 308)

subempleo situación provocada cuando un trabajador debe aceptar un trabajo que requiere menos habilidades que las que él posee (pág. 410)

*unificar unir o juntar (pág. 421)

*exclusivo ser el único en su tipo (pág. 89)

clima urbano patrones climáticos de las ciudades, incluyendo temperaturas más altas y patrones de vientos distintos, al compararse con áreas rurales cercanas (pág. 61)

expansión urbana expansión de asentamientos humanos en áreas naturales (pág. 172)

urbanización crecimiento de las ciudades (págs. 75, 308)

*vary to be different (p. 326)

vaquero Mexican cowhand (p. 234)

*volume amount (p. 411)

*variar ser diferente (pág. 326)

vaquero empleado que trabaja con el ganado en México (pág. 234)

*volumen cantidad (pág. 411)

water cycle system in which water moves from the Earth to the air and back to the Earth (p. 53)

ciclo del agua sistema en el que el agua se mueve de la Tierra hacia el aire y luego de vuelta hacia la Tierra (pág. 53)

Glossary/Glosario

weather changes in temperature, wind speed and direction, and air moisture that take place over a short period of time (p. 56)

weathering process in which rock is broken into smaller pieces by water and ice, chemicals, or even plants (p. 47)

welfare state country where the government is the main provider of support for the sick, needy, and the retired (p. 307)

***widespread** scattered or found in a wide area (pp. 86)

winter solstice day of the year that has the fewest hours of sunlight and the most hours of darkness (p. 38)

clima cambios en la temperatura, velocidad y dirección del viento, y humedad en el aire que duran un período breve (pág. 56)

deterioro por exposición proceso por el cual se rompen las rocas en pedazos más pequeños ocasionado por el agua y el hielo, las químicos o hasta los vegetales (pág. 47)

estado de bienestar país en el que el gobierno es el proveedor principal de ayuda para los enfermos, necesitados y jubilados (pág. 307)

***generalizado** que se distribuye o encuentra en un área amplia (pág. 86)

solsticio de invierno día del año que tiene la menor cantidad de horas de luz diurna y la mayor cantidad de horas de oscuridad (pág. 38)

Glossary/Glosario

Index

Index

Index

Index

Index

Index

Index

Index

Index

Index

Index

Index

Index

Index

Acknowledgments

Text

51-Mark Twain. *Roughing It.* Harper & Brothers Publishers. Originally published by The American Publishing Company. 1871; **148-**Langston Hughes. "I, Too." In *The Collected Poems of Langston Hughes.* Ed. Arnold Rampersad. New York: Vintage Classics. 1995; **222-**"The Hard-Hearted Son." *Folktales of Mexico.* Ed., Trans. Américo Paredes. The University of Chicago Press. 1970; **324-**Charles Dickens. *Hard Times.* In *The Works of Charles Dickens.* New York: Books, Inc. 1854; **381-**Valentin Rasputin. *Farewell to Matyora.* Trans. Antonina W. Bouis. Evanston, IL: Northwestern University Press. 1991.

Photographs

Cover-(tl) CORBIS, (tc) Alan R. Moller/Getty Images, (c) Bill Bachman/Alamy Images, (r) CORBIS, (bl) Paul Thompson/Alamy Images; **ii–1-**NASA/Photo Researchers; **v-**Paul A. Souders/CORBIS; **vi-**(l) Blaine Harrington III/CORBIS, (r) Pete Oxford/Nature Picture Library; **vii-**Walter Bibikow/Getty Images; **viii-**Peter Guttman/CORBIS; **ix-**Markus Scholz/Peter Arnold, Inc.; **x-**AP Images; **xi-**Lucien Aigner/CORBIS; **xii-**(l) Tim Page/CORBIS, (r) Alfredo Maiquez/Getty Images; **xiii-**Klaus Nigge/National Geographic Image Collection/Getty Images; **11-**Cancan Chu/Getty Images; **12–13-**Gavin Hellier/Getty Images; **14-**John Van Hasselt/CORBIS; **15-**Peter Hulme/Ecoscene/CORBIS; **16-**Michael S. Yamashita/CORBIS; **18-**(t) ThinkStock/SuperStock, (cl) Janet Foster/Masterfile, (cr) Mark Tomalty/Masterfile, (bl) Jurgen Freund/Nature Picture Library, (br) age fotostock/SuperStock; **20-**(t) David Young-Wolff/PhotoEdit, (tc) NOAA/CORBIS, (b) The Photolibrary Wales/Alamy Images, (bc) Martin Harvey/Getty Images; **22-**(t) Dorling Kindersley/Getty Images, (b) Steve Skjold/Alamy Images; **34-**NASA/Roger Ressmeyer/CORBIS; **36-**(l) Andrew Parker/Alamy Images, (r) World Perspectives/Getty Images; **39-**(t) Tony West/CORBIS, (cl) imagebroker/Alamy Images, (cr) Kevin George/Alamy Images, (b) StockTrek/Getty Images; **42–43-**Bill Hatcher/National Geographic Image Collection; **44-**David Parker/Photo Researchers; **46-**Anthony West/CORBIS; **48-**Rafiqur Rahman/Reuters/CORBIS; **49-**Paul Bigland/Lonely Planet Images; **50-**Jimmy Chin/National Geographic Image Collection; **51-**John Lemker/Animals Animals; **52-**(l) Tom Bean/Getty Images, (r) James P. Blair/NGS/Getty Images; **54-**Yves Marcoux/Getty Images; **55-**China Newsphoto/Reuters/CORBIS; **57-**John Maier Jr/Argus Fotoarchiv/CORBIS SYGMA; **61-**AFP/Getty Images; **62-**Peter Arnold, Inc./Alamy Images; **63-**Vince Streano/age fotostock; **64-**Norbert Rosing/National Geographic Image Collection; **67-**(tc) age fotostock, (tr) Tom Uhlman/Alamy Images, (bl) Remi Benali/CORBIS, (br) Greg Stott/Masterfile; **70–71-**ML Sinibaldi/CORBIS; **72-**Keren Su/Getty Images; **74-**(l) Cancan Chu/Getty Images, (r) Greg Elms/Lonely Planet Images; **77-**Wayne R. Bilenduke/Getty Images; **78-**Reuters/Jagadeesh NV; **79-**(tl) Reuters/Bobby Yip, (tr) Danita Delimont/Alamy Images, (b) AP Photo; **80-**Reuters/Gary Hershorn; **81-**Baldev/CORBIS; **82-**Erich Schlegel/Dallas Morning News/CORBIS; **84-**Hideo Haga/HAGA/The Image Works; **86-**North Wind Picture Archives/Alamy Images; **87-**Kevin Lee/Getty Images; **89-**age fotostock/SuperStock; **90-**Charles O. Cecil/Alamy Images; **90–91-**W. Cody/CORBIS; **91-**Sean Sprague/The Image Works; **92-**Frederic J. Brown/AFP/Getty Images; **95-**(l) AP World Wide, (r) George Pimentel/wireimage.com; **97-**(tl) Jamal Said/Reuters/Landov, (cl) Richard I'Anson/Lonely Planet Images, (cr) Tom Hanson/Canadian Press/AP Images, (b) Jerry Alexander/Lonely Planet Images; **100-**(t to b) Creatas/SuperStock, AP Images, Jim Zuckerman/CORBIS, Kurt Scholz/SuperStock, Lisa Englebrecht/Danitadelimont.com, Gary Cook/Alamy Images; **100–101-**(bkgd) NASA; **101-**(t to b) Jose Azel/Getty Images, Macduff Everton/CORBIS, AP Images, ITAR-TASS/Vitaly Belousov/Newscom; **105-**(tl) Timothy O'Keefe/Index Stock Imagery, (tr) Christian Heeb/Aurora Photos, (bl) Jim Wark/Lonely Planet Images, (br) Kevin Horan/Getty Images; **113-**Tim Smith/Getty Images; **114–115-**age fotostock/SuperStock; **116-**Ralph Lee Hopkins/Lonely Planet Images; **117-**aerialarchives.com/Alamy Images; **118-**(l) Paul A. Souders/CORBIS, (r) Sarah Leen/National Geographic Image Collection; **119-**SuperStock; **121-**Richard Olsenius/National Geographic Image Collection; **123-**Mona Reeder/Dallas Morning News/CORBIS; **124-**Steve Terrill/CORBIS; **126-**Liz Condo/AP Images; **127-**Franz Marc Frei/CORBIS; **129-**(t) Paul A. Souders/CORBIS, (cl) Walter Bibikow/Getty Images, (cr) Eric Nguyen/Jim Reed Photography/CORBIS, (b) Robert Harding World Imagery/CORBIS; **132–133-**Gunter Marx Photography/CORBIS; **134-**Mark E. Gibson/CORBIS; **136-**(l) The British Museum/HIP/The Image Works, (r) FPG/Getty Images; **137-**(l) Swim Ink 2, LLC/CORBIS, (r) Tim Brakemeier/dpa/CORBIS; **138-**Joseph Barrak/AFP/Getty Images; **139-**Mary Evans Picture Library; **140-**Najlah Feanny/CORBIS; **142-**Ed Andrieski/AP Images; **142–143-**Photodisc/Getty Images; **143-**Max Whittaker/CORBIS; **144-**Oliver Strewe/Lonely Planet Images; **145-**Bob Daemmrich/The Image Works; **146-**Tony Vaccaro/Getty Images; **148-**(tl) CORBIS, (tr) Lucien Aigner/CORBIS, (b) Bettmann/CORBIS; **149-**Alan Marsh/Getty Images; **151-**(t) Roy Rainford/Robert Harding, (b) Bettmann/CORBIS, (bc) Hulton Archive/Getty Images, (br) Tim Smith/Getty Images; **154–155-**Aaron Huey/Polaris; **155-**(tcr) Melanie Acevedo, (tr) Ryan Remiorz/AP Images, (bcr) Roy Morsch/age fotostock, (br) Purestock/Alamy Images; **156–157-**Charles O'Rear/CORBIS; **158-**Ed Kashi/CORBIS; **159-**Julia Malakie/AP Images; **161-**Ted Soqui/CORBIS; **163-**AP Photo; **164-**(l) Beth Dixson/Alamy Images, AP Photo; **165-**AP Photo; **166-**AP Photo; **167-**AP Photo; **168-**Bill Brooks/Alamy Images; **169-**Jason Kryk/AP Images; **170-**The Bill and Melinda Gates Foundation; **171-**Evan Vucci/AP Images; **173-**(t) Adam Pretty/Getty Images, (cl) David Leahy/Getty Images, (bl) John and Lisa Merrill/CORBIS, (br) Mark Elias/Bloomberg News/Landov; **176–177-**Stone/Getty Images; **179-**(tr) Jack Novak/SuperStock, (cl) Ken Fisher/Getty Images, (bl) Jeff Rotman/Getty Images, (br) Hubert Stadler/CORBIS; **189-**Tom Cockrem/Lonely Planet Images; **190–191-**Tony Savino/The Image Works; **192-**Jeremy Horner/CORBIS; **193-**Jon Arnold Images/SuperStock; **194-**Kit Houghton/CORBIS; **195-**Pete Oxford/Nature Picture Library; **197-**(t) Media Bakery, (b) The Bridgeman Art Library; **198-**David Lyons/National Geographic Image Collection; **200-**(l) Tui De Roy/Minden Pictures, (r) Brent Winebrenner/LPI; **203-**(tl) SuperStock, (tr) Trevor Smithers ARPS/Alamy Images, (c) Rodrigo Arangua/AFP/Getty Images, (b) Galen Rowell/Odyssey Productions; **206–207-**Danny Lehman/CORBIS; **208-**Carlos Lopez-Barillas/CORBIS; **209-**Robert Frerck and Odyssey Productions; **211-**Werner Forman/CORBIS; **212-**(l) Charles & Josette Lenars/CORBIS, (r) Brooklyn Museum/CORBIS; **213-**(l) Index, Museo de America, Madrid, Spain/The Bridgeman Art Library, (r) Angelo Cavalli/Getty Images; **214-**(l) H.N. Rudd/CORBIS, (r) Jose Fuste Raga/CORBIS; **216-**Tim Page/CORBIS; **216–217-**Getty Images; **217-**Alfredo Maiquez/Getty Images; **218-**Blaine Harrington III/CORBIS; **219-**Tom Cockrem/Lonely Planet Images; **220-**David Dudenhoefer/Odyssey Productions; **221-**(l) Chris Brandis/AP Images, (r) AM Corporation/Alamy Images; **222-**Robert Holmes/CORBIS; **223-**GM Photo Images/Alamy Images; **225-**(tl) Danny Lehman/CORBIS, (tr) Mario Algaze/The Image Works, (bl) Alfredo Dagli Orti/The Art Archive/CORBIS, (br) Adriano Machado/Reuters/CORBIS; **228–229-**Adriana Zehbrauskas/Polaris, (tr) Danita Delimont/Alamy Images, (cr) Ken Welsh/age fotostock, (br) Luc Novovitch/Alamy Images; **230–231-**Chad Ehlers/Getty Images; **232-**Lynsey Addario/CORBIS; **233-**World Pictures/Alamy Images; **234-**Danita Delimont/Alamy Images; **235-**Danny Lehman/CORBIS; **237-**Oswaldo Rivas/Reuters/CORBIS; **238-**(l) Mark Godfrey c. 2004 The Nature Conservancy, (r) Courtesy Marie Claire Paiz; **239-**Alejandro Ernesto/epa/CORBIS; **241-**AP Photo/Dolores Ochoa; **242-**Peter Arnold, Inc./Alamy Images; **243-**(tl) World Picture Library/Alamy Images, (tc) AP Photo/Alberto Cesar-Greenpeace/HO, (tr) Sue Cunningham Photographic/Alamy Images, (b) Reuters/Carlos Barria; **244-**Reuters/Jamil Bittar; **245-**Reuters/Paulo Whitaker; **246-**Roger Ressmeyer/CORBIS; **247-**Paulo Whitaker/Reuters/Landov; **249-**Vanderlei Almeida/AFP/Getty Images; **250-**Eduardo De Baia/AP Images; **251-**Eliseo Fernandez/Reuters/CORBIS; **253-**(t) Marcelo Sayao/epa/CORBIS, (cl) Marco Ugarte/AP Images, (cr) Juan Barreto/AFP/Getty Images, (b) Jeff Greenberg/age fotostock; **256–257-**Roberto Gerometta/Lonely Planet Images; **259-**(tl) Anthony West/CORBIS, (tr) Jon Arnold Images/Alamy Images, (bl) Owen Franken/CORBIS, (br) Walter Bibikow/Getty Images; **269-**Nicole Duplaix/NGS/Getty Images; **271-**Tim Graham/Getty Images; **272–273-**Richard Nebesky/Lonely Planet Images; **274-**Emile Luider/Getty Images; **275-**age fotostock/SuperStock; **276-**(l) Chase Jarvis/Getty Images, (r) Jon Arnold/SuperStock; **277-**Walter Geiersperger/CORBIS; **278-**age fotostock/SuperStock; **279-**(inset) Andra Maslennikov/Peter Arnold, Inc., Ben Osborne/Getty Images; **281-**Sergei Supinsky/AFP/Getty Images; **282-**Fernand Ivaldi/Getty Images; **286-**Raymond Gehman/CORBIS; **287-**George Simhoni/Masterfile; **289-**(tl) John Garrett/CORBIS, (cl cr) age fotostock/SuperStock, (br) Asgeir Helgestad/Nature Picture Library; **292–293-**Hubert Stadler/CORBIS; **294-**David Tomlinson/Lonely Planet Images; **295-**Ted Spiegel/CORBIS; **297-**(l) Matt Houston/AP Images, (r) Royalty-Free/CORBIS; **298-**C. Steve Vidler/eStock Photo; **299-**National Gallery Collection; By kind permission of the Trustees of the National Gallery, London/CORBIS; **300-**(l) Scala/Art Resource, (r) Royalty-Free/Getty Images; **301-**(l) Ashmolean Museum, University of Oxford, UK/Bridgeman Art Library, (r) Rèunion des Musèes Nationaux/Art Resource; **304-**Homer Sykes/Alamy Images; **304–305-**Royalty-Free/CORBIS; **305-**Robert Fried Photography; **306-**Jeff Morgan/Alamy Images; **307-**Gideon Mendel/CORBIS; **308-**Michel Euler/AP Images; **309-**Simeone Huber/Getty Images; **310-**Daniel Mihailescu/AFP/Getty Images; **313-**(t) Art Resource, (cl) The Art Archive, (cr) Jonathan Smith/Lonely Planet Images, (b) Masterfile; **316–317-**Richard Harbus/Polaris; **317-**(tr) Steven Mark Needham/Picturearts/Newscom, (cr) Franck Fife/AFP/Newscom, (br) Patrick Sheandell O'Carroll/Getty Images; **318–319-**Elliot Daniel/Lonely Planet Images; **320-**The Image Bank/Getty Images; **322-**Manfred Gottschalk/Lonely Planet Images; **323-**Jayanta Shaw/Reuters/CORBIS; **324-**(l) General Photographic Agency/Getty Images, (r) Mary Evans Picture Library/The Image Works; **325-**Gideon Mendel/CORBIS; **326-**scenicireland.com/Christopher Hill Photographic/Alamy Images; **327-**Palmi Gudmundsson/Getty Images; **329-**George F. Mobley/National Geographic Image Collection; **330-**Jack Dabaghian/Reuters/CORBIS; **331-**(l) Eddie Koegh/Reuters Photo Archive/Newscom, (r) Getty Images for Nike; **332-**Reuters/Luis D'Orey; **333-**K.M. Westermann/CORBIS; **334-**Winfried Rothermel/AP Images; **335-**Christian Charisius/Reuters/CORBIS; **336-**Martin Ruetschi/epa/CORBIS; **338-**Getty Images; **339-**age fotostock/SuperStock; **340-**(inset) Charles O'Rear/CORBIS, Jose Manuel Ribeiro/Reuters/Landov; **341-**Peter Adams/Getty Images; **343-**Brian Atkinson/Alamy Images; **344-**Jack Naegelen/Reuters/CORBIS; **345–346-**AP Images; **348-**Sergei Supinsky/AFP/Getty Images; **349-**Reuters/Fabrizio Bensch; **350-**Katarina Stoltz/Reuters/CORBIS; **352-**Sean Gallup/Newsmakers/Getty Images; **353-**Peter Turnley/CORBIS; **355-**Robb Kendrick/Getty Images; **357-**(tl) Alain Nogues/CORBIS, (cl) Tim Graham/Getty Images, (cr) Bob Stern/The Image Works, (bl) Goddard Space Flight Center Scientific Visualization Studio/NASA, (br) Craig Pershouse/Lonely Planet Images; **360–361-**Viktor Korotayev/Reuters/CORBIS; **363-**(tl) Tkachev Andrei/ITAR-TASS/Landov, (tr) age fotostock/SuperStock, (bl) Konstantin Mikhailov/Nature Picture Library, (br) Roshanak.B/CORBIS; **369-**Novosti/Topham/The Image Works; **370–371-**Maria Stenzel/National Geographic Image Collection; **372-**NGS/Getty Images; **373-**Lee Foster/Lonely Planet Images; **376-**Osetrov Yury/ITAR-TASS/Landov; **376–377-**Karl Weatherly/Getty Images; **377-**Klaus Nigge/NGS/Getty Images; **378-**Rashid Salikhov/EPA/epa/CORBIS; **380-**(l) Maria Stenzel/National Geographic Image Collection, (r) SIME s.a.s/eStock Photo; **381-**(r) Marc Garanger/CORBIS, (b) Wolfgang Kaehler/CORBIS; **382-**(inset) Konstantin Mikhailov/naturepl.com, Chris Niedenthal/Time Life Pictures/Getty Images; **383-**(l) Peter Guttman/CORBIS, (r) Peter Turnley/CORBIS, (b) Wade Kahle/Lonely Planet Images; **386–387-**Mark Sykes/Alamy Images; **388-**Stringer/AFP/Getty Images; **390-**(l) Martin Gray/National Geographic Image Collection, (r) Kremlin Museums, Moscow, Russia/The Bridgeman Art Library;